CORE INTERNET
APPLICATION
DEVELOPMENT
WITH ASP.NET 2.0

PRENTICE HALL CORE SERIES

Core J2EE Patterns, Second Edition, Alur/Malks/Crupi

Core PHP Programming, Third Edition, Atkinson/Suraski

Core Lego Mindstorms, Bagnall

Core Python Programming, Second Edition, Chun

Core JSTL, Geary

Core JavaServer Faces, Geary/Horstmann

Core Web Programming, Second Edition, Hall/Brown

Core Servlets and JavaServer Pages, Second Edition, Hall/Brown

Core Java™ 2, Volume I—Fundamentals, Horstmann/Cornell

Core Java™ 2, Volume II—Advanced Features, Horstmann/Cornell

Core C# and .NET, Perry

Core CSS, Second Edition, Schengili-Roberts

Core Security Patterns, Steel/Nagappan/Lai

Core Java Data Objects, Tyagi/Vorburger/McCammon/Bobzin

Core Web Application Development with PHP and MySQL, Wandschneider

CORE INTERNET APPLICATION DEVELOPMENT WITH ASP.NET 2.0

Randy Connolly

PRENTICE
HALL

Upper Saddle River, NJ • Boston • Indianapolis • San Francisco
New York • Toronto • Montreal • London • Munich • Paris • Madrid
Capetown • Sydney • Tokyo • Singapore • Mexico City

Many of the designations used by manufacturers and sellers to distinguish their products are claimed as trademarks. Where those designations appear in this book, and the publisher was aware of a trademark claim, the designations have been printed with initial capital letters or in all capitals.

The author and publisher have taken care in the preparation of this book, but make no expressed or implied warranty of any kind and assume no responsibility for errors or omissions. No liability is assumed for incidental or consequential damages in connection with or arising out of the use of the information or programs contained herein.

The publisher offers excellent discounts on this book when ordered in quantity for bulk purchases or special sales, which may include electronic versions and/or custom covers and content particular to your business, training goals, marketing focus, and branding interests. For more information, please contact:

U.S. Corporate and Government Sales
(800) 382-3419
corpsales@pearsontechgroup.com

For sales outside the United States, please contact:

International Sales
international@pearsoned.com

Visit us on the Web: www.prenhallprofessional.com

This Book Is Safari Enabled

The Safari® Enabled icon on the cover of your favorite technology book means the book is available through Safari Bookshelf. When you buy this book, you get free access to the online edition for 45 days.

Safari Bookshelf is an electronic reference library that lets you easily search thousands of technical books, find code samples, download chapters, and access technical information whenever and wherever you need it.

To gain 45-day Safari Enabled access to this book:

• Go to http://www.prenhallprofessional.com/safarienabled
• Complete the brief registration form
• Enter the coupon code 28N1-15JL-VZ5D-7FL8-21YR

If you have difficulty registering on Safari Bookshelf or accessing the online edition, please e-mail customer-service@safaribooksonline.com.

Library of Congress Cataloging-in-Publication Data

Connolly, Randy, 1964-
 Core Web application development with ASP .NET 2.0 / Randy Connolly.
    p.   cm.
 Includes bibliographical references and index.
  ISBN 0-321-41950-2 (pbk. : alk. paper) 1. Active server pages. 2. Microsoft .NET. 3. Web servers. 4. Web site development. 5. Internet programming. I. Title.

 TK5105.8885.A26C67 2007
 005.2'76—dc22

                                        2006037360

ISBN 0-321-41950-2

Text printed in the United States on recycled paper at Courier in Stoughton, Massachusetts.
First printing, February 2007

To Diana, Alexander, Benjamin, and Norm.
With much love.

Contents

Chapter 2

HOW ASP.NET WORKS   53

Chapter 5
EXCEPTION HANDLING AND
VALIDATION CONTROLS   257

Chapter 6
CUSTOMIZING AND MANAGING YOUR SITE'S APPEARANCE　311

Chapter 7

ASP.NET SITE NAVIGATION   373

PART II
WORKING WITH DATA 445

Chapter 8
DATA BINDING AND REPRESENTATION 447

Chapter 9
USING ADO.NET 503

Chapter 10
DATA CONTROLS   577

Chapter 11
DESIGNING AND IMPLEMENTING WEB APPLICATIONS   665

Chapter 14

PERSONALIZATION WITH PROFILES AND WEB PARTS   833

Chapter 15
WEB SERVICES   905

Preface

"… the highest simplicity of structure is produced, not by a few elements, but by the highest complexity."

—Ralph Waldo Emerson, "Goethe; or, the Writer," *Representative Men*, Chapter 8

In November 2005, version 2.0 of Microsoft's .NET Framework and ASP.NET was released along with a new version of its Visual Studio development environment. This new version of ASP.NET significantly increased its power as well as its complexity. When I first began teaching Web application development back in 1999 with classic ASP, I could teach my students the essentials of ASP in just two weeks. Of course, to create a sample application of even moderate complexity in ASP required the students to do a great deal of coding. Now, with ASP.NET 2.0, it requires almost two-thirds of a semester to teach my students ASP.NET. The students, however, now can create a sample application of substantial complexity. That is, although ASP.NET 2.0 can be complex, it can dramatically improve a Web developer's productivity. Thus, to paraphrase Emerson, after the developer has grasped and comprehended the seeming initial complexity of ASP.NET, he may very well be struck by its ultimate simplicity, even its beauty.

This book endeavors to help the reader make the transition from complexity to simplicity. That is, it tries to make the process of learning how to create realistic Web applications using ASP.NET 2.0 less daunting for readers who are unfamiliar with ASP.NET, as well as for readers who are somewhat familiar with ASP.NET but want to learn how to use it more effectively.

As part of the process of learning how to create realistic Web applications, this book also endeavors to stress the importance of proper programming and design principles. When first learning ASP.NET, a developer is often tempted to focus all of her attention on using the many different Web server controls along with the Visual Studio Designer. This is quite understandable given the range and power of these controls and the simplicity and functionality of Visual Studio. However, as you create more complex "real-world" Web applications, other considerations, such as maintainability, scalability, and adaptability, become progressively more important. As a consequence, this book's ultimate aim is to help the reader (you) become not only proficient with ASP.NET 2.0, but also to help you become a better Web application developer by also focusing on contemporary best practices in Web application development.

Target Audience

This book is intended first and foremost for professional developers who desire to learn how to create Web applications using the latest version of Microsoft's ASP.NET. Because I teach Web development at a college, this book is also intended for potential use in the classroom for upper-level students taking a course in Web application development using ASP.NET.

Prerequisites

This book assumes that the reader already knows the basics of HTML and CSS. It does not assume any knowledge of ASP.NET or C#. The book does assume that you are familiar with programming using an object-oriented language. As a result, this book does not provide detailed coverage of C# (for that, see Stephen Perry's *Core C# and .NET* from Prentice Hall, 2006); instead, the book illustrates how to use C# in conjunction with ASP.NET.

The book also contains the occasional UML diagrams. Although knowledge of the UML (Unified Modeling Language) may increase your understanding, it is by no means a necessity for this book. This book also assumes that you are familiar in general with databases and XML.

Approach

This book tries to provide you with a clear path to learning how to effectively and realistically use ASP.NET 2.0 for creating Web applications. Due to the sheer size of ASP.NET 2.0, a fair amount of book space is used just to teach the very basics of

ASP.NET. This book's approach is to verge on the side of conciseness in regard to the very basics in order to spend more time with the issues you typically face after you master those basics.

As should be no surprise in a book that is about software development, there is a fair amount of programming code in this book. Much of the code consists of very short code snippets. There are, however, the occasional longer code listings. These listings provide a more complex completed example, such as an RSS reader, a file manager for uploading and downloading files, or a sample business object. These listings are all heavily commented so that you can learn not only from the book's text, but also from these longer code listings. Most chapters also contain a few walk-through exercises. These are a set of step-by-step instructions for accomplishing some task in ASP.NET.

There are several possible pathways through each chapter. A reader could focus principally on the main text and its code snippets, and skip over the longer code listings and the walkthrough exercises. Other readers might prefer to first work through a chapter's walkthrough exercises, and then read through the text to extract a fuller understanding of the chapter's content. Other readers might glance through the chapter text, and then "read" the longer code listings.

The book is structured so that a reader with no knowledge of ASP.NET can progress linearly through the chapters, in that material in one chapter builds on knowledge of the material presented in earlier chapters. However, the material is presented in such a way that a reader can take a more "random" approach, skipping forward and backward to the material that is of interest to her.

The approach and sequence of topics in this book were chosen principally as a result of my experience teaching ASP.NET in the classroom to undergraduates, as well as to professional developers. It was also influenced by my own experiences using ASP.NET professionally for real-world clients.

Overview

This book is broken into three principal parts. The first part is "Core ASP.NET," and consists of the first seven chapters of the book. These chapters introduce and explore the key fundamental features of ASP.NET. The second part encompasses the next five chapters: "Working with Data." It focuses on perhaps the most important aspect of any Web application: representing, extracting, manipulating, and presenting data to the user. The third and final part contains four chapters: "Implementing Web Applications." Its focus is the more advanced side of application development with ASP.NET: security, personalization, Web services, and localization and deployment.

Chapter 1 introduces ASP.NET and the .NET Framework. It examines the different components of the .NET platform, compares ASP.NET to other Web development environments, describes the ASP.NET compilation model, examines the event system in ASP.NET, and illustrates how to create simple ASP.NET pages using Visual Studio 2005.

Chapter 2 continues the coverage of the basics of ASP.NET. This chapter examines in depth how ASP.NET works. It describes the event system in ASP.NET, the page lifecycle, and the essential mechanisms of postback and view state. It also covers some more advanced topics that could be skipped and returned to after you become more comfortable with ASP.NET. These topics include the ASP.NET compilation model, the Page class, as well as the application lifecycle.

Chapter 3 provides an overview of ASP.NET's Web server control architecture, covers Web forms syntax, examines how to use the common features of all Web server controls, and provides and illustrates how to use a core subset of the standard Web server controls. Because ASP.NET 2.0 now has so many Web server controls, some of the less frequently used core Web server controls are covered in Chapter 4.

Chapter 4 continues the coverage of the standard Web server controls. The controls covered in this chapter are more complicated. Some of the controls covered in this chapter include the Panel, MultiView, Wizard, FileUpload, and Xml controls. Several of the longest code listings in the entire book are in this chapter.

Chapter 5 covers one of the most important facets of Web application development, namely, how to deal with exceptions, both at the language level and at the ASP.NET level. It also illustrates how to use the ASP.NET validation controls.

Chapter 6 examines how to create complex user interfaces using styles, themes, skins, and master pages. The chapter also covers the creation of your own user controls.

Chapter 7 examines how to describe and create a site's navigation system using the ASP.NET site navigation controls.

Chapter 8 is the first chapter of the second part of the book. ASP.NET 2.0 introduces a new way of working with data and this chapter's focus is on the different ways that data can be represented. It covers data binding, arrays, collections, generics, and data sets.

Chapter 9 continues the material from Chapter 8 by examining how to programmatically and declaratively work with data in databases. This chapter begins by examining how to access and modify data within databases in ASP.NET using the classes of ADO.NET. The chapter also covers the codeless approach to accessing data using the data source controls introduced in version 2.0 of ASP.NET.

Chapter 10 illustrates how to use the various data controls in ASP.NET. It illustrates the use of the Repeater, DataList, FormView, DetailsView, and GridView controls. Each of these controls uses data binding to display (and for some even edit) multiple sets of data in different ways.

Chapter 11 shifts the focus away from individual controls and classes and instead examines some of the issues involved in creating a more complex Web application with ASP.NET. It begins with the design of Web applications and some common layering models for Web applications, and then moves on to implement two sample layered architectures.

Chapter 12 covers an aspect of ASP.NET that is vital for any Web application: managing state. This chapter begins with the various types of ASP.NET state whose data is stored on the client, such as view state and cookies. It then moves on to those state mechanisms whose data is stored in the server: session state, application state, and finally the ASP.NET cache.

Chapter 13 is the first chapter of the final part of the book. It covers security, one of the most important aspects of any Web application. It discusses authentication and authorization in the context of ASP.NET, illustrates how to use the various login control as well as the new provider system, including the membership and role management providers.

Chapter 14 examines two mechanisms in ASP.NET 2.0 for integrating user personalization into a Web application: namely, the profile system and the Web part framework. The profile system allows an application to persist user information across time and multiple pages. The Web part framework provides the developer with a mechanism for creating pages in which the user can customize the placement, appearance, and possibly the behavior of the page's content.

Chapter 15 looks at how to synchronously and asynchronously consume Web services in ASP.NET. The chapter also demonstrates how to construct Web services.

Chapter 16 demonstrates how to plan and adapt an ASP.NET application for an international audience, as well as the various ways to deploy a completed ASP.NET Web application.

The **Appendix** provides a preliminary examination of ASP.NET AJAX, which up until the fall of 2006 was known by the code-name Atlas. ASP.NET AJAX is a free framework from Microsoft that adds Asynchronous JavaScript and XML (AJAX) support to ASP.NET. ASP.NET AJAX encompasses a fairly large set of functionality that integrates client script (Javascript) libraries with ASP.NET server-based pages. It provides an API for working with Javascript, a declarative alternative to working with Javascript, rich client-script components, along with special Atlas server-side controls.

Supplementary Materials

The Web site for this book is http://www.randyconnolly.com/core. It contains

- The source code for all the examples in the book
- All databases, images, and style sheets used in the chapter examples
- Solutions to the practice exercises that are at the end of each chapter
- A list of known errors in the book and the code
- A form for submitting corrections and suggestions
- Downloadable versions of additional or updated appendices

This book is also intended for potential use in the classroom for upper-level students taking a course in Web application development using ASP.NET. For educators who adopt this book for their courses, the following material is available from this same site:

- Powerpoint lectures for each chapter
- Recommended syllabi and detailed lesson plans for half-semester courses
- Assignments and course projects
- Multiple-choice, short-answer, and long-answer examination questions
- Laboratory tutorials

Prentice Hall also maintains a book Web page that contains additional information: www.prenhallprofessional.com/title/0321419502.

Acknowledgments

This book took almost exactly one year to the day to write. During this time, I incurred numerous obligations to which I am now very grateful to have the opportunity to acknowledge. First, I would like to thank my editor Joan Murray for taking a chance and giving me this chance. Thank you as well to some of the other people at Pearson Education who helped with the editing and production of this book, including Jessica D'Amico, Kelli Brooks, Sean Donahue, Vanessa Moore, and Julie Nahil. I am also thankful for the initial encouragement I received from Shannon Bailey, senior sales representative for Pearson Education.

One of the pleasures of writing a book like this is that you receive feedback from technical reviewers. I am thankful to the following reviewers: Robin Pars and Jerry Maresca. Cay Horstmann and J. Ambrose Little were particularly diligent and insightful reviewers, and I am extra grateful to them.

As I wrote this book, I realized that I was ignorant of many things. On numerous occasions, this ignorance was somewhat rectified by the many excellent articles and blogs of the following people: K. Scott Allen, Dino Esposito, Martin Fowler, Scott Guthrie, Jimmy Nilsson, Fritz Onion, Ted Pattison, Scott Mitchell, and Rick Strahl.

During this past year, I continued with my full-time teaching responsibilities. My work life was made more manageable by my two department chairs during this time, Judy Gartaganis and Bill Paterson. My stress levels during the year were thankfully often alleviated by my colleague, Paul Pospisil. I am also thankful for the support of the Mount Royal College 2005/6 Research Reserve Fund, which funded a reduction in my teaching load.

I have had many excellent students over the years. Many of my students have helped, perhaps without realizing it, in both the planning and implementation of this book, and to them I continue to be both inspired and grateful.

Finally, and most importantly, I must acknowledge the support of my family. My wife Diana and my children Alexander and Benjamin saw very little of me the past six months. In the final difficult last three months, I was always motivated by my desire to spend time with them again, as well as continually encouraged to create something worthy of their respect.

— Randy Connolly
January 2007

About the Author

Randy Connolly teaches Computer Science students at Mount Royal College in Calgary, Canada. He has been with the Computer Science and Information Systems department since 1997. He takes great pride in teaching tomorrow's talented young developers. He specializes in teaching Web application development, games development, and object-oriented design. His extensive experience and expertise in ASP.NET comes from a combination of teaching and work in the professional sector. Connolly spent more than eight years developing Web sites for international clients and more than sixteen years doing corporate software development. He has been the recipient of the Canadian Social Science and Humanities Research Council Doctoral fellowship grant and the Petro-Canada Innovation in Research and Teaching Award (1998 and 2003).

Part I

CORE ASP.NET

Chapter 1

Introducing ASP.NET 2.0

"The true beginning of our end."

—William Shakespeare, *A Midsummer Night's Dream*

The end goal of this book is to teach and guide the reader through the increasingly large topic of Web application development using ASP.NET 2.0. The true beginning of this end then is to introduce ASP.NET in a reasonably manageable fashion. This chapter begins this journey by answering the question, "Why ASP.NET?" That is, it explains why ASP.NET was developed and examines the advantages it provides. As part of the answer to this question, the chapter looks at other competing technologies as well as provides an overview of the .NET Framework. The chapter briefly introduces the nature and structure of ASP.NET, illustrates how to use Microsoft Visual Studio 2005, and then finishes with a number of tutorial walkthroughs for creating some sample ASP.NET Web Forms using Visual Studio. In sum, this first chapter is strictly introductory; in-depth coverage of how ASP.NET works is left to the next chapter.

Why ASP.NET?

Released in November 2005, ASP.NET 2.0 is the current version of ASP.NET, Microsoft's powerful technology for creating dynamic Web content. ASP.NET is one

3

of the key components of Microsoft's .NET Framework, which is both a development framework and software platform. ASP.NET 1.0 and 1.1, initially released in 2002, replaced Microsoft's older but still quite popular ASP (Active Server Pages) technology. This section provides an overview of ASP.NET. It begins by describing dynamic server technology in general, moves on to a brief examination of competing dynamic technologies, and then highlights the key features of ASP.NET.

Static Versus Dynamic Web Content

Over the past 10 years, the Internet has evolved from a hypertextual information system offering static information to a marketplace for the buying and selling of goods and services, and now to a widely used infrastructure for the development and hosting of software applications within organizations. Thus, over time, the Internet has moved from principally static page content to dynamically generated content via programs running on Web servers. That is, most Web pages that you view are not static HTML pages but are instead the output from programs that run on servers and that interact with server resources like databases and XML Web services. Figures 1.1 and 1.2 illustrate the differences between static and dynamic Web content.

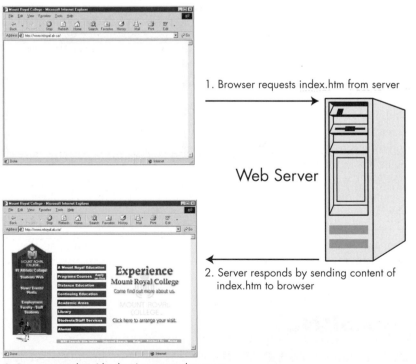

1. Browser requests index.htm from server

Web Server

2. Server responds by sending content of index.htm to browser

3. Browser renders (displays) requested content

Figure 1.1 Static Web content

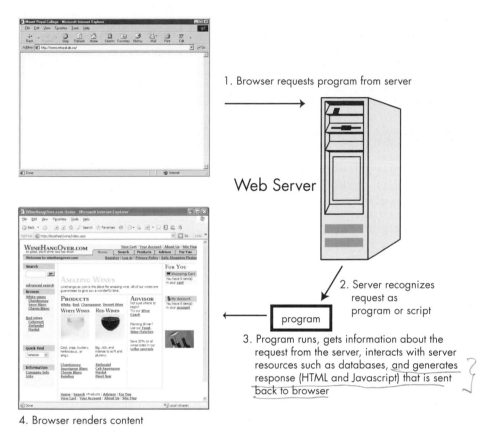

Figure 1.2   Dynamic Web content

Competing Dynamic Server Technologies

There are quite a number of different technologies for dynamically generating Web content. All of these technologies share one thing in common: Using programming logic, they generate HTML on the server and send it back to the requesting browser. Yet despite this essential similarity, we can categorize dynamic technology into three broad types:

- Direct output
- Page scripting
- Hybrid

The first technologies for generating dynamic Web content were of the ***direct output*** type. CGI and Java servlets are examples of this type. With this approach, programmers had to write the code for directly outputting each and every HTML line back to the client, as in the following Java servlet code.

```
public class HelloWorld extends HttpServlet
{
  public void doGet(HttpServletRequest request,
       HttpServletResponse response)
  {
    response.setContentType("text/html");
    PrintWriter out = response.getWriter();
    out.println("<html>");
    out.println("<head><title>Sample</title></head>");
    out.println("<body>");
    out.println("<h1>Date Tester</h1>");
    out.println("The date is ");
    java.util.Date aDate = new java.util.Date();
    out.println(aDate.ToString());
    out.println("</body>");
    out.println("</html>");
  }
}
```

The key advantage of this approach is fast execution time, because these programs could usually be compiled to binary (or byte code for the Java servlets). However, its main drawback is that any change in the design of a Web page, no matter how minor, requires the intervention of a programmer, who must make the change, recompile the code, and perhaps turn off the server to deploy.

For this reason, Web developers largely left the direct output approach behind when a new approach became available in the later 1990s with Microsoft's ASP and the open-source PHP (PHP Hypertext Preprocessor). We might call the approach used in ASP and PHP a **_page scripting_** approach. That is, each Web page is a separate ASP or PHP script file. The key to the page scripting approach is that these script files contain both regular HTML markup as well as programming logic contained within some special tag (`<% … %>` for ASP, `<?php … ?>` for PHP), as shown in the following sample ASP code.

```
<html>
<head><title>Sample</title></head>
<body>
The time is now <b><% = Time %></b><br>
<% if hour(now) < 8 then %>
     It is <i>too</i> early in the morning
<% else %>
     Good day
<% end if %>
</body>
</html>
```

Both ASP and PHP have a fairly quick learning curve and can be used to create quite complex sites. However, the page scripting approach does have a number of drawbacks. The principal of these drawbacks is that as a page (or a whole site of pages) becomes progressively more complex, the page scripting approach can become progressively harder to maintain, change, and debug. The term *spaghetti code* doesn't quite do justice to the tangled labyrinthine convolutions of a two-thousand-line-long ASP or PHP page. A complex, poorly written ASP or PHP page can be a nightmare to maintain, because it usually mixes user interface markup, presentation logic, data access logic, and business or application logic all within the same page (though one can certainly use server-side includes and other mechanisms in ASP or PHP to create more maintainable pages).

Another related drawback is that the languages used in ASP (usually VBScript) and PHP (up until the more recent PHP 5) lack modern programming features such as inheritance and structured exception handling. As well, both VBScript and PHP are interpreted scripting languages. This means that the server has to decode each line of programming code in the page for every single request. As a result, complex ASP or PHP pages with lots of programming logic that are heavily requested could be quite slow (though there are PHP compilers available that can mitigate this particular drawback).

Finally, another drawback (though to many it certainly is an advantage) to the page scripting model is its simplicity. The problem with simplicity here is that both ASP and PHP provide only a bare minimum of built-in functionality and services. This makes these technologies easy to learn; however, almost everything requires programming due to the minimal services they provide the developer. As a result, almost every common task in a dynamic Web page requires programming. The typical ASP or PHP page often has a great deal of repetitive code for common tasks such as populating an HTML `select` list with field values from a database table or for validating form input. In other words, what is lacking in the page scripting approach are simplified abstractions that encapsulate these very common Web development tasks and which would therefore reduce the amount of coding needed to create the typical dynamic Web page.

These drawbacks are addressed (though in different ways) in the most current dynamic server technology approach, which we might call the ***hybrid*** approach. Sun's JSP (JavaServer Pages) and related technologies such as JavaServer Faces and Struts, Adobe's (originally Macromedia's) ColdFusion, open-source Ruby on Rails, and Microsoft's ASP.NET combine, in varying degrees, the programming flexibility and the execution speed of the direct output approach, with the ease of the page scripting model, and add common Web programming functionality via proprietary tags. ColdFusion uses a rich tag-based language that minimizes the amount of necessary coding. JSP initially used a fairly minimal set of built-in tags, although it did provide a mechanism (custom tags) for creating new tags; instead, JSP allows a programmer to use Java to implement contemporary software design best practices to create Web sites that are more maintainable and extensible. ASP.NET also allows the developer to use contemporary software design best practices, but adds a rich set of built-in tags (plus the capability to create new ones) that encapsulate many common Web tasks.

CORE NOTE

You may wonder whether Adobe Flash is also an example of dynamic server technology. It is not. Flash objects are downloaded to the browser, and if the Flash plugin is installed, it executes *on the browser*. Although a Flash object can interact with server resources, it does not execute on the server.

ASP.NET Advantages

ASP.NET provides a number of advantages compared to Microsoft's earlier, "classic" ASP technology. These advantages are

- Better performance
- More powerful development environment
- Easier maintenance
- Smoother deployment and configuration

ASP.NET provides better performance over ASP because ASP.NET pages are compiled (the code compilation model is covered in detail later in Chapter 2). It is also a significantly more powerful development environment. It uses fully object-oriented languages that work with a rich class library along with a very complete set of server-based controls that encapsulate common Web functionality that significantly reduces the amount of coding for Web developers.

ASP.NET sites can be easier to maintain because developers can use current best practices in software design and engineering. As well, because ASP.NET handles much of the logic necessary for producing correct output for different devices (for instance, Internet Explorer, FireFox, or old Netscape browsers), it can reduce the amount of maintenance work required to test and fine-tune your pages for different output devices.

Finally, ASP.NET provides a smooth deployment experience. Due to the architecture of the .NET Framework (covered next), deploying ASP.NET applications now generally only involves uploading files. The .NET applications and components do not need to be registered with the Windows registry, so there is no more "DLL Hell." As well, ASP.NET simplifies the configuration experience by providing XML-based configuration files as well as an integrated security system.

.NET Framework

Many of the advantages that ASP.NET provides in comparison to other dynamic Web technologies are a result of its integration into Microsoft's *.NET Framework*. The

.NET Framework is a ***development framework*** that provides a new programming interface to Windows services and APIs, and integrates a number of technologies that emerged from Microsoft during the late 1990s. The .NET Framework is also a ***software platform*** for the running and deployment of Windows-based software systems (though other operating systems can in theory be targeted).

The core features of the .NET Framework are as follows:

- Language interoperability—A software system can be created using any combination of the available .NET languages. You can thus use the .NET language that you feel most comfortable and productive with (although for this book we use C# only). The .NET Framework makes this possible with a specification called the CTS (Common Type System), to which all .NET compilers must adhere.
- Fully object-oriented languages—To better compete with Java and to better reflect current software development methodologies, all .NET languages are fully object oriented.
- Common runtime engine shared by all languages—For there to be language interoperability, a common runtime engine is needed to locate and load .NET data types, as well as handle memory management, provide security sandboxing, and ensure type-safety.
- Base class library usable by all languages—The .NET Framework provides a rich and consistent set of classes for performing typical software tasks (drawing user interface widgets, interacting with data, communicating across a network, etc).
- Simplified deployment—With .NET, there is no longer any need to register components (via the registry), and thus there are fewer deployment problems in comparison to older Windows-based applications.
- Better security—.NET provides code-access security as well as a general security context via the .NET runtime environment.
- Better performance—.NET languages are compiled into an intermediary machine-independent format, which in turn is Just-In-Time (JIT) compiled into CPU-specific binary code; as such, it provides superior performance. This JIT-compiled code is also optimized for the specific processor(s) on which it is running.

CORE NOTE

In June 2006, Microsoft combined a number of new Windows development technologies and branded them as the *.NET Framework 3.0.* This .NET Framework 3.0 includes Windows CardSpace, Windows Communication Foundation (formerly Indigo), Windows Presentation Foundation (formerly Avalon), Windows Workflow Foundation (formerly

WinFx), as well the **.NET Framework 2.0**. Thus, .NET Framework 3.0 rather confusedly contains the current version of the .NET Framework, which at present is still version 2.0.

Components of .NET Framework

The .NET Framework sits on top of the Windows operating system, and consists of the three fundamental components shown in Figure 1.3.

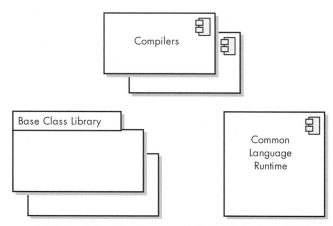

Figure 1.3   Components of the .NET Framework

Language Compilers

Initially, perhaps the most trumpeted aspect of the .NET Framework is that the various .NET languages can interoperate. **Language interoperability** means that you can use multiple .NET languages within a single .NET application. Microsoft provides Visual Basic.NET (VB.NET), C#, JScript.NET, C++, and J++. The two most popular choices are VB.NET and C#. Other .NET languages are available from third parties. Although it is certainly possible to create a .NET application using multiple languages, this does not happen all that frequently. From this author's experience, most .NET applications are written using a single language, because this generally makes an application easier to maintain and support in the long run. Language interoperability is, however, often utilized whenever a .NET application makes use of someone else's compiled class libraries. For instance, the base class library classes that are part of .NET are written in C#, but can be used just as easily by a Visual Basic .NET application as a C# application.

How is this language interoperability possible? It is possible because all .NET language must follow the rules in the **Common Language Specification** (CLS). These rules define a subset of common data types and programming constructs that all .NET languages must support (although a language can contain additional types and constructs that are not specified by the CLS). You can use any CLS-compliant language in a .NET application.

The different .NET languages can work together because they are compiled into a common format. No matter what programming language is used, all code is compiled into **Microsoft Intermediate Language** (MSIL), also called Common Intermediate Language (CIL or simply IL), rather than binary. MSIL is a CPU-independent virtual machine language analogous to Java's bytecode. It consists of CPU-independent instructions for loading/storing information and calling methods.

MSIL is not itself interpreted or executed. Instead, the Common Language Runtime (CLR, covered shortly) converts the MSIL into managed native binary code at runtime using the Just-In-Time compiler as methods are called; alternately, the entire assembly can be precompiled to native code by the runtime at install time. Figure 1.4 illustrates this process.

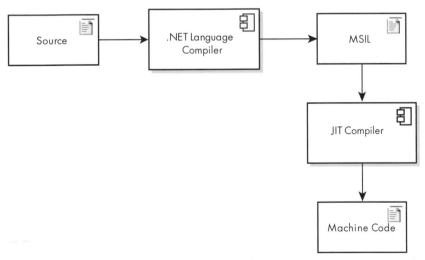

Figure 1.4 General compilation process

MSIL is physically stored within special containers called **assemblies**. Although these assemblies have familiar extensions (e.g., DLL or EXE), they are quite different from traditional Windows DLL or EXE files. A .NET assembly contains not only MSIL instructions; it also contains a collection of metadata that includes type definitions, version information, external assembly references, and other standardized information. This metadata allows different components, tools, and runtimes to work together. The CLR uses this metadata for verification, security enforcement, cross-context marshaling, memory layout, and execution. For this reason, .NET assemblies are said to contain **managed code**, in that the CLR manages the memory utilization and execution of the code.

It should be noted that .NET assemblies (which contain MSIL code) can be decompiled (using, for instance, the `ILDasm.exe` program that is installed with the Framework) and even reverse engineered. This can potentially be a problem if one has proprietary algorithms or important licensing keys that need to be hidden. If you need to protect the intellectual property contained within your source code, you may want to use an **obfuscator** (there are several that are commercially available as well as the free Dotfuscator Community Edition available within Visual Studio 2005). An obfuscator makes the process of reverse-engineering MSIL much more difficult (but not impossible because it does not do any encryption or hiding).

CORE NOTE

Even if you feel that you do not need to use an obfuscator for your applications, do remember that any assembly that is publicly available can be decompiled. Thus, avoid placing security information such as passwords, access codes, or encryption keys into your source code.

Common Language Runtime

The **Common Language Runtime** (CLR) provides a common runtime environment for the execution of code written in any of the .NET languages. It is a software-only, virtual platform that abstracts functionality from the operating system platform. Conceptually, the CLR and Java's JVM (Java Virtual Machine) are similar in that they are both runtime infrastructures that abstract the underlying platform hardware and operating system. However, although the JVM officially supports only the Java language, the CLR supports multiple languages because all .NET languages are compiled into the same MSIL format (although because the JVM executes bytecode, it could, in principle, support languages other than Java). Unlike Java's bytecode, however, MSIL is never interpreted. Another conceptual difference is that Java code runs on any platform with a JVM, whereas .NET code runs only on platforms that support the CLR, which officially at present is only Windows. There are some non-Microsoft efforts at porting the .NET Framework to other environments, such as the Mono project and DotGNU Portable .NET.

The key components of the CLR are as follows.

- A type system that locates, loads, and manages the .NET types and operations found in its programming languages
- A metadata system for persisting and organizing compiled code into a common format called *assemblies*

- An execution system that loads assemblies, performs Just-In-Time compilation, runs programs, performs security checks, and manages garbage collection

.NET Framework Base Class Library

The .NET Framework **Base Class Library** (BCL) provides a rich but standard set of CLS-compliant classes that developers can use in their applications. This library includes classes for working with the base types and exceptions, representing common data structures and collections, performing data access, and constructing Windows and Web interfaces. These classes are hierarchically organized into *logical* containers called **namespaces** (see Figure 1.5). These namespaces are somewhat analogous to Java packages, except that .NET namespaces, unlike Java packages, are not also *physical* containers. Compiled .NET code (i.e., MSIL) is physically stored in assemblies; an assembly can contain classes in multiple namespaces, or classes within a namespace can be physically partitioned across multiple assemblies.

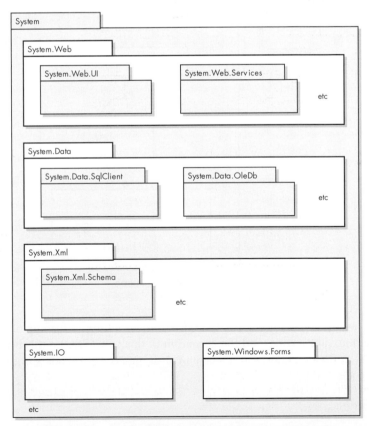

Figure 1.5 Partial .NET Framework class library hierarchy

.NET Execution

As mentioned in the previous section, .NET programs written in a CLS-compliant language are compiled by the appropriate language compiler into MSIL and then persisted into one or more assemblies. These programs may make use of other classes, written by other developers, or provided as part of the .NET Framework itself in the BCL. The CLR is involved in the execution of the MSIL-based programs, as shown in Figure 1.6.

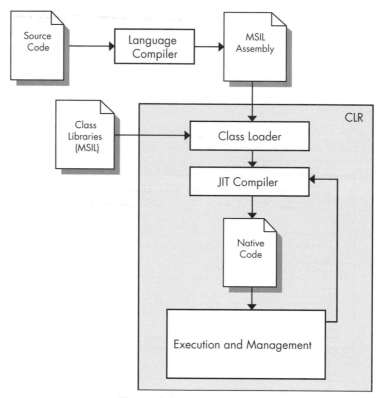

Figure 1.6   .NET execution

As can be seen from Figure 1.6, the CLR is involved in the loading of MSIL, its translation into native code, and the execution of this code. Due to this involvement of the CLR in the execution and management of memory, this code is referred to as managed code.

CORE NOTE

It should be remembered that the .NET Framework runs on a host OS (for now, Windows only). Thus, there must be some interface with the Windows mechanism for program loading and execution. The Windows DLL (not a .NET assembly DLL) `mscorwks.dll` loads the DLLs that actually constitute the CLR: `mscoree.dll` (the execution engine) and `mscorjit.dll` (JIT compiler).

There is certainly much more to learn about the .NET and ASP.NET execution process. This material is covered in Chapter 2. Instead, let us move on and introduce ASP.NET itself.

ASP.NET Web Forms

An ASP.NET Web application consists of a number of Web pages, controls, programming classes, and services running within a single Web server application directory (and any subdirectories within it). The heart (and bones and muscles) of a Web application are its Web pages. These are text files with an `.aspx` extension and are referred to as **Web Forms**. A Web Form consists of two parts.

- The declaratively defined (that is, by markup/tags) visual elements. This consists of both HTML and ASP.NET controls.
- The form's programming logic.

ASP.NET allows the programming logic to exist within either

- The same file as the visual elements.
  This code is contained within a **code declaration block** (i.e., within `<script runat="server">`...`</script>` tags) embedded within the Web Form.
- A separate, fully defined class file.
  This file is usually called a **code-behind file**, although some refer to it as a code-separation file, a code-beside file, or simply a code file.

Listing 1.1 contains the obligatory Hello World example using an embedded code declaration block. The content that is specific to ASP.NET has been emphasized by using a **bold** monospaced font in the listing. Figure 1.7 illustrates how the result will look in the browser.

Listing 1.1   HelloWorldEmbedded.aspx

```
<%@ Page Language="C#" %>

<!DOCTYPE html PUBLIC "-//W3C//DTD XHTML 1.0 Transitional//EN"
   "http://www.w3.org/TR/xhtml1/DTD/xhtml1-transitional.dtd">

<script runat="server">
   protected void Page_Load(object sender, EventArgs e)
   {
      myDate.Text = DateTime.Now.ToShortDateString();
   }
</script>

<html xmlns="http://www.w3.org/1999/xhtml" >
<head>
    <title>Hello World Embedded</title>
</head>
<body>
   <form id="form1" runat="server">
   <h1>Hello World</h1>
   The date is <em>
   <asp:Label ID="myDate" runat="server"></asp:Label>
   </em>
   </form>
</body>
</html>
```

Figure 1.7   HelloWorldEmbedded.aspx in the browser

CORE NOTE

All code examples in the book can be downloaded from my Web site,
http://www.randyconnolly.com/core.

The example in Listing 1.1 begins with the `Page` directive, which is used to define page-specific instructions used by the ASP.NET environment. ***Directives*** are processing instructions for the parser and compilers (these will be covered in more detail in Chapter 2) when they process an ASP.NET page. Although directives can be located anywhere in an `.aspx` file, the standard practice is to place them at the beginning of the file. Directive statements are not case sensitive and quotation marks are not required around the attribute values. In this example, the only attribute in the page directive is to specify which programming language will be used in any of the page's scripting blocks. The default value is `VB`, although this can be changed via the compilation element in the `Web.config` file (covered later in the chapter). Some other possible values are `C#`, `C++`, `VJ#`, and `JScript`.

Notice that the `<script>` element contains a `runat="server"` attribute. This tells the ASP.NET environment that the code within the block is to be executed on the server (i.e., it is not client-side Javascript or VBScript). The language within this script block is C#. The code itself declares a page-level event handler method that sets the `Text` property of a control named `myDate` to a short version of the current date.

In this example's HTML, you should notice an element named `<asp:Label>`. This is a predefined ASP.NET ***Web server control***. We will be discussing server controls in a bit more detail later this chapter. At any rate, the markup for this `Label` control sets its `ID` property to the value `myDate`. As well, it must contain the `runat="server"` attribute; if not, the ASP.NET environment simply passes on the markup to the browser, where it is ignored. This markup is essentially the equivalent to the declaration and instantiation of a variable named `myDate` of the type `Label`. That is, consider the following *markup*:

```
<asp:Label ID="labDate" runat="server"></asp:Label>
```

This markup is equivalent to the following *programming*:

```
Label labDate = new Label();
```

Notice as well that the markup for this `Label` control has a matching end tag. ASP.NET server controls follow XML syntax in that all tags must have an end tag. You can combine the begin and end tags together in a single element as in XML by adding a / at the end of the start tag, as shown in the following.

```
<asp:Label ID="labDate" runat="server" />
```

The other important thing to notice in this listing is the `runat="server"` attribute in the `<form>` element. All ASP.NET pages *must* contain a form element that contains this `runat` attribute. All body content in a Web Form should appear within this special `<form>` element. Visual Studio also adds a `runat="server"` attribute to the `<head>` element as well, although this is not strictly necessary for an ASP.NET page.

CORE NOTE

The example code in Listing 1.1 contains an XHTML DOCTYPE, which specifies that the HTML that is generated from this ASP.NET page will be compliant with that defined by the XHTML 1.0 Transitional DTD. The transitional DTD allows the use of legacy HTML elements and attributes (such as font and iframe) that have been officially removed from XHTML. You can also change the DOCTYPE to xhtml1-strict.dtd or xhtml11.dtd.

Changing the DOCTYPE may affect how the browser renders the document. When Internet Explorer encounters a document that contains a valid XHTML DOCTYPE, it renders it in Standards mode. This means that it uses the standard CSS box model. If the page does not contain a valid DOCTYPE, IE renders it in Quirks mode, meaning that it will use the IE 5.0 CSS box model.

When Mozilla Firefox opens a document with a DOCTYPE that specifies the transitional.dtd, it renders using Almost Standards mode and uses Standards mode for documents using the xhtml1.dtd or xhtml11.dtd. The point worth noting here is that adding the DOCTYPE helps ensure that the different browsers render your pages in a more consistent way. Visual Studio can also flag elements in your page that do not fit the specified DOCTYPE.

Listings 1.2 and 1.3 illustrate the same functional example as the previous listing, but this time there are two separate files: the Web Form and its code-behind file.

Listing 1.2 HelloWorldCodeBehind.aspx

```
<%@ Page Language="C#" AutoEventWireup="true"
    CodeFile="HelloWorldCodeBehind.aspx.cs"
    Inherits="HelloWorldCodeBehind" %>

<!DOCTYPE html PUBLIC "-//W3C//DTD XHTML 1.0 Transitional//EN"
    "http://www.w3.org/TR/xhtml1/DTD/xhtml1-transitional.dtd">

<html xmlns="http://www.w3.org/1999/xhtml" >
<head>
    <title>Hello World Code-Behind</title>
</head>
<body>
    <form id="form1" runat="server">
    <h1>Hello World</h1>
```

```
    The date is <em>
    <asp:Label ID="myDate" runat="server"></asp:Label>
    </em>
    </form>
</body>
</html>
```

Listing 1.3   HelloWorldCodeBehind.aspx.cs

```
using System;
using System.Data;
using System.Configuration;
using System.Collections;
using System.Web;
using System.Web.Security;
using System.Web.UI;
using System.Web.UI.WebControls;
using System.Web.UI.WebControls.WebParts;
using System.Web.UI.HtmlControls;

public partial class HelloWorldCodeBehind : System.Web.UI.Page
{
    protected void Page_Load(object sender, EventArgs e)
    {
        myDate.Text = DateTime.Now.Date.ToString();
    }
}
```

There are several things worth noting about these two listings. First, there is no longer any programming in the .aspx page. It has been replaced by two new attribute references in the Page directive. The CodeFile attribute specifies the path to the code-behind file for the page. This attribute is used together with the Inherits attribute, which specifies the name of the class in the code-behind file.

CORE NOTE

The AutoEventWireup="true" attribute in Listing 1.2 is in fact optional, because the default for ASP.NET is true. If this attribute is set to false, the page must programmatically hook page events to their event handlers; when set to true, the page's events are automatically wired to methods that follow the Page_ naming convention (e.g., the event handler for the Load event is Page_Load, whereas the event handler for the Init event is Page_Init). Thus, with auto-wiring, all you need to do is create a method with the appropriate name (e.g., `Page_Load`) and you do not need worry about binding the event and the method together.

The second thing worth noting is that the code-behind file in Listing 1.3 is a complete (actually *partially* complete, but more on that later) C# class that inherits from the `Page` class. Because it is a class, it contains various `using` statements to reference the various standard .NET namespaces (most of which are in fact unnecessary for this simple example). Although the code-behind class can be given any name, it is a convention to use the same name as the page's filename. Similarly, the code-behind file can have any filename, but the convention is to name the file the same as its Web Form, but with an extra `.cs` (for C#) or `.vb` (for Visual Basic) extension.

At first glance, the advantages of using a code-behind file might not be that apparent. It certainly appears to require more typing! However, the typing difference between the two is not really an issue, because all but one line of the code in Listing 1.3 was created by Visual Studio. The real advantage of separating the code into its own file is that it may lead to more maintainable Web Forms. Earlier in this chapter, we discussed the main drawback of the page scripting model used by, for instance, classic ASP. You may recall that this drawback is the difficulty in maintaining these pages due to the intertwining of presentation (HTML) and programming logic in the same file. One of the main benefits of ASP.NET is that a page's programming logic can be *conceptually* separated from the presentation; by using a code-behind file, a page's programming logic can also be *physically* separated from the presentation/markup.

By placing the programming code into its own file, it is also potentially easier to make use of a division of labor in the creation of the site. For instance, the graphic design team can work on the layout of a page while the programmers can modify the code for the page, because the two pages can be edited separately (although it should be noted that this can be tricky due to the close coupling between the two files).

Although ASP.NET has always supported both the embedded code model and the code-behind model, versions of Visual Studio prior to Visual Studio 2005 only supported the code-behind model. Visual Studio 2005 now supports both the embedded and the code-behind models. When you create a new Web Form in Visual Studio 2005, you can specify whether you want to use a code-behind file by toggling the Place Code in Separate File check box in the Add New Item dialog box (see Figure 1.8).

Ultimately, choosing between the embedded model and the code-behind model is now mainly a matter of developer preference. This book uses the code-behind model partly due to this author's preference (you can insert a saying about leopards and spots here), and partly because it is easier to explain and describe an example by physically separating the code from the markup.

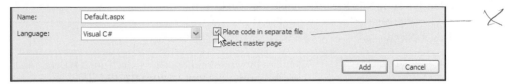

Figure 1.8 Specifying a code separation file in Visual Studio

C# Language

As mentioned previously, ASP.NET applications can be created with any CLS-compliant .NET language. This book uses C#, but you could use VB.NET because the differences between the two languages are mainly just syntax.

For instance, the Visual Basic equivalent for the code in Listing 1.3 is similar to that shown in the following.

```
Partial Class HelloWorldEmbedded
    Inherits System.Web.UI.Page

    Protected Sub Page_Load(ByVal sender As Object,
            ByVal e As System.EventArgs) Handles MyBase.Load

        labDate.Text = DateTime.Now.ToShortDateString()

    End Sub
End Class
```

Visual Basic versions of all the code examples in the book are available from my Web site at http://www.randyconnolly.com/core. You can also download an additional electronic appendix from this site that contains a C# language tutorial and briefly lists the syntax differences between C# and Visual Basic.

Web Application Structure

An ASP.NET Web application can consist simply of a folder containing Web Forms and other files. You can, however, add any number of nested subfolders within this root folder. ASP.NET in fact has a number of reserved application folder names, which are listed in Table 1.1.

Besides Web Forms and other common Web files (such as .gif, .jpg, .js, and .css files), ASP.NET supports a number of other file types, the most notable of which are listed in Table 1.2.

Table 1.1   ASP.NET Reserved Application Folders

Folder Name	Description
App_Browsers	Contains browser definition files (which are XML-based files with the .browser extension) used by this application for identifying and determining the capabilities of browsers. Normally, most applications can simply rely on the global browser definition files instead.
App_Code	Contains any non-code-behind class files to be used by the application. These can be business objects, utility classes, data access objects, and so on, as well as XML schema and Web services definition files. ASP.NET dynamically compiles any classes contained in this folder. Classes contained in this folder are automatically referenced in the application.
App_Data	Contains application data files, such as SQL Server Express data, Microsoft Access files, or XML data.
App_GlobalResources	Contains resource files that are available globally throughout the application. Resource files are typically used for localizing an application for multiple languages or cultures. Resources are covered in Chapter 16.
App_LocalResources	Contains resource files that are associated with a specific page or control.
App_Themes	Contains files that define the appearance of pages and controls in the site. Themes are covered in Chapter 6.
App_WebReferences	Contains files used to define references to external Web services. Web services are covered in Chapter 15.
Bin	Contains compiled .NET assemblies (.DLL files). Any classes contained in these assemblies are automatically referenced in the application. Typically used to house assemblies from external sources or Visual Studio projects that are not part of the Web site project.

Table 1.2   Notable ASP.NET File Types

Extension	Description
.asax	The Global.asax file defines application-level event handlers.
.ascx	Defines a user control (covered in Chapter 6). User controls are used to encapsulate a block of reusable user interface functionality.

Table 1.2   Notable ASP.NET File Types *(continued)*

Extension	Description
.ashx	Defines a custom HTTP handler (discussed in Chapter 2). Handlers are used to implement custom response functionality based on the extension of the request.
.asmx	Defines an XML Web service (covered in Chapter 15).
.aspx	Defines a Web Form.
.axd	Special handlers used to manage Web site administration requests.
.config	An XML-based configuration file (named Web.config) for an application or for the machine itself (machine.config).
.master	Defines a master page that specifies the common layout for other Web Forms. Master pages are covered in Chapter 6.
.resx	Resource file containing resource strings used for localization (covered in Chapter 16).
.sitemap	Defines the navigation structure of the site. These site map files are covered in Chapter 7.
.skin	Defines the visual property settings to be applied to controls in a site's theme. Skin files are covered in Chapter 6.

You will be encountering most of these different file types as you progress through the book. However, there is one file mentioned in Table 1.2 that we should discuss now: the Web.config file. This file is a special XML file that is used to configure the Web application itself. Each folder in the application can also contain its own Web.config file. As well, there is a single machine.config file in the .NET Framework installation folder that defines configuration settings that apply to the entire computer.

Some of the settings that can be configured in the Web.config file include the security settings for the application, additional HTTP handlers, connection strings to databases, and configurations for various ASP.NET services such as session state, Web parts, and the site map system. As you progress through the book, you will encounter many of the possible configuration changes that can be made via the Web.config file.

Now that we have introduced the basics of ASP.NET, we can turn to Visual Studio 2005, a powerful, but not essential, tool for creating ASP.NET applications.

Visual Studio 2005

You can create an ASP.NET site using Notepad (or any other simple text editor) and perhaps some of the command-line tools that come with the .NET Framework. However, Visual Studio does provide several advantages for the ASP.NET developer. These advantages include a drag-and-drop designer, syntax checking, integrated compilation and debugging, various facilities for managing the files in the Web application, and the capability to test your Web applications without IIS via the Visual Studio Web Server.

All the exercises in this book make use of Visual Studio 2005 as the IDE (Integrated Development Environment). You can also use Microsoft's Visual Web Developer 2005 Express Edition, a free, slightly simpler version of Visual Studio 2005 that can only be used for creating and editing Web applications. (Visual Studio 2005 in contrast can also be used to create Windows applications, class libraries, and many other code projects.) You can download Visual Web Developer 2005 Express Edition from `http://www.asp.net/downloads`.

It is important to note that Visual Studio does not create a different kind or type of Web application than one created with a simple text editor. The end result from both is an ASP.NET Web application, as shown in Figure 1.9.

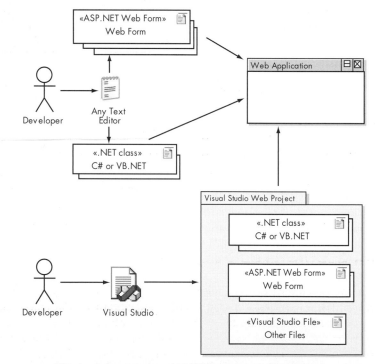

Figure 1.9   Creating ASP.NET pages with Visual Studio

One advantage of using Visual Studio 2005 is that you can always have the ability to create and test an ASP.NET Web application on your computer. If you do not have Visual Studio, you can only test your application on your computer if your machine has Internet Information Services (IIS, which is covered shortly) installed.

With Visual Studio 2005, we could say that your computer is a *development server* (available only to yourself). Alternately, you might upload your work to a *staging server* running IIS for team testing. Of course, if you want others to see this Web application, it must eventually be uploaded to a *production server* (available to your Web application's audience). Figure 1.10 illustrates the relationship between the development team, the eventual Web audience for the Web application, and their servers.

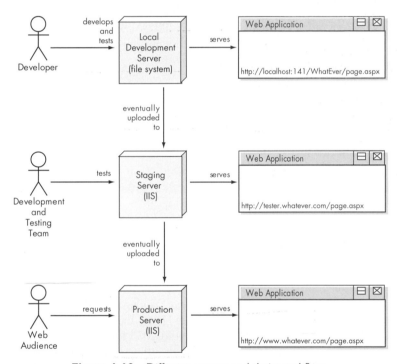

Figure 1.10 Different servers and their workflow

Visual Studio Web Projects

All files, folders, and settings in a Web application created with Visual Studio are contained within conceptual containers called *solutions* and *projects*. Depending upon which way you use Visual Studio to construct your Web application, a solution may contain one or more additional projects as well as additional files and metadata about the project. Visual Studio provides two ways of constructing a Web application with projects.

1. Web site project—This approach uses the content and structure of the site's folder to define the contents of the Visual Studio project. There is no Visual Studio project file; instead, the content of the **Web site project** is directly inferred by Visual Studio from the folder structure and its contents. This approach is new to Visual Studio 2005 and generally is the easiest to use when starting a Web site from scratch and will be used throughout this book.

2. Web application project—Rather than use the file structure of the site, this approach uses a separate Visual Studio project file (with `.csproj` or `.vbproj` extension) to maintain a list of files that belong to the project. An ASP.NET application can even be split across multiple Visual Studio projects. This was the approach used by Visual Studio 2003 and is often the preferred choice when migrating existing Visual Studio 2003 Web projects to Visual Studio 2005. Note: Visual Studio 2005 does not currently come with the Web application project. It must be downloaded (`http://msdn.microsoft.com/asp.net/reference/infrastructure/wap`) and installed separately.

For both of these approaches, Visual Studio saves information about the application as a whole in two files: a solution definition file (`.sln`) and a solution user options file (`.suo`). Unfortunately, these two files are not by default saved in the same location as the rest of the Web site. Instead, Visual Studio saves these files in the Visual Studio Projects folder within `My Documents` (e.g., `C:\Documents and Settings\Randy\My Documents\Visual Studio\Projects`).

Web Server Options

To test or run ASP.NET Web applications, Web server software is necessary. Prior to Visual Studio 2005, you needed to have access to a computer that was running Microsoft's production Web server software, Internet Information Services (IIS). To run IIS, your computer's operating system *must* be Windows 2000, Windows XP Professional (not XP Home), Windows Vista (not Vista Home Basic), or Windows Server 2003.

One of the advantages of using Visual Studio 2005 for ASP.NET development is that your site can be run and tested with or without using IIS. It supports a variety of configurations: local IIS, file system, FTP, and remote IIS sites (see Figure 1.11).

File System Web Sites

If you cannot or do not want to use IIS locally as your Web server, you can now test your ASP.NET pages as a file system Web site if you are using Visual Studio 2005. In a file system Web site, you can create and edit files in any folder you like, whether on your local computer or in a folder on another computer that you access via network share, by using the Visual Studio 2005 Web server. The Visual Studio Web server can

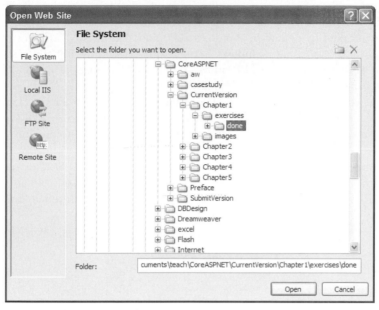

Figure 1.11 Opening a Web project in Visual Studio

run locally on all current versions of Windows, including Windows XP Home. The Visual Studio Web server accepts only localhost requests. It cannot serve pages to another computer, and is therefore suitable only for testing pages locally.

If you create a file system Web site, you can create an IIS virtual directory (covered shortly) later that points to the same file system folder.

CORE NOTE

There are some important differences between the Visual Studio Web server and IIS. One of these differences is the security context in which the respective servers execute the ASP.NET pages. This difference can affect testing because of differences in how the pages run. As a result, if you use the Virtual Studio Web server to test a site, it should also be tested again using IIS.

Local IIS Web Sites

Internet Information Services (IIS) is Microsoft's production Web server software. IIS includes not only a Web server, but also an FTP server, and an SMTP virtual e-mail server. To run IIS, your computer's operating system must be Windows 2000, XP Professional (not XP Home), Vista (not Vista Home Basic), or Server 2003.

IIS is installed by default in Windows 2000 and Windows NT. However, in Windows XP Professional and Windows Server 2003, IIS is not initially installed, but must be added using the Add/Remove Windows Components option of Add or Remove Programs in the Control Panel.

If your computer has Microsoft's IIS installed, you can run a local IIS Web site. When you create a local IIS Web site, the pages and folders for your site are typically (but not necessarily) stored in a folder under the default IIS folder for Web sites, which is `c:\Inetpub\wwwroot`.

There are two ways of using a local IIS Web site with Visual Studio. You can run the Internet Information Services snap-in from the Windows Control Panel and create an IIS *virtual directory*, which is like a pointer that references the physical folder for your Web site, as shown in Figure 1.12.

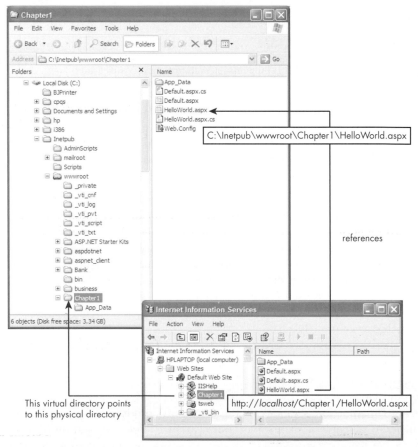

Figure 1.12   Virtual directories versus physical directories

Alternatively, you can let Visual Studio create the IIS virtual directory. In that case, the pages and folders for your Web site can be in any accessible folder and a virtual directory in your local copy of IIS points to the physical folder location.

There are reasons, however, for not using IIS to create your Web site. If your operating system does not support IIS (i.e., Windows XP Home), of course, you cannot use it. You also may decide not to use IIS for security reasons because running IIS requires extra vigilance with security upgrades. As well, corporate or school policy may not allow you to install IIS on your computer.

CORE NOTE

To create a local IIS Web site, you also need administrator privileges on your computer.

FTP Web Sites

Visual Studio allows you to directly open and edit Web sites that are available on an FTP server. This may be a useful approach if your Web site is located on a third-party hosting site and you want to modify files on its server directly within Visual Studio. If you have read and write privileges to your site via FTP, Visual Studio can create, modify, and test pages directly on the server. As an alternative to using an FTP Web site, you can develop your site as a local file system Web site and then FTP the site using Visual Studio's Copy Web Site option (Chapter 16 has more details on possible options for deploying your Web applications).

Remote IIS Web Sites

A remote IIS Web site is a site that uses IIS but is on another computer that you can access over a network. The remote computer must have IIS installed and be configured with FrontPage 2002 Server Extensions from Microsoft. When you create a remote Web site, the pages and folders for your site are stored under the default IIS folder on the remote computer. When you run the pages, they are served using IIS on the remote computer.

Tutorial: Creating ASP.NET Web Forms

In this the final section of the chapter, you will learn how to create a few simple ASP.NET pages using Visual Studio 2005. Although the basics of Visual Studio are covered, neither this section nor this book is intended to comprehensively teach Visual Studio 2005. Rather, the intent of this section is to illustrate how one can create a few simple ASP.NET pages using Visual Studio and to describe how these pages work.

Creating a Web Site in Visual Studio

As previously mentioned, Visual Studio provides two ways to work with a Web application: using a Web site project or using a Web application project. In this section, we will be using the Web site project approach. With this approach, we can create a brand new site using the File →New Web Site menu option, or open an existing Web site using the File →Open Web Site menu option. With both options, you can create or open a file system site, a local or remote IIS site, or an FTP site. Walkthrough 1.1 demonstrates how to create a new file system Web site.

Walkthrough 1.1   *Creating a New Web Site in Visual Studio 2005*

1. Use the File →New Web Site menu option.

    This displays the New Web Site dialog (see Figure 1.13). Visual Studio comes with its own templates; you can also create or download your own templates (the ones visible in the My Templates area of the dialog were downloaded from `http://msdn.microsoft.com/asp.net/ reference/design/templates`).

2. Choose the ASP.NET Web Site template.

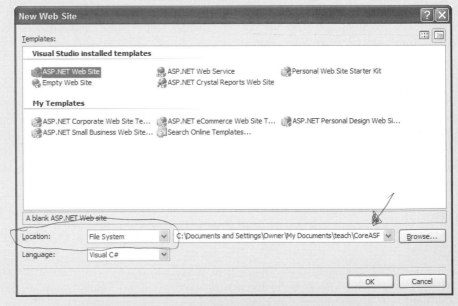

Figure 1.13   New Web Site dialog in Visual Studio 2005

You may be curious as to what is the difference between the `ASP.NET Web Site` and the `Empty Web Site` templates. The `Empty` template is as advertised: It simply creates a folder and leaves the folder completely empty. The `ASP.NET Web Site` template is also fairly minimal. It creates a folder as well, but also creates an empty `App_Data` folder as well as a single Web Form named `Default.aspx` (along with its code-behind file, `Default.aspx.cs`).

3. Be sure the Location drop-down box is set to File System, and the Language is Visual C# (see Figure 1.13).

4. Browse to the location where you want to create your Web site. You can create your site anywhere on your file system, including network drives.

5. Change the name of the project to `Chapter1`. The name of your Web site shows up at the end of the file system path. Visual Studio creates a folder with this name after you click the OK button.

6. Click the OK button. Visual Studio now creates a Web project container. This is visible on the right side of the screen in the Solution Explorer window (see Figure 1.14). All the content in your Web project is visible in this window. You can use it to open, rename, and delete files in your Web project.

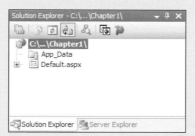

Figure 1.14 Visual Studio Solution Explorer

Adding a New Web Form

After you have created your Web project in Visual Studio, you are now ready to start adding Web content to the project (see Walkthrough 1.2). There are many different types of content that can be added to a Web project in Visual Studio (see Figure 1.15). Initially, the only content you will add to your Web project is ASP.NET Web pages, which you may recall are called ASP.NET Web Forms.

Walkthrough 1.2   *Adding a Web Form to a Web Project*

1. Use the Website → Add New Item menu option (or right-click the `WebSite1` project container in the Solution Explorer and choose the Add New Item menu option from the context menu). This displays the Add New Item dialog box shown in Figure 1.15.

2. Choose the Web Form template and change the name to `HelloWorld.aspx`.

3. Be sure that the Place Code in the Separate File option is checked. This ensures that Visual Studio creates a code-behind file as well. As well, be sure that the language is set to Visual C#.

4. Click the Add button. Visual Studio creates the `HelloWorld.aspx` and the `HelloWorld.aspx.cs` files.

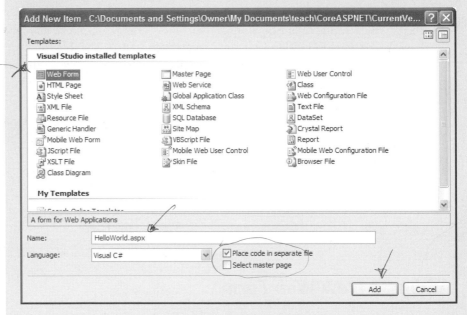

Figure 1.15   Web project content types

Adding HTML Content to a Web Form

Now that your page has been created, you can start to add content to it. There are two ways of adding HTML content to your Web Form in Visual Studio. You can add the text and tags directly in Source view (see Figure 1.16) or in the word processor-like WYSIWYG Design view (see Figure 1.17). Design view lets you visually design Web documents without having to worry about the markup. Of course, you are free to use whichever view you prefer. This book mostly uses Source view because it is generally easier and more concise to explain something in ASP.NET by referencing the markup itself. In Walkthrough 1.3, however, we will illustrate how to work with both Source and Design views.

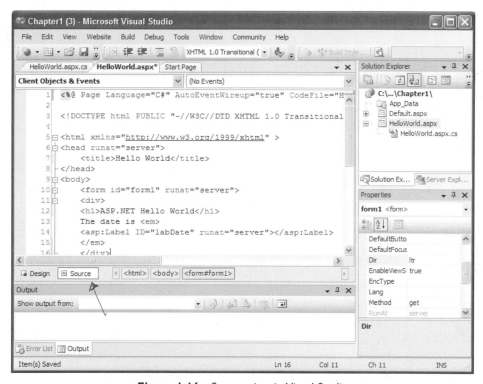

Figure 1.16   Source view in Visual Studio

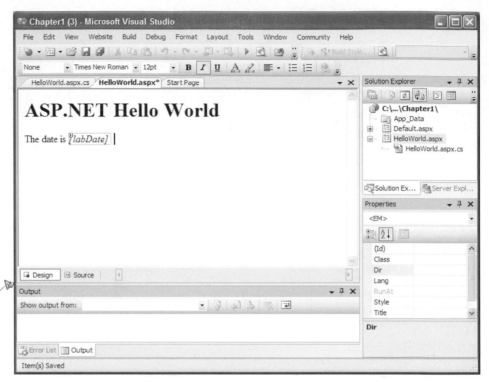

Figure 1.17 Design view in Visual Studio

Walkthrough 1.3 *Adding Markup Content to a Web Form*

1. Click the blank line between the two `<div>` tags.

2. Type in the following:

```
<h1>ASP.NET Hello World</h1>
The date is
<asp:Label ID="labDate" Runat="server" ></asp:Label>
```

As you type the third line, Visual Studio displays an Intellisense drop-down list (see Figure 1.18). You can select an item from the list by pressing the spacebar or Enter key. This line adds an ASP.NET `Label` Web server control, which is described in more detail later in the chapter.

CORE NOTE

Although ASP.NET server controls use the syntax of XML, which is
case-sensitive, Web server control syntax is not case-sensitive.

Figure 1.18   Visual Studio Intellisense

3. Click the Design tab at the bottom of the document window to switch to
Design view. Notice that the label control shows up in brackets along
with its ID in Design view. To see the result of any ASP.NET Web server
control, we must preview the page in a Web browser.

4. If the Toolbox window is not visible (it is generally on the left side of the
window), use the View →Toolbox menu option.

5. From the Standard set, drag the Label option from the toolbox and drop
in the form (see Figure 1.19). This adds a Label control to your form.

Figure 1.19   Toolbox window

CORE NOTE

You can also add a control to your form by double-clicking the control in
the toolbox.

6. Select the `Label` just added to the form by clicking it.

7. In the Properties window, change the `Id` to `labJunk` (see Figure 1.20).

Figure 1.20   Properties window

8. Click the Source tab at the bottom of the document window to switch back to Source view.

9. Click somewhere within the markup for the `Label` control. Notice that you can also use the Properties window within Source view as well.

10. Delete the markup for the `labJunk` label.

11. Switch to Design view, then back to Source view. Notice that the deleted `Label` is also not visible in the designer.

12. Use the File → Save HelloWorld.aspx menu command (or use `Ctrl+S`).

If you do not explicitly save your work, Visual Studio asks if you want to save your work when you attempt to view it.

Viewing a Web Form

Visual Studio's designer gives you a preview of what your Web page will look like after it is in the browser; but to truly test your Web Forms, you must view them in a Web browser. Visual Studio provides three quick methods for testing your Web pages.

- View in Browser—This views the specified page in a browser window.
- Start without Debugging (`Ctrl+F5`)—This views the current page in a browser, but invokes an explicit build (compile) step.

- Start with Debugging (F5)—This views the current page in an external browser with Visual Studio debugging enabled.

Walkthrough 1.4 demonstrates the first two approaches for test viewing your Web Form. Debugging will be covered a bit later in the chapter.

Walkthrough 1.4   *Test Viewing a Web Form*

1. In the Solution Explorer, right-click `HelloWorld.aspx` and select the View in Browser menu command. This command executes the Web page and displays the resulting HTML in your default Web browser (see Figure 1.21).

Figure 1.21   HelloWorld.aspx in Web browser

Notice that the `Label` Web server control does not appear in the browser. You programmatically fill it in the next walkthrough.

CORE NOTE

If you are using Internet Explorer 7, you may get a message in the browser about intranet settings. To prevent this message from always appearing, you can click the message and choose the Don't Show Me This Again option, as shown in Figure 1.22.

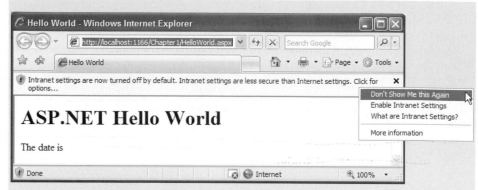

Figure 1.22   Disabling intranet warning in IE 7

2. In the browser, view the source (in Internet Explorer, use the View Source menu command). It should look similar to the following.

```
<!DOCTYPE html PUBLIC "-//W3C//DTD XHTML 1.0
   Transitional//EN"
   "http://www.w3.org/TR/xhtml1/DTD/xhtml1-transitional.dtd">

<html xmlns="http://www.w3.org/1999/xhtml" >
<head><title>Untitled Page</title></head>
<body>
   <form name="form1" method="post" action="HelloWorld.aspx"
     id="form1">
   <div>
   <input type="hidden" name="__VIEWSTATE" id="__VIEWSTATE"
     value="/wEPDwUJODExMDE5NzY5D2QWAgIDD2QWAgIBDw8WAh4EVG
     V4dAUKMDgvMDEvMjAwNmRkZDZPhFHJER4chf3nmlgfL+uq4W58" />
   </div>

   <div>
   <h1>ASP.NET Hello World</h1>
   The date is
   <span id="labDate"></span>
   </div>
   </form>
</body>
</html>
```

Notice that the Label control does not appear in the HTML sent to the browser; instead, it has been rendered as `<span id="labDate"> </span>`. As well, notice that a hidden `<input>` tag named "`__VIEWSTATE`" with a very long value attribute has been added. The meaning of this viewstate will be described in Chapter 2.

CORE NOTE

Web server controls in ASP.NET 2.0 now generally generate XHTML 1.1 compliant markup. The only controls that can generate non-XHTML 1.1 compliant markup are those that use a `Target` property (e.g., `AdRotator`, `BulletedList`, `HyperLink`).

3. Close the Web browser.

4. Switch back to Visual Studio.

5. Use the Debug → Start Without Debugging menu command (or press **Ctrl+F5**). This accomplishes the same thing as the View in Browser menu command.

6. Right-click the `HelloWorld.aspx` file in the Solution Explorer and choose the Browse With ... option. This displays the Browse With dialog (see Figure 1.23) that allows you to view the page with a different browser. If you want, you can add browsers via the Add button.

Figure 1.23   Choosing a different browser

Adding Programming Logic

Earlier in the chapter, you learned that there are two different approaches for managing the visible elements (also called the markup) and the programming code in an ASP.NET Web Form. In one approach, the markup and code are kept together in the same file; the code in this case is contained within an embedded code declaration block using the `<script runat="server">` element. In the other approach, the markup is in one file and the code is in another file (the code-behind file).

Code Render Blocks

You can add code to your markup regardless of whether you are using a code-behind file. ASP.NET allows you to add code via **_code render blocks._** A code render block is used to define self-contained lines of code within your markup, using the following syntax:

```
<% inline code here %>
```

The inline code uses the language defined by the `Page` declaration at the top of the Web Form. An example C# code render block might look like the following.

```
<%
    DateTime theDate = DateTime.Now;
    Response.Write( theDate.ToShortDateString() );
%>
```

This particular code render block outputs the current date as a short date (e.g., 05/12/2007) to the response stream (i.e., it would show up in the browser).

A code render block can also include **_inline expressions_**, which are shortcuts for calling the `Write` method of the `Response` object. The syntax for an inline expression is

```
<%= inline expression %>
```

The previous example could be replaced by the following inline expression.

```
<%= DateTime.Now.ToShortDateString() %>
```

Although the use of code render blocks is familiar to ASP programmers, *their use is very much discouraged in ASP.NET*. In the vast majority of cases, we can replace code render blocks with a combination of server controls and programming within either code declaration blocks or within the page's code-behind file.

You can also add **_server-side comments_** to add comments to your markup. They are called server-side comments because they are not sent back to the browser. The syntax for a server-side comment is

```
<%-- Server-side comment here --%>
```

CORE NOTE

Server-side comments are never sent back to the browser. In contrast, client-side comments, such as the following, are sent to the browser.

```
<!-- Client-side comment here -->
```

Using Server Controls

Normal HTML elements such as `<input>`, `<h1>`, and `<select>` are not processed by the server but are sent to and displayed by the browser. Server controls, in contrast, are tags that are processed by the server. Each ASP.NET server control has an object model containing properties, methods, and events. You can use this object model to programmatically interact with the control.

Server controls are added to a Web Forms page in the same way as any HTML element. That is, you can type the markup code in Source view, or use drag-and-drop from Design view. As well, you can also programmatically add controls at runtime (although we won't be doing this until later in the book). The two possible syntaxes for declaring a server control in your markup are:

```
<tagprefix:tagname ID="aName" runat="server" />
```

```
<tagprefix:tagname ID="aName" runat="server" >
</tagprefix:tagname>
```

ASP.NET 2.0 defines over 60 built-in Web server controls, all of which have a tag prefix of `asp`. For instance, in the example from Walkthrough 1.3, we added a `Label` Web server control that had the following declaration.

```
<asp:Label ID="labDate" Runat="server" ></asp:Label>
```

Much of this book is devoted to explaining and demonstrating these built-in Web server controls. Later in the book, you will also learn about user controls and custom server controls, in which you can define your own tag prefixes and tag names.

HTML Server Controls

ASP.NET provides a special type of server control called the **HTML server control** that has a different syntax from that shown just previously. HTML server controls look like standard HTML tags, except for one thing: They contain a `runat="server"` attribute. HTML server controls are HTML elements that contain attributes that make them programmable on the server. By being programmable on the server, you can programmatically respond to events or bind data. HTML server controls have an object model that maps closely to that of the corresponding HTML elements. As a result, standard HTML attributes are exposed in HTML server controls as properties.

Two sample HTML server controls are shown here. Notice that each HTML server control requires both `id` and `runat="server"` attributes.

```
<input type="text" id="text1" runat="server" />
<p id="para1" runat="server"></p>
```

Because HTML server controls only have as much functionality as the available HTML elements, this book does not in fact spend any time working with them. Instead, it focuses on using the much more powerful Web server controls.

Web Server Controls

Like HTML server controls, **Web server controls** are also created on the server and they require a `runat="server"` attribute to work. Some Web server controls represent traditional HTML elements such as buttons and drop-down lists; other Web server controls represent more complex or abstract elements such as calendars, data lists, data sources, menus, and tree views. These more complex Web server controls usually do not map one-to-one to any existing HTML tags and may in fact be realized by dozens if not hundreds of HTML tags.

In Walkthrough 1.5, you will programmatically set the content of the `Label` Web server control in the code-behind file for `HelloWorld.aspx`.

Walkthrough 1.5   *Adding Programming Logic to a Web Form*

1. In the Solution Explorer, right-click `HelloWorld.aspx` and select the View Code menu command. Alternately, you can use **F7**.

2. Type either of the following (new code for you to enter is **emphasized**) within the `Page_Load` method. We will explain why this code is within a `Page_Load` method in the section "ASP.NET Event Model" beginning on page 53 of Chapter 2.

```
using System;
using System.Data;
using System.Configuration;
using System.Collections;
using System.Web;
using System.Web.Security;
using System.Web.UI;
using System.Web.UI.WebControls;
using System.Web.UI.WebControls.WebParts;
using System.Web.UI.HtmlControls;

public partial class HelloWorld : System.Web.UI.Page
{
    protected void Page_Load(object sender, EventArgs e)
    {
        labDate.Text = DateTime.Now.ToShortDateString();
    }
}
```

3. Save your changes.

4. Use the View in Browser menu command to test the page. The result should look like that shown in Figure 1.24.

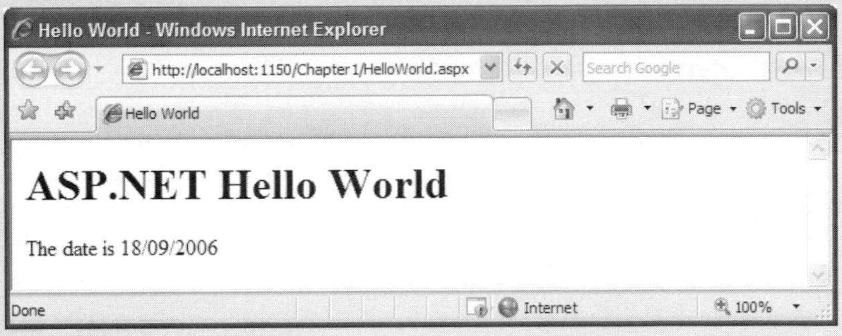

Figure 1.24　Updated HelloWorld.aspx in the Web browser

CORE NOTE

The format of the short date displayed in the browser varies depending upon the locale settings of your computer. I am writing this chapter in Canada, so the date format for my computer is `dd/mm/yyyy`. For example, if your computer's locale is the United States, you will probably see the date displayed as `mm/dd/yyyy`.

Encountering Errors

As you probably well know, errors are a common part of software development. In Walkthrough 1.6, you will introduce some errors (if you haven't already done so) into your page in order to see what happens when Visual Studio and ASP.NET encounter errors.

Walkthrough 1.6　*Adding Errors to Your Page*

1. Remove the period between `labDate` and `Text` from the programming code entered in step 2 from Walkthrough 1.5.

2. Save your changes.

3. Use the View in Browser menu command to test the page. The browser will show that a compile error occurred (see Figure 1.25).

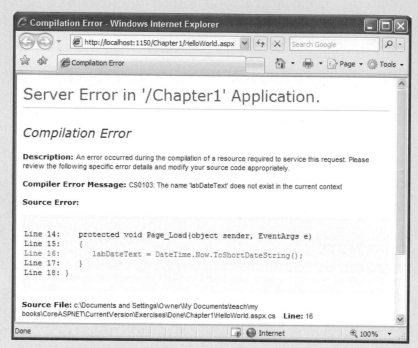

Figure 1.25 Compile error message in the Web browser

4. Close the browser.

Instead of seeing the compile error message in the browser, you could have Visual Studio show the error message before viewing in the browser, which certainly would be quicker.

5. In Visual Studio, use the Build →Web Site menu option.

This displays the compiler error message in two ways. The error is shown in the Error List window. It also is indirectly displayed in the code window itself as a colored "squiggle" underline (see Figure 1.26).

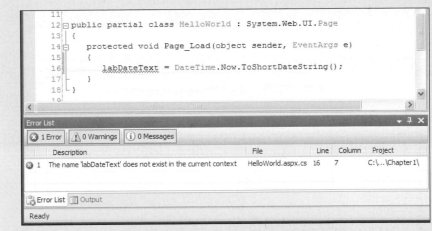

```
11
12  public partial class HelloWorld : System.Web.UI.Page
13  {
14      protected void Page_Load(object sender, EventArgs e)
15      {
16          labDateText = DateTime.Now.ToShortDateString();
17      }
18  }
19
```

Error List				
⊗ 1 Error	⚠ 0 Warnings	ⓘ 0 Messages		
Description		File	Line	Column	Project
⊗ 1 The name 'labDateText' does not exist in the current context		HelloWorld.aspx.cs	16	7	C:\...\Chapter 1\

Error List Output

Ready

Figure 1.26   Build errors in Visual Studio

6. Fix the error by adding back the period between `labDate` and `Text`.

7. Use the Build →Web Site menu option and then test view the page.

Some errors cannot be caught by the compiler, but are caught instead by something called the ASP.NET parser (which we will discuss further in Chapter 2). As such, these parser errors might not be displayed in Visual Studio but only in the browser. Walkthrough 1.7 demonstrates a sample parser error.

Walkthrough 1.7   Adding a Parser Error to Your Page

1. Remove the closing `</asp:label>` tag from `HelloWorld.aspx`.

2. Use the Build →Web Site menu option. Notice that there are no errors in the error list, although eventually a colored squiggle underline will show up under the `Label` control.

3. View page in browser.

   The browser displays a parser error message (see Figure 1.27). Parser errors are usually not detectable until runtime.

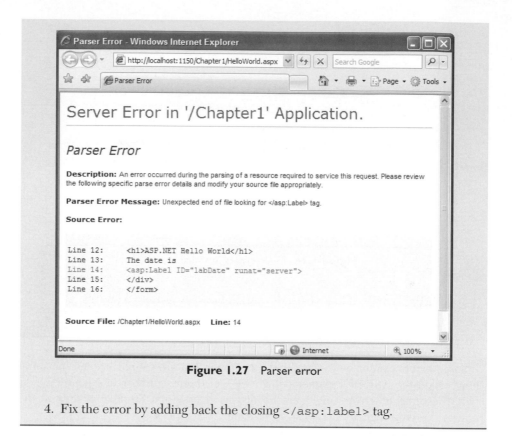

Figure 1.27   Parser error

4. Fix the error by adding back the closing `</asp:label>` tag.

Using the Visual Studio Debugger

Sometimes, a software problem can only be tracked down by examining the state of programming variables while the program is running. You can do this in Visual Studio by using the ***debugger***. It allows you to set ***break points*** for individual lines in your programming code. When a break point is encountered during execution, the program is paused on that line so that you can examine the state of your program's variables.

Walkthrough 1.8 demonstrates how to use the debugger in Visual Studio.

Walkthrough 1.8   *Using the Visual Studio Debugger*

1. Switch to the code-behind class for `HelloWorld.aspx`.

2. Change the `Page_Load` method by adding the following:

```
public partial class HelloWorld : System.Web.UI.Page
{
    protected void Page_Load(object sender, EventArgs e)
    {
        // Get the current month
        int iMonth = DateTime.Now.Month;

        // Increment the month
        iMonth++;

        // Change it to a string
        string sMonth = iMonth.ToString();

        // Set the label to this month value
        labDate.Text = sMonth;
    }
}
```

Notice that in this example there are code comments. Throughout this book, the programming code tends to be heavily commented. Because comments are not essential to make the program run (but do help make it more understandable), you are always free to leave out the comments when you work through any of the book's walkthrough exercises.

3. View the results in the browser. It simply displays the numeric value for the next month after the current month.

4. Close the browser and return to Visual Studio.

5. Add a break point to the first line in our `Page_Load` method by clicking to the left of the line number for that line, as shown in Figure 1.28. Alternately, pressing F9 sets a break point for the current line. After the break point is set, the line is highlighted in red.

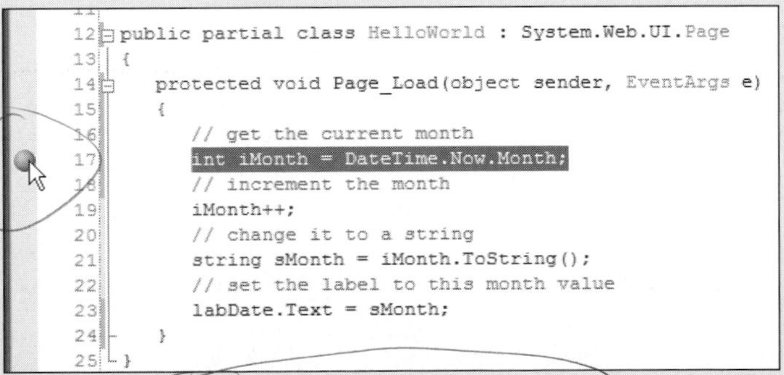

Figure 1.28 Adding a break point

6. Use the Debug → Start Debugging menu command (or press **F5**).

The first time you try debugging in a Web project, Visual Studio informs you that debugging is currently not enabled, as shown in Figure 1.29. To enable debugging, Visual Studio must add a `Web.config` file to your project and change an element within it that enables debugging.

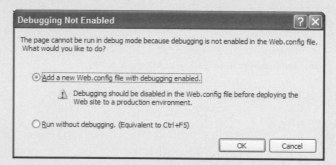

Figure 1.29   Enabling debugging

7. Choose the Add a New Web.config File option and the click the OK button.

8. Eventually, the browser pauses while Visual Studio stops at your break point. Visual Studio now allows you to inspect the state of the application in the Locals window, as shown in Figure 1.30. If the Locals window is not visible, you can use the Debug → Windows → Locals menu command.

9. You can now control the execution of the program via the Debug toolbar, shown in Figure 1.31.

10. Click either the Step Over button or the Step Into button. Either of these buttons executes the current line and steps over to the next line. Notice that the iMonth value in the Locals window has now changed.

Step Into is also used when stopped on a method call; it instructs the debugger to step *into* the method and stops execution on the first line within that method. When stopped on a method call, Step Over instructs the debugger to call the method and stop execution after the method call returns. Step Out instructs the debugger to execute the rest of the current method and then stop execution after returning from the method.

11. Click again on the Step Over or Step Into button.

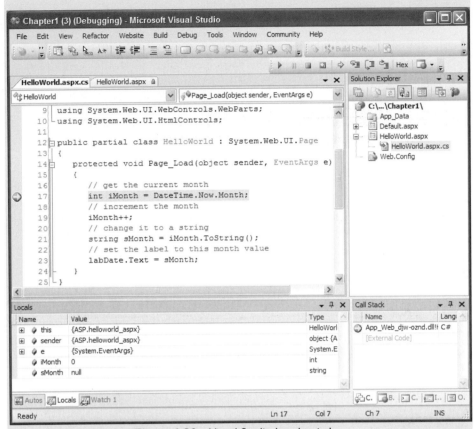

Figure 1.30   Visual Studio Locals window

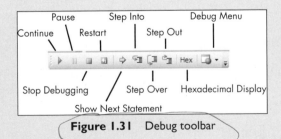

Figure 1.31   Debug toolbar

12. Click the Continue button. Execution continues and the page is displayed.

13. Hit the Refresh button on the browser. Notice that you are back to your original break point, because the `Page_Load` method is called each time the page is requested.

14. Close the browser window.

15. Remove the break point by clicking the red circle to the left of the break-pointed line.

This walkthrough provides only a quick glimpse into the powerful debugging capabilities of Visual Studio 2005. To learn more about debugging with Visual Studio, see the Scott Allen article listed in the references at the end of the chapter.

Summary

This chapter introduced the ASP.NET Web development environment. It looked at the principal advantages of ASP.NET and its integration into the .NET Framework. The chapter also provided some tutorial walkthroughs on creating some sample ASP.NET pages. The next chapter continues this coverage of the basics of ASP.NET. It examines what happens behind the scenes with ASP.NET and describes in detail the overall event model for ASP.NET.

Exercises

The solutions to the following exercise can be found at my Web site, `http://www.randyconnolly.com/core`. Additional exercises only available for teachers and instructors are also available from this site.

1. Create a Web Form that displays your name and address within a single `Label` control. The name and address should be displayed on separate lines.

Key Concepts

- Assemblies
- Base class library (BCL)
- Break points

- Code-behind file
- Code declaration block
- Code render block
- Common Language Runtime (CLR)
- Common Language Specification (CLS)
- Debugger
- Development framework
- Development server
- Direct output dynamic server technology
- Directives
- HTML server control
- Hybrid dynamic server technology
- Inline expression
- Internet Information Services (IIS)
- Language interoperablity
- Managed code
- Microsoft Intermediate Language (MSIL)
- Namespaces
- .NET Framework 2.0
- .NET Framework 3.0
- Obfuscator
- Page scripting dynamic server technology
- Production server
- Server-side comments
- Software platform
- Staging server
- Virtual directory
- Visual Studio projects and solutions
- Web Forms
- Web server control
- Web site project

References

Allen, Scott. "Basic Debugging Features in Visual Studio 2005."
http://www.odetocode.com.

Guthrie, Scott. "Microsoft Visual Studio 2005 Web Project System: What Is It and Why Did We Do It?" http://msdn.microsoft.com.

Guthrie, Scott. "Using IIS with Microsoft Visual Studio 2005 and the New Web Project System." http://msdn.microsoft.com.

Microsoft. "Introduction to Web Application Projects."
    http://msdn.microsoft.com.

Richter, Jeffrey. "Microsoft .NET Framework Delivers the Platform for an Integrated, Service-Oriented Web." *MSDN Magazine* (September 2000).

Thangarathinam, Thiru. "New Files and Folders in ASP.NET 2.0."
    http://www.15seconds.com.

Chapter 2

HOW ASP.NET WORKS

The previous chapter introduced the basics of ASP.NET 2.0. We are now ready to move onto the magic of how ASP.NET works. As mentioned in the last chapter, ASP.NET is a powerful framework for creating dynamic Web applications. Yet, despite this power, an individual ASP.NET page is nothing special; it is simply a text file with an .aspx filename extension. This text file contains content to be sent to the browser as well as content to be used by the ASP.NET environment on the server. The magic of ASP.NET dwells not in the text file itself but behind the "wondrous curtain" of the ASP.NET environment. This chapter steps behind this curtain and examines in some detail how ASP.NET works.

Some of the content in this chapter can be a bit complex and technical. If this is your first time using ASP.NET, you may want to skip some parts of this chapter and then return to them at some point in the future. If you take this strategy of skipping some of the chapter, be sure to read the first section on the ASP.NET event model because knowledge of it is essential.

ASP.NET Event Model

One of the key features of ASP.NET is that it uses an event-based programming model. In the simple Hello World example covered in the previous chapter, we added a small bit of programming to a method named Page_Load. This method is in fact an ***event handler***. An event handler is a method that determines what actions are performed when an event occurs, such as when the user clicks a button or selects an item from a list. When an event is raised, the handler for that specific event is executed. Events can in fact be assigned to multiple handlers. As well, methods that handle particular events can be set or changed dynamically.

In the .NET Framework, all event handlers have a specific method signature—that is, a specific return type and parameters. Event handlers are always `void` methods (or `Sub` methods in Visual Basic). Event handlers always accept two parameters: an `object` parameter and an `EventArgs` parameter (or a subclass of `EventArgs`, such as `CommandEventArgs` or `ImageClickEventArgs`). The `object` parameter references the object that raised the event. If you use the same event handler method for multiple controls, the `object` parameter can be used to determine which control triggered the event. The `EventArgs` parameter (or its subclass) contains information specific to the particular event. For instance, the `ImageClickEventArgs` parameter contains the x and y coordinates of where the user clicked the image.

It is important to note that the event system in ASP.NET operates in a different manner than in a Windows application or from the event system in browser-based Javascript. In a Windows application, for instance, events are raised and handled on the same processor. In contrast, ASP.NET events are raised on the client (the browser) but transmitted to and handled on the server (see Figure 2.1).

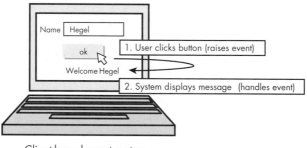

Client-based event system

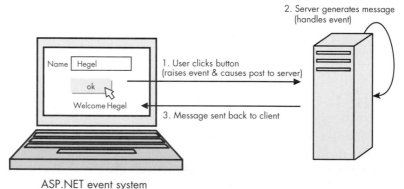

ASP.NET event system

Figure 2.1   Client-based event system versus ASP.NET event system

Because event handling requires a round-trip to the server, ASP.NET offers a smaller set of events in comparison to a totally client-based event system. Events that occur very frequently, such as mouse movement or drag-and-drop events, are not really supported by ASP.NET (although it is still possible to use client-side event handlers for these types of events in Javascript, or to use an AJAX-based API such as ASP.NET AJAX or AJAX.NET).

Postback

The first and foremost thing to learn about the ASP.NET event system is the concept of **postback**. In ASP.NET, postback is the process by which the browser posts information back to itself (i.e., posts information back to the server by requesting the same page). Postback in ASP.NET only occurs within Web Forms (i.e., within a form element with runat=server), and only server controls postback information to the server.

Figure 2.2 illustrates the basic and simplified postback interaction for a simple Web page.

More specifically, the simplified processing cycle for a Web Form is as follows.

1. The user requests an ASP.NET Web Form. In this example, the request uses the HTTP GET method.
2. On the server, the page is run, doing any preliminary processing such as compilation (if necessary), as well as calling other handlers as part of the page and application lifecycle (covered later in the chapter).
3. The Page_Load method of the page is called.
4. The rest of the page executes, which ultimately results in a generated HTML response, which is sent back to the browser. Part of this generated HTML is the view state (discussed shortly) information contained within a hidden HTML input element. As well, the action and method attributes of the <form> element are set so that the page will make a postback request to the same page when the user clicks the Enter button.
5. Browser displays the HTML response.
6. The user fills in the form, then causes the form to post back to itself (perhaps by clicking a button). If the user clicks a link that requests a different page, the following steps are not performed, because with the new page request, we would return back to step 1.
7. The page is posted back to the server, usually using the HTTP POST method. Any form values along with the view state information are sent along as HTTP form variables.
8. On the server, the page is run (no compilation is necessary because it will have already been compiled). The ASP.NET runtime recognizes that this page is being posted back due to the view state information. All user input is available for programmatic processing.

9. The `Page_Load` method is called.
10. Any invoked control event handlers are called. In this case, a click event handler for the button will be called.
11. The generated HTML is sent back to the browser.
12. Browser displays the HTML response.

These steps continue as long as the user continues to work on this page. Each cycle in which information is displayed and then posted back to the server is sometimes also called a *round trip*.

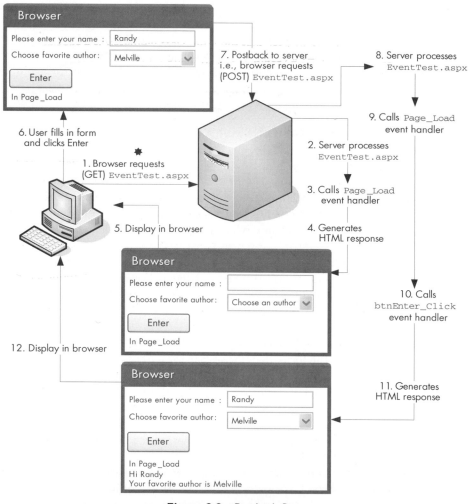

Figure 2.2   Postback flow

Page and Control Events

As can be seen from Figure 2.2, there are two different event types in ASP.NET: *page events* and *control events*. When a page request is sent to the server, a specific series of page events is always triggered in a specific order. Control events are associated with particular controls and are fired in certain circumstances. There are some standard events that all controls share; as well, most controls have unique events particular to that control. For instance, the `DropDownList` Web server control has an event that is triggered when the user selects a new list item.

> ### CORE NOTE
>
> We will see later in the chapter that the `Page` class ultimately is a subclass of the `Control` class. As a result, Web pages and server controls share many of the same events.

View State and Control State

View state is one of the most important features of ASP.NET. It is a specially encoded string that is used to retain page and form information between requests and is stored within a hidden HTML `<input>` element. All page elements not posted back via the standard HTTP `POST` mechanism are stored within this string. The view state thus provides the mechanism for preserving display state within Web Forms. Recall that HTTP is by nature stateless. This means that after the server responds to a request, it no longer preserves any data used for that request. Nonetheless, Web applications very frequently need to retain state on a page between requests. For instance, imagine a page that contains a user registration form. After the user clicks the Submit button, the code running on the server must check first to ensure that this user information doesn't already exist. If it does, it must return to the browser with the appropriate error message. Unless you want the user to curse and be frustrated with your form, you should also redisplay the form so that it contains the previously entered data.

This is an example of the need to maintain state in a Web application. Implementing this kind of state has typically involved cookies or form parameters and was often a real hassle in an older environment such as ASP classic. Although view state is not in fact used by ASP.NET to restore control values in a form, view state is ASP.NET's solution to the general problem of HTTP statelessness.

View state is generated after all the page code has executed but before the response is rendered. The value of each Web server control on the page is serialized into text as a number of Base64-encoded triplets, one of which contains a name-value pair. This view state string is then output to the browser as a hidden

`<input>` element named (as we have already seen in Chapter 1) __VIEWSTATE. When the form is posted back, ASP.NET receives the view state (because it was contained in a form element), deserializes this information, and restores the state of all the controls prior to the post. ASP.NET updates the state of the controls based on the data that has just been posted back, and then calls the usual page and control event handlers.

Because the details of encoding and decoding values from the view state are handled by the ASP.NET runtime, you can generally ignore the view state and simply revel in its benefits. However, sometimes, a developer may want to turn off the view state for a page. For instance, if a very large data set is being displayed, the view state also is quite large, which may significantly lengthen the time it takes the browser to download and render the page (this is especially an issue for mobile browsers). If a page is not going to post back to itself, you can improve page performance by disabling the view state for the page within the Page directive, as shown here.

```
<%@ Page … EnableViewState="false" %>
```

The view state can also be programmatically manipulated within the code-behind class. It is a dictionary object that uses keys to locate and store objects. This use of view state, along with other issues involved in using it, is covered in Chapter 12.

Control state is a new feature in ASP.NET 2.0. It allows the developer to store custom control data between round trips, similar to the view state; unlike the view state, the control state can never be turned off by the developer. It is typically used when creating custom controls that will be used by other developers. Because control state is always available, it can safely be used even when view state is disabled.

Page Lifecycle

Page and control events occur in a certain order, which is called the *page lifecycle*. The precise order and number of events in this lifecycle are shown in Figure 2.3 and described in all their exhaustive glory in Table 2.1.

CORE NOTE

If you want to examine the setup of this pipeline yourself, you can do so by examining the private ProcessRequestMain method of Page. One way to do so is to use Lutz Roeder's .NET Reflector (available from http://www.aisto.com/roeder/dotnet) to examine the code in the System.Web.UI assembly.

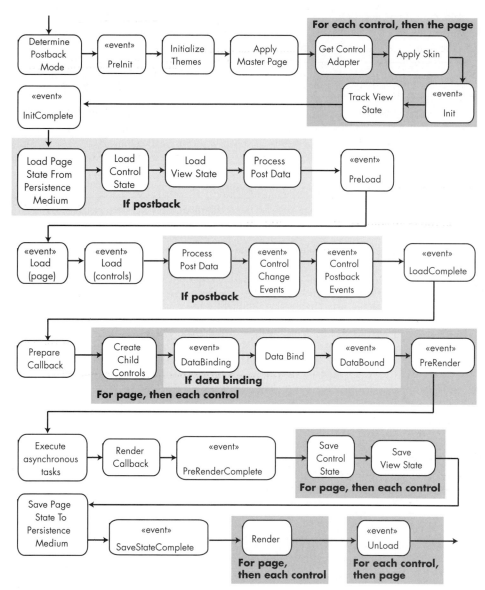

Figure 2.3 Page lifecycle

Table 2.1   Page Lifecycle

Event	Description
Determine postback mode	The `IsPostBack` property is set based on the presence of the view state in the page request. Can be handled by overriding the `DeterminePostBackMode` method.
PreInit	Occurs at the beginning of page initialization. You can use this event to set the master page or theme dynamically.
Initialize themes	The page theme is set and initialized. The private method `InitializeThemes` method of the `Page` class is called.
Apply master page	The page's master page is applied. The private method `ApplyMasterPage` method of the `Page` class is called.
Get control adapter (controls, then page)	Control adapters allow a developer to change the markup produced by server controls. This step gets any control adapter defined in the `App_Browsers` folder for the control.
Apply skin (controls, then page)	Applies any skin defined for the control.
Init (controls, then page)	You cannot access other server controls yet as there is no guarantee that it has been initialized yet. View state information cannot be used yet.
InitComplete	Raised after page initialization is complete. All declared controls on the page are initialized; they do not, however, contain data entered by the user. View state information can still not be used yet.
Page state is loaded from persistence medium	If this is a postback request, load any saved view state information from hidden `<input>` element. You can implement your own custom state mechanism by overriding the `LoadPageStateFromPersistenceMedium` method of the `Page` class.
Control state loaded (controls)	If this is a postback request, load any control state information. Control state exists in a postback request even if view state has been disabled.
View state loaded (page, then controls)	If this is a postback request, load any relevant view state information for this page or control.
Process post data	Loads post data back into any controls. Implemented by the private `ProcessPostData` method of the `Page` class.
PreLoad	Occurs after any view state is restored but before the `Load` event.
Load (page, then controls)	Used to perform most of the processing steps for the page and controls that are to occur for each page request.

Table 2.1   Page Lifecycle *(continued)*

Event	Description
Process post data	Loads post data back into any controls. This is attempted again in order to populate any dynamic controls added in any `Load` handlers.
Control change events	All control change events (such as `TextChanged` for a `TextBox`) are triggered.
Control postback events	All control postback events (such as `Click` for a `Button`) are triggered
`LoadComplete`	Occurs after all `Load` events. You can use this event for any task that requires all controls to be loaded.
Prepare callback	If an asynchronous call back is defined, it is raised.
Create child controls (page, then controls)	If the control contains any child controls, they are created.
Data binding	Data binding (and its events) occurs for any controls that have a `DataSourceID` property set. Data binding is covered in Chapter 8.
`PreRender` (page, then controls)	This event is the last chance to affect the page or controls before they are rendered.
Execute any asynchronous tasks	Starts the execution of any asynchronous tasks that have been defined for the page using the `PageAsyncTask` class and registered using the `RegisterAsyncTask` method.
Render callback	Renders any client-script callback.
`PreRenderComplete`	Indicates that all content for the page has been pre-rendered.
Page state is saved to persistence medium	Saves the page view state and control state to persistence medium. You can implement your own custom state mechanism by overriding the `SavePageStateFromPersistenceMedium` method of the `Page` class.
`SaveStateComplete`	Occurs after the page state has been saved.
`Render` (for page, then controls)	The page's `Render` method is called and then the `Render` method for each control and its children is called. Rendering finally outputs the HTML and other text to be sent to the client.
`Unload` (for controls, then page)	First each control and then the page triggers this event just before calling the `Dispose` method for the control or page. Can be used to perform any final cleanup of resources used by the controls or pages.

This is no doubt a very imposing list of steps. Fortunately, for most development tasks, you can remain blithely ignorant of most of these steps. We can get by initially instead simply by understanding the five general stages in the page lifecycle:

- Page initialization—During this stage, the page and its controls are initialized. The page determines if it is a new request or a postback request. The page event handlers `Page_PreInit` and `Page_Init` are called. As well, the `PreInit` and `Init` methods of any server controls are called. Any themes (covered in Chapter 6) are then applied.
- Loading—If the request is a postback, control properties are loaded with information recovered from special page state containers called the view state and the control state. The `Page_Load` method of the page, as well as the `Page_Load` method of its server controls are called.
- Postback event handling—If the request is a postback, any control postback event handlers are called.
- Rendering—During page rendering, the view state is saved to the page, and then each control along with the page renders themselves to the output response stream. The `PreRender` and then the `Render` method of the page and the controls are called. Finally, the result from the rendering is sent back to the client via the HTTP response.
- Unloading—Final cleanup and disposal of resources used by the page occurs. The `Unload` methods of the controls and the page are called.

Within each of these stages, the ASP.NET page raises events that you can handle in your code. For the vast majority of situations, you only need worry about one page event (`Page_Load`) and certain unique control events. Because page events always happen, you only need write the page event handler in your code using the appropriate naming convention (if `AutoEventWireup` is enabled). The naming convention is `Page_XXXX` where `XXXX` is the event name.

Control events, on the other hand, need to be explicitly wired—that is, you must explicitly bind the handler method to the event. This can be done declaratively in the control definition in the markup, or programmatically in the code-behind. Prior to Visual Studio 2005, the Designer in Visual Studio always used the programmatic approach. The current version of Visual Studio now uses the declarative approach.

To declaratively bind a handler to a control event, you use the appropriate `OnXXXX` attribute of the control, where `XXXX` is the event name. For instance, to bind the event handler method `btnSubmit_Click` to the `Click` event of a `Button` Web server control, you would use

```
<asp:Button id="btnSubmit" runat="server"
    OnClick="btnSubmit_Click" />
```

There must now be an event handler named `btnSubmit_Click` defined in the code for this page. As mentioned earlier, all event handlers in the .NET Framework have a common method signature. The appropriate event handler would thus look like the following:

```
protected void btnSubmit_Click(object sender, EventArgs e)
{
    // Do something
}
```

CORE NOTE

You can get Visual Studio to create the event handler and add the appropriate attribute to the control by double-clicking the appropriate event entry within the Properties window while within Design view, as shown in Figure 2.4.

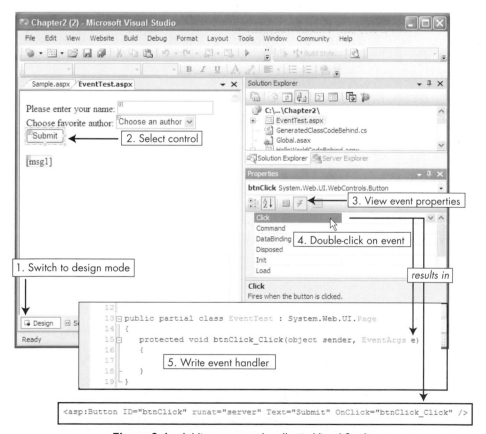

Figure 2.4 Adding an event handler in Visual Studio

CORE NOTE

Many developers (as well as Visual Studio itself) use the `objectname_`
`eventname` naming convention for event handler methods. Using a
consistent naming convention ultimately makes your Web application
easier to understand and maintain.

You can also do the equivalent event binding using programming. Conceptually,
this approach is quite a bit more complicated. It requires that you hook up a **_dele-
gate_** to the appropriate event of the control. A delegate is an object that encapsulates
a method (similar to a function pointer in C and C++) in a type-safe manner. The
analogous code for programmatically wiring the button's `Click` event using a delegate would be

```
btnSubmit.Click += new EventHandler( this.btnSubmit_Click );
```

Because an event can be handled by multiple event handlers, the preceding code
had to add the delegate to its list of delegates for that event (using the += operator).
To better understand how to work with event handlers, Walkthrough 2.1 demonstrates how to implement the example shown in Figure 2.2.

Walkthrough 2.1   _Event-Handling Example_

1. In Visual Studio, create a new Web site called `Chapter2`.

2. Use the Website → Add New Item menu option (or right-click the
   project container in the Solution Explorer and choose the Add New
   Item.

3. Choose the Web Form template and change the filename to `Event-`
   `Test.aspx`.

4. Place the following markup within the `<form>` element. Notice the
   `OnClick` attribute for the `Button` control.

   ```
   Please enter your name:
   <asp:TextBox ID="name" runat="server" />
   <br />
   Choose favorite author:
   <asp:DropDownList ID="myList" runat="server">
       <asp:ListItem>Choose an author</asp:ListItem>
   ```

```
    <asp:ListItem>Atwood</asp:ListItem>
    <asp:ListItem>Austin</asp:ListItem>
    <asp:ListItem>Hawthorne</asp:ListItem>
    <asp:ListItem>Melville</asp:ListItem>
</asp:DropDownList>
<br />
<asp:Button ID="btnEnter" Text="Enter" runat="server"
    OnClick="btnEnter_Click" />
<p><asp:Label ID="msg1" runat="server" /></p>
```

5. Switch to the code-behind file for EventTest by right-clicking Event-Test.aspx and select the View Code menu command or by pressing **F7**.

6. Modify the Page_Load method as shown in the following.

```
protected void Page_Load(object sender, EventArgs e)
{
    msg1.Text = "In Page_Load<br/>";
}
```

7. Add the following method.

```
protected void btnEnter_Click(object sender, EventArgs e)
{
    if (myList.SelectedIndex > 0)
    {
        msg1.Text += "Hi " + name.Text + "<br/>";
        msg1.Text += "Your favorite author is ";
        msg1.Text += myList.SelectedItem;
    }
}
```

This method checks if the user has selected one of the authors from the DropDownList (i.e., it is not still on the Choose an Author list item, which has a SelectedIndex of 0), and if so, it displays a message containing the selected author in the Label control.

8. Save your changes.

9. Use the View in Browser menu command to test the page. Enter something in the textbox, select an item from the list, and select the Enter button. The result should look like that shown in Figure 2.5.

Notice that the Page_Load method is called the first time the page is requested, as well as after the button is clicked. The EnterBtn_Click method is called only after the button is clicked.

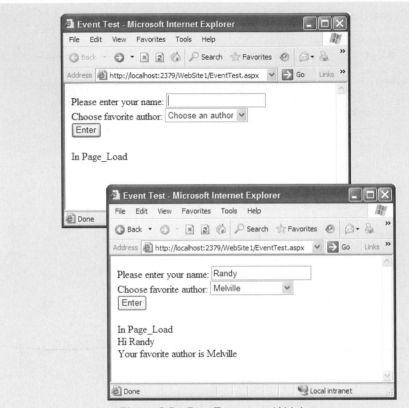

Figure 2.5   EventTest.aspx in Web browser

10. Examine the generated HTML in the browser via the browser's View
Source menu option. It looks something like that shown below. Notice
that the `action` attribute on the `form` element is `EventTest.aspx`.
This means that when you click the Submit button, you are making a
`POST` request to the same page.

```
<!DOCTYPE html PUBLIC "-//W3C//DTD XHTML 1.0
   Transitional//EN"
   "http://www.w3.org/TR/xhtml1/DTD/xhtml1-transitional.dtd">

<html xmlns="http://www.w3.org/1999/xhtml">
<head><title>Event Test</title></head>
<body>
<form name="form1" method="post" action="EventTest.aspx"
   id="form1">
<div>
```

```
<input type="hidden" name="__VIEWSTATE" id="__VIEWSTATE"
    value="/wEPDwUJMzU4OTQyMTQyD2QWAgIDD2QWAgIHDw8WAh4EVGV4
    dAU+SW4gUGFnZV9Mb2FkPGJyLz5IaSBSYW5keTxici8+WW91ciBmYXXZ
    vcml0ZSBhdXRob3IgaXMgTWVsdmlsbGVkZGQUuquBlGDmIzZ2VVPG2a
    Kmu+a81g==" />
</div>
<div>
    Please enter your name:
    <input name="name" type="text" value="Randy" id="name" />
    <br />
    Choose favorite author:
    <select name="myList" id="myList">
      <option value="Choose an author">
        Choose an author</option>
      <option value="Atwood">Atwood</option>
      <option value="Austin">Austin</option>
      <option value="Hawthorne">Hawthorne</option>
      <option selected="selected" value="Melville">
        Melville</option>
    </select>
    <br />
    <input type="submit" name="btnEnter" value="Enter"
        id="btnEnter" />
    <p><span id="msg1">In Page_Load<br/>
    Hi Randy<br/>Your favorite author is Melville</span></p>
</div>
<div>
<input type="hidden" name="__EVENTVALIDATION"
    id="__EVENTVALIDATION"
    value="/wEWCALi/s/8DAL7uPQdAuuUwb8PAqmgr5IGArOL1q0PA
    uny6fcEAoDL04ICApe3wPgBDkQ091kDsBMvJvAv4m1IZpXZsi4=" />
</div></form>
</body>
</html>
```

Detecting Postback

There are times when you may want your page to behave differently the very first time it is requested. One typical example is that you want to read and display values from a database in a list only the first time the page is requested. In subsequent postbacks, the data is preserved by the view state so there is no need to re-read the database.

ASP.NET provides the developer with the ability to test if it is being requested for the first time via the `IsPostBack` property of the `Page` class (recall that this is the base class for all code-behind classes). This property is equal to `false` if the page is being requested for the first time. Thus, you can perform different processing the first time the page is requested using code similar to the following in the `Page_Load` method.

```
protected void Page_Load(object sender, EventArgs e)
{
    ...
    if (! IsPostBack)
    {
        // Do something here for very first request
    }
    ...
}
```

The ! in the if condition is a Boolean NOT in C#. A more verbose but equivalent statement would be

```
if (IsPostBack == false)
```

Postback and Non-Postback Controls

Button-type controls with Click events always generate an immediate postback to the server. But not all control events generate an immediate postback. In fact, most control events by default do not cause a postback. Some controls—for instance, a Label control—never can cause a postback. **Change events** also do not, by default, generate a postback. An example of a change event is selecting an item from a drop-down list or entering text into a text box. However, you may be able to enable postback for change-type events by setting the control's AutoPostBack property to true.

For instance, you could change the example in the previous walkthrough so that the DropDownList control automatically causes a postback. By doing so, you could eliminate the button completely and instead do your message processing in the event handler for the SelectedIndexChanged event. Listings 2.1 and 2.2 illustrate how to change EventTest.aspx to use a DropDownList that automatically posts back to the server when the user changes the selected item in the list.

Listing 2.1   EventTest.aspx

```
<%@ Page Language="C#" AutoEventWireup="true"
   CodeFile="EventTest.aspx.cs" Inherits="EventTest" %>

<!DOCTYPE html PUBLIC "-//W3C//DTD XHTML 1.0 Transitional//EN"
    "http://www.w3.org/TR/xhtml1/DTD/xhtml1-transitional.dtd">
<html xmlns="http://www.w3.org/1999/xhtml">
<head runat="server">
   <title>Event Test</title>
</head>
<body>
<form id="form1" runat="server">
   <div>
      Please enter your name:
      <asp:TextBox ID="name" runat="server" />
```

```
        <br />
        Choose favorite author:
      <asp:DropDownList ID="myList" runat="server"
            AutoPostBack="true"
            OnSelectedIndexChanged="myList_SelectedIndexChanged" >
        <asp:ListItem>Choose an author</asp:ListItem>
        <asp:ListItem>Atwood</asp:ListItem>
        <asp:ListItem>Austin</asp:ListItem>
        <asp:ListItem>Hawthorne</asp:ListItem>
        <asp:ListItem>Melville</asp:ListItem>
      </asp:DropDownList><br />
        <p><asp:Label ID="msg1" runat="server" /></p>
    </div>
</form>
</body>
</html>
```

Listing 2.2   EventTest.aspx.cs

```csharp
using System;
using System.Data;
using System.Configuration;
using System.Collections;
using System.Web;
using System.Web.Security;
using System.Web.UI;
using System.Web.UI.WebControls;
using System.Web.UI.WebControls.WebParts;
using System.Web.UI.HtmlControls;

/// <summary>
/// Code-behind for EventTest.aspx Web Form used in Chapter 1
/// </summary>
public partial class EventTest : System.Web.UI.Page
{
  /// <summary>
  /// Event handler will be called each time page is requested
  /// </summary>
  protected void Page_Load(object sender, EventArgs e)
  {
    msg1.Text = "In Page_Load<br/>";
  }

  /// <summary>
  /// Event handler for the drop-down list
  /// </summary>
  protected void myList_SelectedIndexChanged(object sender,
    EventArgs e)
```

```
    {
      // Ignore first item in list
      if (myList.SelectedIndex > 0)
      {
        msg1.Text += "Hi " + name.Text + "<br/>";
        msg1.Text += "Your favorite author is ";
        msg1.Text += myList.SelectedItem;
      }
    }
  }
}
```

CORE NOTE

The code in Listing 2.2 contains *XML documentation comments*. These are the comments that begin with ///. Visual Studio generates the comment stubs for you when you type in ///. If your comments are in this format, you can generate MSDN-style documentation pages for your classes via a compiler option. As well, Visual Studio's Intellisense feature can use this type of commenting to provide additional information, as shown in Figure 2.6.

```
/// <summary>
/// Returns all the records for this entity          By defining comments in this format ...
/// </summary>
public EntityCollection<T> GetAll()
{
    EntityCollection<T> collection = null;
    if (IsGetAllCached)
        collection = DataCache<T>.RetrieveCollection(CacheName);
    if (collection == null)
    {
        collection = GetCollection(SelectStatement, CommandType.Text, null);
        if (IsGetAllCached)
            DataCache<T>.AddCollection(CacheName, collection);
    }
    return collection;
}
```

```
public EntityCollection<Book> GetAllBooks()
{
    BookDAO dao = new BookDAO();
    return dao.|
}
```
```
    AdaptCollectionToDataTable
    CacheName
    Delete
    Equals
    GetAll                          EntityCollection<Book> AbstractDAO<Book>.GetAll()
    GetByCriteria                   Returns all the records for this entity
    GetByKey
    GetHashCode                     ... we see comments with Intellisense
    GetType
    Insert
```

Figure 2.6   Visual Studio's Intellisense and comments

Cross-Page Posting

Although the postback mechanism is ideal for most page processing situations, there are occasions when you may want to post back to a different page. This was not really possible in ASP.NET 1.x, but version 2.0 now supports ***cross-page posting***, which allows a page to post back to a different page. Cross-page posting is enabled for individual controls by using the `PostBackUrl` property. This property allows you to specify the page that will handle the postback. For instance, we could change the `Button` in Walkthrough 2.1 to the following.

```
<asp:Button ID="btnEnter" Text="Enter" runat="server"
    PostBackUrl="OtherPage.aspx" />
```

Notice that there is now no need to respond to the `Click` event. The handling for this event occurs instead in the `Page_Load` of `OtherPage.aspx`. You might recall that the `Click` event handler in the walkthrough example displayed the user's name entry in the name `TextBox` and the user's selection in the author `DropDownList`. The problem with cross-page posting is that you need to access these control values from the previous page.

Luckily, the `Page` class provides the `PreviousPage` property, which returns a reference to the `Page` object that represents the previous Web Form. With this reference, you can retrieve the state of the `DropDownList` control. To do so requires using the `FindControl` method of this previous class, as shown in the following example.

```
public partial class OtherPage : System.Web.UI.Page
{
    protected void Page_Load(object sender, EventArgs e)
    {
        // First retrieve references to controls on previous page
        TextBox txtName =
            (TextBox)PreviousPage.FindControl("name");
        DropDownList drpAuthors =
            (DropDownList)PreviousPage.FindControl("myList");

        // If the references exist, display their content
        if (drpAuthors != null && txtName != null)
        {
            msg1.Text += "Hi " + txtName.Text + "<br/>";
            msg1.Text += "Your favorite author is ";
            msg1.Text += drpAuthors.SelectedItem;
        }
    }
}
```

ASP.NET Code Compilation

In the last chapter, we created a sample Hello World ASP.NET page. As we saw, creating this page was not complicated. But what happens when the browser/user requests the `HelloWorld.aspx` file? The quick (but partial) answer given in the previous chapter is that the visual elements of the page are parsed into a class, and this class, along with its code, is dynamically compiled (into MSIL), JIT compiled, and then executed on the server, which produces the HTML and Javascript that is sent to the browser. However, the complete answer is a bit more complex. This answer begins with the ASP.NET 2.0 compilation process.

ASP.NET 2.0 introduces a new approach to the coding and compilation process for Web Forms. This new approach fixes two key synchronization problems with the model used in ASP.NET 1.x.

The first of these synchronization problems was a result of the sometimes confusing code-behind model in ASP.NET 1.x. Prior to version 2.0, a Web Form's code-behind class was the base class for the class generated by the runtime from the .aspx file itself (see Figure 2.7). This meant that to programmatically manipulate controls defined in the .aspx file, the controls had to be declared programmatically as `protected` data members in the code-behind class. That is, the controls were declared in the base class (the code-behind) but instantiated in the subclass (the class generated from the .aspx file). Thus, despite the fact that the code-behind was the base class, it was actually dependent upon its subclass, which is very much a counterintuitive relationship to anyone familiar with object-oriented development.

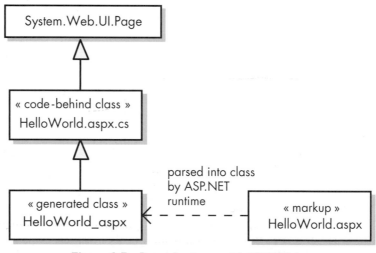

Figure 2.7   Page inheritance with ASP.NET 1.x

This approach thus created a close coupling between the .aspx file and its code-behind that could be quite frustrating. For instance, if one had a control named myControl in the markup, but declared it in the code-behind as yourControl, the error would not be located until runtime. Another consequence of this close coupling was that, in practice, it was often difficult to have different people edit the .aspx file and its code-behind.

The second synchronization problem with the ASP.NET 1.x code-behind and compilation model was that the code-behind classes had to be manually compiled by the developer (by using a command-line compiler or using the Build command in Visual Studio) and then deployed, separate from the .aspx files. That is, all the code-behind class files in the Web application had to be compiled into an assembly, which was then stored in the /bin folder of the application. The .aspx files, on the other hand, did not have to be precompiled. Instead, in ASP.NET 1.x, an .aspx page was parsed at runtime the first time the page was requested into a temporary class, which was in turn compiled and stored in its own temporary assembly, as shown in Figure 2.8.

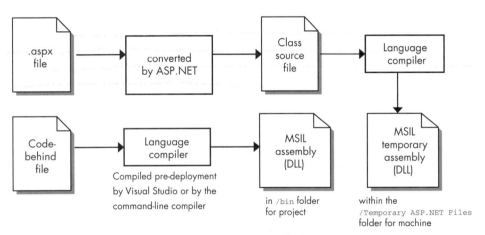

Figure 2.8   Compilation process with ASP.NET 1.x

The synchronization problem that lurked in this approach was that the developer could make a change to the .aspx file without recompiling and uploading the assembly for the code-behinds. This could sometimes result in seemingly bizarre and irrational runtime errors due to the discrepancy between the Web Form and its code-behind class. Indeed, if I had a thousand dollars for each strange bug my students have created over the years as a result of this synchronization problem, I could donate my royalties for this book to charity, secure in the knowledge that I am a rich man!

ASP.NET 2.0 introduces a new coding and compilation model that addresses these synchronization problems with ASP.NET 1.x. The first key change is that the code-behind file is now only a *partial class*. This new programming construct in version 2.0 of the .NET Framework allows a class to be split across multiple files. The files are then merged into a single class either by Visual Studio when you build (compile) the site or by the ASP.NET environment when a page in the site is first requested.

Because the code-behind class in version 2.0 is a partial class, it now no longer needs the control declarations and event wire-ups (that is, as long as the page uses the default `AutoEventWireup` attribute in the `Page` directive) that littered the code-behind classes in ASP.NET 1.x. Instead, the runtime generates the complete code-behind class based on the partial code-behind class that you create, as shown in Figure 2.9.

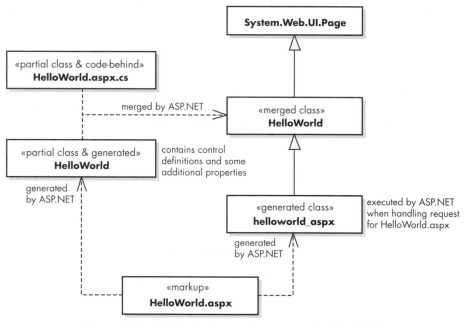

Figure 2.9   Code-behind page inheritance with ASP.NET 2.0

What happens behind the scenes is different if the code is embedded within the .aspx file instead of within a code-behind file. In this case, the generated class is the merged result of the two parts of the Web Form (its code and its markup); this generated class now inherits directly from the Page class (see Figure 2.10).

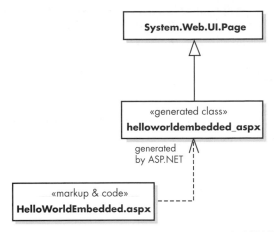

Figure 2.10 Embedded code page inheritance with ASP.NET 2.0

An important benefit of this new compilation model in ASP.NET 2.0 is that you no longer have to worry about the synchronization problems caused by having the separate compilation stage for the code-behind classes. ASP.NET 2.0 can now dynamically compile your entire application at runtime. That is, ASP.NET now compiles not only your code-behinds but *all* your other classes, such as business objects, data access classes, or any other classes for you at runtime as long as these other classes reside within the App_Code folder for the application. With this dynamic compilation model, each folder in the Web application are compiled into a separate dynamic assembly, as shown in Figure 2.11.

CORE NOTE

The path for the generated class files created from the Web Forms along with the temporary assemblies is \[.NET System Directory]\ Temporary ASP.NET Files\[virtual directory]\[x]\[y] where x and y are randomly generated names. For instance, the path for the assembly on my development server was C:\WINDOWS\ Microsoft.NET\Framework\v2.0.50727\Temporary ASP.NET Files\chapter2\7229f9fd\8d0746a9.

Alternately, ASP.NET 2.0 also allows you to precompile your entire application prior to deployment into one or more assemblies. Only the affected assemblies then need to be uploaded to the server. That is, none of your source files need to be uploaded to the server. Although this provides the best performance, security, and intellectual property protection, it does come at the cost of being unable to easily modify and deploy changes. We will cover precompilation in Chapter 16 on deployment and configuration.

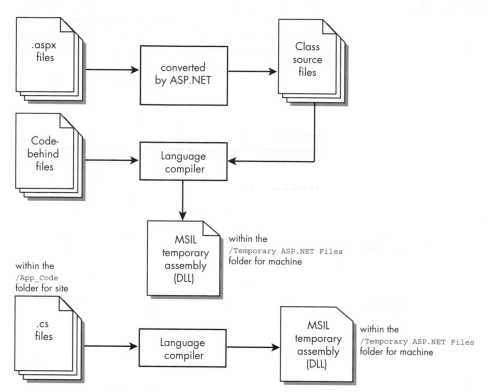

Figure 2.11   Compilation process with ASP.NET 2.0

Compilation Order

ASP.NET compiles the various files in a Web application in a very specific order. There are two separate levels of files that are compiled. The files in the top level are compiled the first time there is a request for an ASP.NET file in the application; after that, files in the top level are only recompiled if there is a specific dependency change. Table 2.2 lists the order in which these top-level items are compiled. Changing any of the files in this top level causes the Web application to *restart*. When an application restarts, ASP.NET recompiles the items in the top level; as well, any other files that have dependencies to these items are recompiled as well.

Table 2.2 Top-Level Compilation Item Order

File/Folder	Description
App_GlobalResources	This folder contains resource files (.resx and .resources) that are compiled into assemblies with global scope. A resource file is an XML file that contains key/value pairs; these pairs are typically strings that will be translated into different languages or paths to images. You generally have a different resource file for each language supported by your application. Resources are covered in Chapter 16.
App_WebResources	This folder contains Web service contract files (.wsdl files), schemas (.xsd files), and other files that define a Web service reference for use within the application. Web services are covered in Chapter 15.
Profile properties	ASP.NET profile properties are defined in the application's Web.config file. They allow your application to track and permanently store user-specific information. These properties are stored in an assembly. Profiles are covered in Chapter 14.
App_Code	This folder contains the source code for any utility classes, business objects, data access classes, or any other classes that you want to compile as part of your application.
Global.asax	File containing application-level event handlers.

After the top-level items have been compiled, ASP.NET then compiles other files as needed (i.e., as a result of requests). Table 2.3 lists the order in which these bottom-level items are compiled.

Table 2.3 Bottom-Level Compilation Item Order

File/Folder	Description
App_LocalResources	This folder contains resource files that are associated with a specific page, user control, or master page in an application.
HTTP handlers	HTTP handlers are compiled, if necessary, when requested. ASP.NET maps HTTP requests to HTTP handlers based on a filename extension. The built in handlers are: individual Web Forms (.aspx), user controls (.ascx), Web service handlers (.asmx), the application's trace handler (trace.acd), and any custom HTTP handlers (.ashx). Handlers are covered later in this chapter.

Table 2.3   Bottom-Level Compilation Item Order *(continued)*

File/Folder	Description
Themes and master pages	Content in the `App_Themes` folder and any master pages are compiled when the referencing Web Form or user control is compiled. Themes and master pages are covered in Chapter 6.

The Page Class

As can be seen in Figures 2.9 and 2.10, all Web Forms ultimately inherit from the Page class, which is defined in the `System.Web.UI` namespace. The Page class inherits from the `TemplateControl` class, which in turn inherits from the `Control` class. As a result, the Page class provides a great deal of functionality exposed as properties and methods that you can make use of in your code-behind classes (or your embedded code blocks if that is your preference). Some of these properties are analogous to the intrinsic global objects of ASP classic, such as `Request`, `Response`, `Session`, and `Server`. Other Page properties provide useful access to information about the page, such as `IsPostBack`, `IsValid`, `Theme`, and `EnableViewState`. The Page class also provides many useful methods, such as `LoadControl`, `Validate`, and `RegisterClientScriptBlock`.

You shall be using many of these properties and methods of the Page class as you progress through the book. Again, because they are defined in the Page class (or in one of its ancestors), they are available to any of your Web Forms. For instance, if you want to make use of the `Redirect` method of the `Response` property (which instructs the browser to request a different page) in a code-behind class, you could use either of the following.

```
public partial class MyExample: Page
{
    ...
    // Use this approach
    Response.Redirect("somePage.aspx");
    ...
    // Or use this approach
    this.Response.Redirect("somePage.aspx");
}
```

CORE NOTE

This book frequently uses ellipses (...) in the code examples. Ellipses indicate that some additional, nonrelevant code has been omitted for brevity's sake.

The C# keyword this can be used to signify the current class and is preferred by some developers for referencing members of the current class (or of one of its parents).

Although we will certainly be using various members of the Page class throughout this book, it is useful now to say a few words about three of its properties: the Request, Response, and Server properties.

Request

The Request property of the Page class returns an HttpRequest object. This HttpRequest represents the HTTP values sent by the browser with its request. It contains members for retrieving query string or form parameters, cookie data, as well as information about the requesting browser. Table 2.4 lists the *notable* properties of the HttpRequest class.

CORE NOTE

Throughout this book, there are tables that display the notable members of a class or control. For space reasons, these tables are often not exhaustive; instead, they list the most useful and commonly used members. The interested reader can always examine the MSDN documentation (either online or within Visual Studio) for a complete member listing.

Table 2.4　Notable Properties of HttpRequest

Property	Description
AnonymousID	Returns an identifier for an unauthenticated user, if anonymous identification is enabled. Anonymous identification is covered in Chapter 13.
ApplicationPath	Returns the virtual path of the application.
Cookies	Returns a collection of cookies sent by the browser. Cookies are covered in Chapter 12.
FilePath	Returns the virtual path of the current page/request.
Form	Returns a collection of form data sent with the request.
Params	Returns a collection that combines the values contained in the Cookies, Form, QueryString, and ServerVariables collections.

Table 2.4   Notable Properties of HttpRequest *(continued)*

Property	Description
PhysicalPath	Returns the physical path of the page/request on the server.
QueryString	Returns a collection of query string data sent with the request.
ServerVariables	Returns a collection of named server variables sent with the request.

Response

Analogous to the just-covered Request property, the Response property of the Page class returns an HttpResponse object. The HttpResponse class represents the server's HTTP response to the current request. Tables 2.5 and 2.6 list some of the notable members of the HttpResponse class.

Table 2.5   Notable Properties of HttpResponse

Property	Description
BufferOutput	Indicates whether to buffer output and only send it back to the client after the entire page has been processed. The default is true.
Cache	Specifies the policy values (such as the expiry time) for the ASP.NET cache. Chapter 12 covers caching in detail.
Cookies	The cookie collection that is sent to the browser as part of the response. Cookies are also covered in Chapter 12.

Table 2.6   Notable Methods of HttpResponse

Method	Description
Redirect	Instructs the client to request a different page.
Write	Writes information to the HTTP response stream.

Server

The Server property of the Page class returns an HttpServerUtility object. The HttpServerUtility class provides various helper methods, many of which we will use in different places throughout the book. Table 2.7 lists the notable methods of this class.

Table 2.7   Notable Methods of HttpServerUtility

Method	Description
CreateObject	Creates a COM object.
HtmlDecode	Decodes the passed HTML-encoded string.
HtmlEncode	HTML-encodes the passed string so that it can be correctly displayed in a browser.
MapPath	Returns the physical file path for the passed virtual application path.
Transfer	Stops execution of the current page and begins execution of the specified page.
UrlDecode	Decodes the passed URL-encoded string.
UrlEncode	URL-encodes the passed string so that it can be correctly transmitted to the browser via the URL.

Response.Redirect Versus Server.Transfer

You may have noticed from Tables 2.5 and 2.6 that there appears to be two different ways of programmatically switching to another page: Response.Redirect and Server.Transfer. The Response.Redirect method sends a message to the requesting client to request a new page. This requires a round trip between the browser and the server, but allows the user to see the new URL in the browser address bar. Server.Transfer is a quicker approach in that ASP.NET simply loads the specified page without the round trip. As a result, the browser's address bar is not updated. This can be particularly useful for pipeline style processes such as a checkout system in which the user does not need to see the URLs of pages within the pipeline.

ASP.NET Application Lifecycle

We've now seen how an ASP.NET page is parsed into a class, compiled into an assembly, and then executed, which results in the page event cycle, the end of which is the rendering/generation of HTML that is sent back to the requesting browser. The word *executed* does hide the fact that there is a lot happening behind the scenes when an ASP.NET page runs. The page lifecycle is just one of several processing steps that occurs as part of the larger ASP.NET *application lifecycle*. Figure 2.12 illustrates the key steps in this lifecycle.

Each of the steps shown in Figure 2.12 is described in more detail in the following sections.

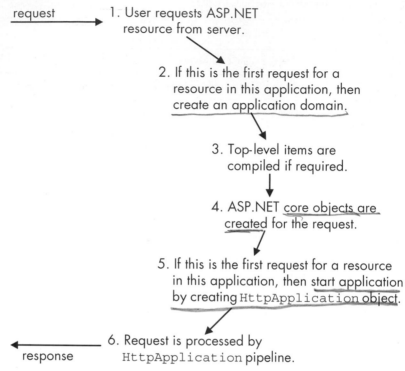

request →

1. User requests ASP.NET resource from server.

2. If this is the first request for a resource in this application, then create an application domain.

3. Top-level items are compiled if required.

4. ASP.NET core objects are created for the request.

5. If this is the first request for a resource in this application, then start application by creating `HttpApplication object`.

6. Request is processed by `HttpApplication` pipeline.

← response

Figure 2.12   Key steps in the ASP.NET application lifecycle

1. User Requests ASP.NET Resource from Server

Like all things dealing with the Web, in the beginning was the request. That is, an ASP.NET application's lifecycle begins when a browser requests an ASP.NET resource from an ASP.NET application on the Web server. ASP.NET resources are just one type of resource that a Web server can handle. Although we have already seen that Visual Studio 2005 provides its own local-only Web server, if an ASP.NET page is going to be available to other users, it must eventually be hosted on a machine running IIS (or some other ASP.NET-capable Web server, such as Cassini). ASP.NET is actually just one of several possible ISAPI (Internet Server API, Microsoft's lower-level programming interface that acts as a bridge between applications and Internet services provided by IIS) extensions and filters running under IIS. An **ISAPI extension** is a Windows DLL that can be directly invoked by a URL and that interacts and works with a request to a Web server; for ASP.NET, the extension is `aspnet_isapi.dll`. An **ISAPI filter**, on the other hand, is a

Windows DLL that modifies the incoming and outgoing data stream to and from IIS; for ASP.NET, the filter is `aspnet_filter.dll`, and is used only to preprocess cookieless session state.

When IIS receives a request, it first examines the extension of the requested resource, and determines which if any ISAPI extension is to handle the request. Requests for static content, such as HTML files and image files, are handled directly by IIS without using an ISAPI extension. When the .NET Framework is installed on the server, it maps `.aspx`, `.asmx`, `.ascx`, `.ashx`, and several other extensions to `aspnet_isapi.dll`. You can view these mappings in IIS via the Configuration option under the Home Directory or Virtual Directory tab (see Figure 2.13).

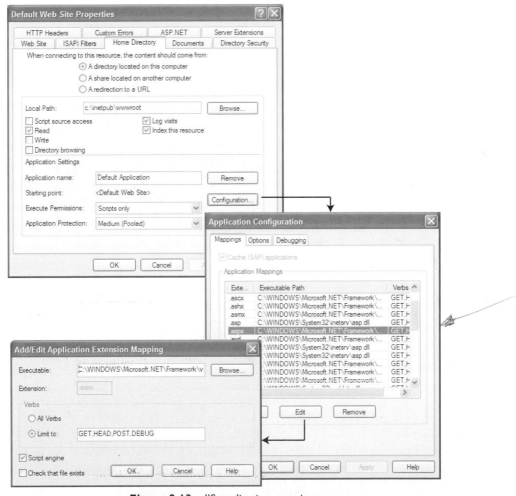

Figure 2.13 IIS application mappings

CORE NOTE

It is also possible within the Web Site properties dialog to specify which version of ASP.NET (and thus `aspnet_isapi.dll`) will be handling ASP.NET requests for the application, as shown in Figure 2.14.

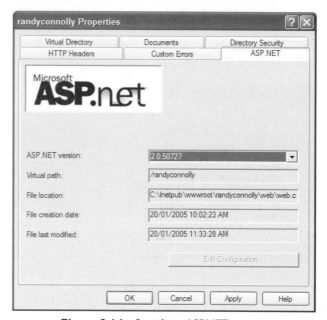

Figure 2.14   Specifying ASP.NET version

Recall that if the filename extension has not been mapped to ASP.NET, ASP.NET does not handle the request. Basic HTML pages and the common image file formats, for instance, are not, by default, mapped to ASP.NET. As a result, ASP.NET security does not apply to these files. (In IIS 6, however, you can use wildcard mapping to map all extensions to `aspnet_isapi.dll`.)

After IIS recognizes a request as an ASP.NET request, the request is passed on to `aspnet_isapi.dll`. How this process occurs and what happens next varies depending upon whether the IIS 5, IIS 6 (Windows Server 2003 only), or IIS 7 (Windows Vista and Longhorn only) processing model is being used.

In the IIS 5 processing model, the `aspnet_isapi.dll` extension is usually hosted directly within the IIS process. When the extension receives the request, it spawns, if not already running, the ASP.NET **_worker process_** (`aspnet_wp.exe`), which then takes over and controls the execution of the request. This worker process is a small Win32 executable that loads and hosts the CLR. Generally, there is only one instance of this process running on the machine; that is, all future requests are routed through this one worker process (see Figure 2.15). However, if there are multiple CPUs on the Web server, each CPU can run a separate single worker process.

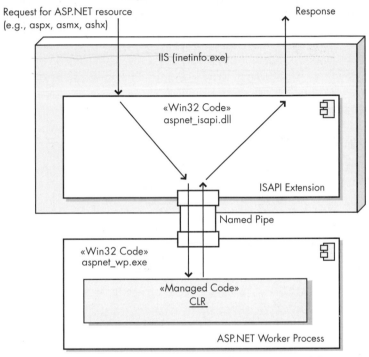

Figure 2.15   ASP.NET and the IIS 5 processing model

In the IIS 6 processing model, IIS no longer hosts any ISAPI extensions. Instead, requests are sent to a generic worker process (named w3wp.exe) for that specific ASP.NET application. This worker process then hosts the aspnet_isapi.dll extension. One advantage of the IIS 6 model is that each Web application process is isolated from every other Web application process (and indeed from every other ISAPI extension), as can be seen in Figure 2.16.

In IIS 6, each worker process can run one or more Web applications. This Web application running within a worker process is called an IIS *application pool*. Figure 2.17 illustrates the configuration of application pools within IIS 6.0.

At any rate, in both IIS 5 and IIS 6, the worker process finally hands over the request to a chain of .NET classes, which continue the request processing.

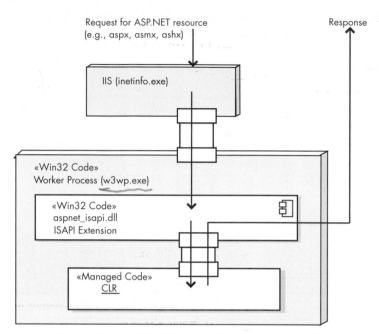

Figure 2.16   ASP.NET and the IIS 6 processing model

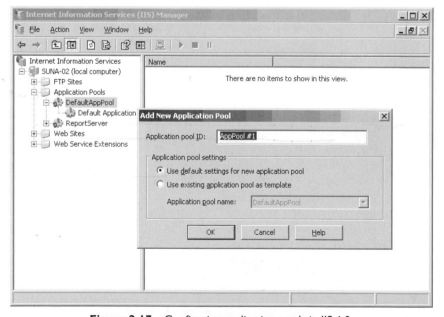

Figure 2.17   Configuring application pools in IIS 6.0

At the time of this book's writing, IIS 7 is currently in beta. In IIS 7, ASP.NET is now integrated into the core server. In both the IIS 5 and IIS 6 process model, ASP.NET requests are first processed by IIS and then forwarded to the ASP.NET ISAPI extension. In IIS 7, ASP.NET processing is handled directly within IIS. ASP.NET modules are now integrated directly into the IIS request pipeline itself. As such, .NET modules can now potentially be used for non-ASP.NET requests. As well, ASP.NET modules can run before or even replace existing IIS functionality. However, using this new IIS 7 integrated mode may require making some changes to the ASP.NET Web application's configuration settings (in the `Web.config` file), if that application uses any custom HTTP modules or HTTP handlers.

If First Request for Any Resource in Application, Create Application Domain

A given Web server can host multiple Web applications. Each Web application typically exists as a separate IIS virtual directory on the server or as the Web site root. When the server receives its first request for an ASP.NET resource for a Web application, a class called `ApplicationManager`, which activates, initializes, and manages the lifetime of all the ASP.NET applications, creates a managed *application domain* as a managed `AppDomain` class. Each ASP.NET application is housed within its own `AppDomain` (see Figure 2.18); this provides each application with its own

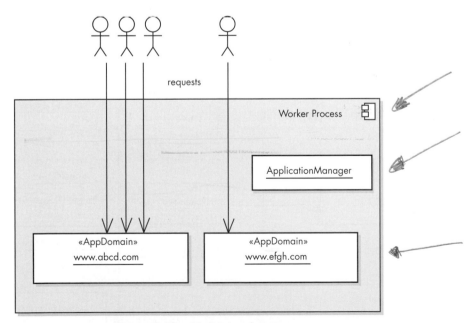

requests

Worker Process

ApplicationManager

«AppDomain»
www.abcd.com

«AppDomain»
www.efgh.com

Figure 2.18 Application domains

memory isolation without the cost of a separate Windows process. Because each ASP.NET Web application is hosted within its own application domain, each application can have its own runtime environment.

After the AppDomain is created, an instance of the HttpRuntime class is created and contained within the AppDomain. The ProcessRequest method of the HttpRuntime object is called.

Top-Level Items Are Compiled If Required

As mentioned in the earlier section on compilation order, top-level resource items are compiled before other ASP.NET items. It is at this point in the lifecycle that the top-level resource items are compiled if they haven't already been compiled or if there has been a change in a top-level item.

ASP.NET Core Objects Are Created for the Request

After the ProcessRequest method of the HttpRuntime object is called, the ASP.NET runtime creates the core objects for processing requests within the ASP.NET environment. The first of these is HttpContext, which represents the context of the current request, and which creates and wraps (i.e., provides programmatic access via properties to) the other core objects for processing a request, namely the HttpRequest, HttpResponse, Cache, HttpApplicationState, HttpSessionState, HttpServerUtility, ProfileBase, and TraceContext objects, as shown in Figure 2.19.

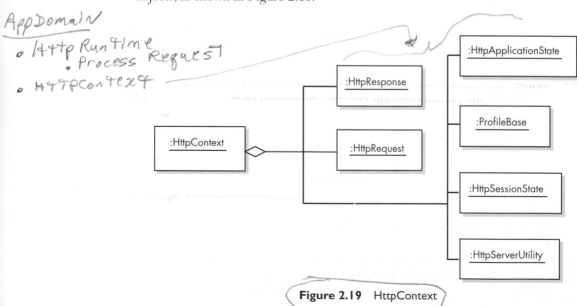

Figure 2.19   HttpContext

Perhaps the two most important of these are the `HttpRequest` and the `Http-Response` objects. The `HttpRequest` class contains all the information about the current request, such as the requesting browser type, cookies for this site contained on the client, and any GET/POST parameter values being sent to the server. The `HttpResponse` class encapsulates all the HTTP response information sent from an ASP.NET operation back to the browser, such as the rendered output (HTML), cookies, and HTTP header information.

5. *Assign HttpApplication Object to Request*

After the core objects are created, the `HttpRuntime` retrieves an application object to fulfill the request. An application object is an instance of the `HttpApplication` class. If the site has a `Global.asax` file (also known as an ASP.NET *application class/file*), ASP.NET creates an instance of the class defined in this file instead of an `HttpApplication` object. The `Global.asax` file is an optional file that contains event handlers for application-level and session-level events raised by ASP.NET or by HTTP modules (see the following discussion on modules). The `Global.asax` file is stored in the root of an ASP.NET application. At runtime, `Global.asax` is parsed and compiled into a dynamically generated class derived from the `HttpApplication` base class.

Each `AppDomain` (through the `HttpApplicationFactory`) maintains a pool of `HttpApplication` objects, as shown in Figure 2.20. Although each instance of the `HttpApplication` class processes many requests in its lifetime, it can only process one request at a time. The size of this pool is dependent upon the application's load (i.e., the number of simultaneous requests).

When the `HttpApplication` object is created, any HTTP modules associated with the application are also created and contained within it, as shown in Figure 2.20. An ***HTTP module*** is an object that is used for *every* request made to an application. HTTP modules are called as part of the `HttpApplication` request pipeline (see "Process Request Using HttpApplication Pipeline" beginning on page 92). ASP.NET HTTP modules are similar to ISAPI filters in that they run for all requests. However, they are written in managed code and are fully integrated with the lifecycle of an ASP.NET application. HTTP modules can also be reused across applications. HTTP modules are thus used to examine incoming requests, take actions based on the request, and examine the outbound response and modify it, if necessary.

ASP.NET uses modules to implement a variety of application features. Some of the built-in modules help implement caching, security authentication, session state services, role management, permissions for accessing URLs and files, as well as error handling (see Table 2.8). Modules can consume application events and can raise events that can be handled in the `Global.asax` file.

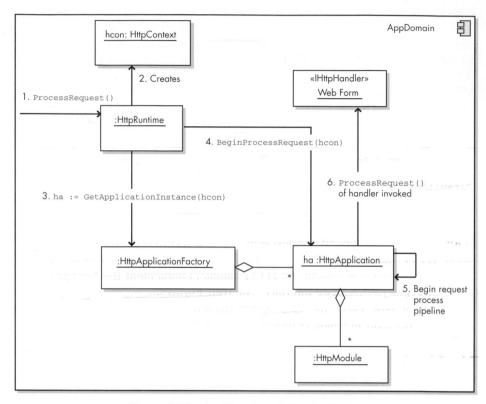

Figure 2.20   AppDomain and HttpApplication

Table 2.8   ASP.NET HttpModules

Module	Description
OutputCacheModule	Handles ASP.NET page-level caching.
SessionStateModule	Manages the session state.
WindowsAuthenticationModule	Authenticates using Windows authentication.
FormsAuthenticationModule	Authenticates using Forms authentication.
PassportAuthenticationModule	Authenticates using Passport authentication.
RoleManagerModule	Manages the roles for the current user.
UrlAuthorizationModule	Authorizes using requested URL.

Table 2.8   ASP.NET HttpModules *(continued)*

Module	Description
FileAuthorizationModule	Authorizes using requested file.
AnonymousIdentificationModule	Manages anonymous identifiers.
ProfileModule	Manages creation of user profile and profile events.
ErrorHandlerModule	Traps errors and displays messages.
DefaultAuthenticationModule	Ensures that an authentication object is present in the context.

Although modules operate against every request received by the ASP.NET application, **HTTP handlers**, on the other hand, operate only against specific requests based on the request extension. All HTTP handlers implement the IHttpHandler or the IHttpAsyncHandler interface. All Web Forms are in fact HTTP handlers because their base class (the Page class) implements IHttpHandler. ASP.NET comes with the built-in handlers shown in Table 2.9.

Table 2.9   ASP.NET HttpHandlers

Handler	Description
.aspx	Handler for regular ASP.NET Web Forms.
.asmx	Handler for ASPNET Web services.
.ascx	Handler for user controls.
Trace.axd	Special handler for ASP.NET trace viewer.

You can also create your own HTTP handlers by creating a class that implements the IHttpHandler or the IHttpAsyncHandler interface. Handlers must also be defined in the HttpHandlers section of the Web.config file.

So why would you want to create a custom handler? The typical reason for using a custom handler instead of simply using a Web Form is for situations in which you want to avoid the overhead involved (such as view state) with ASP.NET Web Form processing. For instance, imagine if you needed to satisfy requests for images being pulled from a database. If these requests do not need to output any HTML, but simply return the retrieved image, it is much quicker (to execute, not to develop) for this functionality to run as an HTTP handler.

6. *Process Request Using HttpApplication Pipeline*

After the `HttpApplication` object has been initialized and retrieved, the request can finally be processed. The request is processed in a certain specific order, and for this reason, it is called a *pipeline*. This request pipeline mainly consists of triggered events. The majority of these events are handled by the `HttpApplicaton` object, whereas others are handled by the various HTTP modules or by the HTTP handler defined for the requested file type. The steps in the pipeline are as follows.

1. Validate the request.

   The request information sent by the browser is initially preprocessed to verify that it contains nothing potentially dangerous in terms of security.

2. Perform URL mapping if necessary.

   The `Web.config` file allows you to map a URL that is displayed to users to a URL that exists in your Web application. This mapping occurs here.

3. `BeginRequest` event triggered.

   This event indicates the creation of any given new request. This event is always raised and is always the first event to occur during the processing of a request.

4. `AuthenticateRequest` event triggered.

   This event is triggered when the authentication mechanism configured (in the `Web.config` file) has authenticated (i.e., established the identity of) the user of the current request.

5. `PostAuthenticateRequest` event triggered.

   This event is triggered after the `AuthenticateRequest` event has occurred (that is, after the identity of the user has been established).

6. `AuthorizeRequest` event triggered.

   This event occurs when ASP.NET has authorized the current request.

7. `PostAuthorizeRequest` event triggered.

   This event is triggered after the `AuthorizeRequest` event has occurred (that is, after the request has been authorized).

8. `ResolveRequestCache` event triggered.

   When this event occurs, any HTTP caching modules can serve requests from the cache, bypassing execution of the rest of this pipeline.

9. `PostResolveRequestCache` event triggered.

   This event is triggered after the request cache has been processed.

10. Based on the filename extension of the requested resource, the appropriate HTTP handler is instantiated.

11. `PostMapRequestHandler` event triggered.

This event is triggered after the current request has been mapped to the appropriate HTTP handler.

12. `AcquireRequestState` event triggered.

This event is triggered when the current state (for example, session state) that is associated with the current request is acquired from the ASP.NET runtime.

13. `PostAcquireRequestState` event triggered.

This event is triggered after the state for the current request is acquired.

14. `PreRequestHandlerExecute` event triggered.

This event is triggered just before the HTTP handler executes.

15. Call the `ProcessRequest` method of the HTTP handler class.

The `ProcessRequest` method enables processing of the requests by the HTTP handler. For Web Forms, this method is defined in the base `Page` class. *In other words, it is during this event that the Web Form executes.* The page lifecycle, as shown in Figure 2.8, can be inserted here.

16. `PostRequestHandlerExecute` event triggered.

This event is triggered after the HTTP handler class has finished executing the `ProcessRequest` method.

17. `ReleaseRequestState` event triggered.

This event is triggered after the application is finished with the request. This event tells any state HTTP modules to save the current state data.

18. `PostReleaseRequestState` event triggered.

This event is triggered after the request state has been saved.

19. Perform response filtering if specified.

The `HttpResponse` object has a `Filter` property that allows a filter to be wrapped around the output sent to the HTTP response stream.

20. `UpdateRequestCache` event triggered.

When this event is triggered, any HTTP caching modules can store responses that will be used to serve subsequent requests from the cache.

21. `PostUpdateRequestCache` event triggered.

This event is triggered after the request cache has been updated.

22. `EndRequest` event triggered.

This event is triggered to indicate that the HTTP request pipeline chain is finished.

CORE NOTE

If you want to examine the setup of this pipeline yourself, you can do so by examining the private `InitInternal` **method of** `HttpApplication`.

Thankfully, for the vast majority of ASP.NET Web applications, the developer can remain blithely unaware of this complex chain of events in the ASP.NET lifecycle. The ASP.NET runtime does a truly wonderful job of hiding the complexity of the environment from the developer.

Summary

This chapter examined the details of how ASP.NET works. It examined how Web Forms are parsed and compiled, the lifecycle of ASP.NET applications, as well as how the ASP.NET event system works.

The next chapter examines in detail the most essential of the standard Web server controls. These controls are the building blocks of most Web Forms; as such, learning how to use them is the essential next step in learning ASP.NET.

Exercises

The solution to the following exercise can be found at my Web site, `http://www.randyconnolly.com/core`. Additional exercises only available for teachers and instructors are also available from this site.

1. Create a Web Form that contains two `TextBox` controls, a `Label` control and a `Button` control. Add an event handler to the `Button` control so that it adds the two numbers entered into the two `TextBox` controls and displays the result in the `Label` control.

Key Concepts

- Application class/file
- Application domain
- Application lifecycle
- Application pool
- Application restart

- Change events
- Control events
- Control state
- Cross-page posting
- Delegate
- Event handler
- HTTP handler
- HTTP module
- `HttpApplication` pipeline
- ISAPI extension
- ISAPI filter
- Page events
- Page lifecycle
- Partial class
- Postback
- Round trip
- View state
- Worker process
- XML documentation comments

References

Allen, Scott. "Design Considerations for Cross-Page Postbacks in ASP.NET 2.0." `http://www.odetocode.com`.

Bustamante, Michele Leroux. "Inside IIS & ASP.NET." `www.theserverside.com`.

Esposito, Dino. "The ASP.NET HTTP Runtime." `http://msdn.microsoft.com`.

Esposito, Dino. "Cross-page Postbacks." *asp.netPRO Magazine* (September 2006).

Microsoft. "ASP.NET Application Life Cycle Overview." `http://msdn.microsoft.com`.

Onion, Fritz. *Essential ASP.NET with Examples in C#*. Pearson Education, Inc, 2003.

Patel, Jayesh, *et al*. "ASP.NET 2.0 Internals." `http://msdn.microsoft.com`.

Strahl, Rick. "A Low Level Look at ASP.NET Architecture." `http://www.code-magazine.com`.

Strahl, Rick. "Understanding Page Inheritance in ASP.NET 2.0." `http://west-wind.com/weblog/posts/3016.aspx`.

Wilson, Paul. "Page Events: Order and Postback." `http://authors.aspalliance.com/PaulWilson/Articles`.

3

WORKING WITH THE STANDARD WEB SERVER CONTROLS

In the two previous chapters, we created several basic ASP.NET pages using a few of the basic Web server controls, such as `Label`, `TextBox`, `Button`, and `DropDown-List`. ASP.NET provides many (over 60) other Web server controls. Although one does not necessarily need to learn the intimate details of every one of these controls, the development of most real Web applications requires a good grasp of a subset of these controls, which are referred to in Visual Studio as the standard Web server controls. This chapter covers these essential Web server controls; subsequent chapters cover the rest.

This chapter is quite long because it covers 19 different controls. Although the controls are presented in an order that starts with the simplest and progresses to the more complex, the reader can also use this chapter more as a reference and jump "randomly" from one control to another.

Introducing Server Controls

Normal HTML tags such as `<input>`, `<H1>`, and `<select>` are not processed by the server but are sent to and displayed by the browser. Server controls, in contrast, are tags that are processed by the server. Each ASP.NET server control has an object model containing properties, methods, and events. You can use this object model to interact with the control.

There are five kinds of server controls:

- HTML server controls
- Web server controls
- Validation server controls
- User controls
- Custom server controls

All five of these different types of controls can be used within a single given Web Form.

HTML Server Controls

Most standard HTML tags can be turned into **HTML server controls** simply by adding the `runat="server"` attribute. This `runat` attribute indicates that the element is to be processed on the server, and as such, you can programmatically respond to events or bind data. Web server controls are almost always preferable to HTML server controls due to their richly typed object model, to the more complex interactions that they allow, to their capability to automatically generate the correct HTML for both downlevel (HTML 3.2) and uplevel (HTML 4.0) browsers, and to their support of data binding. For this reason, this book does not cover HTML server controls, but instead focuses on using Web server controls.

However, HTML server controls can be useful for situations in which you need complete control over how the HTML element will be rendered in the browser, or when migrating an existing ASP page to ASP.NET.

Web Server Controls

Like HTML server controls, **Web server controls** are also created on the server and they require a `runat="server"` attribute to work. Some Web server controls represent traditional HTML form elements, such as buttons and drop-down lists; other Web server controls represent more complex or abstract elements, such as calendars, data lists, data sources, and tree views. These more complex Web server controls do not necessarily map one-to-one (or even at all) to any existing HTML tags and can in fact be realized by dozens if not hundreds of HTML tags and many lines of Javascript code.

Validation Controls

These controls allow you to test a user's input for validity. They are simply a special type of Web server control. Validation controls encapsulate common user input validation checks required by most Web applications: ensuring that a required field is not empty, comparing an input value against another value, checking if a value falls within a range, and verifying that an input value matches a given pattern. Validation controls are covered in Chapter 5.

User Controls

These are developer-created controls that use the same programming techniques used to write Web Forms pages. They typically allow the encapsulation of the functionality of multiple server controls along with other ASP.NET or HTML content in a single unit. User controls are covered in Chapter 6.

Custom Server Controls

A custom server control is a Web server control that you can create. A custom control is a compiled class and may combine multiple existing server controls. A custom control, unlike a user control, contains no declarative elements and can be extended, use templates, support data binding, and be redistributed in a precompiled assembly. Although this book does not have a section dedicated to the construction of custom server controls, two sample custom server controls are created in Chapter 14.

Overview of Web Server Controls

Web server controls are added to a Web Form in the same way as any HTML element. That is, you can type the markup code in Source view or use drag-and-drop from Source or Design view. As well, you can programmatically add controls at runtime (although we won't be doing this until the next chapter). The syntax for creating a Web server control is

```
<asp:controlName id="some_id" runat="server" «other attributes» >
</asp:controlName>
```

Table 3.1 lists the standard Web server controls. Those marked with an asterisk are covered in the next chapter.

Table 3.1   Standard Web Server Controls

Server Control	Description
AdRotator*	Displays an advertisement banner (i.e., a randomly selected image that when clicked navigates to a new Web page).
BulletedList	Displays a bulleted list of items.
Button	Displays a push button that posts a Web Form page back to the server.
Calendar	Displays a month calendar from which the user can select dates.
CheckBox	Displays a check box for selected true or false values.
CheckBoxList	Displays a multiselection check box group.
DropDownList	Displays a drop-down list for selecting a value from a list of values.
FileUpload*	Allows a user to upload a file to the server. Consists of a text box and browse button.
HiddenField	Stores a nondisplayed value in a form that needs to be persisted across posts.
HyperLink	Displays a hyperlink that when clicked requests a different page.
Image	Displays an image.
ImageButton	Displays an image that posts the form back to the server.
ImageMap	Displays an image with predefined hot spot regions that post back to the server or navigate to a different page.
Label	Displays static content that can be set programmatically and whose content can be styled.
LinkButton	Creates a hyperlink-style button that posts the form back to the server.
ListBox	Creates a single- or multiselection list.
Literal	Like the Label, displays static content that is programmable. Unlike the Label control, it does not let you apply styles to its content.

Table 3.1 Standard Web Server Controls *(continued)*

Server Control	Description
MultiView and View*	The MultiView control is a container for groups of View controls. A View control is a container for HTML content and other server controls. The MultiView control displays only a single View at a time.
Panel*	Provides a container for other controls and HTML content so that the content in the Panel can act as a single unit.
PlaceHolder*	A container control used for dynamically loading other controls.
RadioButton	Creates a radio button form element.
RadioButtonList	Creates a group of radio button form elements.
Table	Creates an HTML table; principally used for programmatically constructing a table.
TextBox	Creates a text box form element.
Wizard*	Provides a series of interconnected forms used for collecting information incrementally from the user.
Xml*	Displays an XML file or the results of an XSLT (Extensible Stylesheet Language Transformation) transformation.

Common Members

Learning how to work with all of these controls might seem a daunting prospect. Thankfully, one way the designers of ASP.NET endeavored to make the process of learning how to use Web server controls easier is their object model (see Figure 3.1).

As can be seen in Figure 3.1, most Web server controls inherit from the WebControl class (the exceptions for the standard server controls shown in the diagram are the Literal and Xml controls). This WebControl class in turn inherits from the Control class. Both of these base classes define a variety of properties, methods, and events (most of which modify the formatting and display of the controls) that are available to all controls derived from them. Most of the properties are available at design time, and can thus be set declaratively (i.e., within the tag).

Table 3.2 lists the most notable properties of the WebControl class.

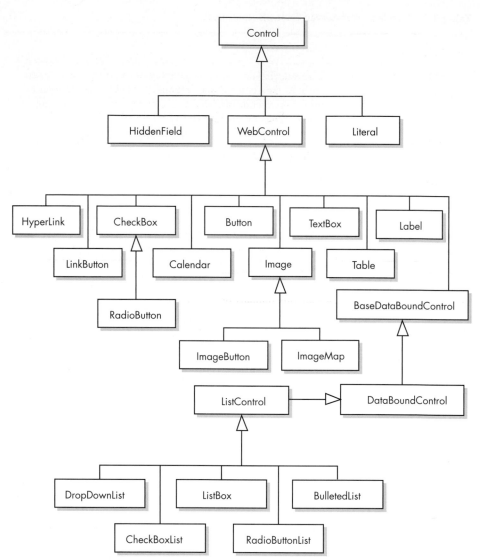

Figure 3.1 Partial object model for standard Web server controls

Table 3.2 Notable Properties of the WebControl Class

Property	Description
AccessKey	The control's keyboard shortcut key (a single letter). The user can press this key in conjunction with the ALT key to access the control.
Attributes	Collection of additional attributes not defined by the control.
BackColor	The background color (either standard HTML color identifier or the name of the color) of the control.
BorderColor	The color of the control's border.
BorderWidth	The thickness (in pixels) of the control's border.
BorderStyle	The style (e.g., dotted, dashed, solid, double, etc.) of the control's border. Possible values are described by the BorderStyle enumeration.
CssClass	The CSS class name assigned to the control.
Enabled	Toggles the functionality of the control; if set to false, the control is disabled.
Font	Font information for the control. This property contains subproperties (see the following Core Note).
Height	The height of the control.
TabIndex	The control's position in the tab order.
ToolTip	The tool tip text (i.e., the text that appears when the mouse rests over control) for the control.
Width	The width of the control.

CORE NOTE

Properties can also have properties; these are called **subproperties**. For instance, the Font property is a complex object with properties of its own, such as Name and Size. When working with subproperties programmatically, you use dot notation (e.g., somecontrol.Font.Size=10;). When working with subproperties declaratively, you use hyphen (-) notation (e.g., <asp:Label id="somecontrol" Font-Size="10" runat="server" />).

The WebControl class itself inherits from another class, the Control class, which also contains some properties that you may need to manipulate to change the appearance of a Web server control. Notable properties of the Control class are summarized in Table 3.3.

Table 3.3   Notable Properties of the Control Class

Property	Description
Controls	Collection of child controls for the control.
EnableViewState	Specifies whether the control persists its view state to the client.
Id	The unique identifier for the control.
Page	A reference to the Web Form that contains this control.
Parent	A reference to the parent control (if any) for this control.
SkinID	A reference to the skin applied to a control. A theme can contain multiple skins; this property specifies which of those skins to apply to the control. Skins are covered in Chapter 6.
Visible	Specifies whether the control is visible.

Manipulating Properties Programmatically

You can retrieve the value of a property or set the value of a property at runtime. These properties are strongly typed and vary depending upon the property. Thus, some properties have a primitive data type such as a Boolean or a numeric, whereas other property values are defined by an enumerated type or some other type, for example:

```
// Using a primitive
myLabel.Text = "Randy";
string abc = myTextBox.Text;
myLabel.Visible = false;

// Using an enumeration
myBulletedList.BulletStyle = BulletStyle.Circle;
TextBoxMode mode = myTextBox.TextMode;
```

Event Properties

All controls support events. You can specify the event handler method for a given event declaratively by affixing the `On` prefix to the event property name. For instance, if you have an event handling method named `btnOne_Click` that you want to run when the user clicks a button, you would use

```
<asp:button id="btnOne" runat="server" OnClick="btnOne_Click" />
```

Event properties can also be set programmatically. This was the method that the Visual Studio 2003 designers used for connecting events to their handlers. (Visual Studio 2005 now uses the declarative approach.) The equivalent programmatic setting of the previous event property would look like

```
btnOne.Click += new EventHandler(btnOne_Click);
```

The type for the `Click` event is `EventHandler`, which is a delegate type. The delegate must be provided with the name of the event handling method (`btnOne_Click`); this method must have the signature specified by `EventHandler`. By convention, all event delegates in the .NET Framework are void methods with two parameters: the source object that raised the event and the data for the event, usually contained within an `EventArgs` object (or an object derived from it). Thus, the method signature of your sample event handler would be

```
void btnOne_Click(object source, EventArgs e)
```

Unit-Based Measurement Properties

Various measurement properties such as `Width`, `Height`, and `Font.Size` are implemented using the `Unit` structure. This `Unit` structure allows you to use any HTML- or CSS-compatible size unit, such as cm, inch, and pixels. These size units are defined in the `UnitType` enumeration. For instance, you can set the `Width` property to 90 pixels using

```
Unit un = new Unit(90);
un.Type = UnitType.Pixel;
labMsg.Width = un;
```

Color-Based Properties

All color-based properties use the `Color` structure. The `Color` structure defines all the HTML 4.0 system-defined colors as well as the color names supported by most browsers (such as `Color.Gold` and `Color.LemonChiffon`), as well as methods for retrieving and specifying color using different color models (such as HSB and RGB). As a result, a color can be specified in at least four different ways, as shown here:

```
// Set the color using predefined value
labMsg.ForeColor = Color.Gold;

// Set the color using a predefined name
labMsg.ForeColor = Color.FromName("Gold");

// Set the color using RGB
labMsg.ForeColor = Color.FromArgb(204, 153, 0);

// Set the color using hexadecimal HTML color
labMsg.ForeColor = Color.FromName("#CC9900");
```

Collection Properties

Some properties are not a single structure, primitive, or enumerated type, but a collection of other objects. An example of such a property is the `Items` collection of the `DropDownList` control; this collection contains zero or more `ListItem` objects. These collection properties have their own methods and properties for determining the size of the collection, as well for adding, retrieving, and removing items from the collection. The following code illustrates how one of these collection properties is typical manipulated.

```
DropDownList drpSample = new DropDownList();

// Create the item, then add to collection
ListItem li = new ListItem("Item 2");
drpSample.Items.Add(li);

// Combine the creation and addition to collection steps
drpSample.Items.Add(new ListItem("Item 1"));
```

Additional Control Attributes

Although each Web server control has a wide variety of properties that encapsulate most of the required functionality of the control, you can also add or read additional **HTML attributes** of the control. Attributes are name-value pairs that are added to the rendered HTML. One of the reasons for using these attributes is to provide additional client-side scripting behavior to a control. For instance:

```
myButton.Attributes.Add("onclick",
   "alert('Posting information...')");
myButton.Attributes["onmouseout"] = "document.bgColor='green';";
myButton.Attributes["onmouseover"] = "document.bgColor='blue';";
```

This code shows two different ways to connect Javascript function calls to client-side events. The first line causes a Javascript alert box to pop up when the user clicks the button; the last two lines change the background color of the browser window when a user moves her mouse over and off the button. These three lines are rendered in the browser as

```
<input type="submit" name="myButton" value="Click Me"
    onclick="alert('Posting information...');" id="myButton"
    onmouseout="document.bgColor='green';"
    onmouseover="document.bgColor='blue';" />
```

CORE NOTE

Notice that the `id` value of the server control is passed down to the client as an HTML `id` attribute (and not the `name` attribute). As a result, if you want to reference this control in the Javascript, it must be fully qualified.

Although using attributes provides a relatively easy way to programmatically attach a few lines of Javascript to a control, it is quite unwieldy for any Javascript more than a few lines long. Debugging a long Javascript script that is placed within a single C# string is not for the faint of heart. A much better approach is to place as much of your Javascript as possible into a client-side script file and limit the code in your attributes to calls to functions in that file.

The Essential Standard Web Server Controls

This section covers the essential standard Web server controls in detail. For each of these controls there are descriptions, property and event summaries, and sample listings that illustrate typical uses of that control. You can download either a starting or a finished version of the files used in the chapter from my Web site, http://www.randyconnolly.com/core.

CORE NOTE

Because all of these controls ultimately inherit from `WebControl` and/or `Control`, only the control's unique properties and events are summarized in any of the following tables in this chapter.

Label Control

The `Label` control is used to display static (that is, users cannot edit it) content on a Web page. A `Label` control is typically used when you want to programmatically change or set the text in a page at runtime. `Label` controls can also be used as child controls of some of the other templated controls such as the `Repeater` and the `GridView`.

Table 3.4 lists the unique properties of the `Label` control.

Table 3.4   Unique Properties of the Label Control

Property	Description
AssociatedControlId	The ID of the control that will be associated with this label. Used to associate the access key for the label with another control (described in the following section, "Assigning An Access Key").
Text	Specifies the text content of the control.

To display text in a `Label` control, one only needs to assign string data to its `Text` property. You can also include HTML tags in this string data, as shown in the following:

```
labMsg.Text = "<p>This is the <i>First</i> line";
labMsg.Text += "<br>" + "This is second line</p>";
```

It may not be all that clear why you would use a `Label` control and not simply type in your static text directly in the HTML. Typically, `Label` controls are used in conjunction with other controls. For instance, you could place a `Label` control on the form that only contains text if some type of error occurs, or is assigned a message after some other postback form event occurs (such as selecting from a list or clicking a button). Many of the examples for the subsequent controls in this chapter use `Label` controls.

`Label` controls are rendered in the browser as static text within an HTML `<span>` element. For instance, the following control,

```
<asp:Label id="labMsg" runat="server" text="hello"/>
```

is rendered as

```
<span id="labMsg">hello</span>
```

Assigning an Access Key

HTML 4.0 supports the use of the `AccessKey` attribute for links and form elements. It allows the user to use a combination of keyboard keys (on Windows machines, usually the ALT key plus some other key) to do a function usually performed by a mouse. Version 2.0 of ASP.NET supports the association of `Label` controls with other controls, so the `AccessKey` of the `Label` moves the focus to the associated control. For instance, in Listing 3.1, two `Label` controls provide hot keys for a `TextBox` and `DropDownList` control. Notice as well that underlines have been added to the label to show the user the access key for accessing the associated control. The result in the browser is shown in Figure 3.2.

CORE NOTE

In this and most of the other Web Form listings in this chapter, some of the markup (for instance, page directives, CSS definitions, and `html`, `head`, `body`, and `form` elements) has been omitted for brevity's sake.

Listing 3.1   LabelHotKeys.aspx

```
<h1>Using AccessKey for Controls</h1>
<asp:Label ID="labName" runat="server"
    AccessKey="N" AssociatedControlID="txtName"
    Text="<u>N</u>ame">
</asp:Label>
<asp:TextBox ID="txtName" runat="server"></asp:TextBox><br />

<asp:Label ID="labMonth" runat="server"
    AccessKey="M" AssociatedControlID="drpMonth"
    Text="<u>M</u>onth">
</asp:Label>
<asp:DropDownList ID="drpMonth" runat="server">
    <asp:ListItem>January</asp:ListItem>
    <asp:ListItem>February</asp:ListItem>
    <asp:ListItem>March</asp:ListItem>
</asp:DropDownList>
```

CORE NOTE

You cannot assign a hot key that is already used by the browser's user interface. For instance, Alt+F is used by Internet Explorer to activate the File menu, so you cannot use F as a hot key.

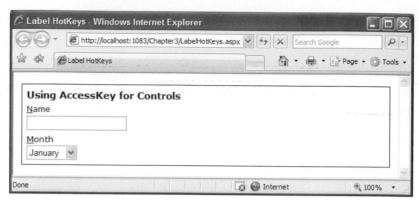

Figure 3.2   LabelHotKeys.aspx

Literal Control

Like the Label control, the Literal control displays static text content on a Web page. Also like the Label control, the Literal control allows for the programmatic manipulation of its content at runtime using server code. However, unlike the Label Web server control, the Literal control does not add any HTML elements to the text. With the Label control, the content is wrapped in an HTML <span> element; with the Literal control, the <span> element is not added.

Unlike most of the other Web server controls covered in this chapter, the Literal control does not inherit from the WebControl class; instead, it inherits from the Control class. This means the various properties listed in Table 3.2 are not available to the Literal control. Table 3.5 lists the unique properties of the Literal control.

Table 3.5   Unique Properties of the Literal Control

Property	Description
LiteralMode	Specifies whether the text content of the control is to be unchanged (PassThrough), HTML-encoded (Encode), or transformed to remove unsupported markup elements (Transform). Possible values are described by the LiteralMode enumeration. The default is Transform.
Text	Specifies the text content of the control.

Listing 3.2 demonstrates the use of these three different literal modes. Figure 3.3 illustrates the result.

Listing 3.2 LiteralTest.aspx

```
<h1>LiteralMode Test</h1>
<h2>PassThrough</h2>
<asp:Literal ID="Literal1" Mode="PassThrough" runat="Server"
    Text="<b>bold</b><br/><i>italic</i><bad>
        unsupported</bad><br/>" >
</asp:Literal>

<h2>Encode</h2>
<asp:Literal ID="Literal2" Mode="Encode" runat="Server"
    Text="<b>bold</b><br/><i>italic</i><bad>
        unsupported</bad><br/>" >
</asp:Literal>

<h2>Transform</h2>
<asp:Literal ID="Literal3" Mode="Transform" runat="Server"
    Text="<b>bold</b><br/><i>italic</i><bad>
        unsupported</bad><br/>" >
</asp:Literal>
```

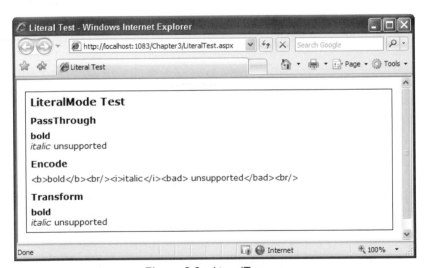

Figure 3.3 LiteralTest.aspx

The code shown in Listing 3.2 generates the following HTML.

```
<h1>LiteralMode Test</h1>
<h2>PassThrough</h2>
<b>bold</b><br/><i>italic</i><bad> unsupported</bad><br/>
```

```
<h2>Encode</h2>
&lt;b&gt;bold&lt;/b&gt;&lt;br/&gt;&lt;i&gt;italic&lt;/i&gt;&lt;
bad&gt;unsupported&lt;/bad&gt;&lt;br/&gt;
<h2>Transform</h2>
<b>bold</b><br/><i>italic</i><bad> unsupported</bad><br/>
```

Notice how the encoded content has been HTML-encoded so that the markup is visible to the user. Notice as well that the Transformed content has not been transformed! The reason the unsupported tag has not been removed is that when the Literal control is rendered on a browser that supports HTML or XHTML, setting the LiteralMode to Transform produces the same behavior as specifying PassThrough.

TextBox Control

The TextBox control is used to display a single-line text box or a multiline text area form element. This text box can contain either a single or multiple lines. Table 3.6 lists the unique properties of the TextBox control.

Table 3.6   Unique Properties of the TextBox Control

Property	Description
AutoCompleteType	Specifies the AutoComplete behavior of the text box. Current browsers support a feature called AutoComplete that allows a user to fill a common text box (such as a last name or phone number) from a list of stored values maintained by the browser. You can set this property to one of the values in the AutoCompleteType enumeration. The default for this property is None. This property is rendered in the browser as the vcard_name attribute.
AutoPostBack	A Boolean value that indicates whether an automatic postback to the server should occur when the user modifies the text in the control and then moves the focus out of the control.
Columns	Controls the display width of the box in characters.
MaxLength	Specifies the maximum number of characters that can be entered in the text box.
Rows	Specifies the number of rows that are displayed in a multiline text area.
TextMode	Specifies whether the text box is single-line (the default), multiline, or password. Can be programmatically set using the TextBoxMode enumeration.
Wrap	A Boolean value that indicates whether the content of a multiline box uses word wrapping.

Listing 3.3 illustrates several examples of the TextBox control.

Listing 3.3   TextBoxTest.aspx

```
<p>
   Name: <br />
   <asp:TextBox ID="txtName" runat="server"
      AutoCompleteType="LastName" />
</p>
<p>
   State: <br />
   <asp:TextBox ID="txtState" runat="server" MaxLength="2"
      Columns="2" AutoCompleteType="HomeCountryRegion" />
</p>
<p>
   Comments: <br />
   <asp:TextBox ID="txtComments" runat="server" Rows="4"
      TextMode="MultiLine" Wrap="true" />
</p>
<p>
Password:
   <br />
   <asp:TextBox ID="txtPass" runat="server" TextMode="Password" />
</p>
```

Figure 3.4 illustrates how these different TextBox controls are rendered in the browser.

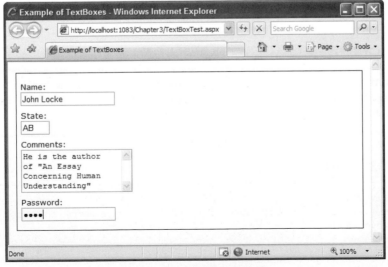

Figure 3.4   TextBoxTest.aspx

The `TextBox` control has one unique event shown in Table 3.7. Like all control events, this event property can be declaratively set using the `OnPropertyName` syntax. This event is raised when the text has changed in the control on a postback to the server. In the example in Listings 3.4 and 3.5, the label for the region control is changed based on the value in the Country text box. Note that the event is only triggered *after* a postback to the server. In the listing, a postback automatically occurs after the text changed event via the `AutoPostBack` property on the `TextBox`.

Table 3.7   Events of the TextBox Control

Event	Description
TextChanged	Raised on a postback when the content of the control is changed and the user tabs out of the control.

Listing 3.4   TextBoxEvent.aspx

```
<h1>TextBox TextChanged</h1>
<p>
   Country: <br />
   <asp:TextBox ID="txtCountry" runat="server"
      OnTextChanged="txtCountry_TextChanged"
      AutoPostBack="true" />
</p>
<p>
   <asp:Label ID="labRegion" runat="server" Text="Region" /><br />
   <asp:TextBox ID="txtState" runat="server" />
</p>
```

CORE NOTE

In this and other code listings in the chapter, some of the code for the class (e.g., the `using` statements and class definition) has been omitted for brevity.

Listing 3.5   TextBoxEvent.aspx.cs

```
/// <summary>
/// Handler for the text changed event of the country text box
/// </summary>
protected void txtCountry_TextChanged(object sender, EventArgs e)
{
```

```
string country = txtCountry.Text.ToLower();
if (country == "canada")
    labRegion.Text = "Province";
else if (country == "united states" || country == "usa")
    labRegion.Text = "State";
else
    labRegion.Text = "Region";
}
```

The result of this listing is shown in Figure 3.5.

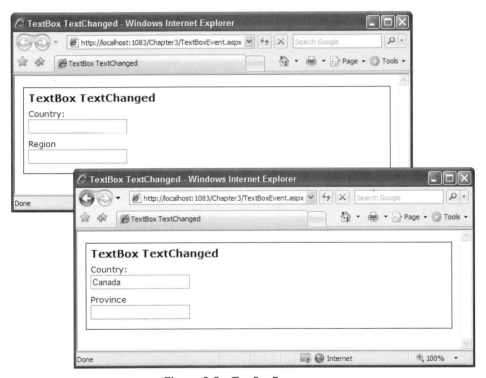

Figure 3.5 TextBoxEvent.aspx

Button-Style Controls

There are three kinds of button controls in ASP.NET.

- Button—Displays a standard HTML submit button.

- LinkButton—Displays a hyperlink that works as a button. Unlike a regular HTML <a> element or the HyperLink control, the LinkButton control causes a postback (and thus allows for post-click processing on the server).
- ImageButton—Displays an image that works as a button and that allows you to determine the image coordinates of the location that was clicked.

All three button controls submit the form to the server when clicked; that is, they cause a postback to the server when clicked.

Button controls can be either *submit* or *command* buttons. By default, buttons are submit buttons. This means that they cause a postback to the server when pushed; this event can then be handled on the server by writing a Click event handler. Command buttons also cause a postback when pushed. However, they also have a command name associated with them. This allows you to use a single event handler (a Command event handler) for multiple buttons on a form. Although the three buttons do not share a common base class (Button and LinkButton inherit from WebControl, whereas ImageButton inherits from Image), they nonetheless share several unique properties and events, as shown in Tables 3.8 and 3.9.

Table 3.8   Unique Properties of the Button, ImageButton, and LinkButton Classes

Property	Description
CausesValidation	Indicates whether validation is performed when button is clicked. Validation is covered in Chapter 5.
CommandArgument	Specifies optional argument to be used in conjunction with the CommandName property.
CommandName	Specifies the command name for the button.
OnClientClick	Specifies the client-side script to be run when the button's click event is triggered.
PostbackUrl	Specifies the URL that the page posts back to when the button is clicked. Normally, a page posts back to the same page as the button. This property allows you to post back to a different page.
Text	The text caption in the button (Button and LinkButton only).
UseSubmitBehavior	Indicates whether the control uses the client browser's submit mechanism or the ASP.NET postback mechanism (Button only). Default is true (use the browser's submit mechanism). If set to false, client-side script is added to the page that posts the form to the server.

Table 3.9   Unique Events of the Button, ImageButton, and LinkButton Classes

Event	Description
Click	Raised when the button is clicked. Used to define a handler for a submit-style button.
Command	Raised when the button is clicked. Used to define a handler for a command-style button.

Listings 3.6 and 3.7 illustrate the use of the three different button controls. The result in the browser is shown in Figure 3.6.

Listing 3.6   ButtonTest.aspx

```
<p>
    <asp:ImageButton ID="imgbtnTest" runat="server"
        ImageUrl="images/navigation.gif"
        AlternateText="Navigation Menu"
        OnClick="imgbtnTest_Click" />
    <br />
    <asp:Label ID="labMessage1" runat="server"></asp:Label>
</p>
<p>
    <asp:Button ID="btnTest" runat="server" Text="Click Me"
        OnClick="btnTest_Click" />
    <br />
    <asp:Label ID="labMessage2" runat="server"></asp:Label>
</p>
<p>
    <asp:LinkButton ID="lnkbtnTest" runat="server"
        OnClick="lnkbtnTest_Click">
      Link to click
    </asp:LinkButton>
    <br />
    <asp:Label ID="labMessage3" runat="server"></asp:Label>
</p>
```

Listing 3.7   ButtonTest.aspx.cs

```
/// <summary>
/// Handler for the image button
/// </summary>
protected void imgbtnTest_Click(object sender,
    ImageClickEventArgs e)
```

```
{
   labMessage1.Text = " ImageButton Clicked Coordinates: " +
      e.X.ToString();
   labMessage1.Text += ", " + e.Y.ToString();
}


/// <summary>
/// Handler for the (regular) button
/// </summary>
protected void btnTest_Click(object sender, EventArgs e)
{
   labMessage2.Text = "Button was clicked";
}


/// <summary>
/// Handler for the link button
/// </summary>
protected void lnkbtnTest_Click(object sender, EventArgs e)
{
   labMessage3.Text = "LinkButton was clicked";
}
```

Figure 3.6   ButtonTest.aspx

Command Event

It is not uncommon for a page to contain multiple buttons that are similar in some way. An example is multiple link buttons in a list—for instance, Add to Cart buttons in a list of products. In such a situation, you do not want separate event handlers for each button, but a single event handler that handles the Click event for all the Add to Cart buttons.

The issue with using a single event handler for multiple buttons is that the event handler usually requires some way of determining which particular button triggered the event. The solution to this problem is the Command event.

When a button is clicked, the form is submitted to the server and both the Click and Command events are raised (Click is raised first). The only difference between the two events is that additional information (such as information that can be used to identify which button triggered the event) can be passed to the Command event via the CommandName and the CommandArgument attributes/properties.

Listings 3.8 and 3.9 use the Command event in conjunction with the CommandName attribute to implement a simple calculator that uses one event handler for four different buttons. The result in the browser can be seen in Figure 3.7.

Listing 3.8 CommandTest.aspx

```
<h1>Simple Calculator</h1>
<div class="box">
   <asp:TextBox ID="txtValue1" runat="server" />
   <asp:Button runat="server" ID="btnAdd"
      Width="30px" Text="+"
      OnCommand="Button_Command" CommandName="add" />
   <asp:Button runat="server" ID="btnSubtract"
      Width="30px" Text="-"
      OnCommand="Button_Command" CommandName="subtract" />
   <br/>
   <asp:TextBox ID="txtValue2" runat="server" />
   <asp:Button runat="server" ID="btnMultiply"
      Width="30px" Text="*"
      OnCommand="Button_Command" CommandName="multiply" />
   <asp:Button runat="server" ID="btnDivide"
      Width="30px" Text="/"
      OnCommand="Button_Command" CommandName="divide" />
</div>
<p><asp:Label ID="labMessage" runat="server" /></p>
```

Listing 3.9   CommandTest.aspx.cs

```csharp
/// <summary>
/// Single Command event handler for all the calculator buttons
/// </summary>
protected void Button_Command(Object o, CommandEventArgs e)
{
    double dVal1 = 0.0;
    double dVal2 = 0.0;

    // Try converting user input into double values
    bool val1okay = Double.TryParse(txtValue1.Text, out dVal1);
    bool val2okay = Double.TryParse(txtValue2.Text, out dVal2);

    if (val1okay && val2okay)
    {
        double result = 0;

        string op = "";
        switch (e.CommandName)
        {
            case "add":
                    op = "+";
                    result = dVal1 + dVal2;
                    break;
            case "subtract":
                    op = "-";
                    result = dVal1 - dVal2;
                    break;
            case "multiply":
                    op = "*";
                    result = dVal1 * dVal2;
                    break;
            case "divide":
                    op = "/";
                result = dVal1 / dVal2;
                break;
        }
        labMessage.Text = txtValue1.Text + op + txtValue2.Text
            + "=" + result;
    }
    else
    {
        labMessage.Text =
            "Unable to compute a value with these values";
    }
}
```

Figure 3.7   CommandTest.aspx

CORE NOTE

Notice the use of the `Double.TryParse` method. This method is used to convert the contents of the `TextBox` controls into `double` values. The `out` keyword indicates that the variable is being passed by reference. This means that the `TryParse` method returns the converted double value within the passed variable.

Working with Client-Side Events

There may be times when you want to associate client-side script events with your buttons. For instance, you want to display a client-side alert box when a button is clicked, or change the CSS or image of a button in response to the mouse's movement. ASP.NET allows you to add client-side attributes to any server control; if the control is not recognized by ASP.NET, it is simply passed to the client. For instance, in the following `ImageButton` control, the `OnMouseOver` attribute is not defined for the `ImageButton` control in ASP.NET.

```
<asp:ImageButton … OnMouseOver="this.src='images/hot.gif'" />
```

Because the attribute is not recognized by ASP.NET, it is simply passed to the client and rendered as an attribute in the destination element. In this case, the resulting code sent to the browser is

```
<input type="image" … OnMouseOver="this.src='images/hot.gif'" >
```

What do you do if the client attribute you want to work with has the same name as a supported property in ASP.NET? For instance, what if you want to display a Javascript alert box in response to a button click? Because both the server-side and the client-side event share the same name (OnClick), you cannot pass an attribute such as OnClick="alert('message')" to the client. The solution to this problem has typically required programmatically adding client-code to the attributes collection, such as

```
myButton.Attributes.Add("onclick",
    "alert('Posting information...')");
```

However, with ASP.NET 2.0, there is a nonprogramming solution to the problem of passing code to the client for the OnClick event of buttons. The different ASP.NET button controls now have an OnClientClick property that allows you to attach Javascript code, which is run when the client event is triggered on the client. You can thus use this property instead of the Attributes collection, as in

```
<asp:ImageButton … OnClientClick="alert(
    'Posting Information...')" />
```

Listing 3.10 illustrates the use of some client-side events in conjunction with a Button control. In the listing, the control uses both an OnClientClick as well as two client-side attributes (OnMouseOver and OnMouseOut) to switch the CSS class of the button when the user moves the mouse over the button. The result in the browser can be seen in Figure 3.8.

Listing 3.10 ClientEvents.aspx

```
<head runat="server">
    <title>Client Events</title>
    <link href="chapterStyles.css" type="text/css"
        rel="stylesheet" />
    <style type="text/css">
    .normal {
        border: 3px double #999999;
        padding: 0.25em;
        background-color: aliceblue;
        color: DimGray;
        font: bold 12px Verdana,Helvetica,Arial,sans-serif;
    }
    .over {
        border: 3px double DarkRed;
        padding: 0.25em;
        background-color: lightcyan;
        color: DarkRed;
        font: bold 12px Verdana,Helvetica,Arial,sans-serif;
    }
```

```
      </style>
</head>
<body>
    <form id="form1" runat="server">
    <div id="container">
    <h1>Using client-side events</h1>
    <asp:Button ID="btnTest" runat="server"
        Text="Click Me" CssClass="normal"
        OnClientClick="alert('posting to server, please wait');"
        OnMouseOver="this.className='over';"
        OnMouseOut="this.className='normal';" />
</div>
</form>
</body>
```

Figure 3.8   ClientEvents.aspx

CheckBox Control

The CheckBox control allows a user to choose between a true or false state. It is rendered on the browser as a check box form element. The CheckBox is usually just a single element within a form; it can, however, be used to cause a postback to the server. The unique properties and events of the check box control are shown in Tables 3.10 and 3.11.

Table 3.10 Unique Properties of the CheckBox Control

Property	Description
CausesValidation	Indicates whether validation is performed (true/false) when button is clicked. Validation is covered in Chapter 5.
Checked	Indicates whether the check box is checked (true).
InputAttributes	Collection of attributes to be rendered by (passed to) the client for the check box part of the control.
LabelAttributes	Collection of attributes to be rendered by (passed to) the client for the label part of the control.
Text	Specifies the text of the label part of the control.
TextAlign	Specifies the alignment (right or left) of the text label in relation to the check box itself.
ValidationGroup	Specifies the name of the validation group for which the control causes validation.

Table 3.11 Unique Events of the CheckBox Class

Event	Description
CheckedChanged	Raised when the check box is checked or unchecked. Note that this event is only raised with a postback.

Listings 3.11 and 3.12 illustrate the usage of the CheckBox control. Notice that Listing 3.11 uses the CheckBox control both as a static element within the form as well as a control that causes a postback. In the later usage, the control's event handler (shown in Listing 3.12) toggles the visibility of other controls on the form (see Figure 3.9).

Listing 3.11 CheckBoxTest.aspx

```
<h1>Check Box Test</h1>
<div class="box">
   <p>Delivery:
   <asp:CheckBox ID="chkDelivery" runat="server"
     OnCheckedChanged="CheckChanged" AutoPostBack="True" />
   </p>
   <p>
      <asp:Label ID="labAddress" runat="server"
         Text="Customer Address: "  Visible="false" /><br />
```

```
        <asp:TextBox ID="txtAddress" runat="server"
          Columns="60" Visible="False" />
    </p>
    <p>
        Pizza Styles: <br />
        <asp:CheckBox ID="chkThin" runat="server"
          Text="Thin Crust" />
        <br />
        <asp:CheckBox ID="chkExtra" runat="server"
          Text="Extra Sauce" />
    </p>
</div>

<asp:Button ID="btnOrder" runat="server"
    Text="Order Pizza" OnClick="btnOrder_Click" />
<p><strong><asp:Label ID="labMessage" runat="server" />
</strong></p>
```

Listing 3.12   CheckBoxTest.aspx.cs

```
/// <summary>
/// Called when user changes the delivery check box
/// </summary>
protected void CheckChanged(object sender, System.EventArgs e)
{
    if (chkDelivery.Checked)
    {
       txtAddress.Visible = true;
       labAddress.Visible = true;
    }
    else
    {
       txtAddress.Visible = false;
       labAddress.Visible = false;
    }
}


/// <summary>
/// Called when user clicks order button
/// </summary>
protected void btnOrder_Click(object sender, EventArgs e)
{
    labMessage.Text = "Pizza Order Styles: <br/>";
    if (chkThin.Checked)
       labMessage.Text += chkThin.Text + "<br/>";
    if (chkExtra.Checked)
       labMessage.Text += chkExtra.Text + "<br/>";
}
```

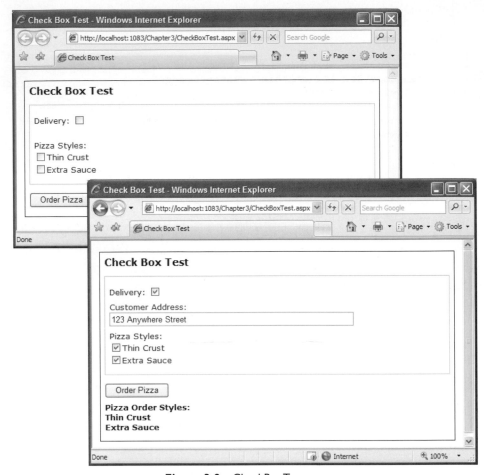

Figure 3.9   CheckBoxTest.aspx

RadioButton Control

The RadioButton control represents a radio button in a form. RadioButton controls can be logically grouped together using the GroupName property. Alternately, multiple radio buttons can be grouped together by using the RadioButtonList (covered separately in the next section).

Programming the RadioButton control is almost the same as programming the CheckBox control, because RadioButton is a subclass of the CheckBox class. The only property that is unique to the RadioButton control is the GroupName property, which is used to logically group separate radio button controls so that they form a set of mutually exclusive buttons (that is, only one radio button in the group can be selected), as in

```
Select a philosopher: <br/>
<asp:RadioButton ID="radPhil1" Runat="server"
   GroupName="phil" Text="Aristotle" />
<asp:RadioButton ID="radPhil2" Runat="server"
   GroupName="phil" Text="Plato"/>
```

List-Style Controls

The `DropDownList`, `ListBox`, `CheckBoxList`, `RadioButtonList`, and `Bulleted-List` controls are list controls with fundamentally similar functionality. All of these classes share the same base class: the `ListControl` class. The `ListControl` class in turn inherits from the `DataBoundControl` class, as shown in Figure 3.10. (Data binding is covered in Chapter 8.)

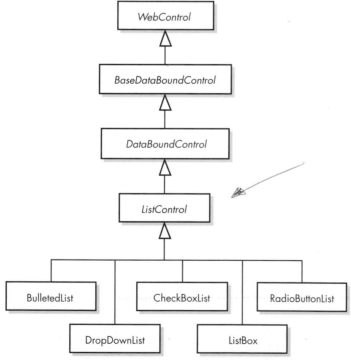

Figure 3.10   List controls class hierarchy

The unique properties and events of the ListControl class are shown in Tables 3.12 and 3.13.

Table 3.12   Unique Properties of the ListControl Class

Property	Description
AppendDataBoundItems	Specifies whether the list is cleared of existing items before data binding. The default is false, which means the list is cleared; setting this value to true preserves existing list values and appends the data bound items to the end of the list.
DataTextField	Specifies the field name of the data source that will provide the textual content for the list.
DataTextFormatString	Specifies the formatting string (see Chapter 10, page 585) that controls the visual display of the list content.
DataValueField	Specifies the field name of the data source that will provide the value for each list item.
Items	The collection of ListItems in the control.
SelectedIndex	The index (starting with 0) of the selected list item(s). For multiple selections, this property returns the lowest ordinal index that was selected. A value of -1 indicates that no item was selected in the list.
SelectedItem	The list item that was selected. For multiple selections, this property returns the item with the lowest index in the control.
SelectedValue	The value of the item that was selected.

Table 3.13   Unique Events of the ListControl Class

Event	Description
SelectedIndexChanged	Raised when the selection of the list control changes. Note that this event is only raised with a postback.

Notice that the ListControl class has a collection of ListItem controls. A ListItem encapsulates both the text and value of an item in a list. Table 3.14 lists the principle properties of the ListItem.

Table 3.14   Properties of the ListItem Class

Property	Description
Attributes	Specifies a collection of attributes to be rendered in browser. Note: These attributes are not in fact rendered in the browser.
Enabled	Indicates whether the list item is enabled. Disabled list items are not visible.
Selected	Indicates whether a list item is selected.
Text	The display text of the list item.
Value	The value of the list item.

You add `ListItem` objects to any of the list controls either declaratively or programmatically. For instance, the following adds list items to a `DropDownList` control declaratively.

```
<asp:DropDownList ID="myDrop" runat="server">
    <asp:ListItem Selected="True">Choose a color</asp:ListItem>
    <asp:ListItem>Red</asp:ListItem>
    <asp:ListItem>Blue</asp:ListItem>
    <asp:ListItem Value="#00FF00">Green</asp:ListItem>
</asp:DropDownList>
```

To add list items programmatically, you must add `ListItem` objects to the control's `Items` collection, as in

```
ListItem li = new ListItem("Choose a color ");
li.Selected = true;
myDrop.Items.Add(li);
myDrop.Items.Add(new ListItem("Red"));
myDrop.Items.Add(new ListItem("Blue"));
// Specify both display text and value
myDrop.Items.Add(new ListItem("Green","#00FF00"));
```

This code snippet illustrates the different ways that you can add items to a list control. Notice that the `ListItem` constructor is overloaded; you can specify just the display text of the item or both the display text and its value.

To programmatically process a multiselection list control, you typically need to iterate through the collection. Listings 3.13 and 3.14 illustrate the markup and code for displaying and iterating through a multiselection list box. Figure 3.11 illustrates the result in the browser window.

Listing 3.13   ListControlProgrammatic.aspx

```
<h1>Choose multiple colors (use ctrl or shift): </h1>
<asp:ListBox ID="myList" runat="server"
    SelectionMode="Multiple" Rows="6">
    <asp:ListItem Value="#FF0000">Red</asp:ListItem>
    <asp:ListItem Value="#FF00FF">Magenta</asp:ListItem>
    <asp:ListItem Value="#FFFF00">Yellow</asp:ListItem>
    <asp:ListItem Value="#00FF00">Green</asp:ListItem>
    <asp:ListItem Value="#00FFFF">Cyan</asp:ListItem>
    <asp:ListItem Value="#0000FF">Blue</asp:ListItem>
</asp:ListBox>
<p><asp:Button ID="myBtn" runat="server" Text="Submit"/></p>
<asp:Label ID="labResult" runat="server" />
```

Listing 3.14   ListControlProgrammatic.aspx.cs

```
/// <summary>
/// Called each time the page loads
/// </summary>
protected void Page_Load(object sender, EventArgs e)
{
    if (IsPostBack)
    {
        labResult.Text = "Colors chosen: <br/>";
        foreach (ListItem li in myList.Items)
        {
            if (li.Selected)
            {
                labResult.Text += "<span style='color:";
                labResult.Text += li.Value + "'>" + li.Text;
                labResult.Text += "</span><br/>";
            }
        }
    }
}
```

List items can also be added implicitly using data binding. Chapter 8 illustrates
the use of data binding with list controls.

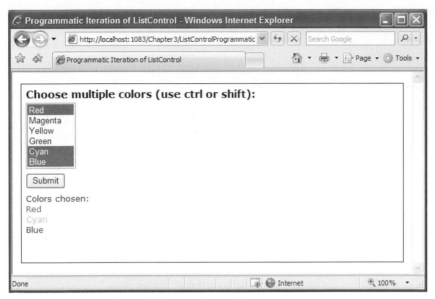

Figure 3.11   ListControlProgrammatic.aspx

BulletedList

The BulletedList control displays a bulleted list of items. This list can be ordered (a numbered list) or unordered (a bulleted list). The style of the bullet or the numbers can be set via properties of the control (see Table 3.15).

Table 3.15   Unique Properties of the BulletedList Control

Property	Description
BulletImageUrl	The path of the image to be used for the bullet if the Bullet-Style is CustomImage.
BulletStyle	The style of the bullets in the list. Possible values are described by the BulletStyle enumeration (Numbered, LowerAlpha, UpperAlpha, LowerRoman, UpperRoman, Disc, Circle, Square, or CustomImage).
DisplayMode	The mode to display the list items. Possible values are described by the DisplayMode enumeration (HyperLink, LinkButton, or Text).

Table 3.15   Unique Properties of the BulletedList Control *(continued)*

Property	Description
FirstBulletNumber	Specifies the numeric value of the first item in an ordered (numbered) bulleted list.
Target	When a hyperlink in a bulleted list item is clicked, the Web page content is displayed in the window or a frame with this name.

Like the `CheckBoxList`, `RadioButtonList`, `DropDownList`, and `ListBox` controls, the `BulletedList` control has the `ListControl` class as its base class. Like in these other classes, individual items can be added declaratively to the list via the `<asp:ListItem>` element, as in the following.

```
<asp:BulletedList id="aList" runat="server"
    BulletStyle="LowerRoman">
  <asp:ListItem>Item 1</asp:ListItem>
  <asp:ListItem>Item 2</asp:ListItem>
  <asp:ListItem>Item 3</asp:ListItem>
</asp:BulletedList>
```

The list's appearance can be changed via the `DisplayMode` property. The default value for this property is `Text`, which simply displays the list items in a bulleted list. Other possible values for this property are `HyperLink` and `LinkButton`. Although both of these settings display the list as a series of hyperlinks (see Figure 3.12), they differ in their behavior after the user clicks the link. `HyperLink` navigates with no postback to the URL specified via the `Value` attribute, whereas `LinkButton` posts back to the server when the link is clicked.

Listings 3.15 and 3.16 illustrate how to use the `BulletedList` and how the `DisplayMode` changes the list's appearance and behavior. It uses a `DropDownList` that lets the user select the `DisplayMode`. The handler for the `DropDownList` then sets the `DisplayMode` programmatically (see Figure 3.12 for the final result).

Listing 3.15   BulletedListTest.aspx

```
<p>Choose a display mode:
<asp:DropDownList ID="drpDisplayMode" runat="server"
    OnSelectedIndexChanged="drpDisplayMode_SelectedIndexChanged"
    AutoPostBack="True">
  <asp:ListItem Selected="True">Text</asp:ListItem>
  <asp:ListItem>HyperLink</asp:ListItem>
  <asp:ListItem>LinkButton</asp:ListItem>
</asp:DropDownList>
</p>
```

```
<asp:BulletedList ID="blCompanies" runat="server"
     DisplayMode="Text"
     BulletStyle="Square" OnClick="blItems_Click">

   <asp:ListItem Value="http://www.microsoft.com">
      Microsoft</asp:ListItem>
   <asp:ListItem Value="http://www.adobe.com">
      Adobe</asp:ListItem>
   <asp:ListItem Value="http://www.oracle.com">
      Oracle</asp:ListItem>

</asp:BulletedList>
<p><asp:Label ID="labMsg" runat="server"></asp:Label></p>
```

Listing 3.16   BulletedListTest.aspx.cs

```
/// <summary>
/// Handler for bullet list click
/// (only called when DisplayMode = LinkButton)
/// </summary>
protected void blItems_Click(object sender,
   BulletedListEventArgs e)
{
   labMsg.Text = "The bullet item index you selected was "
     + e.Index;
}

/// <summary>
/// Handler for drop-down list of display modes
/// </summary>
protected void drpDisplayMode_SelectedIndexChanged(object sender,
     EventArgs e)
{
   // Get the selected value in the drop-down list
   string sMode = drpDisplayMode.SelectedItem.Text;

   // Convert the string to the display mode enum
   BulletedListDisplayMode mode = (BulletedListDisplayMode)
     Enum.Parse(typeof(BulletedListDisplayMode),
        sMode, true );

   // Change the display mode of bulleted list to selected value
   blCompanies.DisplayMode = mode;
}
```

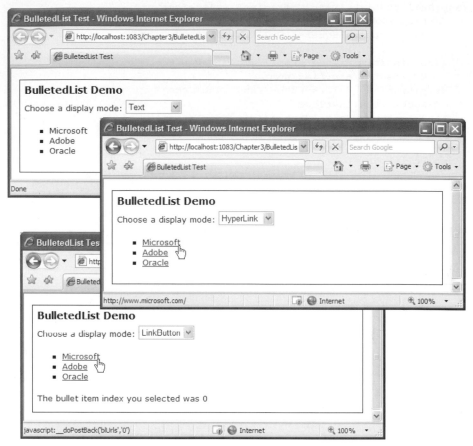

Figure 3.12   BulletedListTest.aspx

Notice that the `drpDisplayMode_SelectedIndexChanged` method in Listing 3.16 uses the `Parse` method of the `Enum` class to convert the string from the selected `DropDownList` to an enumerated value of type `BulletedListDisplayMode`. The more verbose alternative to this approach is to use conditional logic such as

```
string sMode = drpDisplayMode.SelectedItem.Text;
if (sMode == "Text")
   blCompanies.DisplayMode = BulletedListDisplayMode.Text;
else if (sMode == "HyperLink")
   blCompanies.DisplayMode = BulletedListDisplayMode.HyperLink;
else if (sMode == "LinkButton")
   blCompanies.DisplayMode = BulletedListDisplayMode.LinkButton;
```

RadioButtonList and CheckBoxList

The RadioButtonList and CheckBoxList controls encapsulate a list of radio buttons and check boxes. The RadioButtonList allows the user to select one item from a list of mutually exclusive radio buttons. The CheckBoxList allows the user to select multiple items from a list of check boxes.

Table 3.16 lists the unique properties of the RadioButtonList and CheckBoxList controls.

Table 3.16 Unique Properties of the RadioButtonList and CheckBoxList Controls

Property	Description
CellPadding	Specifies the pixel distance between the border and the contents of the table cell (if RepeatLayout is set to Table).
CellSpacing	Specifies the pixel distance between table cells (if using a table for layout).
RepeatColumns	Specifies the number of columns to use to display the list items.
RepeatDirection	Specifies that the list items are displayed horizontally in rows from left to right (Horizontal) or vertically in columns from top to bottom (Vertical). Possible values are described by the Repeat-Direction enumeration.
RepeatLayout	Specifies whether the list is displayed within a table (Table) or not within a table (Flow). If the list is not displayed in a table, the list items are separated by line breaks (\<br/\>). Possible values are described by the RepeatLayout enumeration. Default value is Table.
TextAlign	Specifies the horizontal alignment for items within the list. Possible values are described by the TextAlign enumeration (Left, Right).

The example in Listings 3.17 and 3.18 illustrates the use of both RadioButtonList and CheckBoxList controls. It also demonstrates the runtime setting of the layout and direction of these list controls.

Listing 3.17 CheckAndRadioLists.aspx

```
<div class="layout">
    Repeat Direction:
    <asp:DropDownList ID="drpDirection" runat="server">
```

```
        <asp:ListItem>Horizontal</asp:ListItem>
        <asp:ListItem Selected="True">Vertical</asp:ListItem>
    </asp:DropDownList><br />
    Repeat Layout:
    <asp:DropDownList ID="drpLayout" runat="server">
        <asp:ListItem Selected="True">Table</asp:ListItem>
        <asp:ListItem>Flow</asp:ListItem>
    </asp:DropDownList><br />
    Repeat Columns:
    <asp:DropDownList ID="drpColumns" runat="server">
        <asp:ListItem>1</asp:ListItem>
        <asp:ListItem>2</asp:ListItem>
        <asp:ListItem>3</asp:ListItem>
    </asp:DropDownList>
    <br />
    <asp:Button ID="btnChange" runat="server"
        Text="Change Properties" OnClick="btnChange_Click" />
</div>
<div class="box">
<p>
Crust:
<br>
<asp:RadioButtonList ID="rlstCrust" runat="server" >
    <asp:ListItem>Thin</asp:ListItem>
    <asp:ListItem>Medium</asp:ListItem>
    <asp:ListItem Selected="True">Thick</asp:ListItem>
</asp:RadioButtonList>
</p>
<p>
Toppings:<br>
<asp:CheckBoxList ID="clstToppings" runat="server"
        RepeatColumns="2"
        RepeatDirection="Vertical" RepeatLayout="Table" >
    <asp:ListItem>Ham</asp:ListItem>
    <asp:ListItem>Mushrooms</asp:ListItem>
    <asp:ListItem>Pepperoni</asp:ListItem>
    <asp:ListItem>Tomatoes</asp:ListItem>
    <asp:ListItem>Green Peppers</asp:ListItem>
    <asp:ListItem>Shrimp</asp:ListItem>
    <asp:ListItem>Extra Cheese</asp:ListItem>
    <asp:ListItem>Anchovies</asp:ListItem>
</asp:CheckBoxList>
</p>
<asp:Button ID="btnOrder" runat="server" Text="Order"
   OnClick="btnOrder_Click" />
</div>
<p><asp:Label ID="labMessage" runat="server" /></p>
```

Listing 3.18　CheckAndRadioLists.aspx.cs

```csharp
/// <summary>
/// Handler for change properties button
/// </summary>
protected void btnChange_Click(object sender, EventArgs e)
{
    // Apply the layout settings to the two lists

    // First get the number of columns and apply to lists
    int columns = Convert.ToInt32(drpColumns.SelectedValue);
    rlstCrust.RepeatColumns = columns;
    clstToppings.RepeatColumns = columns;

    // Now get the layout and apply to lists
    string sLayout = drpLayout.SelectedValue;
    RepeatLayout layout = (RepeatLayout)Enum.Parse(
        typeof(RepeatLayout), sLayout, true);
    rlstCrust.RepeatLayout = layout;
    clstToppings.RepeatLayout = layout;

    // Finally get the repeat direction and apply to lists
    string sDirect = drpDirection.SelectedValue;
    RepeatDirection direct = (RepeatDirection)Enum.Parse(
        typeof(RepeatDirection), sDirect, true);
    rlstCrust.RepeatDirection = direct;
    clstToppings.RepeatDirection = direct;
}

/// <summary>
/// Handler for order button
/// </summary>
protected void btnOrder_Click(object sender, EventArgs e)
{
    // Get the crust from the radio list and display
    labMessage.Text = "<b>Pizza Ordered: </b><br>";
    labMessage.Text += rlstCrust.SelectedItem.Text;
    labMessage.Text += " Crust<br/><b>Toppings:</b><br/>";

    // Get all the toppings selected in list and display
    foreach (ListItem topping in clstToppings.Items)
    {
        if (topping.Selected)
        {
            labMessage.Text += topping.Text + "<br/>";
        }
    }
}
```

Figure 3.13 illustrates the result in the browser window. Be sure to use the browser's View Source option and compare how the `RepeatLayout` property changes the rendered HTML.

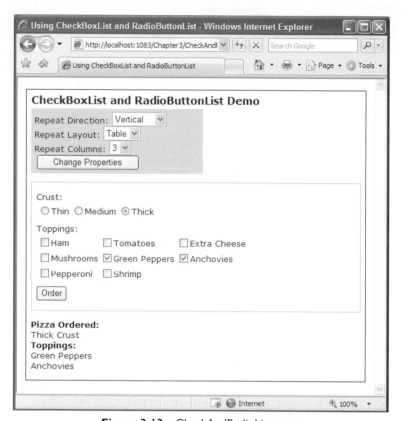

Figure 3.13   CheckAndRadioLists.aspx

Image Control

The `Image` control is used to display an image on the page. It provides the same functionality as the HTML `IMG` element, but allows you to programmatically set image properties in server code. For instance, the image URL can be set at design time or runtime and can even be bound to a value from a database.

Note that the `Image` control simply displays an image; it does not act like a button. If you want an image to have the behavior of a button, you must use the `ImageButton` control. If you need to determine the coordinates of where the image was clicked, use the `ImageMap` control.

Table 3.17 lists the unique properties of the Image control.

Table 3.17   Unique Properties of the Image Control

Property	Description
AlternateText	The text to be displayed when the image is not available or the browser's images are turned off.
DescriptionUrl	Provides additional semantics for image. That is, it provides a further explanation of the meaning of the image for nonvisual browsers. It is rendered in the browser using the longdesc attribute of the HTML <img> element. This is usually set to the URL of a page that contains details about the image in text format.
GenerateEmptyAlternateText	If set to true, adds an empty alt attribute (alt="") to the HTML <img> element. For accessibility reasons, images that do not contribute to the meaning of the page (such as spacer images, bullets, etc.), should have this property set to true.
ImageAlign	The alignment of the image in relation to other elements on the page. Possible values are described by the ImageAlign enumeration (NotSet, Left, Right, Baseline, Top, Middle, Bottom, AbsBottom, AbsMiddle, TextTop). Default is NotSet.
ImageUrl	The path of the image file to be displayed.

Listings 3.19 and 3.20 illustrate how to use the Image control to dynamically change image properties (in this case, the image URL) at runtime based on user input.

Listing 3.19   ImageTest.aspx

```
<h1>Image Control test</h1>
<asp:Image ID="imgTest" runat="server"
   AlternateText="No image chosen yet" />
<br/>
<asp:DropDownList ID="drpImages" runat="server"
     AutoPostBack="True"
     OnSelectedIndexChanged="drpImages_SelectedIndexChanged">
  <asp:ListItem>Select an image to display</asp:ListItem>
  <asp:ListItem Value="0131118269">Core Java</asp:ListItem>
```

```
    <asp:ListItem Value="0131472275">Core C#</asp:ListItem>
    <asp:ListItem Value="0321246756">Framework Design
        Guidelines</asp:ListItem>
</asp:DropDownList>
```

The event handler in Listing 3.20 displays an image based on the user's selection from the drop-down list. The image files in this example are stored in a subfolder named images. The tilde character (~) is used to indicate the root of the Web site.

Listing 3.20   ImageTest.aspx.cs

```
/// <summary>
/// Called when user selects from drop-down list
/// </summary>
protected void drpImages_SelectedIndexChanged(object sender,
        EventArgs e)
{
    // Only display image if user has selected an image
    if (drpImages.SelectedIndex > 0)
    {
        imgTest.Visible = true;
        imgTest.ImageUrl = "~/images/" +
            drpImages.SelectedItem.Value + ".gif";
    }
}
```

However, when this example is viewed in the browser, the result might not be what you want. Figure 3.14 illustrates how this example appears in the browser on the first request.

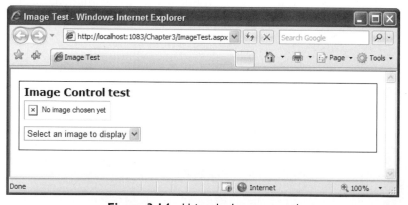

Figure 3.14   Using the Image control

The problem here is that the markup does not, by itself, display an image. Because the URL has not been specified either declaratively or programmatically, the `Image` control displays as an empty image. Notice how the `AlternateText` property can be used to provide alternative text when there is no image URL.

The solution to this problem is to add the following conditional to the `Page_Load` method that hides the `Image` control until the user makes a selection from the list (which generates a postback event).

```
protected void Page_Load(object sender, EventArgs e)
{
    // Hide the image until there is an item selected
    if (drpImages.SelectedIndex == 0)
        imgTest.Visible = false;
}
```

The result in the browser is shown in Figure 3.15.

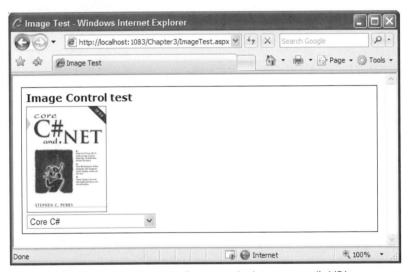

Figure 3.15   Dynamically setting the Image control's URL

ImageMap Control

The `ImageMap` control is a more specialized version of the `Image` control (in fact, it is a subclass of the `Image` control), with which the developer can define hot spot regions (i.e., clickable areas). When a user clicks a hot spot region, the `ImageMap` control can either generate a postback (for additional server-side processing) or simply navigate to the specified URL.

Tables 3.18 and 3.19 list the unique properties and events of the `ImageMap` control.

Table 3.18   Unique Properties of the ImageMap Control

Property	Description
HotSpotMode	Specifies the behavior of the control when a hot spot is clicked. Possible values are described by the `HotSpotMode` enumeration. Choices are `Navigate` (the hot spot navigates to the URL), `Post-Back` (the hot spot generates a postback), and `NotSet`. You can also mix hot spot modes (that is, have one hot spot a postback type and the other a navigate type) by specifying the `HotSpotMode` property of the individual `HotSpot` objects instead.
HotSpots	A collection of `HotSpot` objects that represent the hot spot regions in the `ImageMap`. There are three types of `HotSpot` objects: `CircleHotSpot`, `RectangleHotSpot`, and `PolygonHotSpot`.
Target	Specifies the target window or frame to display the Web content after a hot spot is clicked.

Table 3.19   Unique Events of the ImageMap Classes

Event	Description
Clicked	Raised when a hot spot is clicked.

Each hot spot region is defined as a nested element within the `ImageMap` control, as shown here.

```
<asp:ImageMap ID="imapMenu" runat="server"
    ImageUrl="images/navigation.gif" AlternateText="Menu"
    OnClick="imapMenu_Click" >

  <asp:RectangleHotSpot HotSpotMode="Navigate"
    NavigateUrl="Home.aspx" AlternateText="Go to Home Page"
    Left="0" Top="0" Right="160" Bottom="40" />

  <asp:RectangleHotSpot HotSpotMode="PostBack"
    PostBackValue="Home" AlternateText="Go to the home page"
    Left="115" Top="41" Right="154" Bottom="65" />

</asp:ImageMap>
```

Notice that in this example, the `HotSpotMode` is defined individually for each hot spot. The first hot spot navigates directly to `Home.aspx`, whereas the second generates a postback to the server (which we call the `imapMenu_Click` event handler). The event handler for the image map is passed the value set via the `PostBackValue` property.

CORE NOTE

Be careful that you specify the `HotSpotMode` for each `HotSpot` region (or set it for the `ImageMap` control as a whole), because the default is `HotSpotMode.NotSet` (which navigates to the site root).

Listing 3.21 illustrates how to use the `ImageMap` control to implement a navigation bar (the result is shown in Figure 3.16). Notice that a `PolygonHotSpot` is used to define the hot spot for the page logo. The `Coordinates` property specifies the x and y coordinates of the vertices that make up the polygon. In this example, there are six vertices. The first vertex has an x position of 2 (pixels) and a y position of 3.

Listing 3.21   ImageMapTest.aspx

```
<h1>ImageMap Control Test</h1>
<asp:ImageMap ID="imapMenu" runat="server"
    ImageUrl="images/navigation.gif" AlternateText="Menu"
    OnClick="imapMenu_Click">

    <asp:PolygonHotSpot  HotSpotMode="Navigate"
        NavigateUrl="Home.aspx"
        AlternateText="Go to Home Page"
        Coordinates="2,3,2,39,156,39,158,18,60,18,41,3" />

    <asp:RectangleHotSpot Bottom="65" HotSpotMode="PostBack"
        Left="115" PostBackValue="Home"
        Right="154" Top="41"
        AlternateText="Go to the home page" />

    <asp:RectangleHotSpot Bottom="65" HotSpotMode="PostBack"
        Left="165" PostBackValue="Browse"
        Right="220" Top="41"
        AlternateText="Browse our products" />

    <asp:RectangleHotSpot AlternateText="Do an advanced search"
        Bottom="65" HotSpotMode="PostBack"
        Left="232" PostBackValue="Search"
        Right="285" Top="41" />
```

```
    <asp:RectangleHotSpot AlternateText="Find out more about us"
        Bottom="65" Left="293"
        Right="360" Top="41" />

</asp:ImageMap>
<br />
<asp:Label ID="labMessage" runat="server"></asp:Label>
```

The event handler (shown in Listing 3.22) for this `ImageMap` control simply displays the `PostBackValue` of the hot spot that was clicked by the user.

Listing 3.22   ImageMapTest.aspx.cs

```
/// <summary>
/// Called when hot spot has HotSpotMode=PostBack
/// </summary>
protected void imapMenu_Click(object sender, ImageMapEventArgs e)
{
    labMessage.Text = "You clicked " + e.PostBackValue;
}
```

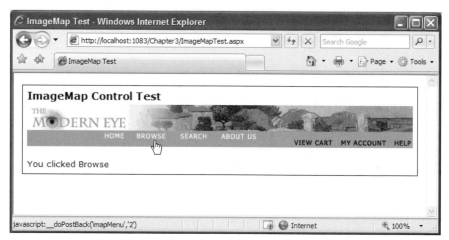

Figure 3.16   Using the ImageMap control

CORE NOTE

Unfortunately, the Visual Studio designer provides no way of visually specifying the hot spot regions. Instead, you must specify the pixel coordinates for the vertices of each hot spot. Unless you are exceptionally talented at gauging pixel positions by eye, you need to use some type of external graphical editor to determine those pixel coordinates.

HyperLink Control

The `HyperLink` control is used to create hyperlinks on a Web page. It provides the same functionality as the HTML `<a>` element, but allows you to programmatically set link properties in server code. This control is typically displayed as text but can also be displayed as an image.

Table 3.20 lists the unique properties of the `ImageMap` control.

Table 3.20 Unique Properties of the HyperLink Control

Property	Description
ImageUrl	The path of the image file to be displayed.
NavigateUrl	The URL to which to navigate when the link is clicked.
Target	Specifies the target window or frame to display the Web content after a link is clicked.
Text	The text caption for the link.

Listing 3.23 demonstrates the capability to dynamically change link properties (in this case, the link destination) at runtime based on user input. The result looks similar to that shown in Figure 3.17.

Listing 3.23 HyperLinkTest.aspx

```
<h1>HyperLink Test</h1>
Use list to specify link:<br/>
<asp:DropDownList ID="drpLinks" Runat="server"
   AutoPostBack="True"
   OnSelectedIndexChanged="drpLinks_SelectedIndexChanged">
```

```
    <asp:ListItem>Select a company</asp:ListItem>
    <asp:ListItem>adobe</asp:ListItem>
    <asp:ListItem>ibm</asp:ListItem>
    <asp:ListItem>microsoft</asp:ListItem>
</asp:DropDownList>
<p>Here is a link:
    <asp:HyperLink ID="hypTest" Runat="server" />
</p>
```

The code-behind class for this example (shown in Listing 3.24) dynamically configures the HyperLink control each time the user selects an item from the DropDownList.

Listing 3.24   HyperLinkTest.aspx.cs

```
/// <summary>
/// Called each time the page loads
/// </summary>
protected void Page_Load(object sender, System.EventArgs e)
{
    // Hide the hyperlink until there is a selection
    if (drpLinks.SelectedIndex == 0)
        hypTest.Visible = false;
}

/// <summary>
/// Called when drop-down list item is selected
/// </summary>
protected void drpLinks_SelectedIndexChanged(object sender,
        System.EventArgs e)
{
    if (drpLinks.SelectedIndex > 0)
    {
        string company = drpLinks.SelectedItem.Text;
        hypTest.Visible = true;
        hypTest.Text = company;
        hypTest.ToolTip = "Go to the web site of " + company;
        hypTest.NavigateUrl = "http://www." + company + ".com";
    }
}
```

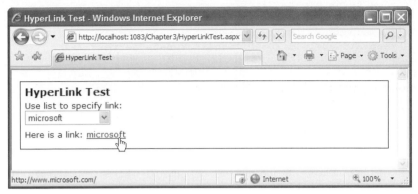

Figure 3.17   Using the HyperLink control

HiddenField Control

The HiddenField control is used to store a value on a page that needs to be per-sisted across posts to the server. In all the examples in this chapter, we have simply relied on the page's view state or control state to maintain the values of form ele-ments between posts. Later in Chapter 12, we use the session and cookie collections to maintain state information for nonform elements. However, if these methods are disabled (for instance, the user has disabled cookies in his browser) or are not avail-able (for instance, for performance reasons, you do not want to use the view state), you can also use the HiddenField control to store state values. The HiddenField control is rendered as an <input type= "hidden"/> HTML element.

The HiddenField control has only one unique property (the Value property, which is used to specify a value for HiddenField control) and one unique event (the ValueChanged event, which is triggered every time the value of the HiddenField control changes between posts to the server).

Listings 3.25 and 3.26 demonstrate a sample usage of the HiddenField control. In it, two ImageButton controls are displayed in the form. The page uses two Hid-denField controls to track how many times the user clicks on each ImageButton (see Figure 3.18). This page works even if the view state is disabled for it.

Listing 3.25   HiddenFieldTest.aspx

```
<h1>HiddenField Test</h1>
<p>Click multiple times on these two images</p>
<div id="left">
    <div class="box">
        <asp:ImageButton ID="ibtnImage1" runat="server"
            ImageUrl="images/0321246756.gif"
```

```
         AlternateText="Click on me"
         OnClick="ibtnImage1_Click" />
      <p><asp:Label ID="labMessage1" runat="server" /></p>
      <asp:HiddenField ID="hfImage1" runat="server" />
   </div>
</div>
<div id="right">
   <div class="box">
      <asp:ImageButton ID="ibtnImage2" runat="server"
         ImageUrl="images/0131472275.gif"
         AlternateText="Click on me"
         OnClick="ibtnImage2_Click" />
      <p><asp:Label ID="labMessage2" runat="server" /></p>
      <asp:HiddenField ID="hfImage2" runat="server" />
   </div>
</div>
```

Listing 3.26   HiddenFieldTest.aspx.cs

```
/// <summary>
/// Called each time the page loads
/// </summary>
protected void Page_Load(object sender, EventArgs e)
{
   // initialize the value in the hidden fields
   if (!IsPostBack)
   {
      hfImage1.Value = "0";
      hfImage2.Value = "0";
   }
}


/// <summary>
/// Click handler for first image button
/// </summary>
protected void ibtnImage1_Click(object sender, EventArgs e)
{
   IncrementCount(hfImage1);
   labMessage1.Text = "# Clicks: " + hfImage1.Value;
}


/// <summary>
/// Click handler for second image button
/// </summary>
protected void ibtnImage2_Click(object sender, EventArgs e)
{
   IncrementCount(hfImage2);
```

```
    labMessage2.Text = "# Clicks: " + hfImage2.Value;
}

/// <summary>
/// Increments the count value in the passed hidden field
/// </summary>
private void IncrementCount(HiddenField hf)
{
    int count = Convert.ToInt32(hf.Value);
    count++;
    hf.Value = count.ToString();
}
```

Figure 3.18   Using the HiddenField control

Table Control

The Table Web server control is used for creating server-programmable tables. Tables can be used for presenting tabular information as well as the layout and design of a Web page (although this last use of tables is now usually discouraged in favor of creating layouts with CSS). Although it is usually easier to use the HTML <table> element for static tables, the Table server control can be used to dynamically add rows or columns to a table at runtime.

Similar to the HTML `table` element, the `Table` server control is a parent container (see Figure 3.19). It contains a collection of `TableRow` elements (that correspond to `<tr>` elements in a HTML table), each of which in turn contains a collection of `TableCell` elements (that correspond to `<td>` elements). Rows and columns can be specified using markup or programmatically added to the `Rows` property of the `Table` and the `Cells` property of the `TableRow`.

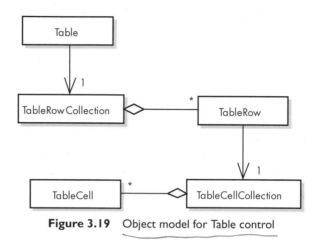

Figure 3.19   Object model for Table control

Tables 3.21, 3.22, and 3.23 list the unique properties of the `Table`, `TableRow`, and `TableCell` controls.

Table 3.21   Unique Properties of the Table Control

Property	Description
BackImageUrl	The URL of the image file to display behind the table.
Caption	The text to display in the rendered table's caption element (`<caption>`). The caption is displayed either above or below the table. The table caption provides accessibility technologies with a description of the table.
CaptionAlign	Specifies where the caption is to appear relative to the table. Possible values are described by the `TableCaptionAlign` enumeration: `Bottom`, `Left`, `NotSet`, `Right`, and `Top`.
CellPadding	Specifes the pixel distance between the border and the contents of the table cell.
CellSpacing	Specifes the pixel distance between table cells.

Table 3.21　Unique Properties of the Table Control *(continued)*

Property	Description
GridLines	Specifies the grid line style to display in the control. Possible values are described by the `GridLines` enumeration (`Both`, `Horizontal`, `None`, `Vertical`).
HorizontalAlign	The horizontal alignment of the control on the page. Possible values are described by the `HorizontalAlign` enumeration (`Centre`, `Justify`, `Left`, `NotSet`, `Right`). Default is `NotSet`.
Rows	The collection of `TableRow` objects that represent the rows in a table.

Table 3.22　Unique Properties of the TableRow Control

Property	Description
Cells	The collection of `TableCell` objects that represent the cells of a row in a table.
HorizontalAlign	The horizontal alignment of the row content. Possible values are described by the `HorizontalAlign` enumeration: `Centre`, `Justify`, `Left`, `NotSet`, `Right`). Default is `NotSet`.
TableSection	Specifies where the table row is placed in the control. Possible values are described by the `TableRowSection` enumeration: `TableBody`, `TableFooter`, `TableHeader`). The default is `TableBody`. This property allows you to build more accessible table elements by adding the `<thead>`, `<tbody>`, and `<tfoot>` elements to the rendered table.
VerticalAlign	The vertical alignment of the row content. Possible values are described by the `VerticalAlign` enumeration (`Bottom`, `Middle`, `NotSet`, `Top`). Default is `NotSet`.

Table 3.23　Unique Properties of the TableCell Control

Property	Description
AssociatedHeaderCellID	A string array that specifies the ID of the header cells related to this table cell. This associates, for accessibility reasons, the table data cell content with its table header cell. For instance, a screen-reader may call out the header's text before each cell. The accessible table example in Listing 3.29 illustrates how to use this property.

Table 3.23   Unique Properties of the TableCell Control *(continued)*

Property	Description
ColumnSpan	The number of table columns the cell spans.
HorizontalAlign	The horizontal alignment of the row content. Possible values are described by the HorizontalAlign enumeration (Centre, Justify, Left, NotSet, Right). Default is NotSet.
RowSpan	The number of table rows the cell spans.
Text	The text contents of the cell.
VerticalAlign	The vertical alignment of the row content. Possible values are described by the VerticalAlign enumeration (Bottom, Middle, NotSet, Top). Default is NotSet.
Wrap	Indicates whether the text contents of the cell wrap. The default is true.

Although the Table control can have rows added programmatically at runtime, it often makes more sense to instead use one of the data controls, such as a Repeater, DataList, or GridView. These data controls are in fact usually rendered in the browser as an HTML <table>, but work with a data source such as a database, and use templates to specify their visual presentation. These data controls are covered in Chapter 10.

Listings 3.27 and 3.28 demonstrate both the markup and programmatic approaches to working with the Table control. In the programmatic approach, TableRow objects are created, and then filled with the appropriate number of TableCell objects. Each TableRow object is then added to the Table control.

Listing 3.27   TableTest.aspx

```
<h1>Using Table Control</h1>
<h2>Table via Markup</h2>
<p>
<asp:Table id="tabMarkup" runat="server" >
  <asp:TableRow HorizontalAlign="Center"
      BackColor="#FFFF80" Font-Bold="True">
    <asp:TableCell Width="100px" Text="First">
    </asp:TableCell>
    <asp:TableCell Width="100px" Text="Second">
    </asp:TableCell>
  </asp:TableRow>
```

```
    <asp:TableRow HorizontalAlign="Center"
          BackColor="#FFFFC0">
      <asp:TableCell Text="10.5"></asp:TableCell>
      <asp:TableCell Text="36.5"></asp:TableCell>
    </asp:TableRow>
    <asp:TableRow HorizontalAlign="Center"
           BackColor="#FFFFC0">
      <asp:TableCell Text="45.3"></asp:TableCell>
      <asp:TableCell Text="16.5"></asp:TableCell>
    </asp:TableRow>
</asp:Table>
</p>
<h2>Table via Programming</h2>
<p>
<asp:Table id="tabProgramming" runat="server"></asp:Table>
</p>
```

Listing 3.28 TableTest.aspx.cs

```
/// <summary>
/// Called each time the page loads
/// </summary>
protected void Page_Load(object sender, EventArgs e)
{
    // -------  Set up table row 1  -------
    TableRow tr1 = new TableRow();

    tr1.BackColor = System.Drawing.Color.Goldenrod;
    tr1.Font.Bold = true;

    // Set up cells for row 1
    TableCell tc1a = new TableCell();
    tc1a.Text = "Author";
    tc1a.Width = 100;
    TableCell tc1b = new TableCell();
    tc1b.Text = "Nationality";
    tc1b.Width = 100;

    // Add cells to row 1
    tr1.Cells.Add(tc1a);
    tr1.Cells.Add(tc1b);

    // -------  Set up table row 2  -------
    TableRow tr2 = new TableRow();
    tr2.BackColor = System.Drawing.Color.LightGoldenrodYellow;
```

```
// Set up cells for row 2
TableCell tc2a = new TableCell();
tc2a.Text = "Milton";
TableCell tc2b = new TableCell();
tc2b.Text = "English";

// Add cells to row 2
tr2.Cells.Add(tc2a);
tr2.Cells.Add(tc2b);

// ------- add rows to table  -------
tabProgramming.Rows.Add(tr1);
tabProgramming.Rows.Add(tr2);
}
```

Figure 3.20 illustrates how the example in Listings 3.27 and 3.28 appears in the browser.

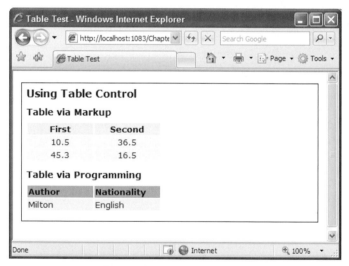

Figure 3.20   TableTest.aspx

Creating Accessible Tables

Understanding the meaning of tabular data within a Web page requires understanding how the individual cell data relate to the header descriptions for each column and/or row in the table. For a sighted visitor, this usually only requires a glance at the table's column and/or row headings. But for those with visual disabilities, this may not be an option. However, HTML 4.0 does provide a number of attributes and elements to help those who use screen readers or assistive technologies to understand a Web page's tables. ASP.NET 2.0 now supports these features, making it easier to create accessible tables.

Although sighted users can generally comprehend the meaning of a table from its context and via a quick scan at its content, users with visual disabilities do not have this option. For this reason, one should set the `Table` control's `Caption` property. This adds a title caption (which can be placed above, below, or beside the table) that should summarize the meaning of the table.

An important way to improve the accessibility of a table is to indicate which cells are header cells. In HTML, we can do this by using the `<th>` element instead of the `<td>` element. We can get ASP.NET to render a table cell as a `<th>` by using the `TableHeaderCell` instead of `TableCell`. There is also a `TableHeaderRow` and a `TableFooterRow` control, which you can use instead of `TableRow`; these two controls strictly serve a readability purpose, as their classes simply inherit from the `TableRow` class. The following example illustrates the use of `TableHeaderRow` and `TableFooterRow`.

```
<asp:Table id="tabAccessible" runat="server" … >
    <asp:TableHeaderRow >
        <asp:TableHeaderCell Text="Full Name"
            AbbreviatedText="Name" />
        <asp:TableHeaderCell Text="Age" />
    </asp:TableHeaderRow>
    …
</asp:Table>
```

This example also illustrates how you can use the `AbbreviatedText` property to provide an abbreviated version of the header text. This property is rendered as the `abbr` attribute of the HTML `<th>` element, which is used by screen readers to read a shortened version of the header for each cell in the table.

Another way to improve the accessibility of a table is to group its rows into header, body, and footer sections. These are rendered as HTML `<thead>`, `<tbody>`, and `<tfoot>` elements. This division allows the browser to support the independent scrolling of the `tbody` rows; as well, it is possible to style the rows for these areas differently. You can indicate the grouping section of a row via the `TableSection` property.

```
<asp:TableHeaderRow TableSection="TableHeader">
```

If the `TableSection` property is not specified for a `TableRow`, the rendered `<tr>` is placed within a `tbody` section by default.

Finally, another way to improve the accessibility of a table is to associate a header cell with each data cell via the `AssociatedHeaderCellID` property of the `Table-Cell` control. This property is used to establish a relationship between a data cell and its header; certain readers will then be able to speak the header name for the cell before speaking the cell data. The `AssociatedHeaderCellID` property takes a comma-delimited list of header cell `ID` values that are to be associated with that data cell. Listing 3.29 illustrates the usage of this property (the result is shown in Figure 3.21).

Listing 3.29 AccessibleTable.aspx

```
<asp:Table id=" tabAccessible" runat="server"
    CaptionAlign="Top" Caption="Timing Results for Running Test">
  <asp:TableHeaderRow TableSection="TableHeader">
    <asp:TableHeaderCell Text="Name" ID="headName" />
    <asp:TableHeaderCell Text="First Trial" ID="headFirst" />
    <asp:TableHeaderCell Text="Second Trial" ID="headSecond" />
  </asp:TableHeaderRow>
  <asp:TableRow>
    <asp:TableCell Text="Fred"
      AssociatedHeaderCellID="headName" />
    <asp:TableCell Text="10.5"
      AssociatedHeaderCellID="headFirst" />
    <asp:TableCell Text="36.5"
      AssociatedHeaderCellID="headSecond" />
  </asp:TableRow>
  <asp:TableRow>
    <asp:TableCell Text="Sue"
      AssociatedHeaderCellID="headName" />
    <asp:TableCell Text="45.3"
      AssociatedHeaderCellID="headFirst" />
    <asp:TableCell Text="16.5"
      AssociatedHeaderCellID="headSecond" />
  </asp:TableRow>
  <asp:TableFooterRow TableSection="TableFooter">
    <asp:TableCell Text="Average"
      AssociatedHeaderCellID="headName" />
    <asp:TableCell Text="27.9"
      AssociatedHeaderCellID="headFirst" />
    <asp:TableCell Text="10.0"
      AssociatedHeaderCellID="headSecond" />
  </asp:TableFooterRow>
</asp:Table>
```

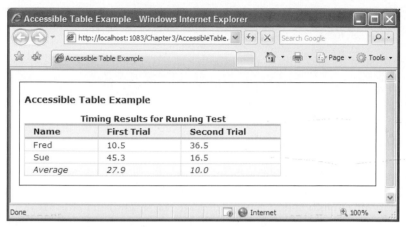

Figure 3.21 Accessible table

This example of an accessible `Table` control is rendered in the browser as shown in the following. Notice how the Caption property of the `Table` control is rendered as an HTML `<caption>` element. Notice as well how the `AssociatedHeader-CellID` property of the `TableCell` control is rendered as the headers attribute of the `<td>` element.

```
<table id="Table1" border="0">
   <caption align="Top">
      Timing Results for Running Test
   </caption>
   <thead>
      <tr>
         <th id="Th1">Name</th>
         <th id="Th2">First Trial</th>
         <th id="Th3">Second Trial</th>
      </tr>
   </thead>
   <tbody>
      <tr>
         <td headers="headName">Fred</td>
         <td headers="headFirst">10.5</td>
         <td headers="headSecond">36.5</td>
      </tr>
      <tr>
         <td headers="headName">Sue</td>
         <td headers="headFirst">45.3</td>
         <td headers="headSecond">16.5</td>
      </tr>
   </tbody>
```

```
<tfoot>
    <tr>
        <td headers="headName">Average</td>
        <td headers="headFirst">27.9</td>
        <td headers="headSecond">10.0</td>
    </tr>
</tfoot>
</table>
```

Calendar Control

The `Calendar` control is perhaps the most complex of the basic server controls covered in this chapter. It displays a single month calendar that allows a user to navigate from month to month and to select dates, weeks, or entire months. It displays the days of the month, day headings for the days of the week, a title with the month and year, links for selecting individual days of the month, and links for moving to the next and previous month. For instance, Figure 3.22 illustrates the appearance of this basic calendar:

```
<asp:calendar id="calTest" runat="server"></asp:calendar>
```

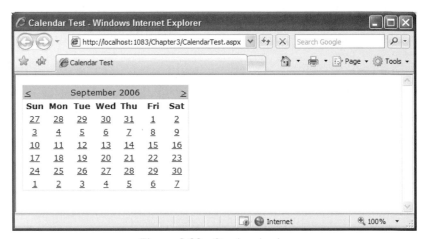

Figure 3.22   Simple calendar

You can customize the appearance of the `Calendar` control by setting the properties that control the style for different parts of the control. For instance, Figure 3.23 illustrates how the calendar appears for the following definition.

```
<asp:calendar id="calTest" runat="server"
    backcolor="PaleGoldenrod" width="400px" height="200px"
```

```
font-size="12px" font-names="Arial"
borderwidth="2px" bordercolor="#000000"
nextprevformat="shortmonth">
```

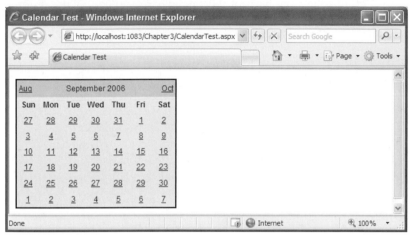

Figure 3.23   Formatted calendar

Formatting the Calendar Using Style Elements

The appearance of the Calendar control can be further customized by setting various *style elements*. Many of the more complex Web server controls in ASP.NET use style elements. These style elements are additional tags that are embedded within the parent control (such as the Calendar control) and allow you to customize the appearance of that control. For each of the Calendar style elements, you can modify the font, border, color, size, or CSS class of the calendar element referenced by the style element. The supported style elements are

- DayHeaderStyle—Specifies the style for the section that displays the days of the week.
- DayStyle—Specifies the style for the dates in the displayed month.
- NextPrevStyle—Specifies the style for the next and previous month links in the title section.
- OtherMonthDayStyle—Specifies the style for the dates that are not in the currently displayed month.
- SelectedDayStyle—Specifies the style for the selected dates on the calendar.
- SelectorStyle—Specifies the style for the week and month date selection column.

- `TitleStyle`—Specifies the style for the title section.
- `TodayDayStyle`—Specifies the style for today's date.
- `WeekendDayStyle`—Specifies the style for the weekend dates.

Figure 3.24 illustrates the parts of the calendar referenced by the different style element elements.

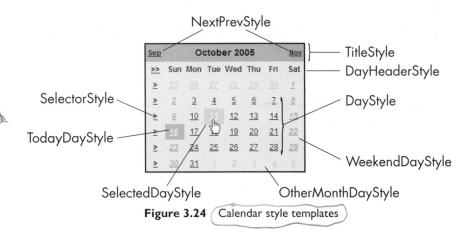

Figure 3.24 Calendar style templates

As mentioned previously, these style elements can be embedded within the opening and closing tags of the `Calendar` element. For example:

```
<asp:calendar id="calTest" runat="server">
  <titlestyle font-size="14px" font-bold="true" />
</asp:calendar>
```

Alternately, each style subproperty can be set within the `calendar` element itself using hyphen notation, as in

```
<asp:calendar id="calTest" runat="server"
  TitleStyle-Font-Size="14px" TitleStyle-Font-Bold="true">
```

Listing 3.30 demonstrates the use of several of these style elements. The result can be seen in Figure 3.25.

Listing 3.30 CalendarTest.aspx

```
<asp:calendar id="calTest" runat="server"
  backcolor="PaleGoldenrod" width="400px" height="200px"
  font-size="12px" font-names="Arial"
  borderwidth="2px" bordercolor="#000000"
  nextprevformat="shortmonth">
```

```
<titlestyle font-size="14px" font-bold="true"
  backcolor="Goldenrod"/>
<dayheaderstyle font-bold="true" />
<todaydaystyle backcolor="Orange" forecolor="#ffffff" />
<othermonthdaystyle forecolor="Tan" />
</asp:calendar>
```

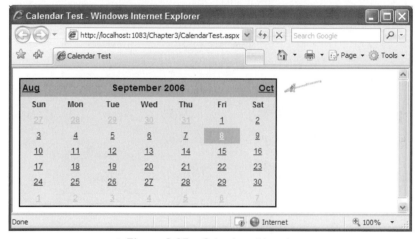

Figure 3.25   Calendar with style

CORE NOTE

As an alternative to specifying each element's style via individual ASP.NET appearance properties such as `font-size` or `forecolor`, you may want to define these instead using CSS and then reference the CSS class via the `CssClass` property of the style element, as shown in the following.

```
<DayHeaderStyle CssClass="dayheader" />
```

Chapter 6 contains more information about working with CSS in ASP.NET.

Visual Studio provides an easy way to format the `Calendar` control (or indeed any other control that uses style elements) via the AutoFormat option while in Design view, as shown in Figure 3.26.

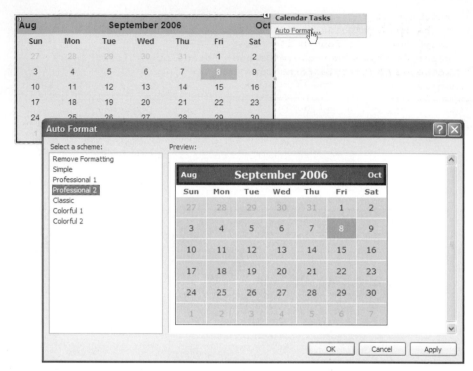

Figure 3.26   Formatting a calendar with Visual Studio

Table 3.24 lists many of the most important properties of the Calendar control. There are several additional properties not listed in this table; you can view the MSDN documentation for a complete listing.

Table 3.24   Notable Properties of the Calendar Control

Property	Description
Caption	The text to display for the calendar's rendered table caption element. The caption is displayed either above or below the calendar. The caption provides accessibility technologies with a description of the calendar, because the Calendar is rendered using an HTML <table> element.
CaptionAlign	Specifies where the caption is to appear relative to the calendar. Possible values are described by the TableCaptionAlign enumeration: Bottom, Left, NotSet, Right, and Top.

Table 3.24 Notable Properties of the Calendar Control *(continued)*

Property	Description
DayNameFormat	The name format for the days of the week. Possible values are described by the DayNameFormat enumeration: FirstLetter, FirstTwoLetters, Full, Short, and Shortest.
FirstDayOfWeek	The day of the week to display in the first day column of the control. Possible values are described by the FirstDayOfWeek enumeration: Sunday, Monday, Tuesday, and so on.
NextMonthText	Provides custom text for the next month link. This property is commonly used along with the PrevMonthText property.
NextPrevFormat	The format for the next and previous month links on the control. Possible values are FullMonth (displays the entire month name), ShortMonth (displays a three-letter abbreviation for the month), and CustomText (to programmatically set the text).
PrevMonthText	Provides custom text for the previous month link. This property is commonly used along with the NextMonthText property.
SelectedDate	The selected date on the calendar.
SelectedDates	Collection of selected dates on the calendar.
SelectionMode	Specifies how dates are selected. Possible values are described by the CalendarSelectionMode enumeration: Day (select a single day), DayWeek (select a single date or entire week), DayWeekMonth (select a single day, week or an entire month), or None (date selection disabled).
SelectMonthText	Allows custom text to be used for the month selection element. This property only applies if the SelectionMode property is set to DayWeekMonth.
SelectWeekText	Allows custom text to be used for the week selection element. This property only applies if the SelectionMode property is set to DayWeek.
ShowDayHeader	Specifies whether the heading for the days of the week is displayed (true or false).
ShowGridLines	Specifies whether the days on the calendar are separated with grid lines (true or false).
ShowNextPrevMonth	Specifies whether the calendar displays the next and previous month navigation elements in the title section (true or false).

Table 3.24   Notable Properties of the Calendar Control *(continued)*

Property	Description
ShowTitle	Specifies whether the title section is displayed (`true` or `false`). Hiding the title section also hides the next and previous month links.
TitleFormat	The format for the title section. Possible values are described by the `TitleFormat` enumeration: `Month` (title displayed with only the month but not the year) and `MonthYear` (title displayed with both the month and the year).
TodaysDate	The value for today's date. Can be programmatically set by assigning it a `DateTime` object.
UseAccessibleHeader	Specifies whether to render the calendar header using the table header element (`<th>`) or just use the regular table data element (`<td>`). For a more accessible calendar, set this value to `true`. The default value is `true`.
VisibleDate	The month to display on the calendar. Can be programmatically set by assigning it a `DateTime` object.

Responding to SelectionChanged Event

In the `Calendar` from the previous listing, each date is displayed as a hyperlink, but nothing happens when it is clicked. We can respond to a user's date selection by responding to the `Calendar` control's `SelectionChanged` event. The `Calendar` control supports a number of additional events, as shown in Table 3.25.

Table 3.25   Unique Events of the Calendar Classes

Event	Description
DayRender	Raised when each day is rendered in the control. Because the `Calendar` control does not support data binding, you can use this event to modify and uniquely format the contents of individual date cells.
SelectionChanged	Raised when a day, a week, or an entire month is selected.
VisibleMonthChanged	Raised when the user clicks on the next or previous month links.

To respond to selection events, you must specify the handler for the Selection-Changed event of the Calendar, as in the following:

```
<asp:calendar id="calTest" runat="server"
    OnSelectionChanged="calTest_SelectionChanged" />
```

The handler for the SelectionChanged event can retrieve the selected date by using the SelectedDate property (which returns a DateTime object). For instance, in the following handler, the selected date is placed within a TextBox on the form.

```
protected void calTest_SelectionChanged(object o, EventArgs e)
{
    txtSelected.Text = calTest.SelectedDate.ToString();
}
```

In this example, the full date and time are displayed in the text box. To change the formatting of the date, you can use one of the other methods of the DateTime class, such as ToShortDateString() or ToLongDateString().

Responding to the DayRender Event

The Calendar control does not support data binding. Thus, if you want to display specific content in any calendar cell, you must programmatically do so via the DayRender event. This event is triggered when each date cell in the control is created. By writing a handler for this event, you can add your own content to any date cell. However, because the DayRender event is raised while the Calendar is being rendered, you cannot add a control that also raises its own events. Thus, you can only add static controls such as LiteralControl, Label, Image, and HyperLink.

Walkthrough 3.1 illustrates how you can add custom content to a calendar. The resulting page in the browser is shown in Figure 3.27.

CORE NOTE

This walkthrough is more complex than any of the walkthroughs from the first two chapters. It uses several features of C# that might be confusing if you are new to ASP.NET and C#. If this is the case, you might want to come back to this walkthrough after working through some of the other chapters in the book.

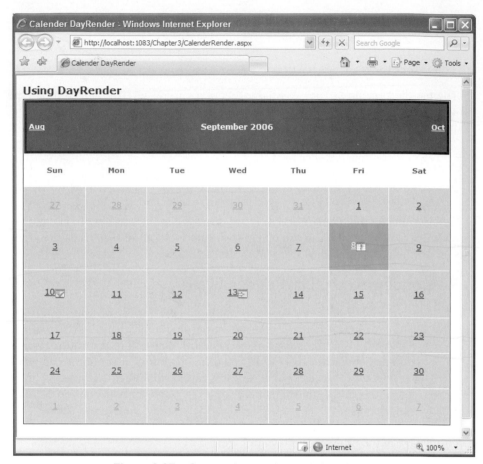

Figure 3.27   Custom date rendering in the calendar

Walkthrough 3.1   *Custom Day Rendering*

This walkthrough uses a custom class named `CalendarEvent` that encapsulates a single calendar event. Individual calendar cells contain `CalendarEvent` data. Custom classes can be used by your Web Forms by creating the class in the `App_Code` folder of your Web site.

1. In Visual Studio, create the `App_Code` folder of your Web site by right-clicking the project container and choosing the Add ASP.NET Folder | App_Code menu option.

2. Add a class to the `App_Code` folder, by right-clicking the `App_Code` folder and choosing the Add New Item menu item.

3. In the Add New Item dialog, choose the Class template and change the name to `CalendarEvent.cs`. Click Add.

4. Change the `CalendarEvent.cs` class to the following.

```csharp
using System;
using System.Data;
using System.Configuration;
using System.Web;
using System.Web.Security;
using System.Web.UI;
using System.Web.UI.WebControls;

using System.Text;

/// <summary>
/// Encapsulates a single calendar event
/// </summary>
public class CalenderEvent
{
    /// <summary>
    /// Represents the possible event types for a date
    /// </summary>
    public enum EventTypes
    {
        AllDayEvent, Appointment, ToDoReminder
    }

    // Data members
    private string _shortDescription;
    private string _fullDescription;
    private DateTime _eventDate;
    private EventTypes _eventType;

    /// <summary>
    /// Constructor for the event
    /// </summary>
    public CalenderEvent(string shortDescription,
        string fullDescription, DateTime eventDate,
        EventTypes eventType)
    {
        _shortDescription = shortDescription;
        _fullDescription = fullDescription;
        _eventDate = eventDate;
        _eventType = eventType;
    }
```

```
/// <summary>
/// Provide a string representation of the event.
/// </summary>
public override string ToString()
{
   // Use StringBuilder for more efficient
   // string concatenation
   StringBuilder sb = new StringBuilder();
   sb.Append(this.Date.ToShortDateString());
   sb.Append(" -- ");
   sb.Append(this.EventTypeString);
   sb.Append("<br/>");
   sb.Append(FullDescription);
   return sb.ToString();
}

/// <summary>
/// The full description of the event.
/// </summary>
public string FullDescription
{
   get { return _fullDescription; }
   set { _fullDescription = value; }
}

/// <summary>
/// The short description of the event.
/// </summary>
public string ShortDescription
{
   get { return _shortDescription; }
   set { _shortDescription = value; }
}

/// <summary>
/// The date of the event.
/// </summary>
public DateTime Date
{
   get { return _eventDate; }
   set { _eventDate = value; }
}

/// <summary>
/// The event type
/// </summary>
```

```
public EventTypes Type
{
    get { return _eventType; }
    set { _eventType = value; }
}


/// <summary>
/// Return a string representation of the event type
/// </summary>
public string EventTypeString
{
    get
    {
        if (this.Type == EventTypes.AllDayEvent)
            return "All Day Event";
        else if (this.Type == EventTypes.Appointment)
            return "Appointment";
        else
            return "To Do Reminder";
    }
}


/// <summary>
/// Return the filename of the icon image for the
/// event type
/// </summary>
public string ImageFile
{
    get
    {
        if (this.Type == EventTypes.AllDayEvent)
            return "cal_allday.gif";
        else if (this.Type == EventTypes.Appointment)
            return "cal_appointment.gif";
        else
            return "cal_todo.gif";
    }
}
}
```

5. Save and build (to check for compile errors).

6. Create a new Web Form named `CalendarRender.aspx`.

This Web Form is quite straightforward. It specifies the names of the two event handlers for the `Calendar`. As well, it contains a `Label` that displays information about the selected date.

7. Add the following to `CalendarRender.aspx`.

```
<h1>Using DayRender</h1>
<asp:Calendar ID="calRender" runat="server" BackColor="White"

    BorderColor="Black" BorderStyle="Solid" CellSpacing="1"
    Font-Names="Verdana" Font-Size="9pt" ForeColor="Black"
    Height="504px" NextPrevFormat="ShortMonth" Width="664px"
    OnDayRender="calRender_DayRender"
    OnSelectionChanged="calRender_SelectionChanged"  >

    <SelectedDayStyle BackColor="#333399" ForeColor="White"
/>
    <OtherMonthDayStyle ForeColor="#999999" />
    <DayStyle BackColor="#CCCCCC" />
    <TodayDayStyle BackColor="#999999" ForeColor="White" />
    <NextPrevStyle Font-Bold="True" Font-Size="8pt"
        ForeColor="White"/>
    <DayHeaderStyle Font-Bold="True" Font-Size="8pt"
        ForeColor="#333333" Height="8pt" />
    <TitleStyle BackColor="#333399" BorderStyle="Solid"
        Font-Bold="True" Font-Size="9pt"
        ForeColor="White" Height="9pt" />
</asp:Calendar>
<p>
<asp:Label ID="labMessage" runat="server" />
</p>
```

8. Add the following code to the code-behind for `CalendarRender.aspx`.

```
public partial class CalenderRender : System.Web.UI.Page
{
    private ArrayList _events;

    protected void Page_Load(object sender, EventArgs e)
    {
        FillCalender();
    }


    /// <summary>
    /// Fills Calendar with events.
    /// </summary>
    private void FillCalender()
    {
        // For now, just hard code the events.
        // In reality, would will be filled from database
        _events = new ArrayList();

        // Create a few sample events. Assign them to
        // today's date, in 2 days from now, and in 5 days
        // from now
```

```csharp
    _events.Add(new CalenderEvent("Doctor Appointment",
        "10am Appointment with Dr. John Locke", DateTime.Now,

        CalenderEvent.EventTypes.Appointment));
    _events.Add(new CalenderEvent("Learn ASP.NET",
        "Learn ASP.NET in preparation for conference",
        DateTime.Now.AddDays(2.0),
        CalenderEvent.EventTypes.ToDoReminder));
    _events.Add(new CalenderEvent("PDA Conference",
        "Microsoft .NET PDA Conference, Seattle",
        DateTime.Now.AddDays(5.0),
        CalenderEvent.EventTypes.AllDayEvent));
}


/// <summary>
/// Handles the calendar day rendering event.
/// </summary>
protected void calRender_DayRender(object sender,
    DayRenderEventArgs e)
{
    // Get the date to be rendered
    DateTime renderDay = e.Day.Date;

    // Check if this date is in our list of events
    foreach (CalenderEvent cEvent in _events)
    {
        // If the date is the same, add appropriate image
        if (renderDay.ToShortDateString() ==
                cEvent.Date.ToShortDateString())
        {
            Image img = new Image();
            img.ImageUrl = "~/images/" + cEvent.ImageFile;
            img.ToolTip = cEvent.ShortDescription;
            img.ImageAlign = ImageAlign.Middle;
            e.Cell.Controls.Add(img);
        }
    }
}


/// <summary>
/// Handles the calendar selection event.
/// </summary>
protected void calRender_SelectionChanged(object sender,
    EventArgs e)
{
```

```
        // Get the selected date
        DateTime selectDay = calRender.SelectedDate;
        string message = "";

        // Check if this date is in our list of events
        foreach (CalenderEvent cEvent in _events)
        {
            if (selectDay.ToShortDateString() ==
                    cEvent.Date.ToShortDateString())
            {
                message = cEvent.ToString();
            }
        }

        // Assign appropriate message to label
        if (message == "") {
            labMessage.Text = "No event scheduled for ";
            labMessage.Text += selectDay.ToShortDateString();
        }
        else
            labMessage.Text = message;
    }
}
```

This `Page_Load` method fills an `ArrayList` collection with sample
`CalendarEvent` objects. (Realistically, you would probably retrieve data
from some external data source like a database or XML file.) The
`DayRender` event handler contains most of the action. It retrieves the date
of the cell to be rendered, loops through the collection of `CalendarEvent`
objects, and if there is a date match, it creates a suitable `Image` control and
adds it to the control. The `SelectionChanged` event handler displays
more information about the event if a date with an event is selected.

This example also uses an `ArrayList` collection class to hold the sample
events. Collections are covered in Chapter 8.

9. Test in browser. The result should be similar to that shown in Figure
   3.27.

CORE NOTE

It should be noted that comparing dates for equality can be a problem
because a `DateTime` object has both a date and a time. If you want only
to compare two `DateTime` objects without the time, you can compare
the `ToShortDateString` values of the objects.

Creating a Pop-Up Calendar

It is not uncommon to have a form that contains multiple date fields for the user to enter. In such a case, multiple `Calendar` controls are not ideal because each calendar uses up so much screen space in the browser. A better approach is to have some type of button that opens the calendar in a pop-up window; after the user selects the date from the calendar, the window closes and the selected date appears in the original form's text box (see Figure 3.28).

To implement this functionality, you need two Web Forms: the form that displays the date text boxes and buttons (in the following example, this is `PopupCalendar-Test.aspx`) and the form that displays the pop-up calendar (`Popup.aspx`). Each of these Web Forms requires a Javascript function to help implement this behavior.

Listing 3.31 shows the markup and Javascript for the sample `PopupCalendar-Test.aspx` page. It contains two `TextBox` controls that contain the selected dates as well as two `ImageButton` controls that are used to open the calendar window. Each button uses the `OnClientClick` property to pass a Javascript function call to the rendered `<input>` button. The Javascript function `PickDate` opens the `Popup.aspx` page and passes the ID of the `TextBox` control that will ultimately receive the user's selected date as a querystring parameter.

Listing 3.31 PopupCalendarTest.aspx

```
<head runat="server">
   <title>Popup Date Selector</title>
   <script language="javascript" type="text/javascript">
   function PickDate(controlName)
   {
      var wnd = null;

      // Set up the look of the popup window
      var settings='width=300,height=200,location=no,menubar=no,
         toolbar=no,scrollbars=no,resizable=yes,status=yes';

      // Pass the control name that will receive the date
      var url = 'Popup.aspx?control=' + controlName;

      // Open the popup window
      wnd = window.open(url,'DatePopup',settings);

      // Give popup window the focus if browser
      // supports this capability
      if (wnd.focus) { wnd.focus(); }
   }
   </script>
</head>
```

```
<body>
    <form id="form1" runat="server">
    <div>
    Start Date:
    <asp:TextBox ID="txtDateStart" runat="server"
        Columns="10"></asp:TextBox>
    <asp:ImageButton ID="btnDateStart" runat="server"
        ImageUrl="~/images/cal_allday.gif"
        OnClientClick="PickDate('txtDateStart')" />

    <br />
    End Date:
    <asp:TextBox ID="txtDateEnd" runat="server"
        Columns="10"></asp:TextBox>
    <asp:ImageButton ID="btnDateEnd" runat="server"
        ImageUrl="~/images/cal_allday.gif"
        OnClientClick="PickDate('txtDateEnd')" />
    </div>
    </form>
</body>
```

Popup.aspx contains most of the magic. This page contains only the Calendar control, as well as a Javascript function that places the selected date in the appropriate TextBox in the calling page (PopupCalendarTest.aspx). The markup for Popup.aspx is shown in Listing 3.32. The most complex part of this page is the Javascript function. It retrieves the control name of the text box to place the date by retrieving the first querystring parameter (via window.location.search.substr(1)) and then retrieving the value of that parameter (via substring(8)). We use the number 8 with the substring() because the parameter name (i.e., control) plus the equal sign (=) is 8 characters long.

Listing 3.32 Popup.aspx

```
<html xmlns="http://www.w3.org/1999/xhtml" >
<head runat="server">
    <title>Select Date</title>
    <script language="javascript">
        function SetDate(dateToSet)
        {
            // Retrieve name of textbox control from querystring
            controlName =
                window.location.search.substr(1).substring(8);

            // Set the text box to the selected date
            window.opener.document.forms[0].
                elements[controlName].value = dateToSet;
```

```
            // Close the window
            self.close();
        }
    </script>
</head>
<body>
    <form id="form1" runat="server">
    <div>
    <asp:Calendar ID="calPopup" runat="server" BackColor="White"
        BorderColor="#999999" CellPadding="4" "
        Font-Names="Verdana" Font-Size="8pt" ForeColor="Black"
        DayNameFormat="Shortest Height="100%" Width="100%"
        OnDayRender="calPopup_DayRender" >

        <SelectedDayStyle BackColor="#666666" Font-Bold="True"
            ForeColor="White" />
        <SelectorStyle BackColor="#CCCCCC" />
        <WeekendDayStyle BackColor="#FFFFCC" />
        <OtherMonthDayStyle ForeColor="#808080" />
        <TodayDayStyle BackColor="#CCCCCC" ForeColor="Black" />
        <NextPrevStyle VerticalAlign="Bottom" />
        <DayHeaderStyle BackColor="#CCCCCC" Font-Bold="True"
            Font-Size="7pt" />
        <TitleStyle BackColor="#999999" BorderColor="Black"
            Font-Bold="True" />
    </asp:Calendar>
    </div>
    </form>
</body>
</html>
```

Looking at the Popup.aspx, you may wonder where the Javascript SetDate function is actually called. The answer to this lies in the event handler for the Calendar control's DayRender event (shown in Listing 3.33). The DayRender event handler replaces the built-in postback links for each day in the Calendar with a HyperLink control that links to the Javascript SetDate function (and passes in the date for that day). The text for the HyperLink control (the day number) is retrieved from the existing text of the cell.

Listing 3.33   Popup.aspx.cs

```
protected void calPopup_DayRender(object sender,
    DayRenderEventArgs e)
{
    HyperLink link = new HyperLink();
```

```
LiteralControl lc = (LiteralControl)e.Cell.Controls[0];
link.Text = lc.Text;
link.NavigateUrl = "javascript:SetDate('" +
   e.Day.Date.ToShortDateString() + "');";
e.Cell.Controls.Clear();
e.Cell.Controls.Add(link);
}
```

Figure 3.28 illustrates how these pages appear in the browser. Notice the URL for the day link in the status bar of Popup.aspx.

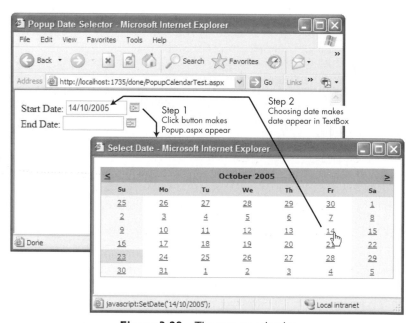

Figure 3.28   The pop-up calendar

CORE NOTE

There are certainly other ways of achieving a pop-up calendar. For instance, we could use the Atlas `PopupControl` (Atlas is Microsoft's AJAX Framework for ASP.NET and is covered in the Appendix), which can turn any ASP.NET control into a lightweight pop-up window. There are also various third-party controls that can achieve similar functionality.

Summary

This chapter examined in some detail the most essential of the standard Web server controls. These controls are the building blocks of most Web Forms; almost any ASP.NET Web Form generally uses one or more of these controls. All of these controls benefit from the advantages of having common class ancestors, namely, the `WebControl` and the `Control` classes. As such, there is a common set of properties, methods, and events that are shared by all controls.

There are still some additional standard Web server controls that were not covered in this chapter. The next chapter covers the remaining, more specialized, standard controls.

Exercises

The solutions to the following exercises can be found at my Web site, http://www.randyconnolly.com/core. Additional exercises only available for teachers and instructors are also available from this site.

1. Create a Web Form that contains a `DropDownList`, `TextBox`, `CheckBox-List`, `Calendar`, and a `Button` control. The two list controls should have multiple items defined. The `Button`'s click event handler should display in a `Label` control the item selected in the `DropDownList`, the text entered in the `TextBox`, the checked items in the `CheckBoxList`, and the selected date in the `Calendar`.

2. Create a Web Form that contains two sets of links. The first set of links should consist of working `HyperLink` controls that navigate to some other page. The second set of links should consist of working `LinkButton` controls. That is, these link buttons should display in a `Label` control information about the button that was clicked.

3. Use the `Table` control to create a data table containing four rows and columns of data, one header row, and one footer row. This data table should be properly accessible.

Key Concepts

- HTML attributes
- HTML server controls
- Style elements
- Subproperties
- Web server controls

References

Allen, Scott. "The Calendar Control and the DayRender Event in ASP.NET."
    http://odetocode.com/Articles/223.aspx.

Bellinaso, Marco. "Creating a Popup Calendar Control."
    http://www.devx.com/vb2themax/Tip/18850.

Homer, Alex. "Accessibility Improvements in ASP.NET 2.0—Part 2."
    http://www.15seconds.com.

Mitchell, Scott. "List Control Items and Attributes."
    http://aspnet.4guysfromrolla.com/articles/091405.aspx.

Thomason, Larisa. "Designing Accessible Tables."
    http://www.netmechanic.com/news/vol4/accessibility_no16.htm.

Chapter 4

THE ADDITIONAL STANDARD WEB SERVER CONTROLS

The previous chapter introduced the most essential of the standard Web server controls. This chapter examines the remaining standard Web server controls. Although you may use these controls less frequently than those covered in the previous chapter, they are still quite useful to know. The controls covered in this chapter can be grouped into two categories: those that are container controls and those that are not. The `Panel`, `MultiView` and `View`, `Wizard`, and `PlaceHolder` controls' basic function is to act as a container or parent for other controls. These container controls have many powerful features that make them an important part of any ASP.NET developer's repertoire. The other controls covered in this chapter (`AdRotator`, `FileUpload`, and `Xml` controls) are not container controls; they perform fairly specialized jobs and as such may not be used nearly as frequently as some other controls. Nonetheless, they do have many unique and useful features that this chapter attempts to demonstrate.

The controls covered in this chapter have a rich set of features that require much longer explanations than the controls covered in the last chapter. To enticingly present these features, this chapter contains several longer demonstration projects: a pizza ordering form, a tabbed panel, a checkout wizard, a file browser, and a RSS reader.

Overview of the Additional Standard Web Server Controls

This chapter covers the additional standard Web server controls in detail. For each of these controls, there are descriptions, property and event summaries, and sample listings that illustrate typical uses of that control. In comparison to the standard Web server controls covered in the previous chapter, the standard Web server controls covered in this chapter are significantly more rich and generalized; they can be used for a very wide range of tasks. As such, many of the controls covered in this chapter are also provided with a more complex, real-world example.

CORE NOTE

You can download either a starting or finished version of the files used in the chapter from my Web site, http://www.randyconnolly.com/core.

Table 4.1 lists the additional standard Web server controls covered in this chapter.

Table 4.1   Additional Standard Web Server Controls

Server Control	Description
AdRotator	Displays an advertisement banner (i.e., a randomly selected image that, when clicked, navigates to a new Web page).
FileUpload	Allows a user to upload a file to the server. Consists of a text box and Browse button.
MultiView and View	The MultiView control is a container for groups of View controls.
Panel	Provides a container for other controls.
PlaceHolder	A container control used for dynamically loading other controls.
Wizard	Provides a series of interconnected forms used for collecting information incrementally from the user.
Xml	Displays an XML file or the results of an XSLT (Extensible Stylesheet Language Transformation) transformation.

All but two of the controls examined in the previous chapter ultimately inherit from the WebControl base class; the other two inherit from Control, the base class of WebControl. As can be seen in Figure 4.1, half of the controls covered in this chapter also inherit from Control, whereas the others inherit (eventually) from the WebControl class.

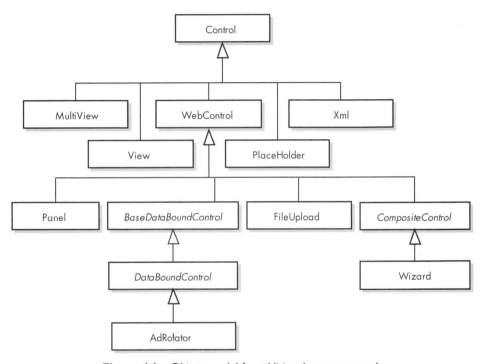

Figure 4.1   Object model for additional server controls

If you compare the members available to the WebControl class with those available to the Control class (see Tables 2.2 and 2.3 on page 77), you will see that the Control class does not have any user interface functionalities other than visibility; rather, it supplies the basic members that all controls need: ID, child control collections, and common control events. The WebControl class, on the other hand, provides the appearance properties and behaviors required by most Web server controls (ForeColor, Height, CssClass, etc.).

The reason that MultiView, View, PlaceHolder, and Xml controls do not inherit from the WebControl base class is that these classes either do not supply a user interface (PlaceHolder) or they provide a user interface that is not related to the base one provided by WebControl (MultiView, View, and Xml).

Panel Control

The `Panel` control is a container control that can be used as a parent container for plain text, HTML elements, and other Web server controls. The `Panel` control is typically used for creating group behavior, for creating a unique look for an area on a page, or to programmatically display and hide groups of controls. For instance, you could set the `BackColor` property of a group of controls at once by setting the `BackColor` property of the `Panel`, as shown in the following.

```
<asp:Panel id="panTest" Runat="server" BackColor="#cccc99" >
   <asp:Label id="labMsg" runat="server"/>
   <asp:DropDownList ID="drpList" Runat="server">
      <asp:ListItem>First</asp:ListItem>
      <asp:ListItem>Second</asp:ListItem>
   </asp:DropDownList>
</asp:Panel>
```

If you want to programmatically hide a group of controls inside a `Panel`, you could easily do so by simply setting the `Visible` property of the `Panel`.

```
panTest.Visible = false;
```

Table 4.2 lists the unique properties of the `Panel` control.

Table 4.2   Unique Properties of the Panel Control

Property	Description
BackImageUrl	The URL of the image to display in the background of the panel (i.e., behind its content).
DefaultButton	Indicates the default button control. This indicates which button is clicked when the `Panel` control has focus and the user presses the Enter key.
Direction	Specifies the direction to display controls that contain text within the panel. Possible values are defined by the `ContentDirection` enumeration (`NotSet`, `LeftToRight`, `RightToLeft`). Used for localization purposes to handle languages that display right to left. Localization is covered in Chapter 16.
GroupingText	Sets the caption for the panel as a whole. Rendered via the HTML `<fieldset>` and `<legend>` elements.
HorizontalAlign	Specifies the horizontal alignment of elements within the panel.

Table 4.2   Unique Properties of the Panel Control *(continued)*

Property	Description
ScrollBars	Specifies the visibility and placement of scrollbars within the panel. Possible values are defined by the ScrollBars enumeration (Auto, Both, Horizontal, None, Vertical).
Wrap	Specifies whether the textual content of the panel has word wrapping (default is true).

The Panel control is rendered to the browser as an HTML <div> element. Thus, you can also use the Panel control for many of the same tasks where you would use a <div> element, such as grouping a block of content together. The Panel control also provides additional functionality over a <div> element, such as applying a style to a group of elements. For instance, let us assume that we have the following style definition:

```
<style> .special { padding: 5 px; margin 10 px; } </style>
```

We can now apply this style to a large number of text and controls by simply placing them within a Panel and then setting the CssClass of the Panel.

```
<asp:Panel id="panTest" Runat="server" CssClass="special">
   Other server controls and html go here
</asp:Panel>
```

Listings 4.1 and 4.2 demonstrate the Panel control at work. In it, several Panel controls are used to selectively hide or show different parts of an order form for a pizza shop. This form has three panels: one for specifying the customer and pizza information, one for displaying the pricing, and the other for showing the order summary. Initially, the last two panels are hidden. To provide a contrast to the Panel approach, this example also illustrates the non-Panel approach to hiding controls, in the individual setting of the Visible property of the customer address controls. After the pizza size is chosen, the pricing panel is displayed; and after the order button is clicked, the first two panels are hidden and the order summary panel is displayed.

Listing 4.1 also uses the GroupingText property of the Panel control. This property adds the little-known HTML <fieldset> and <legend> elements. The <fieldset>element defines a form group that can be used to divide a form into smaller groups; it is rendered in the browser as a rectangle outline. The <legend> element provides a caption for the group of controls. It is rendered in the browser as a text over the top-right rectangle of the <fieldset>. Figure 4.2 illustrates how the GroupingText appears in the browser with a bit of CSS styling. The GroupingText property also improves the accessibility of a form, because voice readers use the <fieldset>and <legend>elements to provide aural orientation within the form.

Listing 4.1   PizzaPanelTest.aspx

```
<div id="left">
   <asp:Panel ID="panPizza" runat="server" Width="25em"
      GroupingText="Pizza Order Form">
      <dl>
         <dt>
            <asp:Label ID="labCustomer" runat="server"
               Text="Customer" AccessKey="C"
               AssociatedControlID="txtCustomer" />
         </dt>
         <dd>
            <asp:TextBox ID="txtCustomer" runat="server" />
         </dd>

         <dt>
            <asp:Label ID="labPhone" runat="server" Text="Phone"
               AssociatedControlID="txtPhone"/>
         </dt>
         <dd>
            <asp:TextBox ID="txtPhone" runat="server"
               Columns="10"/>
         </dd>

         <dt>
            <asp:Label ID="labDelivery" runat="server"
               Text="Delivery"
               AssociatedControlID="chkDelivery"/>
         </dt>
         <dd>
            <asp:CheckBox ID="chkDelivery" runat="server"
               AutoPostBack="True"/>
         </dd>

         <dt>
            <asp:Label ID="labAddress" runat="server"
               Text="Address"
               AssociatedControlID="txtAddress"/>
         </dt>
         <dd>
            <asp:TextBox ID="txtAddress" runat="server"
               Columns="30"/>
         </dd>

         <dt>
            <asp:Label ID="labSize" runat="server" Text="Size"
               AssociatedControlID="drpSize"/>
         </dt>
         <dd>
```

```
            <asp:DropDownList ID="drpSize" runat="server"
               AutoPostBack="True">
               <asp:ListItem Value="U">
                  Choose a size</asp:ListItem>
               <asp:ListItem Value="S">Small</asp:ListItem>
               <asp:ListItem Value="M">Medium</asp:ListItem>
               <asp:ListItem Value="L">Large</asp:ListItem>
            </asp:DropDownList>
         </dd>

         <dt>
            <asp:Label ID="labToppings" runat="server"
               Text="Toppings"
               AssociatedControlID="clstToppings"/>
         </dt>
         <dd>
            <asp:CheckBoxList ID="clstToppings" runat="server"
               AutoPostBack="True" >
               <asp:ListItem Value="0">Ham</asp:ListItem>
               <asp:ListItem Value="1">Pepperoni</asp:ListItem>
               <asp:ListItem Value="2">
                  Extra Cheese</asp:ListItem>
               <asp:ListItem Value="3">Mushrooms</asp:ListItem>
               <asp:ListItem Value="4">
                  Green Peppers</asp:ListItem>
            </asp:CheckBoxList>
         </dd>

         <dt>
            <asp:Label ID="labCrust" runat="server" Text="Crust"
               AssociatedControlID="rlstCrust"/>
         </dt>
         <dd>
            <asp:RadioButtonList ID="rlstCrust" runat="server"
               AutoPostBack="True" >
               <asp:ListItem Selected="True">
                  Normal</asp:ListItem>
               <asp:ListItem>Thin</asp:ListItem>
               <asp:ListItem>Thick</asp:ListItem>
            </asp:RadioButtonList>
         </dd>
      </dl>
   </asp:Panel>
</div>
<div id="right">
   <asp:Panel ID="panPricing" runat="server" Width="18em"
      GroupingText="Pricing">
      <asp:Literal ID="litPricing" runat="server" />
      <p>
```

```
        <asp:Button ID="btnOrder" runat="server" Text="Order Pizza"
          OnClick="btnOrder_Click" />
        </p>
    </asp:Panel>
    <asp:Panel ID="panOrder" runat="server"
      GroupingText="Final Order" Width="18em">
        <asp:Label ID="labOrder" runat="server" />
    </asp:Panel>
</div>
```

The code-behind for this page is more complex than any of the examples from the previous chapters. The Page_Load method must determine the visibility of the various controls by examining the state of the different form elements. Notice that this method is kept rather short as it delegates most of the processing to various helper methods. In general, you should endeavor to keep any individual method short; methods that are overly long can be difficult to understand and modify.

The other interesting part of Listing 4.2 is the generation of the pizza price display. It dynamically creates and populates a container control covered in the previous chapter: the Table control.

Listing 4.2   PizzaPanelTest.aspx.cs

```
public partial class PizzaPanelTest : System.Web.UI.Page
{
  // Data members used by the form

  // M indicates a decimal literal
  private decimal pizzaBase = 0.0M;
  private decimal pizzaToppings = 0.0M;

  /// <summary>
  /// Called each time page is requested or posted back
  /// </summary>
  protected void Page_Load(object sender, EventArgs e)
  {
    // Initialize the visibility of our controls and panels
    txtAddress.Visible = false;
    labAddress.Visible = false;
    panPricing.Visible = false;
    panOrder.Visible = false;

    if (IsPostBack)
    {
      // If delivery check box is checked, show address
      // NOTE: this is what you have to do if not using panels
```

```
    if (IsDelivery())
    {
      labAddress.Visible = true;
      txtAddress.Visible = true;
    }
    // If valid size has been selected, display pricing
    // panel and the pricing table within it
    if (IsValidSize())
    {
      panPricing.Visible = true;
      GeneratePricingTable();
    }
  }
}


/// <summary>
/// Is this a delivery pizza?
/// </summary>
private bool IsDelivery()
{
  if (this.chkDelivery.Checked)
    return true;
  else
    return false;
}


/// <summary>
/// Calculate the price based on the size
/// </summary>
private void CalculatePrices()
{
  // Calculate based on size
  if (this.drpSize.SelectedValue == "S")
    pizzaBase = 10.0M;
  else if (this.drpSize.SelectedValue == "M")
    pizzaBase = 15.0M;
  else if (this.drpSize.SelectedValue == "L")
    pizzaBase = 20.0M;

  // Now add $1.50 for each topping
  foreach (ListItem item in this.clstToppings.Items)
  {
    if (item.Selected)
      pizzaToppings += 1.50M;
  }
}


/// <summary>
/// Was a valid pizza size selected
```

```
///   </summary>
private bool IsValidSize()
{
   if (this.drpSize.SelectedValue != "U")
      return true;
   else
      return false;
}

///   <summary>
///   Generates the pricing table control
///   </summary>
private void GeneratePricingTable()
{
   litPricing.Text = "<dl>";
   CalculatePrices();

   litPricing.Text +=
      CreatePricingRow("Base Price", pizzaBase, false);
   litPricing.Text +=
      CreatePricingRow("Toppings", pizzaToppings, false);
   decimal delivCharge = 0.0M;
   if (IsDelivery())
   {
      delivCharge = 1.00M;
      litPricing.Text +=
         CreatePricingRow("Delivery", delivCharge, false);
   }
   decimal subtotal = pizzaBase + pizzaToppings + delivCharge;
   decimal tax = subtotal * 0.07M;
   litPricing.Text += CreatePricingRow("Tax", tax, false);
   decimal total = subtotal + tax;
   litPricing.Text += CreatePricingRow("Total", total, true);
}

///   <summary>
///   Create a row for the pricing table
///   </summary>
private string CreatePricingRow(string label, decimal value,
   bool isBold)
{
   string s = "<dt id='item'>" + label + "</dt>";
   s += "<dd id='price'>";
   if (isBold) s += "<strong>";
   s += String.Format("{0:c}",value);
   if (isBold) s += "</strong>";
   s += "</dd>";
   return s;
}
```

```
/// <summary>
/// Called when order button is clicked
/// </summary>
protected void btnOrder_Click(object sender, EventArgs e)
{
  // Construct order summary
  String s = "<b>" + drpSize.SelectedItem.Text +
    " Pizza Ordered</b><br/>";
  s += "For " + this.txtCustomer.Text + "<br>";
  if (IsDelivery())
    s += "Deliver to " + this.txtAddress.Text + "<br>";
  s += rlstCrust.SelectedItem.Text + " Crust<br>";
  s += "<b>Toppings:</b><br>";
  foreach (ListItem item in this.clstToppings.Items)
  {
    if (item.Selected)
      s += item.Text + "<br>";
  }

  // Display order summary panel and content
  panOrder.Visible = true;
  labOrder.Text = s;
}
}
```

Figures 4.2, 4.3, and 4.4 illustrate the results of these listings in the browser.

CORE NOTE

In ASP.NET 1.1, the `Panel` control was the only way to programmatically hide and display groups of controls. In ASP.NET 2.0, the `Wizard`, `View`, and `MultiView` controls may be a better choice than the `Panel` control for many of these situations. However, if you want to quickly and easily change the visual appearance of a group of controls the `Panel` control may still be the best choice.

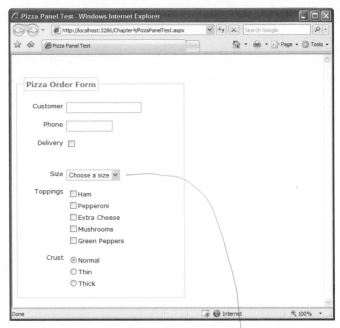

Figure 4.2   PizzaPanelTest.aspx before size selected

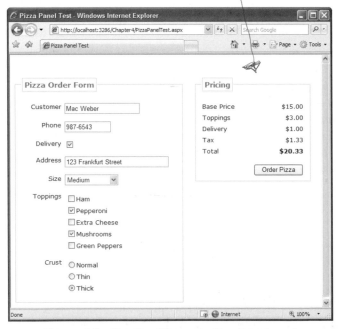

Figure 4.3   PizzaPanelTest.aspx after size selected

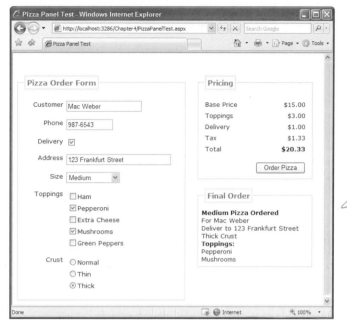

Figure 4.4   PizzaPanelTest.aspx after order button is clicked

MultiView and View Controls

Like the `Panel` control, the `MultiView` control is a container control for other content and controls. In particular, the `MultiView` control is a container for groups of `View` controls. Each of these `View` controls is also a container for other controls and HTML content. The structure of the `MultiView` and `View` controls is as follows:

```
<asp:MultiView ID="aMultiView" runat="Server" >
  <asp:View ID="view1" runat="Server">
    Content for view 1 here
  </asp:View>
  <asp:View ID="view2" runat="Server">
    Content for view 2 here
  </asp:View>
  etc
</asp:MultiView>
```

You can use the `MultiView` and `View` controls as a somewhat easier and more natural way to selectively display and hide groups of controls than by using multiple `Panel` controls in combination with programmatic manipulation of the `Visible` property of the `Panel` controls. Unlike the programmatic manipulation of `Panel` controls, there is complete designer support in Visual Studio for the `MultiView` and `View` controls. Figure 4.5 shows how the designer renders a single `MultiView` control containing three `View` controls.

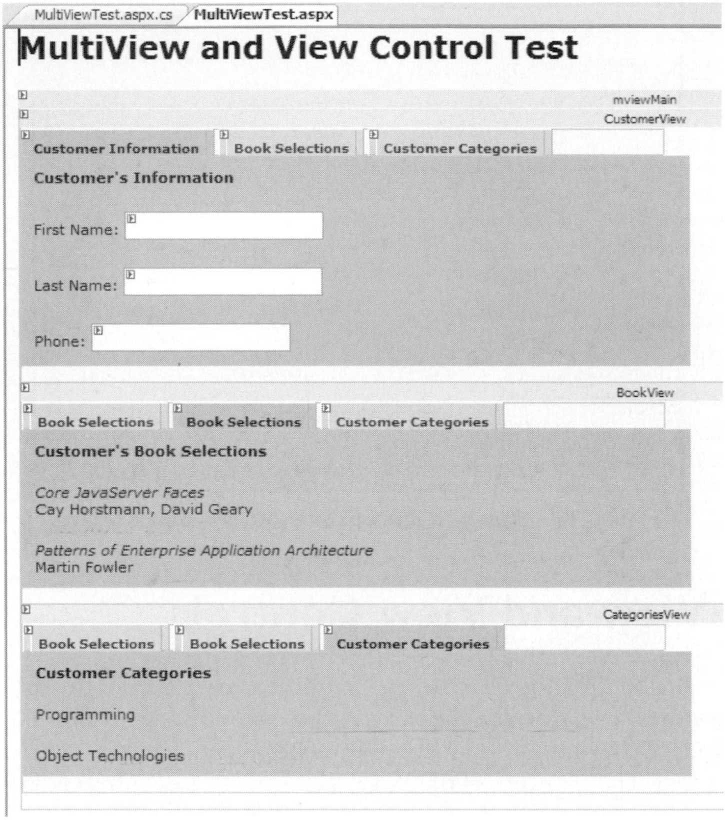

Figure 4.5   Designer support of MultiView and View control

Only one `View` control at a time is active (i.e., displayed) within a `MultiView` control. You can use either the `ActiveViewIndex` property or the `SetActiveView` method to specify which view is active. For instance, if there are three `View` controls defined within the `MultiView` control, you can make the first view active via

```
<asp:MultiView ID="mviewMain" runat="Server" ActiveViewIndex="0">
```

You can also specify the active view programmatically by either setting the view number to display (the `ActiveViewIndex` property) or via the view itself (the

SetActiveView method). For instance, for the MultiView control defined previously, the following code makes a view with an Id of view2 the active view.

mviewMain.SetActiveView(view2);

Table 4.3 lists the unique properties of the MultiView control.

Table 4.3 Unique Properties of the MultiView Control

Property	Description
ActiveViewIndex	Specifies the index of the active view within the MultiView.
Views	The collection of View controls in the MultiView.

Tables 4.4 and 4.5 list the unique events of the MultiView and View controls.

Table 4.4 Events of the MultiView Control

Event	Description
ActiveViewChanged	Raised on a postback when the active view of the MultiView control changes.

Table 4.5 Events of the View Control

Event	Description
Activate	Raised when the view becomes the active view.

Navigation Between Views

The MultiView control also supports the capability to navigate forward and backward between views via command buttons. To add a navigation button that moves to the next view in the control, you add a button with a CommandName of NextView; for a navigation button that moves to the previous view, you add a button with a CommandName of PrevView. To add a button that moves to a specific view, you can add a button with the CommandName of SwitchViewByIndex with the CommandArgument specifying the view to display. In the following example, the View has both next and previous buttons as well as a start over button that returns to the first view.

```
<asp:View ID="view2" runat="Server">
   Content for view 2 here …

   <asp:Button id="view2Prev" Text="Previous" runat="Server"
      CommandName="PrevView">
   </asp:Button>

   <asp:Button id="view2Next" Text="Next" runat="Server"
      CommandName="NextView">
   </asp:Button>

   <asp:Button id="view2Start" Text="Start Over" runat="Server"
      CommandName="SwitchViewByIndex" CommandArgument="0">
   </asp:Button>
</asp:View>
```

Notice that no event handlers are necessary for these command buttons. In a sense, handlers are generated by the MultiView control container by recognizing the reserved command names: NextView, PrevView, and SwitchViewByIndex. You can programmatically discover the names of these reserved command names via the NextViewCommandName, PreviousViewCommandName, and SwitchViewByIndexCommandName fields of the MultiView control.

Creating Tabbed Panels Using a MultiView

One way of using the MultiView control is to create tabbed panels similar to those found in Windows applications, where each View corresponds to a separate tab (see Figure 4.6). To do so, you need to add LinkButton controls to each View that act as the tabs and then use CSS to style the LinkButton controls to look like tabs. As well, a single event handler for the LinkButton controls is necessary; it simply calls the SetActiveView method of the MultiView to the appropriate view.

The key to implement this tabbed MultiView is to group the LinkButton controls in a separate Panel control (or even just an HTML <div> element) and style this tab container Panel. Also, each LinkButton is styled: one style for the currently active tab/view and another style for the inactive views. For instance, the following example defines these three styles.

```
TabContainer
{
   font: bold 0.75em Verdana;
   width: 60em;
   margin-top: 1.5em;
   padding-top: 2em;
}
```

```
.TabItemInactive
{
    border-top: 1px solid white;
    border-left: 1px solid white;
    border-right: 1px solid #aaaaaa;
    border-bottom: none;
    background-color: #d3d3d3;
    text-align: center;
    text-decoration: none;
    padding: 0.75em 0.25em 0 0.25em;
}

.TabItemInactive:hover
{
    background: #808080;
}
.TabItemActive
{
    border-top: 1px solid white;
    border-left: none;
    border-right: 1px solid #aaaaaa;
    border-bottom: none;
    text-decoration: none;
    background-color: #bbbbbb;
    text-align: center;
    padding: 0.75em 0.25em 0 0.25em;
}
```

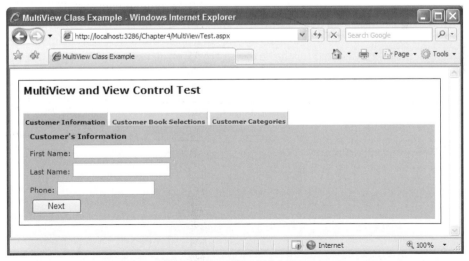

Figure 4.6   Tabbed MultiView

Now, you need to define the tab buttons and apply the styles, as in the following:

```
<asp:MultiView ID="aMultiView" runat="Server" >
  <asp:View ID="view1" runat="Server">
    <asp:Panel ID="panelNavView1" runat="server"
      CssClass="TabContainer">

      <asp:Label ID="labOne" runat="Server" Text="Tab 1"
        CssClass="TabItemActive" >
      </asp:Label>

      <asp:LinkButton ID="lnkb_DefaultBook" runat="Server"
        CssClass="TabItemInactive"
        Text="Tab 2"
        OnCommand="LinkButton_Command"
        CommandName="SecondTab" >
      </asp:LinkButton>

      <asp:LinkButton ID="lnkb_DefaultCategories" runat="server"
        CssClass="TabItemInactive"
        Text="Tab 3"
        OnCommand="LinkButton_Command"
        CommandName="ThirdTab">
      </asp:LinkButton>
    </asp:Panel>
    <!-- Rest of view content here -->
  </asp:View>
  <!--Additional views here -->
</asp:MultiView>
```

Notice that for the active view, this example used a `Label` rather than a `Link-Button` because we want the active view tab to display only, not act as a link. Finally, an event handler is needed for the `LinkButton` controls acting as the tabs. It simply navigates to the appropriate view, as in the following example:

```
protected void LinkButton_Command(object sender,
   CommandEventArgs e)
{
   // Determine which link button was clicked and set
   // the active view to the view selected by the user
   switch ((string)e.CommandName)
   {
      case "FirstTab":
         aMultiView.SetActiveView(view1);
         break;
      case "SecondTab":
         aMultiView.SetActiveView(view2);
         break;
      // Additional cases here
   }
}
```

Listings 4.3 and 4.4 contain the complete markup and code for the tabbed `MultiView` shown in Figure 4.6.

Listing 4.3 MultiViewTest.aspx

```
<h1>MultiView and View Control Test</h1>
<asp:MultiView ID="mviewMain" runat="Server" ActiveViewIndex="0">

    <asp:View ID="CustomerView" runat="Server">
        <asp:Panel ID="panelNavigatonView1" runat="server"
            CssClass="TabContainer">
            <asp:Label ID="labOne" runat="Server"
                CssClass="TabItemActive"
                Text="Customer Information" />
            <asp:LinkButton ID="lnkb_DefaultBook"
                CssClass="TabItemInactive"
                Text="Customer Book Selections" runat="Server"
                OnCommand="LinkButton_Command"
                CommandName="Book" />
            <asp:LinkButton ID="lnkb_DefaultCategories"
                CssClass="TabItemInactive"
                Text="Customer Categories" runat="server"
                OnCommand="LinkButton_Command"
                CommandName="Categories" />
        </asp:Panel>
        <asp:Panel ID="panelView1" runat="server"
            CssClass="ContentPanel">
            <h2>Customer's Information</h2>
            <p>First Name:
            <asp:TextBox ID="txtFirst" runat="server" /></p>
            <p>Last Name:
            <asp:TextBox ID="txtLast" runat="server" /></p>
            <p>Phone:
            <asp:TextBox ID="txtPhone" runat="server" /></p>
            <asp:Button id="view1Next" runat="Server" Width="6em"
                Text="Next" CommandName="NextView" />
        </asp:Panel>
    </asp:View>

    <asp:View ID="BookView" runat="Server">
        <asp:Panel ID="panelNavigatonView2" runat="server"
            CssClass="TabContainer">
            <asp:LinkButton ID="lnkb_BookCustomer" runat="Server"
                CssClass="TabItemInactive"
                Text="Customer Information"
                OnCommand="LinkButton_Command"
                CommandName="Customer" />
```

```
    <asp:Label ID="Label3" runat="Server"
        CssClass="TabItemActive"
        Text="Customer Book Selections" />
    <asp:LinkButton ID="lnkb_BookCategories" runat="server"
        CssClass="TabItemInactive" Text="Customer Categories"
        OnCommand="LinkButton_Command"
        CommandName="Categories" />
</asp:Panel>
<asp:Panel ID="panelView2" runat="server"
        CssClass="ContentPanel">
    <h2>Customer's Book Selections</h2>
    <p>
        <em>Core JavaServer Faces</em>
        <br />Cay Horstmann, David Geary
    </p>
    <p>
        <em>
        Patterns of Enterprise Application Architecture
        </em>
        <br />Martin Fowler
    </p>
    <asp:Button id="view2Back" runat= "Server"
      Text="Previous" CommandName="PrevView" Width="6em" />
    <asp:Button id="view2Next" runat="Server"
      Text="Next" CommandName="NextView" Width="6em" />
</asp:Panel>
</asp:View>

<asp:View ID="CategoriesView" runat="Server">
    <asp:Panel ID="panelNavigatonView3" runat="server"
        CssClass="TabContainer">
    <asp:LinkButton ID="lnkb_CategoriesCustomer"
        runat="Server"
        CssClass="TabItemInactive"
        Text="Customer Information"
        OnCommand="LinkButton_Command"
        CommandName="Customer" />
    <asp:LinkButton ID="lnkb_CategoriesBook" runat="Server"
        CssClass="TabItemInactive"
        Text="Customer Book Selections"
        OnCommand="LinkButton_Command"
        CommandName="Book" />
    <asp:Label ID="Label4" runat="Server"
        CssClass="TabItemActive"
        Text="Customer Categories" />
</asp:Panel>
<asp:Panel ID="panelView3" runat="server"
        CssClass="ContentPanel">
    <h2>Customer Categories</h2>
```

```
      <p>Programming</p>
      <p>Object Technologies</p>
  <asp:Button id="view3Prev" runat= "Server"
    Text="Previous" CommandName="PrevView" Width="6em" />
  <asp:Button id="view3First" runat= "Server"
    Text="Start"
    CommandName="SwitchViewByIndex"
    CommandArgument="0" Width="6em" />
  </asp:Panel>
  </asp:View>
</asp:MultiView>
```

Listing 4.4 MultiViewTest.aspx.cs

```csharp
public partial class MultiViewTest : System.Web.UI.Page
{
    protected void Page_Load(object sender, EventArgs e)
    {
        // The first time the page loads, render the DefaultView.
        if (!IsPostBack)
        {
            // Set CustomerView as the default view
            mviewMain.SetActiveView(CustomerView);
        }
    }
    protected void LinkButton_Command(object sender,
        CommandEventArgs e)
    {
        // Determine which link button was clicked and set the
        // active view to the view selected by the user
        switch ((string)e.CommandName)
        {
            case "Customer":
                mviewMain.SetActiveView(CustomerView);
                break;
            case "Book":
                mviewMain.SetActiveView(BookView);
                break;
            case "Categories":
                mviewMain.SetActiveView(CategoriesView);
                break;
        }
    }
}
```

Container Controls and Naming Containers

Unlike some of the other container controls covered in this book, the `Panel` and `MultiView` controls are not *naming containers*. This is an important concept in ASP.NET. Container controls generate a special ID-based namespace for their child controls; this control namespace is called a naming container. This naming container guarantees that the ID of each of its children is unique within the page. When child controls are created at runtime (for instance, with the Wizard control in this chapter or the data controls covered in Chapter 10) the naming container of the parent is combined with the child control's `Id` to create the control's `UniqueId` property.

The fact that the `MultiView` is not a naming container means that the `Id` of every control contained within all the `View` controls *must* be unique. That is, you cannot have a control named `btnNext` in `view1` and `view2`. This also means that controls in each view are always available for programmatic manipulation. However, the flipside to this functionality is that the view state for all controls in a `MultiView`, regardless of whether they are visible or not, is posted back and forth for every request that uses that `MultiView`.

Wizard Control

Web applications often require some type of wizard-style interface that leads the user through a series of step-by-step forms. A wizard is thus used to retrieve information from the user via a series of discrete steps; each step in the wizard asks the user to enter some subset of information. Some examples of Web-based wizards are the typical user registration procedure for a site or the checkout procedure in a Web store. For instance, the Amazon.com checkout procedure (see Figure 4.7) is not called a wizard but has the features of one: discrete steps separate from the rest of the application/site, an indication of the current step, and a way to move to the next step.

In regular Windows applications, wizards tend to be *modal* in that the user cannot do any other processing while the wizard is active: The user can only move forward, backward, finish, or possibly jump to some other step in the wizard. As well, Windows-based wizards are *pipelines* in that a wizard is a chain of processes in which there is only one entrance and where the output of each step in the process is the input to the next step.

Implementing wizards in Web applications poses several problems. A Windows application can strictly control how a wizard is launched, and can easily ensure users start and exit the wizard in the appropriate way. This is much harder to implement in a Web environment. For instance, a user could bookmark an intermediate step in the wizard and try to return to it at some point in the future; a Web-based wizard must thus be able to maintain the pipeline nature of the wizard and ensure that the user only ever starts the wizard at the first step.

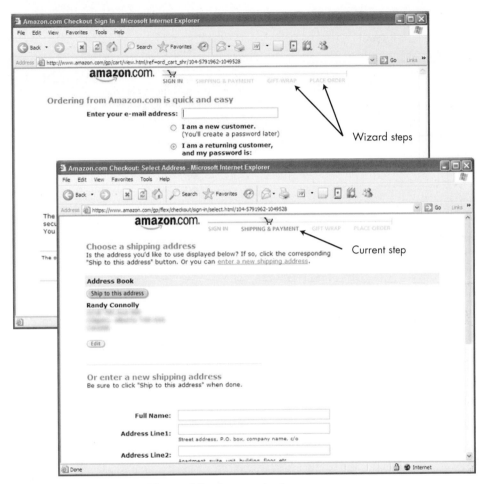

Figure 4.7 Amazon checkout process

Maintaining state information in a multipage Web wizard can also be tricky. Because the intent of a wizard is to gather information from the user in a series of discrete steps, a Web wizard needs to be able to pass information gathered in previous steps onto the next step. This requires repetitive coding for the retrieval and verification of the previous step's data. As well, there is typically a great deal of repetitive code for the handling of navigation within the wizard, as shown in Figure 4.8.

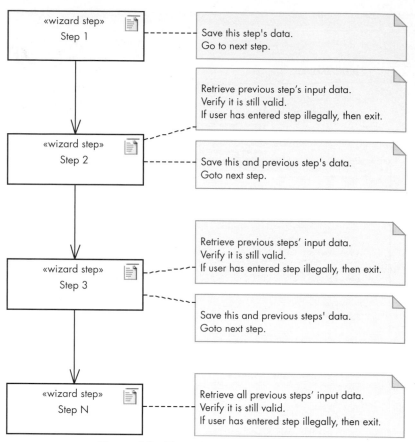

Figure 4.8   Typical Web wizard processing

In ASP.NET 1.1, wizards were implemented using either multiple pages with plenty of duplicate, boiler-plate code (as in Figure 4.8), or within a single page with numerous `Panel` controls, or by dynamically adding user controls to a single page based on the wizard step. The multiple panels within a single page approach eliminates the duplicated code problem of numerous pages; unfortunately, it comes at the cost of plenty of awkward code to toggle the visibility of the panels and buttons and to track the wizard state. I was involved with an ASP.NET 1.1 wizard project with nine discrete steps and more than 20 possible panels all contained within a single ASP.NET page; the conditional logic just for handling the panels and button controls was enough to make even the most hardened ASP spaghetti-code veteran wince in pain.

The new `Wizard` control in ASP.NET 2.0 makes the process of creating a Web wizard significantly easier. This control provides a simpler mechanism for building steps, adding new steps, or reordering the steps. The wizard's navigation can be either linear or nonlinear and can be implemented declaratively without coding. The `Wizard` control eliminates the need to manage the persistence of your data across pages because the control itself maintains state while the user completes the various steps. As well, the `Wizard` control is fully supported by the Visual Studio designer, thus significantly easing the process of creating and modifying your wizard's steps.

Table 4.6 lists some of the notable properties of the `Wizard` control. There are quite a few additional properties not listed in this table; you can view the MSDN documentation for a complete listing.

Table 4.6   Unique Properties of the Wizard Control

Property	Description
ActiveStep	Retrieves the `WizardStepBase` object that is currently displayed.
ActiveStepIndex	The index of the `WizardStepBase` object currently displayed. This property can be used to programmatically set the step to be displayed at runtime.
CancelButtonImageUrl	Specifies the URL of the image displayed for the Cancel button.
CancelButtonText	Specifies the text caption for the Cancel button.
CancelButtonType	Specifies the type of Cancel button. Possible values are defined by the `ButtonType` enumeration (`Button`, `Image`, `Link`).
CancelDestinationPageUrl	Specifies the URL to redirect to when the user clicks the Cancel button.
DisplayCancelButton	Specifies whether the wizard should display the Cancel button (default is `false`).
DisplaySideBar	Specifies whether the sidebar area of the wizard should be displayed. The default is `true`.
FinishCompleteButtonImageUrl	Specifies the URL of the image displayed for the Complete button for the Finish step.
FinishCompleteButtonText	Specifies the text caption for the Complete button of the Finish step.

Table 4.6   Unique Properties of the Wizard Control *(continued)*

Property	Description
FinishCompleteButtonType	Specifies the type of the Complete button of the Finish step. Possible values are defined by the `ButtonType` enumeration (`Button`, `Image`, `Link`).
FinishDestinationPageUrl	Specifies the URL to redirect to when the user clicks the Finish button.
FinishPreviousButtonImageUrl	Specifies the URL of the image displayed for the Previous button of the Finish step.
FinishPreviousButtonText	Specifies the text caption for the Previous button of the Finish step.
FinishPreviousButtonType	Specifies the type of the Previous button of the Finish step. Possible values are defined by the `ButtonType` enumeration (`Button`, `Image`, `Link`).
HeaderStyle	Retrieves the collection of style properties for the Header area of the wizard.
HeaderText	The text caption to display in the header area of the wizard.
SkipLinkText	Specifies the alternate text for a hidden image that allows screen readers to skip the content in the sidebar area. Used for accessibility.
StartNextButtonImageUrl	Specifies the URL of the image displayed for the Next button on the Start step.
StartNextButtonText	Specifies the text caption for the Next button of the Start step.
StartNextButtonType	Specifies the type of the Next button of the Start step. Possible values are defined by the `Button-Type` enumeration (`Button`, `Image`, `Link`).
StepNextButtonImageUrl	Specifies the URL of the image displayed for the Next button.
StepNextButtonText	Specifies the text caption for the Next button.

Table 4.6 Unique Properties of the Wizard Control *(continued)*

Property	Description
StepNextButtonType	Specifies the type of the Next button. Possible values are defined by the ButtonType enumeration (Button, Image, Link).
StepPreviousButtonImageUrl	Specifies the URL of the image displayed for the Previous button.
StepPreviousButtonText	Specifies the text caption for the Previous button.
StepPreviousButtonType	Specifies the type of the Previous button. Possible values are defined by the ButtonType enumeration (Button, Image, Link).

Using the Wizard Control

The Wizard control is composed of a number of separate WizardStep controls. Each WizardStep control represents a single step in the wizard process. The WizardStep control inherits from an abstract class called BaseWizardStep, which in turn inherits from the View control covered in the previous section (see Figure 4.9).

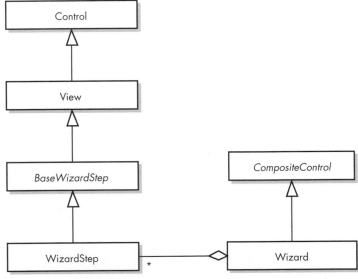

Figure 4.9 Object model for Wizard control

Like the View control, the WizardStep control is a container for HTML markup and other ASP.NET controls. The parent Wizard control manages which Wizard-Step to display and helps maintain the data collected in each step. The following example shows the markup for a simple two-step wizard with some sample content in each of the two steps.

```
<asp:Wizard ID="myWizard" Runat="server"
    HeaderText="Sample Wizard">

  <WizardSteps>

      <asp:WizardStep ID="WizardStep1" runat="server"
          Title="Step 1">
        <b>Step One</b><br />
        <asp:Label ID="label1" runat="server">Email</asp:Label>
        <asp:TextBox ID=" txtEmail " runat="server" /><br />
        <asp:Label ID="label2" runat="server">
          Password
        </asp:Label>
        <asp:TextBox ID="txtPassword" runat="server" />
      </asp:WizardStep>

      <asp:WizardStep ID="WizardStep2" runat="server"
          Title="Step 2">
        <b>Step Two</b><br />
        <asp:Label ID="label3" runat="server">
          Shipping
        </asp:Label>
        <asp:DropDownList ID="drpShipping" runat="server">
          <asp:ListItem>Air Mail</asp:ListItem>
          <asp:ListItem>Fed Ex</asp:ListItem>
        </asp:DropDownList>
      </asp:WizardStep>

  </WizardSteps>

</asp:Wizard>
```

Figure 4.10 illustrates how this example wizard appears in the browser.

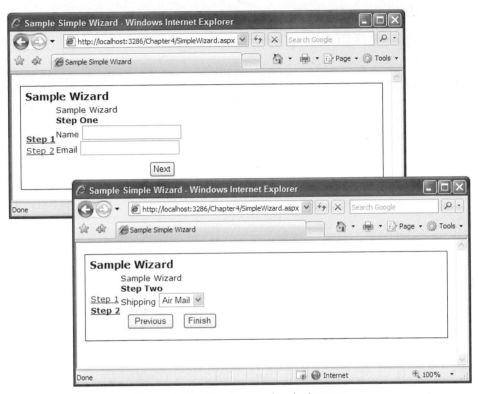

Figure 4.10   Simple wizard in the browser

Table 4.7 lists the notable properties of the WizardStep control.

Table 4.7   Notable Properties of the WizardStep Control

Property	Description
AllowReturn	Indicates whether the user is allowed to return to this step from another subsequent step.
Name	The name of the step.
StepType	The type of navigation interface to display for the step. Possible values are described by the WizardStepType enumeration (Auto, Complete, Finish, Start, Step).
Title	The title of the step.

Understanding the Layout of the Wizard Control

Like the `Calendar` control covered in the previous chapter, the `Wizard` control can be fully customized in terms of its appearance and behavior via properties, style elements, and template elements. ***Style elements*** are used to specify the font, border, color, size, or CSS class of the wizard part referenced by the style element. ***Template elements*** are used to define a custom layout for a given element. Table 4.8 lists the available style and templates for the `Wizard` control.

Table 4.8 Style and Template Elements for the Wizard Control

Name	Description
FinishNavigationTemplate	The layout template for the navigation area for the Finish step.
HeaderStyle	The style properties for the Header area of the wizard.
HeaderTemplate	The template used to define the custom content that is displayed in the header area of the wizard.
NavigationButtonStyle	The style properties for the buttons used in the navigation area of the wizard.
NavigationStyle	The style properties for the navigation area of the wizard.
SideBarButtonStyle	The style properties for the sidebar area buttons.
SideBarStyle	The style properties for the sidebar area of the wizard.
SideBarTemplate	The template used to define the custom content that is displayed in the sidebar area of the wizard.
StartNavigationTemplate	The template used to define the custom content that is displayed in the navigation area of the wizard for the Start step.
StepNavigationTemplate	The template used to define the custom content that is displayed in the navigation area of the wizard.
StepStyle	The style properties for the wizard step area.

To help clarify the relationship between the different style and template elements and the actual `Wizard` control layout areas, Figure 4.11 illustrates these layout areas.

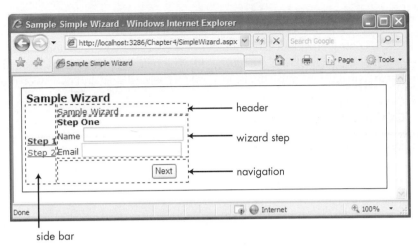

Figure 4.11   Wizard layout areas

The header area in Figure 4.11 is set via the `HeaderText` property of the `Wizard` control. The sidebar area contains a series of links for navigating to each wizard step. This area is optional and can be hidden via the `DisplaySideBar` property of the `Wizard` control. The sidebar can be styled via `SideBarTemplate`, `SideBarStyle`, and `SideBarButtonStyle` (covered shortly). The navigation area contains navigation buttons (the user interface for these buttons can also be an image or a hyperlink) for moving to the next or to the previous step. You have complete control over the appearance of both the next and previous step buttons. You can also add navigation elements for finishing the wizard or canceling the wizard (covered shortly). The `Wizard` control also allows you to customize the appearance of the navigation area for both the first and the final `WizardStep`.

Finally, the wizard step area in Figure 4.11 contains the active `WizardStep` control. A `WizardStep` control can be one of five different types (set via the `StepType` property): `Auto`, `Start`, `Step`, `Finish`, and `Complete`. The default `StepType` is `Auto`, which means the navigation interface for the step is determined by the order in which the step is declared. In a wizard with three steps, the first step is a `Start` step, the second step is a `Step` step, and the third is a `Finish` step. `Start` and `Finish` steps display a different set of navigation buttons than the `Step` step: `Start` does not display a previous button, whereas `Finish` does not display a next button. The `Complete` step is a special type of optional step. It is always displayed last, it collects no data, and contains no navigation. It is useful if you want your wizard to display some type of explicit indication that the wizard is completed.

Customizing the Wizard

The `Wizard` control provides a large number of avenues for customization. You can customize each of the areas shown in Figure 4.11. The following sections discuss and illustrate how to style and customize the header, sidebar, wizard step, and navigation areas.

CORE NOTE

Although the next sections describe how to use the various style and template elements of the `Wizard` control, you may find it easier to use the Visual Studio designer to customize these elements, as shown in Figure 4.12.

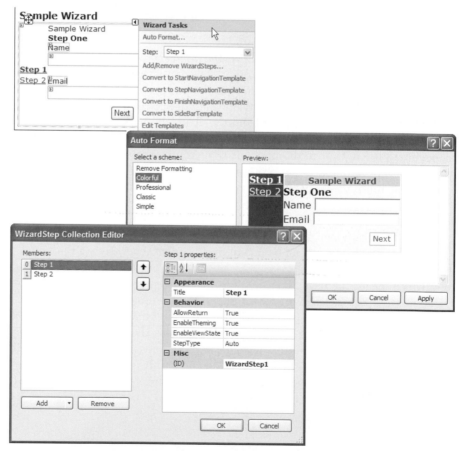

Figure 4.12   Customizing the Wizard with the Visual Studio designer

Styling the Header Area

The wizard header can be customized via the templates HeaderStyle and the HeaderTemplate. The HeaderStyle template allows you to specify the font, color, border, and CSS class to be used for displaying the text in the HeaderText property. Like all template properties, you can set their values within its template tag, or within the parent control via hyphen notation. For instance:

```
<asp:Wizard ID="myWizard" runat="server" HeaderText="Checkout">
   <HeaderStyle BackColor="#CC9966" Font-Bold="true"
      Font-Size="Large"/>
</asp:Wizard>
```

or

```
<asp:Wizard ID="myWizard" runat="server" HeaderText="Checkout"
  HeaderStyle-BackColor="#CC9966" HeaderStyle-Font-Bold="true"
  HeaderStyle-Font-Size="Large">
</asp:Wizard>
```

As mentioned in the previous chapter, you may want to only specify a CSS class within a template rather than specifying appearance properties. Chapter 6 discusses the pros and cons of using CSS versus using appearance properties.

Customizing the Header Area

The HeaderTemplate lets you fully customize not only the formatting but also the content of the header. For instance, the following example (the result can be seen in Figure 4.13) shows how to use information from the Wizard control and the current WizardStep control to display a more useful wizard header. Notice that it uses inline expressions (covered back on page 40 of Chapter 1) to display the current value of various Wizard properties in the page.

```
<asp:Wizard ID="myWizard" runat="server"
      HeaderText="Checkout" ... >

  <HeaderTemplate>
    <div style="margin: 5px 5px 5px 5px">
      <i><%= myWizard.HeaderText %>
      Step <%= myWizard.ActiveStepIndex+1 %> of 2</i><br />
      <b><%= myWizard.ActiveStep.Title%></b>
    </div>
  </HeaderTemplate>

  <WizardSteps>
    <asp:WizardStep ID="WizardStep1" runat="server"
      Title="Login">
    ...
```

```
    <asp:WizardStep ID="WizardStep2" runat="server"
      Title="Address">
    …
  </WizardSteps>
</asp:Wizard>
```

You could also use the `HeaderTemplate` to display an image. The following example demonstrates how this might work. The filename for the image to be displayed in the header is constructed based on the current step index. Notice that it also supplies an `alt` attribute based on the title. The result in the browser can be seen in Figure 4.13, which shows both the text and image header approaches.

```
<HeaderTemplate>
  <div style="margin: 5px 5px 5px 5px">
    <img src=
      'images/title_checkout_step
        <%= myWizard.ActiveStepIndex+1 %>.gif'
        alt='Checkout <%= myWizard.ActiveStep.Title%>' />
  </div>
</HeaderTemplate>
```

Figure 4.13   Using a header template

CORE NOTE

For usability reasons, you should ensure that the total height of the wizard remains constant for each step (thus emulating the behavior of a Windows wizard). Nothing is more annoying than having the navigation button's position jump up and down on the screen as you move through the steps of the wizard!

Styling the Sidebar Area

As mentioned earlier, the sidebar area contains a series of links for navigating to each wizard step. This area is optional and can be hidden by setting the `DisplaySideBar` property of the `Wizard` control to `false`. If you want to ensure that the user only moves linearly through the wizard, it might be best to hide the sidebar area or to disable the links within it.

The sidebar can be styled via the `SideBarStyle` and `SideBarButtonStyle`. The `SideBarStyle` template allows you to specify the font, color, border, and CSS class to be used for displaying the content in the sidebar. The `SideBarButtonStyle` template allows you to specify the font, color, border, and CSS class to be used for displaying the links within the sidebar. The following example illustrates a sample `SideBarStyle` template.

```
<SideBarStyle CssClass="sidebar" />
```

Customizing the Sidebar Area

Just as with the header, you can customize (albeit only partially) the sidebar by using the `SideBarTemplate`. With the `SideBarTemplate`, you *must* use a `DataList` control (covered in detail in Chapter 10, page 587) to contain the links. You can replace the links with any other control that implements the `IButtonControl` interface, such as `ImageButton`, `LinkButton`, or `Button`. For instance, the following sample illustrates how to display buttons rather than links in the sidebar.

```
<SideBarTemplate>
  <asp:DataList ID="SideBarList" runat="server">

    <ItemTemplate>
      <asp:Button ID="SideBarButton" runat="server"
        BackColor="#CCCC99" />
    </ItemTemplate>

    <SelectedItemTemplate>
      <asp:Button ID="SideBarButton" runat="server"
        BackColor="#CCCCCC" />
    </SelectedItemTemplate>
```

```
</asp:DataList>
</SideBarTemplate>
```

Notice how this example uses the `SelectedItemTemplate` of the `DataList` to format the button that corresponds to the currently active step in the wizard differently than the other step buttons.

CORE NOTE

The `DataList` used in the `SideBarTemplate` must follow a few rules. It *must* have its `ID` property set to `SideBarList`. Within the `ItemTemplate`, `SelectedItemTemplate`, or `AlternatingItemTemplate`, it *must* contain a control that implements the `IButtonControl`. Also, this `IButtonControl` control *must* have its `ID` property set to `SideBarButton`.

You can also display images in the sidebar by using the `ImageButton` control. However, to get a unique image for each wizard step, you need to add some programming logic. As well, you need some way to associate the image filenames with the wizard steps. Perhaps the easiest way to do this is to include the wizard step title in the image filename. For instance, let's define a wizard step as follows:

```
<asp:WizardStep ID="WizardStep1" runat="server" Title="Login">
```

In this case, you need to have an image with the title `Login` in the filename, such as `Login.gif`, `step_Login.gif`, or `checkoutStepLoginSelected.gif`. If you have your images thus named, you only need to define a method that constructs the image filename. The following example shows two such methods. The first returns the image filename for the image that to be displayed in the `ItemTemplate`; the second returns the filename for the image to be displayed in the `SelectedItemTemplate`.

```
public object GetStepImage(string title)
{
  return "images/sidebar_" + title + ".gif";
}
public object GetSelectedStepImage(string title)
{
  return "images/sidebar_" + title + "_selected.gif";
}
```

These methods are called when you set the `ImageUrl` property of the `Image-Button` control in the `SideBarTemplate`. For instance, the following illustrates the use of these methods within something called data-binding expressions, which are covered in detail in Chapter 8.

```
<SideBarTemplate>
  <asp:DataList ID="SideBarList" runat="server">
    <ItemTemplate>
      <asp:ImageButton ID="SideBarButton" runat="server"
        ImageUrl='<%# GetStepImage( (string)Eval("Title") )%>'/>
    </ItemTemplate>
    <SelectedItemTemplate>
      <asp:ImageButton ID="SideBarButton" runat="server"
        ImageUrl='<%# GetSelectedStepImage(
          (string)Eval("Title") )%>'/>
    </SelectedItemTemplate>
  </asp:DataList>
</SideBarTemplate>
```

The `DataList` in the sidebar is bound to a collection of `WizardStepBase` objects. Thus, this example passes the contents of the `Title` property (which is defined as an `object` and hence must be cast to a `string`) of the current `WizardStepBase` object in the collection. The result in the browser might look like that shown in Figure 4.14.

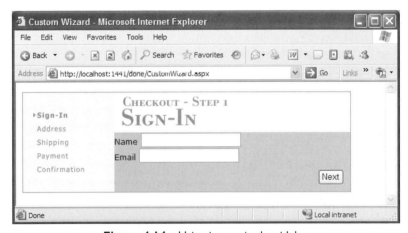

Figure 4.14   Using images in the sidebar

Styling the Wizard Step Area

The content of each wizard step is defined within each step's `WizardStep` element. However, you can specify a consistent style for each step in the wizard by using the `StepStyle` template. Like the other style templates, it allows you to specify the font, color, border, and CSS class to be used for the content of each step. For instance, if you want to provide some padding (i.e., space between the contents of the wizard step and its boundaries) to each wizard step, you could define a CSS style such as

```
<style type="text/css">
   .wizardStepContent { padding: 5px; … }
</style>
```

You could then use that CSS class via the `StepStyle` template.

```
<StepStyle CssClass="wizardStepContent" … />
```

Customizing the Wizard Step Area

Earlier, you saw how the wizard contains a collection of `WizardStep` elements. If you want to have full control over the look and behavior of a wizard step (including the ability to have a completely different navigation system), you could use a `TemplatedWizardStep` instead of a `WizardStep`, as in

```
<asp:Wizard ID="myWizard" Runat="server"
      HeaderText="Sample Wizard">
  <WizardSteps>

      <asp:WizardStep ID="ws1" runat="server" Title="Step 1">
      </asp:WizardStep>
      …
      <asp:TemplatedWizardStep ID="tws1" runat="server"
          Title="Step 2">
        <ContentTemplate>
            …
        </ContentTemplate>
        <CustomNavigationTemplate>
            …
        </CustomNavigationTemplate>
      </asp: TemplatedWizardStep>

  </WizardSteps>
<asp:Wizard>
```

Styling the Navigation Area

Like the other areas of the wizard, the navigation area of the wizard can be fully styled. There are a number of different navigation style tags. With these tags, you can

- Style the entire navigation area (`NavigationStyle`)
- Style all possible buttons (`NavigationButtonStyle`)
- Style the Cancel button for the wizard (`CancelButtonStyle`)
- Style the Next button for the starting wizard step (`StartNextButtonStyle`)
- Style the Complete button for the finished wizard step (`FinishComplete-ButtonStyle`)
- Style the Previous button for the finished wizard step (`FinishPrevious-ButtonStyle`)

- Style the Next button for the regular wizard steps (`StepNextButtonStyle`)
- Style the Previous button for the regular wizard steps (`StepPrevious-ButtonStyle`)

Of course, for most situations, you would probably want to have the same style for all the buttons in the wizard regardless of whether they are Next or Previous buttons. Thus, for most situations, you could just use the `NavigationStyle` and `NavigationButtonStyle` to consistently style your buttons, as in the following:

```
<NavigationStyle BackColor="white" VerticalAlign="Bottom"/>
<NavigationButtonStyle BackColor="#FFFFCC" ForeColor="#666633" />
```

Customizing the Navigation Area

You can also fully customize how the navigation area appears with template tags. There is a navigation template for the `Start`, `Finish`, and regular `Step` step types (`StartNavigationTemplate`, `FinishNavigationTemplate`, and `StepNavigationTemplate`). With these templates, you can completely control what is displayed within the navigation area. For instance, if you decide that you do not want the standard Next and Previous buttons, but would prefer to use `LinkButton` or `ImageButton` controls, you can do so via these templates.

There are some requirements that must be followed with these navigation templates. The `StepNavigationTemplate` *must* contain two `IButtonControl` controls (i.e., `LinkButton`, `ImageButton`, or `Button`). One of these `IButtonControl` controls *must* have its `CommandName` property set to `MoveNext` and the other *must* have its `CommandName` property set to `MovePrevious` to have the wizard navigation work. The `StartNavigationTemplate` *must* have a single `IButtonControl` control with a `CommandName` of `MoveNext`. The `FinishNavigationTemplate` *must* have two `IButtonControl` controls with their `CommandName` properties set to `MovePrevious` and `MoveComplete`.

The following example illustrates the use of the three custom navigation templates. It illustrates how to use images rather than buttons in the navigation area for all three steps. The result can be seen in Figure 4.15.

```
<NavigationStyle BackColor="white" VerticalAlign="Bottom" />
<NavigationButtonStyle BackColor="#FFFFCC" ForeColor="#666633" />

<StartNavigationTemplate>
   <asp:Panel ID="panStart" runat="server"
        CssClass="wizardNavContent">
     <asp:ImageButton runat="server" ID="imgStart"
        ImageUrl="~/images/button_checkout_start.gif"
        CommandName="MoveNext" AlternateText="Sign-In" />
   </asp:Panel>
</StartNavigationTemplate>
```

```
<StepNavigationTemplate>
   <asp:Panel ID="panStep" runat="server"
         CssClass="wizardNavContent">
      <asp:ImageButton runat="server" ID="imgPrev"
         ImageUrl="~/images/button_checkout_previous.gif"
         CommandName="MovePrevious" AlternateText="Previous" />
      <asp:ImageButton runat="server" ID="imgNext"
         ImageUrl="~/images/button_checkout_next.gif"
         CommandName="MoveNext" AlternateText="Next" />
   </asp:Panel>
</StepNavigationTemplate>

<FinishNavigationTemplate>
   <asp:Panel ID="panFinish" runat="server"
         CssClass="wizardNavContent">
      <asp:ImageButton runat="server" ID="imgPrevFin"
         ImageUrl="~/images/button_checkout_previous.gif"
         CommandName="MovePrevious" AlternateText="Previous" />
      <asp:ImageButton runat="server" ID="imgFinish"
         ImageUrl="~/images/button_checkout_finish.gif"
         CommandName="MoveComplete"
         AlternateText="Make Payment" />
   </asp:Panel>
</FinishNavigationTemplate>
```

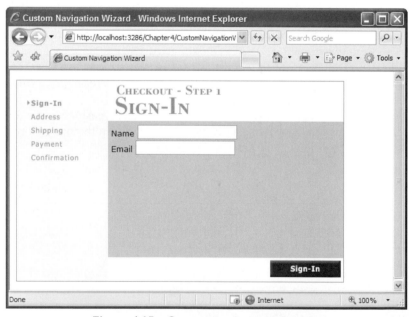

Figure 4.15 Customizing the navigation area

Wizard Event Handling

One of the great things about the `Wizard` control is that it dramatically reduces the amount of coding necessary to implement a step-by-step series. You no longer have to worry, for instance, about coding the navigation logic or the maintenance of the state between steps. Yet, even with the `Wizard` control, some coding is required. After the Finish step, you need to code the processing and (probably) the persistence of the data gathered in the wizard steps. Alternately, you may want to persist the data gathered at each step, and thus need to write code that executes before the wizard moves to the next step. Another reason you may need to write code for the wizard is to override the default linear progression through the wizard steps.

The `Wizard` control supports several unique events (see Table 4.9). Five of the events are associated with click events on the navigation controls. The other event (`ActiveStepChanged`) is triggered when the active view (i.e., the current step) changes. Note that the click events for the navigation buttons are handled *before* the `ActiveStepChanged` handler. This allows you to potentially prevent the view from changing (and thus prevent the `ActiveStepChanged` handler from being called). Thus, you can perform some type of server-side validation on the data gathered in a given wizard step and cancel the step change if the data is not valid.

Table 4.9 Events of the Wizard Control

Event	Description
ActiveStepChanged	Raised on a postback when the user switches to a new step.
CancelButtonClick	Raised on a postback when the user clicks the Cancel button.
FinishButtonClick	Raised on a postback when the user clicks the Finish button.
NextButtonClick	Raised on a postback when the user clicks the Next button.
PreviousButtonClick	Raised on a postback when the user clicks the Previous button.
SideBarButtonClick	Raised on a postback when the user clicks one of the sidebar buttons.

NextButtonClick Event Handler

Because the same navigation click handler is used regardless of the step, the handler typically needs some type of conditional logic using the `ActiveStepIndex` of the wizard. For instance, the following `NextButtonClick` event handler illustrates how you might perform different validation for the different wizard steps.

```
protected void myWizard_NextButtonClick(object sender,
      WizardNavigationEventArgs e)
{
  if (myWizard.ActiveStep == WizardStep1)
  {
     string email = txtEmail.Text;
     string passwd = txtPassword.Text;

     // Check database to see if this user exists
     bool okay = UserBusObject.CheckIfOkay(email, passwd);
     if ( ! okay )
     {
        myLabel.Text += "User does not exist<br/>";
        // Cancel the move to the next wizard step
        e.Cancel = true;
     }
  }
  else if (myWizard.ActiveStep == WizardStep2)
  {
     // Validation for step 2 goes here
  }
  // etc
}
```

This example uses some type of business object, which presumably does some type of database lookup on the email and password values entered by the user. If the email and password do not exist, the move to the next wizard step is cancelled (by setting the `Cancel` property of the passed-in `WizardNavigationEventArgs` object). Notice as well how the `ActiveStep` property of the wizard is compared to the various wizard step objects. An alternative way of doing this comparison is on the step index rather than the step objects themselves, as in

```
myWizard.ActiveStepIndex ==
   myWizard.WizardSteps.IndexOf(WizardStep1)
```

ActiveStepChanged Event Handler

The `ActiveStepChanged` handler is typically used to modify the step order. For instance, in the following example, the `ActiveStepChanged` handler checks if the add address wizard step (which is step 2) is unnecessary; if it is unnecessary, it skips the step and moves to the third step in the wizard.

```
protected void myWizard_ActiveStepChanged(object sender,
   EventArgs e)
{
   // If we are on the first step, then …
   if (myWizard.ActiveStep == WizardStep1)
   {
```

```
    // … check the database to see if we need to
    // enter an address
    if ( UserBusObject.NeedAddress(
        txtEmail.Text,txtPassword.Text) )
    {
        myWizard.MoveTo(WizardStep2);
    }
    else
    {
        myWizard.MoveTo(WizardStep3);
    }
  }
}
```

FinishButtonClick Event Handler

The handler for the Finish button is where you perform the final processing on the data gathered in the wizard. As well, if your wizard has a Complete step, you can then populate its content in this handler. The following example illustrates a sample FinishButtonClick event handler.

```
protected void myWizard_FinishButtonClick(object sender,
     WizardNavigationEventArgs e)
{
    // Gather the data from the various steps
    string email = txtEmail.Text;
    …
    // Gather the data from the various steps
    …
    // Now fill the content of the confirmation wizard step
    myLabel.Text += "FinishButtonClick called<br/>";
    Label labConfirm =
        (Label)myWizard.FindControl("labConfirmation");
    labConfirm.Text = "Order has been processed for " +
        txtEmail.Text;
}
```

Notice that in this example the FindControl method of the Wizard control is used to reference a control within the confirmation wizard step. This is necessary because the confirmation page has not yet been displayed; as a result, you cannot simply directly reference the control like you did with controls on the current or previously visited steps.

FileUpload Control

The FileUpload control provides a mechanism for users to send a file from their computer to the server. The control is rendered in the browser as a TextBox control and a Button control. The user can specify the file to upload by entering the full path to the file on the local computer in the text box of the control, or the user can browse for the file by clicking the button and then locating it in the Choose File dialog box (see Figure 4.16).

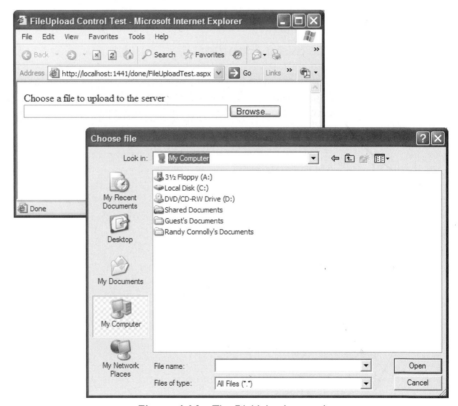

Figure 4.16   The FileUpload control

Table 4.10 lists the unique properties of the FileUpload control.

Table 4.10   Unique Properties of the FileUpload Control

Property	Description
FileBytes	Returns an array of bytes containing the content in the file specified by the user.
FileContent	Returns a `Stream` object containing the content in the file specified by the user.
FileName	The name of the file on the client to upload.
HasFile	Specifies whether the `FileUpload` control contains a file that exists.
PostedFile	Returns the underlying `HttpPostedFile` object for the uploaded file.

The `FileUpload` control does not automatically save a file to the server after the user selects the file to upload. You must explicitly provide a control or mechanism to allow the user to submit the specified file. Perhaps the most common way to do this is by adding some type of upload button to your form, as shown in the following.

```
Choose a file to upload to the server<br />
<asp:FileUpload ID="fupTest" runat="server" Width="400px"/>
<br />
<asp:Button ID="btnUpload" runat="server" Text="Upload File"
   OnClick="btnUpload_Click" />
<br/>
<asp:Label ID="labMessage" runat="server"></asp:Label>
```

The event handler for the upload button must call the `SaveAs` method of the `FileUpload` control to perform the actual upload to the server. The `SaveAs` method requires a full path to the directory on the server in which the file will be saved. Before calling the `SaveAs` method, you should use the `HasFile` property to verify that the control in fact contains a file to upload. The following example illustrates a fairly straightforward event handler for the upload button.

```
protected void btnUpload_Click(object sender, EventArgs e)
{
    if (fupTest.HasFile)
    {
        string path = @"C:\temp\";
        string fullname = path + fupTest.FileName;
        fupTest.SaveAs(fullname);
        labMessage.Text = "File successfully uploaded";
    }
    else
    {
```

```
      labMessage.Text = "File was not specified";
   }
}
```

CORE NOTE

The ASP.NET application must have write access to the directory on the server for the call to `SaveAs` to work.

You could make your file uploading method a little more robust. For instance, you might want to only upload a file if it doesn't already exist. To do so, you need to check for the file and only upload if it doesn't exist. To do so, you can change your event handler as follows:

```
protected void btnUpload_Click(object sender, EventArgs e)
{
    if (fupTest.HasFile)
    {
        string path = @"C:\temp\";
        string fullname = path + fupTest.FileName;
        if ( System.IO.File.Exists(fullname) )
        {
            labMessage.Text =
                "File already exists - uploaded cancelled";
        }
        else
        {
            fupTest.SaveAs(fullname);
            labMessage.Text = "File successfully uploaded";
        }
    }
    else
    {
        labMessage.Text = "File was not specified";
    }
}
```

The `FileUpload` control provides the `PostedFile` property that can be used to provide additional information about the uploaded file. For instance, the following example displays the length and MIME content type of the uploaded file.

```
protected void btnUpload_Click(object sender, EventArgs e)
{
    if (fupTest.HasFile)
    {
        string path = @"C:\temp\";
```

```
    string fullname = path + fupTest.FileName;
    if ( System.IO.File.Exists(fullname) )
    {
       labMessage.Text =
           "File already exists - uploaded cancelled";
    }
    else
    {
       fupTest.SaveAs(fullname);
       labMessage.Text = "File successfully uploaded";

       int contentLength = fupTest.PostedFile.ContentLength;
       string contentType = fupTest.PostedFile.ContentType;
       labMessage.Text += "<br/>";
       labMessage.Text += "Content Type = " + contentType;
       labMessage.Text += "<br/>";
       labMessage.Text += " Content Length = " + contentLength;
    }
  }
  else
  {
    labMessage.Text = "File was not specified";
  }
}
```

Processing the Uploaded File

In some situations, you may want to immediately process the uploaded file. You can do this in a number of different ways. One approach provided by the `FileUpload` control itself is to use either its `FileContent` or `FileBytes` properties. The `File-Content` property provides an input stream that you can programmatically read and manipulate; the `FileBytes` property returns an array of bytes that you can also programmatically read and manipulate.

Using the `FileBytes` property is quite straightforward. You simply need to instantiate a byte array that is the same size as the content length of the uploaded file, and then set it to the `FileBytes` property of the control, as shown in following example.

```
fupTest.SaveAs(fullname);
int contentLength = fupTest.PostedFile.ContentLength;

// Create a byte array to hold the contents of the file.
byte[] input = new byte[contentLength];
input = fupTest.FileBytes;
```

The `FileContent` property returns a `Stream` object, which is an abstracted view into a sequence of bytes. The `Stream` class provides methods for reading a single byte or multiple bytes into an array. The one advantage that the `FileContent` property provides is the capability to sequentially read and process the file; the `FileBytes` property in contrast requires you to read the entire file into memory (into a byte array) before you can process it. The following example illustrates how the `FileContent` stream might be processed.

```
System.IO.Stream myStream = fupTest.FileContent;
int index = 0;
while (index < myStream.Length)
{
    byte aByte = (byte)myStream.ReadByte();
    // Process this byte
    …
    index++;
}
```

Limiting the Size of the Uploaded File

You may want to limit the size of the file that is uploaded to the server, either to preserve disk space or to decrease the risk of denial of service attacks. You can do this by limiting the request length in the application's `Web.config` file. This request length limitation can be made by adding the `maxRequestLength` attribute to the `httpRuntime` element, as shown here.

```
<system.web>
  …
  <httpRuntime maxRequestLength="4096" />
<system.web>
```

This example sets the maximum file upload size to be 4096KB (4MB), which in fact is the default value for the `maxRequestLength` attribute. If you need to allow the user to upload significantly large files, you should also increase the `executionTimeout` attribute of `httpRuntime` as well, as in

```
<httpRuntime maxRequestLength="40000" executionTimeout="2400"/>
```

The `executionTimeout` attribute specifies the number of seconds that a request is allowed to execute before being automatically shut down by the ASP.NET runtime.

CORE NOTE

An upload that exceeds the `MaxRequestedLength` results in an error that cannot be trapped. If the user attempts to upload a file that is too large, the only thing the user sees in her browser is the rather unhelpful and misleading `The page cannot be displayed` message.

PlaceHolder Control

The `Placeholder` Web server control enables you to dynamically add server controls to a page at runtime. The `Placeholder` is an empty container control with no HTML rendering on its own; instead, the control renders any child elements it contains. There are many situations in which it might make sense to add a control dynamically at runtime rather than statically at design time. For instance, a portal application may consist of only a few pages, each containing `Placeholder` controls that are loaded with the appropriate server and user controls at runtime according to some algorithm or some content in a database.

The `PlaceHolder` control has no unique properties; as such, you simply declare the control.

```
<asp:PlaceHolder ID="myPlaceHolder" runat="server" />
```

To add a control to the `Placeholder`, you instantiate the control you want to add, set up its properties, and then add it to the `Placeholder` by calling its `Controls.Add()` method, as shown here.

```
Image img = new Image();
img.ImageUrl = "images/afile.gif";

myPlaceHolder.Controls.Add(img);
```

CORE NOTE

Dynamically added controls need to be added on each request. As a result, it generally makes sense to do so either within, or in some method invoked by, the `Page_Load` method.

You can add HTML content to a `Placeholder` by creating a `LiteralControl` and adding it to the `PlaceHolder`, as in the following:

```
LiteralControl br = new LiteralControl("<br/>");
myPlaceHolder.Controls.Add(br);
```

It should be noted here that controls can be added to *any* container control using the same approach: namely, adding the instantiated control to the `Controls` collection of the container control using its `Controls.Add` method. The `Page` class (and thus any of your Web Forms) is also a container, and can have controls added to it in the same manner.

Creating a File Browser

In the remainder of this section, we use the `PlaceHolder` control (and the `FileUp-load` control) to create a Web Form that allows a user to view and upload files to the server. The markup is simplicity in itself (see Listing 4.5). It contains a `PlaceHolder` control and a `FileUpload` control, both within `Panel` controls. Also, it contains some additional controls for creating a folder. The result in the browser can be seen in Figure 4.17.

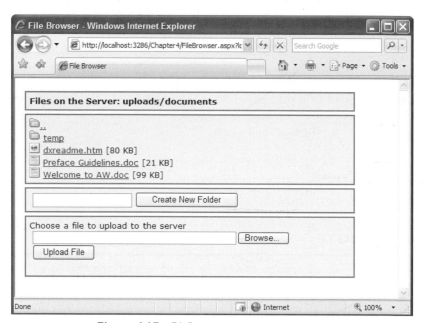

Figure 4.17   FileBrowser.aspx in the browser

Listing 4.5   FileBrowser.aspx

```
<h1 class="boxes">
Files on the Server:
<asp:Literal id="litLocation" runat="server" />
</h1>

<asp:Panel ID="panFiles" runat="server" CssClass="boxes">
    <asp:PlaceHolder ID="myPlaceHolder" runat="server"/>
</asp:Panel>

<asp:Panel ID="Panel1" runat="server" CssClass="boxes" >
    <asp:TextBox ID="txtFolder" runat="server" ></asp:TextBox>
```

```
<asp:Button ID="btnNewFolder" runat="server"
    Text="Create New Folder" OnClick="btnNewFolder_Click"/>
</asp:Panel>

<asp:Panel ID="panUpload" runat="server" CssClass="boxes" >
    Choose a file to upload to the server<br />
    <asp:FileUpload ID="fupTest" runat="server" Width="400px"/>
    <br />
    <asp:Button ID="btnUpload" runat="server" Text="Upload File"
        OnClick="btnUpload_Click" />
    <p>
        <asp:Label ID="labMessage" runat="server"></asp:Label>
    </p>
</asp:Panel>
```

This file browser needs some way to retrieve a list of files in the uploads subfolder of the Web application. Our solution uses the DirectoryInfo class to retrieve a list of files, and then adds them to the PlaceHolder control. The DirectoryInfo class requires the absolute path (e.g., c:\inetpub\wwwroot\myapp\uploads) of the folder that contains the files. Because the absolute path can change as you move from your development machine to the deployment server, you do not want to hard code the path; instead, you use the Server.MapPath method to convert your virtual path into a fully qualified physical path on the server. With the physical path, you can retrieve the filenames and loop though each of them. For each filename, create the appropriate Image control, a HyperLink control for the filename, and the size of the file in kilobytes (KB) as a LiteralControl. All three of these controls are then added to the PlaceHolder control. The HyperLink control allows the user to view/download the specified file. The code for this process looks like

```
// Construct the physical file path to the folder
string path = Server.MapPath("") + "/uploads";
DirectoryInfo dirInfo = new DirectoryInfo(path);

// Get a list of all the files in current path
FileInfo[] files = dirInfo.GetFiles();

// Loop through each file
foreach (FileInfo file in files)
{
    // Get the filename without the path
    string shortname = Path.GetFileName(file.FullName);

    // Add the appropriate file icon
    Image img = new Image();
    img.ImageUrl = GetIconForExtension(file);
    myPlaceHolder.Controls.Add(img);
```

```
        // Add a nonbreakable space
        LiteralControl space2 = new LiteralControl(" ");
        myPlaceHolder.Controls.Add(space2);

        // Add a link to the file so user can download/view it
        HyperLink lnk = new HyperLink();
        lnk.Text = shortname;
        // We may need to remove Url encoding
        lnk.NavigateUrl = Server.UrlDecode(rootpath) + "/" +
            shortname;
        myPlaceHolder.Controls.Add(lnk);

        // Add the file size in kb
        long kb = file.Length / 1000;
        LiteralControl size = new LiteralControl(" [" + kb + " KB]");
        myPlaceHolder.Controls.Add(size);

        // Add a line break
        LiteralControl br2 = new LiteralControl("<br/>");
        myPlaceHolder.Controls.Add(br2);
    }
```

Adding the ability to display and navigate subfolders makes your code-behind quite a bit more complicated. Displaying the subfolders is fairly straightforward and similar to the code for displaying the filenames. Unlike with the files in the folder, however, the HyperLink controls for the folder names link back to the same Web Form, but pass the folder to display as a querystring parameter.

```
// Get a list of all folders
DirectoryInfo[] folders = dirInfo.GetDirectories();
// Loop through the folders
foreach (DirectoryInfo folder in folders)
{
    string shortFolderName = Path.GetFileName(folder.FullName);

    // Add a folder image to the display
    Image img = new Image();
    img.ImageUrl = "images/mime_folder.gif";
    myPlaceHolder.Controls.Add(img);

    LiteralControl space1 = new LiteralControl(" ");
    myPlaceHolder.Controls.Add(space1);

    // The link for the folder must pass the folder name
    HyperLink lnk = new HyperLink();
    lnk.Text = shortFolderName;

    // Because the folder name may contain characters that are
    // not allowed in a querystring, you must URL encode it
```

```
lnk.NavigateUrl = "FileBrowser.aspx?local=" +
    Server.UrlEncode(rootpath + "/" + shortFolderName);
myPlaceHolder.Controls.Add(lnk);

LiteralControl br1 = new LiteralControl("<br/>");
myPlaceHolder.Controls.Add(br1);
}
```

You only need to change the logic for mapping the virtual path to the absolute path by using the passed querystring (if any). The code looks somewhat similar to the following.

```
string localpath = Request.QueryString["local"];

string rootpath;
// If no query string, use uploads folder as the root
if (localpath == null)
    rootpath = "uploads";
else
    rootpath = Server.UrlDecode(localpath);

string path = Server.MapPath("") + "/" + rootpath;
DirectoryInfo dirInfo = new DirectoryInfo(path);
```

Listing 4.6 contains the code-behind for the completed file browser. The majority of the processing logic lies within the GenerateListing method. It loops through all the folders and files and adds the appropriate controls to the PlaceHolder. The rest of the class simply contains other helper methods used by GenerateListing.

Listing 4.6 FileBrowser.aspx.cs

```
using System;
using System.Data;
using System.Configuration;
using System.Collections;
using System.Web;
using System.Web.Security;
using System.Web.UI;
using System.Web.UI.WebControls;
using System.Web.UI.WebControls.WebParts;
using System.Web.UI.HtmlControls;

using System.IO;

/// <summary>
/// Web Form that allows user to view/download files on the
/// server. User can also upload files and create folders.
/// </summary>
```

```csharp
public partial class FileBrowser : System.Web.UI.Page
{
    /// <summary>
    /// Retrieve the path of folder and generate the file listing
    /// </summary>
    protected void Page_Load(object sender, EventArgs e)
    {
        string currentRoot = RetrievePathOfFolderToDisplay();
        litLocation.Text = currentRoot;
        GenerateListing(currentRoot);
    }


    /// <summary>
    /// Displays the content of the specified folder.
    /// </summary>
    private void GenerateListing(string rootpath)
    {
        // First clear out the place holder
        myPlaceHolder.Controls.Clear();

        // Calculate the path to retrieve folders + files
        string path = Server.MapPath("") + "/" + rootpath;

        // Make the "go up a level" link if needed
        MakeUpOneLevelLink(rootpath);

        // Get a list of all folders
        DirectoryInfo dirInfo = new DirectoryInfo(path);
        DirectoryInfo[] folders = dirInfo.GetDirectories();

        // Loop through each folder and display it
        foreach (DirectoryInfo folder in folders)
        {
            DisplayFolder(folder, rootpath);
        }

        // Get a list of all the files in current path
        FileInfo[] files = dirInfo.GetFiles();
        // Loop through each file
        foreach (FileInfo file in files)
        {
            DisplayFile(file, rootpath);
        }
    }

    /// <summary>
    /// Retrieves the path of the folder to be displayed
    /// </summary>
```

```csharp
private string RetrievePathOfFolderToDisplay()
{
    string localpath = Request.QueryString["local"];
    // If no query string, use uploads folder as the root
    if (localpath == null)
        return "uploads";
    else
        // Remove the URL encoding necessary for
        // the querystring
        return Server.UrlDecode(localpath);
}

/// <summary>
/// Displays the appropriate controls for the passed folder
/// </summary>
private void DisplayFolder(DirectoryInfo folder,
    string rootpath)
{
    // Get the folder name without the path
    string shortfolder = Path.GetFileName(folder.FullName);

    // Add a folder icon
    Image img = new Image();
    img.ImageUrl = "images/mime_folder.gif";
    myPlaceHolder.Controls.Add(img);

    // Add a nonbreakable space
    LiteralControl space1 = new LiteralControl(" ");
    myPlaceHolder.Controls.Add(space1);

    // Add a link to the folder so user can display it
    HyperLink lnk = new HyperLink();
    lnk.Text = shortfolder;
    // The link for the folder must pass the folder name.
    // Because the folder name may contain characters that are
    // not allowed in a querystring, we must URL encode it
    lnk.NavigateUrl = "FileBrowser.aspx?local=" +
        Server.UrlEncode(rootpath + "/" + shortfolder);
    myPlaceHolder.Controls.Add(lnk);

    // Add a line break
    LiteralControl br1 = new LiteralControl("<br/>");
    myPlaceHolder.Controls.Add(br1);
}

/// <summary>
/// Displays the appropriate controls for the passed file
/// </summary>
private void DisplayFile(FileInfo file, string rootpath)
{
```

```
    // Get the filename without the path
    string shortname = Path.GetFileName(file.FullName);

    // Add a file icon
    Image img = new Image();
    img.ImageUrl = GetIconForExtension(file);
    myPlaceHolder.Controls.Add(img);

    // Add a nonbreakable space
    LiteralControl space2 = new LiteralControl(" ");
    myPlaceHolder.Controls.Add(space2);

    // Add a link to the file so user can download/view it
    HyperLink lnk = new HyperLink();
    lnk.Text = shortname;
    lnk.NavigateUrl = Server.UrlDecode(rootpath) + "/" +
        shortname;
    myPlaceHolder.Controls.Add(lnk);

    // Add the file size in kb
    long kb = file.Length / 1000;
    LiteralControl size = new LiteralControl(" [" + kb +
        " KB]");
    myPlaceHolder.Controls.Add(size);

    // Add a line break
    LiteralControl br2 = new LiteralControl("<br/>");
    myPlaceHolder.Controls.Add(br2);
}

/// <summary>
/// Returns the filename of the appropriate icon image file
/// based on the extension of the passed file
/// </summary>
private string GetIconForExtension(FileInfo file)
{
    string image = "images/";

    string ext = Path.GetExtension(file.FullName).ToLower();

    if (ext == ".txt")
        image += "mime_text.gif";
    else if (ext == ".doc")
        image += "mime_doc.gif";
    else if (ext == ".pdf")
        image += "mime_pdf.gif";
    else if (ext == ".gif" || ext == ".jpg" || ext == ".wmf")
        image += "mime_image.gif";
    else if (ext == ".html" || ext == ".htm" )
```

```
            image += "mime_html.gif";
    else
            image += "mime_unknown.gif";

    return image;
}


/// <summary>
/// Makes the "go up a level" link (if needed for the
/// current folder) and adds it to the place holder
/// </summary>
private void MakeUpOneLevelLink(string currentFolder)
{
    // Get the previous folder (the next one "up" in
    // the hierarchy)
    string previousFolder = GetPreviousFolder(currentFolder);

    // If there is a previous path, add a link to
    // place holder
    if (previousFolder != "")
    {
        Image imgBack = new Image();
        imgBack.ImageUrl = "images/mime_folder.gif";
        myPlaceHolder.Controls.Add(imgBack);

        HyperLink lnkBack = new HyperLink();
        lnkBack.Text = "..";
        lnkBack.NavigateUrl = "FileBrowser.aspx?local=" +
            Server.UrlEncode(previousFolder);
        myPlaceHolder.Controls.Add(lnkBack);

        LiteralControl br = new LiteralControl("<br/>");
        myPlaceHolder.Controls.Add(br);
    }
}


/// <summary>
/// Gets the previous folder (the next one "up" in the file
/// system hierarchy) from the passed path.
/// If there was no previous folder, return an
/// empty string
/// </summary>
private string GetPreviousFolder(string path)
{
    int posOfLastSlash = path.LastIndexOf("/");
    if (posOfLastSlash < 0)
        return "";
    string stripped = path.Remove(posOfLastSlash);
    return stripped;
}
```

```csharp
/// <summary>
/// Event handler for the upload button for the FileUploader
/// </summary>
protected void btnUpload_Click(object sender, EventArgs e)
{
    // The location for the uploaded file is current path
    string path = RetrievePathOfFolderToDisplay();
    if (fupTest.HasFile)
    {
        string fullname = Server.MapPath(path + "/" +
            fupTest.FileName);
        if (System.IO.File.Exists(fullname))
        {
            labMessage.Text =
                "File already exists - uploaded cancelled";
        }
        else
        {
            fupTest.SaveAs(fullname);
            labMessage.Text = "File successfully uploaded";
            // Recreate the file listing to show the
            // uploaded file
            GenerateListing(path);
        }
    }
    else
    {
        labMessage.Text = "File was not specified";
    }

}

/// <summary>
/// Event handler for the create new folder button
/// </summary>
protected void btnNewFolder_Click(object sender, EventArgs e)
{
    // Get the location for the new folder
    string folderLocation = RetrievePathOfFolderToDisplay();
    string fullPath = Server.MapPath(folderLocation) + "/" +
        txtFolder.Text;
    // Create the folder on the server
    Directory.CreateDirectory(fullPath);
    // Recreate the file listing to show the new folder
    GenerateListing(folderLocation);
}
}
```

AdRotator Control

The AdRotator control displays a randomly selected advertisement banner (a graphic image) on the Web page. The displayed advertisement changes whenever the page refreshes. If a user clicks the ad, he is redirected to the target URL specified by the control. The displayed advertisements can also be priority weighted; this allows certain advertisements to be displayed more often. You can also write your own custom algorithm to control the order and frequency for displaying the advertisements.

The control works by reading advertisement information stored in a separate data source, which is usually an XML file, but could also be any other data source control, such as the SqlDataSource or ObjectDataSource controls (which are covered in Chapter 9). This advertisement data source contains a list of advertisements and their associated attributes. These attributes define the path to an image to display, the URL to link to when the control is clicked, the alternate text to display when the image is not available, a keyword, and display the frequency of the advertisement.

Table 4.11 lists the unique properties of the AdRotator control.

Table 4.11 Unique Properties of the AdRotator Control

Property	Description
AdvertisementFile	The path of the XML file containing the advertisement information.
AlternateTextField	The name of the field in the data source containing the alternate text (i.e., used for the alt attribute of the HTML <img>) for an advertisement.
ImageUrlField	The name of the field in the data source containing the URL of the displayed advertisement image.
KeywordFilter	Each advertisement in the advertisement data source can be assigned a category keyword. Only advertisements containing the keyword specified by this property are displayed by the control.
NavigateUrlField	The name of the field in the data source containing the target URL for an advertisement.
Target	Specifies the name of the browser window or frame that displays the target URL of the advertisement when the control is clicked.

Thus, a typical basic `AdRotator` declaration might look like

```
<asp:AdRotator ID="adTest" runat="server"
    AdvertisementFile="~/App_Data/advert.xml" Target="_blank"/>
```

The `AdvertisementFile` attribute specifies the XML advertisement file to use, whereas the `Target="_blank"` attribute is used so that the navigated URL is opened in a new browser window.

CORE NOTE

For security reasons, you should place any XML files to be processed by your application within the `App_Data` folder of your application.

Advertisement XML File

The `AdRotator` control works in conjunction with advertisement information stored in some type of data source. Perhaps the easiest way to store this information is within an XML file. This XML file has a particular schema (format) that *must* be followed, as illustrated in the following example.

```
<Advertisements>
  <Ad>
    <ImageUrl>~/Images/ads/ad1.gif</ImageUrl>
    <height>240</height>
    <width>65</width>
    <NavigateUrl>
    http://www.aw-bc.com/newpearsonchoices</NavigateUrl>
    <AlternateText>New Pearson Choices</AlternateText>
    <Impressions>2</Impressions>
    <Keyword>books</Keyword>
  </Ad>
  <Ad>
    <ImageUrl>~/Images/ads/ad2.gif</ImageUrl>
    <height>240</height>
    <width>65</width>
    <NavigateUrl>http://www.pearsoned.com</NavigateUrl>
    <AlternateText>Pearson Ed</AlternateText>
    <Impressions>4</Impressions>
    <Keyword>teaching</Keyword>
  </Ad>
  <Ad>
    <ImageUrl>~/Images/ads/ad3.gif</ImageUrl>
    <height>240</height>
    <width>65</width>
```

```
    <NavigateUrl>http://www.etipsforagrades.com</NavigateUrl>
    <AlternateText>First Day Of Class</AlternateText>
    <Impressions>1</Impressions>
    <Keyword>teaching</Keyword>
  </Ad>
</Advertisements>
```

The XML file contains any number of `<Ad>` elements. Each `<Ad>` element has a URL for the image to display, the width and height of the image, the URL to navigate to when the ad is clicked, and the alternative text to display when the image cannot be loaded. The `<Keyword>` element is used to assign a category keyword to the ad. You can use the `<KeywordFilter>` property of the `AdRotator` control so that only advertisements containing the keyword specified by that property are displayed by the control. The `<Impressions>` element controls the appearance frequency of the ad. The number contained in this element determines how often the image is displayed in comparison to the other images. The larger this number is in relation to the impression number of the other ads, the more often the image is displayed.

Although the advertisement XML file could exist anywhere on the server, if you put the XML file into the `App_Data` folder of your Web site, the file automatically has the correct permissions to allow ASP.NET to read the file at runtime. Also, putting your XML file in the `App_Data` folder helps to protect the file from being viewed directly in a browser (because this folder is marked as nonrequestable by the ASP.NET runtime). You can create this special folder directly in Visual Studio by right-clicking the Web project in the Solution Explorer and choosing the Add ASP.NET Folder | App_Data menu option.

Displaying Advertisements from a Database

The `AdRotator` control can read advertisement information from data sources other than an XML file. For instance, if you already have a database table containing information reasonably similar to that stored in the advertisement XML file, you can use that instead by using a *data source control*. Although data source controls are covered in much more detail in Chapter 9, we will illustrate how one can be used in conjunction with an `AdRotator` control (and save the explanation for how the data source control works for Chapter 9).

Assume that you have a Microsoft Access database named `Sample.mdb` that contains a table named `Adverts`. This table contains the following fields: `ID`, `Image-FileName`, `AltDescription`, and `DestinationUrl`. You can then use the following markup to display an `AdRotator` control using this database table.

```
<asp:AdRotator ID="adTest2" runat="server" Target="_blank"
    DataSourceID="ds1Sample"
    ImageUrlField="ImageFileName"
```

```
AlternateTextField="AltDescription"
NavigateUrlField="DestinationUrl" />
```

```
<asp:AccessDataSource ID="ds1Sample" runat="server"
    DataFile="~/App_Data/Sample.mdb"
    SelectCommand="Select * From Adverts"> </asp:AccessDataSource>
```

The `DataSourceID` attribute specifies the ID value of the data source control. Notice as well that you must use the `ImageUrlField`, `AlternateTextField`, and the `NavigateUrlField` attributes to specify which fields in the table contain the image URL, `alt` text, and the navigation URL for each ad.

Programming the AdRotator

If you are unable to use the `Impressions` element of the XML advertisement file (perhaps because you are using a database table as the data source), or you want to use a more sophisticated algorithm for selecting the ad to display in the control, you can write your own event handler for the `AdCreated` event of the `AdRotator` control (see Table 4.12).

Table 4.12   Events of the AdRotator Control

Event	Description
AdCreated	Raised after the creation of the control but before the page is rendered.

To use the `AdCreated` event, you simply need to add the event handler to the control. For instance, the following example specifies the event handler that will display the ad as well as a check box that the event handler will ultimately use to determine which ad to display.

```
<p>This ad is populated programmatically</p>
<asp:AdRotator ID="adTest3" runat="server"
    AdvertisementFile="~/App_Data/advert.xml" Target="_blank"
    OnAdCreated="adTest3_AdCreated"/>
<br />
<asp:CheckBox ID="chkStudent" runat="server"  AutoPostBack="true"/>
I am a student or teacher
```

The `AdCreated` event handler is passed an `AdCreatedEventArgs` object. This object has three properties (`ImageUrl`, `NavigateUrl`, and `AlternateText`) that are used to specify the data needed to render the control. The following event handler uses the current status of the check box to determine which ad to display.

```
protected void adTest3_AdCreated(object sender,
   AdCreatedEventArgs e)
{
   if (chkStudent.Checked)
   {
      e.ImageUrl = "~/Images/ads/ad3.gif";
      e.AlternateText = "First Day Of Class";
      e.NavigateUrl = "http://www.etipsforagrades.com";
   }
   else
   {
      e.ImageUrl = "~/Images/ads/ad2.gif";
      e.AlternateText = "Pearson Ed";
      e.NavigateUrl = "http://www.pearsoned.com";
   }
}
```

Obviously, this is a fairly trivial algorithm. However, one could create a more realistic method that used, for instance, the user's purchasing history, the navigation history of the user within the site, the user's profile information, or some other marketing criteria to determine the ad to display.

It should also be noted that you can select ads based on a keyword by using the `KeywordFilter` property, as in

```
<asp:AdRotator … KeywordFilter="teaching" />
```

For this filtering to work, the ads need to be categorized by keyword. In the XML advertisement file, this is accomplished by using the `Keyword` child element of the `Ad` element.

Xml Control

The `Xml` server control can be used to display the unformatted contents of an XML document or the result of an XSLT transformation in a Web page. The content or transformation result appears in the Web page at the location of the control. Using the control declaratively is simply a matter of declaring the control and specifying the `DocumentSource` attribute, as in

```
<asp:Xml ID="aXml" runat="server"
   DocumentSource="~/App_Data/menu.xml"/>
```

In this example, the control is rendered to the browser simply as the data content; that is, there would be no tags, just the content of the tags, as shown in Figure 4.18. Listing 4.7 contains the contents of this sample `menu.xml` file.

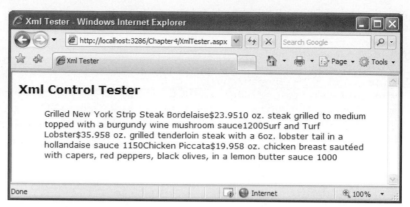

Figure 4.18   Xml control in the browser with no XSLT

Listing 4.7   Menu.xml

```xml
<?xml version="1.0" encoding="utf-8" ?>
<menu>
  <food>
    <name>Grilled New York Strip Steak Bordelaise</name>
    <price>$23.95</price>
    <description>
    10 oz. steak grilled to medium topped with a burgundy wine
    mushroom sauce
    </description>
    <calories>1200</calories>
  </food>
  <food>
    <name>Surf and Turf Lobster</name>
    <price>$35.95</price>
    <description>
    8 oz. grilled tenderloin steak with a 6oz. lobster tail
    in a hollandaise sauce
    </description>
    <calories>1150</calories>
  </food>
  <food>
    <name>Chicken Piccata</name>
    <price>$19.95</price>
    <description>
    8 oz. chicken breast sautéed with capers, red peppers, black
    olives, in a lemon butter sauce
    </description>
    <calories>1000</calories>
  </food>
</menu>
```

The result shown in Figure 4.18 is probably not the kind of output that you want. Luckily, you can control how the XML content is formatted and displayed by using an **XSLT** (Extensible Stylesheet Language Transformation) file. XSLT is a World Wide Web Consortium (W3C) Recommendation that allows one to specify how the content of a source XML document should be transformed into another document that is different in format or structure. An XSLT document is itself an XML document; it is an XML-based programming language for transforming XML documents. The .NET XSLT parser can thus be used to transform an XML document into an XML document with a different structure, a HTML file, a text file, or almost any other type of document (see Figure 4.19).

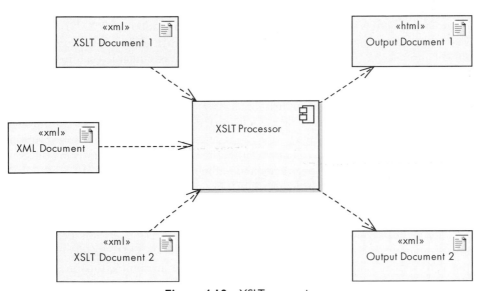

Figure 4.19   XSLT processing

It is certainly beyond the scope of this book to comprehensively discuss XML or XSLT (the References section at the end of the chapter has several useful XSLT references). Instead, this section will try to give you a sense of how to use XSLT and show you some typical XSLT transformations.

Creating an XSLT File

Listing 4.8 contains a sample XSLT file. An XSLT file must be a valid XML file, and thus must begin with the XML declaration. The root element for the XSLT file is the `stylesheet` element. The W3C specification also allows the root element to be named `transform` instead (whereas the .NET XSLT parser supports the `transform` name, Visual Studio marks it as an error). In the listing, the `stylesheet` element also indicates that the prefix `xsl` is an alias for the namespace string `"http://www.w3.org/1999/XSL/Transform"`. The .NET XSLT parser is very particular about this namespace string. If it is not *exactly* the same as shown here, the parser generates a runtime error. Similarly, the version attribute of the `stylesheet` element must be `1.0` or higher. This is not a peculiarity of the .NET XSLT parser but a requirement stated in section 2.3 of the W3C XSLT specification.

The XSLT processing begins with the `template` element. An XSLT document consists of one or more template rules in which you define how the specified XML element (also called a node) is to be transformed. The template element here contains a `match` attribute, which specifies which element in the source XML document is to be transformed by the template rule. This match attribute uses an **XPath** expression. XPath is a language/syntax for finding information in an XML document. Its syntax allows you to navigate through the various XML elements in the XML document and select a given element using a slash (`/`) syntax similar to that used for navigating the file system tree in UNIX or DOS. Our example XPath expression (`/menu`) can be interpreted this way: Select the `menu` element at the root of your XML document and make it the current context for subsequent processing.

Your sample XSLT file also contains a loop. The `for-each` element loops through each element specified by the XPath `select` attribute in the current context (in this case, loop through each `food` element within the `menu` element), outputting the content contained between the beginning and ending of the `for-each` element to your destination (in this case, the browser). The (optional) `sort` element specifies that the collection that you are looping through (the `food` elements) is sorted alphanumerically based on the value of the each `price` element within the `food` element.

The `value-of` element is used to extract the value (i.e., the value between the begin and end tags) of the specified element in your source XML document and output it to your destination. Like the previous `select` attributes, this one also uses XPath syntax to specify which element's value is to be output.

Listing 4.8   Menu.xslt

```
<?xml version="1.0" encoding="UTF-8" ?>
<xsl:stylesheet version="1.0"
    xmlns:xsl="http://www.w3.org/1999/XSL/Transform">

  <xsl:template match="/menu">
    <table width="400">
      <xsl:for-each select="food">
        <xsl:sort select="price" />
        <tr bgcolor="goldenrod">
          <td>
            <b>
              <xsl:value-of select="name" />
```

```
                </b>
            </td>
            <td align="right">
                <xsl:value-of select="price" />
            </td>
        </tr>
        <tr bgcolor="palegoldenrod">
            <td colspan="2">
                <xsl:value-of select="description" />
                <br />
                <i>
                <xsl:value-of select="calories" />
                calories per serving
                </i>
            </td>
        </tr>
    </xsl:for-each>
    </table>
</xsl:template>

</xsl:stylesheet>
```

To use this XSLT file with your XML control, you simply add the `Transform-Source` attribute, as shown here.

```
<asp:Xml ID="aXml" runat="server"
    DocumentSource="~/App_Data/menu.xml"
    TransformSource="~/App_Data/menu.xslt">
```

Figure 4.20 illustrates how this control is rendered in the browser.

CORE NOTE

Rather than containing the XML within an external file, you can also
include the XML inline within the XML control itself, as shown here.

```
<asp:Xml ID="Xml2" runat="server" >
    <menu>
      <food>
        <name>Grilled New York Steak</name>
        <price>$23.95</price>
      </food>
    </menu>
  </asp:Xml>
```

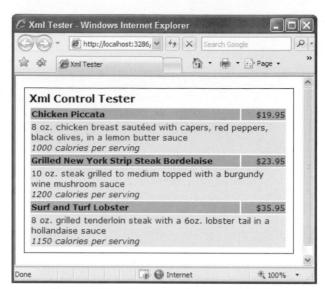

Figure 4.20   XML control using an XSLT file

Table 4.13 lists the unique properties of the Xml control.

Table 4.13   Unique Properties of the Xml Control

Property	Description
Document	The XmlDocument object containing the content to be displayed.
DocumentContent	A string containing the XML content to be displayed.
DocumentSource	The file system path of the XML file to be displayed.
Transform	The XslTransform object that defines the formatting of the displayed output.
TransformArgumentList	Contains a list of optional arguments to be passed to the XSLT file/object.
TransformSource	The file system path of the XSLT file that defines the formatting of the displayed output.
XPathNavigator	Specifies the XPathNavigator object to be used for processing the XML document.

Programming the XML Control

Rather than use the declarative syntax shown so far, you may need to programmatically specify the XML and XSLT documents. In this case, you can simply programmatically set the DocumentSource and TransformSource properties. However, if the XML file does not exist on your file system (for instance, you want to process an XML file available via a URL or process the XML contained within a database), you need to use either the Document or XPathNavigator property. Although the Document property is perhaps somewhat easier to work with, it is marked as obsolete, so you should use the XPathNavigator property instead.

Listing 4.9 illustrates how to programmatically process the XML file used in the previous examples.

Listing 4.9   XmlProgramming.aspx.cs

```
using System;
using System.Data;
using System.Configuration;
using System.Collections;
using System.Web;
using System.Web.Security;
using System.Web.UI;
using System.Web.UI.WebControls;
using System.Web.UI.WebControls.WebParts;
using System.Web.UI.HtmlControls;

using System.Xml;
using System.Xml.XPath;
using System.Xml.Xsl;

public partial class XmlProgramming : System.Web.UI.Page
{
    protected void Page_Load(object sender, EventArgs e)
    {
        // Create the XPathNavigator object for the xml file
        string xmlUrl= Server.MapPath("~/App_Data/menu.xml");
        XPathDocument xpdoc = new XPathDocument(xmlUrl);
        XPathNavigator xnav = xpdoc.CreateNavigator();

        // Setup the xml control
        myXml.XPathNavigator = xnav;
        myXml.TransformSource = "~/App_Data/menu.xslt";
    }
}
```

Notice that in this listing, you must first specify the namespaces for the various XML classes. After that, you simply create the XPathDocument object by passing it the URL (in this case, the full local path) of the XML source file. If you want to use an XML file from an external Web site, you could simply use the URL of the file, as in

```
string xmlUrl =
  "http://www.awprofessional.com/press/events_rss.asp";
```

Processing an RSS Feed

RSS is an XML format used for syndicating (i.e., publishing) content. Many sites now provide some of their online content as an RSS feed. You can thus programmatically read, process, and display this content on your site. Listings 4.10, 4.11, 4.12, and 4.13 illustrate how to process and display a variety of RSS feeds.

The XML in an RSS feed is quite straightforward (see the following code). It contains a channel element that in turn contains the title, link, and description elements plus a few other elements that describe the feed. As well, the channel contains one or more item elements that correspond to the individual content items. (The current RSS specification can be found at http://www.rss-specifications.com).

```
<?xml version="1.0" encoding="utf-8" ?>
<rss version="2.0">
  <channel>
    <title>Fancy RSS Feed</title>
    <link>http://www.anywhere.com/sampleRss.xml</link>
    <description>The most amazing RSS anywhere</description>
    <language>en-us</language>
    <item>
      <title>First great story</title>
      <link>http://www.anywhere.com/story1.html</link>
      <description>Description of story here</description>
      <pubDate>January 23, 2006</pubDate>
    </item>
    <item>
      <title>Second great story</title>
      <link>http://www.anywhere.com/story2.html</link>
      <description>Description of story here</description>
      <pubDate>January 26, 2006</pubDate>
    </item>
    ...
  </channel>
</rss>
```

Of course, to display this RSS feed, you need some type of XSLT transformation to format it. Listings 4.10 and 4.11 contain two different XSLT files that transform a RSS feed in two quite different ways.

Listing 4.10   RssTransform1.xsl

```
<?xml version="1.0" encoding="utf-8"?>
<xsl:stylesheet version="1.0"
    xmlns:xsl="http://www.w3.org/1999/XSL/Transform">

<xsl:template match="/rss/channel">
  <h2 style="font: 14pt Verdana;font-weight:bold;color:#827753;
      background-color:#CFBD84;">
    <xsl:value-of select="title" />
  </h2>
  <p style="font: 10pt Verdana, Helvetica; margin-bottom: 10px;">
    <xsl:value-of select="description" />
  </p>
  <xsl:for-each select="item">
    <h3 style="font: 12pt Verdana, Helvetica; border-bottom: 1px
      solid #A89A6C;"><xsl:value-of select="title" /></h3>
    <p style="font: 10pt Verdana, Helvetica;">
      <xsl:value-of select="description" />
      <br/>
      <a href="{link}">Read more</a>
    </p>
  </xsl:for-each>
</xsl:template>

</xsl:stylesheet>
```

Listing 4.11   RssTransform2.xsl

```
<?xml version="1.0" encoding="utf-8"?>
<xsl:stylesheet version="1.0"
    xmlns:xsl="http://www.w3.org/1999/XSL/Transform">

<xsl:template match="/rss/channel">
  <div style="width:300px;position:absolute;left:350px;top:12px;
      background-color: #DFDFDF; padding: 10px; color: #606060;
      font: Trebuchet MS, Times New Roman, serif;">
    <div style="text-transform: uppercase;">
      <p style="font-size:22px;color:#930000;margin-bottom:2px;">
        <xsl:value-of select="title" />
      </p>
      <p style="font-size: 11px; ">
        <xsl:value-of select="description" />
      </p>
    </div>
    <xsl:for-each select="item">
      <div style="background-color:#D1D1D1;padding:2px;
```

```
        margin-top: 8px;">
      <p style="margin-bottom: 1px; margin-top: 1px;
          font-size: 16px;">
       <a href="{link}" style=" color: #930000;">
       <xsl:value-of select="title" />
       </a>
      </p>
      <p style="font-size:10px;margin-top:1px;margin-
          bottom:1px;border-bottom: 1px dashed #949494;">
       <xsl:value-of select="pubDate" />
      </p>
      <p style="font:11px Verdana, sans-serif;
          line-height:18px;margin-top:1px;margin-bottom:1px;">
       <xsl:value-of select="description" />
      </p>
     </div>
   </xsl:for-each>
  </div>
</xsl:template>

</xsl:stylesheet>
```

Our RSS reader is quite simple. It contains two `DropDownList` controls to let the user select a feed and to select the XSLT file to use, as well as `Button` to perform the read and the `Xml` control to contain the content. The markup for this reader page is included in Listing 4.12.

Listing 4.12   RssReader.aspx

```
<asp:Panel ID="panSelect" runat="server" BorderWidth="1"
     BorderStyle="Solid" BackColor="Beige"
     CssClass="SelectArea">
  <h1>RSS Reader</h1>
  <p>Select a RSS feed<br />
  <asp:DropDownList ID="drpFeeds" runat="server" >
     <asp:ListItem Value=
        "http://rss.cnn.com/rss/cnn_topstories.rss">
     CNN</asp:ListItem>
     <asp:ListItem Value=
        "http://msdn.microsoft.com/rss.xml">
     MSDN</asp:ListItem>
     <asp:ListItem Value=
       "http://newsrss.bbc.co.uk/rss/
          newsonline_uk_edition/technology/rss.xml">
     BBC Technology News</asp:ListItem>
  </asp:DropDownList>
```

```
    </p>
    <p>Select a template<br />
    <asp:DropDownList ID="drpTemplates" runat="server">
        <asp:ListItem Value="~/App_Data/RssTransform1.xsl">
            RssTransform 1</asp:ListItem>
        <asp:ListItem Value="~/App_Data/RssTransform2.xsl">
            RssTransform 2</asp:ListItem>
    </asp:DropDownList>
    </p>
    <p>
    <asp:Button ID="btnRead" runat="server" Text="Read Feed"
        OnClick="btnRead_Click" />
    </p>
</asp:Panel>

<asp:Panel ID="panFeed" runat="server">
    <asp:Xml ID="myXml" runat="server"></asp:Xml>
</asp:Panel>
```

The code-behind for the reader is also quite simple (see Listing 4.13). We simply have to modify the code used in Listing 4.9, so that the source URL and the transform source are those selected by the user.

Listing 4.13   RssReader.aspx.cs

```
using System;
using System.Data;
using System.Configuration;
using System.Collections;
using System.Web;
using System.Web.Security;
using System.Web.UI;
using System.Web.UI.WebControls;
using System.Web.UI.WebControls.WebParts;
using System.Web.UI.HtmlControls;using System.Xml;
using System.Xml.XPath;
using System.Xml.Xsl;

public partial class RssReader : System.Web.UI.Page
{
    protected void btnRead_Click(object sender, EventArgs e)
    {
        // Create the XPathNavigator object
        string xmlUrl = drpFeeds.SelectedValue;
        XPathDocument xpdoc = new XPathDocument(xmlUrl);
        XPathNavigator xnav = xpdoc.CreateNavigator();
```

```
        // Set up the xml control
        myXml.XPathNavigator = xnav;
        string xslFilename = drpTemplates.SelectedValue;
        myXml.TransformSource = xslFilename;
    }
}
```

Figures 4.21 and 4.22 illustrate how the same RSS feed can be dramatically transformed with the XSLT files from Listings 4.10 and 4.11.

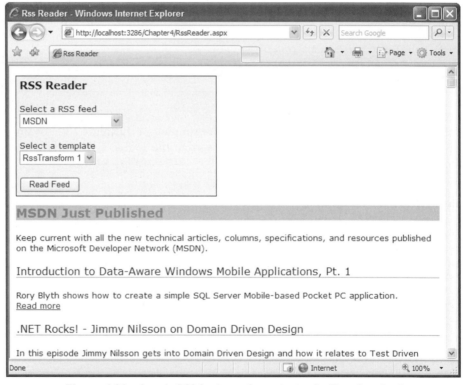

Figure 4.21   Sample RSS feed transformed using RssTransform1.xsl

CORE NOTE

It is possible that the URLs of the RSS feeds may have changed in the time between the writing of this chapter and your reading of it. In this case, a runtime error (The remote name could not be resolved ...) is generated. To fix this error, you must replace the provided URLs with URLs of known, working RSS feeds.

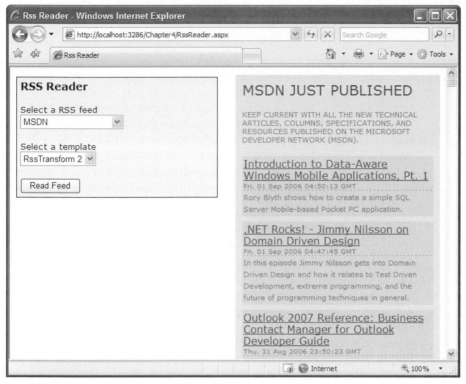

Figure 4.22   Sample RSS feed transformed using RssTransform2.xsl

Summary

This chapter examined the additional standard Web server controls. The first set of these controls—the `Panel`, `MultiView` and `View`, `Wizard`, and `PlaceHolder` controls—are containers for other controls. The second set of controls covered in this chapter—the `FileUpload`, `AdRotator`, and `Xml` controls—are more specialized controls.

The next chapter will cover another type of Web server control, the various validation controls. These controls are used to help the developer with one of the most common tasks of a Web developer: ensuring the user enters valid data. The next chapter also examines exception handling in the ASP.NET.

Exercises

The solutions to the following exercises can be found at my Web site, http://www.randyconnolly.com/core. Additional exercises only available for teachers and instructors are also available from this site.

1. Create a page named PanelTest.aspx. This page should contain three Panel controls. Each of these Panel controls should be 100px in height, contain a few paragraphs of text content, and have scroll bars. The page should contain a CheckBoxList through which the user can toggle the visibility of each Panel control individually.

2. Create a page named MultiViewPizza.aspx. This page should have the same functionality as the PizzaPanelTest.aspx page from Listings 4.1 and 4.2 but use the MultiView control instead of Panel controls.

3. Create a page named CheckoutWizard.aspx. This page should contain a Wizard control that steps the user through the process of checking out or paying for an item in a Web store. The first step should ask the user for a user name and password; if the user name and password are equal to some simple string such as "abcd," proceed to the next step. The second step should ask the user for shipping address information (address, city, region, postal/ZIP). The third step should ask the user for the shipment method (regular mail, air mail, or courier). The fourth step should ask the user for credit card number, card type (Visa, Mastercard, American Express), and expiry month and year. The last step should simply display a message saying the order was successful and displaying shipping address, shipment method, and payment card type.

4. Extend the example in Listing 4.12 by creating a new XSLT file that transforms an RSS feed.

5. Alter Listing 4.12 so that the XSLT files are not hardcoded but are read-in from the App_Data folder. That is, the drpTemplates control should display all XSLT files in the App_Data folder whose filename begins with RssTransform.

Key Concepts

- Data source controls
- Modal
- Naming containers
- Pipelines
- Style elements

- Template elements
- XPath
- XSLT

References

Esposito, Dino. "The ASP.NET 2.0 Wizard Control." *MSDN Magazine* (April 2004).

Holmn, Ken. "What Is XSLT?" `http://www.xml.com`.

Normén, Fredrik. "Change the Button Control of the Wizard Control's SideBar." `http://fredrik.nsquared2.com`.

Refsnes Data. "XSLT Tutorial." `http://www.w3schools.com/xsl/default.asp`.

Chapter 5

EXCEPTION HANDLING AND VALIDATION CONTROLS

"No one is so brave that he is not perturbed by the unexpected."
—Julius Caesar, *De Bello Gallico*, 6.39

This chapter covers one of the most vital topics in Web application development: how to prevent and deal with unexpected errors. Even the best written application may fail. Whether it is due to strange user input, the failure of a remote service, or simple programmer oversight, errors and exceptions happen. Fortunately, the exception handling mechanism in ASP.NET requires forethought, not bravery, on the part of the developer. By planning and coding for exceptions, a developer should be able to face the unexpected with equanimity.

This chapter begins by covering how to plan and code for exceptions in C# and ASP.NET. The chapter then moves on to the various validation controls in ASP.NET. These controls provide a convenient and useful way to construct an application's first line of defense against errors, namely dealing with invalid data.

Error Handling

As already mentioned, even the best written Web application can suffer from run-time errors. Most complex Web applications must interact with external systems such as databases, Web services, RSS feeds, email servers, file system, and other externalities that are beyond your control. A failure in any one of these systems means that your application can also no longer run successfully. It is vitally important that your applications can gracefully handle such problems. The rest of this section discusses and illustrates possible error handling approaches in ASP.NET and C#.

.NET Exception Handling

When an error occurs, something called an ***exception*** is raised, or *thrown* in the nomenclature of .NET. That is, when an error occurs, either the system or the currently executing application reports it by throwing an exception containing information about the error. When thrown, an exception can be handled by the application or by ASP.NET itself. In the .NET exception handling model, exceptions are represented as objects. The ancestor class for all exceptions is `Exception`. This class has several subclasses, such as `ApplicationException` and `SystemException`, which in turn have many subclasses such as `IOException`, `SecurityException`, and `NullReferenceException`. Every `Exception` object contains information about the error.

When an exception is raised but not handled by the application, ASP.NET displays the ***default error page***. This page displays the exception message, the exception type, the line that it occurred on, as well as a stack trace, as shown in Figure 5.1. A ***stack trace*** displays every call, from the original page request down to the line that triggered the exception.

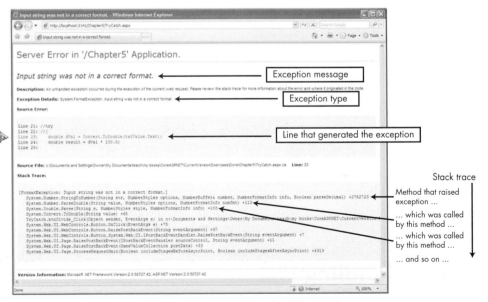

Figure 5.1   ASP.NET exception display

Although this ASP.NET default error page is quite useful when developing and debugging an application, you might not always want to display this page when an exception occurs. Instead, you might want to *handle* the exception. There are three different ways or levels where you can do so.

1. At the class level
2. At the page level
3. At the application level

Exception Handling at the Class Level Using a try...catch Block

All .NET languages provide a mechanism for separating regular program code from exception handling code. In C#, this is accomplished via the try...catch block. If a runtime error occurs during the execution of any code placed within a try block, the program does not crash but instead tries to execute the code contained in one of the catch blocks. In the following example, there are two catch blocks. If an exception occurs, the system searches the associated catch blocks in the order they appear in the code until it locates a catch block that handles the exception. For this reason, the more specific catch exception must appear before the more general catch exception.

```csharp
try
{
    double dVal1 = Convert.ToDouble(txtValue1.Text);
    double dVal2 = Convert.ToDouble(txtValue2.Text);
    double result = dVal1 / dVal2;

    labMessage.Text = txtValue1.Text + "/" + txtValue2.Text;
    labMessage.Text += "=" + result;
}
catch (FormatException ex1)
{
    labMessage.Text = "Please enter a valid number";
}
catch (Exception ex2)
{
    labMessage.Text = "Unable to compute a value with these values";
}
```

CORE NOTE

If your Web application is going to be localized for different languages, you might want to place the actual error messages in local-specific resource files and instead reference the resource keys in the error messages. For more information, see the discussion on localization in Chapter 16.

There may be times when you want to execute some block of code regardless of whether an exception occurred. The classic example is closing a database connection no matter whether the SQL operation was successful or generated an exception. In such a case, you can use the optional `finally` block, as shown in the following partial example.

```
try
{
    // Open a database connection

    // Execute SQL statement
}
catch (DbException ex)
{
    // Handle database exception
}
finally
{
    // Close database connection if it exists
}
```

The Cost of Exceptions

Throwing exceptions is relatively expensive in terms of CPU cycles and resource usage. As a result, one should try to use exceptions to handle only exceptional situations. If your code relies on throwing an exception as part of its normal flow, you should refactor the code to avoid exceptions, perhaps by using a return code or some other similar mechanism instead.

For instance, I was once hired to update an existing ASP.NET application written by a large programming team. In this application, there were pages that needed to interact with a method in a business object that handled customer requests. The method was passed the customer's email and then the business object's data members were populated from a database if the email existed in the database. The problem was that if the email didn't exist, the business object threw an exception. As a result, the code for using this method had to look similar to the following.

```
try
{
    SomeBusinessObject.Login(email);

    // Other code dependent upon a successful login
}
catch (Exception ex)
{
    // Display message that email was not found
}
```

Incorrect user input is not really an exceptional situation. In fact, it is so common that you should design your code to routinely handle it without raising an exception. The better approach would have been to refactor the `Login` method so that it returns some type of flag (such as a `bool` or a `null`) if the customer email does not exist, as shown in the following.

```
bool okay = SomeBusinessObject.Login(email);
if (! okay)
{
    // Display error message on page
}
else
{
    // Other code dependent upon a successful login
}
```

Similarly, the earlier `string-to-int` exception example can be rewritten so as to avoid the exception, by using the `Int32.TryParse` method, as shown in Listing 3.9 from Chapter 3.

Possible Exception Handling Strategies

If you design your code so that exceptions are thrown only in truly exceptional situations, you might wonder what your program should do when one of these exceptional exceptions occurs. There are four possibilities.

- "Swallow" the exception by catching, and ignore the exception by continuing normal execution.
- Completely handle the exception within the `catch` block.
- Ignore the exception by not catching it (and thus let some other class handle it).
- Catch the exception and rethrow it for some other class to handle it.

The first approach is almost never appropriate. It is rare indeed to have a program that can blithely ignore a runtime error that would have crashed the program had it not been trapped by the `try` block. The second approach seems at first glance to make the most sense. If the class that generates the exception can gracefully and sensibly handle the exception, why shouldn't it? Remember that here we are not referring to routine or expected exceptions that are simply the by-product of a poor design, but are referring to truly unexpected exceptions.

If you remember the cost of exceptions, you (the developer) may want to know when an exception occurs in a production application so that you can change the code to prevent it from occurring in the future. In this case, you might not want to catch the exception but instead let some other class "higher" in the calling stack handle it, perhaps by recording the exception to some type of exception log. Even if you are not recording an exception log, you should remember that *in general, you should not catch exceptions in a method unless it can handle them*, such as by logging exception details, performing some type of page redirection, retrying the operation, or performing some other sensible action.

Sometimes, developers catch an exception only to rethrow it so that it is still available to some other class "higher" in the calling stack, as shown in the following.

```
try
{
    // Other code that causes an exception
}
catch (Exception ex)
{
    // Do something with exception

    // Rethrow exception
    throw;
}
```

The cost of rethrowing an exception is quite close to the cost incurred raising it in the first place. Nonetheless, this approach may make sense if you want to decorate the exception message with some type of diagnostic information, as shown in the following.

```
catch (Exception ex)
{
    string myMessage = "Error in Class XXXX";

    // Throw new exception with your additional info
    throw new Exception(myMessage, ex);
}
```

This way, the exception can still get processed by some other "higher" class, but now it has additional information from your class about the exception.

Exception Handling at the Page Level

ASP.NET allows the developer to handle errors on a page basis via the page's Page_Error event handler. The Page_Error event handler is called whenever an uncaught exception occurs during the execution of the page. In the following example, the sample Page_Error event simply displays the error message and then clears the exception.

```
public partial class PageExceptionTest : System.Web.UI.Page
{
```

```
protected void Page_Load(object sender, EventArgs e)
{
   BuggyMethod();
}

private void BuggyMethod()
{
   // Deliberately throw an exception to simulate
   // uncaught exception
   throw new
     ApplicationException(
        "Your buggy code caused an exception.");
}

private void Page_Error(object sender, EventArgs e)
{
   Exception ex = Server.GetLastError();
   Response.Write("<h1>An error has occurred</h1>");
   Response.Write("<h2>" + ex.Message + "</h2>");
   Response.Write("<pre>" + ex.StackTrace + "</pre>");
   Context.ClearError();
}
}
```

The result in the browser is shown in Figure 5.2.

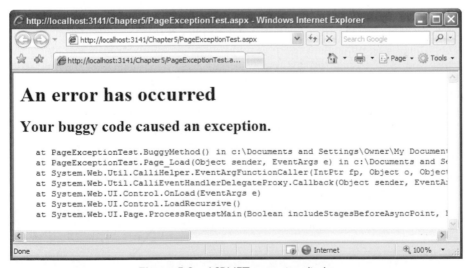

Figure 5.2   ASP.NET exception display

You might wonder why this example uses the `Response.Write` method instead of the usual ASP.NET practice of displaying dynamic text content in a control such as a `Label` control. The reason is that you cannot use controls in the `Page_Error` method because it is called *before* any control instances have been created. The `Context.ClearError` method is also necessary to prevent the default ASP.NET error page (shown in Figure 5.1) from displaying.

The `Page_Error` handler is typically used to handle exceptions not caught and handled by `try...catch` blocks. However, it is often preferable to *not* use the `Page_Error` handler, and instead use the application-wide `Application_Error` handler, which is covered next, for these situations.

Exception Handling at the Application Level

There are two different ways that you can handle an exception at the application level: using a `Application_Error` event handler and using the ASP.NET error page redirection mechanism.

Using the Application_Error Handler

ASP.NET allows the developer to handle errors on an application-wide basis via the `Application_Error` event handler. This handler resides in the application's `Global.asax` file and is often the preferred location to handle uncaught exceptions in an application. The reason why the `Application_Error` event handler is generally preferred over the `Page_Error` event handler is that you often want to do the same thing for all unhandled exceptions in your application: for instance, log them to some type of error log, display a custom message depending upon the role of the user, or send an email to the Web master. Rather than have the same type of error-logging code on every single page, it makes sense to centralize this code into a single spot. This single spot is the `Application_Error` handler.

The following example illustrates an `Application_Error` handler in the `global.asax` file that outputs any exceptions it receives to the Windows Event Log. This log can be viewed by the Event Viewer snap-in (see Figure 5.3 on page 266) that is available via the Administrative Tools option in the Windows Control Panel.

This example creates a new event source category named `WebErrors` if it doesn't already exist, and then outputs the event to this source. Notice as well that it uses the `System.Diagnostics` namespace.

```
<%@ Application Language="C#" %>

<%@ Import Namespace="System.Diagnostics" %>

<script runat="server">
```

```
...

void Application_Error(object sender, EventArgs e)
{
    // Construct the error string
    string msg = "Url " + Request.Path + "Error: " +
        Server.GetLastError().ToString();

    // Need to catch exception just in case you do not
    // have permission to access Event Log
    try
    {
        // Create the WebErrors event source if you need to
        string logName = "WebErrors";

        if (!EventLog.SourceExists(logName))
            EventLog.CreateEventSource(logName, logName);

        // Add a new error event to the log
        EventLog log = new EventLog();
        log.Source = logName;
        log.WriteEntry(msg, EventLogEntryType.Error);
    }
    catch (Exception ex)
    {
        // Not much you can do with this except swallow it
        // or output it to debugger
        Debug.WriteLine(ex.Message);
    }
}

</script>
```

In some situations (such as when a site is hosted on a third-party server), you might not have permission to add to or access the server event log. In such a case, you must use some other mechanism, such as sending an email or logging the exception to some other type of file or database.

To send an exception via email, you can use the `MailMessage` class in the `System.Net.Mail` namespace. The next example, following Figure 5.3, illustrates how this class could be used.

CORE NOTE

To test this example, a valid SMTP server must be available to your Web server.

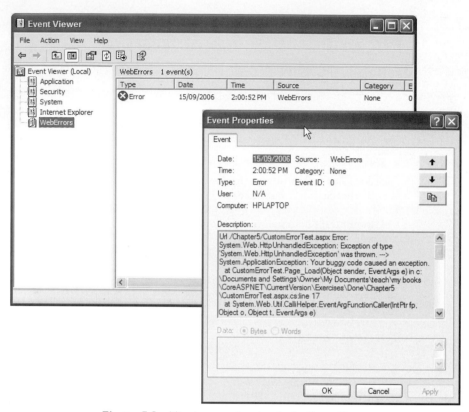

Figure 5.3   Viewing an exception in the Event Viewer

```
<%@ Application Language="C#" %>

<%@ Import Namespace="System.Net.Mail" %>

<script runat="server">

    …

    void Application_Error(object sender, EventArgs e)
    {
        // Construct the mail message
        MailMessage mail = new MailMessage();
        mail.To.Add(new MailAddress(
            "administrator@buggysoftware.com"));
        mail.From = new MailAddress(
            "autogenerated@buggysoftware.com");
```

```
    mail.Subject = "Critical Application Exception";
    mail.IsBodyHtml = true;

    string body = "<html><head></head><body>";
    body += "<h1>" + Request.Path + "</h1>";
    body += "<h2>" + DateTime.Now + "</h2>";
    body += Server.GetLastError().ToString();
    body += "</body></html>";
    mail.Body = body;

    // Send the email
    SmtpClient mailer = new SmtpClient();
    mailer.Host = "host name or IP address goes here";
    try
    {
        mailer.Send(mail);
    }
    catch (Exception ex)
    {
        // Not much you can do with this except output
        // it to debugger
        Debug.WriteLine(ex.Message);
    }
}

</script>
```

As an alternative to hardcoding the email addresses and the IP address, you could define these items in the appSettings section of the Web.config file. The appSettings section can be used to define any custom application-specific values. For instance, you can add the following items to appSettings section.

```
<configuration>
    <appSettings>
        <add key="Error_ToEmail"
            value="administrator@buggysoftware.com"/>
        <add key="Error_FromEmail"
            value="autogenerated@buggysoftware.com"/>
        <add key="Error_SmtpHost"
            value="host name or IP address goes here"/>
    </appSettings>
    ...
</configuration>
```

You can access these values via the ConfigurationManager.AppSettings method (in the System.Configuration namespace). You can change your Application_Error method to use this method to retrieve these values, as shown in the following.

```
string to = ConfigurationManager.AppSettings["Error_ToEmail"];
mail.To.Add(new MailAddress(to));
string from =
   ConfigurationManager.AppSettings["Error_FromEmail"];
mail.From = new MailAddress(from);
…
mailer.Host = ConfigurationManager.AppSettings["Error_SmtpHost"];
```

Finally, another way of handling an application error is to output the exception information to your own custom exception log file. In the example in Listing 5.1, the `Application_Error` handler outputs each exception to a text file in the `App_Data` folder of the application if the `Error_ShouldLogErrors` flag in the `Web.config` file is set to `true`. This flag is defined in the `appSettings` section of the `Web.config` file, as shown here.

```
<add key="Error_ShouldLogErrors" value="true" />
```

Listing 5.1   Global.asax

```
<%@ Application Language="C#" %>

<%@ Import Namespace="System.IO" %>

<script runat="server">

   void Application_Error(object sender, EventArgs e)
   {
      try
      {
         // Get the error log flag from Web.config
         string sLogErrors =
            ConfigurationManager.AppSettings[
               "Error_ShouldLogErrors"];
         bool logErrors = Convert.ToBoolean(sLogErrors);

         // Only log errors if Web.config file tells you to
         if (logErrors)
         {
            // Keep the exception log file in App_Data
            string path =
               Server.MapPath("~/App_Data/ExceptionLog.txt");

            // Append the following to this file
            StreamWriter sw = File.AppendText(path);
            sw.WriteLine("----------------------------------");
            sw.WriteLine(DateTime.Now + " " + Request.Path);
            sw.WriteLine(Server.GetLastError().ToString());
            sw.WriteLine();
```

```
            sw.Flush();
            sw.Close();
        }
    }
    catch (Exception ex)
    {
        // Not much you can do with this except output
        // it to debugger
        Debug.WriteLine(ex.Message);
    }

}

</script>
```

The resulting text file can be seen in Figure 5.4.

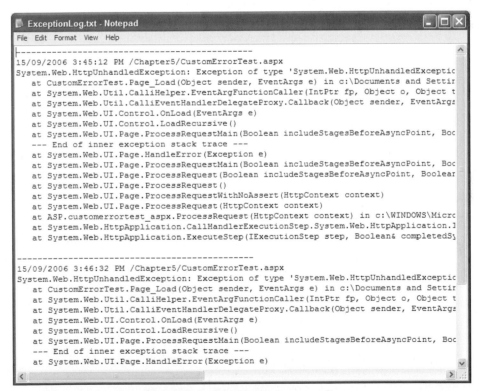

Figure 5.4   Event logging to a text file

Using Custom Error Pages

If you do not use the `Context.ClearError` method in the `Page_Error` or the `Application_Error` handler, ASP.NET redirects to the default ASP.NET error page. By default, ASP.NET only shows this detailed error page to local users (i.e., the developer). Remote users see a different ASP.NET error page that does not contain all the exception details, as shown in Figure 5.5.

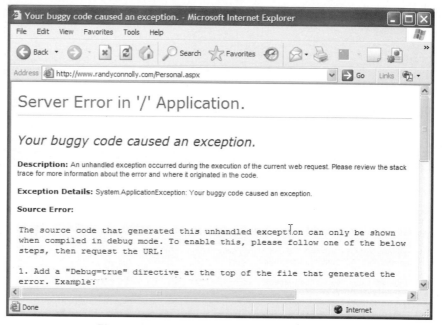

Figure 5.5   Default error page for remote users

You can replace the default ASP.NET error page with your own custom page, as shown in Figure 5.6.

To use a custom error page, you can change the settings of the `<customErrors>` element in the `Web.config` file. In this element, you can specify the custom page that is to be displayed, as shown in the following.

```
<system.web>
   <customErrors mode="On"
      defaultRedirect="FriendlyErrorPage.aspx" />
   ...
</system.web>
```

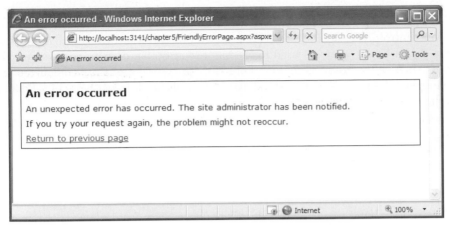

Figure 5.6   Custom error page

Setting the `mode` attribute to `On` means that the ASP.NET details page is not shown, even to local users. If you want local users to still see the default details page, change the `mode` to `RemoteOnly`.

Handling Common HTTP Errors

ASP.NET allows you to create custom error pages for different HTTP error codes. For example, a common feature of many Web sites is to provide custom HTTP 404 (requested page not found) and HTTP 500 (server error) error pages. You can specify custom pages for HTTP error codes within the `<customErrors>` element, as shown in the following.

```
<customErrors mode="On"
      defaultRedirect="FriendlyErrorPage.aspx" >
   <error statusCode="404" redirect="custom404.aspx" />
   <error statusCode="500" redirect="custom500.aspx" />
</customErrors>
```

Using the Validation Server Controls

Data is at the heart of most Web applications. Typically, Web applications require users to fill in form data, which is then used as a basis for other application actions. User data is also often persisted in some form, such as to databases or to XML files. Unfortunately, users can be quite peculiar. They can forget to enter certain important fields in a form, type in something preposterous into a field, or even willfully try to subvert an application's security by entering a rogue script into a form text field.

Fortunately, many of the most common user-input validation scenarios are handled by the ASP.NET **validation controls**. These controls are a special type of Web server control. They significantly reduce some of the work involved in validating user data. In particular, they are used to validate or verify that certain input server controls (such as `TextBox`, `RadioButtonList`, or `DropDownList`) contain correct data. ASP.NET provides different validation controls for different types of validation, such as range checking or pattern matching. For instance, the `RequiredFieldValidator` control can be used to ensure that the user does not leave a form control empty. The `RangeValidator` control can be used to ensure that an input value falls between a minimum and maximum value.

You use validation server controls as you do other server controls. That is, you add the markup to your `.aspx` file where you would like an error indicator to be displayed (typically adjacent to the field it is validating). Each validation control references another input server control elsewhere on the page. For instance, the following example illustrates the use of a `RequiredFieldValidator` validation control.

```
<asp:TextBox ID="txtUserName" runat="server" />

<asp:RequiredFieldValidator Id="reqUser" runat="server"
    ControlToValidate="txtUserName"
    Text="Please enter a User Name" />
```

Notice that the `ControlToValidate` property is used to associate the validation control with the `TextBox` via its `Id`. The `Text` property contains the message that is displayed in this location (i.e., after the `TextBox`) on the page if the `TextBox` is left blank.

There are six different validation controls. These controls provide four of the most common types of validation, a way to construct your own custom validator, and a way to succinctly summarize the display of validation error messages. These validation controls work with the `TextBox`, `DropDownList`, `ListBox`, and `RadioButtonList` server controls (as well as with the `HtmlInputText`, `HtmlSelect`, and `HtmlText-Area` HTML server controls) and can be combined together in one form. For instance, you can use a `RequiredFieldValidator` and a `CompareValidator` to validate the same `TextBox`. The different controls related to validation are listed in Table 5.1.

Table 5.1   Validation Controls

Name	Description
CompareValidator	Compares a user entry against another value or control.
CustomValidator	Validates a user entry using custom validation logic.

Table 5.1 Validation Controls *(continued)*

Name	Description
`RangeValidator`	Checks if a user entry is between a lower and upper boundary.
`RegularExpressionValidator`	Checks if a user entry matches a pattern defined by a regular expression.
`RequiredFieldValidator`	Ensures that the input control is not empty.
`ValidationSummary`	Displays the error messages from all validation controls in a single location.

ASP.NET Form Validation Process

How do these validation controls work? When a form that uses these validators is submitted, the user's input is validated first by using Javascript on the client side if enabled and if supported by the browser. If there is an error, an error message is displayed without a round-trip to the server. If no error (or no Javascript or if client validation is disabled), the data is passed to the server and the data is checked once again on the server side. If the data is not valid, an error message is generated and ultimately sent back to the browser (along with all the other form data).

Why is both client-side and server-side data validation necessary? Client-side validation is useful because it reduces round-trips to the server. This provides immediate feedback to the user as well as improves server performance. Unfortunately, client-side validation by itself is not sufficient. The user could be using a browser that does not support scripting (that is, using an ancient browser or, more commonly, has scripting turned off via the browser preferences). As well, client-side scripting is potentially vulnerable to "script exploits." These can happen when a malicious user enters a Javascript `<script>` block into a text field that can later cause harm when the entered data is echoed back to the browser.

To get the best performance and to protect your application against the problems just mentioned, user data must be validated on both the client and the server side. This used to be quite a bit of work for the developer. Client-side validation requires developing in a different programming language (Javascript), whereas server-side validation often necessitates messy coding to redisplay the form with the user's valid data along with error messages for the invalid data.

Thankfully, ASP.NET's validation controls eliminate most of this work, because they automatically generate the Javascript necessary for client-side validation as well as perform, behind the scenes, the server-side validation.

Client-Side Validation Process

To get a better understanding of how this process works, let us examine the following example. It consists of a text box, a button, and a validator. The `Button` control is necessary because validation only occurs during a postback attempt.

```
User  <asp:TextBox id="txtUserName" runat="server" />

<asp:RequiredFieldValidator id="reqUser" runat="server"
    ControlToValidate="txtUserName"
    Text="Please enter a User Name"/>

<br />
<asp:Button ID="btnTest" runat="server" text="submit"/>
```

The HTML rendered by these controls would look like the following.

```
User  <input name="txtUserName" type="text" id="txtUserName" />

<span id="reqUser" style="color:Red;visibility:hidden;">
Please enter a User Name
</span>

<input type="submit" name="btnTest" value="submit"
    onclick="javascript:WebForm_DoPostBackWithOptions(new
    WebForm_PostBackOptions(&quot;btnTest&quot;,&quot;&quot;,true,
    &quot;&quot;, &quot;&quot;, false, false))" id="btnTest" />
```

The rendered markup (the `<span>` element) for the `RequiredFieldValidator` certainly isn't that special (although the markup for the submit button is more impressive). The functionality of validation controls does not lie, however, within the markup generated by the validation controls but within the Javascript generated by these controls. The Javascript that performs the client-side validation is contained within a number of client-side script blocks that are included in the rendered page, as shown here.

```
<script src="/Chapter5/WebResource.axd?d=gbodNPJ7D4aM6hzCyXZ
    xqMVKlEwlFGeOiL-XDh4oScA1&amp;t=632674287498788464"
    type="text/javascript">
</script>
<script type="text/javascript">
<!--
    function WebForm_OnSubmit() {
        if (typeof(ValidatorOnSubmit) == "function" &&
            ValidatorOnSubmit() == false) return false;
        return true;
    }
-->
</script>
```

```
<script type="text/javascript">
<!--
   var Page_Validators =  new Array(
      document.getElementById("reqUser"));
// -->
</script>

<script type="text/javascript">
<!--
   var reqUser = document.all ? document.all["reqUser"] :
      document.getElementById("reqUser");
   reqUser.controltovalidate = "txtUserName";
   reqUser.evaluationfunction =
      "RequiredFieldValidatorEvaluateIsValid";
   reqUser.initialvalue = "";
// -->
</script>

<script type="text/javascript">
<!--
   var Page_ValidationActive = false;
   if (typeof(ValidatorOnLoad) == "function") {
      ValidatorOnLoad();
   }
   function ValidatorOnSubmit() {
      if (Page_ValidationActive) {
         return ValidatorCommonOnSubmit();
      }
      else {
        return true;
      }
   }
// -->
</script>
```

This Javascript code makes use of several Javascript functions that are not defined in the markup, but are instead contained in Microsoft's client validation Javascript library, referenced in lines 1 and 2. Essentially, the Javascript in this library ultimately changes the CSS visibility of the span containing the error message, depending upon the state of the user's input.

CORE NOTE

The Javascript validation library used to implement these validation controls in ASP.NET 2.0 now uses reasonably standards-compliant Javascript. As a result, the validation controls in ASP.NET 2.0 now work appropriately in FireFox, Opera, and Safari.

It is very important to recognize that this client-side validation only occurs after there has been at least one attempt at a postback. That is, after the user attempts to invoke a postback, the Javascript client-side validation process occurs. If client-side validation fails, the page is not posted back to the server; instead, Javascript is used to display the appropriate validation error message. After the initial message is displayed, the messages automatically disappear without a postback when the user fixes the specified problem.

All of the validation controls provide the capability, via the EnableClient-Script property, to completely disable Javascript validation. As well, a user's browser may not support Javascript (or it might be turned off via the browser's option settings). For this reason, validation on the server is also necessary.

Server-Side Validation Process

As mentioned, validation *may* occur on the client, but *always* occurs on the server. When the user submits a page that passes any client-side validation to the server, the page is initialized and loaded, then each of the validation controls (within the validation group that generated the postback) is checked to see if they are valid. If a validation error is detected in any of these controls, the page is set to an invalid state. Now any control events are called, and the rendered page is finally posted back with any validation error messages now visible. Figure 5.7 illustrates how validation fits into the general page request processing. Validation on the server occurs when the Validation method of the Page base class is called.

It is very important to note that the code for the page still loads and executes normally despite the detection of the validation error! Normally, if client-side validation is enabled, a page with validation errors never gets posted back to the server; however, because client-side validation can be disabled by the user, it is vitally important to check the state of the IsValid property of the page before using any data posted by the client.

For example, let us imagine a Web Form that needs to get the quantity value of an order from the user. After the user enters it and clicks the submit button, the form displays the final price, which is the product of the quantity and the unit cost, in a Label. We can use a CompareValidator control to ensure that the user-entered quantity in the TextBox contains a valid integer, as shown in the following. (Here, we are using the EnableClientScript property to simulate a browser with the Javascript turned off.)

```
Quantity:<br />
<asp:TextBox ID="txtQuantity" runat="server"/>

<asp:CompareValidator ID="compQuantity" runat="server"
   ControlToValidate="txtQuantity"
   Operator="DataTypeCheck"
   Type="Integer"
   EnableClientScript="false"
```

```
   Text="Enter a valid whole number" />

<br />
<asp:Button ID="btnSubmit" Text="Click this to test validation"
   runat="server" OnClick="btnSubmit_Click" />

<br />
<asp:Label ID="labContent" runat="server" />
```

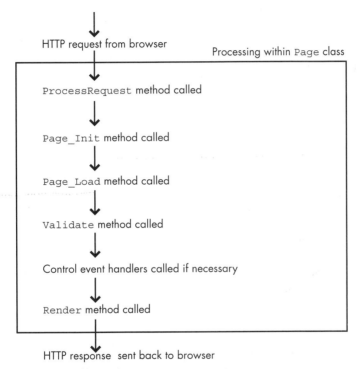

Figure 5.7 Server-side validation process

The event handler for this sample might look like the following.

```
protected void btnSubmit_Click(object sender, EventArgs e)
{
    int quantity = Convert.ToInt32(txtQuantity.Text);
    // In real world, would probably get this value from database
    int unitCost = 5;
    int price = quantity * unitCost;
    labContent.Text = "Price for order is $" + price;
}
```

Unfortunately, because client-side scripting is disabled on the user's browser, this button click event handler is called even if the user entered an invalid quantity (i.e., not a valid integer). The end result in this case is a runtime when the method tries to convert the user-entered value into an integer.

The solution to this problem is to only process the user input if the page's IsValid property is true, as shown here.

```
protected void btnSubmit_Click(object sender, EventArgs e)
{
    // Only process if data is valid
    if (IsValid)
    {
        int quantity = Convert.ToInt32(txtQuantity.Text);
        int unitCost = 5;
        int price = quantity * unitCost;
        labContent.Text = "Price for order is $" + price;
    }
}
```

Common Validation Properties

The five validation controls inherit from a common base, the BaseValidator class, which in turn inherits from the Label control (see Figure 5.8).

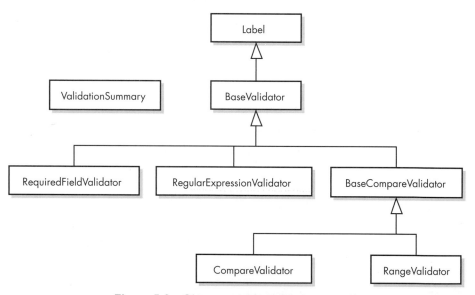

Figure 5.8   Object model for validation controls

The `BaseValidator` class provides several notable properties, which are used in the subsequent examples, as shown in Table 5.2.

Table 5.2 Unique Properties of All Validation Controls

Property	Description
`ControlToValidate`	Indicates the `id` of the input control to validate.
`Display`	Indicates the display behavior of the error message. Possible values are: `None` (validation message is not displayed), `Static` (the space for the message is allocated—that is, it takes up layout space—regardless of whether the message is or is not displayed), and `Dynamic` (the space for the message is dynamically added to the page only if the message is being displayed). The default is `Static`.
`EnableClientScript`	Indicates whether client-side (Javascript) validation is enabled. The default is `true`.
`Enabled`	Indicates whether the validation control is enabled.
`ErrorMessage`	The error message text to be displayed in a `ValidationSummary` control if validation fails.
`ForeColor`	The text color of the error message to be displayed if validation fails. The default is `Color.Red`.
`IsValid`	Indicates whether the validation control passed its validation check. Typically, you do not need to use this property.
`SetFocusOnError`	Indicates whether the focus (i.e., the input cursor) should move to the control specified by the `ControlToValidate` property if validation fails. The default is `false`.
`Text`	The error message text to be displayed if validation fails.
`ValidationGroup`	Specifies the name of the validation group to which the validation control belongs.

Static Versus Dynamic Display of Validation Controls

When a validation control becomes invalid, the content of its `Text` property is displayed at the same position in the markup as the validation control. You can customize this display behavior somewhat by using the `Display` property of any validation control. The `Display` property has three possible values:

- `None`—The validation message text is not displayed.
- `Static`—The space for the error message is allocated regardless of whether the message is displayed.
- `Dynamic`—The space for the message is dynamically added to the page only if validation failed. This only works if client-side validation is enabled.

Figure 5.9 illustrates how the `Display` property changes the rendering of the validation control.

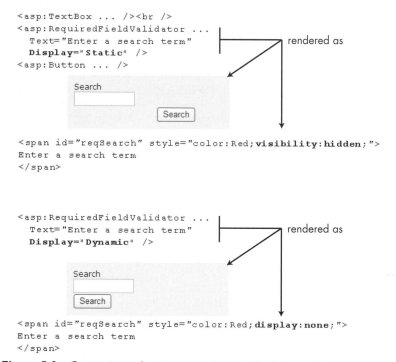

Figure 5.9   Comparison of static versus dynamic display of validation messages

RequiredFieldValidator Control

You can ensure that a user must provide information in a specific input control by using the `RequiredFieldValidator` control. The `RequiredFieldValidator` is most often used to test for an empty text box, although it can test for any value specified by its `InitialValue` property. If the validation fails, the area in the markup taken up by the `RequiredFieldValidator` control is replaced by the contents of the `Text` property of the `RequiredFieldValidator`. Like all the validation controls, you must set the ControlToValidate property of the RequiredField-Validator control to the Id of the control that is to be tested, as shown here.

```
<asp:TextBox ID="txtUserName" runat="server"></asp:TextBox>

<asp:RequiredFieldValidator ID="reqUserName" runat="server"
    ControlToValidate="txtUserName"
    Text="Required field" />
```

A RequiredFieldValidator can appear anywhere in your source document. However, you usually place it quite close to the control that it is validating; that way, the error message within the Text property of the RequiredFieldValidator is displayed close to the control that generated the error.

Because the RequiredFieldValidator control inherits from the BaseValidator control, you can make use of any of the properties listed in Table 5.2. As well, Table 5.3 details the unique properties of the RequiredFieldValidator.

Table 5.3   Unique Properties of the RequiredFieldValidator Control

Property	Description
InitialValue	Indicates the initial value of the associated input control. That is, validation fails if the input control matches the value in this property. The default is an empty string.

The RequiredFieldValidator control can also be used to verify that the user has chosen a list item. In this case, the InitialValue of the RequiredFieldValidator is compared against the Value property of the selected list item, as shown here.

```
<asp:DropDownList ID="lstBooks" runat="server">
   <asp:ListItem Value="0" Selected="True">
      Pick a book
   </asp:ListItem>
   <asp:ListItem Value="1">The Republic</asp:ListItem>
   <asp:ListItem Value="2">Critique of Judgment</asp:ListItem>
   <asp:ListItem Value="3">Theory of Justice</asp:ListItem>
</asp:DropDownList>

<asp:RequiredFieldValidator ID="reqBook" runat="server"
   ControlToValidate="lstBooks"
   Text="Please choose a book from the list"
   InitialValue="0" />
```

ValidationSummary Control

Rather than displaying a detailed error message in the same location as the validation control, you may want to summarize the error messages from all the validation controls in a single location, such as the top or bottom of the form. The `Validation-Summary` control provides this capability. This control can place a summary of the errors in a bulleted list, a simple list, or a paragraph that appears on the Web page or in a pop-up message box.

The unique properties for the `ValidationSummary` control are listed in Table 5.4.

Table 5.4   Unique Properties of the ValidationSummary Control

Property	Description
DisplayMode	Specifies the mode to display the validation error messages. Possible values are specified by the `ValidationSummary-DisplayMode` enumeration: `BulletList` (each error message appears as bulleted item), `List` (each error message appears on its own line), and `SingleParagraph` (each message appears as sentence in a paragraph).
EnableClientScript	Specifies whether the control updates itself using Javascript. The default is `true`.
ForeColor	The foreground color of the validation message.
HeaderText	The header text to be displayed first before the individual error messages.
ShowMessageBox	Specifies whether the error messages show up in a pop-up Javascript alert box. The default is `false`. If `EnableClientScript` is set to false, this property is ignored.
ShowSummary	Specifies whether the error messages show up within the Web page. The default is `true`.
ValidationGroup	Specifies the name of the validation group to which this control belongs.

There are two steps in using the `ValidationSummary` control. The first step is to add an `ErrorMessage` attribute to each of the validation controls. This attribute specifies the message that is to be displayed in the error summary when the validation fails for that control. The second step is to add the control to the location in your page where you want the error summary message to appear and use the `DisplayMode`,

ShowSummary, and ShowMessageBox attributes to indicate how to display the error
summary. The following example illustrates a sample use of this control.

```
<p>Book<br />
<asp:DropDownList ID="lstBooks" runat="server">
   <asp:ListItem Value="0" Selected="True">
      Please pick a book
   </asp:ListItem>
   <asp:ListItem Value="1">The Republic</asp:ListItem>
   <asp:ListItem Value="2">Critique of Judgement</asp:ListItem>
   <asp:ListItem Value="3">Theory of Justice</asp:ListItem>
</asp:DropDownList>

<asp:RequiredFieldValidator ID="reqBook" runat="server"
   ControlToValidate="lstBooks"
   Text="*"
   InitialValue="0" Display="static"
   ErrorMessage="Please choose a book from list"/>
</p>

<p>User Name:<br />
<asp:TextBox ID="txtUserName" runat="server"></asp:TextBox>

<asp:RequiredFieldValidator ID="reqUserName" runat="server"
   ControlToValidate="txtUserName"
   Text="*"
   Display="static"
   ErrorMessage="Please enter a User Name"/>
</p>

<p>Password:<br />
<asp:TextBox ID="txtPassword" runat="server"></asp:TextBox>

<asp:RequiredFieldValidator ID="reqPassword" runat="server"
   ControlToValidate="txtPassword"
   Text="*"
   Display="static"
   ErrorMessage="Please enter a password"/>
</p>

<p>
<asp:ValidationSummary id="valSum" runat="server"
   DisplayMode="BulletList"
   HeaderText="The following errors were found:"
   ShowMessageBox="false"
   ShowSummary="true" />
</p>
```

The result of this code within the browser looks similar to what is shown in Figure 5.10. Notice how the `Text` property of the `RequiredFieldValidator` controls has been set to just an asterisk, whereas the `ErrorMessage` property now contains the longer error message.

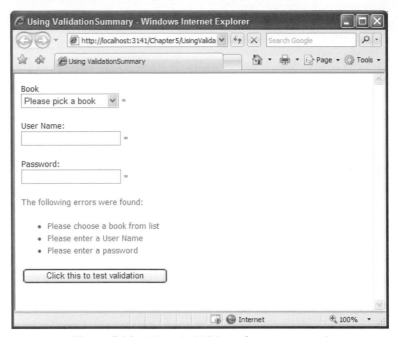

Figure 5.10   Using the ValidationSummary control

CompareValidator Control

The `CompareValidator` control can be used to ensure that a form element is within certain guidelines. With this control, you can

- Compare a form value to a constant
- Verify that a form value is the correct data type
- Compare a form value to a value in another control

Both the `CompareValidator` and the `RangeValidator` controls, which are covered shortly, inherit from `BaseCompareValidator`; as a result, both of these validators have some shared functionality, namely type comparison. Tables 5.5 and 5.6 contain the unique properties of the `BaseCompareValidator` and the `Compare-Validator` controls.

Table 5.5   Unique Properties of the BaseCompareValidator Control

Property	Description
CultureInvariantValues	Indicates whether double, date, and currency values should be converted into a culture-neutral format first before being compared. The default is `false`.
Type	Specifies the data type that the values being compared must match. Possible values are described by the `ValidationDataType` enumeration: `Currency`, `Date`, `Double`, `Integer`, and `String`.

Table 5.6   Unique Properties of the CompareValidator Control

Property	Description
ControlToCompare	Specifies the control that contains the content that is being compared against the content in the `ControlToValidate` control.
Operator	Specifies the comparison operator. Possible values are described by the `ValidationCompareOperator` enumeration: `DataTypeCheck` (a data type comparison only), `Equal`, `GreaterThan`, `GreaterThanEqual`, `LessThan`, `LessThanEqual`, and `NotEqual`. If this property is set to `DataTypeCheck`, the `ControlToCompare` and `ValueToCompare` properties are ignored.
ValueToCompare	Specifies the constant that the `ControlToValidate` control is to be compared against.

As previously mentioned, the `CompareValidator` control can be used in three different ways. The first way it can be used is to compare an input value against a constant contained within the `ValueToCompare` property. The type of comparison is specified using the `Operator` property. Note that the `Operator` is used to indicate the value the data must have. For instance, if you want to ensure that a value entered into a text box is less than or equal to a specific number, you would use the `LessThanEqual` operator, as shown in the following example.

```
Age: <asp:TextBox ID="txtAge" runat="server"></asp:TextBox>

<asp:CompareValidator ID="compAge" runat="server"
   ControlToValidate="txtAge"
   ValueToCompare="18"
   Operator="LessThanEqual"
   Text="You are too old to view this site" />
```

Another way that you can use the CompareValidator control is to ensure that an input value is of the proper type. In this case, you set the Operator property to DataTypeCheck, and use the Type property to indicate the data type that data value must have, as shown in the following example.

```
Sales Date: <asp:TextBox ID="txtDate" runat="server"></asp:TextBox>
<asp:CompareValidator ID="compDate" runat="server"
   ControlToValidate="txtDate"
   Operator="DataTypeCheck"
   Type="Date"
   Text="Enter a valid date" />

<p>
Quantity: <asp:TextBox ID="txtQuantity" runat="server"></asp:TextBox>
<asp:CompareValidator ID="compQuantity" runat="server"
   ControlToValidate="txtQuantity"
   Operator="DataTypeCheck"
   Type="Integer"
   Text="Enter a valid whole number" />
```

The date type check expects a short date as defined in the host computer's regional settings (accessed via the Window's Control Panel). On my Web site's server, situated in Canada, the regional setting for short dates is DD/MM/YYYY. However, I can have ASP.NET ignore the regional setting and use a so-called culture-neutral format by setting the CultureInvariantValues property (defined by the BaseCompareValidator superclass) to true. When this property is enabled, the date format can be either YYYY/MM/DD or MM/DD/YYYY, and the double and currency values will use the US culture format (i.e., use a period (.) for the decimal symbol and dollar sign ($) for the currency symbol). If you need a more flexible date validator that can accept date inputs in a number of different formats, you would have to use a CustomValidator control and program the appropriate date checking.

The last way that you can use the CompareValidator control is to compare one control's content against another control's content. For this type of comparison, you use the Operator and the ControlToCompare properties. The ControlTo-Compare property contains the Id of the control whose content will be compared against, as shown in the following example.

```
Enter Password:<br />
<asp:TextBox ID="txtPass1" runat="server"
   TextMode="password"></asp:TextBox>
<p>
Reenter Password:<br />
<asp:TextBox ID="txtPass2" runat="server"
   TextMode="password"></asp:TextBox>
</p>
```

```
<asp:CompareValidator ID="compPass" runat="server"
   ControlToValidate="txtPass2"
   Operator="Equal"
   ControlToCompare="txtPass1"
   Text="Passwords must match" />
```

In this case, the value contained within the two password text boxes must match; otherwise, validation fails and the error message is displayed.

RangeValidator Control

The `RangeValidator` control can be used to ensure that a form value falls within a range of values. The minimum and maximum values that determine the range can be numbers, dates, or strings. Because this control inherits from the same base class as the `CompareValidator`, the `RangeValidator` control also has the capability to perform data type checks.

Table 5.7 lists the unique properties of the `RangeValidator`.

Table 5.7   Unique Properties of the RangeValidator Control

Property	Description
MaximumValue	Specifies the maximum value of the validation range.
MinimumValue	Specifies the minimum value of the validation range.

Using the `RangeValidator` control is quite similar to using the `CompareValidator`, except that one sets the `MinimumValue` and `MaximumValue` properties along with the `Type` property, as shown in the following example.

```
Enter a number between 1 and 20:<br />
<asp:TextBox ID="txtNumber" runat="server"></asp:TextBox>
<asp:RangeValidator ID="rangeNum" runat="server"
   ControlToValidate="txtNumber"
   MinimumValue="1"
   MaximumValue="20"
   Type="Integer"
   Text="Please enter number between 1 and 20" />

<p>
Enter a valid date from 2006 (YYYY/MM/DD): <br />
<asp:TextBox ID="txtDate" runat="server"></asp:TextBox>
<asp:RangeValidator ID="rangeDate" runat="server"
   ControlToValidate="txtDate"
   CultureInvariantValues="true"
```

```
MinimumValue="2006/01/01"
MaximumValue="2006/12/31"
Type="Date"
Text="Please enter a valid date from 2006" />
```

Note that this example makes use of the `CultureInvariantValues` property so as to have a predictable date format.

RegularExpressionValidator Control

The `RegularExpressionValidator` control can be used to check if a form entry matches that defined by a regular expression. A ***regular expression*** is a set of special characters that define a pattern. These regular expression patterns can then be compared with data contained in a control. This control is often used to verify that a user's input matches a predictable sequence of characters, such as those in a phone number, postal or ZIP code, or email address.

Table 5.8 lists the unique properties of the `RegularExpressionValidator`.

Table 5.8   Unique Properties of the RegularExpressionValidator Control

Property	Description
ValidationExpression	The regular expression that the input must match.

Regular expressions are a type of language that is intended for the matching and manipulation of text. A regular expression consists of two types of characters: literals and metacharacters. A literal is just a character you want to match in the target. A metacharacter is a special symbol that acts as a command to the regular expression parser. Many of these metacharacters begin with the escape character (\) followed by another character. Table 5.9 contains lists several of the more common regular expression metacharacters.

Table 5.9   Common Regular Expression Metacharacters

Regular Expression	Description
^ ... $	If used at the very start and end of the regular expression, it means that the entire string (and not just a substring) must match the rest of the regular expression contained between the ^ and the $ symbols.
\t	Matches a tab character.
\n	Matches a new line character.

Table 5.9   Common Regular Expression Metacharacters *(continued)*

Regular Expression	Description
.	Matches any character other than \n.
[qwerty]	Matches any single character of the set contained within the brackets.
[^qwerty]	Matches any single character not contained within the brackets.
[a-z]	Matches any single character within range of characters.
\w	Matches any word character. Equivalent to [a-zA-Z0-9].
\W	Matches any nonword character.
\s	Matches any whitespace character.
\S	Matches any nonwhitespace character.
\d	Matches any digit.
\D	Matches any nondigit.
*	Indicates zero or more matches.
+	Indicates one or more matches.
?	Indicates zero or one match.
{n}	Indicates exactly *n* matches.
{n,}	Indicates *n* or more matches.
{n,m}	Indicates at least *n* but no more than *m* matches.
|	Matches any one of the terms separated by the | character. Equivalent to Boolean OR.
()	Groups a subexpression. Grouping can make a regular expression easier to understand.

Perhaps the best way to understand regular expressions is to work through the creation of one. For instance, if you want to define a regular expression that would match a North American phone number without the area code, you would need one that matches any string that contains three numbers, followed by a dash, followed by four numbers without any other character. The regular expression for this would be

```
^\d{3}-\d{4}$
```

In this example, the dash is a literal character; the rest are all metacharacters. The ^ and $ symbols indicate the beginning and end of the string; they indicate that the entire string (and not a substring) can only contain that specified by the rest of the metacharacters. The metacharacter \d indicates a digit, whereas the metacharacters {3} and {4} indicate three and four digits, respectively.

A more sophisticated regular expression for a phone number would not allow the first digit in the phone number to be a 1. The modified regular expression for this would be

^**[2-9]**\d{2}-\d{4}$

The [2-9] metacharacter indicates that the first character must be a digit within the range 2 through 9.

You can make your regular expression a bit more flexible by allowing either a single space (440 6061), a period (440.6061), or a dash (440-6061) between the two sets of numbers. You can do this via the [] metacharacter:

^[2-9]\d{2}**[\-\s\.]**\d{4}$

This expression indicates that the fourth character in the input must match one of the three characters contained within the square brackets (\- matches a dash, \s matches a space, and \. matches a period). You must use the escape character for the dash and period because they have a metacharacter meaning when used within the square brackets.

If you want to allow multiple spaces (but only a single dash or period) in your phone, you can modify the regular expression as follows.

^[2-9]\d{2}**\s***[\-\.]**\s***\d{4}$

The metacharacter sequence \s* matches zero or more spaces. You can further extend the regular expression by adding an area code. This is a bit more complicated, because you also allow the area code to be surrounded by brackets (e.g., (403) 440-6061), or separated by spaces (e.g., 403 440 6061), a dash (e.g., 403-440-6061), or a period (e.g., 403.440.6061). The regular expression for this would be

^**\(?\s*\d{3}\s*[\)\-\.]?\s***[2-9]\d{2}\s*[\-\.]\s*\d{4}$

The modified expression now matches zero or one (characters (\(?), followed by zero or more spaces (\s*), followed by three digits (\d{3}), followed by zero or more spaces (\s*), followed by either a), - or . character ([\)\-\.]), finally followed by zero or more spaces (\s*).

Finally, you may want to make the area code optional. To do this, you group the area code by surrounding the area code subexpression within grouping metacharacters—that is, ( )—and then make the group optional using the ? metacharacter.

^**(**\(?\s*\d{3}\s*[\)\-\.]?\s***)?**[2-9]\d{2}\s*[\-\.]\s*\d{4}$

Hopefully, by now you can see that many Web applications could potentially benefit from regular expressions. Table 5.10 contains several common regular expressions that you might use within a Web application.

Table 5.10　Common Regular Expressions

Regular Expression	Description
`^\S{0,8}`	Matches 0 to 8 nonspace characters.
`[a-zA-Z]\w{8,16}`	Simple password expression. The password must be at least 8 characters but no more than 16 characters long.
`[a-zA-Z]+\w*\d+\w*`	Another password expression. This one requires at least one letter, followed by any number of characters, followed by at least one number, followed by any number of characters. You could combine this and the previous two expressions within a single regular expression, or by having two separate `Regular-ExpressionValidator` controls.
`(.+)@([^\.].*)\.([a-z]{2,})`	Email validation based on current standard naming rules.
`((http|https)://)?([\w-]+\.)+[\w]+(/[\w- ./?]*)?`	URL validation. After either `http://` or `https://`, it matches word characters or hyphens, followed by a period, followed by either a forward slash, word characters, or a period.
`4\d{3}[\s\-]d{4}[\s\-]d{4}[\s\-]d{4}`	Visa credit card number (four sets of four digits beginning with the number 4), separated by a space or hyphen.
`5[1-5]\d{2}[\s\-]d{4}[\s\-]d{4}[\s\-]d{4}`	MasterCard credit card number (four sets of four digits beginning with the numbers 51 through 55), separated by a space or hyphen.

CORE NOTE

There are a number of useful regular expression resources available on the Web. Perhaps the best is `http://www.regexplib.com`.

Let's use some of these sample regular expressions with the `RegularExpressionValidator` control. The following example illustrates several sample uses of this control.

```
Phone Number:<br />
<asp:TextBox ID="txtPhone" runat="server"></asp:TextBox>
<asp:RegularExpressionValidator ID="regPhone" runat="server"
    ControlToValidate="txtPhone"
    ValidationExpression=
        "^(\(?\s*\d{3}\s*[\)]\-\.]?\s*)?[2-9]\d{2}\s*[\-\.]\s*\d{4}$"
    Text="Enter a valid phone number" />

<p>
Email:<br />
<asp:TextBox ID="txtEmail" runat="server"></asp:TextBox>
<asp:RegularExpressionValidator ID="regEmail" runat="server"
    ControlToValidate="txtEmail"
    ValidationExpression=
        "^[\w-]+(\+[\w-]*)?@([\w-]+\.)+[\w-]+$"
    Text="Enter a valid email" />

<p>
Web Site URL:<br />
<asp:TextBox ID="txtUrl" runat="server"></asp:TextBox>
<asp:RegularExpressionValidator ID="regUrl" runat="server"
    ControlToValidate="txtUrl"
    ValidationExpression=
        "^((http|https)://)?([\w-]+\.)+[\w]+(/[\w- ./?]*)?$"
    Text="Enter a valid URL" />
```

The Visual Studio 2005 designer also has a regular expression editor that contains many common regular expressions. You can access this editor by clicking the ellipse button for the `ValidationExpression` property in the Properties window.

CORE NOTE

The `RegularExpressionValidator` control operates slightly differently on the client (which uses the Javascript regular expression function) than on the server (which uses the .NET Framework regular expression class). In particular, the .NET regular expression class contains several enhanced metacharacters that are not supported by the Javascript regular expression feature in all browsers.

Using the RegEx Class

There are often times when you may want to use the power of regular expressions without using the `RegularExpressionValidator` control. The `RegEx` class allows you to use regular expressions in your code-behind or other classes. You can use the `RegEx` class to perform not only searches but also to replace one character pattern with another. Even complex programming logic can sometimes be replaced by a simple regular expression.

Listings 5.2 and 5.3 illustrate one sample use of the `RegEx` class. These gather the HTML for a user-entered URL, and then use a regular expression to extract all the headings (e.g., <h1>,<h2>, <h3>, etc.) in the specified page, which are then displayed in a `Literal` control. Besides using the `RegEx` class, Listing 5.3 also uses the `Match` and `MatchCollection` classes. The `Match` class represents a single regular expression match; `MatchCollection` contains a collection of all the matches for the associated regular expression.

Listing 5.2   ScrapeHeadings.aspx

```
<asp:Panel ID="panUrl" runat="server" GroupingText="Search"
     CssClass="myPanel">
  Enter Url:
  <asp:TextBox ID="txtUrl" runat="server" Columns="50" />
  <br />
  <asp:Button ID="btnSearch" runat="server"
     OnClick="btnSearch_Click" Text="Search" />
</asp:Panel>
<p></p>
<asp:Panel ID="panHeadings" runat="server"
     GroupingText="Headings in this Url" CssClass="myPanel">
  <asp:Literal ID="litContent" runat="server" />
</asp:Panel>
```

Listing 5.3   ScrapeHeadings.aspx.cs

```
using System;
using System.Data;
using System.Configuration;
using System.Collections;
using System.Web;
using System.Web.Security;
using System.Web.UI;
using System.Web.UI.WebControls;
using System.Web.UI.WebControls.WebParts;
using System.Web.UI.HtmlControls;
```

```csharp
// Do not forget to add these
using System.Net;
using System.IO;
using System.Text;
using System.Text.RegularExpressions;

public partial class ScrapeHeadings : System.Web.UI.Page
{
  /// <summary>
  /// Each time the page loads, empty the literal control
  /// </summary>
  protected void Page_Load(object sender, EventArgs e)
  {
    litContent.Text = "";
  }


  /// <summary>
  /// Event handler for search button
  /// </summary>
  protected void btnSearch_Click(object sender, EventArgs e)
  {
    // Need to trap error in case of unresponsive URL
    try
    {
      // Use WebClient to download content at URL into a string
      WebClient client = new WebClient();
      string content = client.DownloadString(txtUrl.Text);

      // Match any of the H? tags
      Regex reg = new Regex(@"<h\d>.+</h\d>",
          RegexOptions.IgnoreCase);

      // Get a collection of all the matches
      MatchCollection mc = reg.Matches(content);

      // Iterate through the collection of matches
      foreach (Match m in mc)
      {
        // HTML encode the tag and display in literal
        litContent.Text += HttpUtility.HtmlEncode(m.Value) +
          "<br/>";
      }
    }
    catch
    {
      litContent.Text = "Could not connect to " + txtUrl.Text;
    }
  }
}
```

The call to the `HtmlEncoding` method is necessary because you do not want the browser to render the matching strings as headings; instead, you want to view the matching string as HTML. The `HtmlEncoding` method, for instance, transforms `<h1>WHAT</h1>` into `&lt;h1&gt;WHAT&lt;/h1&gt;`.

An example of the output from the above listings is shown in Figure 5.11.

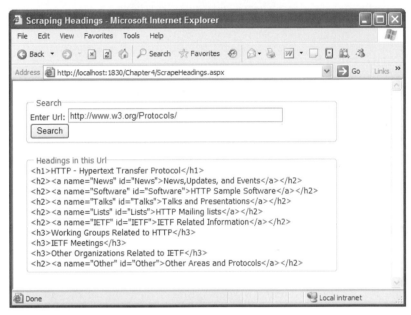

Figure 5.11   Result of Listings 5.2 and 5.3

Regular Expressions and Security

One way to protect your site from so-called injection attacks is to use the `Regular-ExpressionValidator` control for all text input. Injection attacks exploit weak or missing input validation by inserting malicious SQL or Javascript code into form input fields. One small way to protect your site from these attacks is, for instance, to use the `RegularExpressionValidator` control to limit the size of inputted text as well as to ensure that inputted text is limited to alphanumeric fields, spaces, periods, and apostrophes, as shown in the following.

```
<asp:TextBox ID="txtName" runat="server"></asp:TextBox>
<asp:RegularExpressionValidator ID="regName" runat="server"
   ControlToValidate="txtName"
   ValidationExpression="^[a-zA-Z'.\s]{1,50}"
   Text="Enter a valid name" />
```

If the input is coming in from a nonform field source, such as a cookie or querystring, you can use the RegEx class to perform the same type of check.

```
string source = (string)Cookie["someValue"];
RegEx reg = new RegEx("^[a-zA-Z'.\s]{1,50}");
if ( ! reg.IsMatch(source) )
{
    // Some type of error handling would go here
}
```

CORE NOTE

It should be noted that such a use of regular expressions is only one small way of protecting an application from malicious user input.

CustomValidator Control

The ASP.NET validation controls covered so far handle many of the most common validation scenarios. However, there are times when the type of validation you need cannot be handled by these controls. In this situation, you can use the CustomValidator control to provide your own user-defined validation. CustomValidator controls are often used to validate a user's input against some value from an external source such as a database. They can also be used to implement business rules (although my strong preference is keep business logic out of the presentation as much as possible).

Tables 5.11 and 5.12 list the unique properties and events of the CustomValidator.

Table 5.11   Unique Properties of the CustomValidator Control

Property	Description
ClientValidationFunction	Specifies the name of the client-side (Javascript or VBScript) function to be used for client-side validation.
ValidateEmptyText	Indicates whether empty text should be validated. The default is false.

Table 5.12   Events of the CustomValidator Control

Event	Description
ServerValidate	Raised when validation occurs on the server.

In this section, the first CustomValidator is one that ensures that the user enter a date equal to or greater than the current date. The markup for this Custom-Validator is quite straightforward.

```
<asp:TextBox ID="txtDate" runat="server"></asp:TextBox>

<asp:CustomValidator ID="custDate" runat="server"
   ControlToValidate="txtDate"
   ValidateEmptyText="true"
   Text="Enter a valid future date"
   OnServerValidate="custDate_ServerValidate" />
```

Notice that this sample custom control does not perform any client-side validation; it only performs server-side validation. To perform the actual validation on the server, you must provide a handler (in the code-behind) for the ServerValidate event of the CustomValidator control. This event handler is passed a ServerValidateEventArgs object, which contains two useful properties: Value (the string from the input control to be validated) and IsValid (used to set whether the input is valid). The following sample event handler checks if the data entered in the TextBox contains a valid future date.

```
protected void custDate_ServerValidate(object source,
      ServerValidateEventArgs args)
{
   // Retrieve user input
   string sEnteredDate = args.Value;

   // Try converting user input into a valid date
   DateTime dt;
   bool convertSuccessful = DateTime.TryParse(sEnteredDate,
      out dt);

   // If conversion was successful, check if it is in the future
   // and then set the IsValid flag appropriately

   if (convertSuccessful && dt >= DateTime.Today)
      args.IsValid = true;   // valid date
   else
      args.IsValid = false; // not a valid date
}
```

This example uses the TryParse method of the DateTime class. It tries to convert the string to a date. The nice thing about this method is that you do not have to worry about error trapping or the appropriate short date format. It can convert a wide range of date strings (e.g., "02/03/2009" or "May 26 2008") to a DateTime object. The one peculiarity of this method is that it returns a Boolean value indicating the conversion success as well as "returning" the converted DateTime object via the out parameter dt.

Our next example, `CustomValidator`, ensures that the user enters content into at least one of two `TextBox` controls in a form. For instance, imagine a log-in form in which the user must enter either a username or an email address. The `Required-FieldValidator` does not help here because you do not know in advance which of the two text boxes will be empty. Your markup might look like the following:

```
Enter user name:<br />
<asp:TextBox ID="txtUser" runat="server" />
<br />
Enter email:<br />
<asp:TextBox ID="txtEmail" runat="server" />

<asp:CustomValidator ID="OrFieldValidator" runat="server"
   Text="Enter either a user name or a email"
   OnServerValidate="OrFieldValidator_ServerValidate" />
</p>
```

Notice that this `CustomValidator` doesn't bother setting the `ControlTo-Validate` and `ValidateEmptyText` properties because this custom control is in fact validating two different controls.

The server-side event handler for this validator is quite simple. It simply checks the content of two specific `TextBox` controls; if both are empty, the `IsValid` property is set to `false`.

```
protected void OrFieldValidator_ServerValidate(object source,
     ServerValidateEventArgs args)
{
   if (txtUser.Text.Length <= 0 && txtEmail.Text.Length <= 0)
     args.IsValid = false;
   else
     args.IsValid = true;
}
```

Custom Client-Side Validation

At the beginning of this chapter, I described how the various validation controls can perform validation on both the client and the server. The `CustomValidator` control also supports this dual validation strategy, in that validation can occur on the server or on the client. To validate on the client, you must first set the `ClientValidation-Function` property of the `CustomValidator` control. This property is given the name of the client-side function that handles the validation on the client, as shown here.

```
<asp:CustomValidator ID="OrFieldValidator" runat="server"
   Text="Enter either a user name or a email"
   ClientValidationFunction="validateOrFields"
   OnServerValidate="OrFieldValidator_ServerValidate" />
```

You also must implement a client-side function in the markup that performs the same logic as the `OrFieldValidator_ServerValidate` method using Javascript. The signature of the Javascript function *must* be as follows.

```
function name(source,args)
```

Thus, a client-side function that allows only one of two fields to be empty might look like the following.

```
<script type="text/javascript">
  // Javascript function to test if both user and email are blank
  function validateOrFields(source, args)
  {
    var sUser = document.form1.<%= txtUser.ClientID %>.value;
    var sEmail = document.form1.<%= txtEmail.ClientID %>.value;

    if (sUser == "" && sEmail == "")
    {
      args.IsValid = false;
    }
    else
    {
      args.IsValid = true;
    }
    return;
  }
</script>
```

The main trick in this Javascript is how ASP.NET inline expressions are used to reference the content of the two `input` elements that are rendered from the `Text-Box` controls. Here, it is done by using the `ClientID` (the id of the rendered `input` elements) of the `TextBox` controls via an ASP.NET expression. This might make more sense if you examine how this example gets rendered into HTML. First, let us assume that the two `TextBox` controls are rendered as

```
<input name="txtUser" type="text" id="txtUser" />
<input name="txtEmail" type="text" id="txtEmail" />
```

The preceding two lines of Javascript thus are rendered as

```
var sUser = document.form1.txtUser.value;
var sEmail = document.form1.txtEmail.value;
```

Automatic Client-Side Updating

You might have noticed that the standard validation controls update themselves (i.e., display or hide the validation error message) without a postback when the user fixes the content of the control. This effect is achieved by calling one of the Javascript functions contained within Microsoft's client validation script library. You can achieve this same effect with your custom validator by calling this same Javascript function. (This tip is based on Daniel Hac's "CustomValidator Dependent on Multiple Controls," `http://www.codeproject.com`.)

```
<script type="text/javascript">
  // ValidatorHookupControlID function is contained within
  // Microsoft's validation script library
  ValidatorHookupControlID("<%= txtUser.ClientID %>",
     document.getElementById("<%= OrFieldValidator.ClientID
        %>"));
  ValidatorHookupControlID("<%= txtEmail.ClientID %>",
     document.getElementById("<%= OrFieldValidator.ClientID
        %>"));
</script>
```

The Javascript function `ValidatorHookupControlID` is passed, via an ASP.NET expression, the `ClientID` (the `id` of the rendered element) of the `TextBox`, and the `CustomValidator`; everything else is handled by Microsoft's client library.

CORE NOTE

This Javascript snippet must appear at the end of your markup document.

The complete listing for this custom validator is shown in Listings 5.4 and 5.5.

Listing 5.4   UsingCustomValidators.aspx

```
<%@ Page Language="C#" AutoEventWireup="true"
   CodeFile="UsingCustomValidator.aspx.cs"
   Inherits="UsingCustomValidator" %>

<!DOCTYPE html PUBLIC "-//W3C//DTD XHTML 1.0 Transitional//EN"
   "http://www.w3.org/TR/xhtml1/DTD/xhtml1-transitional.dtd">

<html xmlns="http://www.w3.org/1999/xhtml" >
<head runat="server">
   <title>Using a CustomValidator</title>

   <script type="text/javascript">
   // Javascript to test if both user and email are blank
   function validateOrFields(source, args)
   {
      var sUser = document.form1.<%= txtUser.ClientID %>.value;
      var sEmail = document.form1.<%= txtEmail.ClientID %>.value;
```

```
      if (sUser == "" && sEmail == "")
      {
         args.IsValid = false;
      }
      else
      {
         args.IsValid = true;
      }
      return;
   }
   </script>

</head>
<body>
   <form id="form1" runat="server">
   <p>
   Enter user name:<br />
   <asp:TextBox ID="txtUser" runat="server"></asp:TextBox>
   <br />
   Enter email:<br />
   <asp:TextBox ID="txtEmail" runat="server"></asp:TextBox>

   <asp:CustomValidator ID="OrFieldValidator" runat="server"
      Text="Enter either a user name or a email"
      ClientValidationFunction="validateOrFields"
      OnServerValidate="OrFieldValidator_ServerValidate" />
   </p>

   <p>
   <asp:Button ID="btnSubmit"
      Text="Click this to test validation"
      runat="server" />
   </p>
   </form>
</body>
</html>

<script type="text/javascript">
   // ValidatorHookupControlID function is contained within
   // Microsoft's validation script library. Place at end of file.
   ValidatorHookupControlID("<%= txtUser.ClientID %>",
      document.getElementById("<%= OrFieldValidator.ClientID
         %>"));
   ValidatorHookupControlID("<%= txtEmail.ClientID %>",
      document.getElementById("<%= OrFieldValidator.ClientID
         %>"));
</script>
```

Listing 5.5   UsingCustomValidators.aspx.cs

```
public partial class UsingCustomValidator : System.Web.UI.Page
{
   protected void OrFieldValidator_ServerValidate(object source,
      ServerValidateEventArgs args)
   {
      // If either user or email is not empty, then valid
      if (txtUser.Text.Length <= 0 && txtEmail.Text.Length <= 0)
         args.IsValid = false;
      else
         args.IsValid = true;
   }
}
```

Validation Groups

One of the main changes made to the validation controls in ASP.NET 2.0 was the
introduction of validation groups. By default, when a postback occurs, all validation
controls are checked for validity. This can be a problem when a form contains multiple input controls that are not related and have quite unrelated event handlers. Figure 5.12 illustrates this problem. Here, you have a user registration form with various
`RequiredFieldValidator` controls along with a `ValidationSummary` control.
But there is also a search `TextBox` with its own postback-inducing button. In version
1.x (and by default in version 2.0) of ASP.NET, trying to use the search button unfortunately generates the validation error messages shown in Figure 5.12.

Validation groups provide a solution to this problem. Each validation control can
be placed into a validation group as well as the control that causes the postback (e.g.,
`Button`, `DropDownList`, etc.) by setting the control's `ValidationGroup` property
to a common value. When a control within a validation group generates a postback,
only those validation controls in that group are validated. In the following example,
each `Panel` container contains its own validation group.

```
<asp:Panel ID="panContent" runat="server" >
   User Name: <asp:TextBox ID="txtUserName" runat="server" />

   <asp:RequiredFieldValidator ID="reqUserName" runat="server"
         ControlToValidate="txtUserName"
         ValidationGroup="main"
         Text="Enter a user name" />

   Sales Date:<br />
   <asp:TextBox ID="txtDate" runat="server" />

   <asp:CompareValidator ID="compDate" runat="server"
      ControlToValidate="txtDate"
```

```
      Operator="DataTypeCheck"
      Type="Date"
      ValidationGroup="main"
      Text="Enter a valid date" />
</asp:Panel>

<asp:Panel ID="panSearch" runat="server" >
   <asp:TextBox ID="txtSearch" runat="server" Columns="10"/>

   <asp:RequiredFieldValidator ID="reqSearch" runat="server"
      ControlToValidate="txtSearch"
      ValidationGroup="search"
      Text="Enter a search term" />

   <asp:Button ID="btnSearch" runat="server" Text="Search"
      ValidationGroup="search" />
</asp:Panel>
```

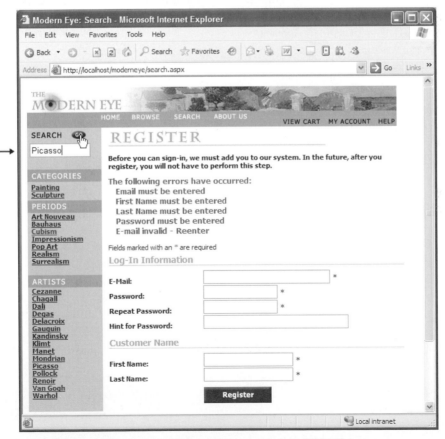

Figure 5.12   Problem with validation controls in ASP.NET 1.x

Listings 5.6 and 5.7 provide a more comprehensive use of validation groups. They also illustrate the use of all of the validation controls covered in this chapter, as well as demonstrate the appropriate "safe" coding approaches for working with validation controls. The result in the browser can be seen in Figure 5.13.

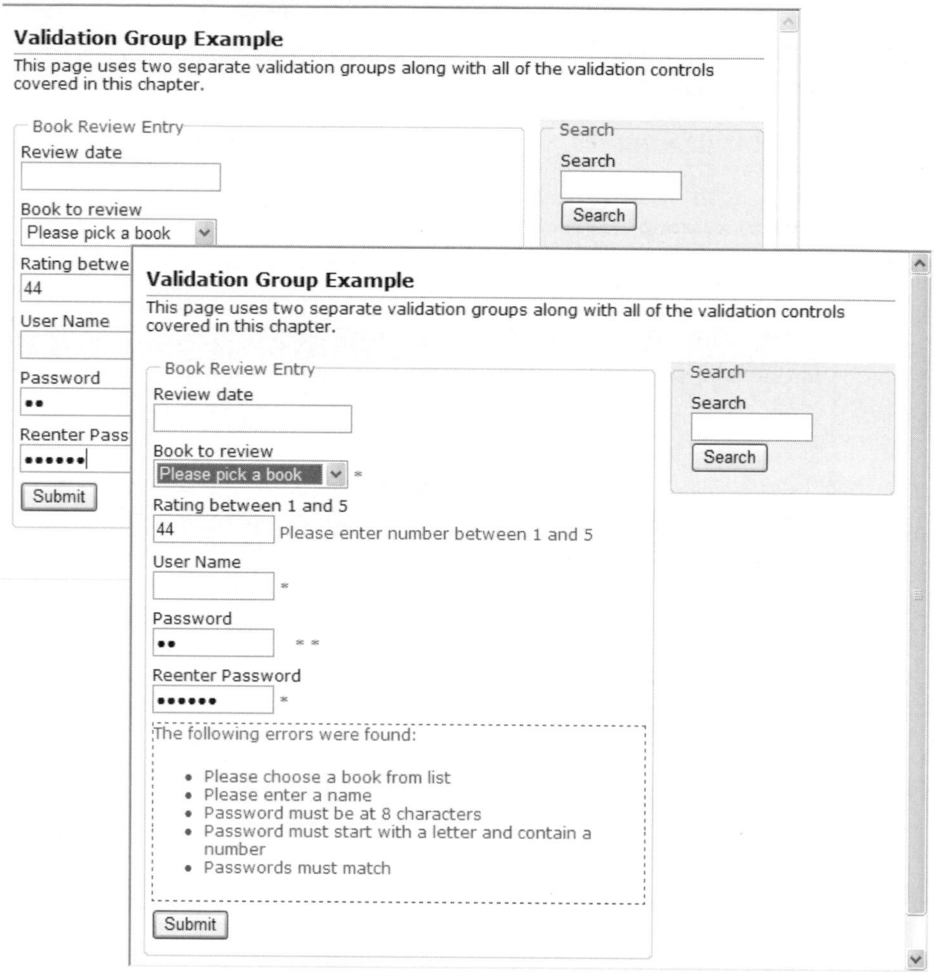

Figure 5.13   GroupingValidators.aspx

Listing 5.6 GroupingValidators.aspx

```
<asp:Panel ID="panHeader" runat="server">
   <h1>Validation Group Example</h1>
   <p>This page uses two separate validation groups along with
      all of the validation controls covered in this chapter.</p>
</asp:Panel>

<%-- Main Book Review Panel --%>
<asp:Panel ID="panContent" runat="server"
      GroupingText="Book Review Entry">
   <p>
   <asp:Label ID="labDate" runat="server" Text="Review date"
      AccessKey="D" AssociatedControlID="txtDate" />
   <br />
   <asp:TextBox ID="txtDate" runat="server"></asp:TextBox>
   <asp:CustomValidator ID="custDate" runat="server"
      ControlToValidate="txtDate"
      ValidateEmptyText="true"
      ValidationGroup="main"
      Text="*" ErrorMessage="Enter a valid future date"
      OnServerValidate="custDate_ServerValidate" />
   </p>

   <p>
   <asp:Label ID="labBook" runat="server" Text="Book to review"
      AccessKey="B" AssociatedControlID="lstBooks" />
   <br />
   <asp:DropDownList ID="lstBooks" runat="server" AccessKey="B" >
      <asp:ListItem Value="0" Selected="True">
         Please pick a book</asp:ListItem>
      <asp:ListItem Value="1">The Republic</asp:ListItem>
      <asp:ListItem Value="2">
         Critique of Judgement</asp:ListItem>
      <asp:ListItem Value="3">Theory of Justice</asp:ListItem>
   </asp:DropDownList>
   <asp:RequiredFieldValidator ID="reqBook" runat="server"
      ControlToValidate="lstBooks" SetFocusOnError="true"
      ValidationGroup="main"
      Text="*" InitialValue="0"
      ErrorMessage="Please choose a book from list"/>
   </p>

   <p>
   <asp:Label ID="labRating" runat="server"
      Text="Rating between 1 and 5" AccessKey="D"
      AssociatedControlID="txtDate" />
   <br />
```

```
<asp:TextBox ID="txtRating" runat="server" Columns="10"
   AccessKey="D"/>
<asp:RangeValidator ID="rangeNum" runat="server"
   ControlToValidate="txtRating"
   MinimumValue="1" MaximumValue="20"
   Type="Integer"
   ValidationGroup="main"
   Text="Please enter number between 1 and 5" />
</p>

<p>
<asp:Label ID="labUser" runat="server" Text="User Name"
   AccessKey="U" AssociatedControlID="txtUserName"   />
<br />
<asp:TextBox ID="txtUserName" runat="server" Columns="10"
   AccessKey="U" />
<asp:RequiredFieldValidator ID="reqUserName" runat="server"
   ControlToValidate="txtUserName"
   ValidationGroup="main"
   Text="*" ErrorMessage="Please enter a name"/>
<asp:RegularExpressionValidator ID="regName" runat="server"
   ControlToValidate="txtUserName"
   ValidationExpression="^[a-zA-Z'.\s]{1,16}"
   Text="Enter a valid name" />
</p>

<p>
<asp:Label ID="labPass1" runat="server" Text="Password"
   AccessKey="P" AssociatedControlID="txtPass1" />
<br />
<asp:TextBox ID="txtPass1" runat="server" TextMode="password"
   Columns="10" AccessKey="P"/>
<asp:RequiredFieldValidator ID="reqPassword" runat="server"
   ControlToValidate="txtPass1"  SetFocusOnError="true"
   ValidationGroup="main" Display="static"
   Text="*" ErrorMessage="Please enter a password"/>
<asp:RegularExpressionValidator ID="regPass1" runat="server"
   ControlToValidate="txtPass1"
   ValidationExpression="^[a-zA-Z]\w{8,}$"
   ValidationGroup="main"
   Text="*" ErrorMessage="Password must be at 8 characters" />
<asp:RegularExpressionValidator ID="regPass2" runat="server"
   ControlToValidate="txtPass1"
   ValidationExpression="^[a-zA-Z]+\w*\d+\w*$"
   ValidationGroup="main"
   Text="*"
   ErrorMessage="Password must start with a letter and contain
      a number" />
</p>
```

```
    <p>
    <asp:Label ID="labPass2" runat="server"
        Text="Reenter Password" AccessKey="R"
        AssociatedControlID="txtPass2" />
    <br />
    <asp:TextBox ID="txtPass2" runat="server" TextMode="password"
        Columns="10" AccessKey="R"/>
    <asp:CompareValidator ID="compPass" runat="server"
        ControlToValidate="txtPass2" Operator="Equal"
        ControlToCompare="txtPass1" ValidationGroup="main"
        Text="*" ErrorMessage="Passwords must match" />
    </p>
    <p>
    <asp:ValidationSummary id="valSum" runat="server"
        ValidationGroup="main"
        BorderStyle="Dashed" BorderWidth="1" BorderColor="red"
        DisplayMode="BulletList"
        HeaderText="The following errors were found:"
        ShowMessageBox="false" ShowSummary="true" />
    </p>
    <p>
    <asp:Button ID="btnSubmit" runat="server"
        ValidationGroup="main"
        Text="Submit" OnClick="btnSubmit_Click"  />
    </p>
</asp:Panel>

<%-- Search Sidebar Panel --%>
<asp:Panel ID="panSidebar" runat="server" GroupingText="Search">
    <div>
    <asp:Label ID="labSearch" runat="server" Text="Search"
        AccessKey="S" AssociatedControlID="txtSearch" />
    <br />
    <asp:TextBox ID="txtSearch" runat="server" Columns="10"/>
    <asp:Button ID="btnSearch" runat="server"
        Text="Search" ValidationGroup="search"
        OnClick="btnSearch_Click"/><br />
    <asp:RequiredFieldValidator ID="reqSearch" runat="server"
        ControlToValidate="txtSearch" Display="Dynamic"
        SetFocusOnError="true" ValidationGroup="search"
        Text="Enter a search term" />
    </div>
</asp:Panel>
```

Listing 5.7 GroupingValidators.aspx.cs

```csharp
public partial class GroupingValidators : System.Web.UI.Page
{
    /// <summary>
    /// Handler for search button
    /// </summary>
    protected void btnSearch_Click(object sender, EventArgs e)
    {
        // only do the redirection if validation group is okay
        if (IsValid)
        {
            Response.Redirect("Search.aspx?search=" +
                txtSearch.Text);
        }
    }

    /// <summary>
    /// Handler for submit button in book review panel
    /// </summary>
    protected void btnSubmit_Click(object sender, EventArgs e)
    {
        // only do the redirection if validation group is okay
        if (IsValid)
        {
            Response.Redirect("ProcessForm.aspx");
        }
    }

    /// <summary>
    /// Handler for custom validator
    /// </summary>
    protected void custDate_ServerValidate(object source,
        ServerValidateEventArgs args)
    {
        // First try converting user input into a valid date
        string sEnteredDate = args.Value;
        DateTime dt;
        bool convertSuccessful = DateTime.TryParse(sEnteredDate,
            out dt);

        // If conversion was successful, check if it is
        // in the future
        if (convertSuccessful && dt >= DateTime.Today)
            args.IsValid = true;
        else
            args.IsValid = false;
    }
}
```

Summary

This chapter examined one of the most important aspects of Web development: the handling of unexpected errors, as well as one important way of preventing them through the use of the ASP.NET validation server controls. These controls provide a mechanism for checking the validity of user input on both the client and on the server.

The next chapter examines how to create complex user interfaces using styles, themes, skins, master pages, and the new site navigation controls.

Exercises

The solutions to the following exercises can be found at my Web site, http://www.randyconnolly.com/core. Additional exercises only available for teachers and instructors are also available from this site.

1. Create a page named CalculatorExceptions.aspx. This page should have the same functionality as the CommandTest.aspx calculator example from Chapter 3, except that rather than using the Int32.TryParse method to convert from a string to an integer, use the Convert.ToInt32 method. This requires using a try...catch block to protect against user input errors.

2. Create a page named CalculatorValidation.aspx. This page should have the same functionality as the CommandTest.aspx calculator example from Chapter 3, except that it should use validation controls to ensure that the user enters a valid number in the TextBox controls.

3. Create a page named FormValidation.aspx. This page should contain the following fields: Last Name, First Name, Phone, Hire Date, Nationality, Email, and Password. All of these fields are required. Phone, Email, and Password should use a regular expression validator. Hire Date should be a valid date after January 1, 2007. The password should be entered twice and should be the same in both. Upon postback, if the data is valid, hide the form and display the data that the user entered. Be sure to make the form as accessible as possible.

Key Concepts

- Default error page
- Exception

- Regular expression
- Stack trace
- Validation controls

References

Bromberg, Peter A. "ASP.NET Production Exception Logging for Dummies."
http://www.eggheadcafe.com.

Hac, Daniel. "CustomValidator Dependent on Multiple Controls."
http://www.codeproject.com.

Howard, Rob. "An Exception to the Rule, Part 2." http://msdn.microsoft.com.

Meier, J. D., *et al*. "How to: Protect from Injection Attacks in ASP.NET."
http://msdn.microsoft.com.

Robillard, Eli. "Rich Custom Error Handling with ASP.NET."
http://msdn.microsoft.com.

Walther, Stephen. "Changes to the Validation Controls in ASP.NET 2.0."
http://msdn.microsoft.com.

6

CUSTOMIZING AND MANAGING YOUR SITE'S APPEARANCE

ASP.NET 2.0 provides a number of ways to customize the style of pages and controls in your Web application. This chapter covers these approaches. It examines the various appearance properties of Web server controls, illustrates how to use CSS with ASP.NET, moves on to themes and master pages, and then finishes with user controls.

Changing the Appearance of Server Controls

The previous chapters introduced many of the standard Web server controls. This section returns to the coverage of Web server controls by demonstrating how to more fully customize the appearance of these controls. The chapter does so in two ways. The first way uses common formatting properties of the Web server controls, whereas the second way uses cascading style sheets.

Using Common Appearance Properties

As mentioned back in Chapter 3, most of the standard Web server controls inherit from the WebControl class. This WebControl class in turn inherits from the Control class. Both of these base classes define properties that can be used to modify the appearance of any Web server control. Table 6.1 lists the principal appearance properties of the WebControl and Control classes.

Table 6.1   Appearance Properties of the WebControl and Control Classes

Property	Description
BackColor	The background color (using either a hexadecimal HTML color identifier or a standardized color name) of the control.
BorderColor	The color of the control's border.
BorderWidth	The thickness (in pixels) of the control's border.
BorderStyle	The style (e.g., dotted, dashed, solid, double, etc.) of the control's border. Possible values are described by the BorderStyle enumeration.
CssClass	The CSS class name assigned to the control.
Enabled	Toggles the functionality of the control; if set to false, the control is disabled.
Font	List of font names for the control.
ForeColor	The color of the text of the control.
Height	The height of the control.
Style	A collection of attributes that is rendered as an HTML style attribute.
Visible	Specifies whether the control is visible.
Width	The width of the control.

Any of the properties listed in Table 6.1 can be set declaratively or programmatically. For instance, the following markup demonstrates how to set the foreground and the background colors of a Label control.

```
<asp:Label id="labTest" runat="server"
    ForeColor="#CC33CC" BackColor="Blue"/>
```

To set the same properties programmatically, you could do so in a number of different ways, two of which are shown here.

```
labTest.ForeColor = Color.FromName("#CC33CC");
labTest.BackColor = Color.Blue;
```

Color is a C# struct that has fields for the predefined color names supported by the major browsers, as well as methods for creating a Color object from a name or from three numbers representing RGB values.

CORE NOTE

To use Color, you must also reference the System.Drawing namespace.

Most of the various appearance properties are rendered in the browser as inline CSS styles. For instance, the Label control from the preceding two examples would be rendered to the browser as

```
<span id="labTest" style="color:#CC33CC;
   background-color:Blue;"></span>
```

Using the Style Class

Setting the various formatting properties for your Web controls, whether through programming or declarative means, is acceptable when there are only one or two properties to set. However, when you have many properties that need to be changed in multiple controls, this approach is not very ideal. A better approach is to use the Style class.

The Style class is ideal for changing multiple properties to multiple controls all at once. It encapsulates most of the formatting properties listed in Table 6.1 and can be applied to multiple Web server controls to provide a common appearance. To use this class, you simply instantiate a Style object, set its various formatting properties, and then apply the style to any server control by using the control's ApplyStyle method. The following example illustrates this usage.

```
Style myStyle = new Style();
myStyle.ForeColor = Color.Green;
myStyle.Font.Name = "Arial";

// Now apply the styles to the controls
myLabel.ApplyStyle(myStyle);
myTextBox.ApplyStyle(myStyle);
```

The Style class is best for situations where you need to programmatically change the appearance of a set of controls all at once. If you simply need to set up a consistent appearance to a series of controls, it is almost always better to use Cascading Style Sheets (CSS) or ASP.NET themes, both of which are covered in this chapter.

Using CSS with Controls

The previous section demonstrated how to use some of the common appearance properties of Web server controls. Although these properties are very useful for customizing the appearance of your Web output, they do not contain the full formatting power of Cascading Style Sheets. Fortunately, you can also customize the appearance of Web server controls using CSS.

There are two ways to harness the power of CSS with Web server controls. The first way is to assign a CSS declaration to the Style attribute/property of a control. For instance, the following example sets the CSS letter-spacing property to increase the whitespace between each letter in the Label to 2 pixels, along with setting the font style to italic.

```
<asp:label id="labMsg" runat="server" Text="hello world"
    style="letter-spacing: 2px; font-style: italic" />
```

To achieve the same effect by programming, you would use

```
labMsg.Style["letter-spacing"] = "2px";
labMsg.Style["font-style"] = "italic";
```

Notice that from a programming perspective, the Style property is a ***named collection***. A named collection acts like an array, except that individual items can be retrieved either through a zero-based index or a unique name identifier.

All styles added to a control, whether declaratively or programmatically, are rendered in the browser as an inline CSS rule. For instance, either of the two previous two examples would be rendered to the browser as

```
<span id="labMsg" style="letter-spacing:2px;font-style: italic">
hello world
</span>
```

The other way to use CSS with Web server controls is to assign a CSS class to the CssClass property of a control. For instance, assume that you have the following embedded CSS class definition.

```
<style type="text/css">
    .pullQuote { background: silver;
                margin: 10px;
                font-family: Verdana, Arial,Helvetica,sans-serif;
                font-size: 10pt; }
</style>
```

You could assign this CSS class via

```
<asp:label id="labMsg2" runat="server" CssClass="pullQuote" />
```

To achieve the same effect by coding, you would use

```
labMsg2.CssClass = "pullQuote";
```

Listings 6.1 and 6.2 demonstrate how to style Web server controls with CSS by using both the `Style` and `CssClass` properties. The markup contains three `Label` controls, each of which contain a paragraph of text. The form also contains two `DropDownList` controls. The first changes the CSS `text-transform` property (which changes the text from uppercase to lowercase) for two of the `Label` controls. The second `DropDownList` control sets the other `Label` control's `CssClass` property to one of two predefined CSS classes, both of which float the paragraph so that it becomes a pull quote relative to the other text (see Figure 6.1).

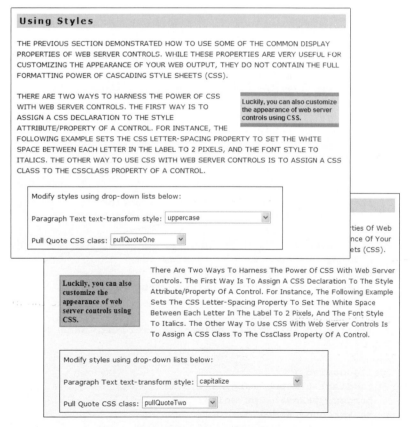

Figure 6.1   Using CSS.aspx

Although the example in Listing 6.1 uses embedded styles (that is, CSS rules within an HTML <style> element), you should generally locate a page's CSS in an external file and then link to it using the <link> element. By doing so, multiple pages in the site can use the same CSS file. As well, using an external CSS file generally reduces the page's bandwidth, because the browser can cache the CSS file.

CORE NOTE

You may notice that in Listing 6.1, the CSS styles use either % or em units rather than pixels. Doing so ensures that the relative font size and spacing work properly even if the user increases or decreases the browser's font size.

Listing 6.1   Using CSS.aspx

```
<html xmlns="http://www.w3.org/1999/xhtml">
<head runat="server">
   <title>Using CSS</title>
   <style type="text/css">
      body {
         background: #fffafa; margin: 1em;
         font: small/1.5em verdana, arial, sans-serif;
      }
      h1 {
         background: gold; color: black;
         font: bold 120% verdana, helvetica, sans-serif;
         letter-spacing: 0.25em; padding: 0.25em;
      }
      .controlPanel {
         padding: 0.5em; border: black 1px solid;
         background: #eee8a; margin: 1.5em; width: 75%;
      }
      .pullQuoteOne {
         padding: 0.25em; margin: 0.25em 1em;
         border: solid 7px #908070;
         border-right-width: 0; border-left-width: 0;
         background: lightgrey;
         float: right; width: 15em;
         font: bold 90% arial, helvetica, verdana, sans-serif;

      }
      .pullQuoteTwo {
         padding: 0.25em; margin: 1.5em;
         border: #82a91b 2px solid;
         background: #adc175;
```

```
         float: left; width: 10em;
         font: bold 105% times new roman, serif;
    }
    </style>
</head>
<body>
    <form id="form1" runat="server">
        <h1>Using Styles</h1>
        <p>
        <asp:Label ID="labOne" runat="server">
    The previous section demonstrated how to use some of the common
display properties of web server controls. While these properties are
very useful for customizing the appearance of your web output, they
do not contain the full formatting power of Cascading Style Sheets
(CSS).
        </asp:Label>
        </p>
        <p>
        <asp:Label ID="labPullQuote" runat="server">
        Luckily, you can also customize the appearance of web
        server controls using CSS.
        </asp:Label>
        </p>
        <p>
        <asp:Label ID="labTwo" runat="server">
    There are two ways to harness the power of CSS with web server
controls. The first way is to assign a CSS declaration to the Style
attribute/property of a control. For instance, the following example
sets the CSS letter-spacing property to set the white space between
each letter in the Label to 2 pixels, and the font style to italics.
The other way to use CSS with web server controls is to assign a CSS
class to the CssClass property of a control.
        </asp:Label>
        </p>

        <div class="controlPanel">
            <p>Modify styles using drop-down lists below:</p>
            <p>Paragraph Text text-transform style:
            <asp:DropDownList ID="drpParagraph" runat="server"
                 AutoPostBack="True" OnSelectedIndexChanged=
                 "drpParagraph_SelectedIndexChanged">
             <asp:ListItem Selected="True">
             Choose a text-transform style</asp:ListItem>
             <asp:ListItem Value="lowercase">
                 lowercase</asp:ListItem>
             <asp:ListItem Value="uppercase">
                 uppercase</asp:ListItem>
             <asp:ListItem Value="capitalize">
                 capitalize</asp:ListItem>
```

```
        </asp:DropDownList>
        </p>
        <p>Pull Quote CSS class:
        <asp:DropDownList ID="drpPull" runat="server"
            AutoPostBack="True" OnSelectedIndexChanged=
            "drpPull_SelectedIndexChanged">
          <asp:ListItem Selected="True">
            Choose a css class</asp:ListItem>
          <asp:ListItem Value="pullQuoteOne">
            pullQuoteOne</asp:ListItem>
          <asp:ListItem Value="pullQuoteTwo">
            pullQuoteTwo</asp:ListItem>
        </asp:DropDownList>
        </p>
      </div>
    </form>
  </body>
</html>
```

The code-behind class (shown in Listing 6.2) for this example is quite straight-forward. It contains selection event handlers for the two `DropDownList` controls. The first of these changes the `text-transform` CSS property of two `Label` controls based on the user's selection; the second sets the CSS class of the pull quote `Label` based on the user's selection.

Listing 6.2 Using CSS.aspx.cs

```
public partial class UsingCSS : System.Web.UI.Page
{
    /// <summary>
    /// Handler for text transform drop-down list
    /// </summary>
    protected void drpParagraph_SelectedIndexChanged(
        object sender, EventArgs e)
    {
        if (drpParagraph.SelectedIndex > 0)
        {
            labOne.Style["text-transform"] =
                drpParagraph.SelectedValue;
            labTwo.Style["text-transform"] =
                drpParagraph.SelectedValue;
        }
    }
    /// <summary>
    /// Handler for pull quote drop-down list
    /// </summary>
```

```
protected void drpPull_SelectedIndexChanged(object sender,
        EventArgs e)
{
    if (drpPull.SelectedIndex > 0)
        labPullQuote.CssClass = drpPull.SelectedValue;
}
}
```

Appearance Properties, CSS, and ASP.NET

The intent of CSS is to separate the visual presentation details from the structured content of the HTML. Unfortunately, many ASP.NET authors do not fully take advantage of CSS, and instead litter their Web server controls with numerous appearance property settings (e.g., BackColor, BorderColor, etc.). Although it is true that these properties are rendered as inline CSS styles, the use of these properties still eliminates the principal benefit of CSS: the capability to centralize all appearance information for the Web page or Web site into one location, namely, an external CSS file. Also, because the appearance properties are rendered as inline CSS, this increases the size and the download time of the rendered page.

By limiting the use of appearance properties for Web server controls within your Web Forms, and using instead an external CSS file to contain all the site's styling, your Web Form's markup becomes simpler and easier to modify and maintain. For instance, rather than setting the Font property declaratively for a dozen Web server controls in a page to the identical value, it makes much more sense to do so via a single CSS rule. And if this CSS rule is contained in an external CSS file, it could be used throughout the site (that is, in multiple Web Forms), reducing the overall amount of markup in the site.

However, ASP.NET 2.0 does provide an additional mechanism for centralizing the setting the appearance of Web server controls on a site-wide basis, called themes and skins, which is our next topic.

CORE NOTE

There are many superb CSS resources available. Two of the best books are Charles Wyke-Smith's *Stylin' with CSS* (Pearson Education, 2005) and Eric Meyer's *Eric Meyer on CSS* (New Riders, 2002).

Using Themes and Skins

The previous section illustrates how you can customize your controls by setting the style properties of the controls themselves. ASP.NET 2.0 introduced the *theme* mechanism. This mechanism allows the developer to style the appearance of Web server controls on a site-wide basis. Like CSS, ASP.NET themes allow you to separate Web server control styling from the pages themselves, but have the additional benefit of having a complete object model that can be manipulated programmatically. Themes still allow you to use CSS for the majority of your visual formatting, and because theme support is built in to ASP.NET, you can dramatically alter the appearance of your Web site with a single line of programming (or a single line in the Web.config file). For instance, Figure 6.2 illustrates how a single Web Form's appearance can be radically transformed using three different themes.

Figure 6.2   Same page—three different themes

An ASP.NET Web application can define multiple themes. Each theme resides in its own folder within the App_Themes folder in the root of your application. Within each theme folder, there are one or more *skin* files, as well as optional subfolders, CSS files, and image files (see Figure 6.3).

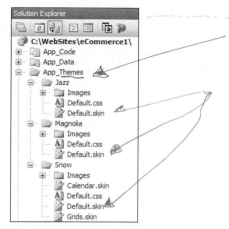

Figure 6.3 Theme file structure

Defining Skins

A skin describes the appearance of one or more control types. For example, a skin file might look like the following.

```
<asp:Label runat="server" ForeColor="Blue" Font-Size="10pt"
    Font-Name="Verdana" />
```

Notice that a skin simply contains a control definition *without* the id attribute. A given skin file can contain multiple control definitions. Alternately, many developers have a separate skin file for each control type (a theme can contain any number of skin files).

Not all properties can be skinned. Generally speaking, only properties relating to appearance (i.e., the properties in Table 6.1 plus additional properties depending upon the control) can be specified in a skin. Referencing a property that is not themeable in a skin file generates an error. As well, certain controls, such as the Repeater, are not themeable, generally because they do not inherit from the WebControl class.

CORE NOTE

It is important to note that property values specified by a skin override the property values set for the control in the aspx and ascx pages. This may seem counterintuitive from an object-oriented programming perspective, because you might expect the more specialized (the page) to override the general (the skin). However, you can make a control in a Web Form or user control ignore the settings in a skin by adding EnableTheming="false" to the control.

There is no Visual Studio designer support for creating skins. That is, the only way to create and modify a skin file is directly in Source view within Visual Studio. Even worse, Visual Studio's Intellisense is not available in Source view when modifying a skin. As an alternative, you could create a temporary Web Form, use the Design view or Source view as needed to add controls and set up their properties, copy and paste the markup to your skin file, and then remove the id attribute from each of the controls.

Creating Themes in Visual Studio

Themes reside in separate folders within the App_Themes folder within your site. You can create this folder yourself in Visual Studio by right-clicking the Web project in the Solution Explorer and choosing Add ASP.NET Folder → Theme option, as shown in Figure 6.4.

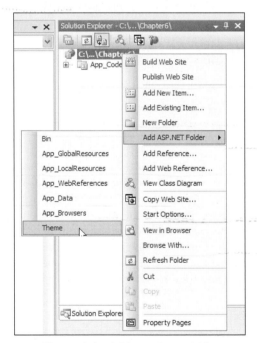

Figure 6.4 Adding a theme folder

Alternately, Visual Studio can automatically create a theme folder for you when you add a skin file via the Add New Item menu option (see Figure 6.5). In general, you probably want to avoid this approach because Visual Studio names the theme folder the same as the skin file.

Figure 6.5   Automatically adding a theme folder

CORE NOTE

Microsoft provides several design templates that use a variety of themes and can be downloaded at `http://msdn.microsoft.com/asp.net/reference/design/templates`.

Walkthroughs 6.1 and 6.2 demonstrate how to create a theme and a skin.

Walkthrough 6.1   *Adding a Theme*

1. Use the Add ASP.NET Folder → Theme menu option in Visual Studio.
2. Name the folder `Cool`.
3. Use the Add ASP.NET Folder → Theme menu option in Visual Studio.
4. Name the folder `Professional`.

Walkthrough 6.2   *Creating a Skin*

1. Right-click the `Cool` theme and choose the Add New Item menu option in Visual Studio.
2. Choose the Skin template and name the file `Label.skin`.
3. Remove the commented example.
4. Add the following code:

   ```
   <asp:Label runat="server" ForeColor="Green" />
   ```
5. Save and close the skin.

Applying a Theme

After a theme has been created (that is, after you've created one or more skin files), you can apply a theme to a page. This can be done in a few different ways. One way is to simply assign the theme using the `Theme=themeName` in the `Page` directive, for instance:

```
<%@ Page … Theme="Cool" %>
```

You can also set the theme for all pages in a site via the `Web.config` file. To do so, simply specify the theme via the `theme` attribute of the `pages` element within the `system.web` element, as shown in the following.

```
<system.web>
    …
    <pages theme="Cool" />
    …
</system.web>
```

CORE NOTE

Themes that are specified via the `Theme` attribute of the `Page` directive override the theme setting in the `Web.config` file.

A page's theme can also be set programmatically. To do so, you can set the `Theme` property (defined in the `Page` base class) for a form in its code-behind class. This is covered in more detail later in the chapter. Finally, another, less common way to set the theme is to set it for all sites on a machine via the `machine.config` file. This file is located at `[windows]\Microsoft.NET\Framework\[version]\CONFIG`. Just as with setting the theme for a site via the `Web.config` file shown earlier, you can set the global theme for the machine as a whole via the `Theme` attribute of the `pages` element within the `system.web` element of this `machine.config` file. The specified theme folder and its contents *must* be located in the global theme space for the machine, located at `[windows]\Microsoft.NET\Framework\[version]\ASP.NETClientFiles\Themes`.

How Themes Work

Now that you have seen how to create and use themes, let us peek under the hood and examine what ASP.NET does to make themes work. Like everything in ASP.NET, it all begins with a request. When a request arrives for a resource from an ASP.NET application that uses themes, the runtime parses and compiles all the skins in each theme. Recall from Chapter 2 that the markup in an `aspx` page is parsed into a class and then compiled into an assembly; an analogous thing happens with the skin files—each theme is parsed and compiled into a separate assembly.

Each theme is realized as a concrete subclass of the `PageTheme` class. This class maintains a collection of `ControlSkinDelegate` objects. This delegate represents or "points to" the actual method that applies the correct skin to the control; this method exists in the class file generated for the skin.

When the runtime executes a page that has a theme, it iterates through the page's `Controls` collection, and if there is a delegate for the control type, it calls the delegated method (in the generated skin class) which then decorates (i.e., changes the properties specified in the skin) the specific control object.

Overriding Themes

As previously mentioned, skin definitions for a control type override any settings for that control type made within a given page. For instance, consider the following skin definition.

```
<asp:Label runat="server" ForeColor="Green" />
```

Now imagine that you use this skin in a page that contains the following markup.

```
<asp:Label runat="server" id="labOne" Text="Hello" />
<asp:Label runat="server" id="labTwo" ForeColor="Blue"
   Text="World" />
```

What text color will the content of these two `Label` controls have when rendered by the browser? In fact, both will be green, because *skin definitions override page definitions*. You can have a control ignore a skin setting via the `EnableTheming` property, as in the following.

```
<asp:Label id="labTwo" … EnableTheming="false" ForeColor="Blue"/>
```

There is another way to have properties defined within individual controls override skin settings. You can do so by changing the `Page` directive of the form and use the `StyleSheetTheme` attribute rather than the `Theme` attribute. Unlike those applied by the `Theme` attribute, the properties applied by the `StyleSheetTheme` are overridden by control properties defined within the page. As such, the `StyleSheetTheme` behaves in a manner more akin to the cascade within CSS. For instance, in the following example, the "World" text is blue.

```
<%@ Page … StyleSheetTheme="Cool" %>
…
<body>
  <asp:Label runat="server" id="labOne" Text="Hello" />
```

```
<asp:Label runat="server" id="labTwo" ForeColor="Blue"
    Text="World" />
</body>
</html>
```

You can also set the `StyleSheetTheme` via the `Web.config` file. To set it in the `Web.config` file, you would use the `styleSheetTheme` attribute (rather than the `Theme` attribute), as in the following.

```
<system.web>
   ...
   <pages styleSheetTheme="Cool" />
   ...
</system.web>
```

Other than the fact that one allows skin properties to be overridden and the other does not, what else is different between the `Theme` and `StyleSheetTheme` attributes? A `Theme` is applied *after* the properties are applied to the server-side control, which is why the properties set by the `Theme` override those of the control. A `StyleSheetTheme` is applied *before* the properties from the server-side control, and are therefore overridden by the properties on the control. As well, the Visual Studio designer displays skins set by the `StyleSheetTheme`, but not by the `Theme`. If you specify both a `Theme` and `StyleSheetTheme`, the `Theme` takes precedence (i.e., control properties are overridden by the theme).

So which should you use? `StyleSheetTheme` is probably ideal during development because the Visual Studio designer displays the skins, and you can make quick changes to the page's Web server control appearance properties as part of your debugging and development. But because one of the primary benefits of themes is that you can change the entire appearance of a site through one simple theme change, it probably makes sense to use the `Theme` property when your site is ready for deployment; by then, you will no longer need the designer support and you will probably want to override any page properties by the formatting specified by the individual skins.

Named Skins

If you need to override the appearance of a skinned control, perhaps a better approach than using `StyleSheetTheme` is to use *named skins*. For instance, you might not want all of your `Label` controls to have the same appearance. You can thus define alternate skin definitions for the `Label` control by giving the different skins separate `SkinID` values. You can then reference this `SkinID` in your Web Form's `Label` controls. For instance, let's define a skin file with the following content.

```
<asp:Label runat="server" ForeColor="Green" Font-Size="10pt" />
```

```
<asp:Label runat="server" ForeColor="Red" Font-Size="14pt"
   Font-Name="Verdana" Font-Bold="True" SkinID="Quote" />
```

To use the named skin in any of your Web Forms, you simply need to add the reference to the `SkinID` in the controls that will use the named skin, for instance:

```
<asp:Label ID="labQuote" runat="server" Text="Hello"
   SkinID="Quote"/>
<asp:Label runat="server" id="labMsg" ForeColor="Blue"
   Text="World" />
```

In this case, the word "Hello" appears in bold, 14pt red Verdana, whereas the word "World" appears as 10pt green text.

CORE NOTE

The `SkinId` does not have to be globally unique. It only needs to be unique for each control within the theme. For instance, each named `Label` control in a theme must have a unique `SkinID`, but a `TextBox` control could have the same `SkinId` as one of the `Label` controls.

Themes and Images

One of the more interesting features of themes is that a given theme folder can also contain images and CSS files. You can thus radically transform a Web page by substituting different images and different style sheets. For instance, different themes could use a different set of images for bullets, image buttons, or for the icons used by the `TreeView` control. The only requirement is that the skin must use a relative URL for the image. This means that the image files must exist somewhere inside the same themes folder as the skin file itself.

For instance, the following skin defines two controls. The first is a named skin that displays the masthead image for the site; the second defines the look for all `BulletedList` controls. The relative path for the images indicates that the files are contained in a subfolder named `images` within this particular theme folder.

```
<asp:Image runat="server" ImageUrl="images/logo.gif"
   AlternateText="Masthead Image" SkinID="logo" />

<asp:BulletedList runat="server" BulletStyle="CustomImage"
   BulletImageUrl="images/bullet.gif" DisplayMode="HyperLink" />
```

To use this skin, your Web Form might look like that shown here. Notice how the resulting code in the Web Form is quite simple, because the additional properties are contained in the skin rather than in the Web Form. Figure 6.6 illustrates how the visual appearance of this form might vary simply by having different images for `logo.gif` and `bullet.gif` in two different themes containing the exact same skin.

```
<asp:Image runat="server" ID="imgLogo" SkinID="logo" />

<asp:BulletedList ID="blstSample" runat="server">
   <asp:ListItem Value="">Home</asp:ListItem>
   <asp:ListItem Value="">Browser</asp:ListItem>
   <asp:ListItem Value="">About</asp:ListItem>
</asp:BulletedList>
```

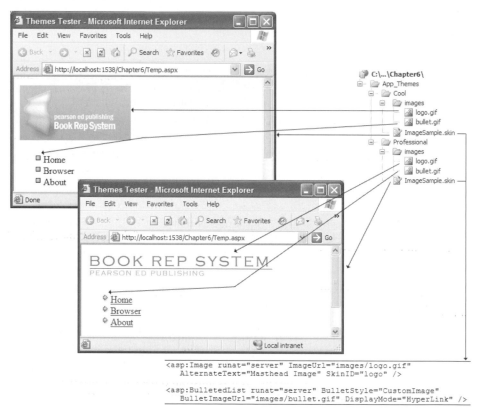

```
<asp:Image runat="server" ImageUrl="images/logo.gif"
    AlternateText="Masthead Image" SkinID="logo" />

<asp:BulletedList runat="server" BulletStyle="CustomImage"
    BulletImageUrl="images/bullet.gif" DisplayMode="HyperLink" />
```

Figure 6.6   Using images in theme skins

Themes and CSS

There is a certain amount of overlap between CSS and ASP.NET skins. Both allow you to specify consistent site-wide formatting. For example, if you want all of your text boxes to have a certain border style and color scheme, you could do so via a skin, as in the following.

```
<asp:TextBox runat="server" BackColor="Beige"
    ForeColor="DarkKhaki" BorderColor="LightGray"
    BorderWidth="1px" />
```

You could achieve the same effect by defining a CSS class in the theme's style sheet.

```
.myTextBoxes { border: 1px solid LightGray; color: DarkKhaki;
    background-color: Beige; }
```

You could then reference this class in the skin.

```
<asp:TextBox runat="server" CssClass="myTextBoxes" />
```

So which approach is better? In general, try to place as much appearance formatting as possible into a theme's CSS files. Many Web sites are created in conjunction with a Web designer, who undoubtedly is familiar already with CSS. A designer can easily modify and even swap the CSS files in any given theme without knowing anything about ASP.NET. If all of a site's formatting is contained within skin files, formatting changes will instead require the intervention of an ASP.NET developer (which is perhaps a good thing if your sole concern is to boost the employment of ASP.NET developers). As well, CSS provides more control over the appearance of a page than is possible with skins, which are limited to those appearance properties exposed by the Web server controls. If you use appearance properties to define the look of the controls in a theme's skin, the downloaded size of the resulting rendered markup will be larger than the CSS approach, because these properties will be emitted in each HTML element. Finally, even with skins, CSS probably is still necessary to format plain HTML text.

Ultimately, then, your site is much more maintainable if as much formatting as possible is contained within CSS. If your site design requires a change in the font or color, it is much more preferable to change just one file (the style sheet), rather than having to change both a style sheet and multiple skins. Finally, another benefit of CSS is that if your Web Forms use CSS rather than HTML tables for layout, different themes could completely change the layout of the site, as was illustrated back in Figure 6.2.

Thankfully, you do not have to choose between CSS and themes. Each theme can in fact contain multiple CSS files. ASP.NET automatically links all of a theme's CSS files into a page by adding the appropriate `<link>` element for each CSS file into the header of a page. Note that each page must have the `runat="server"` attribute in the `<head>` for this to occur, as shown here.

```
<head runat="server">
    <title>Some title here</title>
</head>
```

Despite the benefits of CSS, there are several things that skins can do, which CSS cannot. Some server control properties that are themeable have no CSS equivalent. For instance, you can specify the textual format to display the days of the week in a `Calendar` control or the locations for the hot spots in an `ImageMap` control. As well, because themes are applied on the server side, it is possible to dynamically specify a theme based on user input or configuration information without the bother of Javascript-based CSS file swapping.

In addition, the more complex templated controls, such as `Calendar`, `GridView`, `MultiView`, `Wizard`, and so on, are probably styled more easily through skins, because it is up to ASP.NET to determine exactly what markup to use when rendering these controls. Yet even here, there still is a role for CSS. For example, in the following `GridView` skin definition (we cover the `GridView` control later in Chapter 10), the three style templates contain appearance properties.

```
<asp:GridView runat="server" GridLines="Vertical" >
   <HeaderStyle BackColor="#FF9900" ForeColor="#FFFFFF" />
   <RowStyle BackColor="#FFFFFF" ForeColor="#333333" />
   <AlternatingRowStyle BackColor="#F2F2F2" ForeColor="#333333"/>
</asp:GridView>
```

A better approach is to define the template styling information via CSS classes.

```
.gridHeader
{
   background-color: #FF9900;
   color: #FFFFFF;
}
.gridRow
{
   background-color: #FFFFFF;
   color: #333333;
}
.gridAltRow
{
   background-color: #F2F2F2;
   color: #333333;
}
```

With the CSS classes defined, you could then simply reference these classes in the skin, as shown here.

```
<asp:GridView runat="server" GridLines="Vertical" >
   <HeaderStyle CssClass="gridHeader" />
   <RowStyle CssClass="gridRow" />
   <AlternatingRowStyle CssClass="gridAltRow" />
</asp:GridView>
```

Again, the benefit of this approach is that the typical Web designer, who probably does not know ASP.NET, can still make changes to the visual appearance of the ASP.NET application by modifying the appropriate CSS files.

Dynamically Setting the Theme

One of the key benefits that themes provide to the Web developer is the ability to programmatically change a page's theme. A page's theme can be set programmatically in the code-behind class. However, you may recall from Figure 2.3 in Chapter 2 that theme skins are applied before the controls and page are initialized. Thus, you must set the page's `Theme` property in the `PreInit` event handler for the page, as shown here.

```
protected void Page_PreInit(object o, EventArgs e)
{
    // Set theme for this page
    this.Theme = "Cool";
}
```

The `PreInit` event is new to ASP.NET 2.0. It is raised just before the `Init` event of the page, but after the controls for the page have been instantiated. Of course, with the simple example shown earlier, it makes much more sense to simply set the theme in the `Web.config` or in the `Page` directive. The real advantage of using the programmatic approach is that the page's theme can be set dynamically based on user preferences. This preference can even be persisted in a user profile (covered in Chapter 14), in a session (covered in Chapter 12), or in a database.

Like with the `Theme` property, you can also set the `StyleSheetTheme` property programmatically. However, unlike with setting the `Theme` property, the programmatic setting of the `StyleSheetTheme` property is not done in the `PreInit` method, but is achieved by overriding the property in your code-behind class, as in the following.

```
public override String StyleSheetTheme
{
    get { return "Cool"; }
}
```

Setting the theme dynamically based on user input is not quite so straightforward. The problem lies in the fact that the theme needs to be set in the `PreInit` event of the page, which is before any of the controls have had their values loaded from the view state or the form input data. For example, imagine a page with a drop-down list by which the user can select the theme for the page. The list would have an event handler that would process the user's theme selection, but unfortunately you cannot set the page theme in this event handler. It has to be set *before* the postback event handling in the page's `PreInit` event. Yet during the `PreInit` event, you cannot yet know what the user selected!

The solution to this conundrum is that you need some way to store the user's theme selection in a way that is available to the `PreInit` event, and then reload the page so that the `PreInit` event is invoked again. How then can you store the user's theme selection? Later in Chapter 14, you will learn about the user profile system, which could be used for this problem. An alternative we will use here is to use ASP.NET ***session state*** (refer to Chapter 12 for more detail).

Session state allows you to store and retrieve values for a browser session as the user moves from page to page in the site. Recall that HTTP is a stateless protocol. This means that a Web server treats each HTTP request for a page as an independent request and retains no knowledge of code-behind data members or form values used during previous requests. ASP.NET session state provides a way to identify requests received from the same browser during a limited period of time and provides the ability to persist values for the duration of that session.

ASP.NET session state can be accessed from an ASP.NET Web Form via the `Session` property of the `Page` base class. This property references an object collection that is indexed by name. When you save an object in the session collection, you identify it by using a name, which can be any text string that you want. You can thus use session state to save the user's theme choice in the list event handler, as shown here.

```
protected void drpThemes_SelectedIndexChanged(object o,
    EventArgs e)
{
    // Save theme name in session. You identify this value
    // using "theme" but you could use any name
    Session["theme"] = drpThemes.SelectedItem.Text;

    // Re-execute page so PreInit event can be re-triggered
    Server.Transfer(Request.Path);
}
```

The `PreInit` event handler can now retrieve the user's choice using the following.

```
protected void Page_PreInit(object sender, EventArgs e)
{
    // Retrieve theme from session
    string theme = (string)Session["theme"];

    // Must make sure that session exists
    if (theme != null)
    {
        // Set the page theme
        this.Page.Theme = theme;
    }
    else
    {
        // Set default theme if nothing in session because no theme
```

```
                // has been selected yet (or the session has timed-out)
                this.Page.Theme = "Cool";
        }
}
```

Notice that retrieving the theme name from the session collection requires a casting operation (from object to string). Also, the method cannot assume that the session collection actually contains a theme name. It might be the first time the page has been requested and thus the theme does not exist yet in the session. Alternately, the session may have timed out and thus is empty. For this reason, any time you retrieve an item from session state, you must always verify that the item does exist, typically by comparing it to null.

Creating a Sample Page with Two Themes

To finish our coverage of themes, let's examine an example that demonstrates the dynamic selection of themes. The example page contains a drop-down list that allows the user to select one of two different themes to be applied to that page. The markup for this page is shown in Listing 6.3. Notice that the page contains no appearance markup, only structured content. All formatting is contained in the theme skins and CSS files.

Listing 6.3   ThemeTester.aspx

```
<%@ Page Language="C#" AutoEventWireup="true"
    CodeFile="ThemeTester.aspx.cs" Inherits="ThemeTester"%>

<!DOCTYPE html PUBLIC "-//W3C//DTD XHTML 1.0 Transitional//EN"
    "http://www.w3.org/TR/xhtml1/DTD/xhtml1-strict.dtd">
<html xmlns="http://www.w3.org/1999/xhtml">
<head runat="server">
    <title>Themes Tester</title>
</head>
<body>
    <form id="form1" runat="server">
        <div id="container">
            <div id="header">
                <asp:Image runat="server" ID="imgLogo" SkinID="logo"/>
            </div>
            <div id="menu">
                <asp:BulletedList ID="blstSample" runat="server"  >
                    <asp:ListItem Value="">Home</asp:ListItem>
                    <asp:ListItem Value="">Products</asp:ListItem>
                    <asp:ListItem Value="">About</asp:ListItem>
                </asp:BulletedList>
            </div>
```

```
<div id="content">
   <h1>Technical Books</h1>
   <p>
   Microsoft. Cisco. IBM. Hewlett Packard. Intel. Adobe.
   Macromedia. There's a reason the top technology
   companies choose Pearson Education as their publisher
   partners. Publishing over a thousand new titles each
   year, much of our content is also available online -
   so busy professionals and students can access it from
   any computer, day or night.
   </p>
   <div id="register">
     <fieldset>
         <legend>Contact Us</legend>
         <asp:Label ID="labName" runat="server"
            AssociatedControlID="txtName"
            Text="<u>N</u>ame" />
         <br />
         <asp:TextBox ID="txtName" runat="server"
            AccessKey="n" TabIndex="1" /><br />
         <asp:Label ID="labEmail" runat="server"
            AssociatedControlID="txtEmail"
            Text="E<u>m</u>ail" /><br />
         <asp:TextBox ID="txtEmail" runat="server"
            AccessKey="m" TabIndex="2" /><br />
         <asp:Label ID="labZip" runat="server"
            AssociatedControlID="txtZip"
            Text="<u>Z</u>ip" /><br />
         <asp:TextBox ID="txtZip" runat="server"
            AccessKey="z" TabIndex="3" /><br />
         <asp:Button ID="btnSubmit" runat="server"
            Text="Send" TabIndex="4" AccessKey="d" />
     </fieldset>
   </div>
   <p>
   <asp:DropDownList ID="drpThemes" runat="server"
       AutoPostBack="True"
       OnSelectedIndexChanged=
       "drpThemes_SelectedIndexChanged" >
     <asp:ListItem>Pick a theme</asp:ListItem>
     <asp:ListItem>Cool</asp:ListItem>
     <asp:ListItem>Professional</asp:ListItem>
   </asp:DropDownList>
   </p>
 </div>
</div>
   </form>
</body>
</html>
```

The markup contains a drop-down list that allows the user to select the theme. The code-behind for the page performs this processing, as shown in Listing 6.4.

Listing 6.4   ThemeTester.aspx.cs

```
public partial class ThemeTester : System.Web.UI.Page
{
    /// <summary>
    /// Set the page's theme based on the user's selection
    /// </summary>
    protected void Page_PreInit(object sender, EventArgs e)
    {
        // Retrieve theme from session
        string theme = (string)Session["theme"];

        // Must make sure that session exists
        if (theme != null)
        {
            this.Page.Theme = theme;
        }
        else
        {
            // Set default theme
            this.Page.Theme = "Cool";
        }
    }
    /// <summary>
    /// Process the user's theme choice by saving it in
    /// session state
    /// </summary>
    protected void drpThemes_SelectedIndexChanged(object sender,
        EventArgs e)
    {
        // Ignore the first item ("pick a theme") in list
        if (drpThemes.SelectedIndex != 0)
        {
            // Save theme in session
            Session["theme"] = drpThemes.SelectedItem.Text;

            // Re-request page
            Server.Transfer(Request.Path);
        }
    }
}
```

By keeping your markup devoid of appearance formatting, it can be quite radically transformed by your themes. This example has two different themes: one called Cool and the other called Professional. Figure 6.7 illustrates how this page appears in its two themes (the Cool theme is the one on the right with two layout columns).

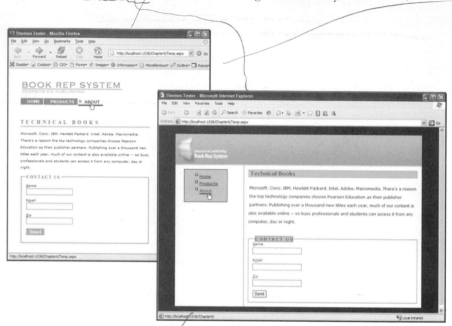

Figure 6.7   ThemeTester.aspx with its two themes

The skins for these two themes (shown in Listings 6.5 and 6.6) are quite similar as well as quite straightforward. Notice that both skins delegate the actual formatting to each theme's CSS file.

Listing 6.5 Cool.skin

```
<asp:Image runat="server" ImageUrl="images/cool.gif"
    AlternateText="Masthead Image" SkinID="logo" />

<asp:BulletedList runat="server"
    BulletStyle="CustomImage"
    BulletImageUrl="images/bullet.gif"
    DisplayMode="HyperLink" />

<asp:TextBox runat="server" CssClass="txtBox" />

<asp:Button runat="server" CssClass="myButton"/>
```

Listing 6.6 Professional.skin

```
<asp:Image runat="server" ImageUrl="images/prof.gif"
    AlternateText="Masthead Image" SkinID="logo" />

<asp:BulletedList runat="server" BulletStyle="NotSet"
    DisplayMode="HyperLink"/>

<asp:TextBox runat="server" CssClass="txtBox" />

<asp:Button runat="server" CssClass="myButton"/>
```

As mentioned, the majority of the heavy lifting for these themes is done by the CSS file for each theme. Listings 6.7 and 6.8 contain the content of each CSS file. The two CSS files are similar in that they use class, ID, and descendant selectors to specify the text formatting and the positioning for the different elements in your Web Form. The `professionalStyles.css` file is the easier of the two to understand because it contains no positioning styles. The only complexity in this style sheet is how the unordered list items are turned into a horizontal menu—that is, by turning off the bullets (`list-item: none`), keeping the list items together on a single line (`display: inline`), and by styling the link and hover pseudo elements.

Listing 6.7 professionalStyles.css

```
body {
    background-color: White;
    font-size: small;
}

h1 {
    margin-top: 3em;
    font-family: Georgia, Times New Roman, serif;
    font-size: 1.2em;
    padding-bottom: 4px;
    border-bottom: 1px solid #cc0000;
    color: #666666;
    text-transform: uppercase;
    letter-spacing: 0.4em;
}

p {
    font:  normal .8em/2.0em Verdana, Arial , sans-serif;
}

#container {
    position: relative;
```

```
        top: 30px;
        left: 30px;
        width: 400px;
    }

    /* style the list as a horizontal menu */
    #menu {
        font-family: Verdana, Arial , sans-serif;
        font-size: 0.9em;
    }

    #blstSample {
        margin-left: 0;
        padding-left: 0;
        white-space: nowrap;
    }

    #blstSample li {
        display: inline;
        list-style: none;
        text-transform: uppercase;
    }

    #blstSample a {
        font-weight: bold;
        padding: 3px 10px 3px 20px;
        margin-right: 2px;
    }

    #blstSample a:link,  #blstSample a:visited {
        text-decoration: none;
        color: white;
        background-color: Gray;

    }
    #blstSample a:hover {
        color: #cc0000;
        border-bottom: 4px solid #cc0000;
        padding-bottom: 2px;
        text-decoration: none;
        background: url(images/bullet.gif) no-repeat 0 50%;
        background-color: white;
    }

    /* style the form elements */
    fieldset {
        border: 1px solid #cc0000;
        padding: 1em;
    }
```

```
.txtBox {
    border:1px solid #666666;
    margin: 0.2em 0 0.8em 0.2em;
}

.myButton {
    border:1px solid gray;
    color:#FFFFFF;
    background-color:#FF9900;
    font-size:1em;
    font-weight: bold;
    margin: 0.2em 0 0.8em 0.2em;
}

label {
    font:  normal 0.8em Verdana, Arial , sans-serif;
    margin: 0.2em 0 0 0.2em;
}

legend {
    font-family: Georgia, Times New Roman, serif;
    font-size: 1em;
    font-weight: bold;
    color: #666666;
    text-transform: uppercase;
    letter-spacing: 0.2em;
}
```

The `coolStyles.css` file is a bit more complex. It uses CSS positioning and margins to place the menu `<div>` and the content `<div>` into two separate columns. The menu `<div>` is floated to the left (`float: left`) of the subsequent content in the form (the content `<div>`) and given a specified width. The content `<div>` is given a left margin that places all of the content to the right of the menu `<div>`. One interesting feature of this CSS file is the use of the so-called Tan Hack to deal with a bug with Internet Explorer 6.0 and earlier. In this case, Internet Explorer is adding the content `<div>` left margin setting to the form's `<input>` elements (the `TextBox` and `Button` controls). To fix this problem, the style sheet uses the `* html` selector (which is only supported by IE) to override the correct margin settings and apply a negative margin. The rest of the CSS is simple text formatting.

Listing 6.8 coolStyles.css

```
body {
    background-color: #0A4581;
    font-size: small;
}
```

```
h1 {
    margin-top: 0;
    padding: 0.2em;
    font-family: Verdana, Tahoma, Helvetica, Arial, sans-serif;
    font-size: 1.2em;
    background-color: #ABC6EE;
    color: #666666;
}

P {
    font: normal .9em/2.2em Verdana, Helvetica, Arial, sans-serif;
}

/* style each of the principle div elements */
#container {
    width: 90%;
    margin: 10px auto;
    background-color: #ffffff;
    color: #333333;
    border: 1px solid gray;
}

#content {
    margin-left: 16em;
    border-left: 1px solid gray;
    padding: 1em;
}

#header {
    padding: 0;
    height: 92px;
    background: url(images/header_background.gif);
}

/* style the list as a vertical list of links */
#menu {
    float: left;
    color: black;
    width: 9em;
    margin: 1em;
    padding: 0.5em;
    border: 1px solid #000;
    font-family: Verdana, Tahoma, Helvetica, Arial, sans-serif;
    background-color: #ABC6EE;
}

#blstSample li {
    padding-top: 0.4em;
}
```

```css
#blstSample a:link,  #blstSample a:visited {
    text-decoration: underline; color: blue;
}
#blstSample a:hover  {
    color: #cc0000;
    border-bottom: 3px solid #cc0000;
    text-decoration: none;
}

/* style the form elements */
#register {
    font-family: Verdana, Tahoma, Helvetica, Arial, sans-serif;
}

fieldset {
    border: 1px solid #666666;
    padding: 1em;
}

legend {
    font-size: 1em;
    font-weight: bold;
    color: #666666;
    text-transform: uppercase;
    letter-spacing: 0.2em;
    background-color: #ABC6EE;
    border: 1px solid #666666;
}

.txtBox {
    border:1px solid #666666;
    margin: 0.3em 0 0.8em 0.2em;
}

/* IE 6 adds the #content margin to the text box and button so we
   must give the text boxes and buttons a negative margin using
   a CSS format only understood by IE (which will override the
   margin set in the .txtBox rule just above).
*/
* html .txtBox { margin-left: -16em; }
* html .myButton { margin-left: -16em; }

label {
    font:  normal 0.8em Verdana, Arial , sans-serif;
}
```

One other feature worth mentioning about these two themes is their use of em units for sizing. By avoiding the use of pixels, these two layouts still work even if users change the display size of the text in their browser (see Figure 6.8). We could have achieved a similar result as well by using percent units (e.g., `font-size: 90%;`) for sizing.

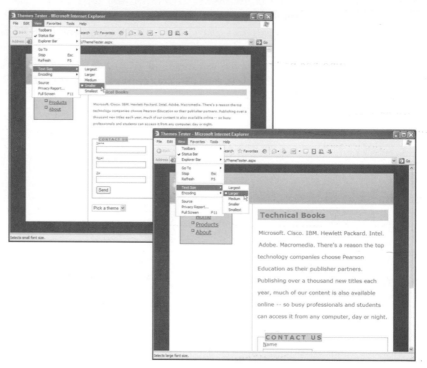

Figure 6.8   Cool theme with different user-selected font sizes

The em unit is the size of the character box for the element's parent. If no other font sizes are specified in other containers, a font size of `1em` is equivalent to the default font size (determined by the browser). The principle used in these styles is to set the default font size in the body to `small`, and then make all other dimensions relative to whatever the browser sets for the `small` font size.

```
body { font-size: small; }
h1 { font-size: 1.2em; }
p { font-size: 0.8em; }
```

If the browser's font size for `small` is 14px, the h1 is displayed at around 17px (14 × 1.2) and the p is displayed at around 11px (14 × 0.8). If the user increases the size of her text through browser preferences, so that `small` is now 18px, the h1 and the p are 21 and 14 pixels, respectively (18 × 1.2 and 18 × 0.8).

Master Pages

ASP.NET 2.0 provided a treasure trove of new features. Perhaps none of these generated as much anticipation as **master pages**. This new feature allows the developer to define the structural layout for multiple Web Forms in a separate file and then apply this layout across multiple Web Forms. You can thus move common layout elements, such as logos, navigation systems, search boxes, login areas, and footers, out of all the individual pages and into a single master page.

Any developer who has had to create and maintain an ASP.NET Web application that consists of more than two or three pages should be able to see the value of this ability. In most Web applications, the individual pages typically share a common structure or a common look and feel across the entire site. For instance, most pages within a site may have a logo in the upper-left corner, a global navigation system across the top, a secondary navigation system down the left side of the page, and a footer at the bottom of the page. It is clearly less than ideal to replicate the markup and code for this common structure across multiple pages.

Master pages provide a solution to this problem. They allow the developer to create a consistent page structure or layout without duplicating code or markup. Master pages are created in much the same way as any other Web Form. They contain markup, server controls, and can have a code-behind class that responds to all the usual page lifecycle events. However, they do have their own unique extension (`.master`) as well as a different directive at the top of the page. As well (and most importantly), they also contain one or more `ContentPlaceHolder` controls.

The `ContentPlaceHolder` control defines a region of the master page, which is replaced by content from the page that is using this master page. That is, each Web Form that uses the master page only needs to define the content unique to it within the `Content` controls that correspond to the `ContentPlaceHolder` controls in the master page, as illustrated in Figure 6.9.

Like any Web server control, each `ContentPlaceHolder` control within a master page must have a unique `Id`.

```
<asp:ContentPlaceHolder id="contentBody" runat="server">
</asp:ContentPlaceHolder>
```

This `Id` is used to link the `Content` controls in the various Web Forms that use the master page. This link is made via the `ContentPlaceHolderId` property of the `Content` control.

```
<asp:Content id="myContent" ContentPlaceHolderId="contentBody"
   runat="server">
</asp:Content>
```

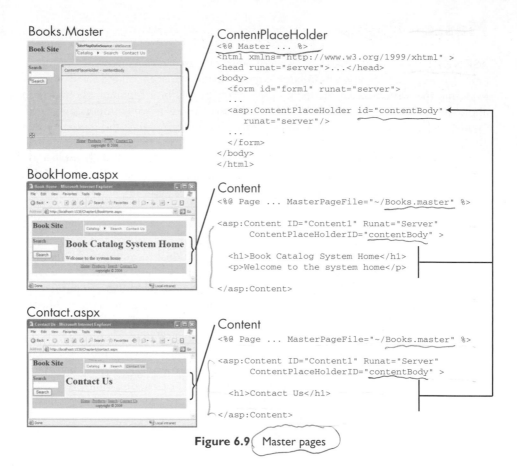

Figure 6.9 Master pages

A master page significantly simplifies the markup for pages that use it. The master page contains the complete XHTML document structure. That is, the html, head, and body elements are contained only within the master page. The .aspx files that use the master page only need define the content that will be inserted into the placeholders in the master page. In fact, these .aspx files can *only* contain content within Content controls. Unlike HTML frames (which perform a somewhat similar function in HTML), master pages are transparent to the user (that is, the user is unaware of their existence) because ASP.NET merges the content of the master page with the content of the requested page.

Visual Studio and its designer completely support master pages. You can visually edit the master page, as well as visually edit the individual aspx pages as they would appear within the master page. Figure 6.10 illustrates the BookHome.aspx page within the Visual Studio designer. Only the contents of the Content control are editable; the master page markup is displayed (ghosted out) but cannot be edited.

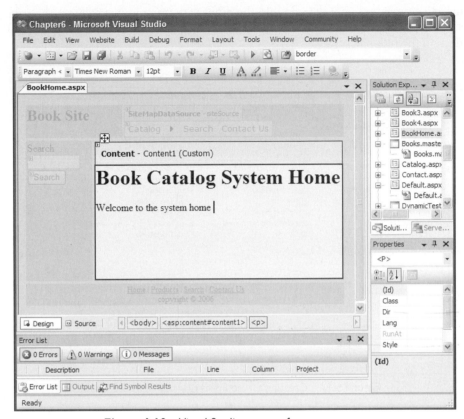

Figure 6.10 Visual Studio support for master pages

You can specify the master page to use when you add a new Web Form in Visual Studio simply by turning on the Select Master Page option in the Add New Item dialog box (see Figure 6.11).

When you choose this Select Master Page option, Visual Studio then displays the Select A Master Page dialog (see Figure 6.12). This dialog displays all the master pages in the Web site (i.e., all the files with the `.master` extension).

Of course, you can use a master page in any Web Form without the intervention of Visual Studio simply by adding the appropriate `MasterPageFile` attribute to the form's `Page` directive, as shown in the following.

```
<%@ Page MasterPageFile="~/Books.master" ... Title="Book Home" %>
```

This example also contains the `Title` attribute. Because the master page must define the `<head>` section, you need some way to specify the page title (which is displayed in the browser's title bar) in the individual pages themselves. The `Title`

directive provides one way to do this; the other is to programmatically set the page's
Title property. If you do not set it, the page is displayed in the browser with "Untitled" in the title bar.

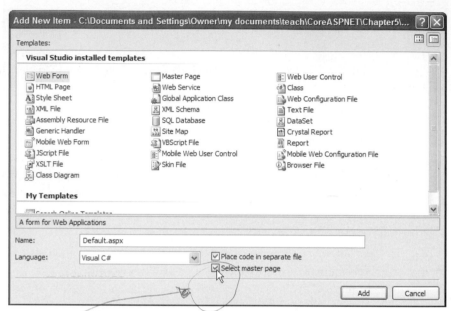

Figure 6.11   Creating a Web Form that uses a master page

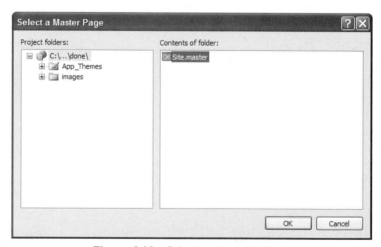

Figure 6.12   Selecting the master page

As an alternative to specifying the `MasterPageFile` attribute on each Web Form in your site, you can specify it at once globally for all pages in the site via the `Pages` element in the `Web.config` file.

```
<system.web>
    ...
    <pages masterPageFile="~/Books.master" />
</system.web>
```

Note that setting the `MasterPageFile` attribute in the Web Form overrides the setting in the `Web.config` file.

Defining the Master Page

As already mentioned, a master page looks like a regular Web Form except that it has a different extension and directive. As well, a master page contains one or more `ContentPlaceHolder` controls. The following example illustrates a sample master page (the positioning and formatting is contained in its style sheet).

```
<%@ Master Language="C#" AutoEventWireup="true"
    CodeFile="Site.master.cs" Inherits="Site" %>

<!DOCTYPE html PUBLIC "-//W3C//DTD XHTML 1.0 Transitional//EN"
    "http://www.w3.org/TR/xhtml1/DTD/xhtml1-strict.dtd">
<html xmlns="http://www.w3.org/1999/xhtml">
<head id="Head1" runat="server">
    <title></title>
    <link rel="stylesheet" type="text/css" href="~/styles.css" />
</head>
<body>
    <form id="form1" runat="server">
        <div id="container">
            <div id="header">
            <asp:Image runat="server" ID="imgLogo"
                ImageUrl="~/images/cool.gif" />
            </div>
            <div id="sideArea">
                <div id="menu">
                    <asp:BulletedList ID="blstSample" runat="server"
                        DisplayMode="HyperLink" >
                    <asp:ListItem Value="BookHome.aspx">
                        Home
                    </asp:ListItem>
                    <asp:ListItem Value="Products.aspx">
                        Products
                    </asp:ListItem>
                    <asp:ListItem Value="Contact.aspx">
```

```
                    Contact Us
                </asp:ListItem>
            </asp:BulletedList>
        </div>
        <div id="sideAreaBox">
            <asp:ContentPlaceHolder ID="sideContent"
                runat="server">
            <p>default side content</p>
            </asp:ContentPlaceHolder>
        </div>
    </div>
    <div id="mainArea">
        <asp:ContentPlaceHolder ID="mainContent"
            runat="server">
        <p>default main content</p>
        </asp:ContentPlaceHolder>
    </div>
    <div id="footer">
        <p>
        This site is not real. It is an example site for Core
        ASP.NET book.
        </p>
    </div>
    </div>
    </form>
</body>
</html>
```

Notice that both `ContentPlaceHolder` controls contain default content. This default content is displayed if the aspx files that use this master page do not provide Content controls for these `ContentPlaceHolder` controls.

Let us now define a Web Form that uses this master page.

```
<%@ Page Language="C#" MasterPageFile="~/Site.master"
    CodeFile="BookHome.aspx.cs" Inherits="BookHome" Title="Book Home"
%>

<asp:Content ID="Content1"
    ContentPlaceHolderID="mainContent"
    Runat="Server">

    <h1>Book Rep System Home</h1>
    <p>Welcome to the book rep system</p>
</asp:Content>

<asp:Content ID="Content2"
    ContentPlaceHolderID="sideContent"
    Runat="Server">
```

```
<h2>New Releases</h2>
<p>Core C#</p>
</asp:Content>
```

By removing the markup for the common elements and placing them into the master page, you are left with a Web Form that is quite striking in its clarity and conciseness. It contains only the content that is unique to this page. The result, using a style sheet quite similar to that shown in Listing 6.8, is shown in Figure 6.13.

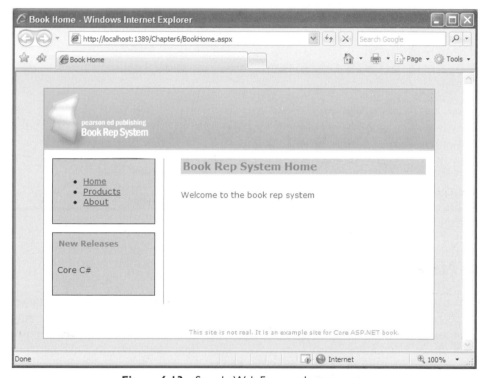

Figure 6.13 Sample Web Form and master page

Notice that all content in this page is contained within either of the two Content controls. Because the Web Form uses a master page, ASP.NET does not allow us to place any markup outside of these two controls. If you do place content outside of a Content control, you will see a Parser Error (see Figure 6.14).

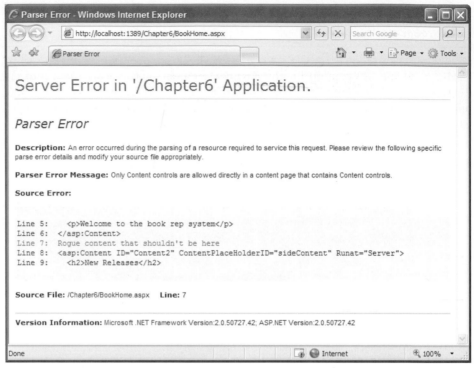

Figure 6.14   Parser error

Nested Master Pages

Master pages can be nested so that one master page contains another master page as its content. This can be particularly useful for Web sites that are part of a larger system of sites. For instance, the master page shown in Figure 6.13 could be just one intranet in a much larger system. You might thus want a way to move between these intranets. Nested master pages provide this mechanism. Figure 6.15 illustrates how the master page in Figure 6.13 can be a child nested inside another parent master page.

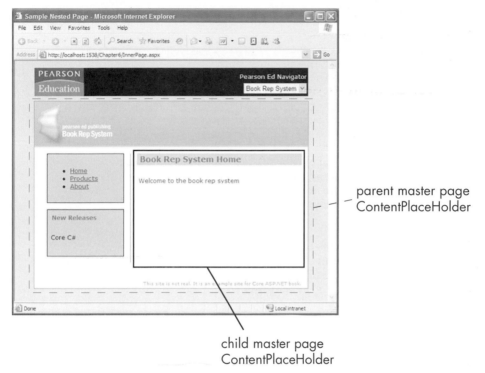

Figure 6.15 Nested master pages

To nest a master page within another master page, the child master page simply needs a Content control that maps to a ContentPlaceHolder control in the parent master page, as well as the appropriate MasterPageFile attribute in the Master directive. For instance, you could modify the previous example of a master page so that it is contained within a Content control, and thus becomes a child master page.

```
<%@ Master MasterPageFile="~/Parent.master"
   CodeFile="Child.master.cs" Inherits="Child" %>

<asp:Content ID="Content1" ContentPlaceHolderID="parentContent"
      Runat="Server">

   <div id="container">
      <div id="header">
      <asp:Image runat="server" ID="imgLogo"
         ImageUrl="~/images/cool.gif" />
```

```
            </div>
            <div id="sideArea">
                <div id="menu">
                    <asp:BulletedList ID="blstSample" runat="server"
                        DisplayMode="HyperLink">
                        <asp:ListItem Value="">Home</asp:ListItem>
                        <asp:ListItem Value="">Products</asp:ListItem>
                        <asp:ListItem Value="">About</asp:ListItem>
                    </asp:BulletedList>
                </div>
                <div id="sideAreaBox">
                    <asp:ContentPlaceHolder ID="sideContent"
                        runat="server">
                    <p>default side content</p>
                    </asp:ContentPlaceHolder>
                </div>
            </div>
            <div id="mainArea">
                <asp:ContentPlaceHolder ID="mainContent" runat="server">
                <p>default main content</p>
                </asp:ContentPlaceHolder>
            </div>
            <div id="footer">
                <p>
                 This site is not real. It is an example site for Core
                 ASP.NET book.
                </p>
            </div>
        </div>
</asp:Content>
```

Your parent master page is quite straightforward with just the one Content-PlaceHolder control. Once again, the formatting and positioning is handled by CSS.

```
<%@ Master Language="C#" AutoEventWireup="true"
    CodeFile="Parent.master.cs" Inherits="Parent" %>

<!DOCTYPE html PUBLIC "-//W3C//DTD XHTML 1.0 Transitional//EN"
    "http://www.w3.org/TR/xhtml1/DTD/xhtml1-transitional.dtd">

<html xmlns="http://www.w3.org/1999/xhtml" >
<head runat="server">
    <title></title>
    <link rel="stylesheet" type="text/css" href="~/styles.css" />
    <link rel="stylesheet" type="text/css" href="~/parent.css" />
</head>
<body>
    <form id="form1" runat="server">
```

```
    <div id="topNav">
       <p>
       Pearson Ed Navigator<br />
       <asp:DropDownList ID="drpPlaces" runat="server">
          <asp:ListItem>Book Rep System</asp:ListItem>
          <asp:ListItem>Addison-Wesley</asp:ListItem>
          <asp:ListItem>Prentice Hall</asp:ListItem>
       </asp:DropDownList>
       </p>
    </div>
    <asp:contentplaceholder id="parentContent" runat="server" />
    </form>
</body>
</html>
```

CORE NOTE

There is no designer support for nested master pages in Visual Studio.

How Master Pages Work

When a page that uses a master page (i.e., a content page) is requested, ASP.NET merges the content page and master page together (assuming of course that both have already been compiled). It does so by inserting the master page's content at the beginning of the content page's control tree. *This means that the master page content is actually a control that is added to the page.* In fact, the master page control is a subclass of the UserControl class (which is covered later in the chapter). Thus, the master page control is the root control in the page's control hierarchy. The content of each individual Content control is then added as a collection of child controls to the corresponding ContentPlaceHolder control in the master page control. This occurs after the PreInit event but before the Init event of the page.

Like any control, master pages have their own sequence of events that are fired as part of the page lifecycle. Because it is the root control in the page's control hierarchy, its events are always fired before the control events in any content pages. As a result, it is important that you do not conceptualize the master page as a "master" in the sense of a "controller" page. That is, the master page should *not* be orchestrating and controlling what happens in the individual content pages it contains. The master page is simply a template page and should control only those server controls it directly contains. Thus, in general, you should endeavor to keep the master page and the content pages as uncoupled as possible.

Referencing Issues with Master Pages

Because master page content is ultimately inserted into the content page's control tree, there are some potential issues to be aware of with external references inside of master pages. Because the user's request is for the content page and not the master page, all URL references are relative to the content page. This can cause some problems when the master page and the content pages are in different folders within the site.

For instance, let us imagine a situation in which your content page is in a folder under the root named content and your master page is contained in a folder under the root named master; inside this master folder, you also have a subfolder named images. Let's say you want to reference an image named logo.gif, which is inside the images folder of master. In such a case, the following references inside your master page do not work.

```
<img src="images/logo.gif" />
body { background-image: url(images/logo.gif); }
<img src="~/master/images/logo.gif" />
```

The first two references in fact refer to /content/images/logo.gif, because all relative references are relative to the content page. The second reference doesn't work either because the application relative symbol (~) only works with server controls.

One alternative to this problem is to use an absolute reference to the site root.

```
<img src="/master/images/logo.gif" />
```

The problem with this approach is its fragility; that is, the reference breaks if the site structure changes. Another approach is to use a server control, as in the following.

```
<asp:Image runat="server" id="a"
    ImageUrl="~/master/images/logo.gif" />
```

This approach works because server controls within master pages that contain URLs have their URLs modified by the ASP.NET environment.

Programming the Master Page

As you have seen, the combined master and content pages appear to the user as a single page whose URL is that of the requested content page. From a programming perspective, the two pages act as separate containers for their respective controls, with the content page also acting as the container for the master page. Yet, because the master page content becomes merged into the content page, you can also programmatically reference public master page members in the content page.

Why would you want to do this? Perhaps your master page contains a control whose content varies depending upon which content page is being viewed. One common example is a master page that contains an advertisement image; the precise advertisement to display in that control might vary depending upon which part of the site is being viewed. The master page might also contain a secondary navigation area that again differs depending upon which part of the site is being visited.

There are two principal ways of accessing content in the master page within the content page. You can do so via the `FindControl` method of the `Master` object or via public members that are exposed by the master page.

Let us begin by examining the `FindControl` approach. The `FindControl` method searches the current naming container for a specified server control and returns a typed reference to it. Thus, you can retrieve a `TextBox` named `txtOne` from the current Web Form via the following.

```
TextBox one = (TextBox)this.FindControl("txtOne");
String contents = one.Text;
```

Notice that the reference returned from the method needs to be cast to the appropriate control type. Of course, it doesn't make too much sense to search the `Page` naming container for the control when you could replace these two lines with the simpler form with which you are accustomed, namely `string contents = txtOne.Text`. Where `FindControl` is truly useful is in those situations where you need to reference a control that is "hidden" within some other naming container, such as a `Wizard` or `GridView` control or within a master page. For instance, imagine that you have the following `HyperLink` control contained within your master page.

```
<asp:HyperLink ID="imgbtnAd" runat="server" />
```

Now, let's say that you want to change the image and the destination URL for this control in each of your content pages. You could so with the following code somewhere in your content page's code-behind class.

```
HyperLink ad = (HyperLink)Master.FindControl("imgbtnAd");
if (ad != null)
{
    ad.ImageUrl = "~/Images/something.gif";
    ad.NavigateUrl = "http://www.somewhere.com";
}
```

Although this approach does work, it is not ideal. A better approach is to safely encapsulate the data you need from the master page into public properties, which you could then access within your content pages. This way, your content pages are not coupled to the implementation details of the master page. The following example adds two properties to the code-behind for the master page. It allows content pages to manipulate the image and navigation URLs of the `HyperLink` control in the master page.

```
public partial class ProgrammedContentMaster :
    System.Web.UI.MasterPage
{
    public string AdImageUrl
    {
        get { return imgbtnAd.ImageUrl; }
        set { imgbtnAd.ImageUrl = value; }
    }

    public string AdNavigateUrl
    {
        get { return imgbtnAd.NavigateUrl; }
        set { imgbtnAd.NavigateUrl = value; }
    }
}
```

Your content pages can now use these properties; to do so requires the use of the
Master property of the Page class. Unfortunately, you cannot simply reference one
of these properties directly from the Master property in your content page
code-behind, as shown here.

```
Master.AdImageUrl = "~/Images/something.gif";
```

You cannot do this because the Master property returns an object of type MasterPage, which is the base class for all master pages. Of course, this general MasterPage class knows nothing of the properties you have just defined in your master
page. Instead, you must cast the Master property to the class name of your master
page, and then manipulate its properties.

```
ProgrammedContentMaster pcm = (ProgrammedContentMaster)Master;

pcm.AdImageUrl = "~/Images/something.gif";
pcm.AdNavigateUrl = "http://www.somewhereelse.com";
```

An alternative to casting is to add the following MasterType directive to your
content pages.

```
<%@ MasterType VirtualPath="~/ProgrammedContentMaster.master" %>
```

This changes the Master property of the Page class so that it is strongly typed
(that is, it is not of type MasterPage, but of type ProgrammedContentMaster).
This eliminates the need for casting the Master property, and thus you can manipulate the custom properties directly.

```
Master.AdImageUrl = "~/Images/something.gif";
Master.AdNavigateUrl = "http://www.somewhereelse.com";
```

Master Pages and Themes

ASP.NET themes provide a centralized way to define the appearance of a Web site. Although your content pages can make use of themes, you can simply use master pages to set the theme for your site as a whole. That is, you cannot use the `Theme` attribute within the `Master` directive at the top of the master page (although you can still do so in the `Page` attribute of each of your content pages).

However, you can use your master page to provide a user interface element that allows the user to browse and dynamically set the theme for your content pages. You may recall back in Listing 6.4, you programmatically set the theme of a page within the `PreInit` event of the page and you used ASP.NET session state to store the currently selected theme. Unfortunately, you cannot set the theme for your content pages within the `PreInit` event of the master page. Instead, you must have the `PreInit` event handler within the content page. If you have hundreds or even thousands of content pages, does that mean you must have the same `PreInit` event handler in all of these content pages?

Fortunately, no; you can make use of some simple object-oriented inheritance so that you only need code the `PreInit` event handler once. Recall that the code-behind class for all Web Forms has the `Page` class as its base class. You can define your own class that inherits from this base class and which contains the `PreInit` event handler that sets the themes. This new class then becomes the base class for the code-behind classes in your site.

The example site contained in Listings 6.9 through 6.13 demonstrates this technique (along with the other material covered in this chapter on master pages). It uses master pages to specify the structure of the site, themes, and CSS to control the appearance of the site's pages. The master page contains both an advertisement banner image that is customized by each content page as well as a theme selector. Figures 6.16 and 6.17 illustrate how the example appears with its two themes.

Listing 6.9 contains the code for the new class that will become the base class for all your Web Forms. Like Listing 6.4, it simply retrieves the theme selected by the user from the session state and applies it to the (content) page. This class file should be saved in your project's `App_Code` folder.

Listing 6.9   ParentPage.cs

```
public class ParentPage: Page
{
    /// <summary>
    /// Sets the theme of the page based on the current
    /// session state
    /// </summary>
    protected void Page_PreInit(object sender, EventArgs e)
    {
        string themeName = (string)Session["themeName"];
```

```
        if (themeName != null)
            this.Page.Theme = themeName;
        else
            this.Page.Theme = "Cool";
    }
}
```

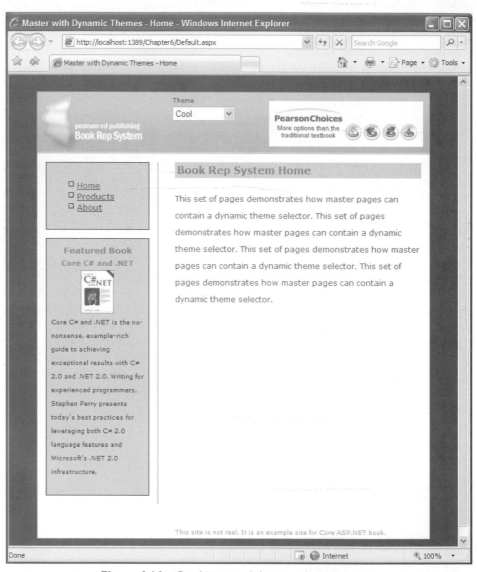

Figure 6.16   Combining cool theme with master pages

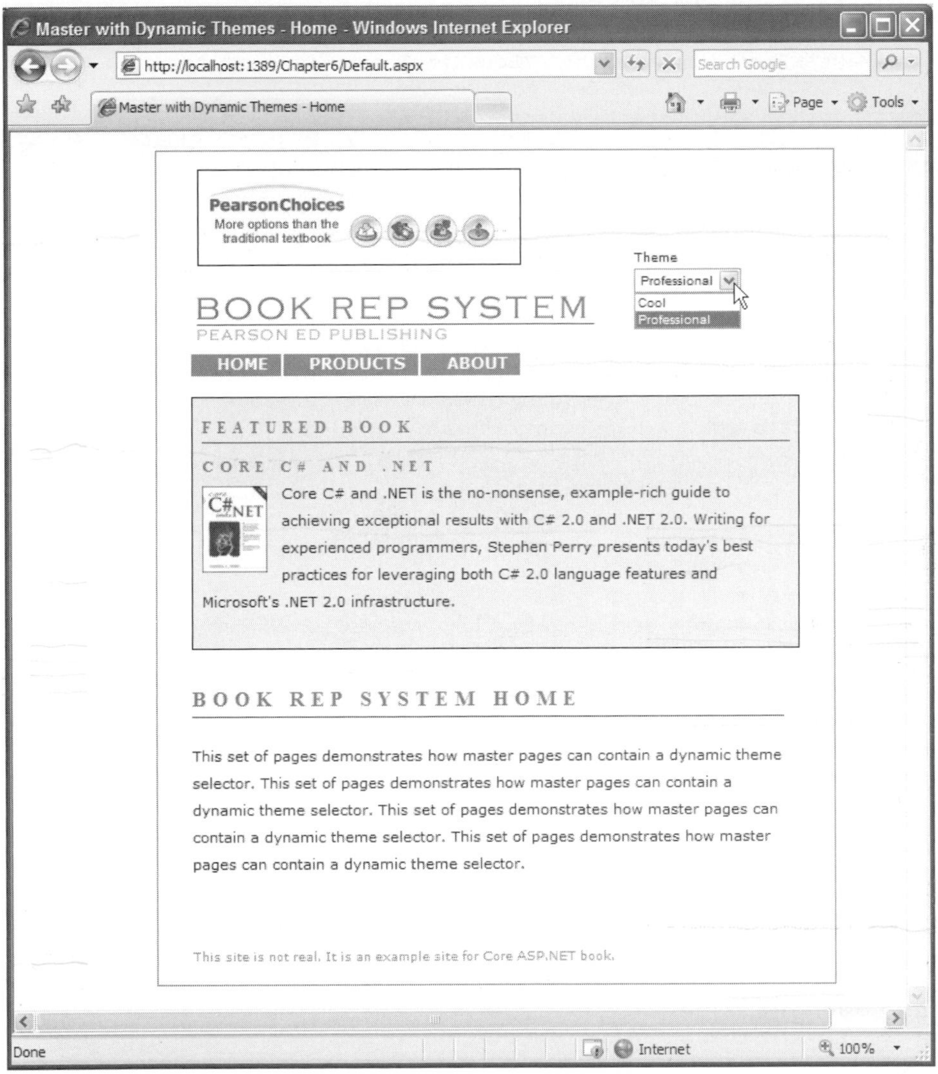

Figure 6.17 Combining professional theme with master pages

I won't bother showing you all the content pages in the site. Listing 6.10 illustrates one sample content page (the home page).

Listing 6.10 Default.aspx

```
<%@ Page Language="C#" MasterPageFile="~/BookWithThemes.master"
   AutoEventWireup="true" CodeFile="Default.aspx.cs"
```

```
    Inherits="Default"
    Title="Master with Dynamic Themes - Home" %>
<%@ MasterType VirtualPath="~/BookWithThemes.master" %>

<asp:Content ID="Content1" ContentPlaceHolderID="sideContent"
    Runat="Server">
  <h2>Featured Book</h2>
  <h3>Core C# and .NET<br />
  <asp:Image ID="imgBook" runat="server" CssClass="sideImage"
    ImageUrl="~/images/0131472275.gif"
    AlternateText="Cover image of Core C# book"/></h3>
  <p>Core C# and .NET is the no-nonsense, example-rich guide to
  achieving exceptional results with C# 2.0 and .NET 2.0. Writing
  for experienced programmers, Stephen Perry presents today's
  best practices for leveraging both C# 2.0 language features and
  Microsoft's .NET 2.0 infrastructure.</p>
</asp:Content>

<asp:Content ID="Content2" ContentPlaceHolderID="mainContent"
    Runat="Server">
  <h1>Book Rep System Home</h1>
  <p>
  This set of pages demonstrates how master pages can contain a
  dynamic theme selector. This set of pages demonstrates how
  master pages can contain a dynamic theme selector. This set of
  pages demonstrates how master pages can contain a dynamic theme
  selector. This set of pages demonstrates how master pages can
  contain a dynamic theme selector.
  </p>
</asp:Content>
```

The code-behind for this sample content page (see Listing 6.11) must be altered to use your ParentPage class as its base class. Notice as well that it modifies properties exposed by the master page to customize the advertisement that appears within the master page.

Listing 6.11   Default.aspx.cs

```
public partial class Default : ParentPage
{
    protected void Page_Load(object sender, EventArgs e)
    {
        Master.AdImageUrl = "~/Images/ads/ad1.gif";
        Master.AdNavigateUrl =
            "http://www.aw-bc.com/newpearsonchoices";
    }
}
```

Listing 6.12 defines the markup for the master page.

Listing 6.12   BookWithThemes.master

```
<%@ Master Language="C#" AutoEventWireup="true"
   CodeFile="BookWithThemes.master.cs"
   Inherits="BookWithThemes" %>

<!DOCTYPE html PUBLIC "-//W3C//DTD XHTML 1.0 Transitional//EN"
   "http://www.w3.org/TR/xhtml1/DTD/xhtml1-strict.dtd">
<html xmlns="http://www.w3.org/1999/xhtml">
<head id="Head1" runat="server">
   <title></title>
</head>
<body>
   <form id="form1" runat="server">
      <div id="container">

         <div id="header">
            <div id="themes">
               <p>Theme <br />
               <asp:DropDownList ID="drpThemes" runat="server"
                  AutoPostBack="true" OnSelectedIndexChanged=
                     "drpTheme_selectedChanged">
               </asp:DropDownList>
               </p>
            </div>
            <div id="bannerAd">
               <asp:HyperLink ID="imgbtnAd" runat="server" />
            </div>
            <div class="clearBreak"></div>
            <div id="logo">
               <asp:Image runat="server" ID="imgLogo"
                  SkinID="logo"/>
            </div>
         </div>

         <div id="sideArea">
            <div id="masterMenu">
               <asp:BulletedList ID="blstSample" runat="server" >
                  <asp:ListItem Value="Default.aspx">
                     Home</asp:ListItem>
                  <asp:ListItem Value="Products.aspx">
                     Products</asp:ListItem>
                  <asp:ListItem Value="About.aspx">
                     About</asp:ListItem>
               </asp:BulletedList>
            </div>
```

```
            <div id="sideAreaBox">
                <asp:ContentPlaceHolder ID="sideContent"
                    runat="server">
                <p>default side content</p>
                </asp:ContentPlaceHolder>
            </div>
        </div>

        <div id="mainArea">
            <asp:ContentPlaceHolder ID="mainContent"
                runat="server">
            <p>default main content</p>
            </asp:ContentPlaceHolder>
        </div>

        <div id="footer">
            <p>
            This site is not real. It is an example site for Core
            ASP.NET book.
            </p>
        </div>
        </div>
    </form>
</body>
</html>
```

Like the other master pages examined in this chapter, this master page contains no formatting. The CSS and skins of your themes control the appearance of each page. The master page contains four main sections: `<div id="header">`, `<div id="sideArea">`, `<div id="mainArea">`, and `<div id="footer">`. The side-Area and mainArea sections contain the two ContentPlaceHolder controls. The header section contains the logo image, an advertisement image, and a DropDown-List that allows the user to change the theme. The theme list is not filled via markup, but instead is filled programmatically in the code-behind class for this master page, as shown in Listing 6.13.

Listing 6.13   BookWithThemes.master.cs

```
using System;
using System.Data;
using System.Configuration;
using System.Collections;
using System.Web;
using System.Web.Security;
using System.Web.UI;
```

```csharp
using System.Web.UI.WebControls;
using System.Web.UI.WebControls.WebParts;
using System.Web.UI.HtmlControls;

// Note that you need to include this namespace reference
using System.IO;

public partial class BookWithThemes : System.Web.UI.MasterPage
{
    /// <summary>
    /// Populate theme list based on themes in App_Themes folder
    /// </summary>
    protected void Page_Load(object sender, EventArgs e)
    {
        // Dynamically load the drop-down list only the first time
        if (!IsPostBack)
        {
            // Themes must be in this location
            string path = Server.MapPath("~/App_Themes");

            // Verify this location exists
            if (Directory.Exists(path))
            {
                // Retrieve array of theme folder names
                String[] themeFolders =
                    Directory.GetDirectories(path);

                // Process each element in this array
                foreach (String folder in themeFolders)
                {
                    // Retrieve information about this folder name
                    DirectoryInfo info = new DirectoryInfo(folder);

                    // Add this folder name to the drop-down list
                    drpThemes.Items.Add(info.Name);
                }

                // Once all the themes are added to the list, you
                // must make the content page's current theme the
                // selected item in the list

                // First search the list items for the page's
                // theme name
                ListItem item =
                    drpThemes.Items.FindByText(Page.Theme);

                // Now set the selected index of the list (i.e.,
                // select that list item) to the index of the list
                // item you just found.
```

```
                    drpThemes.SelectedIndex =
                        drpThemes.Items.IndexOf(item);
                }
            }
        }


        /// <summary>
        /// Event handler for the theme selector
        /// </summary>
        protected void drpTheme_selectedChanged(object s, EventArgs e)
        {
            // Save theme in session
            string theme = drpThemes.SelectedItem.Text;
            Session["themeName"] = theme;

            // Re-request page
            string page = Request.Path;
            Server.Transfer(page);
        }


        /// <summary>
        /// Property to get/set the url of the advertisement image
        /// </summary>
        public string AdImageUrl
        {
            get { return imgbtnAd.ImageUrl; }
            set { imgbtnAd.ImageUrl = value; }
        }


        /// <summary>
        /// Property to get/set the url for the link surrounding the
        /// advertisement image.
        /// </summary>
        public string AdNavigateUrl
        {
            get { return imgbtnAd.NavigateUrl; }
            set { imgbtnAd.NavigateUrl = value; }
        }
}
```

The only remaining files are the skins and CSS for the two themes. For space reasons, I do not include them here (although they can be downloaded from my Web site at http://www.randyconnolly.com/core). They are quite similar to those shown in Listings 6.5 through 6.8.

User Controls

The previous section examined the powerful master page mechanism in ASP.NET. A master page allows the developer to define the structural layout for multiple Web Forms in a separate file and then apply this layout across multiple Web Forms. You can thus move common layout elements out of all the individual pages and into a single master page. As a consequence, the master page feature is a powerful mechanism for reducing code-behind and markup duplication across a Web application.

Yet, it still is possible, even when using a master page, for presentation-level (i.e., user interface) duplication to exist in a site. For instance, consider the page shown back in Figure 6.16. In this example, the feature book box is displayed only on the home page. But imagine that you want this box to appear on several other pages, but not on every page (if it was to appear on every page, you would place it in the master page). Your inner programmer should shirk at the idea of simply copying and pasting the markup and code for implementing this featured book box to multiple pages. Although such a solution is easy in the short term, maintaining this type of approach in the long run is a real headache; every time you have to make a change to this box, you have to change it in multiple places.

User controls are the preferred ASP.NET solution to this type of presentation-level duplication. They provide a cleaner approach to user interface reuse then copying and pasting or using the server-side includes of classic ASP. In addition, user controls in ASP.NET are very simple to create and then use. As well, they follow the same familiar development model as regular Web Forms.

Creating and Using User Controls

User controls are created in a manner similar to Web Forms. As with Web Forms, a user control can contain markup as well as programming logic. Also like Web Forms, the programming for a user control can be contained within the same file as the markup, or contained within a separate code-behind file. After a user control is defined, it can then be used in Web Forms, master pages, or even other user controls.

The markup for a user control is contained in a text file with the `.ascx` extension. This file can contain any necessary programming logic within embedded code declaration block (i.e., within `<script runat="server">...</script>` tags) embedded within this `.ascx` user control file. Alternately, the programming code can be contained in a code-behind class for the user control. However, the code-behind class for a user control inherits from the `UserControl` class, rather than the `Page` class.

Walkthroughs 6.3 and 6.4 demonstrate how to create and then use a simple user control.

Walkthrough 6.3   *Creating a User Control*

1. Use the Website →Add New Item menu option in Visual Studio, or right-click the project in Solution Explorer and choose Add New Item.

2. From the Add New Item dialog box, choose the Web User Control template and name the control `FeatureBookControl.ascx`. Click Add.

   Notice that a blank user control contains no content other than a `Control` directive. Unlike with a Web Form, there is no HTML skeleton with a user control. It is completely up to the developer to decide what markup should appear in the user control.

3. Change the user control so that it has the following content.

   ```
   <%@ Control Language="C#" AutoEventWireup="true"
       CodeFile="FeatureBookControl.ascx.cs"
       Inherits="FeatureBookControl" %>


   <h2>Featured Book</h2>
   <h3>Core C# and .NET</h3>
   <asp:Image ID="imgBook" runat="server" CssClass="sideImage"
       ImageUrl="~/images/0131472275.gif"
       AlternateText="Cover image of Core C# book"/>


   <p>
   Core C# and .NET is the no-nonsense, example-rich guide to
   achieving exceptional results with C# 2.0 and .NET 2.0.
   Writing for experienced programmers, Stephen Perry presents
   today's best practices for leveraging both C# 2.0 language
   features and Microsoft's .NET 2.0 infrastructure.
   </p>
   ```

4. Save the control.

Now that you have created a user control, you can use it in a Web Form, master page, or other user control. To make use of a user control, you must follow two steps:

1. Indicate that you want to use a user control via the `Register` directive, as shown in the following.

   ```
   <%@ Register TagPrefix="SomePrefix" TagName="SomeName"
       Src="someControl.ascx" %>
   ```

   `TagPrefix` determines a unique namespace for the user control, which is necessary to differentiate multiple user controls with the same name. `TagName` is the unique name for the user control, whereas `Src` specifies the virtual path to the user control, such as `MyControl.ascx` or `~/Controls/MyControl.ascx`.

2. After registering the user control, place the user control tag in the markup just as you would with any Web server control (including the `runat="server"` and `Id` properties). For instance, if you had the user control specified in step 1, the following markup adds this control.

```
<SomePrefix:SomeName id="myUC1" runat="server" />
```

CORE NOTE

As an alternative to manually entering these two steps, you can also simply drag-and-drop the user control onto your page while it is in Design view in Visual Studio.

Walkthrough 6.4   *Using a User Control*

1. Create a new Web Form or edit an existing Web Form. For instance, you could use the `Default.aspx` page from Listing 6.10.

2. Add the following `Register` directive to the page.

```
<%@ Register Src="FeatureBookControl.ascx"
    TagName="FeatureBookControl" TagPrefix="uc" %>
```

3. In a sensible spot, add the following markup to the page. If you are using the `Default.aspx` page from Listing 6.10, replace the markup in the first `Content` control with the following.

```
<uc:FeatureBookControl ID="myFeaturedBook" runat="server" />
```

4. Save and test the page. The user control should be displayed in the page.

Adding Data and Behaviors to the User Control

In the user control created in Walkthrough 6.3, the information on the featured book was hardcoded. A more realistic version of this user control would interact with some type of business object or database. Thus, like most Web Forms, most user controls also include some type of programming logic.

You also may want to customize some aspect of the user control, so that it appears or behaves differently when used in different pages or controls. For instance, in the example Featured Book user control, it might be useful to specify the category of book you want to see in the control. You can easily add this type of customization to a control, by adding public properties to the user control. These public properties can then be manipulated declaratively or programmatically by the containing page.

For instance, Listing 6.14 demonstrates the definition of a `FeatureCategory` property in the code-behind class for the `FeatureBookControl` user control. The `Page_Load` in this simplified example modifies the output of the control based on the value of this property.

Listing 6.14   FeatureBookControl.ascx.cs

```
public partial class FeatureBookControl :
    System.Web.UI.UserControl
{
    // Data member for feature category property
    public string _category;

    protected void Page_Load(object sender, EventArgs e)
    {
        // Real-world example would use category values and content
        // from a database or business object. Here you
        // simply hardcode the values

        imgBook.ImageUrl = "~/images/";
        if (FeatureCategory == "Programming")
        {
            labTitle.Text = "Framework Design Guidelines";
            imgBook.ImageUrl += "0321246756.gif";
            labDescription.Text = "This book can improve …";
        }
        else
        {
            labTitle.Text = "Core C# and .NET";
            imgBook.ImageUrl += "0131472275.gif";
            labDescription.Text = "Core C# and .NET is the …";
        }
        imgBook.AlternateText = "Cover image of " + labTitle.Text;
    }

    public string FeatureCategory
    {
        get { return _category; }
        set { _category = value; }
    }
}
```

This code-behind class assumes that the markup for the `FeatureBookControl` user control has been modified, as shown in Listing 6.15.

Listing 6.15 FeatureBookControl.ascx

```
<%@ Control Language="C#" AutoEventWireup="true"
    CodeFile="FeatureBookControl.ascx.cs"
    Inherits="FeatureBookControl" %>

<h2>Featured Book</h2>
<h3><asp:Label ID="labTitle" runat="server"  /></h3>
<asp:Image ID="imgBook" runat="server" CssClass="sideImage" />
<p>
<asp:Label ID="labDescription" runat="server" />
</p>
```

This public property in the user control can now be used wherever you use this user control. For instance, the following example illustrates one way that this property could be used.

```
<uc:FeatureBookControl ID="myFeaturedBook" runat="server"
    FeatureCategory="Programming" />
```

Summary

This chapter examined the different ways to customize the visual appearance of your Web application in ASP.NET 2.0. It began with the simplest, namely the common appearance properties that are available for most server controls. These properties allow you to control colors, borders, and text formatting. Although these properties are very useful for customizing the appearance of your Web output, they do not contain the full formatting power of Cascading Style Sheets. Luckily, ASP.NET server controls fully support styles via the CssClass and the Style properties. I recommended that you minimize the amount of appearance formatting in your server controls as much as possible, and instead externalize appearance settings in your CSS files. The benefit to this approach is that your Web Form's markup becomes simpler, easier to modify, and scales better to different devices.

The chapter also covered two important features of ASP.NET 2.0: themes and master pages. Themes provide a way to customize the appearance of Web server controls on a site-wide basis. Themes can still be integrated with CSS; doing so allows the developer to completely separate style from content. The master pages mechanism provides a much sought-after templating technique to ASP.NET. With master pages, elements that are common throughout a site, such as headers, footers, navigation elements, and the basic site layout itself, can be removed from Web Forms and placed instead within a master page. This significantly simplifies the Web Forms within a site, making the site as a whole easier to create and maintain.

The brief final section in the chapter covered user controls. These are an essential part of most real-world Web sites. User controls provide a consistent, object-oriented approach to user interface reuse in ASP.NET.

The next chapter covers another vital part of your Web site's appearance, its navigation system. It examines how you can programmatically move from page to page as well as the new controls in ASP.NET 2.0 devoted to navigation: the `Menu`, `Tree`, and `SiteMap` controls.

Exercises

The solutions to the following exercises can be found at my Web site, http://www.randyconnolly.com/core. Additional exercises only available for teachers and instructors are also available from this site.

1. Create a page named `PropertyTester.aspx`. This page should allow the user to dynamically change various appearance properties of some sample controls on the page, as shown in Figure 6.18. Ideally, the code-behind class uses an instance of the `Style` class as a data member, whereas event handlers simply modify this instance and apply it to the controls.

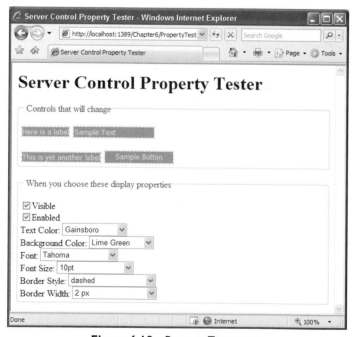

Figure 6.18   PropertyTester.aspx

2. Create a new theme to be used by the `ThemeTester.aspx` example from Listing 6.3.

3. Create a master page named `ThreeColumns.master` that contains a header, three content columns, and a footer. The three columns should each contain a `Content` control. Create a demonstration page that uses this master.

4. Create a user control named `ThemeSelector.ascx` that allows the user to change the theme used on the page. This control should only display themes that exist. Create a demonstration page that uses this user control.

Key Concepts

- Master pages
- Named collection
- Named skins
- Session state
- Skins
- Themes
- User controls

References

Allen, Scott. "Master Pages in ASP.NET." `http://odetocode.com`.

Allen, Scott. "Themes in ASP.NET." `http://odetocode.com`.

Murkoth, Jeevan C. "Master Pages in ASP.NET 2.0." *dotnetdevelopersjournal.com* (December 2004).

Onion, Fritz. "Master Your Site Design with Visual Inheritance and Page Templates." *MSDN Magazine* (June 2004).

Winstanley, Phil. "Skin Treatment: Exploiting ASP.NET 2.0 Themes." *asp.netPro Magazine* (October 2005).

7

ASP.NET Site Navigation

"Agriculture, manufactures, commerce and navigation: the four pillars of our prosperity . . ."

—Thomas Jefferson, First Annual Message to Congress, Dec. 8, 1801

Although navigation may no longer be the pillar of our nations' prosperity, for a Web site, navigation is indeed the pillar of its prosperity. Most usability experts stress that there is a strong correlation between the effectiveness of a site's navigation system and a user's satisfaction with that site. Because all Web applications require some type of navigation system, that is, some mechanism for moving from page to page within a Web site, every ASP.NET developer must spend some time constructing this navigation system. Previous chapters have shown how links and buttons, both with and without postback, can be used to request other pages. This chapter examines some of the unique site navigation features that have been added to ASP.NET 2.0. Although these navigation features may or may not increase your prosperity, they will certainly reduce the amount of development time spent on this most necessary part of Web application development.

ASP.NET Site Navigation Overview

When you begin to design a new Web site, typically one of the very first tasks performed is to design the organization structure for the site. This organization structure is usually some type of hierarchical organization of pages. In this structure, the home page is the "top" page in the hierarchy. A limited number of top-level category pages are then "under" this home page, with each of these top-level pages having a hierarchy of pages below them, as shown in Figure 7.1. This hierarchical structure is generally referred to as a ***site map***.

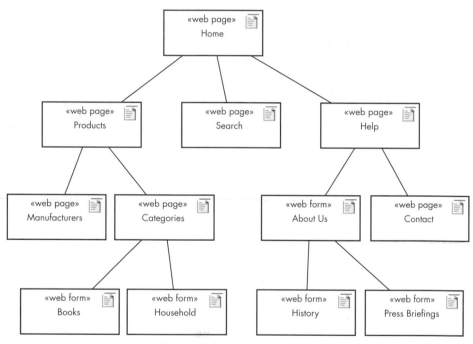

Figure 7.1   Example site map

The site navigation features introduced in ASP.NET 2.0 added new controls for displaying the site map as well as a consistent mechanism to allow the developer to separate the data for the site map from its presentation in these new controls. This last point is quite important. The ASP.NET site navigation system allows all of a site's navigation links to be stored in an external data store; special Web server controls can use this navigation data to render the links in a bulleted list or in one of the new navigation controls, namely, as a menu, tree, or breadcrumb (that is, a series of links that displays the path from the current page back to the home page).

By separating the data of the navigation system (shown in Figure 7.1) from its eventual presentation, the site becomes a great deal easier to maintain and customize. One of the principal design goals of object-oriented programming design in general is to reduce the coupling between components or objects in the system. The architecture of the new site navigation features in ASP.NET accomplishes this goal by reducing the coupling between the organization structure for the site and the way it is presented in the Web page.

In version 1.x of ASP.NET, it was hard to avoid intermeshing the organization structure of the site with its implementation. For example, a typical navigation system for accessing the top-level categories in a site might look like the following.

```
<ul>
  <li><a href="default.aspx" id="current">Home</a></li>
  <li><a href="products.aspx">Products</a></li>
  <li><a href="search.aspx">Search</a></li>
  <li><a href="contact.aspx">Contact Us</a></li>
</ul>
```

Notice how there are two types of information here. One is the structural or site map data (Home/default.aspx, Products/products.aspx, Search/search.aspx, and Contact Us/contact.aspx); the other type of data is the implementation details for the site map (i.e, it uses a <ul> list containing anchor tags to present the navigation and the home link is currently active, and thus might be styled differently). The problem with combining the site map information with its implementation is that making changes to the site map structure necessitates making changes to the implementation (that is, the markup) as well. The site navigation system introduced in ASP.NET 2.0 now lets the developer define the site map independently of its implementation, thus allowing organization changes without markup changes.

Provider Model

The architecture of the new site navigation system in ASP.NET 2.0 is quite easy to use as well as very extensible and powerful. It uses what Microsoft calls the ***provider model***. A provider is a software module that provides a uniform programming interface between a service and a data source. It abstracts the actual storage media so that you can code to the provider API rather than to the specific details of a particular data source. Figure 7.2 illustrates how the provider model is used in the context of the ASP.NET site map architecture.

Three new controls provide the user interface for your navigation system. The `TreeView`, `Menu`, and `SiteMapPath` controls provide different ways of rendering the hierarchical site map information. As well, other controls, such as the `BulletedList` or the `GridView`, can also display site map data. The controls and the pages they are contained in do not directly interact with the site map data source, but with the appropriate site map provider or with the `SiteMap` class itself.

ASP.NET ships with one site map provider, the `XmlSiteMapProvider`, but others (such as, a `SqlSiteMapProvider` or a `FileSystemSiteMapProvider`) could be created that follow the interface specified by `SiteMapProvider`. These unique site map provider classes would handle the actual interaction with the external data sources.

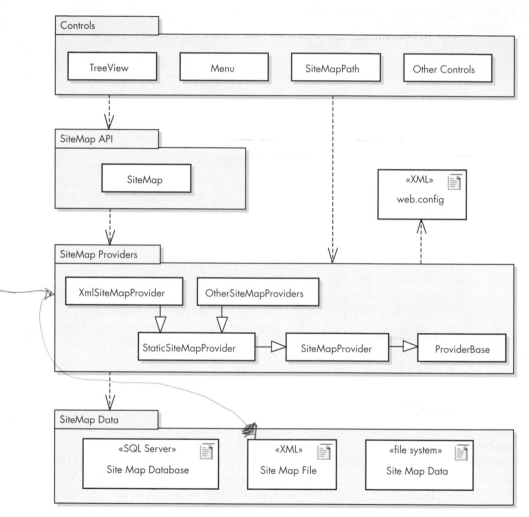

Figure 7.2   Provider model

Finally, one of the great things about the provider model is that the decision for which site map provider to use can be easily changed via the `Web.config` file. The provider model is covered in much more detail in Chapter 13.

XML Site Map

To use the new ASP.NET site navigation controls, you must define the organizational structure of the site in some type of external data source. The source for this data map can be an XML file, a database, or even a file system hierarchy. By default, ASP.NET 2.0 uses the `XmlSiteMapProvider`, which uses a special XML file named `Web.sitemap` to contain the site structure; the navigation controls then consume this file and display its contents as a menu, tree, or breadcrumb. You can create this XML site map file directly within Visual Studio via the Add New Item option.

The format of this XML site map is quite straightforward, as shown in Listing 7.1.

Listing 7.1 Web.sitemap

```xml
<?xml version="1.0" encoding="utf-8" ?>
<siteMap
  xmlns="http://schemas.microsoft.com/AspNet/SiteMap-File-1.0">
  <siteMapNode url="BookHome.aspx" title="Home" >

    <siteMapNode url="Catalog.aspx" title="Catalog" >
      <siteMapNode url="Categories.aspx" title="Categories" >
        <siteMapNode url="List.aspx?cat=1" title="Graphics" />
        <siteMapNode url="List.aspx?cat=2" title="Internet" />
        <siteMapNode url="List.aspx?cat=3" title="Networking" />
      </siteMapNode>
      <siteMapNode url="Series.aspx" title="Series" >
        <siteMapNode url="List.aspx?series=1"
            title="Core Series" />
        <siteMapNode url="List.aspx?series=2"
            title=".NET Series" />
        <siteMapNode url="List.aspx?series=3"
            title="Signature Series"/>
      </siteMapNode>
    </siteMapNode>

    <siteMapNode url="Search.aspx" title="Search" />

    <siteMapNode url="Help.aspx" title="Help" >
      <siteMapNode url="About.aspx" title="About Us" />
      <siteMapNode url="Contact.aspx" title="Contact Us" />
    </siteMapNode>

  </siteMapNode>
</siteMap>
```

single root element

The site map XML file contains any number of nested `siteMapNode` elements contained within the `siteMap` document element. This `siteMap` element must contain a single root `siteMapNode` element. This root element represents the home page and can contain one or more `siteMapNode` elements, which correspond to the main section pages. Each of these `siteMapNode` elements under the root can contain other nested `siteMapNode` elements.

Each `siteMapNode` element must define a destination URL and a title that is displayed for this node when the site map is rendered in a navigation control. Some additional optional attributes for the `siteMapNode` element are listed in Table 7.1.

CORE NOTE

A valid XML site map file must not have any duplicate URLs. However, there can be duplicate empty `url` attributes. This is a restriction of the `XmlSiteMapProvider` (because it uses the `url` attribute value as a key), not of the navigation system itself.

Table 7.1   siteMapNode Attributes

Attribute	Description
description	Provides a tool tip description when mouse is hovered over the rendered node (usually a `Literal` or `Hyperlink`).
resourceKey	Specifies the resource key for the label. This is used for localization. That is, this key is used to retrieve the appropriate localized version of the title from the language resource file. Localization is covered in Chapter 16.
roles	The collection of security roles associated with this node.
title	The title for the site node. This usually is rendered as a `Literal` or `HyperLink` by the navigation controls that consume the site map.
url	The URL that the site node represents. This specifies the destination URL when the site map is used and rendered by a navigation control.

Consuming the XML Site Map

XML site maps (or indeed the site maps of any provider type) are principally intended to be used by the special navigation controls included as part of version 2.0 of ASP.NET. These controls are covered in the next three sections. But before that, I should mention that you can use the XML site map with *any* of the Web server controls that support data binding. Although data binding in all its glory will be covered in some depth over the next few chapters, we can illustrate here how to use this XML site map.

In contemporary CSS-based standards-oriented Web development, developers frequently construct their navigation systems by wrapping their links within XHTML <ul> (list) elements, and then use CSS to style the list. Indeed, we examined a typical example right at the beginning of this chapter. Because the BulletedList Web server control can also render its content as plain XHTML <a> elements within a <ul>, we can illustrate how an XML site map can be used to achieve separation between the site organization (contained in the site map file) and its presentation (contained in the BulletedList and the CSS).

Using the XML site map file in a Web Form is almost criminally easy. There are just two steps. The first step is to add a SiteMapDataSource control to your page, as shown in the following example.

```
<asp:SiteMapDataSource ID="siteSource" runat="server"
    ShowStartingNode="false"/>
```

Other than the obligatory id and runat attributes, there is only the ShowStartingNode attribute that needs to be explained. A value of false for this attribute indicates that you want to skip the root siteMapNode element and display instead the content of that root element. In contrast, a value of true initially displays just the root element. For instance, in the example site map in Listing 7.1, you would only see the Home node. Finally, notice that you do need to specify the name of your site map file. By default, the SiteMapDataSource control uses the Web.sitemap file (although it is possible to use a site map with a different name).

But what exactly is this SiteMapDataSource control? It is an example of a ***data source control***. What are data source controls? These are a new type of control introduced in ASP.NET 2.0 that declaratively encapsulates an external data source. Data source controls connect to and retrieve data from a data source and make it available for other controls to bind to without requiring any programming code. We examine data source controls in considerable detail in Chapter 9.

Now that you have added the SiteMapDataSource control to your page, you can now reference it via the DataSourceID attribute of the Web server control that is to display the data. For instance, to display the XML in the site map in two different BulletedList controls, you could do so with the following.

```
<asp:BulletedList id="bulHoriz" runat="Server"
    DataSourceID="siteSource"
    DisplayMode="HyperLink" />
<asp:BulletedList id="bulVert" runat="Server"
    DataSourceID="siteSource"
    DisplayMode="HyperLink" />
```

The `DataSourceID` attribute references the `id` of your `SiteMapDataSource` control. Notice that no code is necessary. All the messy file opening and reading code is handled, behind the scenes, by the `SiteMapDataSource` control, whereas the output process is handled by the `BulletedList` control.

The result in the browser is similar to that shown in Figure 7.3.

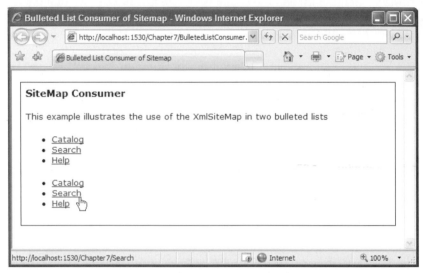

Figure 7.3   Displaying XML site map in a bulleted list

There are a few interesting issues with the result shown in Figure 7.3. The first is that you only see the first level in the site map hierarchy. This is a fairly serious drawback. The `Menu` and `TreeView` controls (covered later in this chapter) address this problem. However, if you only have a single, nonhierarchical list of menu items and you want to avoid using HTML tables (the `Menu` and `TreeView` controls render themselves using nested `<table>` elements), either for accessibility or regulatory or philosophic reasons, using `SiteMapDataSource` with the `BulletedList` approach still gives you the benefits of separating navigation data from its presentation.

The other interesting issue to notice in Figure 7.3 is that the `BulletedList` controls are not using the URL information from the site map file (notice the URL in the browse status bar). This is easily addressed by using the `DataValueField` and `DataTextField` attributes.

```
<asp:BulletedList ID="bulHoriz" runat="Server"
    DataValueField="url" DataTextField="title"
    DataSourceID="siteSource" DisplayMode="HyperLink" />
```

These two attributes tell the `BulletedList` control to use the `url` attribute in your underlying data source (i.e., the `Web.sitemap` file) for the `href` of the hyperlink, and the `title` attribute from the data source as the displayed value in the list.

Because the `id` of each control is rendered as an HTML `id` attribute, you can use CSS styling to make your `BulletedList` controls look quite interesting (see Figure 7.4). Listing 7.2 provides the code for the completed Web Form shown in Figure 7.4.

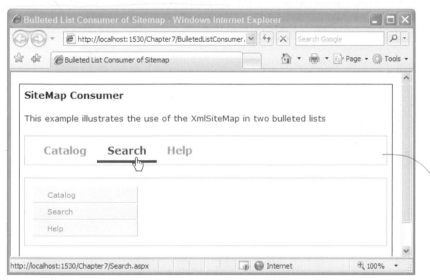

Figure 7.4   Styling the bulleted list

Listing 7.2   BulletedListConsumer.aspx

```
<%@ Page Language="C#" AutoEventWireup="false" %>

<!DOCTYPE html PUBLIC "-//W3C//DTD XHTML 1.0 Transitional//EN"
    "http://www.w3.org/TR/xhtml1/DTD/xhtml1-transitional.dtd">

<html xmlns="http://www.w3.org/1999/xhtml" >
<head runat="server">
    <title>Bulleted List Consumer of Sitemap</title>
    <link href="chapterStyles.css" type="text/css"
      rel="stylesheet"/>
    <style type="text/css">
    /* style the first list horizontally */
    #bulHoriz { border: solid 1pt silver; padding:1em;
        margin-left:0;}
    #bulHoriz ul { text-align: right;   }
```

```
#bulHoriz li { display: inline; list-style-type: none;   }
#bulHoriz a:link, #primary a:visited
{
    color: #3399CC;
    font-size: 120%;
    font-weight: bold;
    border-bottom: solid 4px white;
    padding: 0.5em 1em 0.4em 1em;
    text-decoration: none;
    margin: 0;
}
#bulHoriz a:hover {
  border-bottom: solid 4px #800000;
  color: #800000;}

/* style the second list vertically */
#bulVert { border: solid 1pt silver; padding:1em;
    margin-left:0;}
#bulVert ul { padding: 0; margin: 0; }
#bulVert li { list-style: none; margin: 0; font-size: 80%;}
#bulVert li a
{
    width: 13em;
    display: block;
    background-color: #f7f2ea;
    border-width: 1px;
    border-color: #ffe #aaab9c #ccc #fff;
    border-style: solid;
    color: #777;
    text-decoration: none;
    padding: 0.5em 0 0.5em 2em;
}
#bulVert li a:hover
{
    color: #800000;
    background: #f0e7d7;
}
  </style>
</head>
<body>
   <form id="form1" runat="server">
   <div id="container">
      <h1>SiteMap Consumer</h1>
      <p>This example illustrates the use of the XmlSiteMap in
      two bulleted lists</p>

      <asp:BulletedList ID="bulHoriz" runat="Server"
         DataValueField="url" DataTextField="title"
         DataSourceID="siteSource" DisplayMode="HyperLink" />
```

```
    <asp:BulletedList ID="bulVert" runat="Server"
        DataValueField="url" DataTextField="title"
        DataSourceID="siteSource" DisplayMode="HyperLink" />

    <asp:SiteMapDataSource ID="siteSource" runat="server"
        ShowStartingNode="false" />
</div>
</form>
</body>
</html>
```

Programming the Site Map

Regardless of which data format the site map uses, you can use the `SiteMap` class to programmatically access the site map data. This data is read in its entirety and then stored in memory; the `SiteMap` class provides read-only access to this data. The `SiteMap` class provides several static properties for accessing this navigation data. One of the most useful of these properties is `CurrentNode`. This property retrieves the `SiteMapNode` for the current page. You can then use this property to retrieve the parent node for this page as well as its next and previous siblings (i.e., the next and previous `SiteMapNode` objects at the same level of the site map hierarchy).

One potential usage for this `SiteMap.CurrentNode` property is to provide next, previous, and up/parent links on each page, similar to that shown in Figure 7.5.

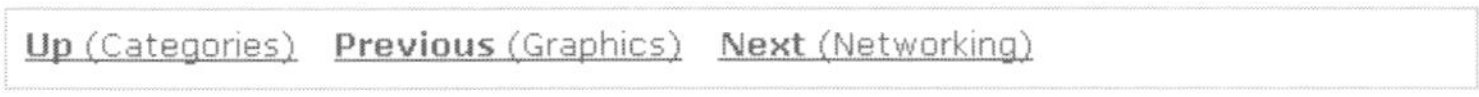

Up (Categories)   **Previous** (Graphics)   **Next** (Networking)

Figure 7.5   Site node buttons

You can do this by adding `HyperLink` controls to your pages that do not have their `NavigateUrl` properties set.

```
<asp:HyperLink ID="lnkPrev" runat="server"  />
<asp:HyperLink ID="lnkNext" runat="server"  />
<asp:HyperLink ID="lnkUp" runat="server"  />
```

Your code-behind can set the `NavigateUrl` property of these controls to the `Url` of the `PreviousSibling`, `NextSibling`, and `ParentNode` of the `CurrentNode`. For instance, if you have three `HyperLink` controls named `lnkPrev`, `lnkNext`, and `lnkUp`, you can then specify their destination URLs via the following.

```
lnkPrev.NavigateUrl = SiteMap.CurrentNode.PreviousSibling.Url;
lnkNext.NavigateUrl = SiteMap.CurrentNode.NextSibling.Url;
lnkUp.NavigateUrl = SiteMap.CurrentNode.ParentNode.Url;
```

The relationship between the SiteMapNode objects within the SiteMap class after reading the site map can be visualized as a tree-like structure. Figure 7.6 illustrates the object hierarchy that would be contained in SiteMap after processing the web.sitemap file from Listing 7.1. If you are currently viewing the page about.aspx, the next sibling would be contact.aspx, and the parent would be help.aspx.

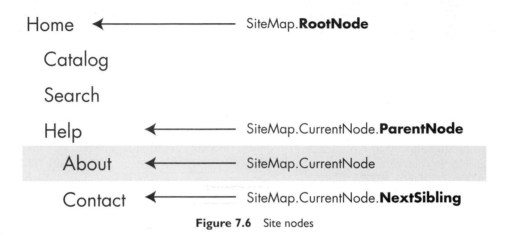

Figure 7.6   Site nodes

What would be the previous sibling for about.aspx? There isn't one. There is also no next sibling for contact.aspx, nor a parent for BookHome.aspx. For these nodes, the simple code shown previously would not work correctly. Instead, you need to verify that the current node in fact has a parent or a next or previous sibling before you perform any assignment, as shown in this example.

```
if (SiteMap.CurrentNode != null)
{
   if (SiteMap.CurrentNode.PreviousSibling != null)
      lnkPrev.NavigateUrl =
         SiteMap.CurrentNode.PreviousSibling.Url;
   else
      lnkPrev.Visible = false;

   if (SiteMap.CurrentNode.NextSibling != null)
      lnkNext.NavigateUrl = SiteMap.CurrentNode.NextSibling.Url;
   else
      lnkNext.Visible = false;

   if (SiteMap.CurrentNode.ParentNode != null)
      lnkUp.NavigateUrl = SiteMap.CurrentNode.ParentNode.Url;
   else
      lnkUp.Visible = false;
}
```

Notice that this code sample first verifies that the `CurrentNode` exists, just in case the current page is not in the current site map. Notice as well how the appropriate `HyperLink` is hidden in those situations where there is no up, previous, or next page.

Using Different Site Maps

The default site map file is named `Web.sitemap` and uses the `XmlSiteMapProvider`. You can easily use a different XML site map file by adding a new `provider` element to the `Web.config` file, as shown in the following.

```
<system.web>
    ...
    <siteMap>
        <providers>
            <add name="WebSiteMap"
                type="System.Web.XmlSiteMapProvider"
                siteMapFile="~/web.sitemap"/>
            <add name="SecondSiteMap"
                type="System.Web.XmlSiteMapProvider"
                siteMapFile="~/second.sitemap"/>
        </providers>
    </siteMap>
</system.web>
```

Notice that the site maps are added as new providers and could, in fact, use a different provider type than the `XmlSiteMapProvider`. Although adding the default site map is not strictly necessary, it may make it clearer to have an explicitly named provider for the default site map.

After you have added the provider to the `Web.config` file, you can now reference its name in any `SiteMapDataSource` control using the `SiteMapProvider` attribute.

```
<asp:SiteMapDataSource ID="siteSource" runat="server"
    ShowStartingNode="false" SiteMapProvider="SecondSiteMap" />
```

The `SiteMapProvider` property can also be set dynamically at runtime. To illustrate this ability, lets use a `DropDownList` control that displays all the site map providers available to us and that programmatically sets the `SiteMapProvider` property of the `SiteMapDataSource` control when the user selects from the list. The markup might look like the following.

```
<asp:DropDownList ID="drpProviders" runat="server"
    AutoPostBack="True"
    OnSelectedIndexChanged="drpProviders_SelectedIndexChanged" />

<asp:BulletedList ID="bulVert" runat="Server"
    DataValueField="url" DataTextField="title"
```

```
    DataSourceID="siteSource" DisplayMode="HyperLink" />

<asp:SiteMapDataSource ID="siteSource" runat="server"
    ShowStartingNode="false"    />
```

Your code-behind only needs to fill the list with the provider names during the page load, as well as handle the list selections. The former can be achieved simply by iterating through the static `Providers` collection of the `SiteMap` class and adding each provider name to the list; the later only requires setting the `SiteMapProvider` property to the selected item.

```
protected void Page_Load(object sender, EventArgs e)
{
    if (!IsPostBack)
    {
        // Iterate through all the defined providers and
        // add to list
        foreach (SiteMapProvider provider in SiteMap.Providers)
        {
            drpProviders.Items.Add(new ListItem(provider.Name));
        }
    }
}

// Event handler for list selection
protected void drpProviders_SelectedIndexChanged(object sender,
        EventArgs e)
{
    siteSource.SiteMapProvider = drpProviders.SelectedItem.Text;
}
```

One reason you want to dynamically set the `SiteMapProvider` is in a situation where the site hierarchy has been split across multiple site map files (generally, to make the Web application's site map easier to work with). For instance, imagine a site with a primary and secondary navigation system in a master page. In this site, the primary navigation system displays the major sections of the site (e.g., Products, Services, and Support). Each major section has its own separate site map file that is displayed in the secondary navigation area of each page in the site. Imagine that both the primary and secondary navigation are implemented as `BulletedList` controls. All you need do when the user switches to a different major section via the primary navigation is to programmatically change the `SiteMapProvider` property of the `SiteMapDataSource` used by the secondary `BulletedList`, as shown in Figure 7.7.

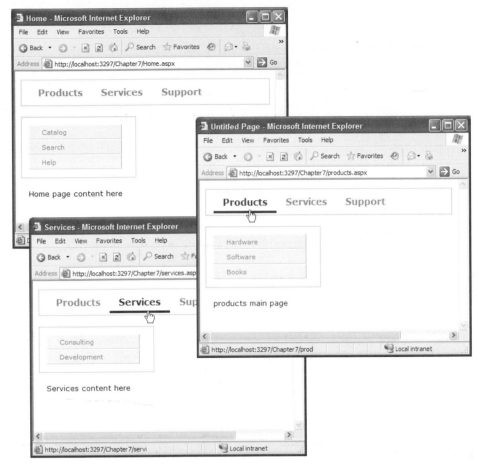

Figure 7.7   Using multiple site map providers

In the last chapter, we looked at how you can add public properties to your master page's code-behind class to allow the individual content pages to programmatically interact with the master page. You can use the same technique here to allow the content pages to modify the `SiteMapProvider` property of the `SiteMapDataSource` used by the secondary navigation system. For instance, assume that your master page (here called `Sample.master`) has the following `SiteMapDataSource` defined for the secondary navigation.

```
<asp:SiteMapDataSource ID="secondarySiteSource" runat="server"
   ShowStartingNode="false" />
```

You can then add the following property to your master page.

```
public partial class Sample : System.Web.UI.MasterPage
{
    public string SecondaryProvider
    {
        set { secondarySiteSource.SiteMapProvider = value;   }
    }
}
```

Your content pages can then simply set this property in their own code-behind classes.

```
Master.SecondaryProvider = appropriate secondary site map name
```

Other Features of the Site Map

The information within a site map can be localized. That is, the displayable information in a site map can be customized for different language environments. In such a case, you can specify a resource key for the SiteMapNode title via the resourceKey attribute of SiteMapNode. The resource key is used to retrieve the appropriate localized version of the title from a language resource file. Localization is covered in Chapter 16.

Site maps are also fully integrated into the security system of ASP.NET. Many Web sites need the capability to hide menu options from unauthenticated users or show certain menu options only to very specific users. ASP.NET security has a role management system that provides a way to restrict access to Web pages based on security roles. Site maps provide a way to hide site map nodes also based on these security roles (called site map security trimming).

SiteMapPath Control

The previous section demonstrated how site map data can be used with other Web server controls. However, to truly use the complete power of the navigation system in ASP.NET, you need to use the dedicated navigation controls: Menu, TreeView, and SiteMapPath. The TreeView and Menu controls allow the user to move forward and backward in the navigation hierarchy, whereas the SiteMapPath allows only backward navigation. All three make use of the ASP.NET site map infrastructure. Because the SiteMapPath control is the simplest of the three, it is perhaps the best place to begin.

The SiteMapPath control displays a navigation path (also known as a **bread-crumb**) that shows the user the current page location and displays links as a path back to the home page, as demonstrated in Figure 7.8. The control is not displayed if it is used on a page that is not specified in the site map data.

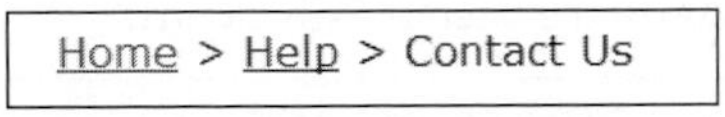

Home > Help > Contact Us

Figure 7.8   Sample SiteMapPath control

You can easily add a `SiteMapPath` control to any page that has a matching `siteMapNode` in your site map, as follows.

```
<asp:SiteMapPath ID="smpBreadcrumb" runat="server" />
```

If this markup was added to `Contact.aspx` and the site was using the site map shown in Listing 7.1, the result would look like that shown in Figure 7.8.

The `SiteMapPath` control consists of a number of `SiteMapNodeItem` objects, where each of these node objects corresponds to an element in the navigation path. Each node is separated by a path separator (by default, the > symbol). The node that represents the currently displayed page is the ***current node***. At the base of the path is the ***root node***. Any other node between the current node and root node is an ***ancestor node***. The most immediate ancestor to any nonroot node is called the ***parent node***. Figure 7.9 illustrates the relationship between these nodes.

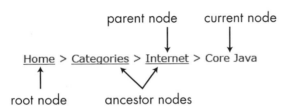

Figure 7.9   SiteMapPath nodes

Each of the nodes displayed by the `SiteMapPath` control is by default rendered as either a `HyperLink` (for the root and ancestor nodes) control or a `Literal` control (for the current node).

Like every control in ASP.NET, the `SiteMapPath` control has various properties that can be set declaratively or manipulated programmatically. Table 7.2 lists the most notable properties of the `SiteMapPath` control. (You can view the MSDN documentation for a complete listing.)

Table 7.2   Notable Properties of the SiteMapPath Control

Property	Description
ParentLevelsDisplayed	Indicates how many levels of parent nodes are displayed by the control "above" the current node. The default is -1, which indicates that all parent and ancestor nodes above the current node are displayed.
PathDirection	Indicates whether the nodes are to be rendered left to right in hierarchical order from the root node to the current node or from the current node to the root node. Possible values are specified by the PathDirection enumeration (CurrentToRoot, RootToCurrent).
PathSeparator	The string that delimits the different nodes in the rendered path. The default is ",".
RenderCurrentNodeAsLink	Indicates whether the current node is rendered as a hyperlink. The default is false (and thus not displayed as a link).
ShowToolTips	Indicates whether a pop-up tool tip should be displayed over the link when the user hovers the mouse over the link. The default is true.
SiteMapProvider	The name of the SiteMapProvider used by the control.
SkipLinkText	The string that is rendered as an alt attribute to the invisible image that is added to the control when it is rendered. This image is used by screen readers as a way to let users skip the links. The default value is Skip Navigation Links.

Styling the SiteMapPath

Like the Calendar and Wizard controls covered in previous chapters, the SiteMapPath control can be customized via style elements or template elements. You can style any of the nodes, change the type of control used to render a node via templates, as well as style or template the path separator.

The following styles are available.

- CurrentNodeStyle—Allows you to style the current node.
- NodeStyle—Allows you to specify the style for all the nodes.
- PathSeparatorStyle—Allows you to style the separator between the nodes.
- RootNodeStyle—Allows you to style the root node.

Each of these style properties has a variety of properties that you can modify. They can be set using subproperty syntax or within a nested style tag. For instance, to change the background color of the root node, you can specify the subproperty within the `SiteMapPath` declaration.

```
<asp:SiteMapPath … RootNodeStyle-BackColor="Yellow">
```

Alternately, you can set it via a nested style tag, as shown here.

```
<asp:SiteMapPath … >
  <RootNodeStyle BackColor="Yellow" />
  …
</asp:SiteMapPath>
```

In most all the examples in the rest of the chapter, you shall use the nested style tag approach because it generally makes for a more manageable `SiteMapPath` declaration.

All of these styles have a fairly similar set of properties. You can adjust the color, border, font, padding, size, and CSS class. If you have several `SiteMapPath` controls that need to be styled identically, you may want to specify this formatting within a skin file.

As we saw in the last chapter, it is often preferable to use CSS to define visual styles; thus, the examples in the book generally specify only the CSS class in these nested ASP.NET style elements, as in the following example.

```
<asp:SiteMapPath … >
  <RootNodeStyle CssClass="someCSSclassName" />
  …
</asp:SiteMapPath>
```

As an example of styling let us create the `SiteMapPath` illustrated in Figure 7.10.

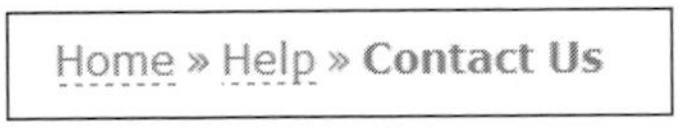

Figure 7.10 Styling the SiteMapPath

To begin, you change the path separator character and then specify the styles for the nodes, the path separator, and the current node.

```
<asp:SiteMapPath ID="smpBreadcrumb" runat="server"
    PathSeparator="&#187;">
  <NodeStyle CssClass="pathNodes" />
  <PathSeparatorStyle CssClass="pathSep" />
  <CurrentNodeStyle CssClass="currentNode" />
</asp:SiteMapPath>
```

Notice the use of the `PathSeparator` attribute. Here, you are using the HTML character code for the » character. Each of these styles simply specifies which CSS class it is going to use. To get the same result as shown in Figure 7.10, you can define the CSS classes as follows (here shown as embedded styles):

```
<style type="text/css">
   .pathNodes {
      color: #666666;
      text-decoration: none;
      border-bottom: dotted 1pt #666666;
    }
   .currentNode {
      font-weight: bold;
      color: #666666;
    }
   .pathSep {
      color: #666666;
      padding-left: 4px;
      padding-right: 4px;
    }
</style>
```

Although you could have used properties of the relevant styles (e.g., `<NodeStyle color="#666666" >`) to define some of the styling, you have no choice but to use CSS to define the bottom border, the text decoration, and the padding.

Customizing the SiteMapPath Output

What if you do not want to use text links for each site map node? The `SiteMapPath` control provides the capability to completely customize the rendering for each node type through the `CurrentNodeTemplate`, `RootNodeTemplate`, `NodeTemplate`, and `PathSeparatorTemplate` elements. These elements allow you to completely override the standard display of each node. For instance, if you want to display an image instead of a character for the path separator, you could do so via the `Path-SeparatorTemplate`.

```
<PathSeparatorTemplate>
   <img src="images/pathSeparator.gif" alt="" />
</PathSeparatorTemplate>
```

You can add almost any markup to these templates. You can also retrieve data about the node via something called a ***data-binding expression***. Data binding refers to the process of dynamically assigning a value or values to a control at either design time or runtime and having the control automatically display the value or values. That is, you only need tell the control where it can find its data, and the control handles the process of displaying it. We examine data binding more thoroughly in the next chapter.

At any rate, you can retrieve the data about the node by using a data binding expression. Within this expression, you use the `Eval` method. This method can be passed the name of the node you want to display. For instance, if you want to display each node as a hyperlinked image, which has a filename that matches the node title (see Figure 7.11), you could use the following:

```
<NodeTemplate>
   <a href='<%# Eval("Url") %>' >
   <img src='images/<%# Eval("Title") %>.gif' %>'/>
   </a>
</NodeTemplate>
```

HOME ⊗ HELP ⊗ Contact Us

Figure 7.11   Using templates with the SiteMapPath

The `Eval` method evaluates late-bound (i.e., runtime) data expressions in the templates of controls that are data bound. At runtime, the `Eval` method calls the `Eval` method of the `DataBinder` object, referencing the current data item of the naming container. The naming container for a given control is the parent control above it in the hierarchy. The `Eval` method takes the name of a data field and returns a string containing the value of that field from the current "record" or object in the data source (in this case, the current object is the current `SiteMapNode`). `Url` and `Title` in the preceding example are properties of the `SiteMapNode` class. The assumption in this example is that we have image files with the same filename as the `Title` of the `SiteMapNode` in your site map.

CORE NOTE

`CurrentNodeTemplate` and `RootNodeTemplate` **override** `NodeTemplate`. Thus, for instance, if you use an image in the `NodeTemplate` but use a text label in the `CurrentNodeTemplate`, the current node is displayed as a text label.

Integrating Query Strings into the SiteMapPath

The `SiteMapPath` control used along with the XML site map file is quite powerful and easy to use. However, for those Web sites that dynamically construct their content from query string information, a fixed XML site map may not be that practical.

For instance, let us imagine a Web site with a product listing page and a single product display page. The listing page displays hundreds of products according to different criteria and displays a brief description for each product along with links to the single product display page. In all likelihood, there are not hundreds of almost identical single product display pages, but just one Web Form that is passed the product identifier via a query string to the request page, which then uses programming logic to retrieve the information for the requested product from some type of external data store and then displays it (see Figure 7.12). In such a case, a fixed site map file is unwieldy because it needs to include *every* possible passed query string value—clearly an unacceptable situation.

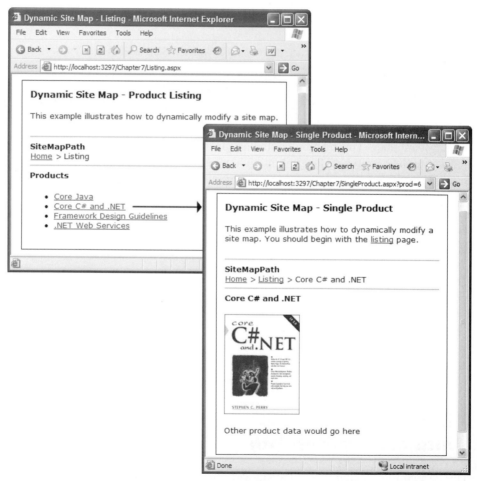

Figure 7.12   Dynamic SiteMapPath based on the query string

CORE WARNING

The following description and example is a bit complex. If you are unfamiliar with application-level event handlers (covered in Chapter 12), you may want to skip this section.

Fortunately, you can use a bit of programming and the `SiteMapResolve` event of the `SiteMap` class to dynamically modify the `SiteMapNode` object based on the requested query string information. The `SiteMapResolve` event is raised any time a `SiteMapNode` is accessed (for instance, by the `SiteMapPath` control) *anywhere* in the application. The handler for this event is passed a `SiteMapResolveEventArgs` object that allows you to examine the query string. As well, this handler returns the (potentially) modified `SiteMapNode` object that then is displayed by your `SiteMap-Path` control. Thus, you need to create a `SiteMapResolve` event handler that examines the query string for the requested page and then modifies any appropriate `SiteMapNode` objects.

Because the `SiteMapResolve` event can be triggered by *any* of your pages that use the site map in your application, the `SiteMapResolve` event handler cannot exist in any individual page's code-behind class. Instead, it must have application-level scope. You may recall from our description of the page and application life cycle in Chapter 2 that not only do pages raise events but the application as a whole does so as well. ASP.NET allows you to handle these application events within a special file named `Global.asax`. You can register a `SiteMapResolve` event handler in the `Application_Start` event handler in `Global.asax`, as shown here.

```
void Application_Start(object sender, EventArgs e)
{
    SiteMap.SiteMapResolve += new
        SiteMapResolveEventHandler(ModifyProductSiteMapNode);
}
```

CORE NOTE

Remember that you can easily create the `Global.asax` file in Visual Studio from the Add New Items dialog.

You now need to create the `ModifySiteMapNode` event handler method. This method can also be defined in the `Global.asax` file. But what should it do? The answer must begin with your site map. Let us assume that you have a site map that looks similar to the following.

```xml
<?xml version="1.0" encoding="utf-8" ?>
<siteMap
   xmlns="http://schemas.microsoft.com/AspNet/SiteMap-File-1.0" >

   <siteMapNode url="Home.aspx" title="Home" >
      <siteMapNode url="Listing.aspx" title="Listing" >
         <siteMapNode url="SingleProduct.aspx" title="Product"/>
      </siteMapNode>
      ...
   </siteMapNode>
</siteMap
```

In the second screen shown in Figure 7.12, `SingleProduct.aspx` is passed the `Id` of the product to display via a query string parameter. Your `SiteMapResolve` event handler thus needs to programmatically change the `Title` property of the `SiteMapNode` for `SingleProduct.aspx` from "Product" to the actual product name (presumably retrieved from a database); if you do not, the last node in the `SiteMapPath` will be "Product" rather than the actual product name. Based on the preceding `Application_Start` event handler, `SiteMapResolve` event handler is called `ModifyProductSiteMapNode` and might look similar to that shown in the complete code for `global.asax` shown in Listing 7.3.

Listing 7.3   Global.asax

```csharp
<%@ Application Language="C#" %>

<script runat="server">
/// <summary>
/// Event handler invoked when application starts (i.e., the
/// first time any page in web app is requested)
/// </summary>
void Application_Start(object sender, EventArgs e)
{
  SiteMap.SiteMapResolve += new
    SiteMapResolveEventHandler(ModifyProductSiteMapNode);
}


/// <summary>
/// Event handler for modifying the product site map node
/// </summary>
public SiteMapNode ModifyProductSiteMapNode(object o,
      SiteMapResolveEventArgs e)
{
   // If the current page is not in site map, ignore it
   if (SiteMap.CurrentNode == null)
      return null;
```

```
    // Make a copy of the SiteMapNode
    SiteMapNode temp = SiteMap.CurrentNode.Clone(true);

    // If this isn't the product node, you can
    // leave it and exit
    if (temp.Title != "Product")
        return temp;

    // Get the product id to retrieve from the query string
    string sId = e.Context.Request.QueryString["prod"];
    // If no query string then leave node as is
    if (sId == null)
        return temp;

    // Use business object to retrieve a populated Product object
    Product prod =
        ProductCatalog.GetProductById(Convert.ToInt32(sId));

    // If you have successfully retrieved a product, change
    // the node's title to match the product name
    if (prod != null)
        temp.Title = prod.Name;

    // Return the modified node
    return temp;
}
</script>
```

Notice that the `ModifyProductSiteMapNode` method makes a copy of the current `SiteMapNode` and checks if it is the product node. If it is, the title of this node is replaced with the title of the actual requested product. In this sample, a populated `Product` entity object is retrieved from a business object named `ProductCatalog`. Of course, this could be replaced by a direct database call or some other logic for looking up the product name from the product ID.

Menu Control

The `Menu` control is one of the navigation controls introduced in version 2.0 of ASP.NET. It displays the navigation hierarchy as links and supports both static and dynamic (pop-up) menu options (see Figure 7.13). The `Menu` control is highly customizable and works with the site map infrastructure covered earlier in the chapter.

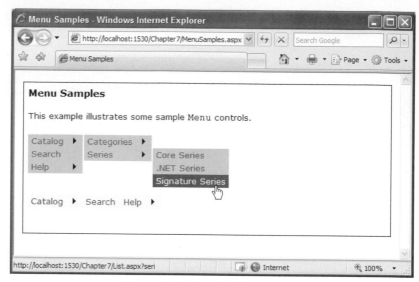

Figure 7.13   Sample Menu controls

We saw back in Chapters 3 and 4 that most Web server controls inherit from the `WebControl` class. The `Menu` control (and the `TreeView` control, which is covered in "TreeView Control" on page 421 of this chapter) inherits instead from the `HierarchicalDataBoundControl` class, which in turn inherits from the `BaseDataBoundControl` class.

As we shall see in more detail in the next chapter, ASP.NET has a control architecture that allows Web server controls to bind to data in an easy and consistent manner. Web server controls that bind to data are referred to as **data-bound controls**, and the controls that facilitate that binding are called data source controls. For instance, in the `BulletedList` example in the first section of this chapter, the `BulletedList` was your data-bound control, and the `SiteMapDataSource` was your data source control. All data-bound controls ultimately inherit from the `Base-DataBoundControl` class, whereas the `HierarchicalDataBoundControl` class is the base class for controls that retrieve and display data from an ASP.NET hierarchical data source control.

Table 7.3 lists the many notable properties of the `Menu` control.

Table 7.3 Notable Properties of the Menu Control

Property	Description
DataBindings	A collection of `MenuItemBinding` objects. These objects allow you to define a custom relationship between a menu item and its data.
DisappearsAfter	The amount of time (in milliseconds) that a dynamic menu is displayed after the mouse pointer is no longer positioned over the menu.
DynamicBottomSeparatorImageUrl	The URL for the image that is displayed at the bottom of each dynamic menu item.
DynamicEnableDefaultPopOutImage	Indicates whether to display the built-in image that indicates that a dynamic menu item has a submenu. The default is `true`. An alternative image can be specified by the `DynamicPopOutImageUrl` property.
DynamicHorizontalOffset	The number of pixels to shift a dynamic menu horizontally from its parent. If the menu is being displayed vertically, this property instead controls the horizontal spacing between the dynamic menu and its parent. The default is `0`.
DynamicItemFormatString	Used to insert additional text into the display of dynamic menu items. The default value for this property is `"{0}"` (that is, no additional text is to be inserted).
DynamicPopOutImageTextFormatString	The alternate text for the image used to indicate that a dynamic menu item has a submenu.
DynamicPopOutImageUrl	The URL for the custom image that is displayed to indicate that the dynamic menu item has a submenu.
DynamicTopSeparatorImageUrl	The URL for the separator image that is displayed at the top of each dynamic menu item. The default is `""`, which means that by default there is no separator image.

Table 7.3   Notable Properties of the Menu Control *(continued)*

Property	Description
DynamicVerticalOffset	If the menu items are being displayed horizontally, this specifies the vertical spacing between the dynamic menu and its parent menu item. If the menu items are being displayed vertically, this specifies the number of pixels to shift the dynamic menu position vertically from its base position.
ItemWrap	Indicates whether the text for menu items should wrap. The default is false.
MaximumDynamicDisplayLevels	The maximum number of menu levels to display for a dynamic menu. The default is 3.
Orientation	Which direction to render the menu. Possible values are described by the Orientation enumeration (Horizontal or Vertical).
PathSeparator	The character used to delimit the path of a menu item. Each menu item in a menu has a value path that specifies the position of the menu item. This value path is a string of delimited characters from the root node to the current menu item.
ScrollDownImageUrl	The URL for the image that is displayed to indicate that the user can scroll down to see additional menu items.
ScrollDownText	The text to be used for the alt attribute of the scroll down image.
ScrollUpImageUrl	The URL for the image that is displayed to indicate that the user can scroll up to see additional menu items.
ScrollUpText	The text to be used for the alt attribute of the scroll up image.
SkipLinkText	The alternate text for a hidden image used by screen readers to provide the capability to skip the list of menu links.

Table 7.3 Notable Properties of the Menu Control *(continued)*

Property	Description
`StaticBottomSeparatorImageUrl`	The URL for the separator image that is displayed at the bottom of each static menu item. The default is `""`, which means that by default there is no separator image.
`StaticDisplayLevels`	The number of static menu levels to display. The default is `1`.
`StaticEnableDefaultPopOutImage`	Indicates whether to display the built-in image that indicates that a static menu item has a submenu. The default is `true`. An alternative image can be specified by the `StaticPopOutImageUrl` property.
`StaticItemFormatString`	Used to insert additional text into the display of static menu items. The default value for this property is `{0}`, which means there is no additional text.
`StaticPopOutImageTextFormatString`	The alternate text for the pop-out image used to indicate that a static menu item has a submenu.
`StaticPopOutImageUrl`	The URL for the custom image that is displayed to indicate that the static menu item has a submenu.
`StaticSubMenuIndent`	The number of pixels to indent submenus within a static menu.
`StaticTopSeparatorImageUrl`	The URL for the separator image that is displayed at the top of each static menu item. The default is `""`, which means that by default there is no separator image.

Using the Menu Control

Hierarchical content can be added to the `Menu` control in two ways: by declaratively or programmatically adding individual `MenuItem` objects/controls and by data binding the control to a data source.

Declaratively adding `MenuItem` controls to a `Menu` control is somewhat similar in approach to adding items to a list control (see page 129 in Chapter 3). For instance, the following example declares a simple two-level menu; Figure 7.14 illustrates the rather uninspiring result in the browser.

```
<asp:Menu id="menuMain" runat="server">
  <Items>
    <asp:MenuItem Text="Home" NavigateUrl="home.aspx" />
    <asp:MenuItem Text="Catalog">
      <asp:MenuItem Text="Categories"
          NavigateUrl="categories.aspx" />
      <asp:MenuItem Text="Series" NavigateUrl="series.aspx" />
    </asp:MenuItem>
    <asp:MenuItem Text="About Us" NavigateUrl="about.aspx" />
  </Items>
</asp:Menu>
```

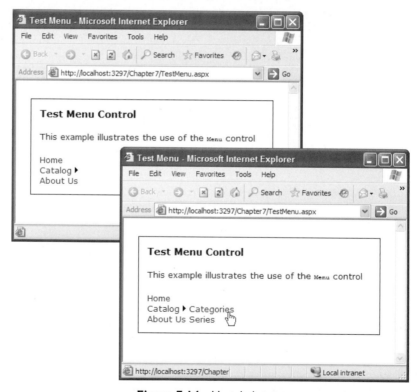

Figure 7.14   Unstyled menu

Notice that the `MenuItem` controls are contained within the `Items` container, which is one of several other elements that can be contained within the `Menu` container. `MenuItem` has various properties that can be used to customize the appearance of any given item in a menu (see Table 7.4). Some of these properties can only be used programmatically.

Table 7.4   Notable Properties of the MenuItem Control

Property	Description
ChildItems	Collection of submenu items for the menu item.
DataBound	Specifies whether the menu item was created through data binding. Default is `false`.
DataItem	Returns the data item that is bound to this menu item.
DataPath	The XPath to the data that is bound to this menu item.
Depth	Returns the depth of the menu item in the menu hierarchy.
Enabled	If set to `false`, the menu item is disabled and no dynamic menus for this item display. If set to `true`, the menu item behaves as normal.
ImageUrl	The URL for the image that is displayed next to the menu item text. The default is an empty string (`" "`), which indicates that this property is not set.
NavigateUrl	The URL to navigate to when the menu item is clicked. The default is an empty string (`" "`), which indicates that this property is not set.
Parent	Returns the parent menu item for this menu item.
PopOutImageUrl	The URL of an image that is displayed in a menu item to indicate that the menu item has a dynamic submenu. The default is an empty string (`" "`), which indicates that this property is not set.
Selectable	Indicates whether menu item can be selectable (i.e., is a link). The default is `true`. If set to `false`, no action occurs when menu item is clicked (but child items are still displayed).
Selected	Specifies whether this menu item is selected. The default is `false`.
SeparatorImageUrl	The URL of a custom image (usually of a line) that is displayed at the bottom of a menu item to separate it from other menu items.

Table 7.4   Notable Properties of the MenuItem Control *(continued)*

Property	Description
Text	The text of the menu item.
ToolTip	The text to be displayed in a tool tip when the mouse pointer is positioned over the menu item.
Value	Used to add supplemental data about the menu item that is not displayed but could be used during postback processing of the menu selection.

Although some of the properties shown in Table 7.4 might not be commonly used, several are quite essential. The following example demonstrates how to use the additional `ImageUrl`, `PopOutImageUrl`, `SeparatorImageUrl`, and `ToolTip` properties. The result in the browser is shown in Figure 7.15.

```
<asp:Menu id="menuMain" runat="server">
  <Items>
    <asp:MenuItem Text="Home" NavigateUrl="home.aspx"
        ImageUrl="images/menuHome.gif"
        SeparatorImageUrl="images/separator.gif"
        ToolTip="Click to return to home page" />
    <asp:MenuItem Text="Catalog"
        PopOutImageUrl="images/menuPopout.gif"
        ImageUrl="images/menuCatalog.gif"
        SeparatorImageUrl="images/separator.gif">

        <asp:MenuItem Text="Categories"
            NavigateUrl="categories.aspx"
            SeparatorImageUrl="images/separator.gif"
            ToolTip="View our books by category" />
        <asp:MenuItem Text="Series" NavigateUrl="series.aspx"
            ToolTip="View our books by series"/>
    </asp:MenuItem>
    <asp:MenuItem Text="About Us" NavigateUrl="about.aspx"
            ImageUrl="images/menuABout.gif"
            ToolTip="Our history and contact info" />
  </Items>
</asp:Menu>
```

You can also add `MenuItem` objects programmatically. For instance, the following example demonstrates the programmatic creation of a menu similar to that shown in Figure 7.14. Notice that the `MenuItem` controls that are nested within the catalog menu item are added via the `ChildItems` collection.

```
protected void Page_Load(object sender, EventArgs e)
{
   menuMain.Items.Add(new MenuItem("Home", "home.aspx"));

   MenuItem catalog = new MenuItem("Catalog");

   // Add the nested catalog menu items
   catalog.ChildItems.Add(new MenuItem("Categories",
      "categories.aspx"));
   catalog.ChildItems.Add(new MenuItem("Series", "series.aspx"));

   // Change one sample menu item property
   catalog.PopOutImageUrl = "images/menuPopout.gif";

   menuMain.Items.Add(catalog);
   menuMain.Items.Add(new MenuItem("About Us", "about.aspx"));
}
```

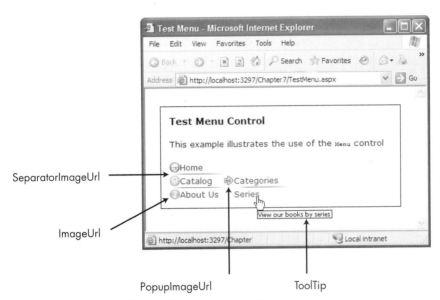

Figure 7.15 Specifying MenuItem properties

Finally, the Menu control can also be populated by data binding the control to a data source. For instance, you can display a menu based on the content of your site map file by linking the DataSourceID property to the ID of our data source, as shown in the following.

```
<asp:Menu id="menuMain" runat="server"
   DataSourceID="siteSource"/>
```

```
<asp:SiteMapDataSource ID="siteSource" runat="server"
   ShowStartingNode="false"/>
```

Changing the Appearance of the Menu

The Menu control is a remarkably flexible control. But as a glance at Table 7.3 indicates, this flexibility comes at the cost of a fair amount of complexity. Almost every aspect of the Menu control's appearance and behavior can be customized. The properties in Table 7.3 can be broken down into three categories, which we will cover in turn:

- Properties pertaining to the appearance and behavior of the Menu element itself
- Nested style tags
- Nested template tags

The properties in Table 7.3 can be categorized along a different axis altogether. Those that relate to **static menu items** and those that relate to **dynamic menu items**. Static menu items are those menu items that are always displayed regardless of the mouse state. Dynamic menu items are child menu items that are normally hidden but dynamically appear when the user hovers the mouse over the parent menu item. There is a parallel set of customization properties for static and dynamic menu items (e.g., StaticMenuItemStyle and DynamicMenuItemStyle).

Finally, you can change the appearance of the menu items based on their level independently of whether they are static or dynamic. Using LevelMenuItem-Styles, LevelSelectedItemStyles, and LevelSubMenuStyles, you can set the appearance of all first level items, and then set the appearance of all second level items, and so on.

Changing the Display Levels and Orientation

You can adjust the number of menu item levels to display via the StaticDisplay-Levels property (the default is 1, meaning the first level under the root is displayed statically). You can also adjust how many dynamic levels can appear with the MaximumDynamicDisplayLevels property. The horizontal or vertical orientation of the menu can be set via the Orientation property.

We can use these three properties with two different Menu controls to create the typical primary and secondary navigation schemes used in most Web sites, as shown in the following example.

```
<asp:Menu id="menuPrimary" runat="server"
   DataSourceID="siteSource"
   Orientation="Horizontal"
   StaticDisplayLevels="1"
   MaximumDynamicDisplayLevels="0" />
```

```
<hr />

<asp:Menu id="menuSecondary" runat="server"
    DataSourceID="siteSource"
    Orientation="Vertical"
    StaticDisplayLevels="3"
    MaximumDynamicDisplayLevels="2" />
```

The first or primary navigation menu is displayed horizontally and displays only the first static level (with no dynamic menu items). The secondary navigation menu is displayed vertically and displays three static levels with no more than two dynamic levels after those three levels. The result in the browser looks similar to that shown in Figure 7.16.

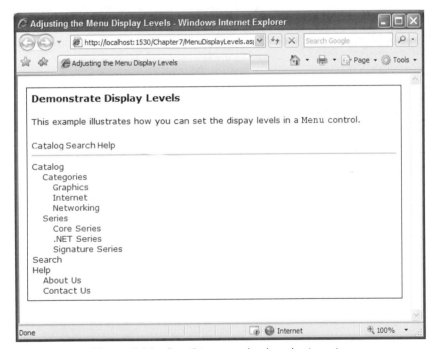

Figure 7.16 Specifying menu levels and orientation

Styling the Menu

As mentioned earlier, you can style both the static and the dynamic menu items separately, and following are the parallel styles to do so.

- `StaticMenuStyle`, `DynamicMenuStyle`—Allows you to style the menu container, but not the menu items.
- `StaticMenuItemStyle`, `DynamicMenuItemStyle`—Allows you to style all the menu items in the menu.
- `StaticSelectedStyle`, `DynamicSelectedStyle`—Allows you to style the selected item in a menu. That is, if the user clicks a given menu item, and the requested URL for that menu item contains this same menu, this menu item can be styled differently.
- `StaticHoverStyle`, `DynamicHoverStyle`—Allows you to style the menu item when the mouse is positioned over the item.

Each of these styles has a variety of properties that you can modify. Just like the `SiteMapPath` control, these styles can be set using subproperty syntax or within a nested style tag.

Listings 7.4 and 7.5 demonstrate how CSS and the `Menu` control can be used together to create an attractive navigation system. These use the same site map as that shown in Listing 7.1. The result when rendered in the browser is illustrated in Figure 7.17.

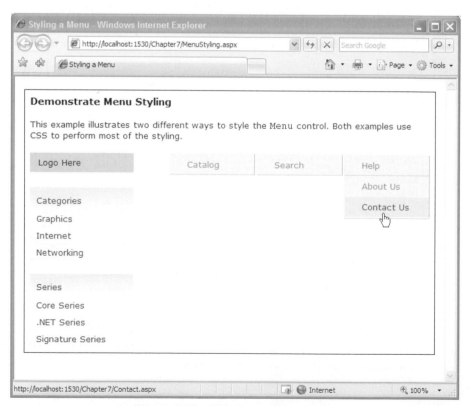

Figure 7.17 CSS menu styling example

The horizontal menu at the top of the page is meant to be the primary navigation system and thus does not show the entire navigation hierarchy. Instead, it has just one static display level and one dynamic display level. It uses both the static and dynamic style tags to specify the appearance of the menu.

The vertical menu on the left side of the browser window is the secondary navigation system for the page. It doesn't replicate the entire navigation hierarchy, but instead displays only the items under the Catalog node. This requires a second SiteMapDataSource control with the StartingNodeUrl attribute set to Catalog.aspx.

You want this secondary menu to display the two levels statically but you want each level to appear differently. Thus, you need to also specify the LevelMenuItemStyles element. The LevelMenuItemStyles element is an alternative to setting the static and dynamic style properties. The styles contained in this element are applied to the menu items based on their menu level. The first style in the element corresponds to the style of menu items in the first level of the menu. The second style in the element corresponds to the style of menu items in the second level of the menu, and so on.

You may notice that menu style elements in the listing simply reference the appropriate CSS class because the CSS class definition contains the actual styling. Some of the CSS styling demonstrates formatting only possible with CSS, such as the background gradient in the secondary menu and the individualized borders in the primary menu.

Listing 7.4 MenuStyling.aspx

```
<h1>Demonstrate Menu Styling</h1>
<p>This example illustrates two different ways to style the
<code>Menu</code> control.
Both examples use CSS to perform most of the styling.</p>

<p id="logo">Logo Here</p>

<asp:Menu id="menuPrimary" runat="server"
   DataSourceID="siteSource1"
   Orientation="Horizontal"
   StaticEnableDefaultPopOutImage="false"
   StaticDisplayLevels="1"
   MaximumDynamicDisplayLevels="1">

   <StaticMenuStyle CssClass="primaryStaticMenu"/>
   <StaticMenuItemStyle CssClass="primaryStaticMenuItem"/>
   <StaticHoverStyle CssClass="primaryStaticHover"/>

   <DynamicMenuStyle CssClass="primaryDynamicMenu" />
   <DynamicMenuItemStyle CssClass="primaryDynamicMenuItem"/>
```

```
      <DynamicHoverStyle CssClass="primaryDynamicHover"/>
</asp:Menu>

<br style="clear:both"/>

<asp:Menu id="menuSecondary" runat="server"
   DataSourceID="siteSource2"
   Orientation="Vertical"
   StaticDisplayLevels="2" StaticSubMenuIndent="0"
   MaximumDynamicDisplayLevels="0" >

   <StaticHoverStyle CssClass="secondaryStaticHover"/>
   <LevelMenuItemStyles>
     <asp:MenuItemStyle CssClass="secondaryLevelOne" />
     <asp:MenuItemStyle CssClass="secondaryLevelTwo" />
   </LevelMenuItemStyles>
</asp:Menu>

<asp:SiteMapDataSource ID="siteSource1" runat="server"
   ShowStartingNode="false" />

<asp:SiteMapDataSource ID="siteSource2" runat="server"
   ShowStartingNode="false" StartingNodeUrl="Catalog.aspx" />
```

Listing 7.5   MenuStyling.css

```
/* style to create a logo placeholder */
#logo {
   float: left;
   width: 10.5em;
   background: #CCCCCC;
   padding: 0.5em 0.5em 0.5em 1em;
   margin: 0;
}
/* styles for the primary menu at top */
.primaryStaticMenu
{
   background-color: transparent;
   float: right;
}
.primaryStaticMenuItem
{
   width: 10em;
   background-color: #f7f2ea;
   border-width: 1px;
   border-color: #efefef #aaab9c #ccc #efefef;
   border-style: solid;
   color: #777777;
```

```
      padding: 0.5em 0 0.5em 1em;
}
.primaryStaticHover
{
      color: #800000;
      background: #f0e7d7;
}

.primaryDynamicMenu
{
      background-color: #f7f2ea;
      border-bottom: solid 1px #ccc;
}
.primaryDynamicMenuItem
{
      width: 10em;
      background-color: #f7f2ea;
      color: #777;
      padding: 0.5em 0 0.5em 1em;
      border-width: 1px;
      border-color: #f7f2ea #aaab9c #f7f2ea #efefef;
      border-style: solid;
}
.primaryDynamicHover
{
      color: #800000;
      background: #f0e7d7;
}

/* styles for the secondary menu down the left */
.secondaryLevelOne
{
      background-color: transparent;
      background-image: url(images/headBackground.gif);
      background-repeat: repeat-x;
      margin: 1.5em 0 0 0;
      padding: 5px 0 0 5px;
      width: 12em;
      height: 35px;
}
.secondaryLevelTwo
{
      background: #FAFBFB;
      padding: 5px 0 5px 5px;
}
.secondaryStaticHover
{
      color: #800000;
}
```

CORE NOTE

Unfortunately, the `DynamicMenuStyle` and `LevelSubMenuStyle` elements do not work properly (dynamic elements do not appear at all) in the Mac Safari browser. This is scheduled to be fixed in one of the first patches or service packs for version 2.0 of the .NET Framework.

Customizing the Menu Output

What if you do not want to use text links for each menu item? The `Menu` control provides the ability to completely customize the rendering for each menu item through the `StaticItemTemplate` and `DynamicItemTemplate` elements. These two elements allow you to completely override the standard appearance and behavior of a menu item. For instance, if you want to display buttons instead of hyperlinks for each static menu item, you could add the following to the `Menu` control.

```
<StaticItemTemplate>
  <asp:Button ID="btnItem" runat="server"
    Text='<%# Eval("Text") %>' />
</StaticItemTemplate>
```

You can add almost any markup to the `StaticItemTemplate` container. The `Text` property of the button in the previous example is set via a ***data-binding expression*** (see the discussion in the previous section, "SiteMapPath Control" beginning on page 388). Of course, to get the buttons to perform your required navigation, you need to add some type of postback event handling that eventually redirects to the URL in your site map. You need to pass this URL to your button event handler. Perhaps the best way to do this is via the `Command` event handler; you can then pass the destination URL in the `CommandName` attribute using data binding.

```
<StaticItemTemplate>
   <asp:Button ID="btnItem" runat="server"
     OnCommand="btnItem_Command"
     CommandName='<%# Eval("NavigateUrl") %>'
     Text='<%# Eval("Text") %>' />
</StaticItemTemplate>
```

The event handler for the button is quite straightforward. It simply redirects to the URL in the `CommandName` property of the `CommandEventArgs` object that is passed to the event handler.

```
protected void btnItem_Command(object sender, CommandEventArgs e)
{
    string url = e.CommandName;
    Response.Redirect(url);
}
```

In fact, you can eliminate the postback event handler altogether by making use of the capability of ASP.NET 2.0 to post back to a different page. In this case, you can simply use the `PostBackUrl` attribute of the `Button` control.

```
<asp:button ID="btnItem" runat="server"
   PostBackUrl='<%# Eval("NavigateUrl") %>'
   Text='<%# Eval("Text") %>' />
```

You can also customize the dynamic menu items in a similar way using the `DynamicItemTemplate` element. For instance, imagine that you want to use image hyperlinks for your dynamic menu items and each menu item has a unique image, as shown in Figure 7.18.

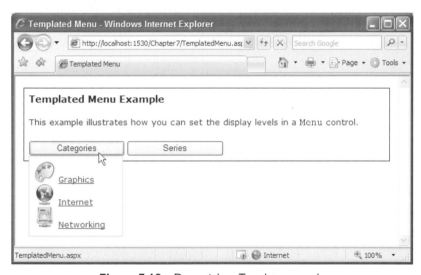

Figure 7.18 DynamicItemTemplate example

One way you can achieve this effect is to use image filenames that can be derived from the `Title` property of the `siteMapNode`. If the image filenames thus match the titles in the site map, you can then calculate the filename for each image using data-binding syntax. For instance, if your site node titles are `Graphics`, `Internet`, and `Networking`, and your filenames are `iconGraphics.gif`, `iconInternet.gif`, and `iconNetworking.gif`, you could set the `DynamicItemTemplate` as follows.

```
<DynamicItemTemplate>
   <asp:hyperlink ID="imgbtnItem" runat="server"
      NavigateUrl='<%# Eval("NavigateUrl") %>'
```

```
    ImageUrl='<%# "images/icon" + Eval("Text") + ".gif" %>'

  ToolTip='<%# Eval("Text") %>' />
<asp:hyperlink ID="lnkItem" runat="server"
  Text='<%# Eval("Text") %>'
  NavigateUrl='<%# Eval("NavigateUrl") %>' />
</DynamicItemTemplate>
```

This approach works because the image filename can be constructed from the `Title` property of the `siteMapNode`.

Handling Menu Events

Earlier, we saw how you can programmatically add menu items to the `Menu` control. Yet, even if you are using a site map to populate your menu, you may still need to programmatically manipulate either the `Menu` control or its underlying site map. For instance, you may want to programmatically manipulate a menu to uniquely customize each menu item, or to alter the `SiteMapDataSource` control to keep multiple menus synchronized. In either case, you need to respond to `Menu` events.

The two principal events that you should be interested in are `MenuItemClick` and `MenuItemDataBound`. The `MenuItemClick` event is triggered when the user clicks any menu item; one use for this event is to synchronize the menu with another control (i.e., modify another control based on which menu item was clicked). The `MenuItemDataBound` event is triggered each time a data value is bound to a menu item; it can be used to modify a menu item before it is rendered.

For instance, imagine a page with two menus that displays the following menu data.

```
<siteMapNode title="Products">
  <siteMapNode title="Hardware" url="Hardware.aspx">
    ...
  </siteMapNode>
  <siteMapNode title="Software" url="Software.aspx">
    ...
  </siteMapNode>
  <siteMapNode title="Books" url="Books.aspx">
    ...
  </siteMapNode>
</siteMapNode>

<siteMapNode title="Services">
  <siteMapNode title="Consulting" url="Consulting.aspx">
    ...
  </siteMapNode>
  <siteMapNode title="Development" url="Development.aspx">
    ...
  </siteMapNode>
```

```
</siteMapNode>

<siteMapNode title="Support">
   <siteMapNode title="Drivers" url="Drivers.aspx">
     . . .
   </siteMapNode>
   <siteMapNode title="Manuals" url="Manuals.aspx">
     . . .
   </siteMapNode>
   <siteMapNode title="Updates" url="Updates.aspx">
     . . .
   </siteMapNode>
</siteMapNode>
```

The first or primary menu has three options (Products, Services, Support). The menu items that are displayed in the secondary menu vary depending upon which menu item the user selects from the primary menu (see Figure 7.19).

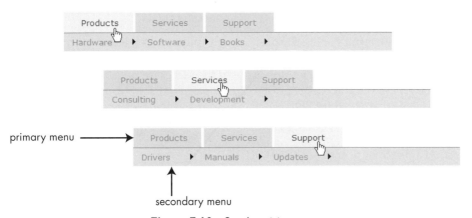

Figure 7.19   Synchronizing menus

The first step to achieve this synchronization is an event handler for the Menu-ItemClick event of the primary menu. It simply sets the StartingNodeUrl property of the SiteMapDataSource used by the secondary Menu control (in this case, it is called siteSecondary).

```
protected void menuPrimary_MenuItemClick(object sender,
   MenuEventArgs e)
{
   string sUrl = "Default.aspx?node=";
   switch (e.Item.Value)
   {
      case "Products":
         siteSecondary.StartingNodeUrl = sUrl + "hardware";
```

```
        return;
    case "Services":
        siteSecondary.StartingNodeUrl = sUrl + "consulting";
        return;
    case "Support":
        siteSecondary.StartingNodeUrl = sUrl + "drivers";
        return;
    }
}
```

The `MenuEventArgs` object that is passed into the event handler can be used to determine which menu item was clicked. This example simply specifies which `SiteMapNode` is the first in the site map hierarchy (i.e., which node level is the first to be displayed by the `Menu` control).

You also have to attach this event handler to your primary menu, as shown here.

```
<asp:Menu id="menuPrimary" runat="server"
    DataSourceID="sitePrimary"
    Orientation="Horizontal" MaximumDynamicDisplayLevels="0"
    OnMenuItemClick="menuPrimary_MenuItemClick" >
```

However, the event handler by itself is not sufficient. Recall that each menu item by default is rendered as a `HyperLink` control. This means that each time the user clicks a menu item, a new request is made to the server for a *different* page. In your case, you do not want to pass control to a new page, but simply do a postback to the *same* page so that the different secondary menu can be displayed. You can achieve this changed behavior by using the `DataBindings` collection of the `Menu` control.

DataBindings and MenuItemBinding

The `DataBindings` collection contains `MenuItemBinding` objects that define the relationship between the menu item and its data. For each `MenuItemBinding` object, you can specify which field in the data is to be mapped to which property of the `MenuItem` object (see Table 7.5). As a result, you can map any data field in your menu's data source to any of the mapping properties of `MenuItemBinding` properties listed in Table 7.5.

Table 7.5   Mapping Properties of MenuItemBinding

Property	Description
`ImageUrlField`	Specifies the data field that is bound to the `ImageUrl` property of a `MenuItem` object.
`NavigateUrlField`	Specifies the data field that is bound to the `NavigateUrl` property of a `MenuItem` object.

Table 7.5 Mapping Properties of MenuItemBinding *(continued)*

Property	Description
TextField	Specifies the data field that is bound to the Text property of a MenuItem object.
ToolTipField	Specifies the data field that is bound to the ToolTip property of a MenuItem object.
ValueField	Specifies the data field that is bound to the Value property of a MenuItem object.

For instance, the following example illustrates how to map the Title attribute of the SiteMapNode element in your site map to the menu items; because there is no NavigateUrlField defined, each menu item does not navigate to a different page but just posts back to the same page (and then executes the menuPrimary_MenuItemClick method).

```
<asp:Menu id="menuPrimary" runat="server"
   DataSourceID="sitePrimary"
   Orientation="Horizontal" MaximumDynamicDisplayLevels="0"
   OnMenuItemClick="menuPrimary_MenuItemClick">

   <DataBindings>
     <asp:MenuItemBinding DataMember="SiteMapNode"
        TextField="Title" />
   </DataBindings>

</asp:Menu>
```

You can also use the DataBindings collection to map a menu to any type of XML file. For instance, assume that you have the legacy XML file shown in Listing 7.6 that you want to use with a Menu control.

Listing 7.6 MenuMapping.xml

```
<?xml version="1.0" encoding="utf-8" ?>
<Books>
   <Category Name="Internet"
        Icon="images/small_iconInternet.gif">
     <Book Title="E-Business">
        <Url>browse.aspx?cat=101</Url>
     </Book>
     <Book Title="Servers">
        <Url>browse.aspx?cat=102</Url>
```

```
        </Book>
        <Book Title="Usability">
            <Url>browse.aspx?cat=103</Url>
        </Book>
    </Category>

    <Category Name="Networking"
            Icon="images/small_iconNetworking.gif">
        <Book Title="Protocols">
            <Url>browse.aspx?cat=201</Url>
        </Book>
        <Book Title="Security">
            <Url>browse.aspx?cat=202</Url>
        </Book>
    </Category>
</Books>
```

In all of our examples in this chapter, we have used the SiteMapDataSource data source control. You may recall that data source controls connect to and retrieve data from an external data source and make it available to other controls for data binding without requiring code. The SiteMapDataSource control is a hierarchical data source control. Another hierarchical data source control is the XmlDataSource control. The XmlDataSource control can read either an XML file or a string containing XML. It can also apply an XSLT (Extensible Stylesheet Language Transformation) transformation to the XML data, as well as filter the data by applying an XPath expression (covered shortly).

You can add an XmlDataSource control to a Web Form in much the same way that you added a SiteMapDataSource control, and then reference it via the DataSourceID attribute of the Web server control that is to display the data, as shown in the following.

```
<asp:XmlDataSource id="xmlSource" runat="server"
    DataFile="menuMapping.xml" />

<asp:Menu id="menuPrimary" runat="server"
    DataSourceID="xmlSource" />
```

The preceding code does not give us exactly what we want. Figure 7.20 illustrates what this example would look like in the browser.

Notice that the menu is displaying the element names of the XML from Listing 7.6. Instead, you want to map the element attributes to the appropriate MenuItem properties by using the DataBindings collection. You use the Name attribute of the <Category> element and the Title attribute of the <Book> element as your menu item titles. You also map the Icon attribute of the <Category> element to the ImageUrlField property for that MenuItem.

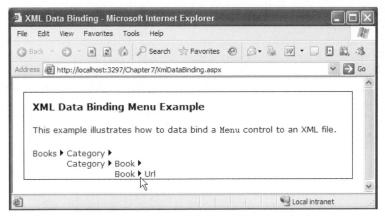

Figure 7.20   Using an XML file without DataBindings

You can achieve this by adding the following `DataBindings` to your `Menu` control.

```
<DataBindings>
  <asp:MenuItemBinding DataMember="Category" TextField="Name"
    ImageUrlField="Icon" />
  <asp:MenuItemBinding DataMember="Book" TextField="Title" />
</DataBindings>
```

In each `MenuItemBinding` element, the `DataMember` attribute is used to specify which element in the XML file contains the data. The `TextField` attribute is used to indicate which XML attribute within the XML element specified by `DataMember` will provide the data for the `TextField` of the `MenuItem`. The result in the browser looks like that shown in Figure 7.21.

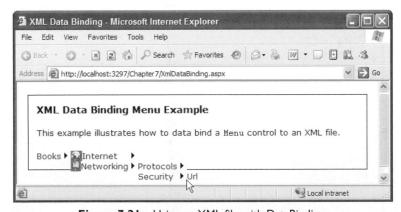

Figure 7.21   Using an XML file with DataBindings

Notice that the Menu in Figure 7.21 begins with the root element (Books) in the XML file. If you want to skip the root element (or indeed any other elements), you can add an **XPath** expression to your XmlDataSource control. XPath is a standardized, platform-independent way to navigate an XML hierarchy. It uses the familiar "slash" file system syntax to navigate down to the element hierarchy. For your example, you could skip the root element in your XML file by adding the following XPath attribute to your XmlDataSource control.

```
<asp:XmlDataSource id="xmlSource" runat="server"
    DataFile="menuMapping.xml" XPath="/Books/Category" />
```

This XPath attribute indicates that the control selects and displays only the <Category> elements within the <Books> root element.

In your example, you also need to specify the URL of the menu items. This requires you to specify the NavigateUrlField attribute of MenuItemBinding. However, unlike with the previous examples, you cannot simply map an XML attribute to NavigateUrlField because the URL data is not within an attribute in your XML file; instead, it is contained within its own nested <Url> element. You can still do this by setting the NavigateUrlField to #innerText (as shown in the following); this maps any text within the Book element to the NavigateUrlField.

```
<asp:MenuItemBinding DataMember="Book"
    TextField="Title" NavigateUrlField="#innerText" />
```

With a bit of styling, your Menu might look like that shown in Figure 7.22.

Figure 7.22   Finished menu using an XML file with DataBindings

TreeView Control

TreeView is a control that can display any type of hierarchical data. Like the Menu and SiteMapPath controls, the TreeView control can be used in conjunction with site maps or it can be used to display other types of hierarchical data (for instance, any type of XML data). Like the Menu control, the TreeView control can be extensively customized via style and template tags as well as be skinned in a theme. Table 7.6 lists the many notable properties of this control.

Table 7.6   Notable Properties of the TreeView Control

Property	Description
AutoGenerateDataBindings	Indicates whether the control automatically generates the bindings between the tree nodes and their data items. The default is true.
CollapseImageToolTip	The alt attribute text for the image displayed for the collapsible node indicator.
CollapseImageUrl	The URL for the custom image used to indicate a collapsible node.
DataBindings	A collection of TreeNodeBinding objects. These objects allow you to define a custom relationship between a menu item and its data.
EnableClientScript	Indicates whether the control renders client-side script to handle the expanding and collapsing of nodes. The default is true.
ExpandDepth	The level of tree nodes to display the first time the tree is rendered. The default is -1, which displays all the nodes.
ExpandImageToolTip	The alt attribute text for the image displayed for the expandable node indicator.
ExpandImageUrl	The URL for the custom image used to indicate an expandable node.
ImageSet	The set of images to be used for the control. Possible values are specified by the TreeViewImageSet enumeration (Arrows, BulletedList, BulletedList2, BulletedList3, BulletedList4, Contacts, Custom, Events, Faq, Inbox, Msdn, Simple, Simple2, WindowsHelp, XPFileExplorer). Default value is Custom.

Table 7.6 Notable Properties of the TreeView Control *(continued)*

Property	Description
LineImagesFolder	The path to the folder that contains the line images used to connect child nodes to their parent node.
MaxDataBindDepth	The maximum number of tree levels to bind the control. Can be used to limit the number of tree levels that appear in the tree. The default is -1, which binds all the levels in the data source to the tree,
NodeIndent	The amount of space in pixels that child nodes are indented from their parent.
Nodes	Collection of all the root TreeNode objects in the tree.
NodeWrap	Indicates whether the text for the node wraps when there is not enough space to display the text in a single line. The default is false.
NoExpandImageUrl	The URL for the custom image used to indicate a nonexpandable node.
PathSeparator	The character used to delimit node values.
PopulateNodesFromClient	Indicates whether the node data is populated on demand from the client. Default is true.
SelectedNode	Returns the TreeNode for the currently selected node.
SelectedValue	Returns the Value property of the selected node.
ShowCheckBoxes	Specifies which node types are displayed with a check box. Possible values are described by the TreeNode-Types enumeration (All, Leaf, None, Parent, Root). The default is None.
ShowExpandCollapse	Indicates whether expansion node indicators are to be displayed. The default is true.
ShowLines	Indicates whether the lines connecting child nodes to their parent are to be displayed. The default is false.
SkipLinkText	The string that is rendered as an alt attribute to the invisible image that is added to the control when it is rendered. This image is used by screen readers as a way to let users skip the tree. The default value is " ".

Understanding the TreeView Control

The TreeView control is made up of individual nodes. Each of these nodes is represented by a TreeNode object. There are three types of tree nodes (see Figure 7.23). A node that contains other nodes is called a **parent node**. A node that contains no other nodes is called a **leaf node**. A parent node that is not contained by any other node but is the ancestor to all the other nodes is the **root node**. Although a typical tree has only one root node, the TreeView control does in fact allow a TreeView to have multiple root nodes, which is useful when you want to display nodes without displaying a single main root node, as in a list of menu items.

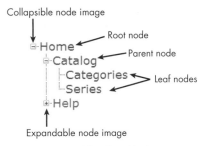

Figure 7.23   TreeNode types

The visual and behavioral properties of the individual nodes in the tree are determined by whether a node is a root, parent, or leaf node. There is a style for each node type (RootNodeStyle, ParentNodeStyle, and LeafNodeStyle). There is also a style that applies to all nodes (NodeStyle), as well as a separate style for selected nodes (SelectedNodeStyle) and for the node that the mouse is above (HoverNodeStyle). Alternately, you can specify node styles based on what level they are within the tree (LevelStyles). The TreeView control also has separate properties for the collapsed and expanded indicators.

Just as with the Menu control, the TreeView control is ultimately rendered in the browser as an HTML <table> element (along with a whole lot of Javascript). As a consequence, these node styles provide not only the usual properties (CssClass, ForeColor, etc.), but also the additional properties listed in Table 7.7. The effects of these style properties are shown in Figure 7.24.

Table 7.7   Additional Style Properties for Node Styles

Property	Description
ChildNodesPadding	The amount of space in pixels above and below the child nodes section of a parent node.
HorizontalPadding	The amount of space in pixels to the left and right of the text in a node.
NodeSpacing	The amount of space in pixels between the node and adjacent nodes at the same level in the tree.
VerticalPadding	The amount of space in pixels to the top and bottom of the text in a node.

Figure 7.24   Additional style properties

As already mentioned, the TreeView control is made up of a number of TreeNode objects. Each of these TreeNode objects can also be customized. Each TreeNode object contains four user interface elements, as shown in Figure 7.25, that can be customized or hidden.

TreeNode has various properties that can be used to customize the appearance of any given item in a menu (see Table 7.8). Some of these properties can only be used programmatically.

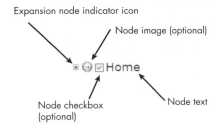

Figure 7.25 TreeNode user interface elements

Table 7.8 Notable Properties of the TreeNode

Property	Description
Checked	Indicates whether the node's check box is selected. The default is `false`.
ChildNodes	Collection of subtree nodes for the tree node.
DataItem	Returns the data item that is bound to this tree node.
DataPath	The XPath to the data that is bound to this tree node.
Depth	Returns the depth of the tree node in the tree hierarchy.
Expanded	Indicates whether the node is expanded.
ImageToolTip	Specifies the tool tip text to display for the image specified by the `ImageUrl` property.
ImageUrl	The URL for the image that is displayed next to the tree node text. The default is an empty string (`""`), which indicates that this property is not set.
NavigateUrl	The URL to navigate to when the menu item is clicked. The default is an empty string (`""`), which indicates that this property is not set.
Parent	Returns the parent node of this node.
PopulateOnDemand	Populates the node's data dynamically (during postback) at request time when the node is expanded. The default is `false`.
Selected	Indicates whether the node is selected. The default is `false`.
ShowCheckBox	Indicates whether a check box is to be displayed next to the node. The default is `false`.

Table 7.8   Notable Properties of the TreeNode *(continued)*

Property	Description
Text	The text of the tree node.
ToolTip	The text to be displayed when the mouse pointer is positioned over the tree node.
Value	Used to add supplemental data about the tree node that is not displayed but could be used during postback processing of the tree node selection.

Using the TreeView Control

Just as with the Menu control, hierarchical content can be added to the TreeView control in two ways: by declaratively or programmatically adding individual Tree-Node objects/controls, and by data binding the control to a data source.

Declaratively adding TreeNode objects to a TreeView control is quite similar to the approach used with the Menu control, except here you add TreeNode rather than MenuItem objects.

```
<asp:TreeView ID="treeMain" runat="server" >
  <Nodes>
    <asp:TreeNode Text="Home" NavigateUrl="home.aspx" >
      <asp:TreeNode Text="Catalog" Expanded="false">
        <asp:TreeNode Text="Categories"
            NavigateUrl="categories.aspx" />
        <asp:TreeNode Text="Series" NavigateUrl="series.aspx" />
      </asp:TreeNode>
      <asp:TreeNode Text="Help" Expanded="false">
        <asp:TreeNode Text="About Us" NavigateUrl="about.aspx" />
      </asp:TreeNode>
    </asp:TreeNode>
  </Nodes>
</asp:TreeView>
```

Figure 7.26 illustrates how the preceding TreeView appears in the browser. Notice that the TreeNode controls are contained within the Nodes container, which is one of several other elements that can be contained within the Nodes container.

Just like the Menu control, the TreeView control can also be populated by data binding. For instance, to data bind your sample TreeView to the Web.sitemap file, you only need to add the appropriate DataSourceID attribute to the control, as in the following example.

```
<asp:TreeView ID="treeMain" runat="server"
  DataSourceID="siteSource">

<asp:SiteMapDataSource ID="siteSource" runat="server" />
```

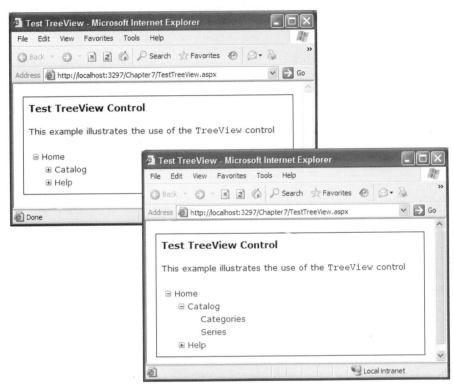

Figure 7.26 Simple TreeView

Changing the Appearance of the TreeView

As you have already seen, there is a wide range of appearance properties and styles available to not only the TreeView control itself but also to the individual TreeNode controls that constitute it. Because we have already looked at how to use styles with the SiteMapPath and Menu controls in this chapter, we will not bother repeating the material here. Instead, we will examine two unique appearance features of the TreeView control: image sets and line sets.

ImageSets

One of the cool features of the `TreeView` is that through the `ImageSet` property, you can select a predefined set of images to give the control a standard look. This property accepts any of the values in the `TreeViewImageSet` enumeration (`Arrows`, `BulletedList`, `Contacts`, `Custom`, `Events`, `WindowsHelp`, etc.).

```
<asp:TreeView ID="treeMain" runat="server" ImageSet="Contacts" />
```

Figure 7.27 demonstrates how most of these image sets appear when rendered in the browser.

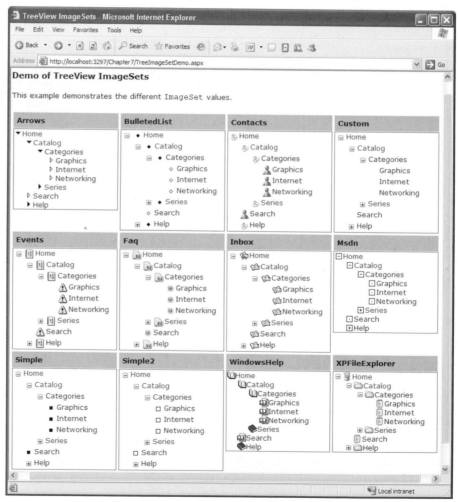

Figure 7.27   Available ImageSets for the TreeView

The default value for `ImageSet` is in fact `Custom`. This means that you can specify your own values for the following `TreeView` properties.

- `CollapseImageUrl`—The URL to a custom image for the collapsible node indicator.
- `ExpandImageUrl`—The URL to a custom image for the expandable node indicator.
- `NoExpandImageUrl`—The URL to a custom image for the nonexpandable node indicator.

For instance, the `TreeView` control definition that follows Figure 7.28 uses `ImageSet="Custom"` along with the preceding properties to create the custom tree shown in Figure 7.28. It also illustrates the use of some of the other styles and properties described in Table 7.7.

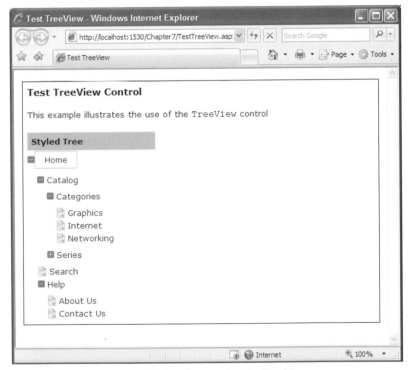

Figure 7.28   Customizing the TreeView

```
<asp:TreeView ID="treeMain" runat="server"
   DataSourceID="siteSource"
   ImageSet="Custom" NodeIndent="15"
```

```
CollapseImageUrl="images/iconCollapse.gif"
ExpandImageUrl="images/iconExpand.gif"
NoExpandImageUrl="images/iconPage.gif" >

  <NodeStyle NodeSpacing="2" ChildNodesPadding="6"
     HorizontalPadding="4" />
  <RootNodeStyle HorizontalPadding="15" VerticalPadding="5"
     BorderStyle="Solid" BorderWidth="1"
     BorderColor="#ACB9B9"/>

</asp:TreeView>
```

LineSets

The TreeView control also allows you to specify whether you want lines connecting the different nodes via the ShowLines property. You can use the default line images or supply your own line images. If you do supply your own, these images must follow a specific naming convention (e.g., Dash.gif, I.gif, L.gif, etc.), and the Line-ImagesFolder property must point to the folder containing these images.

Creating all these images is quite tedious. Thankfully, Visual Studio provides a tool called the TreeView Line Image Generator for creating these images. You can access the tool while in Design view in Visual Studio. Simply choose the Customize Line Images option from the TreeView task panel (see Figure 7.29).

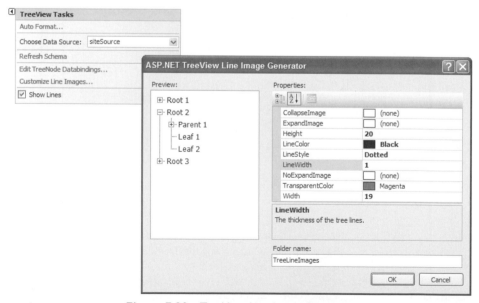

Figure 7.29   TreeView Line Image Generator

Using Other Data with the TreeView Control

Although the previous pages used the `TreeView` control to display site map data (and thus act as a navigation control), the `TreeView` can display other types of data, including XML data and database data.

Using XML Data

In the previous section on the `Menu` control, we demonstrated how that control could display any type of XML data via the `DataBindings` and nested `MenuItemBinding` elements. The `TreeView` control can also display XML data using `DataBindings`, but instead it uses nested `TreeItemBinding` elements, as shown in the following example (which uses the same `MenuMapping.xml` file from Listing 7.6).

```
<asp:TreeView ID="treeMain" runat="server" CssClass="tree"
   DataSourceID="xmlSource" MaxDataBindDepth="1" >

   <DataBindings>
       <asp:TreeNodeBinding DataMember="Category"
          TextField="Name" ImageUrlField="Icon" />
       <asp:TreeNodeBinding DataMember="Book"
          TextField="Title" />
   </DataBindings>

</asp:TreeView>

<asp:XmlDataSource id="xmlSource" runat="server"
   DataFile="menuMapping.xml" XPath="/Books/Category"/>
```

For a more in-depth description of how to use `DataBindings`, refer back to "DataBindings and MenuItemBinding" on page 416.

Using Database Data

The `TreeView` control can easily display data from any other hierarchical data source. However, displaying data from a nonhierarchical data source (such as a database) generally requires a little more programmatic intervention to transform the nonhierarchical data into a hierarchical form. Later in Chapter 11, we create a fairly complex set of business and data classes that encapsulate all of our application and data access logic. Any given Web page could then use these classes to retrieve the data used in the page, thus insulating it from the implementation details of our application's data sources (for instance, Listing 7.3 used a business object to retrieve product information). In such a case, we might then depend upon our business objects to internally represent the relational database data in a hierarchical data structure as well as provide some way of retrieving linked data that we can then add to our Tree-View in a hierarchical manner (see Figure 7.30).

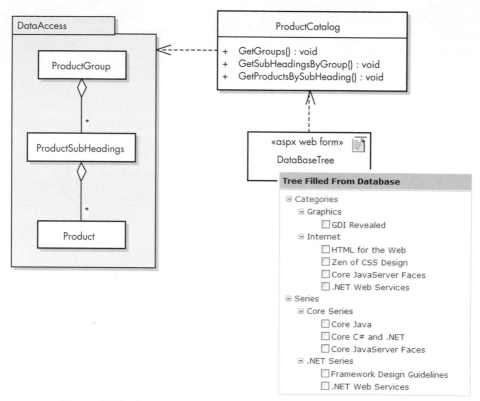

Figure 7.30   Representing relational data in a hierarchical data structure

To create the TreeView shown in Figure 7.30, assume that you already have an existing business object that hides the mundane details of retrieving the data from the database. When the page loads, you retrieve all the product groups and add them as tree nodes to the tree. For each of these product groups, you retrieve all the sub-headings and add them to the tree, and then repeat the process for the products in each subheading. Your loading code would look similar to the following.

```
protected void Page_Load(object sender, EventArgs e)
{
    if (!IsPostBack)
    {
        // Get all the groups from business object
        // and iterate through them
```

```
string[] groups = ProductCatalog.GetGroups();
foreach (string grp in groups)
{
    // Create the node for the group
    TreeNode groupNode = new TreeNode(grp);

    // For each group get their subheadings …
    string[] subheadings =
        ProductCatalog.GetSubHeadingsByGroup(grp);

    // … and process them
    foreach (string sub in subheadings)
    {
        // Create the node for the subheading
        TreeNode subheadingNode = new TreeNode(sub);

        // For each subheading, get their products …
        string[] products =
            ProductCatalog.GetProductsBySubHeading(sub);

        // … and process them
        foreach (string prod in products)
        {
            TreeNode productNode = new TreeNode(prod);
            // Add product node to its parent
            subheadingNode.ChildNodes.Add(productNode);
        }

        // Add subheading node to its parent
        groupNode.ChildNodes.Add(subheadingNode);
    }
    // Add group node to its parent
    treeMain.Nodes.Add(groupNode);
    }
}
}
```

Populate on Demand

The previous example filled the TreeView with *all* the data the first time the page loaded. Although this approach is fine for smaller amounts of data, it is impractical for very large amounts of data. Fortunately, the TreeView supports the capability to populate individual nodes only upon demand; that is, when the user expands the node. This requires specifying a handler for the TreeNodePopulate event as well as setting the ExpandDepth of the TreeView so that it doesn't display all the nodes (this is the default behavior and thus loads all the nodes).

```
<asp:TreeView ID="treeMain" runat="server"
    OnTreeNodePopulate="treeMain_TreeNodePopulate" ExpandDepth="1" >
```

You also need to set the `PopulateOnDemand` property of all nodes (not the `Tree-View` but of the individual `TreeNode` objects) that will be loaded on demand. For instance, from our previous example, you could change the `Page_Load` method so that the subheading nodes are loaded on demand.

```
// Create the node for the group
TreeNode groupNode = new TreeNode(grp);
// For each group get their subheadings and process them
string[] subheadings = ProductCatalog.GetSubHeadingsByGroup(grp);
foreach (string sub in subheadings)
{
    // Create the node for the subheading
    TreeNode subheadingNode = new TreeNode(sub);
    subheadingNode.PopulateOnDemand = true;

    // Add subheading node to its parent
    groupNode.ChildNodes.Add(subheadingNode);
}
```

Finally, you need to create the `TreeNodePopulate` handler. This handler typically retrieves node data from a data source, places the data into a node structure, and then adds this structure to the `ChildNodes` collection of the node being populated. For our example, you load the appropriate product nodes into the subheading node that was just expanded.

```
protected void treeMain_TreeNodePopulate(object sender,
        TreeNodeEventArgs e)
{
    // Get the node that was just chosen to be expanded
    TreeNode subHeadingNode = e.Node;

    // Extract subheading name from node
    string sub = subHeadingNode.Value;

    // For each subheading, get their products
    string[] products =
        ProductCatalog.GetProductsBySubHeading(sub);

    // Loop through each product and add to tree
    foreach (string prod in products)
    {
        TreeNode productNode = new TreeNode(prod);
        // Add product node to its parent
        subHeadingNode.ChildNodes.Add(productNode);
    }
}
```

This event handler is called each and every time the nodes for which `Populate-OnDemand` has been set are expanded. This might mean that if a given node is repeatedly expanded and collapsed, there will be repeated round trips to the server. Luckily, the `TreeView` control also supports client-side node population via the `PopulateNodesFromClient` property of the `TreeView`.

```
<asp:TreeView ID="treeMain" runat="server"
    OnTreeNodePopulate="treeMain_TreeNodePopulate" ExpandDepth="1"
    EnableClientScript="true" PopulateNodesFromClient="true" >
```

What does this property do? After an individual node has been populated on demand (that is, filled by the server), that populated node information is "preserved" by the client (that is, is sent to the client on all future postbacks). Thus, repeatedly expanding and collapsing a node only requires the one trip to the server (for the first expand request). Note as well that the `EnableClientScript` property must be set to `true` (which is the default) for client-side node population to work.

Responding to TreeView Events

The `TreeView` control exposes a variety of events that are raised when either the user interacts with the control or when the control is loaded with data (see Table 7.9).

Table 7.9   TreeView Events

Event	Description
`SelectedNodeChanged`	Raised upon postback when the user selects a tree node.
`TreeNodeCheckChanged`	Raised when a tree node check box changes state upon postback. Note that the user changing the state of the check box does not by itself cause a postback.
`TreeNodeCollapsed`	Raised when a tree node is collapsed.
`TreeNodeDataBound`	Raised when data is bound to a tree node.
`TreeNodeExpanded`	Raised when a tree node is expanded.
`TreeNodePopulate`	Raised when a tree node is expanded in a tree that has its `PopulateOnDemand` property set to `true`.

If the `TreeView` is not simply linked to a site map, one event you almost always need to process is the `SelectedNodeChanged` event. For instance, imagine that you have a `TreeView` containing a list of products. Each time the user selects a tree node containing a product, you then want to display further information about that product (see Figure 7.31). In such a case, you display this other product information in your handler for the `SelectedNodeChanged` event.

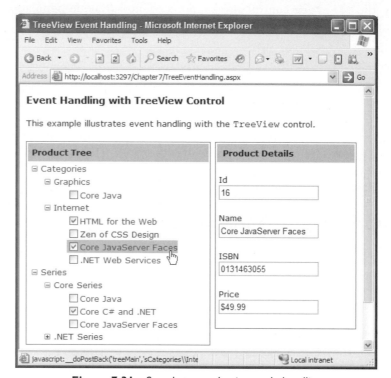

Figure 7.31   Sample tree selection node handling

Like any other event handling, you need to first specify the handler method in the control definition.

```
<asp:TreeView ID="treeMain" runat="server"
   SelectedNodeStyle-BackColor="#A6B4DB"
   ShowCheckBoxes="Leaf"
   OnSelectedNodeChanged="SelectProduct" />
```

You also need to create this event handler. It uses the `SelectedNode` property of the `TreeView` to determine which node was selected, and then if the node is a leaf node (i.e., in our example, the node is a product node), it displays the product information for the selected product. The skeleton for this handler might look like the following.

```
protected void SelectProduct(object sender, EventArgs e)
{
    // Get the tree node that was selected
    TreeNode node = treeMain.SelectedNode;

    // Only process selection if a leaf node was selected
    if (node.ChildNodes.Count == 0)
    {
        ...
    }
}
```

There still is one problem. How do you retrieve the rest of the product information based on your selected tree node? If the `Title` of the `TreeNode` is unique, you have no problem, because presumably you can extract the product information from your business object or database based on that title. However, if it is not unique, you need to use instead the `Value` property of the `TreeNode`. This property allows you to add supplemental data about the tree node that is not displayed but can be used during postback processing of the tree node selection.

To use this `Value` property, you need to set its value when you create the `Tree-Node` objects. For instance, the following sets the `Value` property to the `Id` of the current product object.

```
TreeNode node = new TreeNode(product.Name);
node.Value = product.Id.ToString();
```

Listings 7.7 and 7.8 provide the complete code for the sample `TreeView` selection page, as shown in Figures 7.31 and 7.32. These figures also illustrate that your product nodes will also use check boxes. The user can then check one or more of these boxes, and then click the purchase button. The event handler for the button loops through all the checked nodes, displays the product name and price, and then sums up the total purchase price of all the checked products.

Listing 7.7 TreeEventHandling.aspx

```
<h1>Event Handling with TreeView Control</h1>
<p>This example illustrates event handling with the <code>Tree-
View</code> control.</p>

<div id="products">
    <h2>Product Tree</h2>
    <asp:TreeView ID="treeMain" runat="server"
        OnSelectedNodeChanged="treeMain_SelectedNodeChanged"
        ShowCheckBoxes="Leaf"
        SelectedNodeStyle-BackColor="#A6B4DB" />
</div>
```

```
<div id="details">
   <h2>Product Details</h2>
   <p>Id<br />
   <asp:TextBox ID="txtId" runat="server" /></p>
   <p>Name<br />
   <asp:TextBox ID="txtName" runat="server" /></p>
   <p>ISBN<br />
   <asp:TextBox ID="txtIsbn" runat="server" /></p>
   <p>Price<br />
   <asp:TextBox ID="txtPrice" runat="server" /></p>
</div>

<div id="purchase">
   <asp:Button ID="btnPurchase" runat="server"
      Text="Purchase Checked Products"
      OnClick="btnPurchase_Click"/>

   <p><asp:Label ID="labChoose" runat="server" /></p>
   <p><asp:BulletedList ID="bulSelected" runat="server" /></p>
   <p><b><asp:Label ID="labTotal" runat="server" /></b></p>
</div>
```

Listing 7.8   TreeEventHandling.aspx.cs

```csharp
using System;
using System.Web;
using System.Web.UI;
using System.Web.UI.WebControls;

public partial class TreeEventHandling : System.Web.UI.Page
{
   protected void Page_Load(object sender, EventArgs e)
   {
      if (!IsPostBack)
      {
         // Fill tree with data
         FillTree();

         // Let's begin with all the nodes collapsed as well
         treeMain.CollapseAll();
      }
   }

   /// <summary>
   /// Helper method to fill tree with data
   /// </summary>
   private void FillTree()
   {
```

```csharp
        // Get all the groups and iterate through them
        string[] groups = ProductCatalog.GetGroups();
        foreach (string grp in groups)
        {
            // Create the node for the group
            TreeNode groupNode = new TreeNode(grp);
            // For each group get their subheadings and process them
            string[] subheadings =
                ProductCatalog.GetSubHeadingsByGroup(grp);
            foreach (string sub in subheadings)
            {
                // Create the node for the subheading
                TreeNode subheadingNode = new TreeNode(sub);

                // For each subheading, get their products
                // and process them
                Product[] products =
                    ProductCatalog.GetProductObjectsBySubHeading(sub);

                foreach (Product prod in products)
                {
                    // Create new product tree node
                    TreeNode productNode = new TreeNode(prod.Name);

                    // Set the node's value to the product id
                    productNode.Value = prod.Id.ToString();

                    // Add product node to its parent
                    subheadingNode.ChildNodes.Add(productNode);
                }
                // Add subheading node to its parent
                groupNode.ChildNodes.Add(subheadingNode);
            }
            // Add group node to its parent
            treeMain.Nodes.Add(groupNode);
        }
    }

    /// <summary>
    /// Handles the tree node selection event
    /// </summary>
    protected void SelectProduct(object sender, EventArgs e)
    {
        // Get the tree node that was selected
        TreeNode node = treeMain.SelectedNode;

        // Only process selection if a leaf node selected
        if (node.ChildNodes.Count == 0)
        {
```

```csharp
            // Retrieve the product id that we placed in the node
            int id = Convert.ToInt32(node.Value);

            // From that product id get the product
            Product prod = ProductCatalog.GetProductById(id);

            // If this is a valid product, display details
            if (prod != null)
            {
                txtId.Text = prod.Id.ToString();
                txtIsbn.Text = prod.Isbn;
                txtName.Text = prod.Name;
                txtPrice.Text = String.Format("{0:c}", prod.Price);
            }
        }
    }

    /// <summary>
    /// Handles the purchase button click event
    /// </summary>
    protected void btnPurchase_Click(object sender, EventArgs e)
    {
        // Handle the fact there may be no checked products
        if (treeMain.CheckedNodes.Count <= 0)
            labChoose.Text =
                "You did not choose any products to purchase";
        else
        {
            labChoose.Text =
                "You have selected the following products:";
            double total = 0.0;
            bulSelected.Items.Clear();

            // Loop through each checked node
            foreach (TreeNode node in treeMain.CheckedNodes)
            {
                // Retrieve the product info about this node
                int id = Convert.ToInt32(node.Value);
                Product prod = ProductCatalog.GetProductById(id);

                // If valid product, add it to list
                // and add it to running total
                if (prod != null)
                {
                    string s = prod.Name;
                    s += "(" + String.Format("{0:c}", prod.Price) +
                        ")";
                    ListItem item = new ListItem(s);
                    bulSelected.Items.Add(item);
```

```
            total += prod.Price;
        }
    }
    labTotal.Text = "Total purchase price: ";
    labTotal.Text += String.Format("{0:c}", total);
    }
  }
}
```

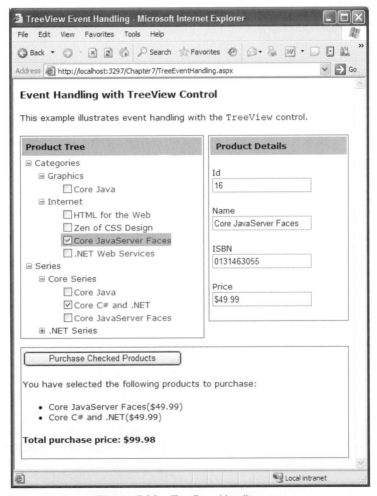

Figure 7.32   TreeEventHandling.aspx

CORE NOTE

Although the navigation controls covered in this chapter are quite powerful, there are also competing third-party navigation controls from companies such as Infragistics, ComponentArt, and ComponentOne that provide additional functionality and flexibility.

Summary

This chapter examined the site navigation features that have been added to version 2.0 of ASP.NET. These features provide several controls to help display your site's navigation system. These controls are the `SiteMapPath`, `Menu`, and `TreeView`. All of these controls support the other main topic of this chapter: the new site map infrastructure. ASP.NET allows you to externalize the site map data and store it in some other external data store, such as an XML file. The principal advantage of separating the data of the navigation system from its eventual presentation is that the site as a whole becomes a great deal easier to maintain and customize.

This chapter provided a glimpse into the new data handling mechanisms in ASP.NET. We are now ready to examine ASP.NET data handling in some detail in the next chapter.

Exercises

The solutions to the following exercises can be found at my Web site, http://www.randyconnolly.com/core. Additional exercises only available for teachers and instructors are also available from this site.

1. Create three XML site map files to represent the menus shown in Figure 7.33 that follows these Exercises.

2. Create three `Menu` controls that use these site map files. At least one of these should appear similar to one of the menus shown in Figure 7.17 on page 408.

3. Use the site map file for the second menu in Figure 7.33 with a `TreeView` control. Be sure to use one of the predefined image sets shown in Figure 7.27 on page 428.

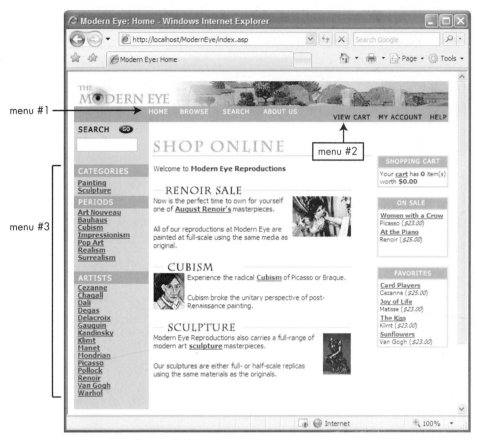

Figure 7.33   Exercise 1 site map structure

Key Concepts

- Ancestor node
- Breadcrumbs
- Current node
- Data-binding expression
- Data-bound controls
- Data source controls
- Dynamic menu items
- Leaf node
- Parent node
- Provider model

- Root node
- Site map
- Static menu items
- XPath

References

Chand, Mahesh. "Working with ASP.NET TreeView Control."
    http://www.c-sharpcorner.com.

Gristwood, David. "Understanding and Extending the Site Navigation System in
    ASP.NET 2.0." http://msdn.microsoft.com.

Mitchell, Scott. "Examining ASP.NET 2.0's Site Navigation, Part 1-3."
    http://aspnet.4guysfromrolla.com.

Prosise, Jeff. "The SQL Site Map Provider You've Been Waiting For." *MSDN
    Magazine* (February 2006).

Walther, Stephen. "Introducing the ASP.NET 2.0 TreeView and Menu Controls."
    http://msdn.microsoft.com.

Part II

WORKING WITH DATA

Chapter 8

DATA BINDING AND REPRESENTATION

"It is a capital mistake to theorize before one has data."

—Sir Arthur Conan Doyle, *The Adventures of Sherlock Holmes*,
   "Scandal in Bohemia"

Although it may very well be a grave mistake for a detective to proceed with his work without data, this book has had no choice heretofore but to present examples without a great deal of data. Because the focus of the earlier chapters in the book was to teach the basics of ASP.NET and its main Web server controls, the examples so far have by necessity been reasonably simple and thus a bit unrealistic. To make our ASP.NET examples more realistic, we need to work with *data*. This chapter is the first of three chapters on working with data in ASP.NET.

The focus in this chapter is on how data can be represented with the .NET Framework and how this data can be displayed using data binding in ASP.NET. Data-binding facilitates the process of displaying data, and as such, is an absolutely vital part of ASP.NET. This chapter begins by introducing data binding in general, and then moves on to how the various classes in the Framework can be used to represent data. It covers arrays, the .NET collection classes (including the generics facility in version 2.0 of the Framework), and then finishes with the powerful `DataSet` class. The chapter concludes by examining the relative merits of each of these approaches for temporary in-memory data storage within an ASP.NET application.

Introducing Data Binding

Almost every Web application displays data from some type of data source. That is, a typical Web page reads data from some external source, usually a database or an XML file, and presents it to the user. Because displaying data is such a common feature of Web applications, the developers of ASP.NET added a feature called ***data binding*** that facilitates this process of displaying data from a data source in a control. Data binding refers to the process of dynamically assigning a value or values to a control at either design time or runtime and having the control automatically display the value or values. That is, you only need tell the control where it can find its data, and the control handles the process of displaying it.

Some Web server controls (e.g., `Label`, `TextBox`) can only display a single value whether they are or are not using data binding. Although data binding is not particularly helpful for this type of control, nonetheless, it is possible to use single-value data binding. Other Web server controls (for instance, those controls that inherit from `ListControl`, such as `ListBox`, `DropDownList`, and `RadioButtonList`) can display multiple values. As well, there are dedicated data controls (see Chapter 10) that also display multiple values. For these controls, multivalue data binding is particularly helpful and powerful. In fact, without data binding, these data controls cannot display anything at all.

How to Use Data Binding

Perhaps the best thing about data binding is how easy and flexible it is to use. Data binding a control to a data source can be achieved in one of two ways:

- Setting the `DataSource` property of the control and then calling the `DataBind` method of the control.
- Setting the `DataSourceId` property of the control to a data source control.

The second approach was introduced in version 2.0 of ASP.NET and will be examined in the next chapter. In this chapter, we focus on the first approach. To use data binding with this approach, you simply have to assign the `DataSource` property of the control to the data and then call the control's `DataBind` method. The control then manages the display of that data. That is, if there are multiple values to display, it loops through the data, extracting and displaying the data based on the settings of the control. For instance, if you have a `DropDownList` control named `drpSample`, you simply do the following.

```
drpSample.DataSource = someDataSource;
drpSample.DataBind();
```

In this example, the `DataSource` property is assigned to *someDataSource*. What kind of object is this?

What Can Be a Data Source?

The object that is to be assigned to the DataSource property of a bindable Web server control must be one that implements, either directly or indirectly, the IEnumerable or the IListSource interface. The following types of objects implement this interface (and thus can be used for data binding):

- Arrays
- In-memory .NET collections classes, such as List and Dictionary
- ADO.NET DbDataReader objects
- ADO.NET DataView, DataTable, or DataSet objects
- Any custom class you create, which also implements the IEnumerable interface

CORE NOTE

The IListSource interface defines a method that ultimately returns a list of IEnumerable data. As a result, you could say that data binding works with any class that implements IEnumerable.

We will cover ADO.NET data readers in the next chapter, and the other ADO.NET DataView, DataTable, or DataSet objects later in the chapter. The next section of this chapter demonstrates how to work with the .NET collection classes as well as how to data bind with them. But before moving onto these collections, let us demonstrate a simple data binding example.

Let us imagine that you have the following DropDownList control.

```
<asp:DropDownList id="drpSample" runat="server" />
```

You could bind an array of strings to this DropDownList simply by adding code similar to the following to the Page_Load method.

```
private void Page_Load(object sender, System.EventArgs e)
{
    string[] names = new string[3] { "Austen","Dante","Goethe" };

    drpSample.DataSource = names;
    drpSample.DataBind();
}
```

This code creates and populates a three-element string array and then makes it the DataSource of the DropDownList. The DataSource property is in fact defined to be of type Object. Although this means that in principle the DataSource property can be assigned to any object, in reality, in the mutator (setter) for this property, the control calls its `ValidateDataSource` method, which in turn verifies that the object is one that can be used for data binding (that is, of type `IEnumerable` or `IListSource`).

Setting the `DataSource` property does not actually cause any visual change in the control. Instead, one must also invoke the `DataBind` method of the control. This method then loads the data from the data source and the control generates the necessary markup for the data.

As previously mentioned, data binding via the `DataSource` property can be used not only with arrays, but also with any of the built-in, in-memory .NET collection classes. The next section examines these collections.

CORE NOTE

Arrays in the .NET Framework are implemented as subclasses of the `Array` base class. This collection class contains various members for examining and manipulating the array elements. As well, this class implements a number of important interfaces (to be discussed in the next section), such as `ICollection`, `IList` and `IEnumerable`.

Using Collections

The previous example demonstrated the use of an array as a source for data binding. The .NET Framework base class library also provides a number of **collection classes** that can also be used for data binding (in fact, an array is just a special type of collection class). A collection class is used to group related objects together. There are a number of different types of collection classes. There are queues, stacks, sorted and unsorted lists, and dictionaries. Some of these collections can hold any type of object, whereas others are strongly typed, such as `StringCollection`, `StringDictionary`, and `NameValueCollection`.

Collection classes provide members for adding, removing, and retrieving data elements. All collections provide a mechanism that makes it easy to iterate through its elements. As well, these collections expand automatically as necessary. In version 2.0 of ASP.NET, there are also special generic versions of the collection classes that allow you to create strongly typed collections.

The main collection classes are contained within the `System.Collections` namespace. The more unique and unusual collections are contained within the `System.Collections.Specialized` namespace, whereas the generic versions are in the `System.Collections.Generics` namespace.

Collection Interfaces

Rather than having a shared base class, both the standard and the generic .NET collection classes share a set of overlapping interfaces. Figure 8.1 illustrates these relationships for the standard collections (the generic collections have a similar set of relationships), whereas Table 8.1 provides an overview of the standard collection classes and interfaces.

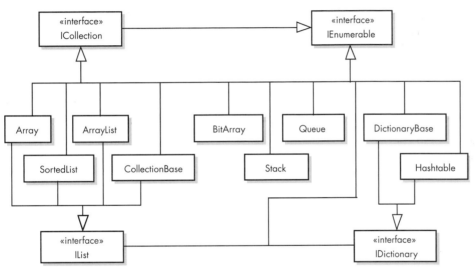

Figure 8.1   .NET collection classes

Table 8.1   Notable Collection Classes and Interfaces

Name	Description
Array	Base class for all arrays.
ArrayList	An array-like collection whose size can dynamically change. Individual elements can be retrieved using an index.
BitArray	A collection of compacted bit values represented as Booleans.
CollectionBase	An abstract base class for implementing your own custom collection.
DictionaryBase	An abstract base class for implementing your own custom key-value collection.

Table 8.1   Notable Collection Classes and Interfaces *(continued)*

Name	Description
Hashtable	A collection of key-value pairs that are organized based on the hash code of the key. Allows for retrieval of individual elements in collection based on the key.
ICollection	The interface for defining the size, enumerators, and synchronization for a collection.
IDictionary	The interface for a collection of key-value pairs.
IEnumerable	The interface for exposing the enumerator of a collection, thus supporting the iteration of a collection.
IList	The interface for a collection of objects that can be individually accessed by an index.
Queue	A collection of first-in, first-out objects.
ReadOnlyCollectionBase	An abstract base class for implementing your own custom read-only collection.
SortedList	A collection of key-value pairs that are sorted by the keys and are accessible by key and by index.
Stack	A collection of first-in, last-out objects.

As you can see from Figure 8.1, all the collection classes implement both IEnumerable as well as the ICollection interfaces. IEnumerable provides a way to iterate a collection, whereas ICollection defines the size and the synchronization capabilities of a collection.

The IEnumerable interface defines a single method (GetEnumerator) that returns an **enumerator**. An enumerator is a type of object that is used to iterate through a collection in a type-safe and dimension-safe manner. It is analogous to a moveable pointer that always indicates the "current" element in the collection. The foreach statement (covered shortly) in C# interacts, behind the scenes, with the enumerator object returned by GetEnumerator.

The ICollection interface extends IEnumerable and provides a Count property that returns the number of elements in the collection. It also defines some synchronization properties as well as a method (CopyTo) that copies the elements of the collection to an array.

Figure 8.1 illustrates that the collection classes can be divided into two basic types: those that implement IList and those that implement IDictionary. The IList interface defines the capabilities for a collection that can be individually accessed by an index, whereas `IDictionary` defines the functionality for a collection of key/value pairs. That is, when using an `IDictionary` collection, the elements are retrieved not by an index but by using a unique key for the element.

Using the Common Collections

Of all the classes listed in Table 8.1, perhaps the two most commonly used by programmers are the `ArrayList` and `Hashtable` collections. The `ArrayList` collection is ideal for situations in which data needs to be principally accessed sequentially (that is, accessed from beginning to end) and where speed of searching for an element is not too vital. The `Hashtable` collection, by contrast, is optimized for quick nonsequential retrieval of elements via a key.

Although these collections can be used to contain groups of primitives (such as integers or Booleans), their true utility lies in using them to store groups of objects, such as strings or your own custom classes. For example, imagine that you have an already existing class called `Customer` (saved in our `App_Code` folder) that encapsulates the common data fields for a customer along with some business logic and that looks similar to that shown in Listing 8.1.

Listing 8.1   Customer.cs

```
/// <summary>
/// Encapsulates the data for a single customer
/// </summary>
public class Customer
{
    // Data members
    private string _id;
    private string _firstName;
    private string _lastName;
    private string _phone;

    // Constructor
    public Customer(string id, string first, string last,
        string phone)
    {
        _id = id;
        _firstName = first;
        _lastName = last;
        _phone = phone;
    }

    // Properties
    public string Id
    {
```

```
      get { return _id; }
      set { _id = value; }
   }
   public string FirstName
   {
      get { return _firstName; }
      set { _firstName = value; }
   }
   public string LastName
   {
      get { return _lastName; }
      set { _lastName = value; }
   }
   public string Phone
   {
      get { return _phone; }
      set { _phone = value; }
   }
   public string Name
   {
      get { return LastName + ", " + FirstName; }
   }

   public bool IsValid
   {
      get
      {
         if (Id.Length > 0 && LastName.Length > 0)
            return true;
         else
            return false;
      }
   }
}
```

With the `Customer` class defined, you can group multiple `Customer` objects using any of the collections shown in Table 8.1. For instance, the following code declares an array of `Customer` objects and then initializes its elements.

```
Customer[] myCustomers = new Customer[] {
   new Customer("334", "Thomas", "Hobbes", "123-4567"),
   new Customer("123", "Jean-Jacques", "Rousseau","456-1267"),
   new Customer("085", "David", "Hume", "564-7823"),
   new Customer("254", "Martin", "Heidegger", "253-6383")
};
```

With this array defined, you can then retrieve an element from it by using an index.

```
Customer c = myCustomers[2];
```

Because arrays and other indexable collections are zero based, the preceding code returns the third customer in the array. You can find out the upper boundary of this array by using its `GetUpperBound` method.

```
int upper = myCustomers.GetUpperBound(0);
```

All the other nonarray collections that implement `ICollection` instead provide the `Count` property as the mechanism for determining the size of the collection.

Iterating Through a Collection

One of the more common tasks you may need to perform with a collection is to iterate through it and process each of its elements. There are several ways to do this common task. The first of these is to use a common `for` loop, as shown in the following example, which loops through the array defined earlier.

```
for (int i=0; i< myCustomers.GetUpperBound(0); i++)
{
    Customer c = (Customer)myCustomers[i];
    string name = c.FirstName;
    ...
}
```

There are quite a few opportunities for mistakes with this type of loop. You could mess up with the index variable, have logical errors in the upper boundary check (for instance, use <= instead of just a <), or make a mistake with the casting or indexing inside the loop. Fortunately, C# provides a safer and more concise way to iterate through a collection via the `foreach` statement, as shown in the following.

```
foreach (Customer c in myCustomers)
{
    string name = c.FirstName;
    ...
}
```

Notice that the `foreach` version of the loop hides the iteration details (the index variable and the boundary check) as well as the assignment of the temporary variable along with its messy type casting. Is this `foreach` loop then simply the equivalent of the `for` loop version? No, it is not. The Microsoft Intermediate Language (MSIL) produced by the compiler for the `foreach` loop is essentially (minus some error trapping and explicit garbage disposal) the MSIL produced by the following, alternate, way to loop through a collection.

```
IEnumerator ie = myCustomers.GetEnumerator();
while (ie.MoveNext())
{
   Customer c = (Customer)ie.Current;
   string name = c.FirstName;
   ...
}
```

What is this code doing? You may recall that all .NET collections implement the IEnumerable interface, which defines the GetEnumerator method. This method returns an IEnumerator object, which is akin to a moveable pointer that

- Indicates the "current" element in the collection
- Can determine if it is pointing at the last element
- Has the capability to move the pointer to the next element

For most situations, the foreach approach is the preferred method of iterating through a collection because it leaves fewer opportunities for bugs and is more readable. However, for some collections (e.g., Hashtable), the foreach loop does not produce the results one generally requires; thus, you must use something closer to this last approach.

ArrayList

The ArrayList is the simplest of the .NET collection classes. One way of thinking about the ArrayList is that it is akin to a more flexible version of an array, in that it provides methods for adding, inserting, and removing elements from the collection. For instance, to add a Customer object to an ArrayList, you might have code that looks similar to the following.

```
ArrayList myList = new ArrayList();
...
Customer c1 = new Customer( ... );
myList.Add( c1 );
```

Notice that you simply need to call the Add method of the ArrayList object and pass it the object that is to be added to the collection. To retrieve a Customer object from this ArrayList of Customer objects, you use code similar to that shown in the following example.

```
int index = ...
Customer c = (Customer)myList[index];
```

Note that the value retrieved from the collection must be cast to the appropriate data type. ArrayList and the other collections in the System.Collections namespace are not strongly typed, but can accept any type of object. For instance, the Add method accepts as a parameter any object of type Object. Recall that the Object class is the ultimate ancestor class for all classes in the .NET Framework. As a result, when you add any object to the collection, the collection simply stores the reference to that object. But when you retrieve an item from the collection, you must let the compiler know what kind of object is being retrieved from the collection. You do this via the cast operation.

CORE NOTE

ArrayList and the other collections in the System.Collections namespace can work with *reference types* (i.e., objects) or *value types* (e.g., int, bool, double, etc., or any struct). However, there is a performance penalty when using value types (instead of reference types) in these collections. Because these collections work with the Object reference type, the compiler must add *box instructions* (which converts the value type into a reference type) or *unbox instructions* (which converts the reference type back into a value type) when using value types in these collections. Although the time cost of this additional boxing/unboxing is not noticeable for small collections, with very large collections, the additional time cost may be noticeable (for instance, see the statistics of Richard Federicho, "Boxing and Performance of Collections," listed in the References section at the end of the chapter).

After you have a populated ArrayList, you can data bind any of your controls that display multiple values to it, using the same technique shown earlier. For instance, if you have a ListBox control named lboxCustomers, you could data bind the ArrayList using the following code.

```
// Create sample customer objects
Customer c1 = new Customer("334", "Thomas", "Hobbes",
    "123-4567");
Customer c2 = new Customer("123", "Jean-Jacques", "Rousseau",
    "456-1267");
Customer c3 = new Customer("085", "David", "Hume", "564-7823");
Customer c4 = new Customer("254", "Martin", "Heidegger",
    "253-6383");

// Create and populate collection
ArrayList myList = new ArrayList();
myList.Add(c1);
myList.Add(c2);
myList.Add(c3);
myList.Add(c4);
```

```
// Data bind collection to control
lboxCustomers.DataSource = myList;
lboxCustomers.DataBind();
```

What would the result of this code look like in the browser? It would look similar to that shown in Figure 8.2.

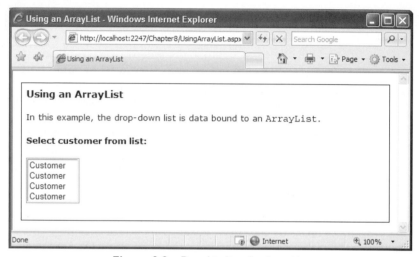

Figure 8.2 Data binding the ArrayList

This is probably not what you want. The ListBox control needs to know which Customer property should be displayed for each Customer object in the control. Because you have not specified this, it is calling each Customer object's ToString method; because this method is not defined in the example shown in Listing 8.1, it uses the ToString method defined in the Object base class, which simply returns the class name of the object.

One solution then is to define our own ToString method in the Customer class that returns the value that you want to see in the ListBox, as shown here.

```
public override string ToString()
{
    return Name;
}
```

This now makes the ListBox display the appropriate data. However, what if you want to display the Name property from Customer in one control, but the Id property in another control? In such a case, you would need the ability to specify the property to display on a control by control basis. As well, you may need the ability to specify different properties for the text to display in the control and the value that each item will have in the control. You can do this via the `DataTextField` and `DataValueField` properties of any list control. For instance, the following definition can be used to define a `ListBox` that displays the `Name` property from the data source, and make each item's value equal to the value of the `Id` property in the data source.

```
<asp:ListBox id="lboxCustomers" runat="server"
    DataTextField="Name"
    DataValueField="Id" />
```

The result in the browser would now look similar to that shown in Figure 8.3.

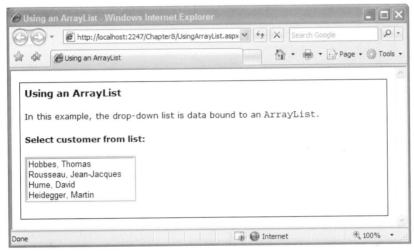

Figure 8.3   Data binding the ArrayList using DataTextField

The rendered HTML for the example shown in Figure 8.3 would be similar to the following. Notice how the content of the `Id` property has been rendered as HTML `value` elements, whereas the content of the `Name` property has been rendered as the text for the `select` options.

```
<select size="4" name="lboxCustomers" id="lboxCustomers">
    <option value="334">Hobbes, Thomas</option>
    <option value="123">Rousseau, Jean-Jacques</option>
    <option value="085">Hume, David</option>
    <option value="254">Heidegger, Martin</option>
</select>
```

You can also use the `ArrayList` of `Customer` objects in any event handling for the data bound control. For instance, imagine that after the user selects a customer from the ListBox, you want the page to display the individual data items for the selected customer, as shown in Figure 8.4.

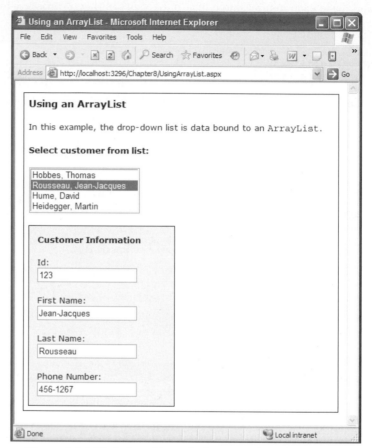

Figure 8.4 Displaying additional information from the customer

To do this, you need to add an OnSelectedIndexChanged event handler for the ListBox to your page. This handler first needs to retrieve the index of the selected item in the ListBox. It then uses that value to index into the ArrayList of Customer objects, and retrieve the selected Customer object. The handler can then assign the Customer properties to the appropriate TextBox controls. The following code illustrates how this event handler might look.

```
/// <summary>
/// Called when user selects an item in the list
/// </summary>
```

```
protected void SelectCustomer(object sender, System.EventArgs e)
{
    // Retrieve the index of the selected customer
    int index = lboxCustomers.SelectedIndex;

    // If the index is valid …
    if (index >= 0 && index <= myList.Count)
    {
        // … then retrieve the Customer object
        // from the Customer's collection
        Customer c = (Customer)myList[index];

        // Populate the form fields
        txtId.Text = c.Id;
        txtFirst.Text = c.FirstName;
        txtLast.Text = c.LastName;
        txtPhone.Text = c.Phone;
    }
}
```

Generics

Generics are a new addition to the .NET programming languages in version 2.0 of the Framework. Generics are a special type of collection, which can be used in many of the same situations as the other collection classes. To help make sense of generics, we should first examine the problem that generics address.

Why Do We Need Generics?

In the last section, we examined the `ArrayList` collection. The `ArrayList`, like the other standard collections in Table 8.1, is quite useful and generalized in that it can work with *any* type of data, whether a reference type (i.e., an object) or a value type (i.e., a `struct` or a primitive such as an `int` or `bool`). These collection classes can do so because they are defined to work with `Object` objects. Because all .NET classes have the `Object` class as their ultimate ancestor, this means that these collections can store and retrieve any .NET object.

Unfortunately, the general nature of the standard .NET collections can also be a drawback. As we have seen, every time you retrieve an object from a collection, you must cast it to the appropriate type. As a result, the code is

- Not as error-free as it could be, because there is a potential for a casting exception if the data in the collection is not of the expected class.
- Not as fast as it could be, because there is a performance penalty for this casting operation.

The lack of compile-time type-safety when using these general .NET collections may be a serious problem. For instance, the following code is compiled with no errors, but the last of these lines generates a runtime exception when this code is executed (see Figure 8.5).

```
ArrayList temp = new ArrayList();
temp.Add( new Customer("085", "David", "Hume", "564-7823") );
temp.Add( "Hello World" );
temp.Add( 25 );

Customer tempC = (Customer)temp[2];
```

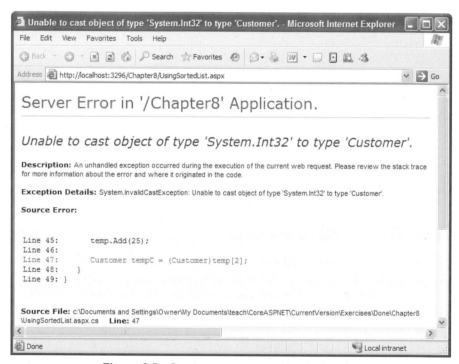

Figure 8.5   Runtime error as a result of miscasting

Some developers endeavor to make their collections type-safe by defining their own custom collection class with appropriately typed members. Although a strongly typed custom collection class deals with the first drawback of the general .NET collection classes, it introduces another problem that is perhaps even worse. Most Web applications need not just one custom collection class but several. That is, what if your application requires not only a CustomerCollection, but a ProductCollection,

`OrderCollection`, and many other custom collection classes as well? It is quite likely that each of these custom collection classes will have almost identical functionality, and thus almost identical code. That is, instead of

```
public void Add(Customer c)
```

you would have

```
public void Add(Product p)
```

Clearly, creating multiple type-specific collection classes is not only tedious and error-prone, it also is difficult to maintain. Any changes in the functionality of any one of these multiple, almost identical, custom collection classes more than likely need to be mirrored to all of them. Developers who sought the design benefits of type-specific collection classes but wanted to avoid the tedium of creating multiple similar collection classes often made use of code generation tools such as CodeSmith or LLBLGen.

Another drawback of the standard .NET collections is the performance penalty that the generalized nature of the .NET collections incurs. This may be noticed when one of these collections is used to store a large collection of value types. You may recall that to make these collections accept value types, the compiler adds box instructions (which convert the value type into a reference type) or unbox instructions (which convert the reference type back into a value type). Certainly, for small collections, the additional time required for this boxing is almost unnoticeable; but for larger collections, the time delay may indeed be noticeable.

In version 2.0 of the Framework, however, there are now generic collections as a solution to some of these problems.

What Are Generics?

Generics let you define a type-safe collection without the maintenance or performance drawbacks that were just described for the more generalized collections. The term *generics* refers to the new capability in version 2.0 programming languages to support the use of placeholders rather than explicit type specifications when defining classes, structures, interfaces, or methods. You can create your own generics as well as use any of the generic collection classes contained within the new `System.Collections.Generics` namespace (see Table 8.2). The support for generics was not a trivial addition to the .NET Framework, as it required not only changes in the underlying programming languages and their compilers, but also changes to the runtime environment and to the Just-In-Time compiler.

Table 8.2   Generic Collection Classes

Name	Description
Dictionary	A strongly typed collection of key-value pairs.
LinkedList	A strongly typed collection that represents a doubly linked list. Can be quickly navigated in either direction.
List	A strongly typed collection of objects that can be individually accessed by an index.
Queue	A strongly typed collection of first-in, first-out objects.
SortedDictionary	A strongly typed collection of key-value pairs contained within a binary search tree that is sorted by the key. Inserts and removes data quicker than SortedList.
SortedList	A strongly typed collection of key-value pairs that are sorted on the keys. Uses less memory than SortedDictionary, and if initially populated with sorted data, it is also faster than SortedDictionary.
Stack	A strongly typed collection of first-in, last-out objects.

CORE NOTE

The syntax for generics is similar to C++ templates, and generics have a similar function as C++ templates. Generics, however, differ behind the scenes in how they are implemented. Most C++ compilers implement templates by simply replacing the parameterized-type code with the type-specific code; this approach can greatly increase the size of the resulting compiled code. Because generics are supported by the MSIL, the runtime that executes it, and the JIT compiler that converts it to machine code, generics are more efficiently rendered into machine code, thus reducing the size of the resulting machine code.

At the beginning of this section on generics, we illustrated the problem of an ArrayList that contains numerous types of objects. The equivalent to an Array-List in the generic collection is List. To use a generic class, you have to specify the type of object that the collection is going to hold when you instantiate it. For instance, the following example creates two list collections: one that holds strings and the other that holds Customer objects.

```
List<int> numbers = new List<int>();

List<Customer> customers = new List<Customer>();
```

list of Customer class objects (handwritten annotation)

Notice that you specify the type within angle brackets (< and >) immediately following the class name. You can now use these collection objects in much the same way as the nongeneric collections. For instance, the following example adds an element to each of these collections.

```
numbers.Add(47);

customers.Add( new Customer("085","David","Hume","564-7823") );
```

If you try to add an element of the wrong type to a generic collection, as in the following example, the code does not compile and you get a compile-time error.

```
numbers.Add("…");   // This does NOT work
```

There is also no longer any need for type casting when retrieving elements from a generic collection, as shown in the following example.

```
int n = numbers[0];

Customer c = customers[0];
```

Generics shift the burden of type-safety away from the developer and give it instead to the compiler. This reduces the possibility of runtime errors and generally makes for cleaner code. As well, the boxing problem with collections of value types described earlier has now been eliminated due to how generics are implemented by the runtime and the JIT compiler.

Dictionary Collections

Recall that with an `ArrayList` or `List` collection, you retrieve an individual element using its ordinal position within the collection. There are times, however, when it is not convenient to retrieve an element by its position in the collection. For instance, if you had a collection of `Customer` objects, it might be much more useful to retrieve a specific customer by using the customer name. You can do so by using a dictionary-style collection such as `Dictionary` or `SortedDictionary` (or the older, nongeneric `Hashtable`).

To perform the same type of retrieval using a dictionary-style collection, you do so using a **key** rather than an index, as shown here.

```
Dictionary<string, Customer> dict =
    new Dictionary<string, Customer>();
…
Customer c = dict[key];
```

In the preceding code snippet, what is this key variable? Very much like the primary key in a database record, the key of a `Dictionary` is a unique identifier for the object in the collection. It can be an object of any type (but in this example, it is a `string`). The key is specified when the object is added to the collection as in the following example.

```
Dictionary<string, Customer> dict =
    new Dictionary<string, Customer>();

String id = "085";
Customer c = new Customer(id, "David", "Hume", "564-7823");
dict.Add(id, c);
```

The great advantage of `Dictionary` over `List` is the speed by which you can search the collection for a given item. For instance, to search through a `List` looking for a particular `Id` would require code similar to the following.

```
List<Customer> myList = new List<Customer>();
...
foreach (Customer c in myList)
{
    if (c.Id == valueToFind) {
      // Do something with this customer
    }
}
```

Notice that to find the requested value, the code can potentially loop through the entire collection looking for a match. This is not a problem in a four-element collection. But in a large collection containing thousands of items, there could be a noticeable delay searching in this linear manner. In contrast, you can do the same thing in a much faster and simpler way with a `Dictionary` using the following code.

```
Dictionary<string, Customer> dict = new Dictionary<string,
    Customer>();

Customer c = dict[valueToFind];
if (c != null) {
  // Do something with this customer
}
```

Although a `Dictionary` is easier and more efficient to search than a `List`, the opposite is true when it comes to iterating through the collection. You may recall that the `foreach` statement uses an enumerator when iterating through a collection. The `Current` property for the enumerator returned by the `GetEnumerator` method of the `Dictionary` does not return an object of the type stored in the collection (e.g., return a `Customer` object). As a result, you cannot simply iterate through a `Dictionary` using the usual `foreach` syntax. That is, the following does *not* work.

```
Dictionary<string, Customer> dict =
   new Dictionary<string, Customer>();

// This does NOT work
foreach (Customer c in dict)
```

Instead of returning an object of the type stored in the collection, the enumerator for the `Dictionary` ultimately returns a `KeyValuePair` value object, which is a structure that defines both the key and value for an item in the `Dictionary`. As a result, to iterate through a `Dictionary`, your looping code would look like the following.

```
foreach (KeyValuePair<string, Customer> pair in dict)
{
   Customer c = pair.Value;
   labMsg.Text += c.Id + "," + c.LastName + "<br/>";
}
```

As well, because the `Dictionary` class has the `Values` property, which returns an `ICollection` of all the values in the collection, you can iterate through it, as shown in the following.

```
foreach (Customer c in dict.Values)
{
   labMsg.Text += c.Id + "," + c.LastName + "<br/>";
}
```

 ADDITIONAL COLLECTIONS

Other than the `Array`, `List`, `Dictionary`, and the sorted versions of the `List` and `Dictionary`, the only other general data structure collection classes provided in the .NET Framework are `Stack` and `Queue` (see Table 8.1). The other collections are more specialized classes for collections of bits or specialized collections, such as `StringDictionary` or `ListDictionary`.

Compared to what is available in Java, the available collections in the .NET Framework are not as complete as they could be. Fortunately, the programmers at Wintellect and Microsoft have created additional collections in the Power-Collections library (available via `http://www.wintellect.com`). This library includes some handy, but perhaps less frequently used, collections such as the ordered and unordered `Set`, the ordered and unordered `Bag`, and a `Dequeue`.

Creating Your Own Generic Collection

We previously mentioned that a typical application may very well have a different collection class for each of the different business entities in the application (such as a product collection and an order collection), and that each of these collections would have similar functionality. With version 2.0 of the Framework, you can now store these different collections in a type-safe manner by simply using one of the generic collections, such as `List` or `Dictionary`. However, it is not uncommon that you may want the collections for your entities to have additional functionality not contained in `List` or `Dictionary`, such as the capability to search for a particular value or check its validity. In such a case, you may decide to create your own generic collection class.

For instance, imagine that you have the following entity classes: `Customer`, `Product`, and `Order`. Each of these classes encapsulates the data for a single customer, product, and order, respectively. You could define a generic custom collection—for instance, named `EntityCollection`—that could contain any of these entities, and which could be used in the following manner.

```
// Create a collection of customers
EntityCollection<Customer> customers =
    new EntityCollection<Customer>();

// Fill collection with data
...
// Data bind to a control
someControl.DataSource = customers;
someControl.DataBind();

// Create a collection of products
EntityCollection<Product> products =
    new EntityCollection<Product>();

// Fill collection with data
...
// Data bind to a control
anotherControl.DataSource = products;
anotherControl.DataBind();
```

To define a generic class, you add a ***type parameter*** to the class definition, for instance:

```
public class EntityCollection<T>
```

The type parameter is the name within the angle brackets that follows the class name (`T` in this case). You can use any name that you want for the type parameter, although by convention, you usually use single letters such as `T` or `K`. This type parameter name can then be used elsewhere within the class wherever you need to reference the type parameter. For instance, if your generic class is to use an internal generic `List` collection as a data member, you could define it as follows.

```
private List<T> _entities;
```

In this case, you are specifying that this `List` contains objects of the same type as the containing class. In a similar manner, you can also define methods that return a generic value or that take a generic parameter. These generic methods reference the same type parameter, as shown in the following example.

```
public void Add(T entity)
{
    _entities.Add(entity);
}
```

The one issue to be aware of when creating your own generic collection class is how to handle the return of a null value. Because generics can be used with value types, a custom generic collection class cannot return a null value. Instead, you can use the `default` operator, which returns a null for reference types, or the default value (usually 0) for value types. The following example illustrates a generic-style **indexer property**. An indexer property is a special property that is necessary for an object to be accessed in the same way as an array.

```
public T this[int index]
{
    get {
        if (index >= 0 && index < _entities.Count)
            return _entities[index];
        else
            return default(T);
    }
}
```

Constraining the Generic Collection

Generics allow a type-safe collection of any reference or value type. However, with your own custom generic collection, you might not want to work with any type, but with a reasonably constrained number of classes. For instance, in the `Entity-Collection` class example, you may want it to store only `Customer`, `Product`, or `Order` objects, and not `int` values or `String` objects. You can do this by adding a **constraint** to your generic collection. A constraint tells the compiler that only objects of the type specified (or derived from the specified type) can be used as the type parameter. The syntax for a constraint is as follows.

```
public class YourClass<T> where T : YourConstraint
```

Typically, this constraint is an interface or an abstract class. Thus, in our example, if you want to constrain our sample `EntityCollection` generic class to only `Customer`, `Product`, or `Order` entity objects, these three entity classes must have a shared base class or interface, and this shared type can be used as the constraint. For instance, imagine that you have the class structure as shown in Figure 8.6.

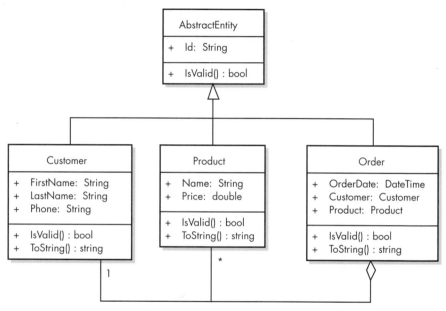

Figure 8.6   Entity class diagram

Given this class structure, our constraint would be as follows.

```
public class EntityCollection<T> where T : AbstractEntity
```

Listings 8.2 and 8.3 contain the completed code for both the `AbstractEntity` and `EntityCollection` classes. The `EntityCollection` class inherits from the `Collection<T>` generic class. This provides a base generic collection implementation so that your collection class only need implement its unique functionality.

Listing 8.2   AbstractEntity.cs

```
using System;

/// <summary>
/// Defines the base interface for any entity
/// </summary>
```

```
public abstract class AbstractEntity
{
    // Data members
    private string _id;

    public AbstractEntity(string id)
    {
        _id = id;
    }

    /// <summary>
    /// Every entity must have an id
    /// </summary>
    public string Id
    {
        get { return _id; }
        set { _id = value; }
    }

    /// <summary>
    /// Each entity will be responsible for determining the
    /// validity of its own state
    /// </summary>
    public abstract bool IsValid
    {
        get;
    }
}
```

Listing 8.3   EntityCollection.cs

```
using System;
using System.Collections;
using System.Collections.Generic;
using System.Collections.ObjectModel;

/// <summary>
/// A generic collection for our application's business entities
/// </summary>
public class EntityCollection<T> : Collection<T>
      where T : AbstractEntity
{

    /// <summary>
    /// Search for the customer with the passed id value
    /// </summary>
    public T FindById(string id)
```

```
{
    foreach (T entity in _entities)
    {
        if (entity.Id == id)
            return entity;
    }
    return null;
}

/// <summary>
/// Checks whether the collection is valid by asking
/// each element in the collection to verify if it is valid
/// </summary>
public bool IsValid()
{
    bool valid = true;
    foreach (T entity in _entities)
    {
        if (!entity.IsValid)
            valid = false;
    }
    return valid;
}

}
```

CORE NOTE

One capability often required of custom collection classes is the capability to dynamically sort on one or more fields, or to filter the collection by some type of criteria. Doing so is not necessarily a trivial task. For more information, see J. Ambrose Little's "Sorting Custom Collections" article that is listed in this chapter's References section.

DataSet

The previous section of this chapter examined several of the in-memory collections available in the System.Collections and System.Collections.Generic namespaces. In the examples from this section, different collections were used to store Customer or Product objects. These Customer and Product classes are custom entity or **domain classes** that encapsulate the data values for a real-world customer or product. The data for these objects could potentially come from any source.

They could be filled from a database table, an XML file, or some other type of external data source.

In this kind of example, there very well may be relationships between the various domain objects. For instance, in the class diagram (also called a domain model) shown in Figure 8.6, the `Order` class contains a single `Customer` object and a collection of `Product` objects, which represent the products being ordered, and the customer who ordered them. It is up to you, the software developer, to implement these relationships modeled in the domain.

This domain-oriented approach has a number of benefits that we will return to later in the chapter. However, there is a more data-oriented alternative to this approach built into the .NET Framework. This alternative is the ***DataSet***.

The `DataSet` is a very rich and complete in-memory data container that mirrors the organization and some of the functionality of a DBMS. That is, a `DataSet` is an in-memory data holder that can store not only data, but also its relational structure, and can perform a variety of useful operations, such as sorting and filtering data, populating itself from XML, and exporting its data and schema to XML.

Given the robust functionality of the `DataSet`, it should not be surprising that it is a very complex class. Table 8.3 and Figure 8.7 illustrate the principle class relations and some of the important members of these classes. These classes are all found within the `System.Data` namespace.

Table 8.3 DataSet Classes

Name	Description
DataColumn	Represents the schema (definition) of a column in a `DataTable`.
DataColumnCollection	The collection of `DataColumn` objects that defines the schema of a `DataTable`. Accessed via the `Collections` property of a `DataTable`.
DataRelation	Relates two `DataTable` objects to each other in a child-parent relationship. This relationship is made between matching columns in the two `DataTable` objects.
DataRelationCollection	A collection of `DataRelation` objects. Accessed via the `Relations` property of the `DataSet`.
DataRow	Represents a row/record of data in a `DataTable`.
DataRowCollection	A collection of `DataRow` objects. Accessed via the `Rows` property of the `DataTable`.
DataTable	Represents a single table of in-memory data.

Table 8.3   DataSet Classes *(continued)*

Name	Description
DataTableCollection	A collection of DataTable objects. Accessed via the Tables property of the DataSet.
DataView	Represents a customized view of a DataTable that can be data bound and that supports sorting and filtering.

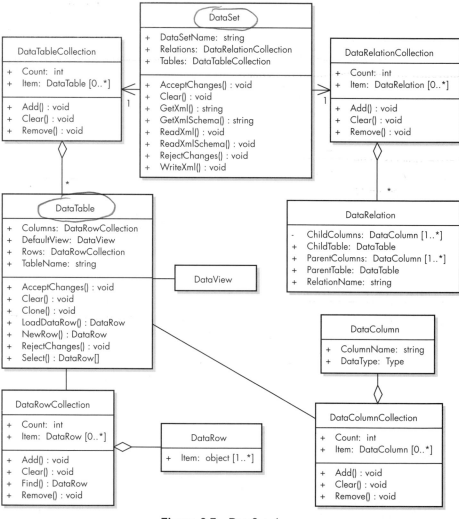

Figure 8.7   DataSet classes

To use a DataSet, you must first fill it with data. There are three ways of populating a DataSet with data.

- Fill it from a database using the appropriate data provider's DataAdapter class.
- Programmatically add DataTable objects to the DataSet.
- Use the ReadXml method of the DataSet to populate data from an XML file or stream.

The first of these approaches is generally the most commonly used. The advantage of this approach is that the DataAdapter defines the schema of the DataTable objects and fills them with data. We demonstrate this first approach in the next chapter (see page 545), where we cover ADO.NET, which is Microsoft's API for working with databases in the .NET Framework. Initially in this chapter we use the second approach, programmatically creating and then filling DataTable objects. The third approach we use at the end of this chapter.

Using the DataTable

As can be seen from Figure 8.7, the heart of the DataSet is its collection of DataTable objects. The DataTable class represents a single table of in-memory data, and can be used outside of the DataSet. Indeed, because the DataSet is such a complex class, and because with Web applications you often need to only retrieve the data from a single table or query, you often may want to work just with the DataTable as a general purpose data container and ignore its containing DataSet. For instance, in the previous section of this chapter, you used various .NET collection classes to contain Customer objects. An alternative approach is to use a DataTable. In this case, you would define the schema of the DataTable via DataColumn objects and then add rows of data to it.

To create a DataTable that can contain similar data as the Customer class shown in Listing 8.1, you need to define the DataColumn objects for the DataTable. For instance, the following example creates the DataTable, defines a single DataColumn for it, and then adds it to the DataTable.

```
DataTable table = new DataTable();

DataColumn firstNameCol = new DataColumn("FirstName",
    typeof(string));
table.Columns.Add(firstNameCol);
```

In this example, you pass two parameters to the constructor of DataColumn. The first of these is the name of the DataColumn, whereas the second is the data type of the data to be stored in this column. As an alternative to specifying these two values in the constructor, you can also set them via properties, as shown in the following example.

```
DataColumn idCol = new DataColumn();

idCol.ColumnName = "Id";
idCol.DataType = typeof(Int32);
idCol.AllowDBNull = false;
idCol.Unique = true;

table.Columns.Add(idCol);
```

Here in this example, you not only specify the name and type of the column, you also specify that the column cannot contain null values and that each row in the DataTable must contain a unique value for this column.

After the schema for the DataTable is finished, data can be added to it. This is most easily accomplished by using the NewRow factory method of the DataTable. This method creates a DataRow object with the correct schema.

```
DataRow r1 = table.NewRow();
```

After the row is created, you can manipulate it by using an index or the column name. For instance, the following fills a row with data (by referencing each column with an index), and then adds it to the DataTable.

```
r1[0] = 1;
r1[1] = "Thomas";
r1[2] = "Hobbes";
r1[3] = "123-4567";

table.Rows.Add(r1);
```

The next example does the same thing, but uses the column name to reference the individual field values.

```
DataRow r2 = table.NewRow();

r2["Id"] = 2;
r2["FirstName"] = "David";
r2["LastName"] = "Hume";
r2["Phone"] = "564-7823";

table.Rows.Add(r2);
```

After this DataTable is created and filled with data, what can you do with it?

A DataTable object can be used as a type of *data transfer object*. That is, a DataTable, unlike a custom class such as the Customer class in Listing 8.1 and its collection version in Listing 8.2, simply contains data; it has no logic, so there is no way to add business rules or other behavior. As such, you could use a `DataTable` to pass information between discrete layers within an application, or if serialized into XML, transported across process boundaries. We discuss layers in Chapter 11 on data architecture.

We can also use `DataTable` objects for data binding. For instance, imagine that you have a `DropDownList` control named `drpCustomer`. You can data bind your `DataTable` to it using the following.

```
DataTable table = new DataTable();
...

drpCustomer.DataSource = table;
drpCustomer.DataBind();
```

You may recall that for data binding to work, the data source must implement the `IEnumerable` interface. The `DataTable` class does not in fact implement this interface, so how then can the preceding code work? It works because the `DataTable` class implements the `IListSource` interface instead of `IEnumerable`. All data bindable Web server controls accept objects that implement `IListSource` as well as objects that implement `IEnumerable`. The `IListSource` interface defines a method named `GetList`, which returns some type of `IList` object (which in turn implements `IEnumerable`). In the case of a `DataTable`, its `GetList` method simply returns its `DefaultView` property, which in turn returns a `DataView` object for the `DataTable`. The `DataView` class is more fully described in the following sections.

Creating Calculated Columns

In the `Customer` class shown back in Listing 8.1, there was a read-only `Name` property that returned the `LastName` and `FirstName` fields concatenated together. You can do the same thing inside of a `DataTable` by using the `Expression` property of the `DataColumn`. This property takes a string that contains a valid expression. For instance, the following example illustrates how to create a calculated column named `FullName` that is equivalent to the aforementioned `Name` property from Listing 8.1.

```
DataColumn firstNameCol = new DataColumn("FirstName",
    typeof(string));
DataColumn lastNameCol = new DataColumn("LastName",
    typeof(string));

DataColumn nameCol = new DataColumn("FullName", typeof(string));
nameCol.Expression = "LastName + ', ' + FirstName";
```

The data type for the expression column must be appropriate for the value that the expression returns. Notice as well that string literals within an expression string must use single quotes.

Filtering and Sorting a DataTable Using the DataView

The `DataView` class represents a data-bindable view of a `DataTable` (it implements `IEnumerable`). A `DataView` allows you to change the sort order of the data in the `DataTable` as well as filter the data within it without requerying the original data. Every `DataTable` contains at least one `DataView`, which is accessed via the `DefaultView` property.

Thus, a `DataView` is somewhat analogous to a database view. Unlike a database view, however, a `DataView` cannot provide a view of different joined `DataTable` objects, nor can it exclude columns (that is, you cannot select a subset of the columns in the `DataTable`) or create new calculated columns.

When working with a `DataView`, you can either create a new instance or modify the `DataTable`'s existing `DataView` via the `DefaultView` of the table. The following example illustrates the two approaches.

```
DataView view1 = new DataView(table);
DataView view2 = table.DefaultView;
```

After you have a `DataView` object, you can change the sort order via the `Sort` property of the `DataView`. This property takes a string that contains the column name followed by `ASC` (ascending) or `DESC` (descending). Multiple sort columns can be specified by separating the column names by commas. For instance, the following two examples illustrate two different types of sorting.

```
view1.Sort = "LastName ASC";
view2.Sort = "Firstname, LastName DESC";
```

You can filter the rows that are displayed by the `DataView` via its `RowFilter` property. This property takes a string that specifies the name of a column followed by an operator and a value to filter on. In other words, the property must be set to a valid SQL where clause. For instance, to display only those rows whose `LastName` begins with the letter `H`, you could use the following.

```
view.RowFilter = "LastName Like 'H%'";
```

You can also create a new `DataTable` from any given view via the `ToTable` method, as shown in the following example.

```
DataTable newTable = view.ToTable();
```

Listings 8.4 and 8.5 demonstrate a sample usage of both the `DataTable` and `DataView` classes. Figure 8.8 illustrates what the result looks like in the browser.

The code-behind in Listing 8.5 creates and populates a `DataTable` and then binds it to a `GridView`. The `GridView` is a Web server control that we have not yet encountered. It is an exceptionally powerful control and is examined in considerable detail in Chapter 11. The main feature of the `GridView` to note here is that it renders a multicolumn data source as an HTML `<table>` element and displays every column and every row in the data source.

Listing 8.4   DataViewTester.aspx

```
<h1>Using a DataView</h1>
<p>
This examples illustrates the use of a <code>DataView</code> as a
way to filter and sort a <code>DataTable</code>
</p>

Choose sort field:
<asp:DropDownList ID="drpSort" runat="server" >
   <asp:ListItem>Id</asp:ListItem>
   <asp:ListItem>FirstName</asp:ListItem>
   <asp:ListItem>LastName</asp:ListItem>
   <asp:ListItem>Phone</asp:ListItem>
</asp:DropDownList><br />

Last Name Filter:
<asp:TextBox ID="txtFilter" runat="server" />

<asp:Button ID="btnSubmit" runat="server"
   OnClick="btnViewData_Click" Text="View Data"/><br />

<hr />
<asp:GridView id="grdCustomer" runat="server" />
```

Listing 8.5   DataViewTester.aspx.cs

```
protected void Page_Load(object sender, EventArgs e)
{
   if (!IsPostBack)
      grdCustomer.Visible = false;
}

/// <summary>
/// Handler for the View Data button
/// </summary>
protected void btnViewData_Click(object sender, EventArgs e)
{
   // Create a populated DataTable
   DataTable table = MakeData();
```

```csharp
    // Make a new view
    DataView view = new DataView(table);
    // Set the sort and filter of the view
    view.Sort = drpSort.SelectedValue + " ASC";
    if (txtFilter.Text.Length > 0)
        view.RowFilter = "LastName Like '" + txtFilter.Text + "'";

    // Now bind the view to the GridView
    grdCustomer.Visible = true;
    grdCustomer.DataSource = view;
    grdCustomer.DataBind();
}

/// <summary>
/// Creates and returns a populated DataTable
/// </summary>
private DataTable MakeData()
{
    DataTable table = new DataTable();

    DataColumn idCol = new DataColumn();
    idCol.ColumnName = "Id";
    idCol.DataType = typeof(Int32);
    idCol.AllowDBNull = false;
    idCol.Unique = true;
    idCol.AutoIncrement = true;

    DataColumn firstNameCol = new DataColumn("FirstName",
        typeof(string));
    DataColumn lastNameCol = new DataColumn("LastName",
        typeof(string));
    DataColumn phoneCol = new DataColumn("Phone", typeof(string));

    table.Columns.Add(idCol);
    table.Columns.Add(firstNameCol);
    table.Columns.Add(lastNameCol);
    table.Columns.Add(phoneCol);

    DataRow r1 = table.NewRow();
    r1[1] = "Thomas";
    r1[2] = "Hobbes";
    r1[3] = "123-4567";
    table.Rows.Add(r1);

    DataRow r2 = table.NewRow();
    r2["FirstName"] = "David";
    r2["LastName"] = "Hume";
    r2["Phone"] = "564-7823";
    table.Rows.Add(r2);
```

```
DataRow r3 = table.NewRow();
r3["FirstName"] = "Martin";
r3["LastName"] = "Heidegger";
r3["Phone"] = "253-6383";
table.Rows.Add(r3);

DataRow r4 = table.NewRow();
r4["FirstName"] = "Jean-Jacques";
r4["LastName"] = "Rousseau";
r4["Phone"] = "456-1267";
table.Rows.Add(r4);

return table;
}
```

Figure 8.8 DataViewTester.aspx

Using the DataSet

The previous discussion focused on the DataTable class, which is the core class of the DataSet. Although the DataTable can be used independently of the DataSet, it is generally more common for the DataTable to be used within the context of a DataSet.

As can be seen in Figure 8.7, a DataSet can contain multiple DataTable objects, which can be accessed via the Tables property of the DataSet. Similarly, you can add DataTable objects to a DataSet via the Add method of Tables, as shown in the following example. (Assume that the `MakeCustomerData` and `MakeProduct-Data` methods each return a filled `DataTable`.)

```
DataSet ds = new DataSet();
ds.Tables.Add( MakeCustomerData() );
ds.Tables.Add( MakeProductData() );
```

You can then retrieve a `DataTable` from its `DataSet` via its index, as shown here.

```
DataTable t1 = ds.Tables[0];
DataTable t2 = ds.Tables[1];
```

As an alternative to using an index, you can name your `DataTable` objects within the `DataSet` and then use that name to access them.

```
DataSet ds = new DataSet();
ds.Tables.Add( MakeCustomerData() );

ds.Tables[0].TableName = "Cust";
...
DataTable dt = ds.Tables["Cust"];
```

There are also times when you may need to manipulate the content of a `DataSet` on a row-by-row or column-by-column basis. You can retrieve any given row in a populated `DataTable` by indexing into its `Rows` property. For instance, in the following example , you are retrieving the first row from the first `DataTable` in a `DataSet`.

```
DataSet ds = new DataSet();
...
DataRow dr = ds.Tables[0].Rows[0];
```

After you have a `DataRow`, you can then retrieve individual data items from it by ordinal or named indexing, as shown in the following. Notice that you must cast the value returned from the `DataRow` to the appropriate data type.

```
string s1 = (string)dr[1];
string s2 = (string)dr["Phone"];
```

You can also combine these two steps together, as in the following example.

```
string s3 = (string)ds.Tables[0].Rows[0]["Phone"];
```

This retrieves the value of the column named `Phone` from the first record of the first table in the `DataSet`. A typical usage of this type of code might be within a loop that needs to process every row in a `DataTable`. For instance, the following example calculates the average for a column named `price` within a `DataTable` named `Products` within a `DataSet`.

```
DataSet ds = new DataSet();
// Populate product DataTable and add it to the DataSet
```

```
...
// Now calculate average price
double sum = 0.0;
int count = 0;
foreach (DataRow dr in ds.Tables["Products"].Rows)
{
    double price = (double)dr["Price"];
    sum += price;
    count++;
}
double average = sum / count;
```

Although the DataSet undoubtedly has a great deal of built-in power and flexibility, the code necessary to manipulate individual items inside it is neither the most attractive nor the most straightforward code possible. Perhaps the best way to see this is to compare what the code might look like if you were using the combination of a Product entity object within a generic collection.

```
EntityCollection<Product> products =
    new EntityCollection<Product>();

// Fill collection with data
...
// Now calculate average price
double sum = 0.0;
int count = 0;
foreach (Product p in products)
{
    sum += p.Price
    count++;
}
double average = sum / count;
```

Not only does the entity object and collection version have a simpler object model for retrieving the data, it also hides the implementation details of our data. That is, it hides the field names of our data as well as eliminates the need for casting (as well as the performance penalty for casting) to the appropriate data types.

Typed DataSets

There is a way to achieve cleaner, type-safe code using the DataSet by using what is known as a ***typed DataSet***. A typed DataSet is not a class within the .NET Framework. Rather, it refers to a series of classes, the main of which inherits from DataSet, that is generated by a special tool (usually you do this within Visual Studio or you can do it yourself from the command line using the XSD.EXE tool). These generated classes expose the data within a DataSet in a type-safe manner and allow for a more domain-oriented naming convention.

For instance, to retrieve the `Price` field from the first row in the `Products` table of a typed `DataSet`, you might use syntax similar to the following.

```
SampleTypedDataSet myDataSet = new SampleTypedDataSet();
...
double price = myDataSet.Products[0].Price;
```

Notice how this example uses a class named `SampleTypedDataSet` rather than `DataSet`. What then is `SampleTypedDataSet`? It is a subclass of `DataSet` that has been generated from an XML schema definition files (XSD). This schema file can be created by the developer from scratch or created from Visual Studio's Add New Item dialog. You can use a series of wizard steps to define a typed `DataSet` directly from a data source such as a database, or you can use the DataSet Designer in Visual Studio to design just the typed `DataSet` structure (see Figure 8.9).

To create the typed `DataSet` shown in Figure 8.9, you simply need to drag-and-drop `DataTables` from the Toolbox in Visual Studio onto the design surface. You can then change the table names, add columns to the tables, change column properties, or add relationships. The result of all this designing is a long schema (XSD) file. The Visual

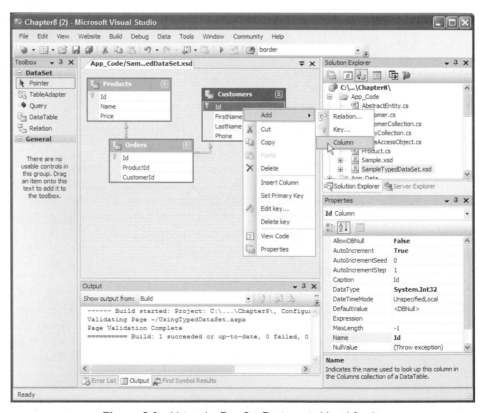

Figure 8.9 Using the DataSet Designer in Visual Studio

Studio extension `MSDataSetGenerator` then generates and compiles the appropriate class (in our example, `SampleTypedDataSet`) from this schema file. You can then use this typed `DataSet` in your code, as shown in the following example.

```
SampleTypedDataSet myDataSet = new SampleTypedDataSet();

// Add a typed row to the products DataTable
SampleTypedDataSet.ProductsRow pr =
    myDataSet.Products.NewProductsRow();
pr.Name = "Book";
pr.Price = 49.99;
myDataSet.Products.Rows.Add(pr);

// Retrieve a column from the first row of the products DataTable
double d = ds.Products[0].Price;

// Data bind the Products DataTable
grdProducts.DataSource = myDataSet.Products.DefaultView;
grdProducts.DataBind();
```

As you can see from this code example, the generated class `SampleTyped-DataSet` also contains a number of nested classes, including `ProductsRow`. Figure 8.10 illustrates how some of the classes generated with a typed `DataSet` are related.

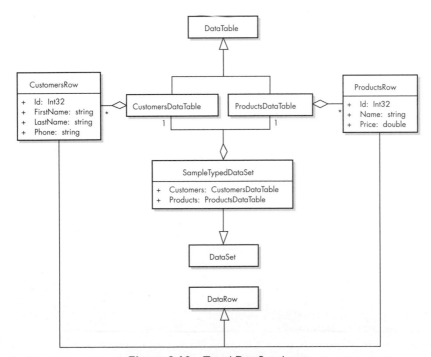

Figure 8.10 Typed DataSet classes

Relating DataTables

If you have a `DataSet` with multiple `DataTable` objects, you can use `DataRela-tion` objects to relate one table to another, navigate through the tables, and return child or parent rows from a related table. For instance, if you have a Book `Data-Table` and an Artist `DataTable`, you can relate them, much like in a database, by specifying the linking columns between the parent and child `DataTables`. For instance, imagine that you define two `DataTable` objects as follows.

```csharp
// First define the artist table
DataTable artistTable = new DataTable();
artistTable.TableName = "Authors";

DataColumn idCol = new DataColumn("AuthorId", typeof(Int32));
DataColumn firstNameCol =
    new DataColumn("FirstName", typeof(string));
DataColumn lastNameCol =
    new DataColumn("LastName", typeof(string));

artistTable.Columns.Add(idCol);
artistTable.Columns.Add(firstNameCol);
artistTable.Columns.Add(lastNameCol);

// Fill with data
...

// Now define book table
DataTable bookTable = new DataTable();
bookTable.TableName = "Books";

DataColumn idCol = new DataColumn("Id", typeof(Int32));
DataColumn authorCol = new DataColumn("AuthorId", typeof(Int32));
DataColumn nameCol = new DataColumn("Title", typeof(string));
DataColumn priceCol = new DataColumn("Price", typeof(double));

bookTable.Columns.Add(idCol);
bookTable.Columns.Add(authorCol);
bookTable.Columns.Add(nameCol);
bookTable.Columns.Add(priceCol);

// Fill with data
...

// Create DataSet and add tables
DataSet ds = new DataSet();
ds.Tables.Add(artistTable);
ds.Tables.Add(bookTable);
```

Notice that the book `DataTable` includes an `AuthorId` column. This column contains a matching ID value from the artist `DataTable`. In database parlance, you would say that the `AuthorId` column in the books table is a foreign key and that there is a one-to-many relationship between the tables, with the artist table being the one table, and the book table the many table. In `DataRelation` terminology, the author `DataTable` is the parent, whereas the book `DataTable` is the child. To set up a `DataRelation`, you give the relation a name and specify both the parent column and the child column; the `DataRelation` is then added to the `Relations` collection of the `DataSet`. The following example illustrates how to set up a `DataRelation` between the author and book tables.

```
DataRelation relation = new DataRelation("Book2Author",
    ds.Tables["Authors"].Columns["AuthorId"],
    ds.Tables["Books"].Columns["AuthorId"]);

ds.Relations.Add(relation);
```

After one or more `DataRelations` have been set up, what can you do with them? Unlike with a SQL join, which combines related fields from multiple tables into a single, separate view, all a `DataRelation` does is make child rows available to a parent row as well as enforce referential integrity constraints when editing, adding, or deleting related rows.

The following example illustrates how child rows are made available to a parent row. It loops through the rows in the parent `DataTable` (in this case, it is the Authors `DataTable`), and displays each related row from the child `DataTable` (the Books `DataTable`).

```
// Loop through each parent row
foreach (DataRow artistRow in ds.Tables["Authors"].Rows)
{
    // Output the author's name
    string fname = (string)artistRow["FirstName"];
    string lname = (string)artistRow["LastName"];
    labReport.Text += "<dt>" + fname + " " + lname;

    // Loop through each child row for this parent
    foreach (DataRow bookRow in artistRow.GetChildRows(relation))
    {
        // Output the book title
        string title = (string)bookRow["Title"];
        labReport.Text += "<dd>" + title;
    }
}
```

XML Integration with the DataSet

At the beginning of this section on the DataSet, we mentioned the three ways in which a DataSet can be populated with data. You have already examined how it can be programmatically created and manipulated. The next chapter on ADO.NET demonstrates how a DataSet can be filled from a database table or query. This section shows how a DataSet can also be filled from an XML stream or file.

A DataSet can use XML data not only for its data but for its schema or structure as well. The DataSet class has the capability to represent its data and schema in its own XML format called a ***DiffGram***. This XML representation can be used, for instance, to transport the DataSet across HTTP for use by another .NET application.

To fill a DataSet with data from an XML file, you would use the ReadXml method of the DataSet. This method is overloaded to accept a number of different arguments. The different overloaded versions of this method allow XML to be read from a file, from an external URL, or even from a string containing XML.

For instance, to populate a sample DataSet from an XML file, you could use code similar to the following.

```
try
{
    DataSet ds1 = new DataSet();
    ds1.ReadXml( Server.MapPath("~/App_Data/somefile.xml") );

    // Use the data set
}
catch (IOException)
{
    // Handle the error
}
```

Because you are accessing an external resource, you should wrap the call to ReadXml within a try...catch block. As well, because ReadXml requires a physical file path, you should use the Server.MapPath method to return the physical file path that corresponds to the virtual path on the Web server.

Instead of reading the XML from a physical file, it can also be read in from a ***stream***. A stream is an abstraction of a sequential flow of bytes from some data source, such as a file, an input/output device, an interprocess communication pipe, or an external HTTP source. For instance, if you want to read in a RSS feed from some other Web site into a DataSet, you might use code similar to that shown in the following example.

```
try
{
    DataSet ds2 = new DataSet();
```

```
XmlTextReader xtr =
    new XmlTextReader("http://somewhere/file.rss");
ds2.ReadXml(xtr);

    // Use the data set
}
Catch ( … )
{
    // Handle the error
}
```

In this case, you are relying on an `XmlTextReader` to make the connection to the external XML file. The `XmlTextReader` provides forward-only, read-only access to a stream of XML data.

What then happens after `ReadXml` is invoked? Recall that the `DataSet` is an in-memory relational structure made up of tables, columns, and relations. An XML document, by contrast, is a hierarchical structure made up of XML elements. How then is this hierarchical structure/schema converted into a relational structure/schema?

When loading a `DataSet` from XML, the schema can be defined inline within the XML file itself using XML Schema definition language, defined externally in a separate XML schema file (`.XSD`), or created through inference from the XML data being loaded.

CORE NOTE

You can improve the speed of the XML processing by specifying whether the schema should be inferred or whether it is contained inline by using the `XmlReadMode` enumeration with the `ReadXml` method. For instance, in our preceding examples, if you are inferring the schema from the data, you should use the following:

```
DataSet ds = new DataSet();
ds.ReadXml("somefile.xml", XmlReadMode.InferSchema );
```

Regardless of whether the schema is defined or inferred, some type of algorithm must be used to translate hierarchical data into relational data. If a schema has been defined, for each `complexType` child element within the schema, a `DataTable` is generated in the `DataSet`, with the table structure determined by the definition of the complex type.

If the schema is inferred from the data, a more complex translation process is involved. The following rules govern the translation of XML data into `DataSet` tables.

- XML elements that have attributes are inferred as DataTable objects.
- XML elements that have child elements are inferred as DataTable objects.
- XML elements that repeat are inferred as a single DataTable.
- If the document element contains no attributes and is not empty it is *not* inferred as a DataTable.

For nested tables, a DataRelation also is generated. After the tables are defined, the following rules determine how the XML data is translated into columns:

- Attributes within an XML element are inferred as DataColumn objects.
- Nonrepeating XML elements that have no attributes or child elements are inferred as DataColumn objects.

What would be the structure of the resulting DataSet after reading the following XML?

```
<?xml version="1.0" encoding="utf-8" ?>
<menu>
  <food>
    <name>Grilled New York Strip Steak Bordelaise</name>
    <price>$23.95</price>
    <description>10 oz. steak grilled to medium </description>
    <calories>1200</calories>
  </food>
  <food>
    <name>Surf and Turf Lobster</name>
    <price>$35.95</price>
    <description>Steak with a 6oz. lobster tail</description>
    <calories>1150</calories>
  </food>
</menu>
```

In this case, there is only one DataTable generated named food. But what if you had the more complex XML file shown here?

```
<?xml version="1.0" ?>
<NavMenu title="GameSystems">
   <MenuItem title="PC" icon="images/icon_4.gif" >
      <Games>
         <Game>
            <name>Game 1</name>
            <price>free</price>
         </Game>
         <Game>
            <name>Game 2</name>
            <price>14.99</price>
         </Game>
      </Games>
```

```
    </MenuItem>
    <MenuItem title="Mac" icon="images/icon_3.gif" >
        <Games>
            <Game>
                <name>Game 3</name>
                <price>49.99</price>
            </Game>
        </Games>
    </MenuItem>
</NavMenu>
```

Figure 8.11 illustrates the `DataSet` schema that would be inferred from the preceding XML.

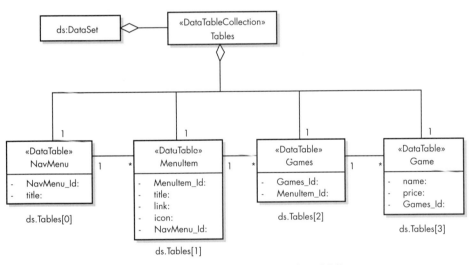

Figure 8.11   Schema generated from XML

Notice how the inference process has added columns to each of the `DataTable` objects. These are linking columns necessary for the `DataRelations` between the `DataTable` objects.

Listings 8.6 and 8.7 demonstrate how to read an XML document (local or remote) into a `DataSet` and then display the contents of each of its `DataTable` objects. The Web Form provides a `TextBox` for entering the path of the XML document and a `Button` to initiate the XML loading. The event handler for the button attempts to create a `XmlTextReader` to the XML document, and if successful, dynamically generates a `GridView` control for each `DataTable` in the `DataSet`. The result looks like that shown in Figure 8.12.

Listing 8.6 ReadXML.aspx

```
<h1>Loading a DataSet with XML</h1>
Enter the filename or the URL for the XML to be loaded:<br />

<asp:TextBox ID="txtXML" runat="server" Columns="60"/>
<asp:Button ID="btnLoad" runat="server" Text="Load XML"
   OnClick="btnLoad_Click" />

<asp:Panel ID="panData" runat="server">
   <p>
   Below you will see a list of <code>GridView</code> controls,
   one for each of the <code>DataTable</code>s generated from
   the XML
   </p>
   <asp:PlaceHolder ID="phData" runat="server" />
</asp:Panel>

<hr />
<asp:Label ID="labMsg" runat="server" CssClass="error"/>
```

Listing 8.7 ReadXML.aspx.cs

```
using System;
using System.Data;
using System.Configuration;
using System.Collections;
using System.Web;
using System.Web.Security;
using System.Web.UI;
using System.Web.UI.WebControls;
using System.Web.UI.WebControls.WebParts;
using System.Web.UI.HtmlControls;

// Don't forget to add these
using System.IO;
using System.Xml;

public partial class ReadXML : System.Web.UI.Page
{
    protected void Page_Load(object sender, EventArgs e)
    {
        if (!IsPostBack)
        {
            panData.Visible = false;
            txtXML.Text = "App_Data/GameSystemsMenu.xml";
        }
```

```csharp
}

/// <summary>
/// Handler for the Load button
/// </summary>
protected void btnLoad_Click(object sender, EventArgs e)
{
    panData.Visible = true;
    string path = "";
    try
    {
        DataSet ds1 = new DataSet();
        path = txtXML.Text;

        // If user input doesn't begin with http then
        // assume a local file
        if (! path.StartsWith("http",
                StringComparison.CurrentCultureIgnoreCase))
            path = Server.MapPath(path);

        // Create the reader and load it into DataSet
        XmlTextReader xtr = new XmlTextReader(path);
        ds1.ReadXml(xtr, XmlReadMode.InferSchema);

        // Loop through each DataTable and output contents
        foreach (DataTable table in ds1.Tables)
        {
            // Dynamically output the name of table
            Literal caption = new Literal();
            caption.Text = "<h2>Table: " + table.TableName +
                "</h2>";
            phData.Controls.Add(caption);

            // Dynamically create a grid view
            GridView grid = new GridView();

            // Set up its look and data bind it to the DataTable
            grid.CellPadding = 3;
            grid.DataSource = table.DefaultView;
            grid.DataBind();

            // Add this GridView to PlaceHolder
            phData.Controls.Add(grid);
        }
    }
    catch (IOException)
    {
        panData.Visible = false;
        labMsg.Text = txtXML.Text + " not found";
```

```
        }
        catch
        {
            panData.Visible = false;
            labMsg.Text = path + " unable to be accessed";
        }
    }
}
```

Figure 8.12   ReadXML.aspx

Outputting a DataSet as XML

A `DataSet` can output its content (with or without its schema) to XML. This XML can be written to a file, a stream, an `XmlWriter`, or a string. To output the XML representation (without the schema) of the `DataSet` to a string, you can simply use the `GetXml` method. To output the schema to a string, you can use the `GetXmlSchema` method.

```
DataSet ds = new DataSet();
...
string s1 = ds.GetXml();
string s2 = ds.GetXmlSchema();
```

To output the content of a `DataSet` to a file, stream, or `XmlWriter`, you can use its `WriteXml` method.

```
ds.WriteXml("output.xml");
```

Like the `ReadXml` method, `WriteXml` is overloaded to accept a number of different arguments. The different overloaded versions of this method specify whether the XML is to be written to a file, a stream, or an `XmlWriter`.

Choosing a Data Container

In this chapter, we have examined several different in-memory containers for data that are available to ASP.NET developers. Because almost every ASP.NET application needs to work with data in some form or another, it is important to have some sense of the relative merits of the different ways in which you can store data programmatically.

For most applications, data is external to the application. That is, data is stored in some format, such as a database, an XML file, or a Web service, that is external to the application. This external data also needs to be read in and manipulated and possibly stored internally within the application. The use of the ADO.NET `DataReader` and the new data source controls in ASP.NET (both covered in the next chapter) may eliminate the need to internally store data for many situations. Yet, even with the `DataReader` and the data source controls, it is not unusual for an ASP.NET application to require some way to store data internally. After all, not all data used within a Web page comes from an external source. A shopping cart, for instance, might not be generated from an external data source at all; thus, some type of internal data container is necessary to store the information within the cart.

Similarly, later in Chapter 11, we will look at some common application architectures that are used in real-world Web applications. You will find then that it is a common best practice to not have your code-behind classes do all the work, but rather it is best to use a variety of different classes that help your code-behind classes. These different classes can often be conceptually grouped together based on their functionality. These conceptual groups are usually referred to as *layers*. A very common layering scheme is to conceptually divide the application classes into three layers: presentation, business logic, and data access. These layers often need to pass data between them, and so you need to choose a data container approach for the application.

Given that most applications need to use an internal data container at some point, what options are available? In this chapter, we have worked with the four main possibilities, namely .NET collections, custom collections, the `DataSet` (or just its main constituent, the `DataTable`), and the typed `DataSet`. Each of these has its particular strengths and weaknesses, which will be summarized in the following discussion. The one you choose really depends upon the application context, the size of the data to be stored, its perceived lifetime, the programming paradigm you are comfortable with, and the relative importance of maintainability or rapid application development times.

.NET Collections as Data Containers

As we saw earlier in this chapter, the .NET Framework comes with a variety of classes that help you store data, such as the array, as well as other collection classes, such as the `ArrayList`, `Hashtable`, and `SortedList`. These classes are general-purpose in that they can be used to store any type of data. The generic versions of these collections, such as `Dictionary` and `List`, can also be used to store any data, but have the advantage of being strongly typed. These collections also implement all the interfaces necessary for data binding or XML serialization.

When used in conjunction with custom classes that represent entities in the business or application domain, the .NET collections, especially the generic versions, can be a particularly easy yet powerful way to organize the data used in your application. They allow you to model the problem space of the application using the language of the problem domain, rather than the language of .NET.

The main drawback for these .NET collections is that these collections are general purpose. That is, the functionality they provide is limited to the general behaviors of a collection, such as adding elements, retrieving elements, and removing elements. You may have to write the code yourself for other behaviors, such as filling these collections from an external data source, searching for elements, sorting elements, or persisting the values back to the data source.

Custom Collections as Data Containers

When using custom classes to represent entities in the problem domain, you may want to create your own custom collection classes as data containers. This approach takes a fair amount of time if you develop the collection mechanism completely from scratch. However, as shown in the sample `EntityCollection` class in Listing 8.3, there is another way. Rather than reimplement the functionality of a collection, you could decide instead to inherit from the `Collection<T>` base class. The advantage with this approach is that you do not have to "reinvent the wheel" by reimplementing the functionality that exists within one of the built-in .NET collection classes. Instead, you can focus on adding the functionality that the domain requires. For instance, a `ProductCollection` class might add a method that calculates the average price of all products, searches for a particular product, loads itself from a data source, or outputs its content to XML.

As well, custom collections along with custom entities allow you to create code that closely models the problem domain. This tends to make the code more meaningful, and as some have argued (for instance, see Evans or Fowler in the References section) creates a more maintainable and adaptable application. This author prefers this approach, and in Chapter 11 we will explore it further.

The disadvantage to this approach is of course the necessity for implementing the extra functionality yourself. For instance, adding sorting or dynamic filtering yourself in a custom collection is not completely trivial. As well, not every programmer is comfortable with the domain-focused, object-oriented development paradigm. For programmers who are more comfortable with a procedural paradigm or who prefer a database-centric approach in the design of their applications, custom collections and entities may not be the best choice. Instead, they may prefer to use `DataSets`. Finally, we should mention that there is a variety of third-party code-generation or object-relational mapping tools that can help the developer that wants to use this domain-oriented approach.

DataSets as Data Containers

The `DataSet` is a very powerful class. It allows your internal data to mirror the structure of your relational data. It can be easily populated from a data source (and can also write itself back out to the data source); has the capability to search, sort, or filter data; has support for concurrency control; and can be easily output to (and read in from) XML. As well, Visual Studio provides a great deal of support for the `DataSet`; thus, a developer can often work more quickly using a `DataSet`. It can take a great deal of programming to implement all the functionality that is there for "free" inside the `DataSet`. In situations where rapid development times are paramount, the `DataSet` may be an ideal choice.

Although the `DataSet` undoubtedly has a great deal of built-in power and flexibility, the code necessary to manipulate individual items inside it is neither the most attractive, the most efficient, nor the most maintainable code possible. As we saw early in the chapter, the object model for manipulating a `DataSet` is a bit awkward, as well as untyped.

The great power of the `DataSet` is often overkill for many scenarios. Most ASP.NET pages, for instance, generally do not need a disconnected data container that caches multiple changes to the data. In contrast to a Windows Forms application, where such a capability is very helpful, Web applications typically involve very little state. Web Forms react from request to request. A Web Form generally reads data to process a single request, manipulate the data somehow, and then display it. Alternately, a form might send a request that requires the database to write some data. In such situations, the complexity of a data container that manages both the reading and writing of data makes less sense in the usual Web application situation of discrete single requests.

If all we generally need is temporary storage for some data for the life of a request, all the extra memory used by the `DataSet` and its ancillary classes will have an effect on performance for no corresponding gain. In fact, when retrieving data from a database, the `DataSet` can be several magnitudes of speed slower than other alternatives (see the Davis article in the References section). `DataSet`s are also very much less than ideal if they are to be returned from a Web service that is being consumed by a non-.NET client.

Finally, using a `DataSet` often leads to code that is a bit less maintainable than code that does not. When loading a `DataSet` from a data source, the field names (in the case of a database table) or the element names (in the case of an XML document) from the data source are propagated to the `DataSet`, and thus to any code that uses it. It is usually considered a best practice to insulate your presentation layer (i.e., your Web Forms and their code-behind classes) from database implementation details; if you do have database details (such as field name indexers to access data in our `DataSet`'s `DataRows`) in your presentation layer, changes made to the database will cascade to your Web Forms. That is, changes to the database structure also require changes to your Web Forms. Some of these problems are mitigated by the typed `DataSet`.

Typed DataSets as Data Containers

A typed `DataSet` has all the advantages of the untyped `DataSet`. As well, the typed `DataSet` provides a much simpler and easier object model than does the regular untyped `DataSet`. Its strongly typed members usually reduce runtime errors as they allow the compiler to catch type and index mismatches that can easily happen when programmatically manipulating an untyped `DataSet`.

Yet despite these advantages, you should keep in mind that a typed `DataSet` is still just a data container. Although it may use the names of your data, like the regular untyped `DataSet`, it does not contain any behaviors (although some behaviors can be implemented as `DataColumn` expressions or can be implemented using the `DataView`'s filtering, sorting, and searching capabilities).

Typed DataSets by and large impose a database-centric approach to your application. (This is related to what Fowler calls the Table Module approach.) For many developers, this is by no means a problem as it is the approach they are most comfortable with. Other developers (including myself) prefer instead to center their application development around the core domain objects (also called business objects or simply entities) of the application itself. For these developers, the typed DataSet (and indeed the untyped DataSet) may very well be avoided in favor of custom collection classes (ideally using generics) containing custom entities.

Finally, another potential problem with typed DataSets is that the schema needs to be refreshed whenever the underlying data structure changes. Generally, a typed DataSet is generated from a database. That is, the different DataTable objects in the typed DataSet mirrors the different tables in the database. Then, if the database schema changes in any way, the schema file for the typed DataSet must be regenerated and the project recompiled. Given that a typical Web application very often has several or even many typed DataSets (because it is impractical from a performance and memory standpoint to use a single monolithic typed DataSet that contains all the data for an application), a change in the database schema usually necessitates regeneration of all these schema files. In such a case, it is quite easy to forget to regenerate one of these files.

Summary

This chapter began this book's coverage of working with data in ASP.NET. Unlike the previous chapters that focused on different Web server controls, this chapter focused on the different ways that data can be initially represented and stored in an ASP.NET application and the data-binding mechanism that allows for the easy display of data within many Web server controls.

The next chapter explores ADO.NET, which is the series of classes in the .NET Framework devoted to the accessing of external data sources.

Exercises

The solutions to the following exercises can be found at my Web site, http://www.randyconnolly.com/core. Additional exercises only available for teachers and instructors are also available from this site.

1. Create a sample Web Form named TestDataBinding.aspx. This page should contain two ListBox controls. Both of these controls should be data bound to two different sample string arrays.

2. Create two classes in the App_Code folder named Product.cs and Order.cs. These two classes should be defined as shown in Figure 8.6. If you haven't already created the AbstractEntity class, do so now.

3. Create a Web Form named TestGenericDataBinding.aspx. This page should contain two ListBox controls. The first ListBox should be bound to a List collection of sample Product objects and should display the product name; the other should be bound to a Dictionary collection of sample Order objects.

4. Create a sample Web Form named TestDataSetDataBinding.aspx. This page should contain two ListBox controls. Both of these controls should be data bound to two different sample DataTable objects.

Key Concepts

- Box instructions
- Collection classes
- Constraint
- Data binding
- Data transfer object
- DataSet
- DiffGram
- Domain classes
- Enumerator
- Generics
- Indexer property
- Key
- Layers
- Reference types
- Stream
- Type parameter
- Typed DataSet
- Unbox instructions
- Value types

References

Davis, Craig. "A Speed Freak's Guide to Retrieving Data in ADO.NET." http://www.devx.com.

Druyts, Jeffrey. "DataSets Are Not Evil." http://jelle.druyts.net.

Esposito, Dino. "Collections and Data-Binding." *MSDN Magazine* (May 2005).

Esposito, Dino. "DataSets vs. Collections." *MSDN Magazine* (August 2005).

Evans, Eric. *Domain-Driven Design: Tackling Complexity in the Heart of Software*. Addison-Wesley, 2004.

Fowler, Martin. *Patterns of Enterprise Application Architecture*. Pearson Education, 2003.

Federicho, Richard. "Boxing and Performance of Collections." `http://www.c-sharpcorner.com`.

Little, J. Ambrose. "Sorting Custom Collections." `http://www.code-magazine.com`.

Lowy, Juval. "An Introduction to C# Generics." `http://msdn.microsoft.com`.

Microsoft. *Designing Data Tier Components and Passing Data Through Tiers*. Microsoft, 2002.

Mitchell, Scott. "Why I Don't Use DataSets in My ASP.NET Applications." `http://aspnet.4guysfromrolla.com`.

Mitchell, Scott. "More On Why I Don't Use DataSets in My ASP.NET Applications." `http://aspnet.4guysfromrolla.com`.

Seguin, Karl. "On the Way to Mastering ASP.NET: Introducing Custom Entity Classes." `http://msdn.microsoft.com`.

Chapter 9

USING ADO.NET

This chapter covers how to programmatically and declaratively work with data in databases. Most contemporary professional Web sites are data-driven in that they retrieve and display data usually from some type of a database. This chapter begins by examining how to access and modify data within databases in ASP.NET using the classes of ADO.NET. The chapter concludes with coverage of the codeless approach to accessing data using data source controls.

Introducing **ADO.NET**

ADO.NET refers to the various classes in the .NET Framework that provide data access. ADO.NET is typically used to access relational databases but can be used as well to access other external data such as XML documents. The classes in ADO.NET fall into two categories: *data containers* and *data providers* (see Figure 9.1).

The previous chapter examined the principal data containers within ADO.NET, namely the `DataTable` and the `DataSet`. The ADO.NET data providers are a handful of .NET classes that are used for connecting to a database, executing data commands, populating a `DataSet`, and providing fast, forward-only, read-only access to data. The four main classes within a data provider are the `DbConnection`, `DbCommand`, `DbDataAdapter`, and `DbDataReader` classes.

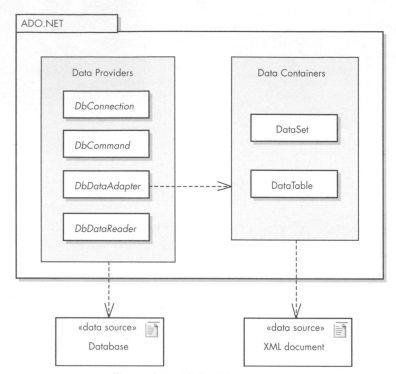

Figure 9.1   ADO.NET architecture

The key point about .NET data providers is that *each database type has its own version of these classes*. Because DbConnection, DbCommand, DbDataAdapter, and DbDataReader are abstract classes, each provider implements its own concrete version of these classes. For instance, there is a data provider for Microsoft SQL Server databases and there is a separate data provider for Oracle databases; as a consequence, there is a SqlConnection class defined in the SQL Server data provider and an Oracle-Connection class defined in the Oracle data provider. Each data provider's version of the required classes in a data provider adds its own prefix to the basic class name.

Table 9.1 provides a short description of each of these four essential ADO.NET abstract base classes.

Table 9.1   Abstract Base Classes of a Data Provider

Class	Description
DbCommand	Executes a data command, such as a SQL statement or a stored procedure.
DbConnection	Establishes a connection to a data source.

Table 9.1 Abstract Base Classes of a Data Provider *(continued)*

Class	Description
`DbDataAdapter`	Populates a `DataSet` from a data source.
`DbDataReader`	Represents a read-only, forward-only stream of data from a data source.

Besides the common four base classes, there are a set of interfaces that each data provider must implement, as shown in Figure 9.2.

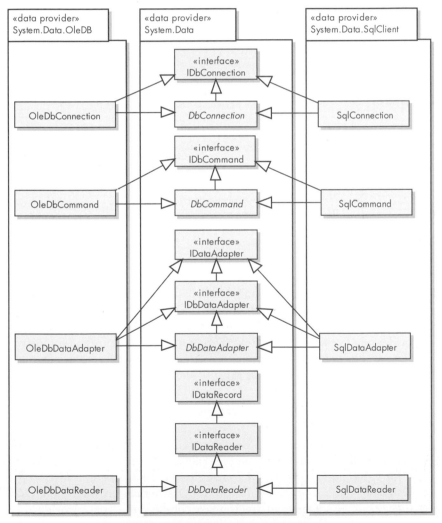

Figure 9.2 ADO.NET data providers

The advantage of the approach illustrated in Figure 9.2 is that each provider can have its own internal optimizations, yet you can still code in a provider-independent fashion by programming to these interfaces or abstract classes.

A data provider also contains additional helper classes that are used a bit less frequently. The additional provider classes are listed in Table 9.2.

Table 9.2   Additional Classes of a Data Provider

Class	Description
DbCommandBuilder	Automatically generates single-table database commands for updating, deleting, or inserting data.
DbConnectionStringBuilder	Provides a way to create and modify connection strings.
DbDataPermission	Ensures user has the appropriate security level for accessing data.
DbException	The base class for all exceptions thrown by the data provider.
DbParameter	Represents a data parameter to a DbCommand.
DbTransaction	Allows the grouping of commands into ADO.NET transactions. This allows you to roll back and undo changes made to a database.

Each data provider has its own namespace within the System.Data namespace of ADO.NET, as shown in Figure 9.3.

The data provider namespaces shown in Figure 9.3 are those that ship with the .NET Framework. Several other vendor-supplied data providers are also available. For instance, Oracle has its own ADO.NET data provider (ODP.NET) that has better support for Oracle features as well as better performance than Microsoft's own data provider for Oracle (unfortunately, there is no support at present for distributed transactions within System.Transaction). There are also third-party data providers for open-source databases such as MySQL and PostgresSQL.

Choosing a Data Provider

Given that there are different data providers to choose from, which data provider should you use? This depends both on the database that is being accessed and your concern for speed and flexibility. Of course, if you are accessing a Microsoft SQL Server database, you are not going to use the Oracle data provider! Table 9.3 discusses the various advantages and disadvantages of the various data providers.

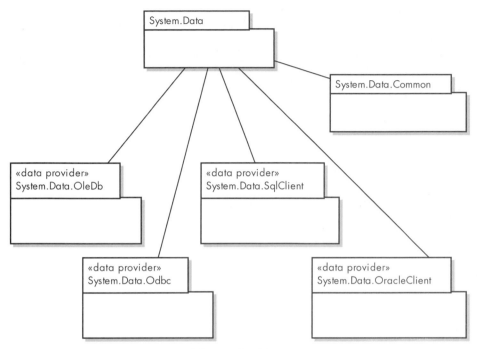

Figure 9.3   ADO.NET namespaces

Table 9.3   ADO.NET Data Providers

Provider	Description
SqlClient	Recommended for accessing Microsoft SQL Server databases (version 7 and later). Provides the significantly fastest access to SQL Server data.
Odbc	Recommended for accessing legacy data sources for which there is no native ADO.NET data provider or any OLE DB driver.
OleDb	Recommended for accessing data sources without a native ADO.NET data provider but which have an OLE DB driver (OLE DB is Microsoft's older COM-based database API used in the original ADO). Typically used for accessing Microsoft Access or Microsoft SQL Server 6.5 data.
	Can also be used instead of the Oracle or SqlClient data providers to make your data access code database independent. However, doing so incurs a substantial performance penalty. There are other preferred approaches (i.e., programming to the abstract base classes) to achieving database-independent code that are covered later in the chapter.

Table 9.3   ADO.NET Data Providers *(continued)*

Provider	Description
Oracle	Recommended for accessing Oracle databases (version 8.1.7 and later). Provides the significantly faster access to Oracle data in comparison to the ODBC and OLE DB providers. Provides support for several unique features of Oracle.
	Oracle's own data provider for Oracle databases provides additional support for Oracle features, and may provide faster, more efficient data retrieval. This provider can be downloaded from Oracle's Web site.

Data Provider Classes

As mentioned earlier in the chapter, each data provider must supply its own version of each of the classes listed in Tables 9.1 and 9.2. The four most important of these classes are those representing a connection, a command, a data adapter, and a data reader. We will refer to these classes from now on by the name of their abstract base class: DbConnection, DbCommand, DbDataAdapter, and DbDataReader.

The process for using these classes is as follows.

1. Create a DbConnection to the database via a connection string.
2. Create and execute a DbCommand for the database.
3. [Optional] Fill a DataSet from the database using a DbDataAdapter, or use a DbDataReader to retrieve data from the database.

The following sections illustrate how to work with each of these four classes.

DbConnection Classes

These classes represent a ***connection*** to a data source through which commands are passed to the data source and through which data is returned. Before you can access a database, you must first create a connection to it. Database commands then "travel" across the connection to the database, as does any data returned from a database.

Each DbConnection class has members for opening and closing a connection, setting and retrieving properties of a connection, and handling connection-related events. Table 9.4 summarizes the notable properties of each DbConnection class.

Table 9.4   Notable Properties of the DbConnection Classes

Property	Description
ConnectionString	The connection string used to specify to which database you are connecting. The contents of this string vary depending upon the provider and the actual database.
ConnectionTimeout	The number of seconds to wait for a connection to open.
Database	Retrieves the name of the database as specified in the connection string.
State	Retrieves the current state (opened, closed, etc.) of the connection. Possible values are described by the Connection-State enumeration.

CORE NOTE

The properties listed in Table 9.4 are those for the abstract base class (DbConnection) for the different connection classes. Each provider's version of this class (e.g., SqlConnection, OleDbConnection, etc.), may add members to those defined in the base class.

Connection Strings

To create a connection, you must specify a ***connection string***. A connection string is a string that specifies the initialization and connection information needed to connect to a data source. It can contain information such as the database name or location, driver type, user name, password, and even connection pooling and timeout information. Connection strings are based on ODBC connection string syntax consisting of name-value pairs separated by semicolons.

```
name1=value1; name2=value
```

A connection string for a Microsoft Access database specifies the OLE DB driver along with the physical location of the database file. An example might look like

```
Provider=Microsoft.Jet.OLEDB.4.0;Data Source=c:\data\abc.mdb;
```

A connection string for connecting to a Microsoft SQL Server database indicates the database name along with security information. A connection string for connecting to a SQL Server database on the same machine as the ASP.NET application might look like

```
Server=localhost;database=books;uid=webuser;pwd=asprules;
```

The name-value pair `server=localhost` indicates the following: the database is on the same machine as that running the code, the database name is `books`, the user is `webuser`, and the password for the user is `asprules`. This example uses **SQL Server Authentication**.

An example of a connection string to a SQL Server database that instead uses **integrated security** (usually called **Windows Authentication** because it uses the currently logged-in user's credentials to access the database) is

```
Data Source=(local);Initial Catalog=books;Integrated Security=SSPI
```

In this example, the `Data Source=(local)` has exactly the same meaning as `Server=localhost` in the previous string. Similarly, the `Initial Catalog=books` refers to the database name in same way as the previous `database=books`.

Using Windows Authentication

SQL Server Authentication makes use of user information contained within SQL Server itself. Instead, Windows Authentication uses security information from the Windows user accounts. In general, SQL Server Authentication is not as secure as Windows Authentication, because Windows Authentication does not expose the user and password information.

On the other hand, Windows Authentication can be quite difficult to deploy. Windows Authentication requires that the logged in Windows user has the appropriate authorization to access the database. When you are using the integrated Visual Studio test server, you are using your Windows account, which probably has all the necessary permissions for accessing any database on your machine. However, after an application is deployed on a Web server running IIS, the user account is no longer your account, but the more limited ASPNET (IIS 5) or NETWORK SERVICE (IIS 6) account. In this case, this ASPNET or NETWORK SERVICE account must be given permission within the DBMS to access the database. If the DBMS is on a different computer than the ASP.NET application, it becomes even more complex. In this case, the Windows identity must travel across the network to the DBMS; enabling this may require making changes to the `machine.config` file for the server. Chapter 13 covers security in more detail and provides more information about using Windows Authentication.

Programming a DbConnection

To create a connection, you simply instantiate the relevant `DbConnection` object (passing it your connection string) and call its `Open` method. The `DbConnection` object is now available for use. After you no longer need the connection, you must close it. The following example demonstrates how to open and close a connection to a sample Microsoft Access database.

```
// Must use @ since string contains backslash characters
string connString = @"Provider=Microsoft.Jet.OLEDB.4.0;Data
    Source=c:\data\abc.mdb;"

OleDbConnection conn = new OleDbConnection(connString);
conn.Open();

// Now use the connection
...

conn.Close();
```

CORE NOTE

The `OleDbConnection` class is in the `System.Data.OleDb` namespace, so you need to import it via

```
using System.Data.OleDb;
```

There are a few things that are less than ideal with the preceding code sample. For one, it is possible that something could go wrong when you try to make the connection; in this case, a runtime exception is generated. In general, any time your pages need to access an external resource, it is possible that an exception could occur. As a consequence, you should wrap the code within a `try...catch` block, as shown in the following example.

```
string connString = ...
OleDbConnection conn = new OleDbConnection(connString);
try
{
    conn.Open();

    // Now use the connection
    ...
}
catch (OleDbException ex)
{
```

```
    // Handle or log exception
}
finally
{
    if (conn != null)
        conn.Close();
}
```

Notice that the call to the `Close` method of the `DbConnection` object is contained within a `finally` block. This ensures that `Close` is called regardless of whether an exception does or does not occur.

CORE NOTE

It must be stressed that connections are a critical and limited resource. Connections represent overhead for the database and so there is always a limited supply of them. As a result, connections must be carefully managed to ensure that an application performs well and can handle increases in the number of users. *It is vitally important to explicitly close a connection when it is no longer needed.* Connections should be opened as late as possible and closed as soon as possible. One way to achieve this is whenever possible use a connection only for the life of a method call.

There is an alternate programming pattern for using a connection that uses the C# `using` statement. This statement defines a scope for a block of code; after the block of code is finished executing, any objects defined in the `using` statement are automatically disposed. For instance, the previous code could be rewritten as follows.

```
using (OleDbConnection conn = new OleDbConnection(connString))
{
    conn.Open();

    // Now use the connection
    ...
}
```

Notice that there is no longer an explicit call to close the connection, nor is there any error catching. The compiler converts the preceding code into something equivalent to the following.

```
OleDbConnection conn = new OleDbConnection(connString);
try
{
    conn.Open();
    ...
```

```
}
finally
{
    conn.Dispose();
}
```

Notice that in the `finally` block, the compiler inserts a method call to `conn.Dispose`, which in turn calls `conn.Close`.

Another way that you could improve this code is to change the connection string so that the path of the database file is not hard-coded within it. You could change the connection so that the path is not contained within, but instead uses the current path of the Web application (via `Server.MapPath`). For instance, in the following example, the sample database file `abc.mdb` is in the `App_Data` subdirectory of the Web application.

```
string connString =
    "Provider=Microsoft.Jet.OLEDB.4.0;Data Source=";
connString += Server.MapPath("~/App_Data/abc.mdb") + ";";
```

Even with this change, it is less than ideal to have the connection string hard-coded within the program code. If confidential user and password information is contained in the string, remember that the resulting Microsoft Intermediate Language (MSIL) can potentially be disassembled by someone with access to the MSIL (this wouldn't be the user of the page because MSIL is not served back to client). Even if you are not concerned about this particular security risk, you generally want to avoid hard-coding connection information to avoid needless code duplication. Because it is quite likely that more than one page in your Web application may need to access the same database, it makes sense to define the connection string only once. You can do this by defining the connection string within the `Web.config` file for the site.

Storing Connection Strings

In ASP.NET 2.0, you can define connection strings for your application in the `connectionString` section of the `Web.config` file. This section is contained within the root `configuration` element of the `Web.config` file. You can add connection strings to the file by using the `add` element, as shown in the following.

```
<configuration>
    <connectionStrings>
        <add name="Books" connectionString="Provider=…" />
        <add name="Sales" connectionString="Data Source=…" />
    </connectionStrings>

    <system.web>
```

```
...
   </system.web>
</configuration>
```

Notice that each element requires not only the connection string, but also a unique name for identifying it. This name can be used when programmatically retrieving the connection string from this file. This can be done via the `Connec-tionStrings` collection property of the static `WebConfigurationManager` class. This collection returns an object of type `ConnectionStringSettings`, which provides properties for retrieving the connection string, as shown here.

```
string connString =
   WebConfigurationManager.ConnectionStrings["Books"].
      ConnectionString;
```

Because the `WebConfigurationManager` class is in the `System.Web.Config-uration` namespace, you may need to add a reference to it via

```
using System.Web.Configuration;
```

CORE NOTE

In ASP.NET 2.0, you can encrypt connection strings (or any other information) within the `Web.config` file. For more information, see Microsoft, "Encrypting and Decrypting Configuration Sections," in the References section at the end of the chapter.

Using the ConnectionStringBuilder

In the previous examples, the connection string was either a hard-coded constant in the programming code, or contained as a constant within the `Web.config` file. Occasionally, the connection string is not a constant, but is dynamically generated, usually based on user input. One such example might be an application with SQL Server authentication that uses a generated connection string based on user input from a user login form. In such a case, you might be tempted to do something like the following.

```
string connString = "server=localhost;database=books;uid=";
connString += txtUser.Text + ";pwd=" + txtPass.Text + ";";
```

Unfortunately, such an approach leaves the page vulnerable to an injection attack (e.g., a user could type in additional connection string information into the password field that could allow the user to bypass the credential check). As an alternative to the preceding code, in ASP.NET 2.0, you can instead use the `DbConnectionString-Builder` class (each provider must implement its version of this class) to dynamically construct your connection string. The `DbConnectionStringBuilder` uses properties to modify and return the connection string. For instance, the following example shows how to use the SQL Server provider's `DbConnectionStringBuilder` to dynamically construct a connection string in a safe manner.

```
SqlConnectionStringBuilder builder =
    new SqlConnectionStringBuilder();

builder.DataSource = "localhost";
builder.InitialCatalog = "Books";
builder.UserID = txtUser.Text;
builder.Password = txtPass.Text;

string connString = builder.ConnectionString;
```

Connection Pooling

As mentioned earlier, database connections are a precious, finite commodity. As well, creating and opening a connection to a database is a relatively slow process, because your application needs to communicate interprocess (or even across a network) to the database server, be authenticated, and then return the connection. In a typical real-world Web site with many simultaneous requests, you can improve the performance and scalability of your application by reducing the number of times you connect to the database by sharing, or pooling, your connections to a data source.

Connection pooling is in fact handled automatically behind-the-scenes by the ADO.NET providers. For some of the providers (such as the SQL Server provider), you can customize how the pooling works or even turn it off, via various options in the connection string. As well, different providers `DbConnection` class (such as that for SQL Server and Oracle) also provide additional members for clearing the pool of connections.

DbCommand Classes

These classes represent a SQL statement or a stored procedure that is executed by the data source. Each `DbCommand` class has members for representing a SQL statement, for creating data parameters, and executing SQL *commands* that either return data (e.g., `SELECT`) or do not return data (e.g., `INSERT`, `DELETE`, or `UPDATE`). The `DbCommand` class can also be used to run stored procedures if the database supports them.

Tables 9.5 and 9.6 summarize the notable members of each `DbCommand` class.

Table 9.5   Notable Properties of the DbCommand Classes

Property	Description
CommandText	The text of the database command. This string is a SQL statement or the name of a stored procedure.
CommandTimeout	The amount of time in seconds to wait for the command to execute.
CommandType	Specifies whether the command text is to be interpreted as a SQL statement or a stored procedure name. Possible values are described by the CommandType enumeration.
Connection	The Connection object to be used by the command.
Parameters	The collection of data parameters to be used for containing criteria values.
Transaction	The transaction within which this command executes.
UpdatedRowSource	Specifies how command results are applied to the DataRow being updated. This only applies when a DbDataAdapter updates data in a DataSet. Possible values are described by the UpdateRowSource enumeration.

Table 9.6   Notable Methods of the DbCommand Classes

Methods	Description
Cancel	Tries to cancel the execution of the current command at the DBMS.
CreateParameter	Factory method for creating a strongly typed parameter object.
ExecuteNonQuery	Executes a command that does not return any data rows. Typically used for UPDATE, INSERT, and DELETE commands.
ExecuteReader	Executes a command that returns a data reader.
ExecuteScalar	Executes a command that returns the first column of the first row in the result set.
Prepare	Creates a compiled version of the command in the DBMS.

Creating a DbCommand

To create a command, you instantiate the relevant DbCommand object and pass it your database DbConnection object. This DbConnection can be set via the constructor or the DbConnection property of the DbCommand. The DbCommand object also needs a database command contained in a string. This command string can also be set via the constructor or the CommandText property of the DbCommand. The following example illustrates how to create a DbCommand object.

```
string connString = "…"
OleDbConnection conn = new OleDbConnection(connString);

// Create a command using SQL text
string cmdString = "SELECT Id,Name,Price From Products";
OleDbCommand cmd = new OleDbCommand(cmdString, conn);

conn.Open();
...
conn.Close();
```

In this example, the command string is a SQL SELECT command. Some of the other, typically used SQL commands are UPDATE, INSERT, and DELETE, all of which are briefly discussed in the next section.

SQL Commands for Retrieving, Adding, Updating, or Deleting Data

To retrieve records from a table, you use the SQL SELECT command. The syntax for the basic SELECT command is shown here (optional values are enclosed in square brackets).

```
SELECT field_names FROM table_names
[WHERE search_criteria]
[ORDER BY field_names [ASC | DESC]]
```

The following sample illustrates four SELECT commands.

```
SELECT id, firstname, lastname FROM Employees
SELECT * FROM Employees
SELECT id, lastname FROM Employees WHERE id < 10
SELECT COUNT(id) FROM Employees WHERE city LIKE 'L%'
```

CORE NOTE

The second example in the preceding code uses a wildcard field select (i.e., SELECT *). In general, this should be avoided in production code. One reason for this is that it can be inefficient; it returns all the columns regardless of whether they are needed. The second reason is that it potentially makes your code dependent upon the field order in the database table. For instance, if field data is accessed via an index into a DbDataReader or a DataRow, changing the field order in the database probably breaks the application. However, the book does occasionally use the wildcard select in the some of the code samples only for brevity reasons.

Although the SQL keywords shown in the preceding examples are in uppercase, SQL is not case sensitive. It is a common convention, nonetheless, to put the SQL key words in uppercase.

The last of the preceding sample SELECT commands uses a SQL aggregate function (COUNT) and a wildcard criterion (%), which returns a single value that is the count of the number of employees whose city begins with the letter L.

To append a new record to a database table, you use the SQL INSERT command. The syntax for the INSERT command is as follows.

```
INSERT INTO table_name (field1,field2,...) VALUES (value1,value2,...)
```

Most databases support the automatic generation of numeric primary keys when inserting new records. In Microsoft Access, these fields are called AutoNumber fields, and in Microsoft SQL Server, these fields are referred to as *identity fields*. A common requirement of applications that insert new records is the need to retrieve the database-generated primary key of the new record. The way to retrieve this database-generated key value differs depending upon the type of database being used. If you are using SQL Server along with stored procedures, the generated key number can be returned via an output parameter (see the example beginning on page 523). If you are using Access, you can run a SELECT @@IDENTITY query (see "Executing a DbCommand" on page 520).

To update data in a database, you use the SQL UPDATE command. The syntax for the UPDATE command is as follows.

```
UPDATE table_name SET field1 = value1, field2 = value2...
    WHERE criteria
```

To delete data in a database, you use the SQL DELETE command. The syntax for the DELETE command is as follows.

```
DELETE FROM table_name WHERE criteria
```

Stored Procedures

A **stored procedure** is a predefined, reusable collection of SQL statements that is stored within a database. It can accept input parameters, output parameters, and can return single or multiple result sets. Stored procedures are executed by referencing their name and they allow the use of user-declared variables, conditional logic, and other powerful programming features. There is a certain amount of controversy about stored procedures. Some developers use stored procedures to encapsulate not only data access logic but a certain amount of business logic as well; other developers believe strongly that business and data logic belongs within business logic and data access classes in the Web application. Some DBMS cache the execution plan of the stored procedure, which does offer a performance benefit over straight SQL statements; however, for SQL Server, execution plans are cached for all commands, whether they are stored procedures or plain SQL statements.

Not all DBMS support stored procedures, but for those providers that do support them (e.g., SQL Server and Oracle), you can use them by setting the `CommandText` property of `DbCommand` to the stored procedure name, and its `CommandType` property to `CommandType.StoredProcedure`, as shown in the following example. The `CommandType` property specifies how the `CommandText` is to be interpreted, either as the name of a stored procedure or as a SQL statement (the default).

```
SqlConnection conn = new SqlConnection(connString);

// Create a command using a stored procedure name
SqlCommand cmd = new SqlCommand();
cmd.Connection = conn;
cmd.CommandText = "RetrieveAllBooks";
cmd.CommandType = CommandType.StoredProcedure;

conn.Open();
...
conn.Close();
```

What does a stored procedure look like? For Microsoft SQL Server, stored procedures are written using T-SQL (Transact-SQL) and are stored within the database. However, you can create a stored procedure in your SQL Server database directly within Visual Studio via the Server Explorer (see Figure 9.4). Note that you must first create a connection to the database in the Server Explorer before you can do this.

A T-SQL stored procedure begins with the command CREATE PROCEDURE. If an existing procedure is being modified, the keyword ALTER is used instead of CREATE. The following example illustrates a simple T-SQL stored procedure. A more complicated stored procedure is shown later in the example beginning on page 523.

```
CREATE PROCEDURE dbo.RetrieveAllBooks
AS
    SELECT ISBN,Title,PublisherId,Year FROM Books
    RETURN
```

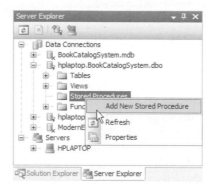

Figure 9.4 Creating a stored procedure in Visual Studio

Executing a DbCommand

After a DbCommand object has been instantiated and its command text, command type, and connection set, the command can be run by calling one of the Execute methods of the DbCommand class (see Table 9.6). The ExecuteNonQuery method is for commands that do not return any record data, such as a SQL INSERT or DELETE. ExecuteScalar is for SELECT commands that return a single value (actually the value of the first column in the first row), such as an aggregate value. ExecuteReader is for SELECT commands that return multiple results. How are these results returned? The ExecuteReader returns a DbDataReader (covered shortly), an object that is a read-only, forward-only cursor, which is used to retrieve the actual data values.

The following example illustrates the use of the ExecuteNonQuery and ExecuteScalar methods of the DbCommand class. It uses the ExecuteNonQuery to add a record to a table using the SQL INSERT command, then uses ExecuteScalar to return the auto-generated key value of the just-inserted record.

```
OleDbConnection conn = new OleDbConnection(connString);

// Construct the SQL to insert a record
string sql = "INSERT INTO Artists (FirstName,LastName,Nationality)";
sql += "VALUES ("Pablo","Picasso","Spain") ";

// Create the command object
OleDbCommand cmd = new OleDbCommand(sql, conn);
```

```
conn.Open();

// Execute the command
cmd.ExecuteNonQuery();

// Retrieve the key of the inserted record
string sIden = "SELECT @@IDENTITY";
OleDbCommand cmdIden = new OleDbCommand(sIden, conn);

// Because this query returns a single row with a single value,
// you can execute the command with its ExecuteScalar method

// ExecuteScalar returns an object so you need to data convert
int autoKey = Convert.ToInt32(cmdIden.ExecuteScalar());
```

Of course, in any real example, you would not hard-code the data to be written, but use data from some source such as user-entered data from a form. But to do this properly, you need to learn about the DbParameter classes.

Using DbParameters

These classes represent a parameter to a command. **Parameters** are used to specify criteria to a query; that is, they are used to construct **parameterized queries**. They are a more secure alternative to simply building a query with criteria via string building. An example of a query constructed from string building is shown in the following example. It uses the value entered by a user into a text box to construct the SQL query.

```
// Do NOT do this!
string sql = "SELECT * FROM Users WHERE User='" + txtUser.Text + "'";
```

In an ideal world, such an example would be perfectly acceptable. Unfortunately, in the less-than-ideal real world, filled with clumsy typists and clever, sometimes malicious users, building a query directly from user input is very much a practice to be avoided. If the user has entered invalid data, this might result in a runtime exception. Even worse, this type of coding is vulnerable to the so-called **SQL injection attack**. In this type of attack, a user enters SQL into a data entry form in order to extract additional information from the database that you want hidden or even to submit surreptitiously nasty commands to the DBMS.

For instance, what would be the resulting SQL string from the previous code if the user entered the following into the txtUser text box?

```
' or 1=1 --
```

With this user input, the resulting SQL string would be

```
SELECT * FROM Users WHERE User='' OR 1=1 --'
```

Because two dashes indicate a SQL comment, the DBMS ignores the final single quote. Because the Boolean OR requires only one expression to be true and because 1=1 evaluates to true, this query selects *all* the records in the Users table, which might be problematic if the query results are being data bound to a control that can display multiple records.

If the user enters the following into the text box, worse might happen.

```
'; DROP TABLE customers; --
```

In this case, if the DBMS supports batch commands *and* the database contains a table named customers *and* the permissions are not set to read-only for Web requests, this input sends a command to the DBMS that deletes the entire customers table!

Some of the dangers of SQL injection attacks can be avoided by using DbParameter objects to construct commands that use criteria constructed from user input. A DbParameter is simply an object that represents a name-value pair, where name is the identifier for the parameter and value is the actual data for the parameter.

Creating a command using a DbParameter involves three steps:

1. Modify the SQL WHERE clause so it uses parameter names instead of values. You could rewrite the previous SQL SELECT command to use a parameter as shown in the following code.

    ```
    string s = "select * from Users where UserId=@user";
    ```

    In this example, @user is the name of the parameter. All parameter names must begin with the @ character.

2. Create the appropriate DbParameter objects and assign them the appropriate names and values.

    For instance, you could create a DbParameter for the SQL Server data provider by assigning the name and value via the constructor.

    ```
    SqlParameter param =
        new SqlParameter("@user",txtUser.Text);
    ```

    Or, you can set the name and value using the appropriate property values.

    ```
    SqlParameter param = new SqlParameter();
    param.ParameterName = "@user";
    param.Value = txtUser.Text;
    ```

3. Add the created DbParameter objects to the DbCommand object's Parameters collection. This step must be done before calling any of the DbCommand object's Execute methods.

    ```
    SqlCommand cmd;
    ...
    cmd.Parameters.Add(param);
    ```

CORE NOTE

You can combine steps 2 and 3 by using the `AddWithValue` method of the `Parameters` collection. For example:

```
cmd.Parameters.AddWithValue("@user", txtUser.Text);
```

Table 9.7 summarizes the notable properties of the `DbParameter` classes.

Table 9.7 Notable Properties of the DbParameter Classes

Property	Description
DbType	Specifies the data type of the parameter. Possible values defined by the `DbType` enumeration.
Direction	Specifies whether the parameter is input-only, output-only, both (bidirectional), or a return value from a stored procedure. Possible values defined by the `ParameterDirection` enumeration.
IsNullable	Specifies whether the parameter can contain a null value.
ParameterName	Specifies the name of the parameter. This name is used to identify the parameter.
Size	Specifies the maximum size of the parameter data in bytes.
SourceColumn	Specifies the name of the source column of the `DataSet` that contains the parameter value. Used only if using a `DataSet` for the data source of a parameter.
Value	Specifies the data value of the parameter.

`DbParameter` objects can also be used in conjunction with stored procedures, which support both input and output parameters. For instance, the following SQL Server stored procedure inserts a new publisher to the `Publishers` table. It accepts an input parameter that contains the name of the publisher to add. It also defines an output parameter that contains the identity value for the `PublisherId` field of the just-inserted record, as well as returns the number of affected rows.

```
CREATE PROCEDURE dbo.CreatePublisher
    (
        @pubName nvarchar(128),
        @pubId int OUTPUT
    )
AS
```

```
INSERT INTO Publishers (PublisherName) VALUES (@pubName)
SET @pubId = SCOPE_IDENTITY()
RETURN @@ROWCOUNT
```

CORE NOTE

In SQL Server, it is preferable to use the SQL function `SCOPE_IDENTITY()` rather than `@@IDENTITY` to retrieve the identity value of the inserted record. The former returns the last identity value produced on this connection in the current scope (which would be this stored procedure), whereas the latter returns the last identity value produced on this connection, regardless of the table that produced it, or the scope that created it.

With this stored procedure defined, you can now make use of it with ADO.NET. As can be seen in the following example, you have to define both the input and the output parameters. The names of these parameters must match the names of the parameters as defined in the stored procedure. As well, the `Direction` property of the output parameter must be set to `ParameterDirection.Output` and its `SqlDbType` property set to match the data type defined in the stored procedure. After the command is executed, you can retrieve the value of the output parameter via its `Value` property.

```csharp
SqlCommand cmd = new SqlCommand();
cmd.Connection = conn;
cmd.CommandText = "CreatePublisher";
cmd.CommandType = CommandType.StoredProcedure;

// Define input parameter with value from a TextBox
cmd.Parameters.AddWithValue("@pubName", txtName.Text);

// Define output parameter that will contain identity value
SqlParameter param = new SqlParameter();
param.ParameterName = "@pubId";
param.Size = 4;
param.SqlDbType = SqlDbType.Int;
param.Direction = ParameterDirection.Output;
cmd.Parameters.Add(param);

conn.Open();

// Run the store procedure
int nrows = cmd.ExecuteNonQuery();
```

```
// Extract the identity value of inserted record
string msg = nrows + " row was added<br/>";
int id = (int)param.Value;
msg += "PublisherId of new record=" + id;

conn.Close();
```

Using Transactions

As you saw in the section on the DbCommand classes, modifying data in a database is a common task in a Web application. What might not have been apparent, however, is that it also is a potentially hazardous task. Of course, modifying data is not exactly hazardous to your health (although a database administrator might try to cause you bodily harm if you seriously mess up the integrity of an important database). Rather, in a Web application, there are many things that can potentially go wrong when modifying data.

For instance, in a Web storefront, you eventually need to get the customer to pay for his purchases. Presumably, this occurs as the last step in the checkout process after the user has verified the shipping address, entered a credit card, and selected a shipping option. What actually happens after the user clicks the final Pay for Order button? For simplicity's sake, let us imagine that the following steps need to happen.

1. Write order record to database
2. Check credit card service to see if payment is accepted
3. If payment is accepted, send message to legacy ordering system.
4. Remove purchased item from warehouse inventory table and add it to the order shipped table.

At any step in this process, errors could occur. For instance, the credit card service could be unresponsive, the credit card payment declined, or the legacy ordering system could be down. **Transactions** provide a way to gracefully handle errors and keep your data properly consistent when errors do occur.

Transactions can be implemented both in ADO.NET as well as within the DBMS. For example, take the process mentioned previously in step 4. What would happen if the DBMS or the Web server crashed after it removed the item from the warehouse inventory table but before it added the purchased item to the order shipped table? The data would no longer be properly consistent.

One way to solve this particular problem is to use an ADO.NET *local transaction*. A local transaction affects operations that target a single database, and is ultimately mapped to the transaction mechanism within the DBMS. The steps involved in working with a local transaction are as follows.

1. Create a DbTransaction object by calling the BeginTransaction method of the DbConnection class.

2. Assign the `DbTransaction` object to each `DbCommand` object being executed as part of the transaction via its `Transaction` property.
3. Execute each `DbCommand`.
4. Commit (i.e., save the database changes) if everything worked okay or roll back (i.e., undo any database changes) if an exception occurred. If the connection is closed before a commit or a roll back (for instance, caused by a crash in the DBMS or the Web server), the transaction would be rolled back.

To demonstrate these steps, Listing 9.1 illustrates how to work a local transaction. It first deletes a specific publisher from the `Publishers` table, and then tries to delete all the records for that publisher from the `Books` table. However, due to the fact that the SQL for the second deletion step in the code is incorrect, a runtime database error occurs. The exception handler then rolls back the first delete step. If you change the table name in the second SQL statement to the correct value (i.e., change to `DELETE FROM` **Books**), both deletes are committed.

Listing 9.1   LocalTransactions.aspx.cs

```
// Specifies database connection. Change this if needed
string connString =
  ConfigurationManager.ConnectionStrings["BookCatalog"].
    ConnectionString;

// Hard-code the publisher to delete
int pubIdToDelete = 3;

// Get the connection to your database
SqlConnection conn = new SqlConnection(connString);

SqlTransaction trans = null;
try
{
    // Create the transaction
    trans = conn.BeginTransaction();

    // Construct first sql
    string sqlA = "DELETE FROM Publishers ";
    sqlA += " WHERE PublisherId=@pubid";

    // Make the first command object and pass it the transaction
    SqlCommand cmdA = new SqlCommand(sqlA, conn, trans);

    // Add parameter
    cmdA.Parameters.AddWithValue("@pubId", pubIdToDelete);
```

```
    conn.Open();

    // Execute the first command
    cmdA.ExecuteNonQuery();

    // Construct second sql with an intentional error
    // that demonstrates transaction rollback
    string sqlB = "DELETE FROM NonExistentTable ";
    sqlB += " WHERE PublisherId=@pubid";

    // Make the second command object and pass it the transaction
    SqlCommand cmdB = new SqlCommand(sqlB, conn, trans);

    // Add parameter
    cmdB.Parameters.AddWithValue("@pubId", pubIdToDelete);

    // Execute the second command
    cmdB.ExecuteNonQuery();

    // Commit the database changes
    trans.Commit();
    labMsg.Text = "Database updated successfully";
}
catch (Exception ex)
{
    labMsg.Text = "[btnUpdate_Click] ";
    labMsg.Text += "Error occurred accessing the database";
    labMsg.Text += "<br/>" + ex.Message;
    if (trans != null)
    {
        // Roll back the changes
        trans.Rollback();
        labMsg.Text += "<br/>" + "Changes rolled back";
    }
}
finally
{
    conn.Close();
    conn = null;
}
```

Local transactions are for actions performed against a single database. A *distributed transaction* is a transaction that affects not just a single database, but multiple resources. In the order processing example mentioned earlier, a distributed transaction is involved because an order requires not only a database, but also the credit card processor, and the external legacy ordering system. Because there are multiple external resources involved, distributed transactions are much more complicated than local transactions.

Distributed transactions are handled by classes in the System.Transaction namespace and may also involve working with nonmanaged APIs such as Microsoft Message Queue (MSMQ) or COM+. Working with these external transaction services is beyond the scope of this book. However, we can demonstrate how to use the TransactionScope class to create a reasonably straightforward distributed transaction.

The TransactionScope class allows you to create and manage both local and distributed transactions. When you create a TransactionScope object, it initially creates a local transaction. If the first database connection is to a SQL Server 2005 database, the scope of the transaction remains local. If a second connection to a different database is made, the scope is promoted to a distributed transaction. As well, if the first connection is to something other than a SQL Server database, the transaction scope also is distributed.

The TransactionScope object defines a block of code that participates in a transaction. If the block of code completely executes successfully, an invocation of the Complete method of the TransactionScope object tells the transaction manager working behind the scenes to commit the transaction; otherwise, it rolls any changes back. The code for using a TransactionScope object might look like the following. Notice that in this example you are using the implicit closing of your connections by embedding the connections within using blocks.

```
bool isConsistent = false;
using (TransactionScope scope = new TransactionScope())
{
    // Open connection to SQL database. This transaction will
    // be local
    using (SqlConnection connA = new SqlConnection(connStrngA))
    {
        // Use this connection
        ...
    }

    // Open connection to Access database, which changes
    // transaction to distributed scope
    using (SqlConnection connB = new SqlConnection(connStrngB))
    {
        // Use this connection
        ...
        // All done
        isConsistent = true;
    }

    // Commit all transactions within this scope
    if (isConsistent)
        scope.Complete();
}
```

To use the classes in System.Transaction namespace, you need to add a reference to the System.Transactions.dll. In Visual Studio, you can do so by right-clicking the solution in the Solution Explorer and choosing the Add Reference option (see Figure 9.5). Within the resulting Add Reference dialog box, select System.Transactions and click OK.

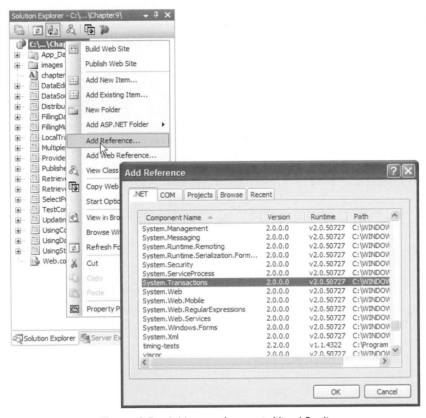

Figure 9.5 Adding a reference in Visual Studio

DbDataReader Classes

Recall that Web applications operate on a stateless server that processes requests, reads data necessary for servicing the requests, and then outputs the response back to the clients. The **data reader** (DbDataReader) is optimized for the fast retrieval of a read-only stream of records and is thus ideal for Web applications. It should be stressed that the DbDataReader is not a data container like the DataSet, but a kind of pointer to a record in a *result set* (that is, a set of records returned from a database query). DbDataReader also implements the IEnumerable interface so multi-value Web server controls can be data bound to it.

Programming a DbDataReader

DbDataReader objects are not created using the C# new operator. Instead, you use the ExecuteReader method of DbCommand. The following example illustrates the creation and data binding of a DbDataReader. Notice that the reader must be closed after using it.

```
string connString = "…"
OleDbConnection conn = new OleDbConnection(connString);

string cmdString = "SELECT Id,ProductName,Price From Products";
OleDbCommand cmd = new OleDbCommand(cmdString, conn);

conn.Open();
OleDBDataReader reader = cmd.ExecuteReader();

someControl.DataSource = reader;
someControl.DataBind();

reader.Close();
conn.Close();
```

The previous example used a DbDataReader by *data binding* it to a control. There are often times when the data binding approach is not possible (nor desired). For instance, you might want to programmatically retrieve the individual column values from the reader and then do something with those values (such as process them, load them into a collection, or display them in different controls). If you are processing multiple records, you need to loop through the records. You can use the Read method of DbDataReader to move the read cursor to the next record in the result set.

```
OleDBDataReader reader = cmd.ExecuteReader();
while ( reader.Read() )
{
    // Process the current record
}
reader.Close();
```

If the reader is only retrieving a single record (or you are only interested in the first record in the result set), you must still use the Read method to position the reader on the first record. This is generally achieved by wrapping the call within a conditional (just in case the result set is empty).

```
OleDBDataReader reader = cmd.ExecuteReader();
if ( reader.Read() )
{
    // Process the first record
}
reader.Close();
```

Field data can be retrieved from the current record in the reader because the reader object acts like a collection, with each element in the collection corresponding to a field in the record. For instance, assume that you are using the following SQL command.

```
SELECT Id,ProductName,Price FROM Products
```

You could retrieve the field data using any of the following three approaches.

```
// Retrieve using column name
int id = (int)reader["Id"];
string name = (string)reader["ProductName"];
double price = (double)reader["Price"];

// Retrieve using a zero-based column ordinal
int id = (int)reader[0];
string name = (string)reader[1];
double price = (double)reader[2];

// Retrieve a typed value using column ordinal
int id = reader.GetInt32(0);
string name = reader.GetString(1);
double price = reader.GetDouble(2);
```

Notice that in the first two approaches the data being retrieved must be cast to the appropriate data type. The various GetX methods of DbDataReader eliminate the need for the casting; however, it only allows you to specify the field using the column ordinal. In all three approaches, the data type of the method or the casting must match the data type of the field in the database.

Handling Nulls

Most database tables allow certain fields to contain no data. This absence of data (also called a **database null**) in a database field is *not* equivalent to the null value in a .NET programming language. As a result, you *cannot* simply test if a field contains no data using this type of code.

```
// This will not work properly
if (reader[1] == null)
    name = "";
else
    name = reader.GetString(1);
```

Instead, you must use the `IsDBNull` method of the `DbDataReader` to test if a field value contains a database null.

```
// This will work properly
if (reader.IsDBNull(1))
   name = "";
else
   name = reader.GetString(1);
```

Implicit Connection Closing

While the `DbDataReader` is being used, the `DbConnection` associated with it cannot be used for any other database operations. Because each database provider performs a certain amount of connection pooling, it is essential to close the reader and its connection directly after it is used. As a consequence, the programming associated with a reader in general follows this pattern.

```
// Create the command
...
// Open the connection
...
// Create the reader
...
// Use the reader
...
// Close the reader
...
// Close the connection
...
```

Although this is the preferred approach, in practice, it can sometimes be difficult to achieve. For instance, a page or class may need to create multiple readers. For performance reasons, it is best to use a single connection for these readers. Furthermore, these readers might be created in separate methods (for instance, one reader in the `Page_Load` method and the other reader in an event handler method). In such a case, it might be messy, from a programming perspective, to close the connection directly after closing the reader.

In such a case, you can implicitly close the connection when you close the reader, by using a different overload of the `ExecuteReader` method of `DbCommand`, as shown in the following.

```
reader = cmd.ExecuteReader(CommandBehavior.CloseConnection);
// Process the record
..
// Close the reader and the connection
reader.Close();
```

This overload of ExecuteReader takes a parameter of type CommandBehavior. Besides CloseConnection, another useful CommandBehavior is SingleRow. Specifying this may improve performance when the query is only going to return a single record of data. But what if you want to specify two or more CommandBehavior values? You can do this via a bitwise combination, as shown in the following.

```
CommandBehavior cb;
cb = CommandBehavior.CloseConnection | CommandBehavior.SingleRow;
reader = cmd.ExecuteReader(cb);
```

Multiple Result Sets

The examples so far have used the DbDataReader to contain the results from a single SQL SELECT command. The data reader does support the processing of multiple result sets. Some data providers (such as the SQL Server provider) allow separate commands to be batched together, either via stored procedures or by combining multiple SELECT commands into a single command string separated by semicolons. You can use the NextResult method of DbDataReader to advance to the next result set. The example that follows illustrates this approach.

```
conn = new SqlConnection(connString);
conn.Open();

// Set up commands
string sql = "SELECT * FROM Authors; SELECT * FROM Books;";
SqlCommand cmd = new SqlCommand(sql, conn);

reader = cmd.ExecuteReader();

// Use the first result set
grdAuthors.DataSource = reader;
grdAuthors.DataBind();

// Get the next result set
reader.NextResult();

// Use the second result set
grdBooks.DataSource = reader;
grdBooks.DataBind();

// Close the reader and connection manually
reader.Close();
conn.Close();
```

Notice that the ExecuteReader call does not make use of CommandBehavior.CloseConnection, because it would close the connection after the first result set is finished processing, but before the call to NextResult.

Tutorial: Reading and Updating Data

The next several walkthroughs provide a practical example that uses a DbConnection, DbCommand, and the DbDataReader. In this example, the user is first presented with a list of books in a ListBox. After the user selects an item in this list, the page then displays the data for several fields of the selected record within a form (see Figure 9.6 for the result in the browser). The user can edit the data in the form and then save any changes back to the database by clicking the update button.

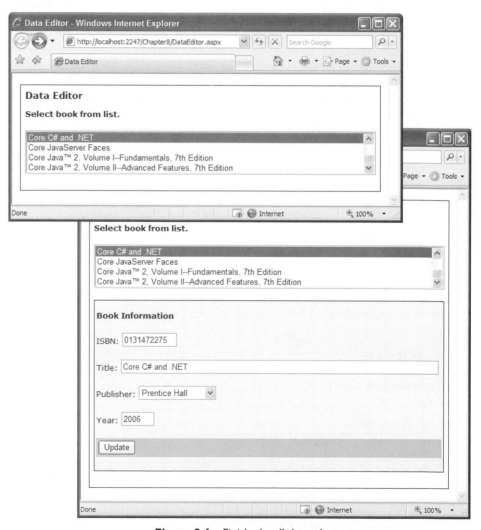

Figure 9.6   Finished walkthrough

The database schema for this example is shown in Figure 9.7.

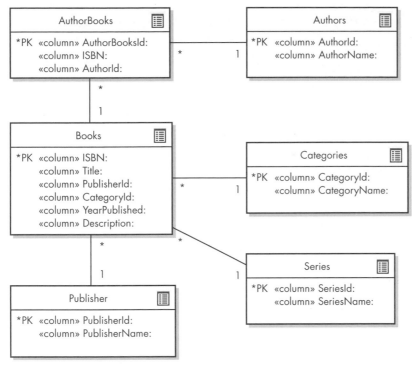

Figure 9.7 Database schema

Walkthrough 9.1 *Adding Markup Content to a Web Form*

1. Create a Web Form named `DataEditor.aspx`.
2. Add the following markup to the page.

```
<h1>Data Editor</h1>
<h2>Select book from list</h2>
<p>
<asp:ListBox id="lboxBooks" runat="server"
    DataTextField="Title" DataValueField="ISBN"
    AutoPostBack="true"
    OnSelectedIndexChanged="SelectBooks" />
</p>
```

```
<asp:Panel id="panBook" runat="server">
   <h2>Book Information</h2>
   <p>ISBN:
   <asp:TextBox id="txtIsbn" runat="server" Columns="9"
      ReadOnly="true"/></p>
   <p>Title:
   <asp:TextBox id="txtTitle" runat="server" Columns="80"/>
      </p>
   <p>Publisher:
   <asp:DropDownList id="drpPublisher" runat="server"
     DataTextField="PublisherName"
     DataValueField="PublisherID" /></p>
   <p>Year:
   <asp:TextBox id="txtYear" runat="server" Columns="3"/></p>

   <p>
   <asp:Button id="btnUpdate" runat="server" Text="Update"
      OnClick="UpdateBook" />
   <asp:Label ID="labUpdate" runat="server" />
   </p>
</asp:Panel>

<p><asp:Label ID="labMsg" runat="server" /></p>
```

Notice that the markup contains a `ListBox` that contains a list of books as well as a `Panel` that contains form elements that display the selected book data.

Walkthrough 9.2 *Setting Up the Page*

1. Switch to `DataEditor.aspx.cs` and add the following references.

   ```
   using System.Data.OleDb;
   using System.Data.Common;
   ```

   For simplicity's sake, this example uses the `BookCatalogSystem.mdb` Access database (which can be downloaded from my Web site, `http://www.randyconnolly.com/core`), and so we will use the `OleDb` data provider.

2. Define the following single data member within the `DataEditor` class.

   ```
   OleDbConnection _conn = null;
   ```

   We use this data member to ensure that this page only has a single connection open.

3. When the page loads for the first time, you want to fill the `ListBox` with all the available books and hide the form element panel. To do so, add the following to the `Page_Load` method. We will create `LoadAllBooks()` in the next step.

```
/// <summary>
/// Handler for loading page
/// </summary>
protected void Page_Load(object sender, EventArgs e)
{
    if (!IsPostBack)
    {
        LoadAllBooks();
        panBook.Visible = false;
    }
}
```

Walkthrough 9.3   *Adding the Helper Methods*

1. Add the following two methods.

```
/// <summary>
/// Data binds the drop-down list of books
/// </summary>
private void LoadAllBooks()
{
    OleDbDataReader reader = GetReader(GetBookSql(),
        null, true);
    lboxBooks.DataSource = reader;
    lboxBooks.DataBind();
    if (reader != null)
        reader.Close();
}


/// <summary>
/// Return the sql string for selecting book info
/// </summary>
private string GetBookSql()
{
    return
      "SELECT ISBN,Title,YearPublished,PublisherId FROM Books";
}
```

The first of these methods uses another helper method named `GetReader` (to be defined) to retrieve a data reader, which in turn is bound to the `ListBox`, then closed. Because we also need to use a data reader and the same select statement for the event handler for the ListBox, we have placed both of these tasks into separate helper methods to reduce code duplication.

2. Create a method named GetReader, which looks like that shown here.

```
/// <summary>
/// Retrieves the data reader for the passed sql string
/// </summary>
/// <param name="sql">
/// Contains sql statement to use for command</param>
/// <param name="param">
/// Optional parameters to add to command</param>
/// <param name="addClose">
/// If true, add close behavior to reader</param>
/// <returns>Data reader containing requested sql
/// data</returns>
private OleDbDataReader GetReader(string sql,
        OleDbParameter[] parameters, bool addClose)
{
    // Get the connection to your database
    OleDbConnection conn = GetConnection();
    OleDbDataReader reader = null;
    try
    {
        // Make the command object using the passed sql
        OleDbCommand cmd = new OleDbCommand(sql, conn);

        // Add data parameters if you have been passed any
        if (parameters != null)
        {
            foreach (OleDbParameter param in parameters)
                cmd.Parameters.Add(param);
        }

        // The CommandBehavior.CloseConnection indicates
        // that the connection will be closed when the
        // reader is closed

        if (addClose)
            reader = cmd.ExecuteReader(
                CommandBehavior.CloseConnection);
        else
            reader = cmd.ExecuteReader();
    }
    catch (Exception ex)
    {
```

```
            labMsg.Text =
                "[GetReader] Error occurred accessing the database";
            labMsg.Text += "<br/>" + ex.Message;

            if (reader != null)
                reader.Close();
            if (conn != null)
                conn.Close();
        }


        // Return the resulting reader
        return reader;
    }
```

This method first opens a connection (performed in another helper
method named `GetConnection`) and then creates a command using the
SQL statement that is passed to the method. It loops through the passed
array of parameters and adds them to the command. It then creates the
data reader and returns it. Notice the exception handling for the method:
It displays an error message in a `Label` control and closes up the objects.

3. Create the last of our helper methods, `GetConnection`.

```
/// <summary>
/// Returns a connection object to your database
/// </summary>
/// <returns></returns>
private OleDbConnection GetConnection()
{
    // If your data member is null or closed, create
    // connection and open it; otherwise, return existing
    // open connection
    if (_conn == null || _conn.State == ConnectionState.Closed)
    {
        // Specifies database connection. Change this if needed
        string connString =
            ConfigurationManager.ConnectionStrings["Books"].
                ConnectionString;

        try
        {
            // Get the connection to the database
            _conn = new OleDbConnection(connString);

            // Open the connection
            _conn.Open();
        }
        catch (Exception ex)
        {
```

```
                labMsg.Text = "[GetConnection] ";
                labMsg.Text += "Error occurred accessing the
                    database";
                labMsg.Text += "<br/>" + ex.Message;
                if (_conn != null)
                    _conn.Close();
        }
    }
    return _conn;
}
```

This method reuses the current open connection, if there is one. If there is none, it retrieves the connection string from the Web.config file.

Walkthrough 9.4   *Adding the Event Handlers*

1. Add the following code for the ListBox selection event handler.

```
/// <summary>
/// Handles the selection of the art work
/// </summary>
protected void SelectBooks(object sender, EventArgs e)
{
    // Make panel visible
    panBook.Visible = true;

    // Retrieve the ISBN of book selected by user
    string sId = lboxBooks.SelectedValue;

    // Construct sql for specified ISBN
    string sql = GetBookSql();
    sql += " WHERE ISBN=@Id";

    // Set up parameters to query
    OleDbParameter[] param = {
        new OleDbParameter("@ID", sId)
    };

    // Get a data reader containing book data
    OleDbDataReader reader = GetReader(sql, param, true);

    try
    {
        // If you have a reader, continue
        if (reader != null)
        {
```

```
            // Position cursor to first record
        if (reader.Read())
        {
            // Retrieve the column data from the reader
            // using the database field names or an ordinal
            // and assign them to form fields
            txtIsbn.Text = (string)reader["ISBN"];

            if (!reader.IsDBNull(1))
                txtTitle.Text = reader.GetString(1);
            else
                txtTitle.Text = "";

            if (!reader.IsDBNull(2))
                txtYear.Text = reader.GetInt32(2).ToString();
            else
                txtYear.Text = "";

            // The publisher ID is more complicated, because
            // it is a value in a drop-down list
            int publisherId = reader.GetInt32(3);
            MakePublisherDropDown(publisherId);

            labUpdate.Text = "";
        }
    }
}
catch (Exception ex)
{
    labMsg.Text = "[lboxBooks_SelectedIndexChanged] ";
    labMsg.Text += "Error occurred accessing the database";
    labMsg.Text += "<br/>" + ex.Message;
}
finally
{
    reader.Close();
}
}
```

When the user selects a book from the list, the `SelectedValue` property of the list contains the ISBN of the selected book. The method retrieves the record for that ISBN and displays several of the record values in various form elements. The one tricky element is the `PublisherId`. You want the form to display not the ID value, but the publisher name, which is contained in the `Publishers` table. From a usability standpoint, the best solution is to use a `DropDownList` of publisher names to display the `PublisherId`. You use a method named `MakePublisherDropDown` to create that list.

2. Create the method that creates a `DropDownList` of publisher names.

```
/// <summary>
/// Data bind a drop-down list with data from publisher
/// table and then make the passed publisherId the selected
/// item in the list
/// </summary>
private void MakePublisherDropDown(int publisherId)
{
    string sql = "SELECT PublisherId, PublisherName ";
    sql += " FROM Publishers ORDER BY PublisherName";

    // Data bind list to the publishers
    OleDbDataReader reader = GetReader(sql, null, false);
    drpPublisher.DataSource = reader;
    drpPublisher.DataBind();

    // Make the passed publisherId the selected item in list
    drpPublisher.SelectedValue = publisherId.ToString();
    reader.Close();
}
```

3. Add the following code for the update button event handler.

```
/// <summary>
/// Handler for updating book data
/// </summary>
protected void UpdateBook(object sender, EventArgs e)
{
    // Retrieve the ISBN of book selected by user
    string sId = lboxBooks.SelectedValue;

    // Construct SQL for specified ISBN
    string sql =
      "UPDATE Books SET Title=@title, YearPublished=@yearPub,";
    sql += "PublisherId=@pubId WHERE ISBN=@isbn";
    labUpdate.Text = sql;

    // Get the connection to your database
    OleDbConnection conn = GetConnection();

    try
    {
```

```
        // Make the command object
        OleDbCommand cmd = new OleDbCommand(sql, conn);

        // Add parameters
        cmd.Parameters.Add(new OleDbParameter("@title",
            txtTitle.Text));
        cmd.Parameters.Add(new OleDbParameter("@yearPub",
            txtYear.Text));
        // Can also use AddWithValue as an alternative
        // to the above
        cmd.Parameters.AddWithValue("@pubId",
            drpPublisher.SelectedValue);
        cmd.Parameters.AddWithValue("@isbn", txtIsbn.Text);

        // Execute the command
        cmd.ExecuteNonQuery();

        labUpdate.Text = "Record updated successfully";
    }
    catch (Exception ex)
    {
        labMsg.Text = "[btnUpdate_Click] ";
        labMsg.Text += "Error occurred accessing the database";
        labMsg.Text += "<br/>" + ex.Message;
    }
    finally
    {
        conn.Close();
        conn = null;
    }
}
```

CORE NOTE

Although this example's principal purpose is to illustrate the nontrivial use of the ADO.NET classes covered so far in the chapter, it is by no means an illustration of best programming practice. I strongly discourage placing this type of data access logic in the code-behind of a Web Form. At the end of this chapter, I illustrate an approach that uses separate data access classes to contain the ADO.NET programming.

DbDataAdapter Classes

The *data adapter* (DbDataAdapter) classes represent a bridge between the DataSet container (covered in the previous chapter) and an underlying database. Each DbDataAdapter class provides a Fill method for filling a DataSet (or just a DataTable) with data from the database and an Update method for outputting any changes made to the data in the DataSet back to the database. Thus, unlike the DbDataReader, which provides a read-only, forward-only pointer into a result set, the DbDataAdapter reads all data in a result set into the in-memory DataSet container. The DbDataAdapter can also persist changes made to the in-memory data by writing the changes back to the database.

Tables 9.8 and 9.9 list the notable members of the DbDataAdapter classes.

Table 9.8   Notable Properties of the DbDataAdapter Classes

Property	Description
DeleteCommand	The DbCommand to be used for deleting data as a result of a call to Update.
InsertCommand	The DbCommand to be used for inserting new data as a result of a call to Update.
SelectCommand	The DbCommand to be used for retrieving data as a result of a call to Fill or FillSchema.
UpdateCommand	The DbCommand to be used for updating existing data as a result of a call to Update.

Table 9.9   Notable Methods of the DbDataAdapter Classes

Method	Description
Fill	Fills a DataSet or a DataTable with data from a database.
FillSchema	Adds a DataTable to a DataSet with the schema specified by SelectCommand. This DataTable does not contain data.
GetFillParameters	Returns an array of IDataParameter objects that contains the previously specified parameters for the SelectCommand.
Update	Saves the current data in the DataSet by invoking the appropriate commands specified by DeleteCommand, InsertCommand, and UpdateCommand.

It should be noted that the `DbDataAdapter` is not the only way to fill a `DataSet` with data from an external data source. Recall from the last chapter that a `DataSet` can also be filled from a database or an XML document, as shown in Figure 9.8.

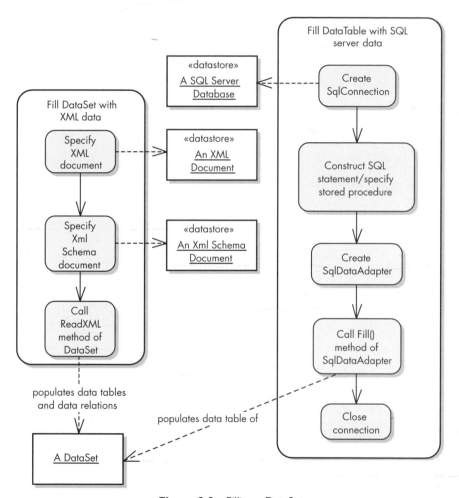

Figure 9.8 Filling a DataSet

Filling a DataSet

The `Fill` method of `DbDataAdapter` is used to fill a `DataSet` or `DataTable` with data from a database. Because this method is so heavily overloaded, we only illustrate a few possible ways it can be used. The simplest use of `Fill` is to supply it with a `DataSet,` as shown in the following example.

```
DataSet ds = new DataSet();

// Create a connection
SqlConnection conn = new SqlConnection(connString);

string sql = "SELECT Isbn,Title,Price FROM Books";
SqlDataAdapter adapter = new SqlDataAdapter(sql, conn);

try
{
    // Read data into DataSet
    adapter.Fill(ds);

    // Use filled DataSet
}
catch (Exception ex)
{
    // Process exception
}
```

What is the result after the call to Fill? The DataSet has a new DataTable named Table that is filled with all the selected data from the Books table. If you want to specify the name of the resulting DataTable, you could use instead a different version of Fill.

```
adapter.Fill(ds, "BooksTable");
```

You might then reference this DataTable name in subsequent programming code.

```
DataRow dr = ds.Tables["BooksTable"].Rows[0];

txtIsbn.Text = Convert.ToString(dr["Isbn"]);
txtTitle.Text = (string)dr["Title"];
```

What about the state of the connection after the call to Fill? The Fill method of the DbDataAdapter opens the connection specified in the connection string and then closes it after the data has been read. For this reason, the first DbDataAdapter code example wrapped the call to Fill within a try...catch block.

If your page needs to invoke the Fill method multiple times, you probably want to avoid opening the connection multiple times. If you open the connection yourself, the DbDataAdapter uses that open connection and does not close it (you then have to close it yourself). This type of approach typically uses separate DbCommand objects (rather than passing the command text in the DbDataAdapter constructor as in the previous example), as illustrated in the following example.

```
DataSet ds = new DataSet();

try
{
    // Set up and open connection
    SqlConnection conn = new SqlConnection(connString);
    conn.Open();

    SqlDataAdapter adapter = new SqlDataAdapter();

    // Set up first command
    string sqlBooks = " SELECT Isbn,Title,Price FROM Books";
    SqlCommand cmdBooks = new SqlCommand(sqlBooks,conn);
    adapter.SelectCommand = cmdBooks;

    adapter.Fill(ds, "BooksTable");

    // Set up second command
    string sqlAuthors =
        "SELECT AuthorId,AuthorName FROM Authors";
    SqlCommand cmdAuthors = new SqlCommand(sqlAuthors,conn);
    adapter.SelectCommand = cmdAuthors;

    adapter.Fill(ds, "AuthorsTable");

    // Use filled DataSet
    ...

    // All finished, so close connection
    conn.Close();
}
catch (Exception ex)
{
    // Process exception
}
```

Updating Data

The Update method of the DbDataAdapter writes back to the database any data
that has changed in the DataSet. When the method is called, it checks each
DataRow (via its RowState property, which indicates whether the row is new, has
been deleted, or a column value within it has been modified) in each DataTable
to see if it has been changed. If the data in the row has changed, it invokes the command specified via the UpdateCommand, DeleteCommand, or InsertCommand properties of the DbDataAdapter. These updates are not performed as a batch process,

but one row at a time. Thus, if 10 existing rows have been modified, two new rows added, and one row deleted, 13 separate write commands are issued to the database.

Creating the commands for updating, deleting, and inserting data is a bit more complicated than the examples shown back in the section "DbCommand Classes" on page 515. In those examples, we simply created a parameterized query (we could have also used stored procedures) and then set up the appropriate DbDataParameter objects. In those cases, we knew which data value was to be associated with the parameter name (it was usually some type of user-entered form value). In the case of a DataSet and the DbDataAdapter, you need to set up a more generalized parameter that uses the appropriate data in the DataSet for the parameter values. To do so requires setting the SourceColumn property of the parameter to the name of column in the DataTable that contains the updated data. As well, the SourceVersion property of the parameter needs to be set to indicate that the current value of the column in the DataTable should be persisted to the database; you can do this by setting the property to DataRowVersion.Current.

The following example illustrates how to set up this parameter via the SourceColumn and SourceVersion properties.

```
// Set up connection
OleDbConnection conn = new OleDbConnection(connString);

// Create adapter
OleDbDataAdapter adapter = new OleDbDataAdapter();

// Set up select command for adapter
string sqlSelect = " SELECT AuthorId,AuthorName FROM Authors";
OleDbCommand cmdSelect = new OleDbCommand(sqlSelect, conn);
adapter.SelectCommand = cmdSelect;

// Set up parameter for insert command
OleDbParameter param = new
OleDbParameter("@name",OleDbType.VarChar);
// Get the value for parameter from the column
// name in SourceColumn
param.SourceColumn = "AuthorName";
// Use the current value in the row for the data
// (this is default)
param.SourceVersion = DataRowVersion.Current;

// Set up insert command for adapter
string sqlInsert = "INSERT INTO Authors (AuthorName)";
sqlInsert += "VALUES (@name) ";
OleDbCommand cmdInsert = new OleDbCommand(sqlInsert, conn);

// Add the parameter just created
cmdInsert.Parameters.Add(param);
```

```
adapter.InsertCommand = cmdInsert;

// Read the data using the SelectCommand
adapter.Fill(ds, "AuthorsTable");

// Add some new rows to the DataTable
DataRow dr1 = ds.Tables["AuthorsTable"].NewRow();
dr1["AuthorName"] = "Randy Connolly";
ds.Tables["AuthorsTable"].Rows.Add(dr1);

DataRow dr2 = ds.Tables["AuthorsTable"].NewRow();
dr2["AuthorName"] = "Alexander Connolly";
ds.Tables["AuthorsTable"].Rows.Add(dr2);

// Write the changed DataSet data to the database
adapter.Update(ds, "AuthorsTable");
```

If you are updating only a single table, you can use a `DbCommandBuilder` object as an alternative to hand-coding the SQL for the insert, update, and delete commands. The `DbCommandBuilder` automatically generates the commands for single-table updates as long as a SELECT command has also been specified, as shown in the following example.

```
OleDbConnection conn = new OleDbConnection(connString);

OleDbDataAdapter adapter = new OleDbDataAdapter();

// Set up select command
string sqlSelect = " SELECT AuthorId,AuthorName FROM Authors";
OleDbCommand cmdSelect = new OleDbCommand(sqlSelect, conn);
adapter.SelectCommand = cmdSelect;

// Create the command builder and pass it the adapter
OleDbCommandBuilder cb = new OleDbCommandBuilder(adapter);

adapter.Fill(ds, "AuthorsTable");

// Modify some of the data in the DataTable

// Update
DataRow dr3 = ds.Tables["AuthorsTable"].Rows[0];
dr3["AuthorName"] = "Benjamin Connolly";

// Delete
ds.Tables["AuthorsTable"].Rows[1].Delete();

// Now write the changes
adapter.Update(ds, "AuthorsTable");
```

Of course, by using the `DbCommandBuilder`, you have little control over the quality of the SQL that is generated. As well, it executes slightly slower than if you had created the commands yourself because `DbCommandBuilder` generates the commands at runtime.

Finally, it should be stressed that the `DbDataAdapter` is not the only way to write data to a database. As you saw in Walkthroughs 9.1 through to 9.4, you can also use `DbCommand` objects along with data parameters to output data. The `DbDataAdapter` still uses `DbCommand` objects internally to specify how data is to be updated.

In my experience, the two-way communication capability of the `DbDataAdapter` and the `DataSet` makes more sense in a Windows Forms application than in an ASP.NET application. Using this update capability in the stateless HTTP environment of Web applications requires caching the modified `DataSet` (generally either in session state or in viewstate) from request to request until the data is finally committed to the database via a call to `Update`.

Data Provider-Independent ADO.NET Coding

Although the data provider architecture of ADO.NET has several advantages, it does have one substantial disadvantage in terms of the way we have used it so far in this chapter: namely, the amount of programming work that is required to switch to a different data provider. For instance, the example page in the earlier walkthroughs used the `OleDb` provider. To switch to the SQL Server provider requires not only a change in the connection string but also requires changing every occurrence of `OleDb` with `Sql`. Although you could certainly use the search and replace option in Visual Studio to do this, it is quite unmanageable if you need to change dozens or hundreds of pages or classes.

A better approach than a manual search and replace is to do your ADO.NET coding in a data ***provider-independent*** manner. You can partially achieve this aim by coding to the abstract base classes used by the specific provider classes (as shown in Figure 9.2). For instance, in the previous examples in the chapter, we have created a `SqlConnection` object in the following manner.

```
SqlConnection conn = new SqlConnection(connString);
```

You could change this code to use the base class instead.

```
DbConnection conn = new SqlConnection(connString);
```

Of course, you still have a specific data provider in the instantiation, so you are only part way to data provider independence. One solution that some developers use is to create a so-called ***factory class***. Typically, this is a class that contains methods that return the appropriate provider object, usually based on some type of information in a configuration file, that looks similar to the following example.

```
public class DataAccessFactory
{
    public static DbConnection MakeConnection()
    {
        // Find out which provider from configuration file
        string provType = GetProviderFromConfiguration();

        // Return appropriate connection
        if (provType == "Sql")
            return new SqlConnection();
        else if (provType == "OleDb")
            return new OleDbConnection();
        ...
    }

    // Other static methods for creating other provider objects
    ...
}
```

Using this factory class, you can create provider objects in a provider-independent fashion.

```
DbConnection conn = DataAccessFactory.MakeConnection();
```

The advantage of this type of factory is that the database provider type can be changed at runtime, so that you could, for instance, test locally with an Access database and then use SQL Server on the production Web server, simply by making a change in a configuration file. (In reality, there are often implementation differences between different provider types that make the ideal of completely database-independent coding elusive).

Rather than make the developers repeatedly create this type of factory themselves, ADO.NET 2.0 has added the `DbProviderFactory` and `DbProviderFactories` classes as a way to instantiate provider objects in a provider-independent manner. The `DbProviderFactories` class is a factory for creating **provider factories**. That is, it is used to create a factory object that is used to create the different data provider objects. It provides a `GetFactory` method, which is passed a string that specifies which provider factory you want to use. The method returns an object of type `DbProviderFactory`, which can be used in turn to create the appropriate connection, command, and other provider objects.

```
DbProviderFactory factory =
    DbProviderFactories.GetFactory("System.Data.OleDb");
```

The `GetFactory` method is passed what is called the **_invariant name_** of the desired provider type. The different invariant names are specified in the `DbProviderFactories` element within the `machine.config` file. This element specifies all the registered data providers on the machine; to help remember it, the invariant name for each provider is the same as its namespace.

Of course, it is more than likely that you do not want to hard-code the invariant name as shown in the preceding example. Instead, you likely want to define it within your `Web.config` file. For instance, the following sample illustrates one possible way of specifying this information in your Web application's `Web.config` file, by using the `providerName` attribute of the `add` element.

```
<connectionStrings>
  <add name="Catalog"
    connectionString="Provider=Microsoft.Jet.OLEDB.4.0;
      Data Source=C:\…\App_Data\BookCatalogSystem.mdb"
    providerName="System.Data.OleDb" />
</connectionStrings>
```

With this information in the `Web.config` file, you can then use the `DbProviderFactories` class as follows.

```
// Retrieve database connection and provider name
ConnectionStringSettings setting =
  WebConfigurationManager.ConnectionStrings["Catalog"];

string connString = setting.ConnectionString;
string invariantName = setting.ProviderName;

// Get appropriate provider factory
DbProviderFactory factory =
  DbProviderFactories.GetFactory(invariantName);
```

CORE NOTE

You also have to add the following import statement to your class to use the provider factory classes.

```
using System.Data.Common;
```

Ideally, you could make your code more robust by verifying that the invariant name specified in the `Web.config` file is supported by the provider factory infrastructure. You can do this by using the `GetFactoryClasses` method of `DbProviderFactories`. This method returns a `DataTable` of all supported providers. You can then search the `DataTable` for the specified invariant name, as shown in the following example.

```
// Verify that this provider name is supported
DataTable providers = DbProviderFactories.GetFactoryClasses();
DataRow[] foundArray =
    providers.Select("InvariantName='"+invariantName+"'");

if (foundArray.Length == 0)
{
    throw new Exception(
        "Data Provider " + invariantName + " not found");
}

// Get appropriate provider factory
DbProviderFactory factory =
    DbProviderFactories.GetFactory(invariantName);
```

After you have the appropriate provider factory, you can use it to create the provider objects. This `DbProviderFactory` class has static methods for returning new instances of the connection, command, data adapter, and parameter classes. For instance, to create a new connection and command, you could use the following.

```
DbProviderFactory factory =
    DbProviderFactories.GetFactory(invariantName);

DbConnection conn = factory.CreateConnection();
conn.ConnectionString = connString;

DbCommand cmd = factory.CreateCommand();
cmd.CommandText = "SELECT * FROM Authors";
cmd.Connection = conn;
```

Notice that the various `Create` methods of the `DbProviderFactory` class take no arguments. This means that the provider objects must be set up via properties after they are created.

In conclusion, it should be noted that although provider-independent database-access code is a very worthy goal, completely provider-independent code can be difficult to achieve for high-load, high-performance Web applications. In such a situation, it is sometimes necessary to use features that are unique to the specific providers. Only you can decide whether having more generalized, more maintainable code is more important than (potentially) higher performance code.

There are ways to still access some of these unique properties and methods of the providers while still using provider-independent code by casting the object to the provider-dependant version. For instance, imagine that you are creating a number of data access classes that will contain all of your ADO.NET code. Furthermore, you want to make use of SQL Server's unique capability to retrieve a result set from a SELECT command as an XML stream, yet still make use of provider-independent coding. In such a case, you could use the C# `is` statement along with some data casting to create a method that might look like the following.

```
public XmlReader GetXml(DbCommand cmd)
{
   if (cmd is SqlCommand)
   {
      SqlCommand sqlCmd = (SqlCommand)cmd;
      return sqlCmd.ExecuteXmlReader();
   }
   else
      // Create an XmlReader from scratch for other providers
      ...
}
```

Data Source Controls

This chapter has covered how you can use ADO.NET to retrieve and modify data from a database. When combined with the data binding material from the last chapter, it is possible to retrieve data from a database table and display it as a Web server control with only 10 to 20 lines of programming code. With **data source controls**, it is possible to manipulate external data with *no* programming code. Data source controls provide a declarative approach (i.e., use markup) for accessing external data. Unlike almost all the other server controls encountered so far in the book, data source controls do not have a user interface. Instead, they declaratively encapsulate an external data source; thus, they are a type of intermediary between the data store and its presentation.

CORE NOTE

We have already used a data source control. We did so back in Chapter 7 when we used the `SiteMapDataSource` control in conjunction with the `Menu` and `SiteMap` controls and the `XmlDataSource` control with the `TreeView` control.

There are five different data source controls that come with ASP.NET.

- `AccessDataSource`—Provides simplified access to a Microsoft Access database. It inherits from `SqlDataSource`.
- `SqlDataSource`—Provides access to any database that uses SQL. This includes Microsoft SQL Server, any OLE DB database (including Microsoft Access), an ODBC database, or an Oracle database.
- `ObjectDataSource`—Allows you to use your own custom class (such as a business object or a data access object) to access data.

- `SiteMapDataSource`—Used by the site navigation controls to access the XML-based site map file.
- `XmlDataSource`—Provides access to any XML document.

Using these controls is simple. To define an `AccessDataSource`, you add something like the following to your page.

```
<asp:AccessDataSource ID="dsBooks" runat="server"
   DataFile="App_Data/BookCatalogSystem.mdb"
   SelectCommand="Select AuthorId,AuthorName from Authors" />
```

In this example, the `DataFile` attribute specifies the location of the database file, whereas the `SelectCommand` attribute specifies to which data the control provides access. Because the `SqlDataSource` and `AccessDataSource` controls can only have one `SelectCommand`, you can think of these controls as a single view into a data source. If you want another view—for instance, all of the `Book` records as well as the related `Author` data—we would have to add an `AccessDataSource` declaration with a different `SelectCommand`.

CORE NOTE

You can use the Visual Studio Designer to generate the markup for your data source controls by dragging and dropping the appropriate data source control on to the page. The Designer uses a Configure Data Source Wizard to help guide you through the process of configuring the control, as shown in Figure 9.9. You can access this wizard at any time in the Designer via the Configure Data Source option in the Task menu.

With the data source control defined, you can now display the data in any data-bindable control simply by setting the `DataSourceID` property to the `ID` of the data source control. For instance, to display the `AuthorName` field from the `Authors` table in a drop-down list, you can use the following.

```
<asp:DropDownList ID="drpAuthors" runat="server"
   DataSourceID="dsBooks" DataTextField="AuthorName" />
```

If you use a `SqlDataSource` control instead, your markup is similar, except you specify a connection string rather than a filename, as well as a provider name.

```
<asp:SqlDataSource ID="dsArt" runat="server"
   ConnectionString="Data Source=local;Initial Catalog=Books;
      Integrated Security=SSPI"
   ProviderName="System.Data.SqlClient"
   SelectCommand="Select AuthorId,AuthorName From Authors" />
```

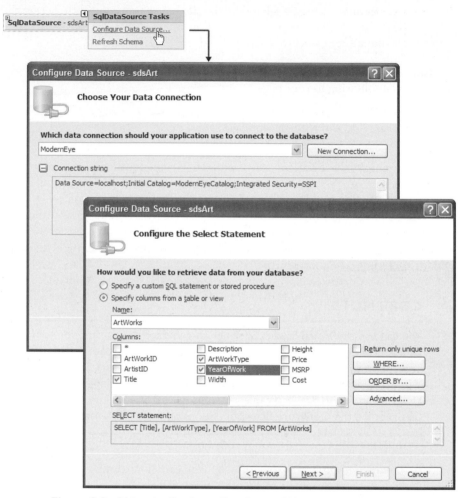

Figure 9.9   Using the Configure Data Source Wizard in Visual Studio

If you want to use a connection string that is defined in your Web.config file, you could replace the connection string in the preceding example with an ***ASP.NET expression*** that looks like the following.

```
<asp:SqlDataSource ID="dsArt" runat="server"
  ConnectionString="<%$ ConnectionStrings:Books %>"
  ProviderName="System.Data.SqlClient"
  SelectCommand="Select AuthorId,AuthorName From Authors" />
```

ASP.NET expressions have the following syntax.

```
<%$ expressionPrefix: expressionValue %>
```

In the connection string example, the expression prefix is `ConnectionStrings`, which refers to the element name of a section in the `Web.config` file (see the following example), whereas `Books` is the expression value, which is the name of the relevant connection string.

```
<connectionStrings>
   <add name="Books"
      connectionString="Data Source=localhost;Initial Catalog=
         BooksCatalog;Integrated Security=SSPI"
      providerName="System.Data.SqlClient"/>
</connectionStrings>
```

Using Parameters

You may not always want to retrieve every record in a database table. In SQL, you can use the WHERE clause to filter the retrieved records. In "Using DbParameters" on page 521, you learned how to use `DbParameter` objects to dynamically filter data at runtime based on user input. You can accomplish the same thing with your data source controls by adding a nested `SelectParameters` element to your data source declaration. This `SelectParameters` element can contain any number of parameter control definitions within it.

```
<asp:SqlDataSource ID="dsArt" runat="server"
   ConnectionString="<%$ ConnectionStrings:Books %>"
   SelectCommand="Select AuthorId,AuthorName From Authors" >

   <SelectParameters>

   Parameter control definitions go here

   </SelectParameters>

</asp:SqlDataSource>
```

In a Web application, the values for a parameter could come from a variety of sources. You might want to use a value from another control on the form, a value from a querystring, or a value from a cookie or a session variable. To support this need, there are a number of different parameter control types that you can use within the `SelectParameter` element (see Table 9.10).

Table 9.10   Parameter Control Types

Type	Description
ControlParameter	Sets the parameter value to a property value in another control on the page.
CookieParameter	Sets the parameter value to the value of a cookie.
FormParameter	Sets the parameter value to the value of an HTML form element.
ProfileParameter	Sets the parameter value to the value of a property of the current user profile.
QuerystringParameter	Sets the parameter value to the value of a querystring field.
SessionParameter	Sets the parameter value to the value of an object currently stored in session state.

All of the parameter control types listed in Table 9.10 inherit from the same base class (Parameter), and as such share the properties listed in Table 9.11.

Table 9.11   Notable Properties of Parameter Class

Property	Description
ConvertEmptyStringToNull	Specifies whether the value of the parameter should be null if the value is an empty string.
DefaultValue	Specifies a default value for the parameter if the value is null or cannot be found. Should be used for parameter types that cannot guarantee a value, such as a Cookie-Parameter or a QuerystringParameter.
Name	Specifies the name of the parameter.
Type	Specifies the data type of the parameter. Possible values are described by the TypeCode enumeration.

To see how to use one of the parameter controls, imagine a page in which the user selects a publisher from a DropDownList and then the page displays all the books by that publisher in a GridView control (see Figure 9.10).

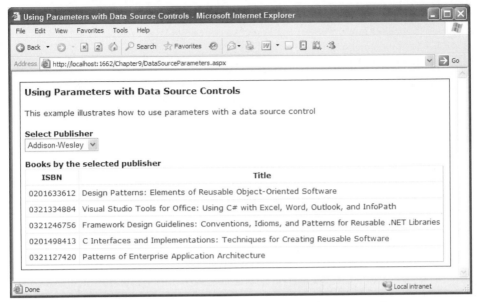

Figure 9.10 Using data source controls with two controls

First, you define a data source control, which selects all the publishers.

```
<asp:SqlDataSource ID="dsPublisher" runat="server"
   ProviderName="System.Data.OleDb"
   ConnectionString="<%$ ConnectionStrings:Catalog %>"
   SelectCommand=
      "Select PublisherId,PublisherName From Publishers" />
```

You then need a DropDownList that displays the publisher names selected in this data source control.

```
<asp:DropDownList ID="drpPublisher" runat="server"
   DataSourceID="dsPublisher" DataValueField="PublisherId"
   DataTextField="PublisherName" AutoPostBack="True"/>
```

You now need another data source control that displays only those books whose PublisherId field matches that selected in the DropDownList. This requires a SelectCommand with a parameter along with a ControlParameter.

```
<asp:SqlDataSource ID="dsBooks" runat="server"
   ProviderName="System.Data.OleDb"
   ConnectionString="<%$ ConnectionStrings:Catalog %>"
   SelectCommand=
      "SELECT ISBN, Title FROM Books WHERE PublisherId=@Pub">
```

```
<SelectParameters>
    <asp:ControlParameter ControlID="drpPublisher"
        Name="Pub" PropertyName="SelectedValue" />
</SelectParameters>
</asp:SqlDataSource>
```

Notice that the `ControlParameter` defines a `ControlID` property. This property is set to the `ID` of the `DropDownList`, because that control contains the selected `PublisherId` value. The `Name` property indicates to which parameter name in the `SELECT` statement the value is mapped, whereas `PropertyName` indicates the `SelectedValue` property of the `DropDownList` that contains the value for the parameter.

All that is left is the `GridView` control that contains the book data.

```
<asp:GridView ID="grdBooks" runat="server"
    DataSourceID="dsBooks" />
```

Using Querystring Parameters

What if the book's `GridView` was on a separate page (let's name this page `PublisherBooks.aspx`) from the publisher's `DropDownList`? In such a case, you would probably pass the selected `PublisherId` within a querystring. For instance, the event handler for the `DropDownList` might look like the following example. It simply redirects to the other page and puts the selected publisher in a querystring parameter named `pubid`.

```
protected void drpPublisherSelected(object sender, EventArgs e)
{
    string pub = drpPublisher.SelectedValue;
    Response.Redirect("PublisherBooks.aspx?pubid=" + pub);
}
```

Within `PublisherBooks.aspx`, you need to change your data source control to use a `QueryStringParameter` rather than a `ControlParameter`.

```
<SelectParameters>
    <asp:QueryStringParameter QueryStringField="pubid"
        Name="Pub" DefaultValue="1"/>
</SelectParameters>
```

Modifying Data

Data source controls can be used not only for retrieving data, but also for updating, inserting, and deleting data. This capability can be used by the data controls added in ASP.NET 2.0, namely the `GridView`, `FormView`, and `DetailsView` controls (we examine these controls in the next chapter). Just as you used the `SelectCommand` property along with the nested `SelectParameter` element, there are `DeleteCommand`, `InsertCommand`, and `UpdateCommand` properties, as well as `DeleteParameter`, `InsertParameter`, and `UpdateParameter` elements.

You use the capability to modify data with a data source control in the next chapter when you delve into the `GridView`, `FormView`, and `DetailsView` controls.

How Do Data Source Controls Work?

Data source controls allow you to perform common data retrieval tasks with no programming. But how do they work? What goes on behind the curtain?

The SQL and Access data source controls are merely a declarative encapsulation of the ADO.NET coding that was covered in the first part of the chapter. For instance, the `SqlDataSource` control delegates most of its work to the `SqlDataSourceView` class. This class has methods for selecting, updating, deleting, and inserting data. It has a `Select` method, which is ultimately called by the server control that is using the data source control each and every time the page is requested (this includes postback requests as well). In this method, the following actions (plus a whole lot of exception handling) are performed.

1. `DbProviderFactory` is used to create a `DbConnection`, which is then opened.
2. `DbProviderFactory` is used to create a `DbCommand` using the provided select statement.
3. `DbProviderFactory` is used to create any `DbParameter` objects based on the `SelectParameter` element.
4. Depending upon on how the `DataSourceMode` property of the `SqlDataSource` control has been set, either a `DbDataReader` is executed or a `DataSet` is filled using a `DbDataAdapter`.
5. If the data has been retrieved into a `DataSet`, its data is also saved into an internal cache (covered in the following section, "Problems with SqlDataSource").
6. The connection is closed.

As you can see from the preceding list, the `SqlDataSource` control uses the same ADO.NET classes and processes that we were programmatically doing earlier in the chapter. Of course, the advantage is that with the `SqlDataSource`, you don't have to do any of the programming!

Problems with SqlDataSource

Although the `SqlDataSource` control eliminates the need for the typical repetitive ADO.NET programming code, there is some controversy about it among developers. The main issue revolves around the suitability of having data access details in the presentation layer. Many ASP.NET developers prefer to keep their Web Forms free of database implementation details such as connection strings, stored procedure names, or SQL statements. The main reason for this preference is to improve maintainability. A large Web application with dozens or even hundreds of Web pages each with multiple `SqlDataSource` controls is very difficult to maintain if implementation details about data access ever needs to be changed. Instead, developers often prefer to encapsulate database access into separate classes (often called **data access objects**) that are used by the Web Forms or other "higher-level" classes such as business objects. (Chapter 11 examines this type of design in more detail.)

Another potential issue with the `SqlDataSource` control is that its `Select` command is invoked every time the page is requested. For a page with multiple postback possibilities, this is an unnecessary load on the DBMS. One way to mitigate this problem is by setting the `DataSourceMode` to `DataSet` and then enabling caching via the `EnableCaching` property.

```
<asp:SqlDataSource ID="dsWhatEver" runat="server"
    DataSourceMode="DataSet" EnableCaching="True"
    … />
```

Of course, if you prefer to use a `DbDataReader` for performance or efficiency reasons, you are out of luck in terms of caching. However, there is still a way to have the declarative advantages of data source controls with the design benefits of data access objects or business objects: the `ObjectDataSource` control.

Using the ObjectDataSource

Like the other data source controls, the **ObjectDataSource** control provides a codeless way to display and manipulate data. Unlike with the `AccessDataSource` or `SqlDataSource` controls, the `ObjectDataSource` control is not an intermediary for a database but for some other class. As previously mentioned, many developers prefer to design their Web applications so that their Web Forms are only concerned with presentation details; other classes are used to implement data access logic, business logic, and application logic. The `ObjectDataSource` allows developers to maintain this type of application architecture and keep the benefits of codeless data binding.

Using an `ObjectDataSource` control is quite straightforward. For instance, imagine that you have a class named `PublisherDA` that contains a method named `GetAll`, which returns a `DataTable` containing publisher data. You could define an `ObjectDataSource` as follows.

```
<asp:ObjectDataSource ID="objCatalog" runat="server"
    SelectMethod="GetAll" TypeName="PublisherDA" />
```

The `TypeName` property specifies the class name of the object that provides the data, whereas the `SelectMethod` property specifies which method in this class is called when the control needs to retrieve data. The `ObjectDataSource` control also supports the `UpdateMethod`, `InsertMethod`, and `DeleteMethod` properties.

The `ObjectDataSource` control has certain expectations with the class specified by `TypeName` and the method specified by `SelectMethod`. The class ideally should have a default constructor (that is a constructor with no parameters) or no constructor (because the compiler adds an empty default constructor if none is defined). It is possible for the control to work with a constructor that takes parameters, but this requires that you define your own `ObjectCreating` event handler for the control. Because the control generally creates an instance of the class specified by `TypeName` each time it needs to use a method of the class, the class should be stateless. The method defined by `SelectMethod` can return any of the following.

- A `DataTable`, `DataSet`, or `DataView`
- An object that implements `IEnumerable`
- Any other `object`

If the method returns an object that is not `IEnumerable`, or a `DataTable`, `DataSet`, or `DataView`, the control places the object into a single element array of that type (which makes the object `IEnumerable`) and returns the array.

The methods that are passed to the control can be either instance methods or static methods. If it is a static method, an instance of the class is not created. If it is an instance method, the control creates an instance of the object, and then after this method is finished executing, the instantiated object is disposed. You can override this instantiation behavior by defining your own `ObjectCreating` event handler.

Like the other data source controls, the `ObjectDataSource` control supports parameters. In this case, the various parameter elements (e.g., `SelectParameters`) are used to specify the parameters to the methods for selecting, updating, deleting, and inserting. For instance, if you want to define an `ObjectDataSource` control that retrieves the books for a publisher that has been selected in a `ListBox` named `drpPublisher`, it might look like the following.

```
<asp:ObjectDataSource ID="dsBooks" runat="server"
  SelectMethod="GetBooksByPublisher" TypeName="BookDA" >

  <SelectParameters>
    <asp:ControlParameter ControlID="drpPublisher"
      Name="id" PropertyName="SelectedValue"
      Type="Int32" />
  </SelectParameters>

</asp:ObjectDataSource>
```

The Name property of the ControlParameter specifies the name of the argument to the method GetBooksByPublisher, a sample version of which is shown here.

```
public DataTable GetBooksByPublisher(int id)
{
   // Set up parameterized query statement
   string sql = SelectStatement + " WHERE PublisherId=@id";

   // Construct array of parameters
   DbParameter[] parameters = new DbParameter[] {
      MakeParameter("@id", id)
   };

   // Return result
   return GetDataTable(sql, parameters);
}
```

The interesting thing about this method is not its implementation but its method signature. Each parameter in SelectParameters must match the name and data type of the arguments to this method. The same approach must be followed for modifying data as well. If you want the ObjectDataSource control to be able to update data, you need to specify an UpdateMethod and any required UpdateParameter elements.

```
<asp:ObjectDataSource ID="objBook" runat="server"
   SelectMethod="GetBooksByIsbn" TypeName="BookDA"
   UpdateMethod="UpdateBook" >

   <SelectParameters>
      <asp:ControlParameter ControlID="lboxBooks"
         Name="isbn" PropertyName="SelectedValue"
         Type="String" DefaultValue="a"/>
   </SelectParameters>

   <UpdateParameters>
      <asp:Parameter Name="isbn" Type="String" />
      <asp:Parameter Name="title" Type="String" />
      <asp:Parameter Name="yearPublished" Type="Int32" />
   </UpdateParameters>

</asp:ObjectDataSource>
```

The definition of UpdateBook might look like the following.

```
public void UpdateBook(string isbn, string title, int yearPublished)
{
   string sql =
      "UPDATE Books SET Title=@title, YearPublished=@yearPub";
```

```
sql += " WHERE ISBN=@isbn";

// Construct array of parameters
DbParameter[] parameters = new DbParameter[] {
    MakeParameter("@isbn", isbn, DbType.String),
    MakeParameter("@title", title, DbType.String),
    MakeParameter("@yearPub", yearPublished, DbType.Int32)
};

// Run the specified command
RunNonQuery(sql, parameters);
}
```

ObjectDataSource Caching

It should be stressed that the `ObjectDataSource` control does not retain the instance of its object across multiple requests. Each time the `SelectMethod` (or `UpdateMethod`, etc.) method is invoked (generally by the Web controls that are data bound to it), the relevant object is instantiated and then disposed. This behavior may be less than ideal for a frequently requested page.

Luckily, the `ObjectDataSource` control supports the caching of data if the `SelectMethod` returns a `DataSet`, `DataTable`, `DataView`, or returns `IEnumerable` data that is not a `DbDataReader`. The ASP.NET *cache* is an area of server memory that is available to all requests for a given application. This application cache is volatile, meaning it is not stored in memory for the life of the application. Instead, it is managed by ASP.NET, which removes items when they expire or become invalidated, or when memory runs low. Chapter 12 covers the ASP.NET cache in more detail. To enable caching, you need to set the `EnableCaching` property of the `ObjectDataSource` to `true`. You can customize the way the `ObjectDataSource` control's caching operates via its `CacheDuration` and `CacheExpirationPolicy` properties.

ObjectDataSource Example

The real benefit of using the `ObjectDataSource` control (in comparison with the `SqlDataSource`) is that your Web pages can remain unconcerned with where the data is actually stored. By localizing the data access details within just a few separate classes, you can enjoy both the codeless benefits of the data source controls as well as the maintainability benefits of a design that contains no database-specific details in your Web Forms.

Listings 9.2 through 9.4 demonstrate these benefits. The first of these listings is a slightly simplified version of the book data editor example, which began with Walkthrough 9.1. For the display and editing of the individual book record fields, this example uses a simplified `DetailsView` control. The next chapter provides more information about the use of this control, which not only displays a single record of

data but also has built-in editing support of that data. Figure 9.11 illustrates how
these listings appear in the browser.

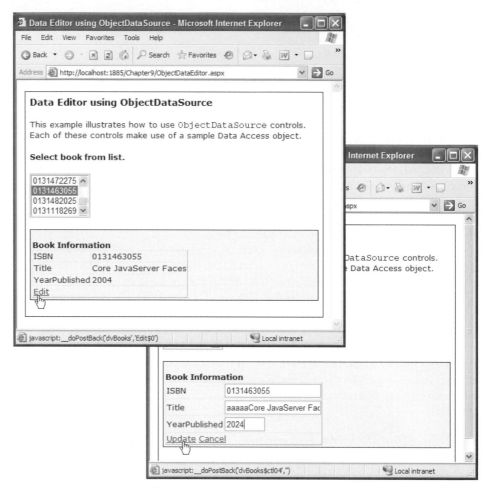

Figure 9.11   ObjectDataEditor.aspx

Listing 9.2   ObjectDataEditor.aspx

```
<h1>Data Editor using ObjectDataSource</h1>
<p>This example illustrates how to use <code>
ObjectDataSource</code> controls. Each of these controls make
use of a sample Data Access object.</p>
<h2>Select book from list.</h2>
<p>
```

```
<asp:ListBox id="lboxBooks" runat="server"
   DataTextField="Isbn" DataValueField="ISBN"
   AutoPostBack="true"  DataSourceID="objAllBooks" />
</p>
<asp:Panel id="panBook" runat="server" CssClass="books">
   <h2>Book Information</h2>
   <asp:DetailsView ID="dvBooks" runat="server"
      DataSourceID="objBook"
      AutoGenerateEditButton="true" />
</asp:Panel>

<asp:ObjectDataSource ID="objAllBooks" runat="server"
   EnableCaching="true"
   SelectMethod="GetAll" TypeName="BookDA" />

<asp:ObjectDataSource ID="objBook" runat="server"
      SelectMethod="GetBooksByIsbn" TypeName="BookDA"
      UpdateMethod="UpdateBook" >

   <SelectParameters>
      <asp:ControlParameter ControlID="lboxBooks"
         Name="isbn" PropertyName="SelectedValue"
         Type="String" DefaultValue="a"/>
   </SelectParameters>
   <UpdateParameters>
      <asp:Parameter Name="isbn" Type="String" />
      <asp:Parameter Name="title" Type="String" />
      <asp:Parameter Name="yearPublished" Type="Int32" />
   </UpdateParameters>
</asp:ObjectDataSource>
```

Both `ListBox` and `DetailsView` controls are data bound to two different `ObjectDataSource` controls. Each of the `ObjectDataSource` controls make use of methods defined in a class named `BookDA`. You might call `BookDA` a data access object because the retrieval and modification of data for each table needed by the application is encapsulated within a separate class. Martin Fowler in his important *Patterns of Enterprise Application Architecture* book refers to this approach as the **Table Module** pattern. In the listings that follow, the data access objects return table data by containing it within a `DataTable` object.

To reduce data duplication within each data access class, common functionality can be extracted into separate data helper classes or within a common base class (as is the case in this example). The class diagram shown in Figure 9.12 illustrates the functionality for two sample data access classes.

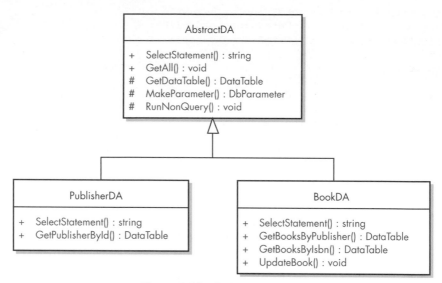

Figure 9.12 Data access classes

Listing 9.3 contains the source code for `AbstractDA`, which is the base class for all the data access classes in this application. It handles almost all of the actual ADO.NET coding. As well, because it uses the provider-independent coding techniques described earlier in the chapter, you can easily switch your database from a Microsoft Access database to a SQL Server database. Notice that it defines an abstract property named `SelectStatement`, which returns the SQL SELECT string for retrieving the data for the table; this property is implemented in each of the subclasses for `AbstractDA`.

Listing 9.3 AbstractDA.cs

```
using System;
using System.Data;
using System.Configuration;
using System.Data.Common;
using System.Web.Configuration;

/// <summary>
/// Encapsulates most of the ADO.NET functionality needed
/// by your data access classes
/// </summary>
public abstract class AbstractDA
{
```

```csharp
/// <summary>
/// Returns all the data for the data source
/// </summary>
public DataTable GetAll()
{
    string sql = SelectStatement;
    return GetDataTable(sql, null);
}


/// <summary>
/// Defines the basic select statement for retrieving data
/// without criteria. Implemented by the concrete subclasses.
/// </summary>
protected abstract string SelectStatement
{
    get;
}


/// <summary>
/// Creates a provider-independent DbParameter object
/// </summary>
protected DbParameter MakeParameter(string name, object value,
        DbType paramType)
{
    DbParameter param = Factory.CreateParameter();
    param.ParameterName = name;
    param.Value = value;
    param.DbType = paramType;
    return param;
}


/// <summary>
/// Returns a filled DataTable specified by sql and parameters
/// </summary>
protected DataTable GetDataTable(string sql,
        DbParameter[] parameters)
{
    DataTable dt = null;
    try
    {
        // Creates provider-independent connection
        DbConnection conn = Factory.CreateConnection();
        conn.ConnectionString =
            ConnectionSetting.ConnectionString;

        // Creates provider-independent data adapter
        DbDataAdapter adapter = Factory.CreateDataAdapter();
```

```csharp
        // Creates provider-independent SELECT command
        DbCommand cmd = Factory.CreateCommand();
        cmd.Connection = conn;
        cmd.CommandText = sql;
        adapter.SelectCommand = cmd;

        // Adds parameters if there are any
        if (parameters != null)
        {
            foreach (DbParameter p in parameters)
                adapter.SelectCommand.Parameters.Add(p);
        }

        // Fills a new data table with data from adapter
        dt = new DataTable();
        adapter.Fill(dt);

    }
    catch (Exception ex)
    {
        // Errors are handled by a custom exception handler
        DataAccessExceptionHandler.HandleException(ex.Message);
    }
    return dt;
}

/// <summary>
/// Runs a SQL query that does not return data
/// </summary>
protected void RunNonQuery(string sql, DbParameter[]
    parameters)
{
    // Creates provider-independent connection
    using (DbConnection conn = Factory.CreateConnection())
    {
        conn.ConnectionString =
            ConnectionSetting.ConnectionString;

        // Creates provider-independent command
        // and adds parameters
        DbCommand cmd = Factory.CreateCommand();
        cmd.Connection = conn;
        cmd.CommandText = sql;

        if (parameters != null)
        {
            foreach (DbParameter p in parameters)
                cmd.Parameters.Add(p);
        }
```

```
    try
    {
        // Opens connection and execute command
        conn.Open();
        cmd.ExecuteNonQuery();
    }
    catch (Exception ex)
    {
        DataAccessExceptionHandler.HandleException(
            ex.Message);
    }
    finally
    {
        if (conn != null) conn.Close();
    }
    }
}


/// <summary>
/// Returns connection string setting from Web.config
/// </summary>
private ConnectionStringSettings ConnectionSetting
{
    get
    {
        return
          WebConfigurationManager.ConnectionStrings[
            "BookCatalog"];
    }
}


/// <summary>
/// Returns appropriate DbProviderFactory
/// </summary>
private DbProviderFactory Factory
{
    get
    {
        string connString = ConnectionSetting.ConnectionString;
        string invariantName = ConnectionSetting.ProviderName;

        // Verifies that this provider name is supported
        DataTable providers =
            DbProviderFactories.GetFactoryClasses();
        DataRow[] foundArray =
            providers.Select("InvariantName='" +
                invariantName + "'");
        if (foundArray.Length == 0)
        {
```

```
        string msg = "[AbstractDA] Data Provider " +
            invariantName + " not found";
        DataAccessExceptionHandler.HandleException(msg);
    }

    // Gets appropriate provider factory
    return DbProviderFactories.GetFactory(invariantName);
    }
  }
}
```

Because the vast majority of the actual data access coding is contained within AbstractDA, the data access classes for the individual tables are quite straightforward. Listing 9.4 contains the code for the BookDA class.

Listing 9.4 BookDA.cs

```
using System;
using System.Data;
using System.Data.Common;

/// <summary>
/// Data Access class for the Books table.
/// </summary>
public class BookDA: AbstractDA
{
    /// <summary>
    /// Specifies SQL for retrieving book data
    /// </summary>
    protected override string SelectStatement
    {
        get {
            // We only return some data for brevity sake
            return "SELECT ISBN,Title,YearPublished FROM Books";
        }
    }

    /// <summary>
    /// Returns a data table containing book table info for this
    /// ISBN. Note that this data set contains either 0 or 1
    /// rows of data.
    /// </summary>
    public DataTable GetBooksByIsbn(string isbn)
    {
        // Sets up parameterized query statement
        string sql = SelectStatement + " WHERE ISBN=@isbn";
```

```csharp
    // Constructs array of parameters
    DbParameter[] parameters = new DbParameter[]
    {
        MakeParameter("@isbn", isbn, DbType.String)
    };
    // Returns result
    return GetDataTable(sql, parameters);
}

/// <summary>
/// Updates the selected book values
/// </summary>
public void UpdateBook(string isbn, string title,
    int yearPublished)
{
    string sql = "UPDATE Books SET Title=@title,";
    sql += "YearPublished=@yearPub WHERE ISBN=@isbn";

    // Constructs array of parameters
    DbParameter[] parameters = new DbParameter[]
    {
        MakeParameter("@isbn", isbn, DbType.String),
        MakeParameter("@title", title, DbType.String),
        MakeParameter("@yearPub", yearPublished, DbType.Int32)
    };
    // Runs the specified command
    RunNonQuery(sql, parameters);
}
}
```

In Chapter 11, you will again make use of the `ObjectDataSource`. In that chapter, you will use a different data access approach than the Table Module pattern that you used in this chapter. With the Table Module pattern, your data access classes returned data from the database within `DataTable` objects. In the approach used in Chapter 11 (which Fowler calls the Domain Model pattern), you will use business objects that return strongly typed domain objects somewhat similar to the `Customer` and `EntityCollection` classes we defined in Chapter 8. You will find in that chapter that the `ObjectDataSource` control can work just as well with business objects as with data access objects.

Summary

This chapter demonstrated how to use ADO.NET for accessing and modifying data within databases. The classes in ADO.NET pertain to either its own data containers or to the different data providers. The ADO.NET data providers define a handful of .NET classes that are used for connecting to a database, executing data commands, populating a `DataSet`, and providing fast, forward-only, read-only access to data. The four main classes within a data provider are subclasses of the `DbConnection`, `DbCommand`, `DbDataAdapter`, and `DbDataReader` abstract classes. As you saw, each database provider has its own concrete subclass of these classes. As well, the chapter covered data source controls, the codeless approach to working directly with databases or indirectly with data via any type of class that returns data.

The next chapter returns to the coverage of ASP.NET Web server controls. More particularly, the next chapter covers the different multivalue Web server controls: `Repeater`, `DataList`, `GridView`, `DetailsView`, and `FormView`. Each of these controls uses data binding to display (and for some even edit) multiple sets of data in different ways.

Exercises

The solutions to the following exercises can be found at my Web site, `http://www.randyconnolly.com/core`. Additional exercises only available for teachers and instructors are also available from this site.

1. Modify the example used in Walkthroughs 9.1 to 9.4 so that it not only updates the data for the selected book, but also deletes the book as well. This example should use ADO.NET classes covered in the chapter.

2. Modify the example used in Walkthroughs 9.1 to 9.4 so that it uses data provider-independent coding.

3. Create a Web Form named `AuthorBooks.aspx` that displays a list of authors in a `ListBox`. When the user selects an author, the page should display another `ListBox` that displays the book titles for the selected author. When the user selects a book from this second list, the page should redirect to another page named `BookDetails.aspx` that displays the `ISBN`, `Title`, `PublisherId`, `SeriesId`, `CategoryId`, and `Year` fields from the `Book` table for the selected book. This example should use ADO.NET classes covered in the chapter. This exercise uses the `BookCatalogSystem.mdb` database.

4. Create a page named `DistributedTransaction.aspx` that lets the user select a book from a list. After the user selects the book, delete this book from the `Books` table. As well, delete any matching records (i.e., with the same ISBN) from the `CustomerBooks` table of the `Customer-Management.mdb` database. Both deletes should be wrapped within a `TransactionScope`.

5. Create a Web Form named `AuthorBooksDataSource.aspx` that has similar functionality to exercise 3, but which uses data source controls rather than ADO.NET coding.

6. Create a data access class similar to that shown in Listing 9.3 to retrieve data from the publisher table. It should also define a method named `GetPublisherById` that returns a `DataTable` containing the publisher data for the passed integer ID value. Create a test Web Form that demonstrates that it works.

7. Convert the example in Listings 9.2 and 9.3 to use stored procedures rather than SQL text. Be sure to create the necessary stored procedures.

8. Create a data access class similar to that shown in Listing 9.3 to retrieve data from the Artists and ArtWorks table. This exercise uses the `ModernEye-Catalog` database.

Key Concepts

- ADO.NET
- ASP.NET expression
- Cache
- Commands
- Connection pooling
- Connection string
- Connections
- Data access objects
- Data adapters
- Database null
- Data binding
- Data containers
- Data providers
- Data readers
- Data source controls
- Distributed transactions
- Factory class
- Identity fields

- Integrated security
- Invariant name
- Local transactions
- `ObjectDataSource`
- Parameterized queries
- Parameters
- Provider factories
- Provider-independent coding
- Result set
- Stored procedures
- SQL
- SQL injection attack
- SQL Server Authentication
- Table Module pattern
- Transactions
- Windows Authentication

References

Beauchemin, Bob. "Generic Coding with the ADO.NET 2.0 Base Classes and Factories." `http://msdn.microsoft.com`.

Carpentiere, Christa. "Protecting Your Data Integrity with Transactions in ADO.NET." `http://msdn.microsoft.com`.

Fowler, Martin. *Patterns of Enterprise Application Architecture*. Addison-Wesley, 2003.

Homer, Alex. "Writing Provider-Independent Data Access Code with ADO.NET 2.0." `http://www.devx.com`.

Litwin, Paul. "Stop SQL Injection Attacks Before They Stop You." *MSDN Magazine* (September 2004).

Microsoft. "Encrypting and Decrypting Configuration Sections." `http://msdn.microsoft.com`.

Mosa, Muhammad. "Managing Distributed Transactions with ADO.NET 2.0 Using TransactionScope." `http://www.c-sharpcorner.com`.

Papa, John. "ADO.NET and System.Transactions." *MSDN Magazine* (February 2005).

Chapter 10

DATA CONTROLS

The previous two chapters demonstrated the ease of working with data in ASP.NET. This chapter continues the broader topic of working with data in ASP.NET by focusing on how to work with ASP.NET's powerful multivalue data controls: the `Repeater`, `DataList`, `FormView`, `DetailsView`, and `GridView`. Each of these controls uses data binding to display (and for some, even edit) multiple sets of data in different ways.

Introducing the Multivalue Data Controls

The majority of our data-binding examples so far in the book have used either the `ListBox` or `DropDownList` controls. Although these are certainly useful controls, they are hardly the only control that can display multiple data values. ASP.NET includes five controls dedicated to the display of multiple values from a data source.

ASP.NET 1.1 had three multivalue data controls: the `DataList`, the `Repeater`, and the `DataGrid`. ASP.NET 2.0 introduced two brand new controls (the `Details-View` and `FormView` controls) as well as a new replacement for the `DataGrid` control (the `GridView` control). These controls have several similarities. They all use template tags to separate the control data from its presentation. That is, the control

577

does not provide a user interface; rather, the user interface is customized by the developer via nested template elements. They also all support data binding. In fact, these controls can only display content via data binding. These data controls vary in their flexibility, features, and speed.

CORE NOTE

Because the `DataGrid` control has been replaced in ASP.NET 2.0 with the `GridView` control, this chapter does not cover the `DataGrid` control, even though it is still available for backward compatibility with ASP.NET 1.1.

The `DataList` control displays rows of data as items in a list. The presentation of the data can be customized via templates. Inline editing and deleting of data is also supported by this control. Figure 10.1 illustrates several sample `DataList` layouts.

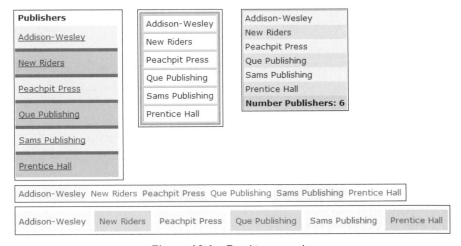

Figure 10.1   DataList examples

The `Repeater` control also provides a list of data. It is unique in that it provides complete flexibility in regard to the HTML presentation of the data. However, because there is no default look, the developer must completely describe via templates how the data is to be rendered. Figure 10.2 illustrates several example `Repeater` controls.

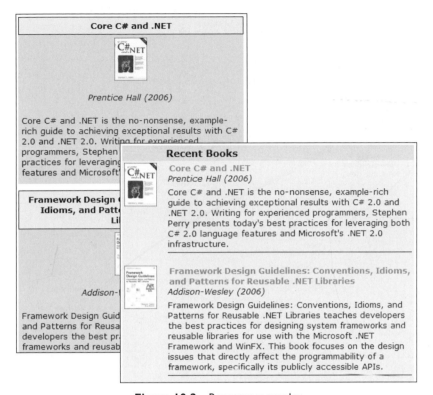

Figure 10.2   Repeater examples

The `DetailsView` control displays a single record of data at a time. It provides buttons for navigating from record to record. As well, it supports the updating, insertion, or deletion of records. It can be used in conjunction with the `GridView` control to provide a master-detail view of your data. In such a case, the `GridView` displays multiple records in the master table; when the user selects a record in the master, the `DetailsView` control displays more detail for the selected record.

Like the `DetailsView` control, the `FormView` control displays a single record of data at a time and supports the editing of the record. Unlike the `DetailsView` control, the `FormView` control requires the use of templates to define the rendering of each item, so the developer can completely customize the appearance of the record. Figures 10.3 and 10.4 illustrate some examples of `DetailsView` and `FormView` controls.

Figure 10.3　FormView examples

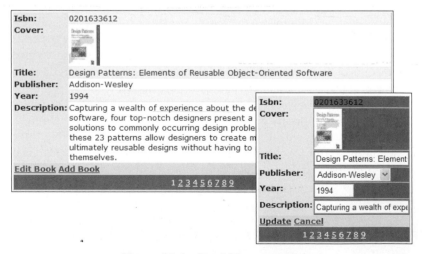

Figure 10.4　DetailsView examples

The `GridView` control displays data in a tabular (row-column) grid. It provides the most features of the data controls. It not only supports the editing and deleting of data, it also supports the sorting and paging of data. Although it also uses templates to customize the appearance of the data, customizing the presentation requires more work than the `DataList`. There is a default look to the `GridView`, so little work is required to displaying an entire table of data. Figure 10.5 illustrates some example `GridView` controls.

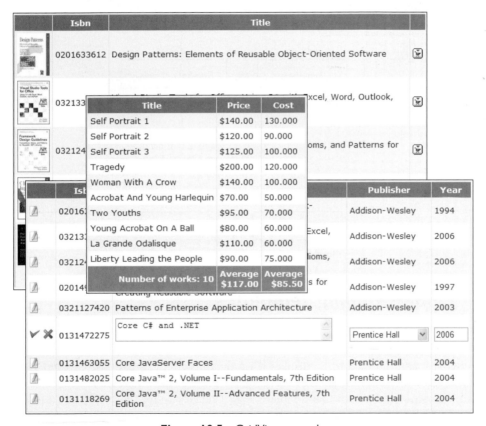

Figure 10.5 GridView examples

Figure 10.6 illustrates the class relationships of these controls. `FormView`, `DetailsView`, and `GridView` were introduced with ASP.NET 2.0, and are based on a different class hierarchy than the older `DataList` and `DataGrid` controls. As a consequence, only the new `FormView`, `DetailsView`, and `GridView` controls support both the viewing *and* editing features of the data source controls.

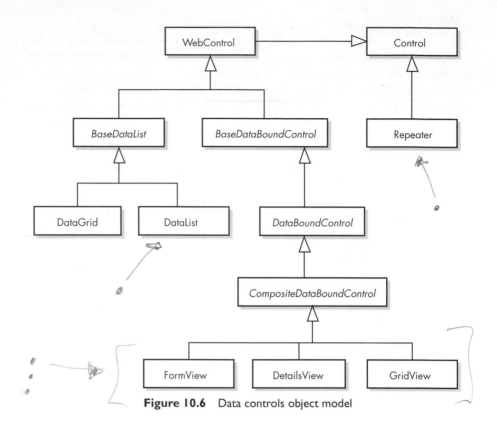

Figure 10.6   Data controls object model

Understanding Templates

The content and layout of list items in these controls are defined using ***templates***. A template defines the HTML elements, the ASP.NET controls, the layout of these controls, and the data to be displayed via data-binding expressions (covered in the next section). Style formatting of a template, such as fonts and colors, is set via the unique style element for that template (e.g., `ItemStyle` for the `ItemTemplate`).

Table 10.1 lists the available general templates (others specific to the `GridView` are covered later). As well, some of these templates are not available to all the controls.

Table 10.1   General Templates for Data Controls

Name	Description
`ItemTemplate`	Specifies the content and layout of items within a list.
`AlternatingItemTemplate`	Specifies the content and layout of alternating items.

Table 10.1   General Templates for Data Controls *(continued)*

Name	Description
SeparatorTemplate	Specifies what should appear between items (and alternating items).
SelectedItemTemplate	Specifies the content and layout of selected items.
EditItemTemplate	Specifies the content and layout of edited items.
HeaderTemplate	Specifies the content and layout of the header of the list.
FooterTemplate	Specifies the content and layout of the footer of the list

Figure 10.7 illustrates how these general templates relate to each other when used in these controls.

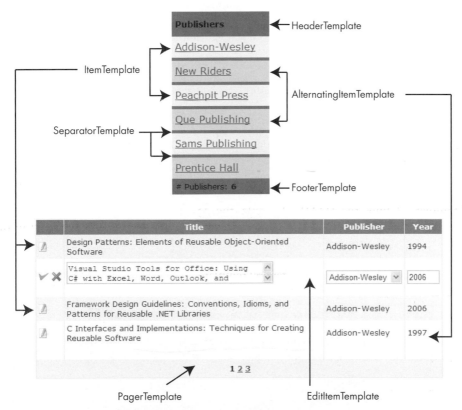

Figure 10.7   General templates for data controls

Data-Binding Expressions

Within the various item templates (e.g., ItemTemplate, EditItemTemplate), you need to specify which data source fields you want to display. ASP.NET provides a special declarative syntax for specifying data elements, generally referred to as *data-binding expressions*. The syntax for a data-binding expression is

```
<%# expression %>
```

The expression within the tags can be anything that evaluates to a value (that is, any method that returns a value, any property, or any programming expression). The expression is evaluated only when the control's DataBind method is invoked. Data-binding expressions can be used anywhere within the <form>...</form> element of the Web Form (and not just within template tags).

In most of the following examples in this chapter, the data-binding expressions refer to a field in a database table, or a column in a DataTable. In some of the examples in the latter chapters, the data-binding expression refers instead to a property in an object. Accessing these values can result in some messy type-casting. For instance, if you want to display the LastName field from the Author table within the ItemTemplate of a DataList, the code might look like the following.

```
<asp:DataList ID="dlstSample" Runat="server">
  <ItemTemplate>
    <%# ((DataRowView)Container.DataItem)["LastName"] %>
  </ItemTemplate>
</asp:DataList>
```

The data item container in the data source must be type-cast to a DataRowView and then the LastName field can be retrieved from it. If you need to convert from an integer to a string, or you need some other type of formatting (such as currency or date formatting), the data-binding expression becomes even more complex.

```
<%#
String.Format("{0:c}",((DataRowView)Container.DataItem)["Price"])
%>
```

Luckily, ASP.NET provides a somewhat easy syntax via the static Eval method of the DataBinder class. This syntax is

```
<%# DataBinder.Eval(Container.DataItem, "expression") %>
```

ASP.NET 2.0 provides a shortcut for DataBinder.Eval; you can instead simply reference the Eval method of the page.

```
<%# Eval("expression") %>
```

In either case, *expression* usually is a field name from a database table or a column name in a DataRow. It can also be a property name of a class. Thus, the data-binding expression for the earlier data-binding example would look like the following:

```
<%# Eval("LastName") %>
```

One of the overloads for the Eval method takes an additional parameter that specifies the formatting to be applied to the value. The syntax for this overload is

```
<%# Eval("expression", "format") %>
```

The format parameter is a string value that uses something called value placeholder replacement syntax. An example of this might look like

```
<%# Eval("Price", "{0:c}") %>
```

In this example, the "{0:c}" is a composite *formatting string*. The 0 in that string is an indexed placeholder that corresponds to a list of values to be formatted. (There is only one item in the list, so it will always be 0.) The c after the colon is one of the predefined characters (such as C for currency, or D for the long version of the date) that indicate how to format the indexed value.

Tables 10.2 and 10.3 specify many of the common format string predefined characters.

Table 10.2 Common Numeric Format Strings

String Value	Description
C or c	The number is displayed as a string representing a currency amount.
D or d	The number is converted to a string of decimal digits (0–9), prefixed by a minus sign if the number is negative. This format is supported for integral types only.
E or e	The number is converted to a string of the form "-d.ddd...E+ddd" or "-d.ddd...e+ddd", where each d indicates a digit (0–9).
F or f	The number is converted to a string of the form "-ddd.ddd..." where each d indicates a digit (0–9). The precision specifier indicates the desired number of decimal places.
P or p	The number is converted to a string that represents a percent. The converted number is multiplied by 100 in order to be presented as a percentage.
X or x	The number is converted to a string of hexadecimal digits. The case of the format specifier indicates whether to use uppercase or lowercase characters for the hexadecimal digits greater than 9.

Table 10.3   Common Date and Time Format Strings

String Value	Description
d	Displays a short date.
D	Displays a long date.
t	Displays a short time.
T	Displays a long time.
f	Displays a combination of the long date and short time patterns, separated by a space.
g	Displays a combination of the short date and short time patterns, separated by a space.
G	Displays a combination of the short date and long time patterns, separated by a space.

Composite formatting can also use a custom format string (instead of the predefined characters) made up of a combination of text and formatting characters. An example of a custom format string is

```
<%# Eval("SalesDate", "{0:dddd d MMMM YYYY}") %>
```

This indicates that the SalesDate value should display the day of the week, the day number, the month, and then the year—for instance Tuesday April 24 2005. Tables 10.4 and 10.5 show many of the common custom format characters.

Table 10.4   Common Custom Numeric Format Strings

String Value	Description
0	If the value being formatted has a digit in the position where the 0 appears in the format string, that digit is copied to the result string.
#	If the value being formatted has a digit in the position where the # appears in the format string, that digit is copied to the result string. Otherwise, nothing is stored in that position in the result string.
.	The first . character in the format string determines the location of the decimal separator in the formatted value; any additional . characters are ignored.

Table 10.4   Common Custom Numeric Format Strings *(continued)*

String Value	Description
,	If the format string contains a , character between two digit placeholders (0 or #) and to the left of the decimal point if one is present, the output will have thousand separators inserted between each group of three digits to the left of the decimal separator.
%	Causes a number to be multiplied by 100 before it is formatted. The appropriate symbol is inserted in the number itself at the location where the % appears in the format string.

Table 10.5   Common Custom Date/Time Format Strings

String Value	Description
d	Displays the current day (number between 1...31) of the month
ddd	Displays abbreviated name of the day
dddd	Displays the full name of the day
M	Displays the month as a number between 1...12
MMM	Displays abbreviated name of the month
MMMM	Displays the full name of the month
y	Displays the year as a two-digit number
yyyy	Displays the year as a four-digit number

DataList Control

The **DataList control** displays data items in a repeating list. The developer must specify which particular data items in the data source to display in this list. This is done by using data-binding expressions within the `ItemTemplate` element.

For instance, assume that your page contains the following data source control.

```
<asp:SqlDataSource ID="dsPubs" runat="server"
    ProviderName="System.Data.SqlClient"
    ConnectionString="<%$ ConnectionStrings:BookCatalog %>"
    SelectCommand=
        "Select PublisherId, PublisherName From Publishers" />
```

CORE NOTE

For simplicity and brevity sake, many of the examples in this chapter make use of the `SqlDataSource` or the `ObjectDataSource` controls. For more information on these controls, see Chapter 9.

You can now define a `DataList` control that displays the `PublisherName` field in a list.

```
<asp:DataList ID="dlstPub" runat="server" DataSourceID="dsPubs">
   <ItemTemplate>
      <%# Eval("PublisherName") %>
   </ItemTemplate>
</asp:DataList>
```

The `DataList` must contain an `ItemTemplate` that specifies the content for the item and its layout. This template simply contains a data-binding expression that references the `PublisherName` field from the data source. The result in the browser looks like that shown in Figure 10.8.

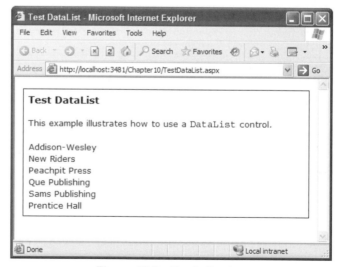

Figure 10.8   Simple DataList

If you view the source for this page in the browser, you will see that this `DataList` has rendered itself as an HTML `<table>`. You can change this rendering by adding the `RepeatLayout` attribute.

```
<asp:DataList ID="dlstPub" runat="server" DataSourceID="dsPubs"
    RepeatLayout="Flow">
```

Using flow layout renders the list using HTML <span> and <br> elements. If you change the list back to using tables, you can add some grid lines as well as change the orientation of the list and the number of list columns, using the GridLines, RepeatDirection, and RepeatColumns attributes. The result in the browser looks like that shown in Figure 10.9.

```
<asp:DataList ID="dlstPub" runat="server" DataSourceID="dsPubs"
    RepeatLayout="Table" RepeatDirection="Horizontal"
    RepeatColumns="2" GridLines="Both">
```

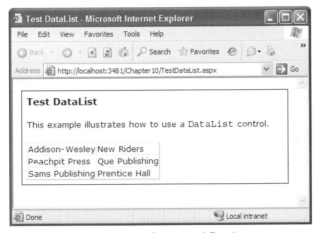

Figure 10.9 Customized DataList

Table 10.6 lists the notable properties (not including the template elements and their styles) of the DataList control.

Table 10.6 Notable Properties of the DataList Control

Property	Description
ExtractTemplateRows	Specifies whether the rows of a Table control defined in each template of a DataList control are extracted and displayed. All rows extracted from the templates of the DataList control are displayed in a single table. Default is false.
GridLines	The grid line style for the list. Possible values are described by the GridLines enumeration (Both, Horizontal, None, Vertical).

Table 10.6 Notable Properties of the DataList Control *(continued)*

Property	Description
RepeatColumns	The number of columns to display in the list.
RepeatDirection	Specifies whether the items are displayed horizontally or vertically.
RepeatLayout	Specifies whether the items are rendered as an HTML <table> or as simple HTML elements. Possible values are described by the RepeatLayout enumeration (Flow, Table).
ShowFooter	Specifies whether the footer template should be displayed.
ShowHeader	Specifies whether the header template should be displayed.

Of course, you can improve the look of this rather plain looking DataList by changing some of the styling attributes of the DataList, as shown in the following example.

```
<asp:DataList ID="dlstPub" runat="server" DataSourceID="dsPubs"
   RepeatLayout="Table" RepeatDirection="Vertical"
   GridLines="Both" RepeatColumns="2" CellPadding="5"
   BackColor="Khaki" ForeColor="Brown" BorderColor="Goldenrod">
```

The appearance of the DataList control (and all the other controls covered in this chapter) can be further customized by setting various templates and style elements. There is a style template for each data template supported by the DataList. Thus, there is a style element for each general template (e.g., ItemStyle, HeaderStyle, FooterStyle for ItemTemplate, HeaderTemplate, and FooterTemplate).

For each of these DataList style templates, you can modify the font, border, color, and size of the element referenced by the template. However, as we discussed back in Chapter 6, it might be advantageous to instead define the styling within an external CSS file. For instance, imagine that you have the following style template.

```
<ItemStyle BackColor="Khaki" ForeColor="Red" Font-Size="Small"/>
```

Rather than define the color and font styling within the ItemStyle, you could do so in a CSS class.

```
.myDataListItem { background-color: Khaki; color: Red;
                  Font-size: small; }
```

With this CSS class defined, you can now reference it within the style template using the CssClass attribute.

```
<ItemStyle CssClass="myDataListItem" />
```

Alternately, you could also define an ASP.NET skin for your `DataList` control as another way of removing repetitive styling attributes from your page's markup.

It should be noted that you also can use the Auto Format option in the Visual Studio Designer to apply a predefined set of templates and styles to your `DataList` (or any of the other controls in this chapter), as shown in Figure 10.10. This figure also shows that the Properties window within the Designer (see Figure 10.10) can also facilitate the customization of a `DataList`.

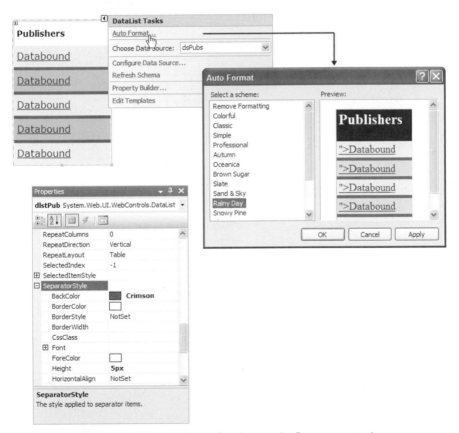

Figure 10.10   Modifying a DataList via the Properties window

Using General Templates

All the controls in this chapter support the general templates described in Table 10.1. The following sample `DataList` demonstrates the use of some of these different templates.

```
<asp:DataList ID="dlstPub" runat="server" DataSourceID="dsPubs"
    CellPadding="5" RepeatLayout="Table">

  <HeaderTemplate>
    <h2>Publishers</h2>
  </HeaderTemplate>

  <ItemTemplate>
    <%# Eval("PublisherName") %>
  </ItemTemplate>

  <ItemStyle BackColor="AntiqueWhite" ForeColor="Brown"
      Font-Size="Medium" Width="150" Height="25" />

  <AlternatingItemStyle BackColor="silver" />
  <SeparatorStyle BackColor="crimson" Height="5" />
  <SeparatorTemplate></SeparatorTemplate>
</asp:DataList>
```

The result in the browser looks similar to that shown in Figure 10.11.

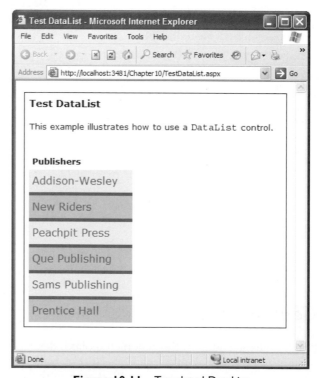

Figure 10.11   Templated DataList

Notice that the `ItemStyle` settings are inherited by the alternating item values. The empty `SeparatorTemplate` is necessary for the `SeparatorStyle` settings to be applied.

The `ItemTemplate` can also be used to contain an embedded HTML `<table>` element. Recall that the `DataList` is by default rendered as an HTML `<table>` with multiple rows but only a single column. This means that all content specified within the `ItemTemplate` are rendered within the table's `<td>` elements. Thus, you can embed a table within the `ItemTemplate`, as shown in the following example.

```
<ItemTemplate>
    <table>
        <tr>
            <td>
                <img src="images/<%# Eval("ISBN") %>.gif"
                    alt="<%# Eval("Title") %>"/>
            </td>
            <td valign="top">
                <p><b><%# Eval("Title") %></b></p>
            </td>
        </tr>
    </table>
</ItemTemplate>
```

In this example, you could replace the `<img>` tag with an `Image` control. However, to do so requires a somewhat more complicated data-binding expression.

```
<asp:Image ID="imgBook" runat="server"
    ImageUrl='<%# String.Format("images/{0}.gif",
        Eval("ISBN")) %>'
    AlternateText='<%# Eval("Title")%>' />
```

Notice that the `ImageUrl` attribute uses the `Format` method to construct the image filename. What happens if you simply try to combine the `Eval` method call within the filename, as shown in the following?

```
ImageUrl='images/<%# Eval("ISBN") %>.gif'
```

Unfortunately, the data-binding expression is not recognized by the ASP.NET parser, and so it thus renders the `Image` control, as follows.

```
<img src="images/<%# Eval("ISBN") %>.gif" alt="…">
```

Linking Pages with the DataList

The previous examples demonstrated the templates and styling options available to the `DataList`. In fact, within the `ItemTemplate`, any valid HTML content or structuring tags are allowed. For instance, if you want to display both the `FirstName` and

`LastName` fields from some data source on separate lines, you could do so by using the following.

```
<asp:DataList ID="dlstPub" runat="server" DataSourceID="dsPubs">
   <ItemTemplate>
      <%# Eval("FirstName") %>
      <br/>
      <%# Eval("LastName") %>
   </ItemTemplate>
</asp:DataList>
```

You can use this capability to turn `DataList` items into links to other pages, simply by adding an HTML `<a>` element to the `ItemTemplate`. This approach is generally used in conjunction with a querystring for passing data from one page to another. Figure 10.12 illustrates this process.

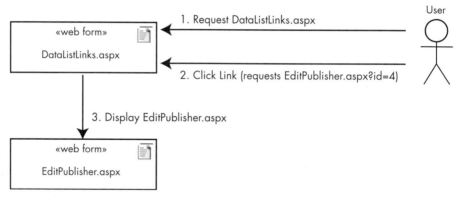

Figure 10.12   Passing information between a DataList and another page

You can implement this flow by extending your earlier `DataList` that displayed all the publisher names, so that each name in the list is a link to a page named `Edit-Publisher.aspx` that allows the user to edit publisher information.

```
<asp:DataList ID="dlstPub" runat="server" DataSourceID="dsPubs">
   <ItemTemplate>
      <a href="EditPublisher.aspx?id=<%# Eval("PublisherId") %>">
      <%# Eval("PublisherName") %>
      </a>
   </ItemTemplate>
</asp:DataList>
```

In this example, each link passes the current `PublisherId` to the `EditPub-lisher.aspx` page via a querystring parameter.

Although the `DataList` supports the editing and selecting of data, this chapter does not demonstrate these capabilities. We instead demonstrate the selecting and editing of data later in this chapter's sections on the `FormView`, `DetailsView`, and `GridView` controls.

Repeater Control

Like the `DataList` control, the ***Repeater control*** displays items in a repeating list. Unlike the `DataList` control, the `Repeater` does not have an inherent look—for example, it does not by default create a vertical list of data or a HTML `<table>` element. Instead, you must provide the layout for the control via templates. The `Repeater` only creates the HTML that you specify within the `ItemTemplate` element. Although this usually means more work (by the developer) is required to display a simple list of data, it may be preferred to the `DataList` by developers who prefer the complete control that the `Repeater` provides over the generated HTML.

Just like the `DataList`, the `Repeater` output is specified by using templates. However, the `Repeater` control only supports `HeaderTemplate`, `ItemTemplate`, `AlternatingItemTemplate`, `SeparatorTemplate`, and `FooterTemplate`. The `Repeater` does *not* support any of the style elements (e.g., `ItemStyle`, `Header-Style`), nor does it support the editing of data.

The following example illustrates one possible use of the `Repeater` control. It outputs a list of images and textual information as shown in Figure 10.13.

This type of list could have been generated by embedding a `<table>` element within the `ItemTemplate` of a `DataList` control. However, many designers prefer to only use HTML tables for data tables and not for layout; instead, they prefer to use CSS to lay out this type of list. One popular, nontable-based approach for such a layout is to use an HTML definition list `<dl>` element. The `<dl>` element can be used to tie together items that exist in a direct relationship with one another. It contains a list of definition term `<dt>` elements; each definition term can be followed by multiple definition description `<dd>` elements. Thus, you could mark up the list shown in Figure 10.13 by using the following definition list (as well as some CSS classes to implement the actual layout).

```
<dl>
   <dt>book title</dt>
   <dd class="bookImage">
      Book image here
   </dd>
   <dd class="publisher">
      Publisher info here
   </dd>
   <dd>
```

```
    Book description here
  </dd>
  ...
</dl>
```

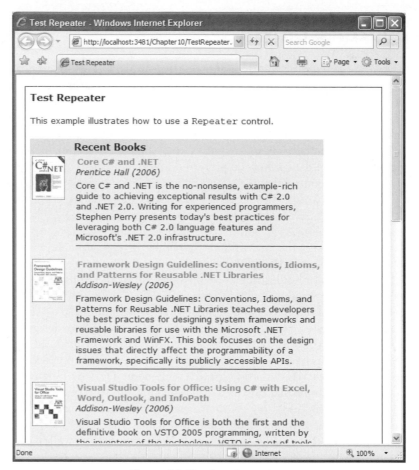

Figure 10.13   Sample repeater

Because in this case you want ASP.NET to emit your list using very particular markup, the `Repeater` is the ideal control to use. For this example, the `Repeater` looks like that shown in the following example.

```
<asp:Repeater ID="rptArtists" runat="server"
   DataSourceID="dsBooks">
```

```
<HeaderTemplate>
    <h2 class="listHeading">Recent Books</h2>
    <dl>
</HeaderTemplate>

<ItemTemplate>
    <dt><%# Eval("Title") %></dt>
    <dd class="bookImage">
      <asp:Image ID="imgBook" runat="server"
        ImageUrl='<%#
           String.Format("images/{0}.gif",Eval("ISBN")) %>'
        AlternateText='<%# Eval("Title")%>' />
    </dd>
    <dd class="publisher">
        <%# Eval("PublisherName") %>
        (<%# Eval("YearPublished") %>)
    </dd>
    <dd>
        <%# Eval("BriefDescription") %>
    </dd>
</ItemTemplate>

<FooterTemplate>
    </dl>
</FooterTemplate>
</asp:Repeater>
```

Although you could style this particular definition list any way that you please, the example shown in Figure 10.13 uses the following CSS.

```
dl { width: 450px; padding: 3px; background-color: #EDECEA;
    margin: 0px;}
dt { float:right; padding: 0; color: #D76600; margin: 0;
    width: 380px; font-weight: bold; font-size: 13px; }
dd { margin: 0;  margin: 0 0 20px 68px;
    border-bottom: 1px solid black;
    padding-bottom: 5px;}
.bookImage { float:left; margin:0;  border-bottom: 0;}
.publisher { border-bottom: 0; font-style: italic;
    margin: 0 0 0 68px;}
.listHeading { background-color: #DDD9CD; margin: 0;
    width: 385px; font-size: 15px;
    padding: 3px 3px 3px 68px; }
```

By changing the CSS to the following, you could change the resulting output to look like that shown in Figure 10.14.

```
dl { margin: 0; padding: 0; width: 40em}
dt { background-color: #EDECEA; padding: 0.5em 0.5em;
```

```
    margin-top: 1em; font-weight: bold; text-align: center;
    border: 1px solid black;}
dd { margin: 0; background-color: #DDD9CD; padding: 1em 0.5em;}
.bookImage { text-align: center; padding: 0.5em;}
.publisher { text-align: center; font-style: italic; }
.listHeading { margin: 0; border-bottom: 1px solid #DDD9CD;
               font-size: 1.2em; text-align: center;}
```

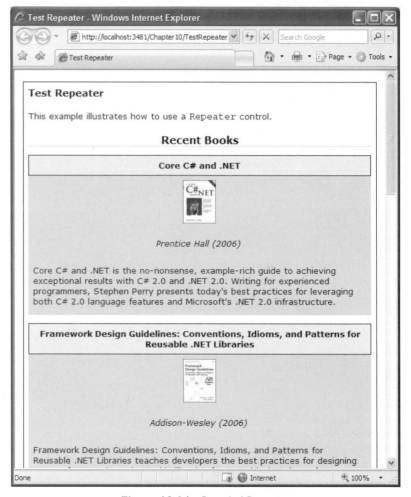

Figure 10.14   Restyled Repeater

The first two controls covered in this chapter provide two ways of displaying multiple data records. The next two controls to be covered (`FormView` and `DetailsView`) provide two ways of displaying a single data record.

FormView Control

The ***FormView control*** displays a single record of data. It provides a built-in mechanism for navigating from record to record; as well, it supports the updating, insertion, and deletion of a record. As a result, the `FormView` control provides a way to create a Web-based data-entry form somewhat analogous to the forms in a program like Microsoft Access or Oracle Forms.

In the previous chapter, there was a series of walkthrough exercises that created a Web Form that displayed a single record of book data that the user could then edit and save to the database. The `FormView` control provides an alternate, completely markup-based approach to creating this same functionality. It also uses the same template approach as the `Repeater` control.

Let us assume that the control is data bound to the following `SqlDataSource` control.

```
<asp:SqlDataSource ID="dsBooks" runat="server"
    ConnectionString="<%$ ConnectionStrings:Books %>"
    SelectCommand=
        "SELECT ISBN,Title,PublisherName,Books.PublisherId,
            YearPublished,BriefDescription FROM Books
            INNER JOIN Publishers ON
            Books.PublisherId=Publishers.PublisherId" />
```

You can now define a `FormView` control as follows. The result (with some CSS styling) in the browser might look like that shown in Figure 10.15.

```
<asp:FormView ID="frmvBooks" runat="server"
    DataSourceID="dsBooks"
    CssClass="entireForm">

    <HeaderTemplate>
        <h2>Book Details</h2>
    </HeaderTemplate>

    <HeaderStyle CssClass="singleBookTitle" />

    <ItemTemplate>
        <div class="singleBook">
        ISBN: <br />
        <asp:Label ID="labIsbn" runat="server"
            Text='<%# Eval("ISBN") %>' CssClass="dataValues" />
        <br />
        Title:<br />
        <asp:Label ID="labTitle" runat="server"
            Text='<%# Eval("Title") %>' CssClass="dataValues" />
        <br />
        Publisher:<br />
```

```
    <asp:Label ID="labPublisher" runat="server"
       Text='<%# Eval("PublisherName") %>'
       CssClass="dataValues" />
    <br />
    Year:<br />
    <asp:Label ID="labDesc" runat="server"
       Text='<%# Eval("YearPublished") %>'
       CssClass="dataValues" />
    <br />
    Description:<br />
    <asp:Label ID="Label1" runat="server"
      Text='<%# Eval("BriefDescription") %>'
      CssClass="dataValues" />
    <br />
    </div>
  </ItemTemplate>
</asp:FormView>
```

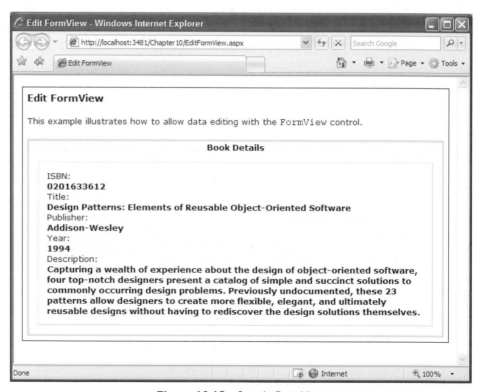

Figure 10.15   Sample FormView

CORE NOTE

Unlike the somewhat similar single record editor example from the previous chapter, the `FormView` control can be quite inefficient if it is being used as a way to browse through a set of records. The reason for this is that, for each postback, the control retrieves the full set of data, even though it only displays a single record.

Just like the `Repeater` control covered earlier in this chapter, the `FormView` requires you to specify the layout of the data values via the `ItemTemplate` element. The `HeaderTemplate` and the `FooterTemplate` can be used to add a header and footer to the control. Anything placed in these templates is rendered within its own row in an HTML `<table>` element. As well, just like the `Repeater`, the `FormView` control supports an equivalent style element for each template. For instance, in the preceding example, there is a `HeaderStyle` element for customizing the appearance of the content within the `HeaderTemplate`.

Table 10.7 lists the notable properties (not including the template elements and their styles) of the `FormView` control.

Table 10.7 Notable Properties of the FormView Control

Property	Description
AllowPaging	Specifies whether the control's paging is enabled.
BackImageUrl	URL of image to display in background of control.
Caption	The text to render as table caption. The caption provides accessibility technologies with a description of the form.
CaptionAlign	Specifies where the caption is to appear relative to the form. Possible values are described by the `TableCaptionAlign` enumeration (`Bottom`, `Left`, `NotSet`, `Right`, and `Top`).
CellPadding	The amount of space in pixels between the contents of a cell and the cell's border.
CellSpacing	The amount of space in pixels between cells.
DataItem	The actual data object that is bound to the control.
DataItemCount	The number of items in the underlying data source.
DataItemIndex	The index of the currently displayed record in the data object.

Table 10.7   Notable Properties of the FormView Control *(continued)*

Property	Description
DataKey	The DataKey collection that contains the primary keys for the current record.
DataKeyNames	The field names for the fields that will be stored in the DataKey collection.
DefaultMode	Specifies the initial data-entry mode for the control. Possible values are described by the FormViewMode enumeration (Edit, Insert, ReadOnly).
EmptyDataText	The text that appears in the control if the data source has no data.
FooterText	The text to appear in the footer area of the control.
GridLines	The grid line style for the list. Possible values are described by the GridLines enumeration (Both, Horizontal, None, Vertical).
HeaderText	The text to appear in the header area of the control.
HorizontalAlign	The horizontal alignment of the control on the page.
PageIndex	The index of the currently displayed record.
SelectedValue	The key value of the current record.

Moving from Record to Record

Although the FormView control displays a single record of data, it can accept a data source containing multiple records. In the example shown in Figure 10.15, only the first record of the data source is displayed. However, you can allow the user to move from record to record by setting the control's AllowPaging property to true.

```
<asp:FormView ID="frmvBooks" runat="server"
  DataSourceID="dsBooks" CssClass="entireForm"
  AllowPaging="true">
```

The result in the browser is shown in Figure 10.16.

You can modify the styling of the record navigation by adding a PagerStyle element. You can also customize the way the paging works via the PagerSettings element. For instance, the following PagerSettings element reduces the number of page numbers to just three, and adds either a first or last page button as well as a button to move to the next three records, as shown in Figure 10.17.

```
<PagerSettings Mode="NumericFirstLast" PageButtonCount="3"/>
```

Figure 10.16　FormView with default paging enabled

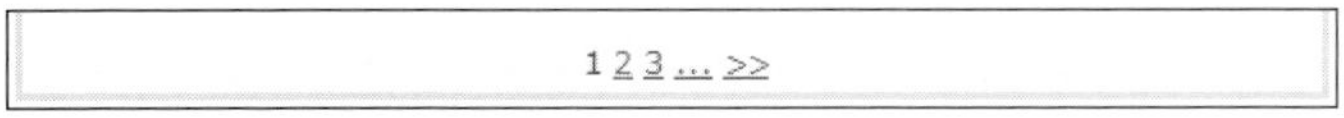

1 2 3 ... >>

Figure 10.17　FormView with pager settings

If you want to replace the navigation record numbers with buttons to move forward and back a record at a time, you could change the Mode property to NextPrevious or to NextPreviousFirstLast (this also provides buttons for moving to the first and last record), as shown in Figure 10.18.

You can replace the default text for the next, previous, first, and last buttons via the NextPageText, PreviousPageText, and so on properties. You can also replace the text entirely for these buttons and use images instead, as shown in the following. The result in the browser is shown in Figure 10.19.

```
<PagerSettings Mode="NextPreviousFirstLast"
   FirstPageImageUrl="images/page_first.gif"
   LastPageImageUrl="images/page_last.gif"
```

```
NextPageImageUrl="images/page_next.gif"
   PreviousPageImageUrl="images/page_previous.gif"/>
```

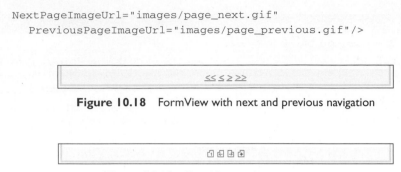

Figure 10.18 FormView with next and previous navigation

Figure 10.19 FormView with navigation images

You can also customize the layout of the navigation buttons by using the Pager-
Template. In such a case, you simply add the appropriate Button controls and set
their CommandName to Page and their CommandArgument to First, Next, Previous,
or Last. For instance, the following PagerTemplate places the next and previous
buttons on top of the first and last buttons. The result in the browser is shown in
Figure 10.20.

```
<PagerTemplate>
   <asp:ImageButton id="ibtnPrev" runat="server"
      CommandName="Page" CommandArgument="Previous"
      ImageUrl="images/page_previous.gif" />
   <asp:ImageButton id="ibtnNext" runat="server"
      CommandName="Page" CommandArgument="Next"
      ImageUrl="images/page_next.gif" />
   <br />
   <asp:ImageButton id="ibtnFirst" runat="server"
      CommandName="Page" CommandArgument="First"
      ImageUrl="images/page_first.gif" />
   <asp:ImageButton id="ibtnLast" runat="server"
      CommandName="Page" CommandArgument="Last"
      ImageUrl="images/page_last.gif" />
</PagerTemplate>
```

Figure 10.20 FormView with custom navigation

Modifying Data

The FormView control can also be used to provide the user with the ability to edit
the data in a single record. To do so requires three steps:

1. Adding one or more buttons to the `ItemTemplate` that changes the `Form-View` to edit, insert, or delete mode. The buttons must have a `CommandName` of `New`, `Edit`, or `Delete`.
2. Define an `EditItemTemplate` and/or `InsertItemTemplate` template that allows the user to edit existing data or enter new data. These templates typically include controls that take user input, such as `TextBox`, `CheckBox`, or `DropDownList` controls. These templates also require buttons that commit or cancel the changes. If you do not supply an `InsertItemTemplate`, it simply uses the layout defined by `EditItemTemplate`.
3. Specify the `DataKeyNames` property of the `FormView` control. This property indicates the field name that represents the key field in the data source.

The ability to modify data with the `FormView` requires that it be bound to a data source control for your data binding (i.e., it uses `DataSourceId` and not data binding programmatically via the `DataSource` property). This data source control must have its `UpdateCommand` (and/or `InsertCommand` and `DeleteCommand`) set appropriately. For instance, to allow us to modify the book data from our example, you could add the following to the `SqlDataSource` control.

```
UpdateCommand="UPDATE Books SET Title=@Title,
   YearPublished=@YearPublished,BriefDescription=@BriefDescription
   WHERE ISBN=@ISBN"
```

You do not need to specify the `UpdateParameters` because the control assumes that the parameter names match the field names. After the data source control has been set up, you can implement these three steps. The first is the simplest. To provide an editing interface to your current example, you only need to add an edit `LinkButton` somewhere within the `ItemTemplate`.

```
<asp:LinkButton ID="lbtnEdit" runat="server" CommandName="Edit"
   Text="Edit Book" />
```

By adding a `Button` with this `CommandName` to the `ItemTemplate`, the `Form-View` automatically handles the event handling for the `Button`. This built-in event handler displays the control as defined in the `EditItemTemplate`. The following example illustrates an `EditItemTemplate` for your sample data.

```
<EditItemTemplate>
   <div class="singleBook">
   ISBN:
   <br />
   <asp:Label ID="labEditIsbn" runat="server"
      CssClass="dataValues"
      Text='<%# Eval("ISBN") %>' /><br />
```

```
Title:<br />
<asp:TextBox ID="txtTitle" runat="server"
    CssClass="dataValues"
    Text='<%# Bind("Title") %>' Columns="75" /><br />
Year:<br />
<asp:TextBox ID="txtYear" runat="server"
    CssClass="dataValues"
    Text='<%# Bind("YearPublished") %>' Columns="4" /><br />
Description:<br />
<asp:TextBox ID="txtDesc" runat="server"
    Text='<%# Bind("BriefDescription") %>'
    CssClass="dataValues"
    Columns="60" Rows="5" TextMode="MultiLine" /><br />

<asp:RequiredFieldValidator ID="reqTitle" runat="server"
    ControlToValidate="txtTitle"
    ErrorMessage="Title can not be blank" />

<div class="actionBar">
    <asp:LinkButton ID="lbtnUpdate" runat="server"
        Text="Save Changes" CommandName="Update" />
    <asp:LinkButton ID="lbtnCancel" runat="server"
        Text="Cancel Changes" CommandName="Cancel" />
</div>
</div>
</EditItemTemplate>
```

There are several things worth noting about the preceding code. The first notable thing is that this template now uses controls (TextBox controls, in this case) for gathering user input. Because you are updating existing data, you need to populate the controls with the current values for the record; you do this via the Text property of the TextControl. Another important point with this example is that the ISBN value is not user modifiable in a TextBox but is simply displayed in a Label control. Although some database tables may allow you to change key values, often the key field in a database table cannot be updated, either because of referential integrity reasons or because the field is an identity field (that is, the database itself generates its value when the record is first created). As well, notice that this code also uses a validation control to ensure that the user does not leave the Title field empty.

This example also illustrates that the EditItemTemplate requires another button control that tells the control to perform the update. The CommandName property of this button must be set to Update for this to work.

Finally, the other notable point about this example is that the data-binding expressions for populating the controls use the Bind method rather than the Eval method. This method is necessary for enabling the two-way data-binding mechanism introduced with ASP.NET 2.0.

Two-Way Data Binding Using Bind

The `EditItemTemplate` requires not only the reading and display of field data from a data source but also the writing of that field data. ***Two-way data binding*** (see Figure 10.21) refers to the capability for runtime data-binding expressions to indicate not only the data value to read but also the control property that contains the value to be used when writing the data value. Two-way data binding only works with the `FormView`, `DetailsView`, and `GridView` controls.

How does this work? Recall the previously defined `UpdateCommand` for the `Sql-DataSource` control. It contained a SQL `UPDATE` command for three fields (`Title`, `YearPublished`, `BriefDescription`) from the `Books` table. Each of these fields is set to a parameter whose name matches the field name (e.g., `Title=@Title`). When

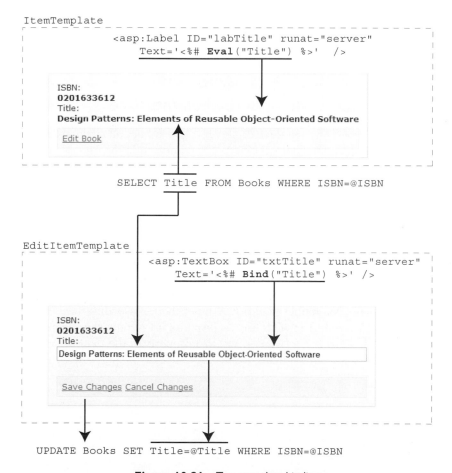

Figure 10.21   Two-way data binding

the `FormView` control is ready to update (e.g., after the user clicks the Update button), it uses whatever control property that was populated by the `Bind` method (e.g., the `Text` property of the `TextBox` control named `txtTitle`) to populate the update parameter (e.g., `@Title`) that matches the field name that was used within the `Bind` method.

The SQL `UPDATE` command does not update every record in the `Books` table but only a single record. Of course, you want to only update the record whose ISBN value matches the ISBN value for the edited record. Your SQL command used a `WHERE` clause with a parameter (e.g., `WHERE ISBN=@ISBN`). This parameter value is populated at update time to the current value of the database field specified by the `DataKeyNames` property of the `FormView` control.

```
<asp:FormView ID="frmvBooks" runat="server"
   DataSourceID="dsBooks" CssClass="entireForm"
   AllowPaging="true" DataKeyNames="Isbn">
```

Because the user cannot change the ISBN value in your database two-way data binding is not necessary for your key field. As a result, the example displays the value in a `Label` control using the `Eval` method.

Using a DropDownList in the Edit Interface

You may have noticed that the `EditItemTemplate` did not allow the user to modify the publisher for the edited book. The `SELECT` command in the example data source control used a SQL `INNER JOIN` to retrieve the appropriate publisher name from the `Publishers` table. However, this approach does not work when editing (or inserting) data. You cannot simply use a `TextBox` for the publisher name because the table being edited (the `Books` table) does not contain the publisher's name but the `PublisherId`, a foreign key linked to the `Publishers` table (see Figure 10.22).

Your editing interface thus must allow the user to specify the `PublisherId` of the publisher. Using a `TextBox` to get this `PublisherId` is not at all appropriate, however, because this `PublisherId` value may not have any meaning to the user. As well, allowing the user to enter the `PublisherId` in a `TextBox` makes it difficult to maintain the data's referential integrity. A much better user interface choice is to instead use a `DropDownList`. This list can display a list of publisher names from the `Publishers` table (using the `DataTextField` property of the `DropDownList`), but use the `PublisherId` as the value (using the `DataValue` property of the list), as shown in Figure 10.23.

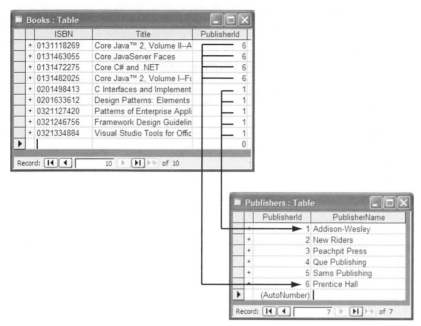

Figure 10.22 Table relationships

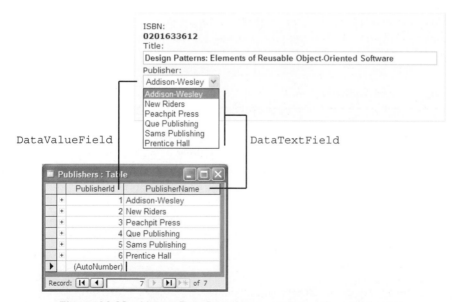

Figure 10.23 Using a DropDownList to maintain referential integrity

Adding this publisher `DropDownList` requires several changes in our example. First, you must change the data source control so that it updates the `PublisherId`.

```
UpdateCommand="UPDATE Books SET
   Title=@Title,PublisherId=@PublisherId,
   YearPublished=@YearPublished,
   BriefDescription=@BriefDescription
   WHERE ISBN=@ISBN"
```

You need to also define a second data source control that populates the `Drop-DownList` with a list of publisher names.

```
<asp:SqlDataSource ID="dsPublisher" runat="server"
   ConnectionString="<%$ ConnectionStrings:Books %>"
   SelectCommand=
      "Select PublisherId,PublisherName From Publishers" />
```

Finally, you need to add the `DropDownList` to your `EditItemTemplate`.

```
Publisher:<br />
<asp:DropDownList ID="drpPublisher" runat="server"
   DataSourceID="dsPublisher" DataValueField="PublisherId"
   DataTextField="PublisherName"
   SelectedValue='<%# Bind("PublisherId") %>' />
```

Notice that the `DataValueField` and `DataTextField` properties are set to the `PublisherId` and `PublisherName` fields. Notice as well that the two-way binding is mapped to the `SelectedValue` property of the list.

Listing 10.1 contains the complete markup for this example, the result of which is shown in the browser in Figure 10.24.

Listing 10.1   EditFormView.aspx

```
<h1>Edit FormView</h1>
<p>
This example illustrates how to allow data editing with the
<code>FormView</code> control.
</p>
<asp:FormView ID="frmvBooks" runat="server"
   DataSourceID="dsBooks"
   CssClass="entireForm" AllowPaging="true" DataKeyNames="Isbn">

   <HeaderTemplate>
      <h2>Book Details</h2>
   </HeaderTemplate>
   <HeaderStyle CssClass="singleBookTitle" />
   <ItemTemplate>
      <div class="singleBook">
```

```
    ISBN: <br />
    <asp:Label ID="labIsbn" runat="server"
      Text='<%# Eval("ISBN") %>' CssClass="dataValues" /><br />
    Title:<br />
    <asp:Label ID="labTitle" runat="server"
      Text='<%# Eval("Title") %>' CssClass="dataValues" />
    <br />
    Publisher:<br />
    <asp:Label ID="labPublisher" runat="server"
      Text='<%# Eval("PublisherName") %>'
      CssClass="dataValues" />
    <br />
    Year:<br />
    <asp:Label ID="labYear" runat="server"
      Text='<%# Eval("YearPublished") %>'
      CssClass="dataValues" />
    <br />
    Description:<br />
    <asp:Label ID="txtDecs" runat="server"
      Text='<%# Eval("BriefDescription") %>'
      CssClass="dataValues" />
    <br />
    <div class="actionBar">
       <asp:LinkButton ID="lbtnEdit" runat="server"
         CommandName="Edit"
         Text="Edit Book" />
    </div>
    </div>
</ItemTemplate>
<EditItemTemplate>
    <div class="singleBook">
    ISBN:
    <br />
    <asp:Label ID="labEditIsbn" runat="server"
        Text='<%# Eval("ISBN") %>' CssClass="dataValues" />
    <br />
    Title:<br />
    <asp:TextBox ID="txtTitle" runat="server"
      CssClass="dataValues"
      Text='<%# Bind("Title") %>' Columns="75" /><br />
    Publisher:<br />
    <asp:DropDownList ID="drpPublisher" runat="server"
      DataSourceID="dsPublisher" DataValueField="PublisherId"
      DataTextField="PublisherName"
      SelectedValue='<%# Bind("PublisherId") %>' />
    <br />
    Year:<br />
    <asp:TextBox ID="txtYear" runat="server"
      CssClass="dataValues"
```

```
            Text='<%# Bind("YearPublished") %>' Columns="4" /><br />
        Description:<br />
        <asp:TextBox ID="txtDesc" runat="server"
           Text='<%# Bind("BriefDescription") %>'
           CssClass="dataValues"
           Columns="60" Rows="5" TextMode="MultiLine" /><br />
        <asp:RequiredFieldValidator ID="reqTitle" runat="server"
           EnableClientScript="false"
           ControlToValidate="txtTitle"
           ErrorMessage="Title can not be blank" />
        <div class="actionBar">
            <asp:LinkButton ID="lbtnUpdate" runat="server"
               Text="Save Changes" CommandName="Update" />
            <asp:LinkButton ID="lbtnCancel" runat="server"
               Text="Cancel Changes" CommandName="Cancel" />
        </div>
        </div>
    </EditItemTemplate>
    <PagerStyle CssClass="singleBookTitle" />
    <PagerSettings Mode="NextPreviousFirstLast"
       FirstPageImageUrl="images/page_first.gif"
       LastPageImageUrl="images/page_last.gif"
       NextPageImageUrl="images/page_next.gif"
       PreviousPageImageUrl="images/page_previous.gif"/>
</asp:FormView>

<asp:SqlDataSource ID="dsBooks" runat="server"
  ProviderName="System.Data.OleDb"
  ConnectionString="<%$ ConnectionStrings:Books %>"
  SelectCommand="SELECT ISBN,Title,PublisherName,
    Books.PublisherId,YearPublished,BriefDescription FROM Books
    INNER JOIN Publishers ON
    Books.PublisherId=Publishers.PublisherId"
  UpdateCommand="UPDATE Books SET Title=@Title,
    PublisherId=@PublisherId,YearPublished=@YearPublished,
    BriefDescription=@BriefDescription WHERE ISBN=@ISBN" />

<asp:SqlDataSource ID="dsPublisher" runat="server"
  ProviderName="System.Data.OleDb"
  ConnectionString="<%$ ConnectionStrings:Books %>"
  SelectCommand=
      "Select PublisherId,PublisherName From Publishers" />
```

Figure 10.24   Finished EditItemTemplate with DropDownList

Modifying Data with an ObjectDataSource Control

You saw in the previous chapter that an `ObjectDataSource` control can be used instead of a `SqlDataSource` control in order to provide a more architecturally sound solution. However, there are a few "tricks" when modifying data using the `ObjectDataSource` control. To demonstrate, assume that you have the following `ObjectDataSource` control defined in your page.

```
<asp:ObjectDataSource ID="dsBooks" runat="server"
   TypeName="BookDA"
   SelectMethod="GetAll"
   UpdateMethod="UpdateBook"

   <UpdateParameters>
      <asp:Parameter Name="isbn" Type="String" />
      <asp:Parameter Name="title" Type="String" />
      <asp:Parameter Name="publisherId" Type="Int32" />
      <asp:Parameter Name="yearPublished" Type="Int32"  />
      <asp:Parameter Name="briefDescription" Type="String" />
   </UpdateParameters>
</asp:ObjectDataSource>
```

With this definition, the `FormView` control expects the method `UpdateBook` to have a very specific method signature. It expects that this `UpdateBook` method takes parameters with names that match the names specified within the various `Bind` method calls used in the data-binding expressions within the `EditItemTemplate`. As a result, your `UpdateBook` method *must* have the following method signature.

```
public void UpdateBook(string isbn, string title,
    int publisherId, int yearPublished, string briefDescription)
```

DetailsView Control

Like the `FormView` control, the ***DetailsView control*** displays a single record of data at a time, provides a way to navigate from record to record, and supports the updating, insertion, or deletion of a record. The `DetailsView` control differs from the `FormView` control in that it does not require the use of templates for defining the look of the control. Instead, it renders each field in the data source as a row in an HTML `<table>` element. As well, it uses a different approach than that used by the `FormView` for specifying the fields that appear in the control. This approach is also used by the `GridView` control.

Assuming you are using the same data source control we defined in the section "FormView Control" on page 599, you can define the simplest `DetailsView` control as follows.

```
<asp:DetailsView ID="detvBooks" runat="server"
   DataSourceID="dsBooks" />
```

The result in the browser looks similar to that shown in Figure 10.25.

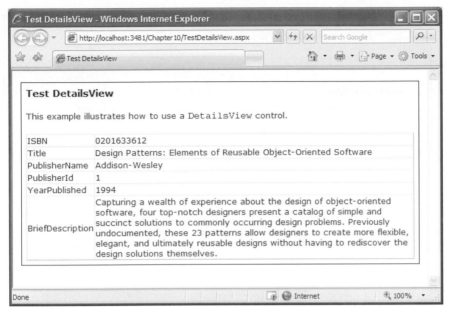

Figure 10.25 Simple DetailsView control

Although quite easy to use, clearly the `DetailsView` control needs some additional customization to make it a bit more useful. For a visual standpoint, you can customize the appearance of the control via its own properties or via style elements, such as `RowStyle`, `HeaderStyle`, and `EditRowStyle`, as shown in the following example (which for illustration purposes uses both the CSS approach and the individual property approach). The result is shown in Figure 10.26.

```
<asp:DetailsView ID="detvBooks" runat="server"
    DataSourceID="dsBooks" GridLines="None"
    AllowPaging="true" CellPadding="4" ForeColor="#333333" >

    <RowStyle VerticalAlign="Top" BackColor="#EFF3FB"/>
    <PagerStyle CssClass="detailsPagerStyle" />
    <FieldHeaderStyle BackColor="#DEE8F5" Font-Bold="True" />
    <HeaderStyle CssClass="detailsHeaderStyle"/>
    <AlternatingRowStyle BackColor="White" />
</asp:DetailsView>
```

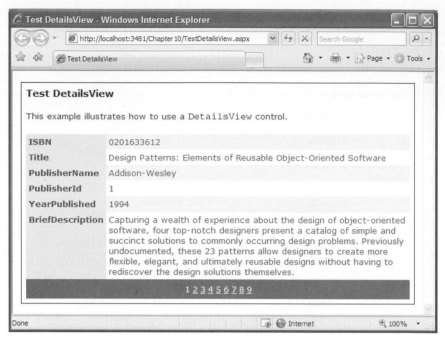

Figure 10.26   Styled DetailsView control

Table 10.8 lists the notable properties (not including the template elements and their styles) of the `DetailsView` control.

Table 10.8   Notable Properties of the DetailsView Control

Property	Description
`AllowPaging`	Specifies whether the control's paging is enabled.
`AutoGenerateDeleteButton`	Specifies whether the control should display a built-in button for deleting current record.
`AutoGenerateEditButton`	Specifies whether the control should display a built-in button for switching control to edit mode.
`AutoGenerateInsertButton`	Specifies whether the control should display a built-in button for switching control to insert mode.
`AutoGenerateRows`	Specifies whether the control should generate a row for each field in the data source.

Table 10.8 Notable Properties of the DetailsView Control *(continued)*

Property	Description
BackImageUrl	URL of image to display in background of control.
DataItem	The actual data object that is bound to the control.
DataItemCount	The number of items in the underlying data source.
DataItemIndex	The index of the currently displayed record in the data object.
DataKey	The DataKey collection that contains the primary keys for the current record.
DataKeyNames	The field names for the fields that are stored in the DataKey collection.
DefaultMode	Specifies the initial data-entry mode for the control. Possible values are described by the DetailsViewMode enumeration (Edit, Insert, ReadOnly).
EmptyDataText	The text that appears in the control if the data source contains no data.
EnablePagingCallbacks	Specifies whether paging operations are performed using client-side callback functions. When enabled, paging is performed using the callback feature, which prevents the need to repost the entire page back to the server when moving from record to record. This means that the paging is done on the client rather than on the server.
FooterText	The text to appear in the footer area of the control.
GridLines	The grid line style for the list. Possible values are described by the GridLines enumeration (Both, Horizontal, None, Vertical).
HeaderText	The text to appear in the header area of the control.
PageIndex	The index of the currently displayed record.
SelectedValue	The key value of the current record.

Customizing the DetailsView Fields

You can also customize the fields that appear in the DetailsView control. The first two examples of the DetailsView control simply displayed every field from the data source in the order that they appeared in the data source. However, you can customize this display. There are two steps in getting the DetailsView to display only a subset of the fields in the data source. The first is to change the AutoGenerateRows property of the DetailsView to false.

```
<asp:DetailsView AutoGenerateRows="false" … />
```

The AutoGenerateRows property indicates whether the control should or should not automatically generate a table row for each field. The second step is to explicitly specify which fields you do want to display via the Fields element within the DetailsView control. The Fields element can contain any of the following field types listed in Table 10.9.

Table 10.9 Field Types

Name	Description
BoundField	Displays the value of the field as text.
ButtonField	Displays a command button.
CheckBoxField	Displays the value of a field as a CheckBox control.
CommandField	Displays built-in Command buttons for edit, insert, and delete commands.
HyperLinkField	Displays the value of a field as a HyperLink control.
ImageField	Displays an image.
TemplateField	Displays the field using a user-defined layout.

All of the field type classes inherit from the DataControlField base class. This base class represents the common functionality needed for any of these concrete field types in Table 10.9. The notable properties for the DataControlField are listed in Table 10.10.

Table 10.10   Notable Properties of the DataControlField

Property	Description
AccessibleHeaderText	Text that is output as the abbr attribute in the rendered table (only for fields within GridView).
ControlStyle	The style settings for any controls contained within the field.
FooterStyle	The style settings for the footer for the field.
FooterText	The text to appear in footer for the field.
HeaderImageUrl	The URL of the image to appear in header for the field.
HeaderStyle	The style settings for the header for the field.
HeaderText	The text to appear in header for the field.
InsertVisible	Sets whether the field is visible when parent control is in insert mode.
ItemStyle	The style settings for textual content displayed for the field.
ShowHeader	Specifies whether the header for the field is displayed.
SortExpression	The sort expression for the field that may be used by the parent control to control sorting.
Visible	Specifies whether the field is visible.

CORE NOTE

The subproperties within ControlStyle, FooterStyle, HeaderStyle, and ItemStyle can be set within the field element itself or within embedded elements. This example illustrates the first approach.

```
<asp:BoundField … HeaderStyle-BackColor="green" />
```

This next example illustrates the use of an embedded element.

```
<asp:BoundField … >
    <HeaderStyle BackColor="green"/>
</asp:BoundField>
```

The Fields element of the DetailsView control thus acts as a container for the different field types. The GridView control covered later in this chapter has a Columns element that also can contain these same field types. The following example illustrates how this `Fields` element can be used to customize the fields that appear in the `DetailsView` control.

```
<asp:DetailsView ID="detvBooks" runat="server"
   DataSourceID="dsBooks"
   AutoGenerateRows="false" CellPadding="5">

   <Fields>
      <asp:BoundField DataField="ISBN" HeaderText="Isbn:" />
      <asp:BoundField DataField="Title" HeaderText="Title:" />
      <asp:BoundField DataField="PublisherName"
         HeaderText="Publisher:" />
      <asp:BoundField DataField="YearPublished"
         HeaderText="Year:" />
      <asp:BoundField DataField="BriefDescription"
         HeaderText="Description:" />
   </Fields>
</asp:DetailsView>
```

This `DetailsView` control displays just the five fields defined by its five `Bound-Field` controls. Within the `BoundField` element, the `DataField` property specifies the field name in the data source that is to be displayed; the `HeaderText` property specifies the label for the data field.

Besides the properties listed in Table 10.10, `BoundField` also includes the additional properties shown in Table 10.11.

Table 10.11 Notable Properties of the BoundField

Property	Description
ApplyFormatInEditMode	Specifies whether the `DataFormatString` should be used when parent control is in edit mode. The default is `false`.
ConvertEmptyStringToNull	Indicates whether empty string values are converted to database nulls when data is updated. The default is `true`.
DataField	The field name from the data source that is displayed in the field.
DataFormatString	The composite format string (see Tables 10.2 through 10.5) for the field is ignored if `HtmlEncode` is set to `true`.
HtmlEncode	Indicates whether the data source value for this field should be HTML-encoded before it is rendered in the control. The default is `true` (which prevents `DataFormatString` from being applied).

Table 10.11 Notable Properties of the BoundField *(continued)*

Property	Description
NullDisplayText	The text displayed if the data source field contains a null.
ReadOnly	Indicates whether the field can be modified in edit mode.

Using the ImageField

The ImageField type can be used to display an image file whose filename is in some part constructed from a value from the data source. Besides the properties listed in Table 10.10, ImageField also includes the properties shown in Table 10.12.

Table 10.12 Notable Properties of the ImageField

Property	Description
AlternateText	The text to be rendered as an alt attribute in the resulting <img> element. This is to be used when the alt attribute is not retrieved from the data source.
ConvertEmptyStringToNull	Indicates whether empty string values are converted to database nulls when data is updated. The default is true.
DataAlternateTextField	The field name from the data source for the field that contains the values that are used for the alt attribute in the resulting <img> element.
DataAlternateTextFormatString	The format string to be used for the alt attribute in the resulting <img> element.
DataImageUrlField	The field name from the data source for the field that contains the values that are used for the filename for the resulting <img> element.
DataImageUrlFormatString	The format string to be used for the filename for the resulting <img> element.
NullDisplayText	The text to be displayed if the data source field contains a null.
NullImageUrl	The URL of the image to be displayed when the field specified by DataImageUrlField is null.
ReadOnly	Indicates whether the field can be modified in edit mode.

You can add an `ImageField` type to your example so as to display an image of the book cover, as shown in the following example.

```
<asp:ImageField HeaderText="Cover:" DataImageUrlField="Isbn"
    DataImageUrlFormatString="images/{0}.gif"
    DataAlternateTextField="Title"
    DataAlternateTextFormatString="Book cover for {0}" />
```

In this example, the filename for the image is specified by the `DataImageUrl-FormatString` property. The `0` within the format string is a placeholder for the data field value specified by the `DataImageUrlField` property. The `DataAlternate-TextFormatString` and `DataAlternateTextField` properties are for specifying the rendered `<img>` element's `alt` attribute. For the first record in your sample `BooksCatalog` database, the preceding field is rendered as shown here.

```
<img src="images/0201633612.gif" alt="Book cover for Design
    Patterns: Elements of Reusable Object-Oriented Software" />
```

Modifying DetailsView Data

Like the `FormView` control, the `DetailsView` control supports the in-place editing of data. Also like the `FormView` control, the `DetailsView` control uses the update capability of the underlying data source control to perform the writing of data to the data source. The `DetailsView` control does differ from the `FormView` control in that the control itself generates default user interface elements (`TextBox` controls) for the fields.

The `DetailsView` control can automatically add Edit, Delete, or Insert buttons via the `AutoGenerateEditButton`, `AutoGenerateDeleteButton`, and `Auto-GenerateInsertButton` properties.

```
<asp:DetailsView ID="detvBooks" runat="server"
    DataSourceID="dsBooks"
    AllowPaging="true" AutoGenerateRows="false"
    DataKeyNames="Isbn"
    AutoGenerateEditButton="True"
    AutoGenerateInsertButton="true" >
```

This adds a row before the page navigation row with an `Edit` and an `Insert` link. Notice as well that you will also have to indicate the key field in the data record via the `DataKeyNames` property (just as you did when modifying data using the `Form-View` control).

If you want to customize this row, you could disable the auto-generation of the buttons, and add a `CommandField` to the `Fields` element.

```
<asp:DetailsView ID="detvBooks" runat="server"
    DataSourceID="dsBooks" AllowPaging="true"
```

```
AutoGenerateEditButton="False"
AutoGenerateInsertButton="False">

<Fields>
  <asp:BoundField … />

  …

  <asp:CommandField EditText="Edit Book"
     ShowEditButton="True"
     ShowInsertButton="true" NewText="Add Book"/>
</Fields>

…

<asp:DetailsView
```

CommandField adds a row that contains command buttons for signaling the selection, updating, insertion, or deletion of data. Figure 10.27 illustrates how the preceding example might appear in the browser in normal, edit, and insert mode.

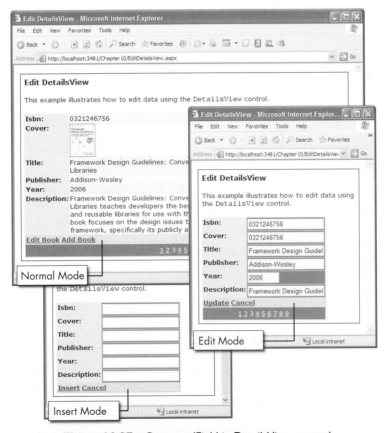

Figure 10.27   CommandField in DetailsView control

Besides the properties listed in Table 10.10, CommandField also includes the properties listed in Table 10.13.

Table 10.13   Notable Properties of the CommandField

Property	Description
ButtonType	Specifies the button type to use for the different buttons in the field. Possible values are described by the ButtonType enumeration (Button, Image, Link).
CancelImageUrl	Image to display for the Cancel button.
CancelText	Text caption to display for Cancel button.
CausesValidation	Specifies whether validation is to be performed when user clicks a button in the field. Default is true.
DeleteImageUrl	Image to display for the Delete button.
DeleteText	Text caption to display for the Delete button.
EditImageUrl	Image to display for the Edit button.
EditText	Text caption to display for the Edit button.
InsertImageUrl	Image to display for the Insert button (which is displayed when control is in insert mode and which commits the new record).
InsertText	Text caption to display for the Insert button.
NewImageUrl	Image to display for the New button (which switches control to insert mode).
NewText	Text caption to display for the New button.
SelectImageUrl	Image to display for the Select button.
SelectText	Text caption to display for the Select button.
ShowCancelButton	Specifies whether a Cancel button is. This button is displayed when control is in edit or insert mode.
ShowDeleteButton	Specifies whether a Delete button is displayed. This button deletes the current record.
ShowEditButton	Specifies whether an Edit button is displayed. This button changes the control to edit mode.

Table 10.13 Notable Properties of the CommandField *(continued)*

Property	Description
ShowInsertButton	Specifies whether an Insert button is displayed. This button changes the control to insert mode.
ShowSelectButton	Specifies whether a Select button is displayed. Selecting a record is generally more useful with the GridView control.
UpdateImageUrl	Image to display for the Update button (which is displayed when control is in edit mode).
UpdateText	Text caption to display for the Update button.
ValidationGroup	The validation group name of the controls to validate when a button is clicked.

Customizing the Edit and Insert Interface

The DetailsView control provides a quick and easy way to allow the user to edit the data in a record. However, it is a bit harder to customize the edit and insert interface than with the FormView control.

If you look at the edit and insert interface shown in Figure 10.27, you can see that it simply uses a TextBox control for each field in the data source (or each Bound-Field in the Fields collection). If using BoundField, you can at least hide some elements when modifying data. For instance, in the example shown in Figure 10.27, you may not want to allow the user to edit the ISBN field (because it is a primary key) or the Cover field (because it is an image field meant to only display the book cover). You can do this by setting the ReadOnly and InsertVisible properties of the BoundField to false.

```
<asp:BoundField DataField="ISBN" HeaderText="Isbn:"
   ReadOnly="true" InsertVisible="false" >
```

What if you do not want to use a TextBox control for a given field when editing or inserting data? For instance, in the example shown in Figure 10.27, the control uses a TextBox for the PublisherName field, when it should actually use a TextBox (or even better, a DropDownList) for the PublisherId foreign key. In such a case, you need to define the field using a TemplateField rather than a BoundField. The TemplateField allows you to define any layout that you want for the field when viewing, editing, or inserting. The TemplateField is thus somewhat analogous to the ItemTemplate used with the DataList, Repeater, and FormView controls, except it only specifies the layout for a single field (rather than for an entire record as with these other controls).

With the `TemplateField`, you can define separately how the field looks in the different modes of the control, via `ItemTemplate`, `EditItemTemplate`, and other template elements. By using a `TemplateField`, you can also make use of validation controls. For instance, you could change your publisher `BoundField` to the following `TemplateField`.

```
<asp:TemplateField HeaderText="Publisher:">

   <ItemStyle CssClass="fieldData" />
   <HeaderStyle CssClass="fieldLabel" />

   <ItemTemplate>
      <%# Eval("PublisherName") %>
   </ItemTemplate>

   <EditItemTemplate>
      <asp:DropDownList ID="drpPublisher" runat="server"
        DataSourceID="dsPublisher" DataValueField="PublisherId"
        DataTextField="PublisherName"
        SelectedValue='<%# Bind("PublisherId") %>' />
   </EditItemTemplate>
</asp:TemplateField>
```

If you need to use a `TemplateField` to define each of your fields, it would probably be much easier to simply use the `FormView` control instead.

GridView Control

The ***GridView control*** provides a way to display data in a tabular (row-column) grid. Like the `DetailsView` control, you can use the different field types (from Table 10.9 on page 618) to customize the visual display of the data within the grid. Also like the `DetailsView` control, the `GridView` supports the paging of data as well as the automatic modification and saving of data when bound to a data source control. The `GridView` also allows the user to sort or select data rows.

Despite the rich functionality of the `GridView` control, it is easy to quickly display tabular data due to its predefined look. Assuming that you are using a data source control named `dsBook` that retrieves data from the `Books` table, you can define the simplest `GridView` control as follows.

```
<asp:GridView ID="grdSample" runat="server"
   DataSourceID="dsBooks" />
```

The result in the browser looks similar to that shown in Figure 10.28.

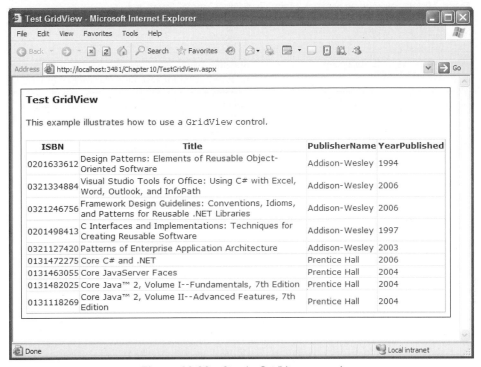

Figure 10.28   Simple GridView control

Table 10.14 lists the notable properties (not including the template elements and their styles) of the `GridView` control.

Table 10.14   Notable Properties of the GridView Control

Property	Description
`AllowPaging`	Specifies whether the control's paging is enabled.
`AllowSorting`	Specifies whether the control's sorting is enabled.
`AutoGenerateColumns`	Specifies whether the control should generate a column for each field in the data source.
`AutoGenerateDeleteButton`	Specifies whether the control should display a built-in button for deleting a current record.

Table 10.14　Notable Properties of the GridView Control *(continued)*

Property	Description
AutoGenerateEditButton	Specifies whether the control should display a built-in button for switching control to edit mode.
AutoGenerateSelectButton	Specifies whether the control should display a built-in button for selecting a record.
BackImageUrl	URL of image to display in background of control.
DataKey	The DataKey collection that contains the primary keys for the current record.
DataKeyNames	The field names for the fields that are stored in the DataKey collection.
DefaultMode	Specifies the initial data-entry mode for the control. Possible values are described by the DetailsViewMode enumeration (Edit, Insert, ReadOnly).
EmptyDataText	The text that appears in the control if the data source contains no data.
EnableSortingAndPagingCallbacks	Specifies whether paging operations are performed using client-side callback functions. When enabled, paging is performed using the callback feature, which prevents the need to repost the entire page back to the server when moving from record to record. This means that the paging and sorting is done on the client rather than on the server.
FooterText	The text to appear in the footer area of the control.
GridLines	The grid line style for the list. Possible values are described by the GridLines enumeration (Both, Horizontal, None, Vertical).
HeaderText	The text to appear in the header area of the control.
PageIndex	The index of the currently displayed record.
PageSize	The number of records to display on each page.

Table 10.14   Notable Properties of the GridView Control *(continued)*

Property	Description
SelectedDataKey	Gets the DataKey object that contains the primary keys for the selected record.
SelectedIndex	The index of the selected row.
SelectedRow	The GridViewRow object for the selected row.
SelectedValue	The data key value for the selected row.
ShowFooter	Specifies whether to display the footer for the control.
ShowHeader	Specifies whether to display the header for the control.
SortDirection	The sort direction for the column.
SortExpression	The sort expression for the column being sorted.

Customizing the GridView Columns

Just like the DetailsView control, the GridView control usually needs some additional customization to make it more useful as well as more pleasing to the eyes. The GridView control is visually customized in almost the exact same manner as the DetailsView control. This means that you can customize the appearance of the GridView via its own properties or via style elements, such as RowStyle, Header-Style, and EditRowStyle. Similar to the approach used with the DetailsView control, you can customize the columns that appear in the GridView by setting its AutoGenerateColumns property to false and then specifying the columns you want to appear in the control by using the same field types listed back in Table 10.9 on page 618.

The one difference here between customizing the GridView and DetailsView controls is that with the GridView, these custom field types are contained within a Columns element (rather than a Fields element, as with the DetailsView control). The following example illustrates a sample customized GridView control. The result in the browser is shown in Figure 10.29.

```
<asp:GridView ID="grdSample" runat="server"
   DataSourceID="dsBooks"
   AutoGenerateColumns="False" BackColor="White"
   BorderColor="#DEDFDE" BorderStyle="None" BorderWidth="1px"
   CellPadding="4" GridLines="Vertical" ForeColor="Black">
```

```
<Columns>
    <asp:ImageField HeaderText="" DataImageUrlField="Isbn"
        DataImageUrlFormatString="images/{0}.gif"
        DataAlternateTextField="Title"
        DataAlternateTextFormatString="Book cover for {0}"
        ReadOnly="True" />
    <asp:BoundField DataField="ISBN" HeaderText="Isbn"
        ReadOnly="True"/>
    <asp:BoundField DataField="Title" HeaderText="Title"/>
    <asp:BoundField DataField="PublisherName"
        HeaderText="Publisher"/>
    <asp:BoundField DataField="YearPublished"
        HeaderText="Year"/>
</Columns>

<RowStyle CssClass="gridRow" />
<HeaderStyle CssClass="gridHeader" />
<AlternatingRowStyle CssClass="gridAlt" />
</asp:GridView>
```

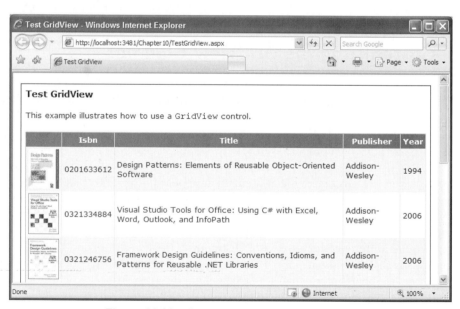

Figure 10.29   Customized GridView control

Using the HyperLinkField

Table 10.9 listed the field types that you can use within the Columns element. The HyperLinkField type can be used to display a hyperlink that is constructed from field data in your data source. Besides the properties listed in Table 10.10, `Hyper-LinkField` includes the additional properties shown in Table 10.15.

Table 10.15   Notable Properties of the HyperLinkField

Property	Description
DataNavigateUrlField	The field name from the data source for the field that contains the values that are used for the `href` attribute for the resulting <a> element.
DataNavigateUrlFormatString	The format string to be used to construct the URL for the resulting <a> element.
DataTextField	The field name from the data source for the field that contains the values that are used to construct the URL for the link.
DataTextFormatString	The format string to be used to construct the link text for the resulting <a> element.
NavigateUrl	The URL for each hyperlink. To be used if the URL is not dynamically retrieved from the data source.
Target	The target window or frame for the link.
Text	The text to display for each hyperlink. To be used if the link text is not dynamically retrieved from the data source.

You can add a `HyperLinkField` to your example to implement what Susan Fowler and Victor Stanwick (see the References at end of the chapter) have called the *list-to-object interaction pattern*. In this pattern, the user views a list of data; by clicking a link, the user then views the details for that data item (generally on a separate page), as shown in Figure 10.30.

In the example list shown in Figure 10.30, the `HyperLinkField` is displaying information from the `Title` field of each displayed record in your data source. The `DataTextField` property of the `HyperLinkField` is used to specify which field data to use as the text of the link.

The base URL for these links is a page called `BookDetails.aspx`. However, as can be seen from Figure 10.30, this page is passed the ISBN of the book to display via a querystring parameter. In other words, the URL for each link in the list is constructed from the ISBN of the record that is being displayed. This can be accomplished by using the `DataNavigateUrlField` and `DataNavigateUrlFormatString` properties of the `HyperLinkField`, as shown in the following example.

```
<asp:HyperLinkField HeaderText="Title" DataTextField="Title"
    DataNavigateUrlFormatString="BookDetails.aspx?id={0}"
    DataNavigateUrlFields="Isbn" />
```

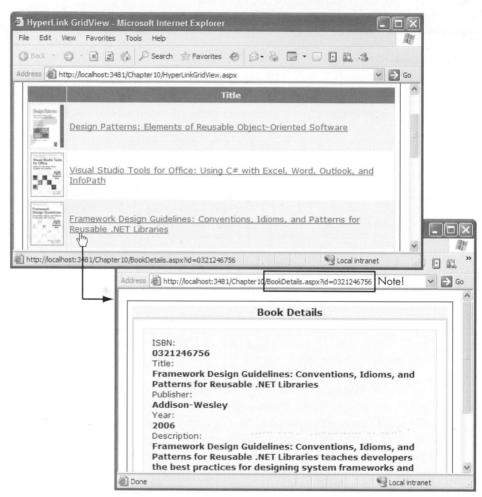

Figure 10.30   List-to-object interaction

The BookDetails.aspx page in this example could use a FormView or a DetailsView control similar to that shown earlier in the chapter but with a somewhat modified data source control, as shown in the following example. Notice that this data source uses a QueryStringParameter to provide the parameter content for the @isbn parameter.

```
<asp:SqlDataSource ID="dsBookDetail" runat="server"
   ConnectionString="<%$ ConnectionStrings:BookCatalog %>"
   SelectCommand=
      "SELECT ISBN,Title,PublisherName,Books.PublisherId,
      YearPublished,BriefDescription FROM Books INNER JOIN
      Publishers ON
      Books.PublisherId=Publishers.PublisherId WHERE ISBN=@isbn">

   <SelectParameters>
      <asp:QueryStringParameter Name="isbn"
         QueryStringField="id" />
   </SelectParameters>

</asp:SqlDataSource>
```

You might also want to add a template to the `DetailsView` or `FormView` control
that handles the possibility that the ISBN value passed via the querystring does not
exist. Remember that cunning users can always modify the querystring, so you should
be able to handle this eventuality. You can do so by adding an `EmptyDataTemplate`,
which describes what the `DetailsView` or `FormView` control displays when its data
source contains no data.

```
<asp:FormView ID="frmvBooks" runat="server"
   DataSourceID="dsBooks" >

   <EmptyDataTemplate>
      Sorry, no book matched this ISBN
   </EmptyDataTemplate>
   …
</asp:FormView>
```

Using the ButtonField

The `ButtonField` adds a button (that is, a text or image link or a push button) for
each record that is displayed. This button is generally used by the user to initiate
some type of custom action on that row. For instance, a `GridView` displaying products in an e-commerce site might have a `ButtonField` for adding the product in
that row to the shopping cart; a `GridView` displaying appointments in an online
appointment manager might have `ButtonField` columns for viewing, printing, or
hiding the appointment in that row.

Unlike the previous field types, a `ButtonField` requires some event handling
code because the button click generates a postback. When the `ButtonField` is
clicked, the form is submitted back to the server, and the `RowCommand` event handler
is called. Thus, you need to create this method, as well as tell the `GridView` the
name of the `RowCommand` event handler method.

Walkthroughs 10.1 through 10.3 demonstrate how to create a `ButtonField` column as well as the event handler for it. The walkthroughs use an image button (you could change this to a regular push button) that adds the book in the row to a cart.

Walkthrough 10.1 *Adding Markup Content to a Web Form*

1. Create a Web Form named `ButtonGridView.aspx`.

2. Add a `SqlDataSource` similar to the following to the form.

```
<asp:SqlDataSource ID="dsBooks" runat="server"
   ProviderName="System.Data.SqlClient"
   ConnectionString="<%$ ConnectionStrings:BookCatalog %>"
   SelectCommand="SELECT ISBN,Title FROM Books" />
```

3. Add a `GridView` control to your form similar to the following.

```
<asp:GridView ID="grdSample" runat="server"
   DataSourceID="dsBooks"
   AutoGenerateColumns="False"
   AllowPaging="true" PageSize="5"   >

   <Columns>
     <asp:ImageField DataImageUrlField="Isbn"
        DataImageUrlFormatString="images/{0}.gif"
        DataAlternateTextField="Title"
        DataAlternateTextFormatString="Book cover for {0}"
        ReadOnly="True" />
     <asp:BoundField DataField="ISBN" HeaderText="Isbn" />

        <asp:BoundField DataField="Title" HeaderText="Title"/>
        <asp:ButtonField ButtonType="Image" CommandName="AddCart"
           ImageUrl="images/btn_addToCart.gif"   />

   </Columns>
</asp:GridView>
```

4. Add the following attributes (shown in emphasis) to the `GridView`.

```
<asp:GridView ID="grdSample" runat="server"
   DataSourceID="dsBooks"
   AutoGenerateColumns="False"
   OnRowCommand="grdSample_RowCommand"
   DataKeyNames="Isbn,Title"
   AllowPaging="true" PageSize="5"   >
```

The OnRowCommand specifies the method name that handles the row command event, which is triggered when the user clicks a row's Add to Cart button. As well, you use DataKeyNames to specify which fields' values are added to the control's DataKeys collection (see Figure 10.31). This collection provides your RowCommand event handler with access to the ISBN and Title data values for the row.

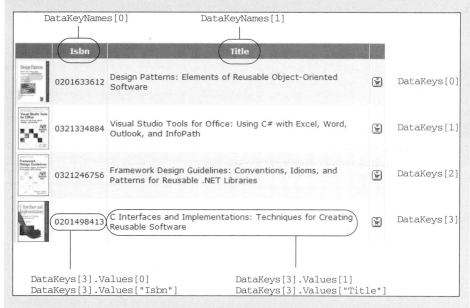

Figure 10.31 DataKeys and DataKeyNames

Although all the cart really requires is the unique identifier for the book (i.e., the ISBN), for demonstration purposes, we will also add the book title to the cart.

5. Add another GridView control that you will use to display the cart contents.

```
<asp:GridView ID="grdCart" runat="server"
   AutoGenerateColumns="false">

   <Columns>
      <asp:BoundField DataField="Isbn" HeaderText="Isbn" />
      <asp:BoundField DataField="Title" HeaderText="Title" />
   </Columns>
</asp:GridView>
```

Walkthrough 10.2 *Adding the RowCommand Event Handler*

1. Add the following event handler to this page's code-behind class.

```
protected void grdSample_RowCommand(object sender,
    GridViewCommandEventArgs e)
{
    // Check which command generated this event
    if (e.CommandName == "AddCart")
    {
        // Retrieve index of the row that generated the event
        int rowIndex = Convert.ToInt32(e.CommandArgument);

        // Get the row's collection of data key values
        DataKey rowKeys = grdSample.DataKeys[rowIndex];

        // Retrieve isbn and title from these data key values
        string isbn = (string)rowKeys.Values["Isbn"];
        string title = (string)rowKeys.Values["Title"];

        // Now add book to cart
        AddBookToCart(isbn, title);
    }
}
```

This event handler first checks that your `ButtonField` generated this event because other user actions (such as moving to a different page within the `GridView`) can also generate this event. The `CommandName` property of the `GridViewCommandEventArgs` object that is passed to the event handler must thus match the `CommandName` that you specified in the markup for your `ButtonField`.

If there is a match, the handler then adds the ISBN and title of the book on that row to the cart. The `CommandArgument` property of the `GridViewCommandEventArgs` object contains the index of the row that generated the event. The method uses that index to retrieve the field values that you specified in the `DataKeyNames` attribute of the `GridView` (see Figure 10.31).

2. Add the following method to your code-behind class. This method performs the actual adding of the book to the cart. This cart needs to persist across multiple requests and be unique to each person using the page. You use the ASP.NET `Session` object to implement this functionality. (We cover session state thoroughly in Chapter 12.)

```
private void AddBookToCart(string isbn, string title)
{
    // Retrieve the cart for this session
    ArrayList cart = (ArrayList)Session["cart"];

    // If cart wasn't in session, create it
    if (cart == null)
    {
        cart = new ArrayList();
    }

    // Ensure this isbn is not already in cart
    foreach (CartItem ci in cart)
    {
        if (ci.Isbn == isbn)
            return;
    }

    // Create cart item and add to cart
    CartItem item = new CartItem(isbn, title);
    cart.Add(item);

    // Preserve updated cart in session
    Session["cart"] = cart;

    // Bind the GridView to the cart
    grdCart.DataSource = cart;
    grdCart.DataBind();
}
```

This method begins by retrieving the cart from session state. If it doesn't exist yet (i.e., it is null), the method creates it. As you can see, the cart is simply an ArrayList of CartItem objects. The method searches this cart to ensure this ISBN is not already on the cart; if it is, it simply exits. If the ISBN does not exist in the cart, it creates a CartItem object (to be defined yet), adds it to the ArrayList, and then resaves the collection in session state. Finally, the method programmatically data binds the collection to the second GridView control so that the user can see the updated cart.

Walkthrough 10.3   *Adding a CartItem Class*

1. Create a new class named `CartItem` in the `App_Code` folder.

2. Add the following code to your class.

```
/// <summary>
/// Represents a single book cart item
/// </summary>
public class CartItem
{
    private string _isbn;
    private string _title;

    public CartItem(string isbn, string title)
    {
        _isbn = isbn;
        _title = title;
    }

    public string Isbn
    {
        get { return _isbn; }
        set { _isbn = value; }
    }

    public string Title
    {
        get { return _title; }
        set { _title = value; }
    }
}
```

You should now be able to test your page. With a bit of additional styling, your page might look similar to that shown in Figure 10.32.

Figure 10.32   Finished ButtonGridView.aspx walkthrough

Selecting Rows

Earlier in the chapter, we demonstrated the use of some of the CommandField types with the DetailsView control. One of the CommandField types that we did not use then was the Select button, because it is not as useful with the DetailsView control. With the GridView control, the Select button is much more useful because it can be used to select a row of data in the control. This selected row can be styled differently from the other rows in the control, and more importantly, the selection can be used to implement another type of list-to-object interaction, often called a ***master-details form***, in which the user can view a list of data (in the GridView), select a row in the list, and then see either more details about the selected row (in a DetailsView or FormView), or some other related list (perhaps in another GridView). Figure 10.33 illustrates one possible master-details form.

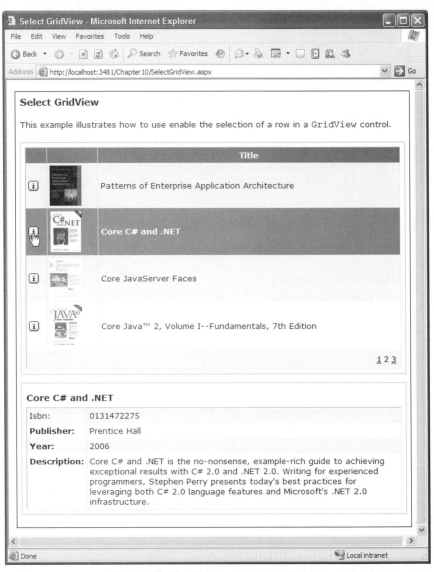

Figure 10.33 Sample master-details form

To enable the selection of a row in the `GridView`, you simply need to add a Select button via a `CommandField`.

```
<asp:CommandField ShowSelectButton="true" SelectText="See More"/>
```

Like the other `CommandField` types, you can configure this one to appear instead as a push button or an image.

```
<asp:CommandField ShowSelectButton="true" ButtonType="Image"
    SelectImageUrl="images/btn_select.gif"/>
```

Clicking the Select button generates a postback. The control then renders the selected row differently to indicate its selected state. You can customize the appearance of the selected row via the `SelectedRowStyle` element.

Master-Details Form

We can use the selection capability of the `GridView` to create a master-details form. Besides the master `GridView` control, this type of form requires some other control to contain the details of the selected record as well as a second data source control. Listing 10.2 provides an example of a master-details form. (Figure 10.33 illustrates how the listing appears in the browser.) It uses a `DetailsView` control to display the details of the book selected in the `GridView`.

Like the shopping cart walkthrough exercise, you need to use the `DataKeyNames` collection of the `GridView` control to provide the link between the master control and the details control. In your case, the `DataKeyNames` collection contains the name of the `Isbn` field.

```
<asp:GridView … DataKeyNames="Isbn" >
```

You can then retrieve the value of this ISBN field for the selected row via the `GridView`'s `SelectedDataKey` property. You might typically do this within a `ControlParameter` for the data source control used by the control that displays the details data.

```
<SelectParameters>
    <asp:ControlParameter ControlID="grdBookList" Name="isbn"
        PropertyName="SelectedDataKey.Values[0]" />
</SelectParameters>
```

In this example, the actual ISBN data value for the selected row is contained within the `Values` collection of the `SelectedDataKey` property. Because `DataKeyNames` can contain more than one key field, the `[0]` retrieves the data value for the first key name (which in this case is the `Isbn` field because that it is the first key field you specified).

You may also want to programmatically handle a selection event. This requires adding a handler for the `SelectedIndexChange` event of the `GridView`, and then within the handler you can programmatically retrieve data from the row. Within this handler, you not only can use the `SelectedDataKey` property, you can also use the `SelectedRow` property of the `GridView`. This property allows you to access the contents of each cell in the selected row.

```
string title = grdBookList.SelectedRow.Cells[2].Text;
```

Figure 10.34 illustrates how these properties are related.

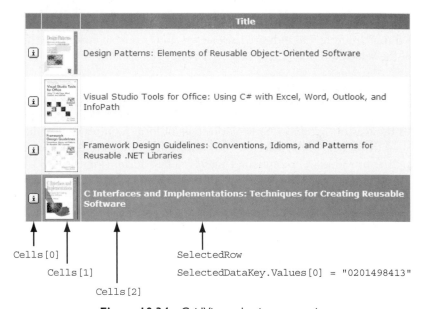

Figure 10.34   GridView selection properties

Listing 10.2   SelectGridView.aspx

```
<h1>Select GridView</h1>
<p>
This example illustrates how to use enable the selection of
a row in a <code>GridView</code> control.
</p>
<div class="box">
   <asp:GridView ID="grdBookList" runat="server"
   AutoGenerateColumns="False"  AllowPaging="true" PageSize="4"
   DataKeyNames="Isbn" DataSourceID="dsBooks"
   Width="600" CssClass="bookList"
   OnSelectedIndexChanged="grdBookList_SelectedIndexChanged"
   CellPadding="4" GridLines="Vertical" >
```

```
        <Columns>
            <asp:CommandField ShowSelectButton="true"
                ButtonType="Image"
                SelectImageUrl="images/btn_select.gif"/>
            <asp:ImageField HeaderText="" DataImageUrlField="Isbn"
                DataImageUrlFormatString="images/{0}.gif"
                DataAlternateTextField="Title"
                DataAlternateTextFormatString="Book cover for {0}"
                ReadOnly="True" />
            <asp:BoundField DataField="Title"
                HeaderText="Title"/>
        </Columns>
        <RowStyle CssClass="bookListRow" />
        <SelectedRowStyle CssClass="bookListSelected" />
        <PagerStyle  CssClass="bookListPager"
            HorizontalAlign="Center"/>
        <PagerSettings Mode="NextPrevious" NextPageText=">"
            PreviousPageText="<" />
        <HeaderStyle CssClass="bookListHeader" />
        <AlternatingRowStyle CssClass="bookListAlt" />
    </asp:GridView>
</div>

<div class="box">
    <h2><asp:Label ID="labSelected" runat="server" /></h2>
    <asp:DetailsView ID="detvBook" runat="server"
        DataSourceID="dsSingleBook" AutoGenerateRows="False"
        CssClass="detail" CellPadding="4"
        GridLines="Vertical" Width="600">
        <Fields>
            <asp:BoundField DataField="ISBN" HeaderText="Isbn:"
                HeaderStyle-CssClass="detailLabel" />
            <asp:BoundField DataField="PublisherName"
                HeaderText="Publisher:"
                HeaderStyle-CssClass="detailLabel"/>
            <asp:BoundField DataField="YearPublished"
                HeaderText="Year:"
                HeaderStyle-CssClass="detailLabel" />
            <asp:BoundField DataField="BriefDescription"
                HeaderText="Description:"
                HeaderStyle-CssClass="detailLabel" />
        </Fields>
        <RowStyle VerticalAlign="Top" CssClass="detailRow" />
        <HeaderStyle CssClass="detailHeader" />
        <AlternatingRowStyle CssClass="detailAlt" />
    </asp:DetailsView>
</div>
```

```
<asp:SqlDataSource ID="dsBooks" runat="server"
   ProviderName="System.Data.SqlClient"
   ConnectionString="<%$ ConnectionStrings:BookCatalog %>"
   SelectCommand="SELECT ISBN,Title FROM Books" />

<asp:SqlDataSource ID="dsSingleBook" runat="server"
   ProviderName="System.Data.SqlClient"
   ConnectionString="<%$ ConnectionStrings:BookCatalog %>"
   SelectCommand=
      "SELECT ISBN,Title,PublisherName,Books.PublisherId,
         YearPublished,BriefDescription FROM Books
         INNER JOIN Publishers ON Books.PublisherId=
         Publishers.PublisherId WHERE ISBN=@isbn">

   <SelectParameters>
      <asp:ControlParameter ControlID="grdBookList" Name="isbn"
        PropertyName="SelectedDataKey.Values[0]" />
   </SelectParameters>
</asp:SqlDataSource>
```

Listing 10.3 demonstrates a sample GridView selection handler. It simply retrieves the book title of the selected book from the Cells collection and displays it within a Label control.

Listing 10.3   SelectGridView.aspx.cs

```
using System.Data;
using System.Configuration;
using System.Collections;
using System.Web;
using System.Web.Security;
using System.Web.UI;
using System.Web.UI.WebControls;

public partial class SelectGridView : System.Web.UI.Page
{
   protected void grdBookList_SelectedIndexChanged(
      object sender, EventArgs e)
   {
      // Retrieves the title value for this row from the grid
      string title = grdBookList.SelectedRow.Cells[2].Text;

      // Sets the label to this title
      labSelected.Text = title;
   }
}
```

GridView Pagination

As some of the examples have already demonstrated, the GridView control supports *pagination*. That is, rather than display all the records in the data source, pagination lets the control break its listing up into multiple, smaller pages displaying a subset of the complete data; the user can then move to a specific page of data via pagination navigation buttons.

Pagination can be enabled for any GridView, FormView, or DetailsView control by enabling its AllowPaging property. The number of records to appear in each page can be set via the PageSize property. As you have already seen with the FormView and DetailsView controls, the appearance of the paging mechanism can be customized via the PagerStyle and PagerSettings elements.

```
<asp:GridView … AllowPaging="true" PageSize="10" >
   …
   <PagerStyle  … />
   <PagerSettings Mode="NextPrevious" NextPageText=">"
      PreviousPageText="<" />
   …
</asp:GridView>
```

How does this paging mechanism actually work? The answer depends on what type of data source control is being used by the GridView, FormView, or DetailsView control that is displaying the pages. If a SqlDataSource control is being used, pagination effectively operates at the control level; if an ObjectDataSource control is being used, pagination must be implemented by the data source control.

For instance, the GridView examples have all used a SqlDataSource control similar to the following to retrieve data from a Books table.

```
<asp:SqlDataSource ID="dsBooks" runat="server"
   …
   SelectCommand="SELECT ISBN,Title FROM Books" />
```

If a GridView with pagination is using this data source control, *all* the records that match this SELECT statement are read and stored into an internal DataSet every time the page is requested or posted back, regardless of whether pagination is enabled or not enabled. If the SELECT statement returns 100,000 records, but the GridView only displays 10 records per page, this is clearly an inefficient approach for a frequently requested page. You can reduce the load on the database somewhat by setting the SqlDataSource's EnableCaching property to true. Unfortunately, this means that you now are trying to store 100,000 records of data within a cached, in-memory DataSet, which probably is an unacceptable use of memory on the server. However, if you are retrieving a fairly small set of data using the SqlDataSource, the built-in, automatic pagination of the GridView may very well be sufficiently efficient, especially if caching is enabled.

CORE NOTE

The `GridView` control supports the `EnableSortingAndPagingCallbacks` property. Setting this property to `true` makes the control use client callbacks (i.e., use client-side Javascript) for paging. This eliminates the need for the page to post back to the server when the user requests a different page in the `GridView`. However, this property is not allowed for `GridView` controls with selection buttons or template fields.

Pagination with the ObjectDataSource

If you are instead using the `ObjectDataSource` control as the input into a `GridView` with pagination, it is possible to implement a more efficient and scalable pagination approach. For this to work, you need your `ObjectDataSource` control to interface with a data access or business object that supports pagination.

You may recall from the last chapter that when you use the `ObjectDataSource` control, you specify the method name that is used to handle the SELECT command. You can then set up any parameters that need to be passed to this method within the `SelectParameters` element, as shown here.

```
<asp:ObjectDataSource ID="dsBooks" runat="server"
   SelectMethod="GetAll" TypeName="BookDA" >

   <SelectParameters>
      …
   </SelectParameters>

</asp:ObjectDataSource>
```

For pagination to work, the class used by `ObjectDataSource` control must have an overloaded version of the select method that accepts two additional parameters: the maximum number of records to retrieve per page and the index of the first record to retrieve. The names of these two method parameters must be set in the `ObjectDataSource`'s `MaximumRowsParameterName` and `StartRowIndexParameterName` properties.

As well, to get the `GridView`'s page navigation buttons to work properly with the `ObjectDataSource` pagination, the class referenced by `ObjectDataSource` also needs to implement a method that returns the total number of records in the SELECT command without pagination. This method must then be identified in the `ObjectDataSource` by its `SelectCountMethod` property.

You could modify the `BookDA` class created at the end of the previous chapter by adding the following methods.

```
/// <summary>
/// Returns all the books
/// </summary>
public DataTable GetAll(int startRowIndex, int rowsToRetrieve)
{
    // Uses a stored procedure to retrieve just the data you need
    string storedProc = "GetAllBooksByPage";

    // Constructs array of parameters
    DbParameter[] parameters = new DbParameter[] {
        MakeParameter("@startRowIndex", startRowIndex,
            DbType.Int32),
        MakeParameter("@rowsToRetrieve", rowsToRetrieve,
            DbType.Int32)
    };

    // Returns result
    return GetDataTable(storedProc, CommandType.StoredProcedure,
        parameters);
}


/// <summary>
/// Returns the total number of book records
/// </summary>
public int CountBooks()
{
    string sql = "SELECT COUNT(*) FROM Books";

    return (int)RunScalar(sql, null);
}
```

With the methods defined, you can now define the pagination-enabled Object-DataSource control that is used by your GridView.

```
<asp:ObjectDataSource ID="dsBooks" runat="server"
    TypeName="BookDA" SelectMethod="GetAll"
    EnablePaging="true" SelectCountMethod="CountBooks"
    MaximumRowsParameterName="rowsToRetrieve"
    StartRowIndexParameterName="startRowIndex" />
```

Creating a Stored Procedure to Implement Custom Pagination

In the example jut covered, the GetAll method made use of a stored procedure named GetAllBooksByPage. What would this stored procedure look like? With versions of SQL Server prior to 2005, the approach generally followed was to have the stored procedure copy all the table data into a new temporary table with an additional identify (i.e., autonumbering) field. The stored procedure then returned the records in which the new identity field's value fell in between the requested range. Fortunately, with SQL Server 2005 and Oracle, there are built-in functions or operators that can be used to return a range of rows without the bother and inefficiency of creating temporary tables.

The SQL Server 2005 stored procedure to retrieve only those records required for the current page might look like the following.

```
CREATE PROCEDURE GetAllBooksByPage
    @startRowIndex INT,
    @rowsToRetrieve INT
AS
BEGIN
    WITH PagedBooks AS (
      SELECT ROW_NUMBER() OVER (ORDER BY Isbn ASC) AS
          Row, Isbn, Title
      FROM Books
    )

    SELECT Isbn, Title
    FROM PagedBooks
    WHERE Row Between @startRowIndex AND
        @startRowIndex+@rowsToRetrieve
END
```

GridView Sorting

The GridView control allows the user to change the visual sort order of the data displayed within the control. When sorting is enabled for the GridView (by setting the AllowSorting property of the control to true), the user can change the sort order of the data by clicking the hyperlinked column header for that field. Furthermore, the user can toggle between an ascending or descending sort order. That is, if you click a column header once, it sorts on that column in ascending order; clicking the column header again sorts it in descending order.

You can specify which columns in the control are to be sortable by setting the SortExpression of each column to the name of the sort field for that column (which is usually the same as the data field name for that column).

```
<asp:GridView ID="grdSample" runat="server"
    DataSourceID="dsBooks"
    AutoGenerateColumns="False" CellPadding="4"
    GridLines="Vertical" CssClass="bookList"
    AllowSorting="true" >

    <Columns>
        <asp:BoundField DataField="ISBN" HeaderText="Isbn"
            SortExpression="Isbn" />
```

```
    <asp:BoundField DataField="Title" HeaderText="Title"
        SortExpression="Title" />
    <asp:BoundField DataField="PublisherName"
        HeaderText="Publisher"
        SortExpression="PublisherName" />
    <asp:BoundField DataField="YearPublished"
        HeaderText="Year"
        SortExpression="YearPublished" />
    </Columns>
    ...
</asp:GridView>
```

The result in the browser can be seen in Figure 10.35.

Figure 10.35 GridView sorting

How does GridView sorting work? The control only provides the user interface for the sorting; it relies on the underlying data source control to perform the actual data sorting. However, the SqlDataSource control does not rely on the DBMS to perform the sorting; instead, it retrieves the unsorted data into a DataSet, and then calls the Sort method of the DataSet to perform the sort within server memory. Although this approach is fine for relatively small amounts of data, it is noticeably slower and less memory efficient for large amounts of data (as always, enabling caching within the SqlDataSource improves performance). That is, when dealing with many records, sorting is generally best performed by the DBMS as these programs have highly optimized sorting algorithms.

Sorting with the ObjectDataSource

If you are using the `ObjectDataSource` control in conjunction with a sortable `GridView` control, it is possible to implement a more efficient and scalable sorting solution that lets the DBMS handle the sorting. You can do this by creating an overloaded version of the selection method in your data-access or business object that supports sorting. This overloaded version contains an additional string argument that contains the sort expression (i.e., the field name of the column to sort on) that you added to your `BoundColumns`.

```
/// <summary>
/// Returns all the specified page of data
/// </summary>
public DataTable GetAll(string sortExpression)
{
    string sql = SelectStatement;

    // Implements sorting by modifying the SQL
    if (sortExpression.Length > 0)
        sql += " ORDER BY " + sortExpression;
    return GetDataTable(sql, null);
}
```

With this overloaded version of the method, you simply need to tell the `Object-DataSource` the name of this additional argument via the `SortParameterName` property.

```
<asp:ObjectDataSource ID="dsBooks" runat="server"
    TypeName="BookDA" SelectMethod="GetAll"
    SortParameterName="sortExpression" />
```

CORE NOTE

If you want to use an `ObjectDataSource` control that supports both custom pagination and custom sorting, you must modify this `GetAll` method so that both the `ORDER BY` logic and the pagination logic are within a stored procedure.

Editing Data within the GridView

Like the `FormView` and `DetailsView` controls covered earlier in the chapter, the `GridView` control supports the in-place editing of data within a row by the user. In fact, you can add editing to a `GridView` control in almost *exactly* the same manner as with the `DetailsView` control (the key difference is that you cannot insert new data with the `GridView`). That is, you can automatically provide Edit or Delete buttons via the `AutoGenerateEditButton` and `AutoGenerateDeleteButton` properties of the `GridView`. Setting any of these properties to `true` adds a special column with the appropriate `Edit` and/or `Delete` links or buttons (see Figure 10.36). Similar to the `DetailsView` control, if you need to customize this command column, you could disable the auto-generation of the buttons and add a `CommandField` to the `Columns` element.

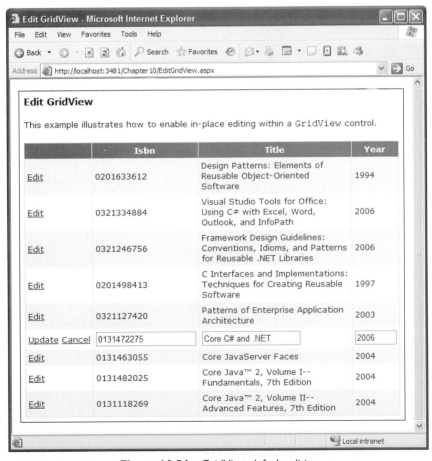

Figure 10.36   GridView default editing

The default editing interface provided by the GridView control (as shown in Figure 10.36) can be customized. Just as you saw with the editing interface of the Details-Control, you may want to use controls other than a TextBox, or you may want to add validation controls, or not place all of your controls along a row. In such a case, you want to use a TemplateField instead of a BoundField for the columns. As you saw in "Customizing the Edit and Insert Interface" on page 625, the TemplateField allows you to customize both the editing and nonediting display of a column.

Listing 10.4 contains an example of a GridView with a customized edit interface. It uses three TemplateField controls, a read-only column, a validation control, and a customized command column using image buttons rather than text. Notice that the SqlDataSource control used by the GridView control in this listing explicitly specifies the parameters for the SQL UPDATE via the UpdateParameter element.

Figure 10.37 illustrates the result in the browser.

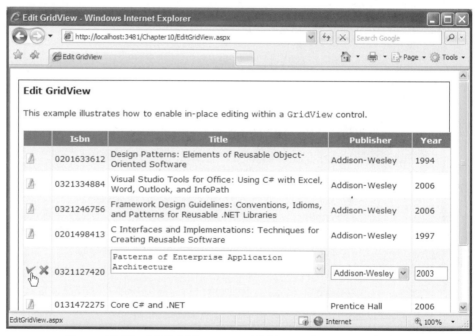

Figure 10.37   EditGridView.aspx—GridView with customized editing

Listing 10.4   EditGridView.aspx

```
<h1>Edit GridView</h1>
<p>
This example illustrates how to enable in-place editing within a
<code>GridView</code> control.
```

```
</p>
<asp:GridView ID="grdSample" runat="server"
  DataSourceID="dsBooks"
  AutoGenerateColumns="False"
  DataKeyNames="ISBN"
  AutoGenerateEditButton="false"
  AllowPaging="true" PageSize="4"
  CssClass="bookList" ShowFooter="true" ShowHeader="true"
  CellPadding="4" GridLines="Vertical" >

  <Columns>
      <asp:CommandField ButtonType="Image"
          ShowEditButton="true"
          EditImageUrl="images/btn_edit.gif"
          CancelImageUrl="images/btn_cancel.gif"
          UpdateImageUrl="images/btn_update.gif" />

      <asp:BoundField DataField="Isbn" HeaderText="Isbn"
          ReadOnly="true" />

      <asp:TemplateField HeaderText="Title">
          <ItemTemplate>
             <%# Eval("Title") %>
          </ItemTemplate>
          <EditItemTemplate>
            <asp:TextBox ID="txtTitle" runat="server"
              Columns="40" Rows="2"
              TextMode="MultiLine"
              Text='<%# Bind("Title") %>' />
            <br />
            <asp:RequiredFieldValidator ID="reqTitle"
                runat="server"
                ControlToValidate="txtTitle"
                ErrorMessage="You must enter a title" />
          </EditItemTemplate>
      </asp:TemplateField>

      <asp:TemplateField HeaderText="Publisher">
          <ItemTemplate>
             <%# Eval("PublisherName") %>
          </ItemTemplate>
          <EditItemTemplate>
            <asp:DropDownList ID="drpPublisher" runat="server"
              DataSourceID="dsPublisher"
              DataValueField="PublisherId"
              DataTextField="PublisherName"
              SelectedValue='<%# Bind("PublisherId") %>' />
          </EditItemTemplate>
      </asp:TemplateField>
```

```
    <asp:TemplateField HeaderText="Year">
        <ItemTemplate>
            <%# Eval("YearPublished") %>
        </ItemTemplate>
        <EditItemTemplate>
            <asp:TextBox ID="txtYear" runat="server" Columns="3"
                Text='<%# Bind("YearPublished") %>' />
        </EditItemTemplate>
    </asp:TemplateField>
</Columns>
<RowStyle CssClass="bookListRow" />
<SelectedRowStyle CssClass="bookListSelected" />
<PagerStyle  CssClass="bookListPager"
    HorizontalAlign="Center"/>
<PagerSettings Mode="NextPrevious" NextPageText=">"
    PreviousPageText="<" />
<HeaderStyle CssClass="bookListHeader" />
<AlternatingRowStyle CssClass="bookListAlt" />
</asp:GridView>


<asp:SqlDataSource ID="dsBooks" runat="server"
    ProviderName="System.Data.OleDb"
    ConnectionString="<%$ ConnectionStrings:Books %>"
    SelectCommand=
        "SELECT ISBN,Title,PublisherName,Books.PublisherId,
          YearPublished,BriefDescription FROM Books INNER JOIN
          Publishers ON Books.PublisherId=
          Publishers.PublisherId"
    UpdateCommand="UPDATE Books SET Title=@Title,
        PublisherId=@PublisherId,YearPublished=@YearPublished,
        BriefDescription=@BriefDescription WHERE ISBN=@ISBN">

    <UpdateParameters>
        <asp:Parameter Name="ISBN" Type="String" />
        <asp:Parameter Name="Title" Type="String" />
        <asp:Parameter Name="PublisherId" Type="Int32" />
        <asp:Parameter Name="YearPublished" Type="Int32" />
        <asp:Parameter Name="BriefDescription" Type="String" />
    </UpdateParameters>

</asp:SqlDataSource>

<asp:SqlDataSource ID="dsPublisher" runat="server"
    ProviderName="System.Data.OleDb"
    ConnectionString="<%$ ConnectionStrings:Books %>"
    SelectCommand=
        "Select PublisherId,PublisherName From Publishers" />
```

CORE NOTE

The order of the `Parameter` elements must match the order of the fields in your UPDATE statement if you are using the `OleDb` provider.

Other GridView Tasks

If you have worked your way through all of these discussions on the `GridView`, you may already have the sense that the `GridView` is a full-featured control. Yet, much of the `GridView`'s flexibility and functionality is available with very little or no programming. In this final section, we examine some relatively common `GridView` display tasks that do require a bit more programming: programmatic row customization, displaying the results of calculations involving data from multiple rows, and using multiple `GridView` controls.

Programmatic Row Customization

Sometimes, the default capabilities of the `GridView` control are not sufficient for all display tasks. Fortunately, the `GridView` has a robust event model that allows the developer to further customize how the control operates. One of the more common ways that a developer can customize the `GridView` is to programmatically customize how a row of data is displayed. For instance, you may want to modify the formatting of a row or a cell based on a data value within the row. To achieve this custom formatting, you can write an event handler for either the `RowCreated` or the `RowDataBound` events.

The `RowCreated` event is raised when each row in the `GridView` is created. This event is fired for *all* rows: header row, item rows, pager rows, and footer rows. The `RowDataBound` event is raised *after* each row is bound to the values in the appropriate data record. This event is also fired for all rows.

Imagine that you want to modify a `GridView` displaying book data so that it highlights those books whose publication year is equal to the current year. Because you need access to the data in the row, you should perform the conditional formatting in the `RowDataBound` event. You need to set up this event in your `GridView` definition.

```
<asp:GridView ID="grdSample" runat="server"
   DataSourceID="dsBooks"
   ...
   OnRowDataBound="grdSample_RowDataBound" >
```

You can now create this event handler.

```
protected void grdSample_RowDataBound(object sender,
   GridViewRowEventArgs e)
{
   // First verify this is data row
   if (e.Row.RowType == DataControlRowType.DataRow)
   {
      // Get the publication year from the row
      int pubYear = (int)DataBinder.Eval(e.Row.DataItem,
         "YearPublished");

      // We will hard-code the year only so this example
      // always works with our sample database, but in a real
      // example, we would programmatically determine the
      // current year using:
      //
      // int currentYear = DateTime.Now.Year;

      int currentYear = 2006;

      // If the current year, change the formatting
      if (pubYear == currentYear)
      {
         e.Row.BackColor = System.Drawing.Color.PaleGoldenrod;
         e.Row.Cells[3].Font.Bold = true;
      }
   }
}
```

This handler is passed a `GridViewRowEventArgs` object that allows you to retrieve the data of the current row via its `Row.DataItem` property. This property returns an `object` that represents the underlying data record. To extract the actual field values from this `object`, you can use the `DataBinder.Eval` method. This is the exact same `Eval` method that you have used in your data-binding expressions in this chapter. Finally, if the publication year of the book matches the current year, this example changes the background color of the row and changes the publication year column to bold (the result in the browser is shown in Figure 10.38).

Performing Calculations

A common requirement of data reports is to perform multiple-row calculations, such as totaling or averaging. A `GridView` (or the `DataList` or `Repeater`) is also a type of reporting tool. Many Web applications use the templated data controls to display data, and then have the user print the data. Although the `GridView` does not support the type of functionality needed in a pure reporting engine (such as grouping and subtotaling, although you can "fake" these with a fair bit of programming), it is relatively straightforward to add a calculation in the footer of the `GridView`.

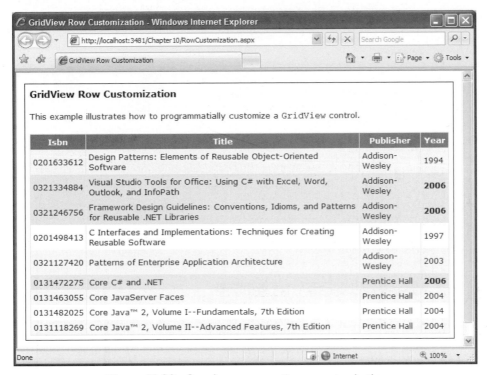

Figure 10.38 Sample programmatic row customization

The next example (the finished version is shown in Figure 10.39) demonstrates how to calculate a running total in the footer of the grid. Unfortunately, there is no "simple" way to do this task. The approach that you need to take is to once again handle the RowDataBound event. The event handler needs to extract data values from the cells in the row and perform the required running total calculation. The event handler also needs to populate the grid footer with the results of the calculation.

Assume that you have the following GridView control.

```
<asp:GridView ID="grdSample" runat="server" DataSourceID="dsArt"
    AutoGenerateColumns="False"
    CssClass="list" ShowFooter="true"
    CellPadding="4" GridLines="Vertical"
    OnRowDataBound="grdSample_RowDataBound" >

    <Columns>
        <asp:BoundField DataField="Title" HeaderText="Title" />
        <asp:BoundField DataField="Price" HeaderText="Price"
            DataFormatString="{0:c}" HtmlEncode="false" />
```

```
        <asp:BoundField DataField="Cost" HeaderText="Cost"
        DataFormatString="{0:c}" HtmlEncode="false" />

    </Columns>
    <RowStyle CssClass="listRow" />
    <HeaderStyle CssClass="listHeader" />
    <AlternatingRowStyle CssClass="listAlt" />
    <FooterStyle CssClass="listFooter" HorizontalAlign="Right"/>
</asp:GridView>
```

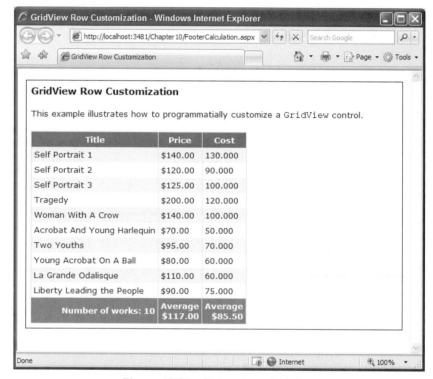

Figure 10.39   Performing calculations

CORE NOTE

Notice that the `Price` and `Cost BoundField` elements use the
`DataFormatString` property to format the output as a currency value.
However, you must also set the `HtmlEncode` to `false` to actually get the
`GridView` to use the `DataFormatString`. When the `HtmlEncode` is set
to `true` (the default), the field is encoded to HTML before the formatting
string is applied.

You can create your event handler as shown in the following example. Notice that it uses three data members to hold the running totals. It updates the running totals if the row is a data row. If it is the footer row, it programmatically inserts the calculations into the footer cells (the footer row has the same number of cells as the data rows).

```
public partial class FooterCalculation : System.Web.UI.Page
{
    int _count = 0;
    decimal _sumPrice = 0.0M;
    decimal _sumCost = 0.0M;

    protected void grdSample_RowDataBound(object sender,
        GridViewRowEventArgs e)
    {
        // Verifies this is data row.
        if (e.Row.RowType == DataControlRowType.DataRow)
        {
            // Gets the price and cost from row
            decimal price = (decimal)DataBinder.Eval(e.Row.DataItem,
                "Price");
            decimal cost = (decimal)DataBinder.Eval(e.Row.DataItem,
                "Cost");

            // Updates running totals
            _sumPrice += price;
            _sumCost += cost;
            _count++;
        }
        else if (e.Row.RowType == DataControlRowType.Footer)
        {
            // Generates footer text
            e.Row.Cells[0].Text = "Number of works: ";
            e.Row.Cells[0].Text += _count;

            e.Row.Cells[1].Text = "Average<br/>";
            decimal avgPrice = _sumPrice / _count;
            e.Row.Cells[1].Text += String.Format("{0:c}", avgPrice);

            e.Row.Cells[2].Text = "Average<br/>";
            decimal avgCost = _sumCost / _count;
            e.Row.Cells[2].Text += String.Format("{0:c}", avgCost);
        }

    }
}
```

CORE NOTE

From a programming design perspective, the approach used in this example is not ideal. Rather than having the presentation layer calculate these values, it is better to have the database or your business layer do it. As well, if you add paging to your `GridView`, this code does not work because it only subtotals the values from the rows in the current page.

Nested GridView Controls

All the examples in this chapter have displayed data from a single data source. In this final section, we look at how to display data in a `GridView` from two tables that exist in a one-to-many relationship. This type of `GridView` is also sometimes referred to as a grouped report, in that each record in the one table is displayed, with all the related records in the many table grouped "underneath" it.

The next example demonstrates how to create this type of `GridView`. The master data comes from the `Publishers` table (the one table), whereas the detail data comes from the `Books` table (the many table). The grid displays each publisher on a separate row, with all the books for that publisher displayed in that same row.

The technique for doing this is perhaps somewhat devious. It makes use of a `GridView` nested within another `GridView`. The inner `GridView` (displaying data from `Books` table) is contained within a `TemplateColumn` of the outer `GridView` (displaying data from `Publishers` table).

```
<asp:GridView ID="grdPublishers" runat="server"
    DataSourceID="dsPublisher" DataKeyNames="PublisherId"
    AutoGenerateColumns="False"
    Width="600" CssClass="publisherList"
    CellPadding="4" GridLines="Vertical"
    OnRowDataBound="grdPublishers_RowDataBound" >

    <Columns>
        <asp:BoundField DataField="PublisherName"
            HeaderText="Publisher"
            ItemStyle-VerticalAlign="top"/>
        <asp:TemplateField>
            <ItemTemplate>
                <asp:GridView ID="grdBookList" runat="server"
                    AutoGenerateColumns="False"
                    ShowHeader="false" CssClass="bookList"
                    CellPadding="4" GridLines="None"   >
```

```
            <Columns>
            <asp:BoundField DataField="Title" />

            </Columns>
            <RowStyle CssClass="bookListRow" />
          </asp:GridView>
        </ItemTemplate>
      </asp:TemplateField>
  </Columns>
  <RowStyle CssClass="publisherRow" />
  <HeaderStyle CssClass="publisherHeader" />
  <AlternatingRowStyle CssClass="publisherAlt" />
</asp:GridView>
```

Notice that the inner GridView is not yet data bound. The inner GridView is data bound during the outer grid's OnRowDataBound event, which is shown here.

```
protected void grdPublishers_RowDataBound(object sender,
   GridViewRowEventArgs e)
{
   if (e.Row.RowType == DataControlRowType.DataRow)
   {
      // Retrieves the publisher id for row from the data keys
      int rowIndex = e.Row.DataItemIndex;
      int pubId = (int)grdPublishers.DataKeys[rowIndex].Value;

      // Retrieves the nested GridView on this row
      GridView grdBooks =
         (GridView)e.Row.FindControl("grdBookList");

      // Gets list of books for publisher
      BookDA bda = new BookDA();
      DataTable books = bda.GetBooksByPublisher(pubId);

      // Manually data binds the inner grid
      grdBooks.DataSource = books;
      grdBooks.DataBind();
   }
}
```

Notice that this event makes use of a method in your books data access class to retrieve a DataTable of books for the row's PublisherId; this DataTable is then bound to the inner GridView. The result is shown in Figure 10.40.

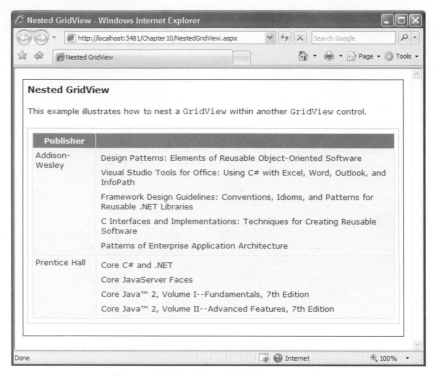

Figure 10.40 Nested GridView controls

 CSS CONTROL ADAPTERS

With all the controls covered in this chapter (with the exception of the `Repeater` control), the developer has limited control over the parent HTML element that is emitted by the controls. In fact, all of these controls render as an HTML `<table>` element. This is also true of some of the other complex controls covered in the book (such as the `Menu` and `TreeView` from Chapter 7, and the various security controls covered in Chapter 13).

As we have mentioned at various times in this book, many developers and designers are currently endeavoring to avoid using HTML `<table>` elements for layout and instead use other HTML elements in conjunction with CSS.

Fortunately, ASP.NET provides a mechanism for changing the HTML rendered by a control using **control adapters**. Although a discussion of how to create control adapters is beyond the scope of this book, there is a free set of CSS-friendly, table-less control adapters for the `GridView`, `DetailsView`, `Menu`, and other complex controls, available from Microsoft at `http://www.asp.net/CSSAdapters`.

Summary

This very long chapter examined in detail the key multivalue data controls in ASP.NET 2.0. All of these controls use templates and/or data-binding expressions. The simple DataList control can be used to quickly output a simple list or single column table of data. The Repeater allows the user to completely customize the output of a series of data values. The DetailsView and FormView controls can be used to display a single record of data, as well as update, insert, or delete data. The FormView is analogous to the Repeater in that the user can highly customize how the control is rendered in the browser. The DetailsView control has a built-in layout, which can be customized on a field-by-field basis using field types. The GridView is the most full-featured of the data controls. It displays data as a table of rows and columns. Like the DetailsView, it can be customized by field types and supports the editing of data as well as pagination and sorting.

The next chapter steps back from our coverage of ASP.NET controls and examines the larger topic of designing and implementing Web applications.

Exercises

The solutions to the following exercises can be found at my Web site, http://www.randyconnolly.com/core. Additional exercises only available for teachers and instructors are also available from this site.

1. Create a page named Authors.aspx that displays all the records in the Authors table within a DataList. The list should display the name of the author. The author's name should be a link that takes the user to the page called AuthorBooks.aspx; the AuthorId should be passed to AuthorBooks.aspx in a querystring parameter named author.

2. Create a page named AuthorBooks.aspx that uses a Repeater to display all the books by the author specified by the querystring parameter named author (which contains the AuthorId). This page should display the author's name in a heading, and then each book's ISBN, title, cover, category name, year published, and description.

3. Modify the FormView example so that the ItemTemplate displays the series and category name, and the EditItemTemplate includes the SeriesId and CategoryId fields as DropDownList controls.

The next two exercises use the ModernEyeCatalog database.

4. Create a page named EditArtWork.aspx that uses a DetailsView control to view a single work of art (from the ArtWorks table) at a time. It should display the title, its artist's name, description, year of work, price, and

cost. This control should include a pager that allows the user to move from work of art to work of art. It should also allow the user to edit these data values.

5. Create a page named `ArtWorks.aspx` that uses a `GridView` control to display the art work title, year of work, price, cost, and the artist's name. This `GridView` must have paging, sorting, and editing enabled.

6. Modify the `ButtonGridView.aspx` page by adding a `ButtonField` to the cart `GridView` that removes that row's book from the cart.

7. Create a `SeriesDA` and `CatalogDA` classes similar in functionality to the `BooksDA` or `PublishersDA`. Create two pages that use a FormView control and an `ObjectDataSource` control that demonstrates these two classes' capability to retrieve and update data from the `Series` and `Catalog` tables.

Key Concepts

- ADO.NET
- Control adapters
- Data-binding expressions
- `DataList` control
- `DetailsView` control
- Formatting string
- `FormView` control
- `GridView` control
- List-to-object interaction pattern
- Master-details form
- Pagination
- `Repeater` control
- Templates
- Two-way data binding

References

Fowler, Susan and Stanwick, Victor. *Web Application Design Handbook: Best Practices for Web-Based Software*. Morgan Kaufmann, 2004.

Guthrie, Scott. "Paging Through Lots of Data Efficiently (and in an Ajax Way) with ASP.NET 2.0." http://weblogs.asp.net/scottgu.

Mitchell, Scott. "GridView Examples for ASP.NET 2.0." http://msdn.microsoft.com.

11

DESIGNING AND IMPLEMENTING WEB APPLICATIONS

"Design . . . is a recognition of the relation between various things. . . . You can't invent a design. You recognize it, in the fourth dimension. That is, with your blood and your bones, as well as with your eyes."

—D. H. Lawrence, *Art & Morality*

ASP.NET is such a full-featured Web development technology that it is quite tempting to focus exclusively on examining the individual features that make up ASP.NET. This chapter shifts the focus away from individual controls and classes and instead examines some of the issues involved in creating a more complex Web application with ASP.NET. The chapter begins with the design of Web applications and some common layering models for Web applications and then moves on to implement a sample layered architecture.

Although a good design may indeed be, as D.H. Lawrence asserts, not completely amenable to rationale articulation, there is substantial literature on the topic of software design that does provide many guidelines and precepts that can help you design a Web application. It is beyond the scope of this book to discuss contemporary software design in detail. The References section at the end of chapter includes several particularly useful works on this very broad topic. Instead, the principle point of this chapter is to discuss various best practices in the design of Web applications and then illustrate some sample implementations of these designs.

Designing an Application

ASP.NET has many features that aid in the rapid development of a Web application. Powerful declarative controls enable the developer to create sophisticated interfaces for the display and editing of data with little or no programming. The convenience and power of the Visual Studio Designer also encourages the developer to rapidly implement Web pages. ASP.NET and Visual Studio seemingly encourage the developer to "stop wasting time designing and planning," and instead to "start dragging and dropping and get the project finished!" This ability to rapidly develop a site is particularly enticing when creating a Web site with a limited number of *use cases*, that is, with a limited set of functional requirements.

The functionality in many "real" Web applications, however, cannot be described in only a few use cases. Instead, there very well may be dozens and dozens, or even hundreds, of use case descriptions that necessitate the efforts of several or many developers working over a substantial time frame to implement them all. It is when working on this type of Web application that this rapid style of development can actually slow the overall process of development.

Real software projects are notoriously vulnerable to shifting requirements; Web projects are probably even more so. This means that the functionality for a Web application is rarely completely specified before development begins. New features are added and other features dropped. The data model and its storage requirements change. As the project moves through the software development lifecycle, the execution environment changes from the developers' laptops to a testing server to a production server to perhaps a farm of Web servers. The developer may test initially against an Access database, then migrate to SQL Server, and then after a company merger, migrate again to an Oracle database. Weeks before alpha testing, the client may make a change that necessitates working with an external Web service rather than a local database for some information. Usability analysts may severely criticize the site's pages, which in turn may require a substantial reworking of the pages' user interface.

It is in this type of Web development environment that rapid development practices may cause more harm than benefit. However, it is also in this environment that following proper software design principles begins to pay handsome dividends. Spending the time to create a well-designed application infrastructure can make your Web application easier to modify and maintain, easier to grow and expand in functionality, less prone to bugs, and ultimately, easier to create. This first section of the chapter endeavors to provide some insight into designing this application infrastructure.

Using Layers

One of the most important benefits of ASP.NET over pure page scripting technologies such as classic ASP or PHP is the possibility of creating a more maintainable application by using current object-oriented software design best practices. Perhaps the most important of these best practices is to structure your application design into discrete logical layers.

What is a layer? A *layer* is simply a group of classes that are functionally or logically related. A layer is a conceptual grouping of classes. Using layers is a way of organizing your software design into groups of classes that fulfill a common purpose. Thus, a layer is not a thing, but an organizing principle. That is, layers are a way of broadly designing an application.

The reason why so many software developers have embraced layers as the organizing principal of their application designs is that a layer is not a random grouping of classes. Rather, each layer in an application should be **cohesive** (that is, the classes should roughly be "about" the same thing and have a similar level of abstraction). Cohesive layers and classes are generally easier to understand, reuse, and maintain.

The goal of layering is to distribute the functionality of your software among classes so that the **coupling** of a given class to other classes is minimized. Coupling refers to the number of other classes that a given class uses. When a given class uses another class, it is dependent upon the class that it uses; any changes made to the used class's interface may affect the class that is dependent upon it. When an application's classes are highly coupled, changes in one class may affect many other classes. As coupling is reduced, a design becomes more maintainable and extensible.

Of course, some coupling is necessary in any application; otherwise, the classes are not interacting. By organizing an application's classes into layers, you hopefully end up with lower coupling than you otherwise might have without using layers as an organizing principle. A layer may have dependencies to another layer's *interface*, but should be independent of another layer's *implementation*.

In this approach, each layer has a strictly limited number of dependencies. A *dependency* (also referred to as the uses relationship) is a relationship between two elements where a change in one affects the other. In the illustration in Figure 11.1, the various layers have dependencies with classes only in layers "below" them—that is, with layers whose abstractions are more "lower-level" or perhaps more dependent upon externalities such as databases or Web services.

Please note what a dependency means in regard to layers. It means that the classes in a layer "above" use classes and methods in the layer(s) "below" it, but not vice versa. Indeed, if the layers have dependencies with each other, you lose entirely the benefits of layering.

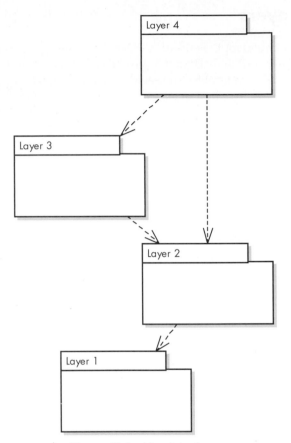

Figure 11.1   Visualizing layers

CORE NOTE

The layering scheme shown in Figure 11.1 is an *open*, or relaxed layering scheme, in that some layers have dependencies with more than one layer. In a *closed* or opaque layering scheme, each layer is dependent only upon the one layer below it. Although a closed layer scheme is perhaps ideal, in practice, it is sometimes difficult to achieve. As Martin Fowler has noted in his *Patterns of Enterprise Application Architecture*, "most [layered architectures] are mostly opaque."

Finally, I should also mention that some authors use the term **tier** in the same sense that I use the term *layer*. However, most contemporary writing on software architecture and design tends to use the term tier in a completely different sense. In this other sense, a tier refers to a processing boundary. These different tiers most often refer to different places in a network. For example, a typical Web application can be considered a three-tier architecture: the user's workstation is the user-interface tier, the Web server is the application tier, and the DBMS running on a separate data server is the database tier, as shown in Figure 11.2. In the remainder of the book, we use the word tier in this latter sense, and use the word layer when referring to the conceptual grouping of classes within an application.

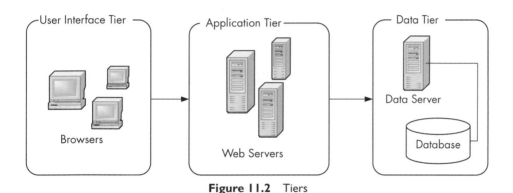

Figure 11.2   Tiers

Consequences of Layering

There are many advantages to be gained by designing an application using layers. The first and most important benefit of using layers is that the resulting application should be significantly more maintainable and adaptable by reducing the overall coupling in the application. If there is low coupling between the layers combined with high cohesion within a layer (along with a well-defined interface for accessing the layer), a developer should be able to modify, extend, or enhance the layer without unduly affecting the rest of the application. As Craig Larman has noted in his *Agile and Iterative Development*, modifying and maintaining applications usually constitutes the majority of development time on a project. As a result, increasing the maintainability of an application is a vital advantage.

Another benefit of layering is that a given layer may be reusable in other applications, especially if it is designed with reuse in mind. This author has used a slightly more complex version of the layers that are implemented later in this chapter in dozens of Web applications. Finally, another benefit of layers is that application functionality contained within a layer can be tested separately and independently of other layers.

However, there are some disadvantages to using layers. One of these disadvantages is that applications may become somewhat more complex to understand and develop by developers who are only familiar with the page scripting development model. Although the advantages of layering are generally worth this cost, in very simple Web applications of only a few pages, the use of numerous layers of abstraction would probably not be worth the cost.

Another disadvantage of using layers is that the extra levels of abstraction can incur a small performance penalty at runtime. However, given the time costs of computer-to-computer communication across a network, the time costs of extra object communication within a computer are relatively unimportant.

The final disadvantage of layering is the difficulty in establishing the proper layering scheme to use. If the application has too few layers, with each layer doing too much, the full benefits of layering may not be realized; if the application has too many layers, the resulting application probably is too complex and thus perhaps less maintainable and understandable. The next few sections try to address this disadvantage by examining several sample layering architectures.

There is a decided lack of a standard nomenclature when it comes to naming layers. Examining the literature, there appears to be dozens and dozens of different layering schemes. But this is not the case. As Eric Evans notes in his *Domain-Driven Design*, through experience and convention, the object-oriented software development industry has converged on layered architectures in general, along with a set of fairly standard layers, albeit with nonstandardized names. The next three sections detail three of the most common layer models.

Two-Layer Model

As we have seen in the last chapter, it is quite possible to create a data-driven ASP.NET Web application with almost no programming thanks to the `SqlData-Source` control and the rich data controls such as the `DetailsView` and `GridView`. Nonetheless, as mentioned in Chapter 9, many developers dislike placing database access details within their Web Forms, even if within the declarative form of the `SqlDataSource` control. In Chapter 9, we created a series of related classes that handled the database access details via ADO.NET programming, and then made use of these classes in our Web Forms via the `ObjectDataSource` control. This was an example of a two-layer architecture.

In the two-layer model, data access details are contained within separate classes that are distinct from the Web Forms themselves. You could name the two layers in this model the presentation layer and the data access layer.

The ***presentation layer*** provides the application's user interface and handles the interaction between the user and the application. In this book, the presentation layer consists of ASP.NET pages and their code-behind classes as well as any additional user or custom controls. The ***data access layer*** provides communication with external systems such as databases, messaging systems, or external Web services, as illustrated in Figure 11.3.

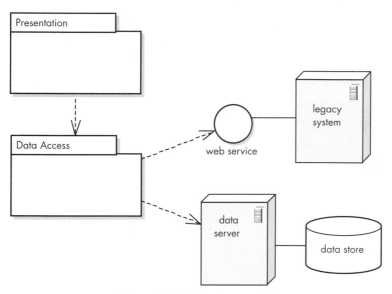

Figure 11.3 Two-layer model

The data access layer in Chapter 9 contained all the ADO.NET programming. Each of the classes within the layer was responsible for ***CRUD*** (Create, Retrieve, Update, and Delete) interaction with a single table in the database. Figure 11.4 illustrates two sample data access classes and their common base class.

Notice that when data is retrieved from the database in the data access layer, it is wrapped within a `DataTable` (although it could have used a `DataSet` instead) and passed to the presentation layer.

The advantage of the two-layer model is that it is quite lightweight and relatively straightforward to implement. However, the two-layer model may not be ideal if the site's application logic becomes more complex. ***Application logic*** refers to the cross-domain logic or process flow of the application itself. An example of application logic is the workflow in an online store for an order. After the user clicks the submit order button, this Web application must create the order in the database, contact the payment system, and submit the payment. If it fails, it must roll back the order and notify the user; otherwise, the order must be committed, the fulfillment system must be sent a message, and the successful order page must be displayed. This workflow has several steps with multiple sets of conditional logic.

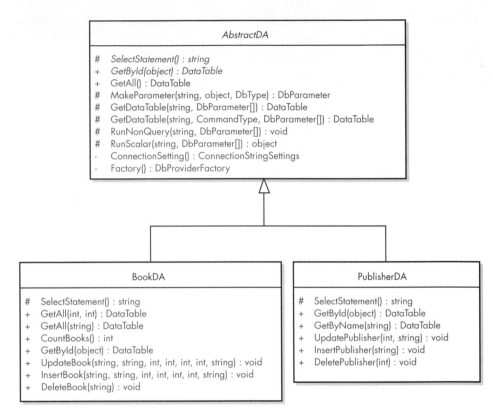

Figure 11.4   Data access layer

The two-layer model may also be less than ideal if you need to add more complex business rules to the application. ***Business rules*** refers to the standard types of input validation you encountered in Chapter 5 as well as to more complex rules for the data that are often specific to an organization's methods for conducting its business.

In sites where the application logic or business rules are complex, this extra complexity generally has to be implemented within the presentation layer when the two-layer model is used. As a consequence, the code-behinds usually become too complex and too filled with repetitive business and application logic coding. I once refactored a client's two-layer ASP.NET Web application in which the code-behind classes for each of the application's 30-plus Web Forms were more than 4,000 lines long each; as a consequence, each was a nightmare to modify due to its length and complexity. The solution in this particular case was to rearchitect the site to a three-layer model.

Three-Layer Model

In the three-layer architecture, a new layer is added to the two-layer model. This new layer is generally called the *business layer*, as shown in Figure 11.5.

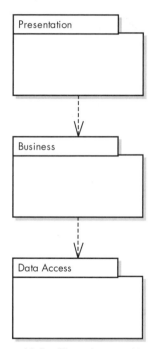

Figure 11.5   Three-layer architecture

The most important change from the two-layer model is that you no longer need to package data from your database within `DataTable` objects. Recall with the two-layer model, data is returned from your sample data access classes within `DataTable` objects (you could have instead used `DataSet` objects). When a `Data-Table` or `DataSet` is being bound directly to a control, they are a supreme convenience. However, there are times when you need to programmatically retrieve and manipulate the individual data items within the `DataSet` or `DataTable`. As you saw in Chapter 8, the code for this is a bit messy. For instance, if you need to retrieve the `LastName` field value from the first `DataRow` of the first `DataTable` in the `DataSet`, your code would be

```
txtLastName.Text = myDataSet.Tables[0].Rows[0]["LastName"];
```

Even worse, because the `DataTable` probably mirrors the table design of your database, you will have introduced database-dependent code into your presentation layer. Furthermore, even if you are not programming against a filled `DataTable` or `DataSet`, this two-layer approach still ensures that a great deal of database-specific markup is contained in your Web Forms. For instance, consider the following `Grid-View` definition.

```
<asp:GridView ID="grdSample" runat="server"
   DataSource="someSource" >

   <Columns>
      <asp:BoundField DataField="Isbn" HeaderText="Isbn" />
      <asp:TemplateField HeaderText="Title">
         <ItemTemplate>
           <%# Eval("Title") %>
         </ItemTemplate>
      </asp:TemplateField>
   </Columns>
</asp:GridView>
```

This markup has references to two implementation details from your database, namely that you have two fields named `Isbn` and `Title`. The two-layer model (or even worse, the one layer model) sprinkles such database details throughout your Web Forms. By making your Web Forms tightly coupled to the database implementation, you significantly decrease their maintainability. This means that any changes to your database (such as a change in the field names) probably result in plenty of time spent making changes to all Web Forms that use that database. Although this might be okay if you are being paid by the hour by a generous and forgiving client, it is undoubtedly unacceptable for most real-world clients!

Designing and Implementing a Business Object

The advantage of the three-layer approach is that you can better insulate the presentation layer from potential changes in the database. Instead of your Web Forms interacting with database-specific `DataTable` or `DataSet` objects, they interact with classes generally referred to as *business objects*. In this approach, each record is represented by a separate instance of the relevant business class. The field values from a record are stored in data members within the business object; these data values are made visible via properties, as shown in the following example.

```
public class SampleBusinessObject
{
```

```
// Data members
private int _id;
private string _name;

...

// Properties
public int Id
{
    get { return _id; }
    set { _id= value; }
}
public string Name
{
    get { return _name; }
    set { _name = value; }
}

...

}
```

Your Web Forms can thus access the data for a record through the much cleaner property syntax. These properties can be accessed programmatically, as shown here.

```
txtName.Text = aCustomer.Name
```

The properties can also be referenced declaratively and within data-binding expressions.

```
<asp:GridView ID="grdSample" runat="server"
    DataSource="someSource" >

    <Columns>
        <asp:BoundField DataField="Id" HeaderText="Id" />
        <asp:TemplateField HeaderText="Name">
            <ItemTemplate>
              <%# Eval("Name") %>
            </ItemTemplate>
        </asp:TemplateField>
    </Columns>
</asp:GridView>
```

The principle advantage of this approach is that the presentation layer is no longer dependent upon the database implementation details, because you are referencing an object property rather than a field name in the DataTable. As well, by eliminating the DataSet or DataTable, the code is certainly much more clean and readable.

CORE NOTE

If you want to have compile-time type verification for your data-binding expressions, you could use the more verbose `Container.DataItem` alternative to the `Eval` method, as shown in the following example.

```
<ItemTemplate>
  <%# ((Book)Container.DataItem)Book.Name %>
</ItemTemplate>
```

Thus, the business layer implements and represents the business or application functionality/logic/processes/data. Depending upon the application, the classes in this layer may encapsulate

- Business/application data in various custom classes
- Validation logic/business rules for the application
- Business/application process or workflow, such as an order process and fulfillment pipeline or a customer support workflow

By removing the business rules and application logic from the presentation layer, your Web Forms can become much simpler. The Web Forms now contain only markup and user-interface event handling. Everything else is contained in these other classes.

Figure 11.6 illustrates some of the classes that might be used within a business layer for a sample Book Catalog application.

It should be noted here that business objects should not just be containers for data about the object. Business objects should also contain logic. For instance, they might contain methods for retrieving or saving its data (by using classes from a data access layer), implementing application logic, authorizing access, as well as validating data against business rules.

Another point to notice in Figure 11.6 is that you need additional business objects to represent collections of the business objects. Again, these business collection classes should not be just containers of data, but should contain logic as well. In the example illustrated in Figure 11.6, the business collection classes contain the capability to load themselves from a data source (using classes from your data access layer), as well as to update or add themselves to the data source.

It is most likely that an application's business objects have some shared functionality. This shared functionality can be placed in a common base class. In Figure 11.6, this is the `AbstractBO` class, whose code is contained in Listing 11.1. It has data members that keep track of whether an object is new, whether it has been modified, and whether a subclass's data is valid against its business rules. Because classes that use these business objects may want to be able to determine which business rules are broken, the `AbstractBO` class maintains a collection of broken rules as well as methods for adding and retrieving the collection, which, for simplicity sake, are a list of strings in this example. Because each individual business object knows how to determine whether its data is valid, `AbstractBO` defines an abstract member `CheckIfSubClassStateIsValid`, which is implemented by each of its concrete subclasses.

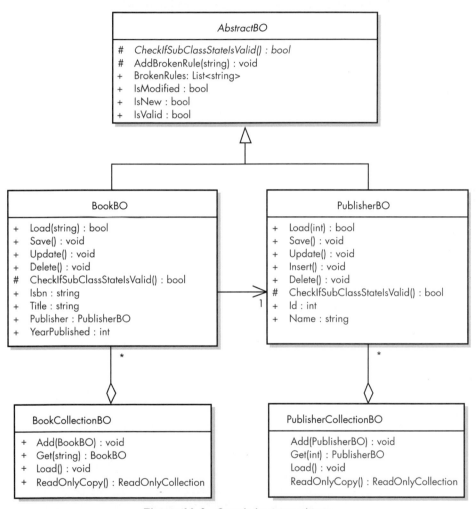

Figure 11.6 Sample business objects

CORE NOTE

In this example, each business object is responsible for checking its business rules. Another more complicated but more adaptable approach is to encapsulate these rules within their own object hierarchy, which could then be acted upon by some type of separate rule management class. For more information on this type of approach, see Jimmy Nilsson's *Applying Domain-Driven Design and Patterns*.

Listing 11.1   AbstractBO.cs

```
using System;
using System.Data;
using System.Collections.Generic;

namespace ThreeLayer.Business
{
    /// <summary>
    /// Represents the base class for all business objects
    /// </summary>
    public abstract class AbstractBO
    {
        // Data members
        protected const int DEFAULT_ID = 0;
        // Flags for whether object is new or has been modified
        private bool _isNew = true;
        private bool _isModified = false;
        // Collection of descriptions of all broken rules
        private List<string> _brokenRules = new List<string>();

        /// <summary>
        /// Each subclass is responsible for checking if its
        /// own state (data members) has any broken business rules
        /// </summary>
        protected abstract bool CheckIfSubClassStateIsValid
        {
            get;
        }

        /// <summary>
        /// Subclasses need capability to add broken rule description
        /// </summary>
        protected void AddBrokenRule(string rule)
        {
            _brokenRules.Add(rule);
        }
```

```csharp
/// <summary>
/// Return the descriptions of any broken rules
/// </summary>
public List<string> BrokenRules
{
    get { return _brokenRules; }
}

/// <summary>
/// Is the business object valid
/// </summary>
public bool IsValid
{
    get
    {
        _brokenRules.Clear();
        return CheckIfSubClassStateIsValid;
    }
}

/// <summary>
/// Has the business object been modified since last save
/// </summary>
protected bool IsModified
{
    get { return _isModified; }
    set { _isModified = value; }
}

/// <summary>
/// Is this business object new or does it contain
/// data that exists in database
/// </summary>
protected bool IsNew
{
    get { return _isNew; }
    set { _isNew = value; }
}

    }
}
```

I don't provide the code for all the classes in Figure 11.6 (although you can get it from my Web site, http://www.randyconnolly.com/core). However, I do provide the code for the PublisherBO business class in Listing 11.2.

This class encapsulates the data for a single publisher and the methods necessary for loading, updating, inserting, and deleting a publisher (by using a data access class similar to that shown at the end of Chapter 9). This business class also needs the capability to determine if its data breaks any of its business rules. The protected `CheckIfSubClassStateIsValid` property ensures that the publisher name is not empty and that the publisher ID is not less than zero. As well, when adding a publisher, this property also ensures that a publisher with the same name doesn't already exist. Any broken rules are added to the `BrokenRules` collection (defined in `AbstractBO`).

Listing 11.2 PublisherBO.cs

```csharp
using System;
using System.Data;

using ThreeLayer.DataAccess;

namespace ThreeLayer.Business
{
    /// <summary>
    /// Business object for publisher information
    /// </summary>
    public class PublisherBO: AbstractBO
    {
        // Data members
        private int _id = DEFAULT_ID;
        private string _name = "";

        // Constructors
        public PublisherBO() { }
        public PublisherBO(int id, string name)
        {
            _id = id;
            _name = name;
            IsNew = false;
            IsModified = true;
        }

        /// <summary>
        /// Loads the object with data based on the passed ID
        /// </summary>
        /// <returns>
        /// True if successfully loaded with valid data,
        /// false otherwise
        /// </returns>
        public bool Load(int id)
        {
```

```csharp
    PublisherDA da = new PublisherDA();
    DataTable table = da.GetById(id);

    // If the table has no data, load failed
    if (table.Rows.Count == 0)
    {
        AddBrokenRule("Publisher with id=" + id +
            " was not found");
        return false;
    }

    // Set the data members to retrieved data
    Id = (int)table.Rows[0]["PublisherId"];
    Name = (string)table.Rows[0]["PublisherName"];
    IsNew = false;

    // Make sure loaded data is valid according to rules
    return IsValid;
}

/// <summary>
/// Saves the object's data. If this is a new object,
/// insert the data; otherwise, update the data
/// if it has changed
/// </summary>
public void Save()
{
    if (IsNew)
        Insert();
    else
        Update();
}

/// <summary>
/// Only updates the data
/// </summary>
public void Update()
{
    if (IsValid)
    {
        if (IsModified)
        {
            PublisherDA da = new PublisherDA();
            da.UpdatePublisher(Id, Name);
            IsModified = false;
        }
    }
}
```

```csharp
/// <summary>
/// Only inserts the data
/// </summary>
public void Insert()
{
    IsNew = true;
    if (IsValid)
    {
        PublisherDA da = new PublisherDA();
        da.InsertPublisher(Name);
    }
}


/// <summary>
/// Deletes the data
/// </summary>
public void Delete()
{
    PublisherDA da = new PublisherDA();
    da.DeletePublisher(Id);
}


/// <summary>
/// Checks if the internal state of the business
/// object is valid
/// </summary>
protected override bool CheckIfSubClassStateIsValid
{
    get
    {
        bool valid = true;
        if (Name.Length == 0)
        {
            AddBrokenRule("Publisher Name can not be empty");
            valid = false;
        }
        if (Id < 0)
        {
            AddBrokenRule(
                "Publisher Id can not be less than zero");
            valid = false;
        }
        // This is an example of a more complex rule
        if (IsNew)
        {
            // Ensure this title doesn't already exist
            PublisherDA da = new PublisherDA();
            DataTable dt = da.GetByName(Name);
            if (dt.Rows.Count > 0)
```

```
            {
                AddBrokenRule("Publisher name already exists");
                valid = false;
            }
        }
        return valid;
    }
}

// Properties

public int Id
{
    get { return _id; }
    set {
        _id = value;
        IsModified = true;
    }
}
public string Name
{
    get { return _name; }
    set {
        _name = value;
        IsModified = true;
    }
}
    }
}
}
```

CORE NOTE

In this and other examples in this chapter, I have significantly simplified the code for explanatory purposes. For instance, this class should have more error checking, support for transactions, and perhaps a decoupled rule defining mechanism.

Using Namespaces

Notice that the examples in these listings make use of the C# namespace keyword. This keyword is used to organize your classes by defining a globally unique type definition. The .NET Framework class library makes use of namespaces to ensure there are no naming conflicts. For instance, there is an Image class in the System.Drawing and System.Web.UI.WebControls namespaces. When you add the using directive to the top of your classes, you are indicating that you will reference classes from that namespace without specifying a fully qualified name.

Thus, if you want to use the `PublisherBO` class in a Web Form code-behind class, you have to add a reference.

```
using ThreeLayer.Business;
...
PublisherBO pub = new PublisherBO();
```

Alternately, you would have to use a fully qualified name.

```
ThreeLayer.Business.PublisherBO pub = new
   ThreeLayer.Business.PublisherBO();
```

Using the Business Object Programmatically

To use this business object in your Web Form, you can use it in an `ObjectData-Source` or you can use it programmatically. For instance, to display the collection of publishers within a `GridView`, you could programmatically bind its read-only collection to the control's `DataSource` property.

```
PublisherCollectionBO pubs = new PublisherCollectionBO();

grdPublishers.DataSource = pubs.ReadOnlyCopy();
grdPublishers.DataBind();
```

Imagine that this same `GridView` has a select button on each row. When the user selects a row, you display the contents of the selected publisher. The code for this might look similar to the following.

```
// Determine ID of selected publisher
int pubId = (int)grdPublishers.SelectedDataKey.Values[0];

// Create the publisher business object and load its data
PublisherBO pub = new PublisherBO();
if (pub.Load(pubId))
{
   panPublisher.Visible = true;
   labId.Text = pub.Id.ToString();
   txtName.Text = pub.Name;
}
```

In this example, you create the publisher business object and tell it to load itself with the data for the selected `PublisherId`. If the load was successful, you can retrieve the field values via properties of the business object.

To update the data in the database, you can also use this same business class. The following example illustrates how a new `PublisherBO` object is created and populated from the Web Form data. It then asks the object to update itself; if the update was unsuccessful due to a broken business rule, it displays the collection of broken rule strings in some control on the form.

```
// Grab the ID and title values
int id = Convert.ToInt32(labId.Text);
string name = txtName.Text;

// Create the publisher business object and try to update it
PublisherBO pub = new PublisherBO(id, name);
pub.Update();

// See if update was successful
if (!pub.IsValid)
{
    // Update was unsuccessful so show any broken business rules
    grdErrors.DataSource = pub.BrokenRules;
    grdErrors.DataBind();
}
```

Using Business Objects with the ObjectDataSource

As you saw in the last chapter, you can bind data controls to any class using the `ObjectDataSource` control. Indeed, you can display the publishers in the `PublisherCollectionBO` class reasonably easily with the `ObjectDataSource`.

```
<asp:ObjectDataSource ID="dsBusiness" runat="server"
    TypeName="ThreeLayer.Business.PublisherCollectionBO"
    SelectMethod="ReadOnlyCopy" >
```

However, you run into some trouble using the `PublisherBO` business object with the `ObjectDataSource`. Unfortunately, the way this control is designed may cause problems for the typical single item business object. The first issue that you may run across is that if you want to use the `ObjectDataSource` control to display and manipulate a business object within a data control such as the `DetailsView`, you may find it difficult to use the business object's own load, update, and insert functionality. When you design a business object, you typically encapsulate not only its data but its capability to load and save its data (by using classes from the data access layer). This typical design can cause some problems when you try to use this functionality in an `ObjectDataSource` control.

For instance, assume that you have a Web Form with a `DetailsView` control that displays and updates data from the `PublisherBO`. Each `PublisherBO` object has the capability to populate its own data members from the database via its `Load` method. However, recall that the method specified by the `SelectMethod` of the `ObjectDataSource` control must return the data that you want to display in the control. This means that you need a method that returns an already populated `PublisherBO` object. Thus, you need some *other* class that returns the populated business object you require (you might call this type of class an ***adapter***, based on the Adapter design pattern). Alternately, you need to add a static method to the business object that returns a populated business object, as shown in the following.

```
public class PublisherBO: AbstractBO
{
    ...
    public static PublisherBO RetrievePublisher(int pubId)
    {
        PublisherBO pub = new PublisherBO();
        if (pub.Load(pubId))
            return pub;
        else
            return null;
    }
}
```

You have a similar problem with the update. Each `PublisherBO` object has the capability to save or update the database via its `Save` or `Update` method. However, the `ObjectDataSource` control expects its specified update method to take either a `PublisherBO` object as a parameter or a list of parameters that correspond to the data values being updated. Again, you need some other class that has an update method that takes a `PublisherBO` object as a parameter (and which simply invokes the business object's own update method), or you need to add a static method to the business object that updates the passed `PublisherBO` object.

```
public class PublisherBO: AbstractBO
{
    ...
    public static void UpdatePublisher(PublisherBO pub)
    {
        pub.Update();
    }
}
```

Your `ObjectDataSource` control might thus look similar to that shown in the following example (it uses a querystring parameter to determine which publisher to display).

```
<asp:ObjectDataSource ID="dsBusiness" runat="server"
   TypeName="ThreeLayer.Business.PublisherBO"
   SelectMethod="RetrievePublisher"
   UpdateMethod="UpdatePublisher"
   DataObjectTypeName="ThreeLayer.Business.PublisherBO">

   <SelectParameters>
      <asp:QueryStringParameter Name="pubId"
         QueryStringField="id" />
   </SelectParameters>

</asp:ObjectDataSource>
```

In this example, you need to also specify the `DataObjectTypeName` property of the control. This property is used to specify the class name of the object the control uses for a parameter in an update, insert, or delete operation.

In this example, the select and update method are contained within the business object; alternately, you could have created a separate adapter class that would have contained the `RetrievePublisher` and `UpdatePublisher` methods, which would have changed your `ObjectDataSource` as follows.

```
<asp:ObjectDataSource ID="dsBusiness" runat="server"
   TypeName="SomeAdapterClass"
   SelectMethod="RetrievePublisher"
   UpdateMethod="UpdatePublisher"
   DataObjectTypeName="ThreeLayer.Business.PublisherBO">
```

Another potential issue with business objects and the `ObjectDataSource` control is that the internal logic within a typical business object may not integrate well with the control. For instance, a common pattern that is often followed with business objects is to use a custom factory class for the creation and customization of the different business objects in the application. However, the `ObjectDataSource` control instantiates any object used with it by using the object's default constructor. As well, when using the `DataObjectTypeName` property of the control to pass a business object to a update, insert, or delete method, it creates a new instance of the business object, populates some of its properties, and then passes it to the appropriate method (see Figure 11.7).

This behavior may cause problems for business objects that make use of internal logic to decide whether to update or insert its data. For instance, your business object can figure out if it needs to update an existing record or insert a new record based on the state of its `IsNew` property, which, unfortunately for `ObjectData-Source` compatibility, is set to `true` in the default constructor.

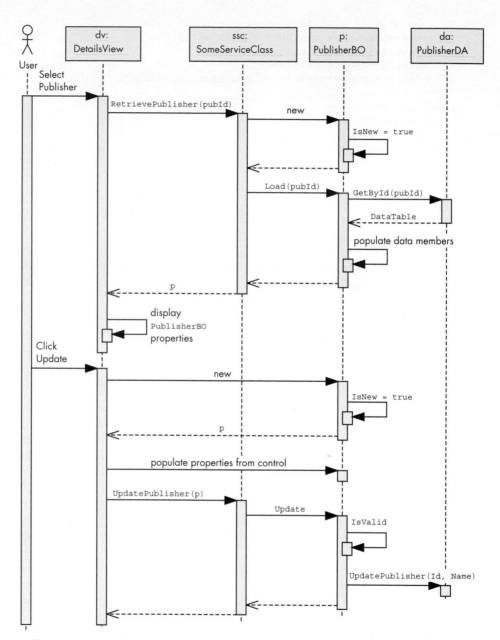

Figure 11.7 Interaction between list control, ObjectDataSource, and a business object

You could certainly redesign your business objects to work better with the `ObjectDataSource`. In fact, you need to do so in order to support paging and sorting for the collection-based business objects. However, some software designers may find the idea of redesigning the business layer to suit the needs of the presentation layer to be one that is very much an anathema to them. In other situations, there may be existing business objects that cannot be redesigned without breaking other existing applications. In such a case, you need to create a façade or an adapter class that provides an interface more suitable for the `ObjectDataSource`. Of course, you may decide to forgo the use of the `ObjectDataSource` all together and simply perform your data binding and data processing the "old-fashioned" ASP.NET 1.1 way via short programming snippets in the code-behind.

As an alternative to the three-layer model, you could instead use a four-layer model. This four-layer model has several advantages, one of which is that potentially it is easier to integrate the four-layer model with the `ObjectDataSource`.

Four-Layer Model

In the basic three-layer model, the business layer is not particularly cohesive, in that it might encapsulate business data, business rules, as well as application logic and processes. To make the business layer more cohesive, some programmers place the application logic and processes in the presentation layer; this unfortunately often results in a very messy and hard to modify presentation layer.

Designing a Four-Layer Architecture

A better approach is to separate the application processes and logic away from both the presentation layer and the business data and operations as shown in Figure 11.8.

In this scheme, the presentation and data access layers are much the same as in the three-layer scheme. The difference in the four-layer model is how the business layer is divided into two: the domain layer and the application logic layer. This follows a common scheme in that the two types of business logic—domain logic and application logic (sometimes also called workflow logic)—are placed into two separate layers.

The *application logic layer* is responsible for coordinating and controlling the application logic and processes; that is, it controls the software in the jobs the software is meant to do. The operations in this layer very often align with specific use cases. You may find this layer referred to as a service layer (Fowler or Nilsson), a controller layer, a management layer, or a business workflow layer (Microsoft).

The application logic layer's objects should contain no state data about the business, but may have state data about the application processes. It delegates most of the business data related work to the *domain layer*, which is responsible for representing the data and rules of the business/application.

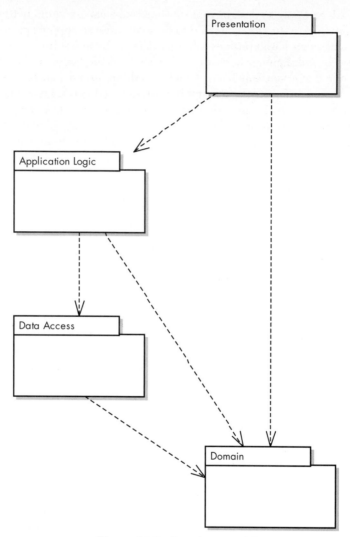

Figure 11.8   Four-layer model

Because this domain layer contains these rules and data, it is very much the focus of the initial design of the application. The classes in this layer are also sometimes referred to as ***entities***. Although the classes within the domain layer may align with the tables in the database (which can be seen later in Figure 11.10), this is by no means necessary. Instead, the classes in the entity layer are meant to represent the concepts in the problem domain of the application. In fact, you already encountered a domain class with the `Customer` class back in Chapter 8.

The final thing to note about the four-layer model shown in Figure 11.8 is that the classes in the domain layer are used by the other three layers. The rationale for this approach is that the entity classes in this model are used to package data as it is passed between the layers. Therefore, they play the role that the `DataTable` played in the two- and three-layer models. You may recall that in the two- and three-layer model, the different data access classes packaged requested data retrieved from the database within a `DataTable` and returned it the requestor. As a result, the user of any of the data access classes had to manipulate the ADO.NET `DataTable`, even though it was not itself a data access class.

As an alternative, in the four-layer model shown in Figure 11.8, the data access classes create and populate the entity classes themselves. For those situations in which multiple data records are being retrieved, the data access classes create multiple instances of the appropriate entity class and then place them within an `EntityCollection`, the same generic-using collection class that we created back in Chapter 8.

Figure 11.9 illustrates some sample classes for your domain layer. Notice that each domain class is a subclass of the `AbstractEntity` class, which is similar to the one that you encountered in Chapter 8, and has some of the same functionality as `AbstractBO`, the base class for all the business classes in the three-layer model.

The different domain classes share some of the same functionality as the business object classes shown in Figure 11.5. The main difference is that the domain classes lack the capability to interact with the database. As a result, these domain classes are reasonably equivalent to what some designers in the Java world call a ***data transfer object***. This term refers to a class that contains just data members with properties for accessing the data members. The main difference between a data transfer object and one of your domain classes is that your domain class also contains behavior for checking and validating business rules.

Finally, note the relationships between the different domain classes in Figure 11.9. Like the business objects in the three-layer model, the entities in the four-layer model represent concepts or things in your application's problem domain. In the example book application, a book has a publisher, a series, a category, and multiple authors. Thus, a `Book` entity has a `Publisher` entity, a `Series` entity, a `Category` entity, and a collection of `Author` entities. Although these relationships follow the data model in your database, they are not identical. For instance, a book entity has a `Publisher` entity object, whereas a `Books` record has a `PublisherId` foreign key; a book entity has a collection of `Author` entity objects, whereas the authors for a given book record are contained in the `AuthorBooks` and `Authors` tables.

It is beyond the scope of this chapter to cover how to best design a domain model. For readers interested in learning more about this topic, see the Evans, Fowler, and Nilsson books cited in the References section at the end of the chapter.

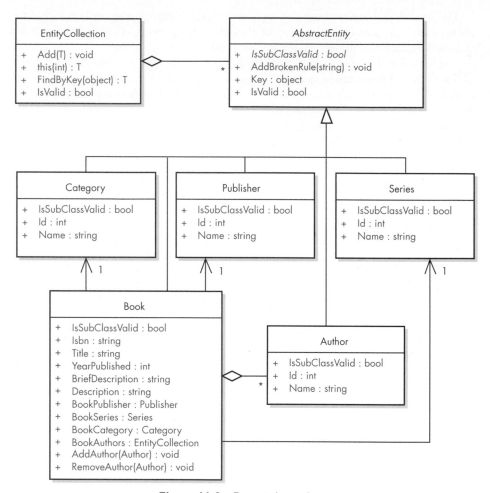

Figure 11.9 Domain layer classes

Modifying the Data Access Layer

In the four-layer model, the business entity classes are used to transport data between the layers. As a result, you have to make some changes to the data access classes that you created at the end of the last chapter. Your data access classes still implement basic CRUD functionality and inherit from an abstract base class; the difference with this version of these classes is that they take entities as parameters and return data within these same entities.

For instance, the two-layer `BookDA` class (a version of which was shown at the end of Chapter 9) contained an `UpdateBook` method. This method was passed each of the data values that needed to be saved, as shown here.

```
public void UpdateBook(string isbn, string title,
    int publisherId, int categoryId,
    int seriesId, int yearPublished,
    string briefDescription, string description)
```

In the new four-layer approach, this method simply is passed a populated `Book` entity object.

```
public void Update(Book book)
```

Similarly, the methods for retrieving data change as well. The old `BookDA` class had the following method that returned a `DataTable` containing one row of data.

```
public DataTable GetBookByIsbn(string isbn)
```

The new version now simply returns a populated `Book` entity.

```
public Book GetBookByIsbn(string isbn)
```

The change to entities does seem to simplify the data access layer. However, there is some complexity that must be added to your layer to modify the `GetAll` method. In the two-layer data access layer, the `GetAll` method was implemented in the base class `AbstractDA`. It simply returned a filled `DataTable` for the relevant `SELECT` command.

```
public DataTable GetAll()
{
    string sql = SelectStatement;
    return GetDataTable(sql, null);
}
```

Here is the problem: What does this method return in the four-layer version? Ideally, it returns a strongly typed version of `EntityCollection` that contains the appropriate entity objects. The trouble is this method was defined in the base class. Because the old version just returned a filled `DataTable`, it didn't need to concern itself with the type of data being returned. Now, however, if you want to return a strongly typed collection, your base class seemingly needs to know which type of data is to be returned. Of course, you could implement the `GetAll` method in each of your data access classes; unfortunately, this adds a great deal of almost identical code to each of data access classes.

The solution to this problem lies in using the C# generics covered in Chapter 8 along with the ***Template Method pattern***. This pattern is often used to eliminate repetitive coding in subclasses by defining the main steps of an algorithm in a base class and let the subclasses implement only those parts of the algorithm that varies from subclass to subclass.

Look at the algorithm that you need to implement for your `GetAll` method. The basic steps in this algorithm are as follows.

1.   Create a connection object
2.   Configure select command string
3.   Create and configure a command object
4.   Open connection
5.   Execute a data reader
6.   Create an entity collection object
7.   For each record in data reader:
8.1 Retrieve field values from record
8.2 Create appropriate business entity object
8.3 Populate entity with field values
8.4 Add entity to entity collection
9.   Close reader and connection
10. Return entity collection

Which of these steps vary from one data access subclass to another? Step 2 and steps 8.1 through 8.3 vary from subclass to subclass. All the other steps in the algorithm are fixed and independent of the data being retrieved. In the existing `AbstractDA` class, you handled the variable step 2 via the following.

```
string sql = SelectStatement;
```

You may recall from Chapter 9 that the property `SelectStatement` is defined in `AbstractDA`, and is implemented in each of the subclasses. This is an example of the Template Method pattern! All you need to do then is define an abstract method in `AbstractDA` that performs steps 8.1, 8.2, and 8.3, and then implement this method in each of your subclasses. Because this method is responsible for creating a single entity and populating it with field values from the current record, you define it as follows.

```
protected abstract AbstractEntity CreateAndFillEntity(DbDataReader
    reader)
```

What might this method look like when it is implemented? The following example illustrates how this method might look in the data access class for the publishers.

```
protected override AbstractEntity CreateAndFillEntity(
    DbDataReader recordJustRead)
{
    // Grab the record values and put them
    // into temporary variables
    int id = (int)recordJustRead["PublisherId"];
```

```
string name = (string)recordJustRead["PublisherName"];

// Build and populate object from the data
Publisher pub = new Publisher(id, name);
return pub;
}
```

CORE NOTE

To simplify this and other code snippets in this chapter for easier comprehension, some exception handling and other details have been left out. The complete versions are available from my Web site, http://www.randyconnolly.com/core.

Now that we have a sample version of the template method implemented, let us turn to the implementation of the GetAll algorithm within AbstractDA. To simplify, we will only look at steps 5 through 10.

```
EntityCollection<AbstractEntity> collection;
Collection = new EntityCollection<AbstractEntity>();

DbDataReader reader = cmd.ExecuteReader();
while (reader.Read())
{
    collection.Add( CreateAndFillEntity(reader) );
}
reader.Close();
conn.Close();
return(collection);
```

Because you are returning a collection and not a DataTable, there is no need to incur the overhead of using a DataAdapter to fill a DataSet; instead, you can use the much faster DataReader. You can simply loop through the returned data reader, get each subclass to read the record, create and fill the appropriate entity, and then add this entity to the collection.

However, there is a problem with the preceding example. If you recall from Chapter 8, the EntityCollection class is defined using generics to make it a strongly typed collection, yet in the preceding example, you are returning a collection of AbstractEntity objects. This means that any class that manipulates this collection still needs to cast the entities to the appropriate type, as shown here.

```
PublisherDA dao = new PublisherDA();
EntityCollection<AbstractEntity> collection = dao.GetAll();
Publisher pub = (Publisher)collection[0];
```

Because the `EntityCollection` class supports generics, you should modify your `AbstractDA` so that it uses generics as well. First, you can change its class definition so that it accepts a constrained type parameter that is similar to the one you used for `EntityCollection` in Chapter 8.

```
public abstract class AbstractDA<T> where T : AbstractEntity
```

Within `AbstractDA`, you use the type parameter wherever you were previously referencing `AbstractEntity`. Thus, the abstract `CreateAndFillEntity` definition changes to the following.

```
protected abstract T CreateAndFillEntity(DbDataReader reader);
```

The creation of the collection (i.e., step 5 in the algorithm) changes as well.

```
EntityCollection<T> collection = new EntityCollection<T>();
```

Finally, you need to modify each of your subclasses so that they supply the appropriate entity class name wherever you use the T type parameter in `AbstractDA`.

```
public class PublisherDA: AbstractDA<Publisher>
{
    protected override Publisher CreateAndFillEntity(…)
    {
        …
    }
    …
}
```

Creating a Complex Domain Entity

You have seen that the `CreateAndFillEntity` template method has the responsibility for creating the appropriate entity type, extracting record values, and then populating the entity from these record values. The example of this method for the `PublisherDA` class was quite straightforward. The version of this method for `BooksDA` needs to be more complicated, however, because the `Book` entity contains not just primitive data types but also other business entities (see Figure 11.9). Handling the `Book` entity's `Publisher`, `Category`, and `Series` entities is fairly straightforward, because the `Books` table exists in a many-to-one relationship with the `Publisher`, `Category`, and `Series` tables (see Figure 11.10).

If you include the fields for each of these additional tables in the SELECT statement for the books (see the following example), you can simply instantiate and fill a `Publisher`, `Category`, and `Series` entity after you read the book record.

```
protected override string SelectStatement
{
    get {
```

```
    return "SELECT ISBN,Title,YearPublished,BriefDescription,
        Description,PublisherName,Books.PublisherId As
        BookPublisherId,SeriesName,Books.SeriesId As
        BookSeriesId,CategoryName,Books.CategoryId As
        BookCategoryId FROM Series INNER JOIN
        (Publishers INNER JOIN (Categories INNER JOIN
        Books ON Categories.CategoryId = Books.CategoryId)
        ON Publishers.PublisherId = Books.PublisherId)
        ON Series.SeriesId = Books.SeriesId";
    }
}
```

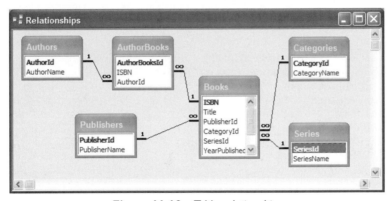

Figure 11.10 Table relationships

Handling the authors for a book is a more complicated matter because the `Books` and `Authors` tables exist in a many-to-many relationship. You use the `GetAuthors-ForIsbn` method of the `AuthorDA` class to retrieve a collection of `Author` objects for the current `ISBN`. Each `Author` entity in this collection is then added to your `Book` entity, as shown here.

```
protected override Book CreateAndBuildEntity(DbDataReader
    recordJustRead)
{
    // Grab the record values and put them
    // into temporary variables
    string isbn = (string)recordJustRead["ISBN"];
    string title = (string)recordJustRead["Title"];
    int yearPub = (int)recordJustRead["YearPublished"];
    string brief = (string)recordJustRead["BriefDescription"];
    string desc = (string)recordJustRead["Description"];
    string pubName = (string)recordJustRead["PublisherName"];
    int pubId = (int)recordJustRead["BookPublisherId"];
    string seriesName = (string)recordJustRead["SeriesName"];
    int seriesId = (int)recordJustRead["BookSeriesId"];
```

```
string catName = (string)recordJustRead["CategoryName"];
int catId = (int)recordJustRead["BookCategoryId"];

// Build and populate object from the data
Book book = new Book(isbn, title, yearPub, brief, desc);

// Create child entities
Publisher publisher = new Publisher(pubId, pubName);
Category category = new Category(catId, catName);
Series series = new Series(seriesId, seriesName);

// Add child entities to book
book.BookPublisher = publisher;
book.BookCategory = category;
book.BookSeries = series;

// Get all the authors for this book
AuthorDA dao = new AuthorDA();
EntityCollection<Author> authors =
    dao.GetAuthorsForIsbn(isbn);

// Add each author to the book
foreach (Author author in authors)
{
    book.AddAuthor(author);
}

return book;
}
```

The `GetAuthorsForIsbn` method in `AuthorDA` queries the `AuthorBooks` and `Authors` tables and returns a list of `Author` entities for the passed `ISBN` value.

```
public EntityCollection<Author> GetAuthorsForIsbn(string isbn)
{
    EntityCollection<Author> collection =
      new EntityCollection<Author>();

    using (DbConnection conn =
        DatabaseActions.Factory.CreateConnection())
    {
        conn.ConnectionString =
            DatabaseActions.ConnectionSetting.ConnectionString;
        conn.Open();

        DbCommand cmd = DatabaseActions.Factory.CreateCommand();
        cmd.Connection = conn;
        cmd.CommandText =
            "SELECT AuthorBooks.AuthorId,AuthorName,ISBN
              FROM Authors INNER JOIN AuthorBooks ON
```

```
        Authors.AuthorId = AuthorBooks.AuthorId ";
    cmd.CommandText += " WHERE ISBN=@ISBN";
    cmd.CommandType = CommandType.Text;

    // Add parameters
    cmd.Parameters.Add(DatabaseActions.MakeParameter(
        "@ISBN",isbn));

    DbDataReader reader = cmd.ExecuteReader();
    if (reader != null)
    {
        while (reader.Read())
        {
            // Create author entity and add to collection
            collection.Add(CreateAndBuildEntity(reader));
        }
        reader.Close();
        conn.Close();
    }
}
return collection;
}
```

Finally, you would have to modify the `Update` and `Insert` methods for `BookDA` in a similar fashion so that any child tables are updated as well.

Creating the Application Logic Layer

Now that you have examined some of the classes within the business entity and the data access layers, you can finally construct your application logic layer. You may recall that this layer is intended to encapsulate the required functionalities and processes of the application, and as such it tends to mirror the functionality specified within use cases. The class methods in this layer are often quite thin in that they generally delegate most of their actual functionality to the underlying domain and data access layers.

Imagine that you are designing an application layer for a Web application that is using not only the entities from Figure 11.9 but other entities as well, such as `Customer`, `CustomerAddress`, `Order`, `Payment`, `CreditCard`, and some other classes pertaining to ordering or the customer. You may decide that your application layer is based on three classes that encapsulate the three basic subsystems of functionality in your application: `BookCatalogLogic`, `CustomerServiceLogic`, and `OrderLogic`.

After examining your use cases, you may decide that you need the following functionality in your `BookCatalogLogic` class:

- Get a list of all publishers
- Get a list of all book categories

- Get a list of all book series
- Get a list of all books
- Get a book by its ISBN
- Get a list of all books for a specified publisher
- Get a list of all books for a specified series
- Get a list of all books for a specified category
- Update a book

If this is the only functionality that you require, then, you can design your `Book-CatalogLogic` class as shown in Figure 11.11.

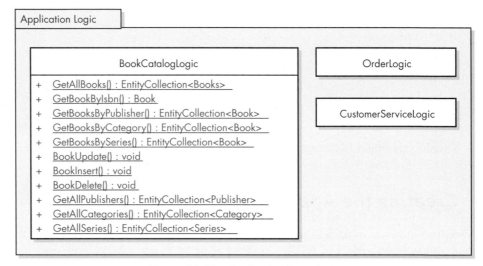

Figure 11.11   Application layer design

CORE NOTE

This example application logic layer is mainly a service layer in that it doesn't contain any examples of more complex application or process logic. If this chapter was going to show the `OrderLogic` class, you would see more process-oriented methods, for instance, `CheckOutPipeline` or `MoveProductFromDistributorToInventory`.

As already mentioned, the classes in the application logic layer contain little if any state and delegate most of its functionality to other layers. Listing 11.3 illustrates a sample implementation for your `BookCatalogLogic` class for the functionality listed previously.

Listing 11.3 BookCatalogLogic.cs

```csharp
using System;
using System.Data;
using System.Collections.Generic;

using FourLayer.BusinessEntity;
using FourLayer.DataAccessObject;

namespace FourLayer.ApplicationLogic
{
    /// <summary>
    /// Handles all the application logic for book catalog
    /// </summary>
    public class BookCatalogLogic
    {
        // --------------------------------------------------
        // Book methods
        // --------------------------------------------------
        public static EntityCollection<Book> GetAllBooks()
        {
            BookDAO dao = new BookDAO();
            return dao.GetAll();
        }

        public static Book GetBookByIsbn(string isbn)
        {
            BookDAO dao = new BookDAO();
            Book b = dao.GetByKey(isbn);
            return b;
        }

        public static EntityCollection<Book>
            GetBooksByPublisher(Publisher pub)
        {
            BookDAO dao = new BookDAO();
            return dao.GetByCriteria("PublisherId", "=", pub.Id);
        }

        public static EntityCollection<Book> GetBooksByCategory(
            int catId)
        {
            BookDAO dao = new BookDAO();
            return
                dao.GetByCriteria("Books.CategoryId", "=", catId);
        }

        public static EntityCollection<Book>
            GetBooksBySeries(int seriesId)
```

```
{
    BookDAO dao = new BookDAO();
    return
        dao.GetByCriteria("Books.SeriesId", "=", seriesId);
}

public static void UpdateBook(Book book)
{
    if (book.IsValid)
    {
        BookDAO dao = new BookDAO();
        dao.Update(book);
    }
}

// -------------------------------------------------
// Publisher, series, categories, authors methods
// -------------------------------------------------
public static EntityCollection<Publisher>
    GetAllPublishers()
{
    PublisherDAO dao = new PublisherDAO();
    return dao.GetAll();
}

public static EntityCollection<Series> GetAllSeries()
{
    SeriesDAO dao = new SeriesDAO();
    return dao.GetAll();
}

public static EntityCollection<Category> GetAllCategories()
{
    CategoryDAO dao = new CategoryDAO();
    return dao.GetAll();
}
    }
}
```

Using the Architecture in the Presentation Layer

Now that you have created a layer infrastructure, you can make use of it in your
Web Forms. Walkthroughs 11.1 through 11.5 use these layers to create the Book-
Portal.aspx page shown in Figure 11.12. This page consists of four GridView

controls and one `DetailsView` control. All interaction with the data is performed via a number of `ObjectDataSource` controls that communicate with an application logic layer.

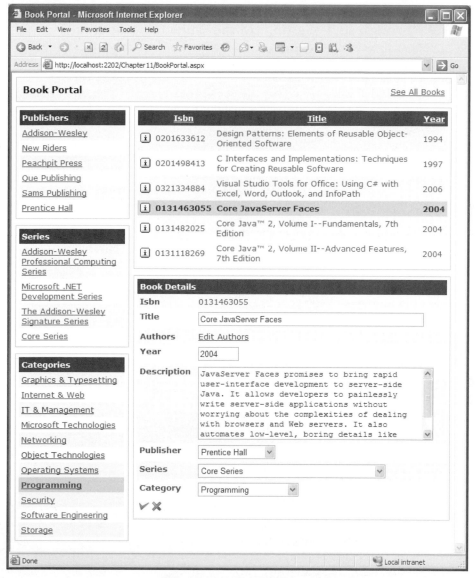

Figure 11.12 BookPortal.aspx

The links in the left column change the list of books visible in the GridView at the top of the right column. Selecting a book in this list displays the complete book information within a DetailsView control shown in the lower-right column. This control also allows the user to edit the book data, as shown in Figure 11.12.

Walkthrough 11.1 *Setting Up the ObjectDataSource Controls*

The first walkthrough exercise sets up several ObjectDataSource controls that will interact with the BookCatalogLogic class. After these are set up, the rest of the page is mainly additional markup.

1. Create a Web Form named BookPortal.aspx.

2. Add the following ObjectDataSource controls to the form. These ObjectDataSource controls are used by the four GridView controls.

```
<asp:ObjectDataSource ID="dsBooks" runat="server"
    TypeName="FourLayer.ApplicationLogic.BookCatalogLogic" />

<asp:ObjectDataSource ID="dsSeries" runat="server"
    TypeName="FourLayer.ApplicationLogic.BookCatalogLogic"
    SelectMethod="GetAllSeries" />

<asp:ObjectDataSource ID="dsPublishers" runat="server"
    TypeName="FourLayer.ApplicationLogic.BookCatalogLogic"
    SelectMethod="GetAllPublishers" />

<asp:ObjectDataSource ID="dsCategories" runat="server"
    TypeName="FourLayer.ApplicationLogic.BookCatalogLogic"
    SelectMethod="GetAllCategories" />
```

3. Create an additional ObjectDataSource control.

```
<asp:ObjectDataSource ID="dsBookSingle" runat="server"
    TypeName="FourLayer.ApplicationLogic.BookCatalogLogic"
    DataObjectTypeName="FourLayer.BusinessEntity.Book"
    SelectMethod="GetBookByIsbn"
    UpdateMethod="UpdateBook">

    <SelectParameters>
      <asp:ControlParameter ControlID="grdBooks"
          Name="isbn" Type="string"
          PropertyName="SelectedDataKey.Values[0]" />
    </SelectParameters>
</asp:ObjectDataSource>
```

This control is used by the `DetailsView` control that displays the complete contents of a single book. Notice that its select method (`GetBooksByIsbn`) requires a string parameter named `isbn` that contains the ISBN of the book to retrieve. The control populates this parameter from the ISBN value of the row selected in the books `GridView` control (to be defined yet). The `DataObjectTypeName` property must also be set because the specified update method is passed a populated `Book` object.

CORE NOTE

In these walkthrough exercises, only the bare outline of the controls and their functionality is described. The styling of the controls is left to the reader. You can download the finished version of the page, complete with styling, from my Web site, `http://www.randyconnolly.com/core`.

Walkthrough 11.2 *Adding GridView Controls to a Web Form*

Now that you have defined the controls that will interact with your application logic layer, you can set up the user interface for your Web Form. The next walkthrough adds the four `GridView` controls to the form.

1. Add a `GridView` control to your form that is used to display a list of books.

```
<asp:GridView ID="grdBooks" runat="server"
   DataSourceID="dsBooks" DataKeyNames="Isbn"
   EmptyDataText="No books found"
      AutoGenerateColumns="False" >

   <Columns>
      <asp:CommandField
         SelectImageUrl="images/btn_select.gif"
         ButtonType="Image" ShowSelectButton="true" />
      <asp:BoundField DataField="Isbn" HeaderText="Isbn" />
      <asp:BoundField DataField="Title" HeaderText="Title" />
      <asp:BoundField DataField="YearPublished"
         HeaderText="Year" />
   </Columns>
</asp:GridView>
```

2. Add a `GridView` control to your form that is used to display a list of all possible book publishers.

```
<asp:GridView ID="grdPublisher" runat="server"
   DataSourceID="dsPublishers" DataKeyNames="Id"
   AutoGenerateColumns="False"
   OnSelectedIndexChanged=
      "grdPublisher_SelectedIndexChanged" >

   <Columns>
      <asp:TemplateField HeaderText="Publishers">
         <ItemTemplate>
            <asp:LinkButton ID="btnSelectPublisher"
               runat="server"
               Text='<%# Eval("Name") %>'
               CommandName="Select" />
         </ItemTemplate>
      </asp:TemplateField>
   </Columns>
</asp:GridView>
```

Notice that the `GridView` uses a selection event handler. When the user selects a publisher, the selection event handler (to be defined yet) changes the books displayed in the book's `GridView` control to only those books whose publisher matches the selected publisher.

For this example, you don't want a separate select column in the `GridView`. Instead, you want this `GridView` to consist of a single column containing the publisher names as links; the links in this case operate as selection buttons. Unfortunately, you cannot use a `CommandField` column because you need different `SelectText` for each row. As the example code illustrates, you can achieve this effect by using a `TemplateField` column containing a `LinkButton` with the `CommandName` set to `Select`.

3. Add a `GridView` control to your form that is used to display a list of the possible series names for the book.

```
<asp:GridView ID="grdSeries" runat="server"
   DataSourceID="dsSeries" DataKeyNames="Id"
   AutoGenerateColumns="False"
   OnSelectedIndexChanged="grdSeries_SelectedIndexChanged" >
   <Columns>
      <asp:TemplateField HeaderText="Series">
         <ItemTemplate>
            <asp:LinkButton ID="btnSelectSeries" runat="server"
               Text='<%# Eval("Name") %>'
               CommandName="Select" />
         </ItemTemplate>
      </asp:TemplateField>
   </Columns>
</asp:GridView>
```

4. Add a `GridView` control to your form that is used to display a list of the possible book category names.

```
<asp:GridView ID="grdCategories" runat="server"
   DataSourceID="dsCategories" DataKeyNames="Id"
   AutoGenerateColumns="False"
   OnSelectedIndexChanged="grdCategory_SelectedIndexChanged">

   <Columns>
      <asp:TemplateField HeaderText="Categories">
         <ItemTemplate>
            <asp:LinkButton ID="btnSelectCategory"
               runat="server"
               Text='<%# Eval("Name") %>'
               CommandName="Select" />
         </ItemTemplate>
      </asp:TemplateField>
   </Columns>
</asp:GridView>
```

5. Add a link that rerequests the page. This resets the page state so that the page no longer is in postback mode.

```
<a href="BookPortal.aspx">See All Books</a>
```

Walkthrough 11.3 *Adding Event Handlers to the Web Form*

Now that you have created the controls, you can add the selection event handlers. Each of these handlers programmatically alter the `ObjectDataSource` control used by the `GridView` for the book data.

1. Add the following event hander methods to the form.

```
protected void grdPublisher_SelectedIndexChanged(
   object sender, EventArgs e)
{
   dsBooks.SelectMethod = "GetBooksByPublisher";
   dsBooks.SelectParameters.Clear();
   Parameter p = new ControlParameter("pubId", "grdPublisher",
      "SelectedDataKey.Values[0]");
   dsBooks.SelectParameters.Add(p);
}

protected void grdSeries_SelectedIndexChanged(object sender,
   EventArgs e)
```

```
{
    dsBooks.SelectMethod = "GetBooksBySeries";
    dsBooks.SelectParameters.Clear();
    Parameter p = new ControlParameter("seriesId", "grdSeries",
      "SelectedDataKey.Values[0]");
    dsBooks.SelectParameters.Add(p);
}

protected void grdCategory_SelectedIndexChanged(
    object sender, EventArgs e)
{
    dsBooks.SelectMethod = "GetBooksByCategory";
    dsBooks.SelectParameters.Clear();
    Parameter p = new ControlParameter("catId", "grdCategories",
      "SelectedDataKey.Values[0]");
    dsBooks.SelectParameters.Add(p);
}
```

Notice that each event handler simply changes the book `ObjectDataSource` control's select method to the appropriate `GetBooksByX` method of the `BookCatalogLogic` class. Because the `GetBooksByX` method takes a parameter, each event handler must populate this parameter from the selected value of the publisher, series, or category `GridView` control.

2. Add the following to the `Page_Load` method of the form.

```
protected void Page_Load(object sender, EventArgs e)
{
    if (!IsPostBack)
    {
        dsBooks.SelectMethod = "GetAllBooks";
    }
}
```

The first time the page loads (and each time the user clicks the `See All Books` link), you want the `ObjectDataSource` control for the books `GridView` to use the `GetAllBooks` method, which returns a collection of all books in the database.

3. You can now test this page in the browser. It should display the publisher, series, and category listings, as well as the list of books. Each time you select a publisher, series, or category, the book list should change.

Walkthrough 11.4 *Add Ability to View and Edit Single Book Data*

We use a `DetailsView` control to display and edit all the data for the selected book.

1. Add the following `DetailsView` control to your Web Form.

```
<asp:DetailsView ID="dvEditBook" runat="server"
    DataSourceID="dsBookSingle" DataKeyNames="Isbn"
    AutoGenerateRows="False" >

    <HeaderTemplate>Book Details</HeaderTemplate>
    <Fields>
        <asp:BoundField DataField="Isbn" HeaderText="Isbn"
            ReadOnly="true"/>

        <asp:TemplateField HeaderText="Title">
            <ItemTemplate><%# Eval("Title")%></ItemTemplate>
            <EditItemTemplate>
                <asp:TextBox ID="txtTitle" runat="server"
                    Columns="55"
                    Text='<%# Bind("Title") %>' />
            </EditItemTemplate>
        </asp:TemplateField>

        <asp:TemplateField HeaderText="Authors">
            <ItemTemplate>
                <asp:GridView id="grdAuthors" runat="server"
                    AutoGenerateColumns="false" ShowHeader="false"
                    DataSource='<%# Bind("Authors") %>'>

                    <Columns>
                        <asp:BoundField DataField="Name" />
                    </Columns>

                </asp:GridView>
            </ItemTemplate>
            <EditItemTemplate>
                <a href='EditAuthors.apx?book=<%#
                    Eval("ISBN") %>'>
                Edit Authors
                </a>
            </EditItemTemplate>
        </asp:TemplateField>

        <asp:BoundField DataField="YearPublished"
            HeaderText="Year" />
```

```
<asp:TemplateField HeaderText="Description">
   <ItemTemplate>
      <%# Eval("BriefDescription")%>
   </ItemTemplate>
   <EditItemTemplate>
      <asp:TextBox ID="txtBrief" runat="server"
         TextMode="multiLine" Columns="45" Rows="7"
         Text='<%# Bind("BriefDescription") %>'/>
   </EditItemTemplate>
</asp:TemplateField>

<asp:TemplateField HeaderText="Publisher">
   <ItemTemplate>
      <%# Eval("BookPublisher.Name") %>
   </ItemTemplate>
   <EditItemTemplate>
      <asp:DropDownList ID="drpPublisher" runat="server"
         DataSourceID="dsPublishers" DataValueField="Id"
         DataTextField="Name"
         SelectedValue='<%# Bind("PublisherId") %>' />
   </EditItemTemplate>
</asp:TemplateField>
<asp:TemplateField HeaderText="Series">
   <ItemTemplate>
      <%# Eval("BookSeries.Name") %>
   </ItemTemplate>
   <EditItemTemplate>
      <asp:DropDownList ID="drpSeries" runat="server"
         DataSourceID="dsSeries" DataValueField="Id"
         DataTextField="Name"
         SelectedValue='<%# Bind("SeriesId") %>' />
   </EditItemTemplate>
</asp:TemplateField>

<asp:TemplateField HeaderText="Category">
   <ItemTemplate>
      <%# Eval("BookCategory.Name") %>
   </ItemTemplate>
   <EditItemTemplate>
      <asp:DropDownList ID="drpCategory" runat="server"
         DataSourceID="dsCategories" DataValueField="Id"
         DataTextField="Name"
         SelectedValue='<%# Bind("CategoryId") %>' />
   </EditItemTemplate>
</asp:TemplateField>
```

```
        <asp:CommandField ButtonType="Image"
            ShowEditButton="true" ShowCancelButton="true"
            CancelImageUrl="images/btn_cancel.gif"
            EditImageUrl="images/btn_edit.gif"
         UpdateImageUrl="images/btn_update.gif" />


    </Fields>
</asp:DetailsView>
```

Notice that the book's authors are displayed in a nested `GridView` control, but that the editing of the authors is delegated to a separate Web Form. It is much easier to edit the authors on a separate page because you need the ability to not only choose a different author, but to add and remove authors as well.

As well, this control makes use of several child properties of the `Book` object. For instance, the publisher name is retrieved within a data binding expression using the following dot notation:

```
<%# Eval("BookPublisher.Name") %>
```

Walkthrough 11.5 *Handling Invalid Business Rules*

Before you update the book, you need to verify that the user's input does not break any business rules for the `Book` entity. Because the book `ObjectDataSource` invokes the Update method, you must check for broken rules in the control's `OnUpdating` event. This event is triggered before the update method is called, but after the data object to be passed to the update method is created and populated.

1. Add the following `GridView` to the page. This control displays any broken business rules.

```
<asp:GridView ID="grdErrors"
    runat="server" ShowHeader="false" />
```

2. Add the following to the book `ObjectDataSource` control.

```
<asp:ObjectDataSource ID="dsBookSingle" runat="server"
    TypeName="FourLayer.ApplicationLogic.BookCatalogLogic"
    DataObjectTypeName="FourLayer.BusinessEntity.Book"
    SelectMethod="GetBookByIsbn"
    UpdateMethod="UpdateBook"
    OnUpdating="dsBookSingle_Updating" >
```

3. Add the following event handler to the form.

```
/// <summary>
/// Triggered when book ObjectDataSource tries to update data
/// </summary>
protected void dsBookSingle_Updating(object sender,
    ObjectDataSourceMethodEventArgs e)
{
    // Retrieve populated update parameter
    Book bk = (Book)e.InputParameters[0];

    // Ask entity if there are any broken business rules
    if (!bk.IsValid)
    {
        // There were broken rules, so cancel the update
        e.Cancel = true;
    }
    // Display broken business rules (which
    // are empty if valid)
    grdErrors.DataSource = bk.BrokenRules;
    grdErrors.DataBind();
}
```

This event handler retrieves the populated book entity that eventually is passed to the Update method from the ObjectDataSourceMethod-EventArgs parameter. It then asks the book entity if it has any broken rules. If it does, it binds the list of broken rule messages to the errors GridView control.

4. Test Web Form in browser. It should cancel the update if there are any broken business rules, and display the broken rule messages in the errors GridView control, as shown in Figure 11.13.

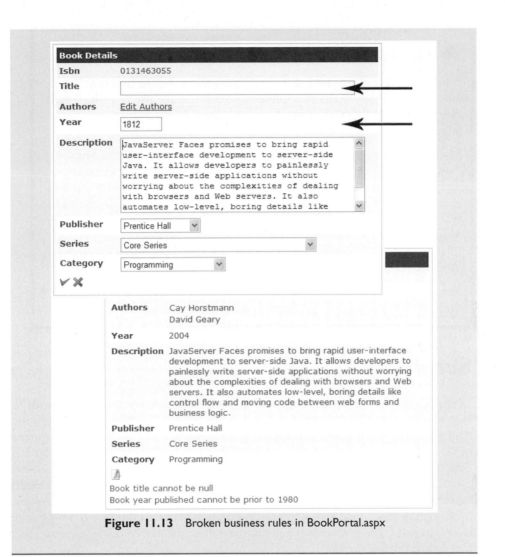

Figure 11.13 Broken business rules in BookPortal.aspx

USING THIRD-PARTY DESIGN RESOURCES

Constructing a full-featured, multilayer application architecture is not a trivial task. Some developers may prefer instead to make use of a third-party resource to help them construct their application infrastructure.

Existing data access and application architecture libraries such as Microsoft Data Access Application Block (also referred to as the Microsoft Enterprise Library) or NHibernate can be plugged into an existing or a new Web application. Code generation tools like LLBLGEN or MyGenerator can generate production-quality data access or business logic classes for you. Alternately, some developers may prefer to use an Object-Relational Mapper (ORM) to handle the linkage between their domain model and a relational database. Some popular ORMs for .NET are EasyObjects.NET, ORM.NET, EntityBroker, and DataObjects.NET.

For a good overview of some of the issues involved with using these types of third-party resources, see the Bouma article listed in the references.

Summary

This chapter focused on the design and implementation of layered architectures for Web applications. The rationale for a well-designed application infrastructure is that the creation of Web applications can be a complex endeavor. A "real" Web application may very well contain dozens and dozens, or even hundreds, of use case descriptions that necessitate the efforts of many developers. It is with this type of real Web application that proper software design principles are so important. This chapter examined one of the most important ideas in the development of modern complex software: the conceptual division of the application's classes into related but separate layers. In particular, it described and implemented a two-layer, three-layer, and then four-layer Web application.

The next chapter examines some of the additional capabilities of ASP.NET that are vital for any Web application: state management and using the ASP.NET cache.

Exercises

The solutions to the following exercises can be found at my Web site, http://www.randyconnolly.com/core. Additional exercises only available for teachers and instructors are also available from this site.

1. Create a Book business object using the `PublisherBO` example from Listing 11.2 as your model. You can use the supplied `BookDA` data access object to perform the interaction with the database. Create a test page that demonstrates this new class's functionality.

2. Add the following functionality to the `BookCatalogLogic` class: get a list of books for the specified author ID, update publisher, insert publisher, and delete publisher. Create a test page that demonstrates this new functionality.

The next two exercises use the `ModernEyeCatalog` database.

3. Design and implement a business object layer for this database. You can use the example in Listing 11.2 as a guide. Be sure to create a business object named `ArtWorkBO`.

4. Design and implement a four-layer model for this database.

Key Concepts

- Adapter
- Application logic
- Application logic layer
- Business layer
- Business object
- Business rules
- Cohesive
- Coupling
- CRUD
- Data access layer
- Data transfer object
- Dependency
- Domain
- Domain layer
- Entity
- Layer
- Presentation layer
- Template Method pattern
- Tier
- Use cases

References

Bouma, Frank. "Solving the Data Access Problem: to O/R Map or Not to O/R Map." http://weblogs.asp.net/fbouma.

Buschmann, Frank, *et al*. *Pattern-Oriented Software Architecture: A System of Patterns*. John Wiley & Sons, 1996.

Evans, Eric. *Domain-Driven Design: Tackling Complexity in the Heart of Software*. Addison-Wesley, 2004.

Fowler, Martin. *Patterns of Enterprise Application Architecture*. Addison-Wesley, 2003.

Larman, Craig. *Agile and Iterative Development: A Manager's Guide*. Addison-Wesley, 2003.

Microsoft. *Application Architecture for .NET: Designing Applications and Services*. Microsoft, 2003.

Nilsson, Jimmy. *Applying Domain-Driven Design and Patterns*. Addison-Wesley, 2006.

Chapter 12

MANAGING
ASP.NET STATE

> "Everything is in a state. . . . "
> —Marcus Aurelius, *Meditations*, ix. 19

This chapter is about state management in ASP.NET. State management is essential to any Web application, because every Web application has information that needs to be preserved from page to page. ASP.NET provides a number of mechanisms for preserving and managing this information. Although you certainly do not need to store *everything* in your application in state, a judicious use of these state features can dramatically improve the usability and performance of a Web application.

The vast majority of Internet applications operate using the HTTP protocol. This protocol has many advantages. From an application developer's perspective, it does have one significant drawback. HTTP is **stateless**. This means that each request for a page is treated as a new request by the server. As a result, information from one request is generally not available to the next request. There are times, however, when it is quite helpful, or even necessary, for information from one request to be available to another. For this reason, most server-side dynamic Web technologies include some mechanism for managing and preserving state.

This chapter begins with the various types of ASP.NET state whose data is stored on the client. It then moves on to those state mechanisms whose data is stored in the server: session state, application state, and finally the ASP.NET cache.

Client-Stored State

ASP.NET includes a number of features for managing state on both a per-page basis and an application-wide basis. These features are

- View state
- Control state
- Hidden fields
- Querystrings
- Cookies
- Profile properties
- Application state
- Session state

View state, control state, hidden fields, cookies, and querystrings all store data on the client, whereas application state, session state, and profile properties are stored in server memory. Each of these state options acts as data containers (albeit some with limited storage capacity and type support) that can be filled with whatever content the application developer deems necessary. As well, each of these state options has its own advantages and disadvantages.

View State

You saw back in Chapter 2 that ASP.NET preserves the state of the page's controls between postbacks by packaging and encoding it within a hidden HTML <input> element with the name __VIEWSTATE. This view state feature can also be used programmatically to preserve additional information between postbacks for the same page. The ViewState property of the page provides access to the page's view state via a dictionary-style collection (i.e., each item added to the collection is associated with a key) called a StateBag, where each item is indexed by a unique name. For instance, in the following example, an integer value is placed into the ViewState.

```
ViewState["RequestCount"] = count;
```

The string "RequestCount" is the dictionary key that is used to retrieve this object from the collection, as shown in the following. Notice that because the ViewState stores a collection of objects, retrieving values requires an explicit cast.

```
int count = (int)ViewState["RequestCount"];
```

The information in the view state collection is serialized by the runtime into XML. *Serialization* refers to the process of converting an object into a series of bytes in order to persist it to memory, a database, or a file. Its main purpose is to save the state of an object to be able to recreate it later. The reverse process is called *deserialization*.

You can add any custom type that can be serialized into XML to the view state, as well as any string, primitive number, Boolean, array, ArrayList object, or Hashtable object. To make a class serializable, you simply need to add the Serializable attribute to the class definition.

```
[Serializable]
public class Category : AbstractEntity
```

Attributes are a descriptive declaration that can be added to programming elements such as classes, methods, and properties, which provide extra information about the code. This additional information is placed into the metadata by the compiler and can be extracted at runtime using reflection.

It should be noted that if you did want to make this Category class serializable, you would also need to add the Serializable attribute to its AbstractEntity base class. As well, all of its internal state (i.e., its private data members) must also be serializable. For instance, if you want to make the Book class serializable, you not only need to add the Serializable attribute to it, but also to Publisher, Category, Series, and EntityCollection.

The following example illustrates the ViewState collection at work. The markup contains two buttons and a Panel with some Label controls within it.

```
<asp:Button ID="btnRequest" runat="server" Text="Postback"
   OnClick="btnRequest_Click" />
<asp:Button ID="btnShow" runat="server" Text="Show Count"
   OnClick="btnShow_Click" />
<asp:Panel ID="panCount" runat="server">
   Number of times page requested:
   <asp:Label ID="labCount" runat="server" /><br />
   Book:
   <asp:Label ID="labBook" runat="server" />
</asp:Panel>
```

The three event handlers in the code-behind class do all the work.

```
protected void Page_Load(object sender, EventArgs e)
{
   if (!IsPostBack)
   {
      panCount.Visible = false;

      // Initialize view state variables
      ViewState["PostbackCount"] = 0;
```

```
        Book book = new Book();
        book.Isbn = "0000000001";
        book.Title = "A Thousand Ways to Use ViewState";
        ViewState["Book"] = book;
    }
}

protected void btnRequest_Click(object sender, EventArgs e)
{
    int count = (int)ViewState["PostbackCount"];
    count++;

    ViewState["PostbackCount"] = count;
}

protected void btnShow_Click(object sender, EventArgs e)
{
    panCount.Visible = true;

    int count = (int)ViewState["PostbackCount"];
    labCount.Text = count.ToString();
    Book book = (Book)ViewState["Book"];
    labBook.Text = book.ToString();
}
```

The first time the page is requested, it initializes two view state variables: an `int` that contains the count of the number of times the page has been posted back, as well as a partially populated `Book` variable. The event handler for the postback button retrieves the `PostbackCount` variable, increments it, and resaves it to the view state. The other button makes the `Panel` visible and sets the two `Label` controls to the values of the two view state variables. The result in the browser is shown in Figure 12.1.

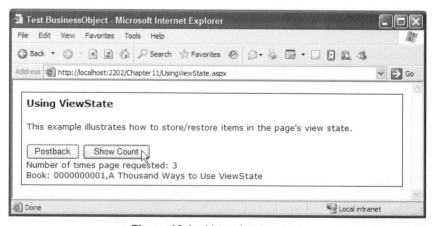

Figure 12.1 Using the view state

Uses and Misuses of View State

The view state collection is ideal for storing page-specific information of limited size. Because the information is stored entirely within the view state sent to the client, it consumes no server memory. Because the hash format (SHA/1) of the view state information is base-64 encoded, the information in it is generally not meaningful to most users and hence is a bit more hidden than if it was in an HTML hidden field or in a querystring parameter. However, even though the view state information is encoded, it is not encrypted and because it is still on the client, it can be tampered with by curious or malicious users. You can prevent a tampered view state from causing any potential problems by adding the `EnableViewStateMac` attribute to the `Page` directive.

```
<%@ Page … EnableViewStateMac="true" %>
```

When you set the `EnableViewStateMac` attribute to `true`, the page calculates a checksum value based on the current state of the view state. When the page is posted back, it verifies the posted-back view state by recalculating the checksum to see if it matches the expected checksum.

If you need to prevent users from comprehending your view state information, it is possible to encrypt it. You can do this for an individual page by setting the `ViewStateEncryptionMode` attribute of the `Page`.

```
<%@ Page … ViewStateEncryptionMode="Always" %>
```

Although the ability to secure the view state is nice, the main potential issue with view state is not really its security. Rather, the problem with view state is the fact that it can significantly add to the download size of the page. Remember that everything in the view state is serialized, hashed, base-64 encoded, and then placed into a hidden `<input>` element. The view state maintains information on every control on the page; as well, every child control of a parent control has information maintained in view state. Recall the book portal page in Figure 11.12 on page 703; when downloaded to the browser, its total size is 17K. Of that 17K, the view state consumes 5K. For this reason, you should be cautious with further increasing the downloaded page size by programmatically storing large amounts of additional data in the view state.

It should also be mentioned that it is possible to disable view state for a page by using the `EnableViewState` attribute within the `Page` directive.

```
<%@ Page … EnableViewState="false" %>
```

You can also disable view state on a control-by-control basis, via the `EnableViewState` property of any Web server control. The reason you may want to disable the page's view state is to decrease the download size of pages that do not post back to the server. Similarly, if your page does not handle any server control events and if the page's server controls have no dynamic data binding (or you are programmatically binding on every request), you may want to disable the page's view state.

Finally, it should be mentioned that a very large view state can cause problems with some firewalls and proxy servers. You can get ASP.NET to break up the view state information into multiple `<input>` elements via the `maxPageStateField-Length` attribute within the `pages` element of the `Web.config` file.

```
<pages maxPageStateFieldLength="1000"></pages>
```

This attribute represents the number of bytes of view state to be stored in each `<input>` element. You can also use this `pages` element to set the view state encryption mode and other values for the entire site rather than on a page-by-page basis.

```
<pages maxPageStateFieldLength="1000" enableViewStateMac="true"
    viewStateEncryptionMode="Always"></pages>
```

Control State

The **control state** collection, added in ASP.NET 2.0, is similar in many respects to the view state collection, except that it can be used to preserve state for control data between postbacks. Control state information is maintained even when the view state for a page is disabled. This is particularly essential for developers creating custom controls that need to preserve their state information. As well, control state allows developers to better customize the rendered page size on a control-by-control basis. However, control state is more complex to use than view state. It is a custom-persistence mechanism that requires additional programming to handle the loading and saving of control state for each control. Due to space limitations, we will not cover the use of control state. The references at the end of the chapter list some useful articles on how to use control state when creating custom controls.

Hidden Fields

Back in Chapter 3, we introduced the `HiddenField` control as a means of persisting a page value across multiple requests. The `HiddenField` control is rendered as an `<input type= "hidden"/>` HTML element. You can use `HiddenField` controls to maintain control state even if the view state is disabled. Like the view state, the values of any `HiddenField` controls are maintained on the client. However, unlike the view state, the value of any `HiddenField` can potentially be viewed by the user and even tampered with. Again, this may raise a security vulnerability if the `Hidden-Field` control value returned from the client is not evaluated on the server for user misuse.

Another limitation of the `HiddenField` control is that it essentially is limited to storing simple primitives, because the `Value` property of the control is of type `string`. As well, storing very large strings within a `HiddenField` control may be blocked by some firewalls and proxies.

Querystrings

A querystring is the information that is appended to the end of a URL request. It begins with the ? character and is followed by name=value parameters separated by the & character. The querystring is ***URL encoded***. This means that special characters such as the space character and punctuation are replaced by either a % character followed by its two-digit hexadecimal representation, or a special reserved symbol (e.g., spaces are encoded with +). For instance, the parameters page=resumé (with an accent) and name=John Locke might appear as the following in a querystring.

```
http://www.whatever.com/file.aspx?page=resum%E9&name=John+Locke
```

A querystring can be used to submit data back to the same page or to another page through the URL. Thus, querystrings provide a simple, universally supported but limited way of maintaining *some* state information. The maximum allowable length of a querystring varies from browser to browser. Internet Explorer limits the entire URL (which includes the domain address as well as the querystring) to about 2K, so clearly querystrings cannot be used to store anything more than a few simple primitive values.

A serious potential problem with querystrings is that the information contained within them is completely visible to the user in the browser's address bar. Some users quite commonly experiment by modify the querystring when making requests, so it is important to verify any information retrieved from a querystring.

Cookies

Cookies are a client-side approach for persisting state information. They are name-value pairs that are saved within one or more files that are managed by the browser. These pairs accompany both server requests and responses within the HTTP header (see Figure 12.2).

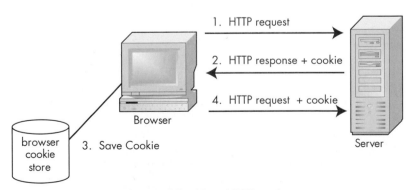

Figure 12.2 Using HTTP cookies

Cookies are not associated with a specific page but with the page's domain, so the browser and server exchanges cookie information no matter what page the user requests from the site. The browser manages the cookies for the different domains so that one domain's cookies are not transported to a different domain.

Although cookies can be used for any state-related purpose, they are principally used as a way of maintaining continuity over time in a Web application. One typical use of cookies in a Web site is to "remember" the visitor, so that the server can customize the site for the user. Some sites use cookies as part of their shopping cart implementation so that items added to the cart remain there even if the user leaves the site and then comes back.

There are limitations to the amount of information that can be stored in a cookie (around 4K) and to the number of cookies for a domain (Internet Explorer limits a domain to 20 cookies). Cookies can also expire. That is, the browser deletes a cookie if it is beyond its expiry date, which is a configurable property of a cookie.

The most important limitation of cookies is that the browser may be configured to refuse them. As a consequence, sites that use cookies should not depend on their availability for critical features. Similarly, the user can also delete cookies or even tamper with the cookies, which may lead to some serious problems if not handled. Several years ago, there was an instructive case of a Web site selling stereos and televisions that used a cookie-based shopping cart. The site placed not only the product identifier but also the product price in the cart. Unfortunately, the site then used the price in the cookie in the checkout. Several curious shoppers edited the price in the cookie stored on their computer, and then purchased some big screen televisions for only a few cents!

Reading and Writing Cookies

Although the browser maintains the actual cookies, you can write a cookie value to the HTTP response stream by adding a `HttpCookie` object to the `Cookies` collection of the `Page` class's `Response` property.

```
HttpCookie cookie = new HttpCookie("Name",txtName.Text);

// Set expiry date to 1 day, 12 hours from now
cookie.Expires = DateTime.Now + new TimeSpan(1, 12, 0, 0);
Response.Cookies.Add(cookie);
```

`Cookies` is a dictionary-style collection that can be accessed by index or by the cookie name. The following example illustrates how to read the cookie.

```
HttpCookie cookie = Request.Cookies["name"];
labCookie.Text = cookie.Value;
```

Application State

Querystrings, view state, control state, and cookies are all client-based state approaches. Application state is a server-stored state mechanism that allows you to store global data in a dictionary-style collection that is accessible from all pages in the Web application.

Application state is stored in server memory, but unlike session state (covered shortly), which is specific to a single user browser session, application state applies to all users and sessions of the Web application. Thus, application state is ideal for storing relatively small, frequently used sets of data that do not change from user-to-user or request-to-request.

Application state is stored as an instance of the HttpApplicationState class. As you saw in Chapter 2, an instance of this class is created the first time a user accesses any URL resource in an application. The HttpApplicationState class can be accessed via the Application property of the Page class, or through the Current.Application property of the HttpContext class.

```
Application["SiteRequestCount"] = 0;
HttpContext.Current.Application["SiteName"] = "www.site.com";
...
int count = (int)Application["SiteRequestCount"];
string name = (string)Application["SiteName"];
```

Items placed in application state remain there until the application restarts (for instance, because of a change to the Web.config file or due to ASP.NET's process recycling). When should items in application state be initialized? Because we generally cannot predict the first page to be requested in a Web application, one approach to initialize application variables is to use *lazy initialization* before you access any application variable. This approach requires you to check if the application variable exists; and if it doesn't, initialize it.

```
if (Application["SiteRequestCount"] == null) {
    Application["SiteRequestCount"] = 0;
}

int count = (int)Application["SiteRequestCount"];
count++;
Application["SiteRequestCount"] = count;
```

Note that this kind of approach can result in synchronization problems if multiple requests execute this code simultaneously. To prevent any potential synchronization problems, you can lock the application state when it is being updated.

```
Application.Lock();
if (Application["SiteRequestCount"] == null) {
    Application["SiteRequestCount"] = 0;
}

int count = (int)Application["SiteRequestCount"];
count++;
Application["SiteRequestCount"] = count;
Application.Unlock();
```

Because application state is instantiated when the application starts, it might make more sense to populate it at this point in the application lifecycle. You can do this via the `Application_Start` event handler in the `Global.asax` file.

The Global.asax File

The `Global.asax` file contains application-level event handlers and can be created directly from Visual Studio's Add New Item dialog.

```
<%@ Application Language="C#" %>

<script runat="server">

    void Application_Start(object sender, EventArgs e)
    {
        // Code that runs on application startup
        Application["SiteRequestCount"] = 0;
        HttpContext.Current.Application["SiteName"] =
            "www.somesite.com";
    }
    …
</script>
```

Note that anything placed in application state is actually global to the worker process on the individual server machine. In multiprocessor machines or in multiserver environments, each processor or server has its own application state (see Figure 12.3). As a consequence, you cannot rely on application state to store site-unique values or update global counters in these configurations.

As mentioned at the beginning of this discussion, application state is best used for small, frequently used, very infrequently changed singletons that are global to the entire application and that must be available to all user sessions. Later in the chapter, we cover the ASP.NET cache. Generally, using the cache instead of application state is preferable because cache memory can be reduced in times of large memory load, whereas application state cannot.

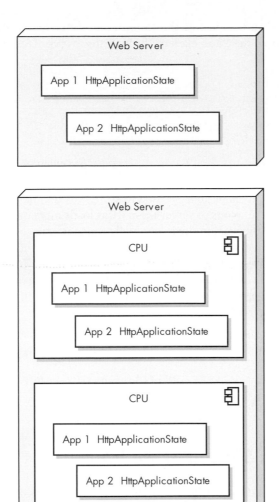

Figure 12.3   Application state

Session State

Like application state, session state is a server-based state mechanism that allows you to store data in a dictionary-style collection. However, session state is scoped to the current browser session. That is, each user or browser session has a different session state. Session state only lasts for a limited finite amount of time (usually around 20 minutes). Thus, if a user leaves the application and then returns later, the second user session has a different session state from the first.

Session state is an instance of the `HttpSessionState` class accessed via the `Session` property of the `Page` class or through the `Current.Session` property of the `HttpContext` class.

```
Session["NumCartItems"] = 0;
HttpContext.Current.Session["Cart"] = new ShoppingCart();
...
int count = (int)Session["NumCartItems"];
ShoppingCart cart = (ShoppingCart)Session["Cart"];
```

Session state is typically used for storing information that needs to be preserved across multiple requests by the same user. Because each user session has its own session state collection, it should not be used to store large chunks of information; this consumes very large amounts of server memory as loads increase.

Because session information does eventually timeout, you should always check if an item retrieved from session state still exists before using the retrieved object. If the session object does not yet exist (either because it is the first time the user has requested it or because the session has timed out), one might generate an error, redirect to another page, or create the required object using the lazy initialization approach you saw earlier with application state objects.

```
if (Session["Cart"] == null) {
    Session["Cart"] = new ShoppingCart();
}
ShoppingCart cart = (ShoppingCart)Session["Cart"];
```

Alternately, you can use the `Session_Start` method of the `global.asax` file to initialize any session objects.

How Does Session State Work?

You may recall from Chapter 2 that all requests are processed within the `Http-Application` pipeline. This pipeline consists of different events, some of which are handled by `HttpApplication` itself, whereas other events are handled by different HTTP modules. Session state processing is managed by the `SessionStateModule` after the `HttpApplication.AcquireRequestState` event is triggered. This module's first principle duty is to generate or obtain the **session ID**. This unique, 15-byte string is used by ASP.NET to identify each current session. It enables an ASP.NET application to connect a specific browser with its session data on the Web server.

By default, the session ID value is transmitted between the browser and the server in a cookie. However, you can configure the application to use cookieless sessions via a setting in the `Web.config` file.

```
<sessionState cookieless="UseUri" />
```

When cookieless sessions are enabled, the session ID is inserted into the URL.

```
http://.../Ch12/(S(hlxh3ibe2htriazpxdne3b55))/Sample.aspx
```

It should be noted that ASP.NET can insert the session ID *only* for relative paths. Thus, of the next two links, only the first has the correct session ID inserted; the second absolute path gets a newly generated session ID.

```
<a href="UsingSessionEnd.aspx">relative link gets correct
    session id</a>

<a href="/Chapter12/UsingSessionEnd.aspx">absolute link won't
    work</a>
```

Although cookieless sessions ensure session support even when the client's cookie support is disabled, having the session ID in the URL can be a potential security risk. The potential problem can occur when an external site such as a search engine references a link with an inserted session ID. When ASP.NET receives a request for a URL with a session ID that has timed out, it "recycles" the session ID and creates a new session using the same session ID supplied in the URL. If another request then comes in from a different user with that same previously expired, but now active, session ID, then ASP.NET assume that this request is part of the same session. Thus, you now have two different users sharing the same session!

To prevent this situation from occurring, you can set the regenerateExpired-SessionId flag to the sessionState element in the Web.config file.

```
<sessionState cookieless="UseUri"
    regenerateExpiredSessionId="true"/>
```

Setting the regenerateExpiredSessionId flag to true forces ASP.NET to always generate a brand new session ID when creating a new session.

So what happens besides the generating or obtaining of a session ID after a new session is started? For a brand new session, the SessionStateModule assigns an initially empty dictionary-style collection that can be used to hold any state values for this session. When the request is finished processing, the session state is saved to some type of state storage mechanism, called a ***state provider***. Finally, when a new request is received for an already existing session, the SessionStateModule fills the session's dictionary collection with the previously saved session data from the state provider. Figure 12.4 illustrates the different steps in this process.

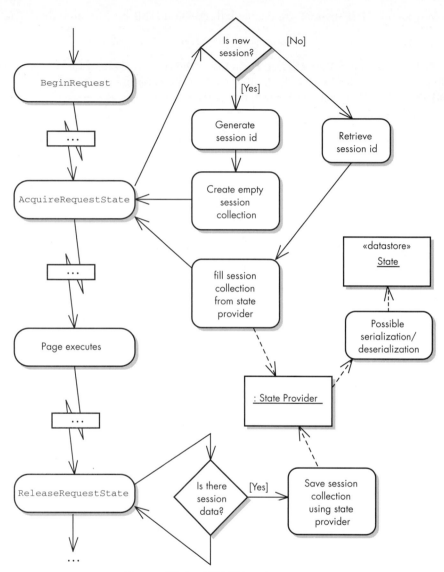

Figure 12.4   ASP.NET session process

Session State Providers

ASP.NET supports three different session state providers, as well as the infrastructure for creating a custom state provider. You can specify which state provider is to be used in your application via the mode attribute in the sessionState element in the Web.config file.

```
<configuration>
   <system.web>
      …
      <sessionState … mode="InProc"/>
   </system.web>
</configuration>
```

In-Process Session Provider

By default, state data is saved on the Web server within the Web application's in-memory cache (we cover the ASP.NET cache in the last section of this chapter). This default state provider is called the `InProc` (or **in-process**) provider, because it is run in the same process as the Web application itself (see Figure 12.5).

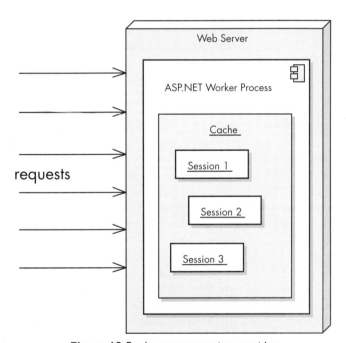

Figure 12.5   In-process session provider

`InProc` provides the fastest access to session state. If your site is going to run on a single Web server and there is a fairly modest number of concurrent sessions, the in-process state provider provides the best performance.

State Server Session Provider

There are situations in which in-process state provider is not an ideal choice. If there are a large number of concurrent sessions, the Web application may run out of memory because in-process session state uses the same memory as the application. As well, in-process session state is lost whenever the application process is recycled (recall that the ASP.NET worker process is periodically restarted). Finally, higher-volume Web applications often run on a multiprocessor Web server in which each processor handles a separate worker process (sometimes called a ***Web garden***) or on multiple Web servers (also called a ***Web farm***). For these situations, in-process session state does not work, because one processor or server may service one request for a particular session, and then a completely different processor or server may service the next request for that session.

For situations in which it is unacceptable to lose session state during process recycling or for multiprocess or multiserver deployments, you need to use one of the other state providers. The other state providers store the session's state data in the out-of-process Win32 state service (`StateServer` provider), or in a special SQL Server database (`SQLServer` provider). For instance, you can also create a custom state storage provider if you want to use Oracle or use a legacy SQL Server state database whose schema is different than that used by the built-in `SQLServer` provider.

The `StateServer` provider uses the session state service, which is a Win32 service (`aspnet_state.exe`) that must be running on the Web server or on a remote server (generally preferable) that is accessible by all the Web servers in the Web farm. Because the session state service runs as a separate process, it is insulated from IIS failures or to ASP.NET process recycling (see Figure 12.6).

Although the session state service is installed as part of ASP.NET, you do need to start the service. You can do this via the Services option in the Windows Control Panel (see Figure 12.7).

The `Web.config` file also has to be modified for the application to use the session state service. The following provides a sample configuration in which the session state service is on the local machine using the default session state service port (42424). If the session service is running on a different machine than the Web server, you can replace `localhost` with the IP address of that machine.

```
<sessionState …
    mode="StateServer"
    stateConnectionString="tcpip=localhost:42424" />
```

CORE NOTE

There are also third-party session state servers available for ASP.NET, such as ScaleOut's StateServer.

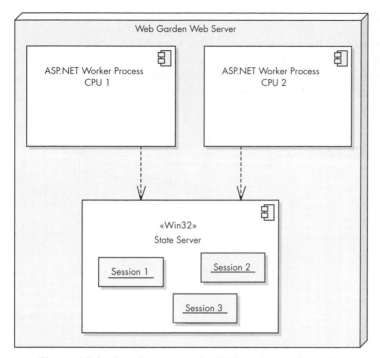

Figure 12.6   StateServer provider Web garden configuration

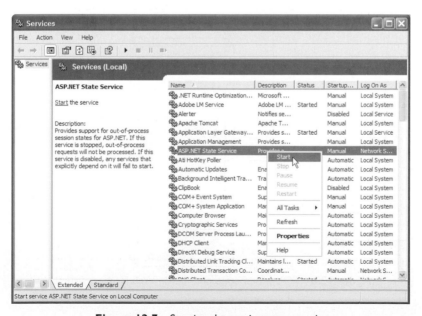

Figure 12.7   Starting the session state service

SQL Server Session Provider

The capability to store session state within a special SQL Server database provides a very reliant alternative to the session state service. Because the session data is stored in a database table, it is preserved even if the Web server crashes. However, because the session is being persisted to a database, it certainly will be slower than the other two state providers (see Figure 12.8).

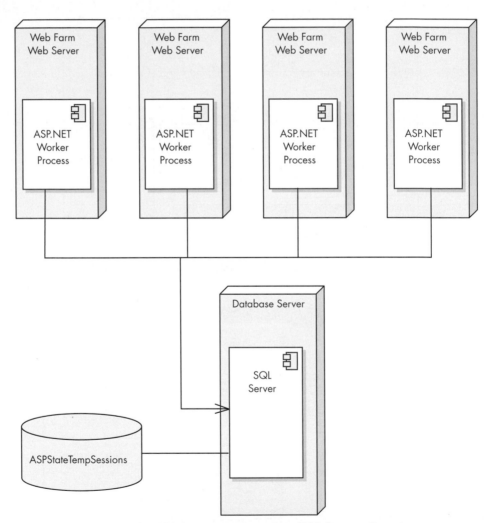

Figure 12.8   SQL Server state provider in Web farm configuration

Using the SQL Server state provider involves two steps. The first is to change the `Web.config` file so that it indicates that you will be using the SQL Server state provider.

```
<sessionState ...
   mode="SQLServer"
   sqlConnectionString="server=localhost;integrated
   security=SSPI" />
```

The second step is to ensure that you have created the special SQL Server database to be used. In the .NET Framework folder (`\Windows\Microsoft.NET\Framework\[version]`), there is a program named `aspnet_regsql.exe`, which steps you through the process of configuring SQL Server for a variety of ASP.NET services (such as memberships, profiles, and Web parts) that we encounter in the next few chapters. However, to configure just the session state database, you need to run this program in command-line mode. To create the session state database, you must enter the following from the command line (the `-E` indicates that the program authenticates with SQL Server using current Windows authentication, whereas `-ssadd` adds the session support database).

```
aspnet_regsql -ssadd -E
```

This creates a database named `ASPState`, which contains no tables but several stored procedures for creating the tables in the `tempdb` system database. For each session, a new record is added to the `ASPStateTempSessions` table (see Figure 12.9).

The `aspnet_regsql.exe` program also defines a SQL Server job named `ASPState_JobSchedule_DeleteExpiredSessions`, which deletes expired session records from this table. By default, this job runs once a minute. As well, the `ASPState` database is removed each time SQL Server restarts. If you do not want this behavior, you can modify your earlier command line to the following, which makes the `ASPState` database permanent.

```
aspnet_regsql -E -ssadd -sstype p
```

Optimizing Session State

Although session state is an invaluable tool for constructing modern Web applications, it does have a performance cost that requires careful configuration. One of the more important of these is the `Timeout` attribute of the `sessionState` element in the `Web.config` file. This attribute allows you to specify the amount of time in minutes that ASP.NET waits before it times out an inactive session. If the number is too large, too much server memory is used for storing expired session data (especially if you are using the in-process state provider); if the number is too small, sessions may time out before the user is finished. As well, to prevent any problems with your security settings, the session state timeout value should be the same as that set for the form's authentication timeout (this also is covered in the next chapter).

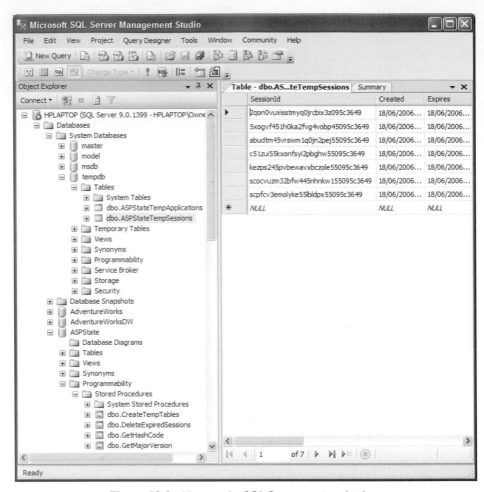

Figure 12.9   Viewing the SQL Server session database

It is important to note that when the in-process provider is used the session data is stored in its "native" format. That is, because session data is stored in a collection contained in the same process's memory space, it can contain any type of data in its native, managed state. This is not the case with the other state providers. Because both the state server and the SQL Server state provider reside in a different process (in fact, usually on a completely different machine) than that of the Web application, the session data must be serialized when it is saved, deserialized when it is read, and then perhaps sent over the network to another machine. Recall from our earlier discussion of serialization (see "View State" on page 718), a class (and any child objects that it contains) must be marked with the `Serializable` attribute for it to be serialized. Because it takes time to serialize and deserialize, you should ideally place fairly simple objects into session state if possible to reduce the total amount of data that is serialized.

You can also improve session performance by disabling it on pages that do not need it. You can do this via the `EnableSessionState` attribute of the `Page` directive.

```
<%@ Page … EnableSessionState="false" %>
```

Another way to optimize session state is to set the `EnableSessionState` attribute to `ReadOnly` for pages that access session data but do not modify it.

```
<%@ Page … EnableSessionState="ReadOnly" %>
```

Because it is possible for more than one page to modify the same session (for instance, when the user creates multiple browser windows after starting the session), ASP.NET must make two calls to the state provider for each request: one that marks the session as locked and reads the session data and the other to unlock the session and write the session data. Setting the `EnableSessionState` to `ReadOnly` eliminates the need for the last call to the state provider. Although this does not result in much of a performance gain for the in-process provider, it certainly improves performance for the other two providers (especially the SQL Server provider).

Profile Properties

Often, the kind of state information that a Web application needs to preserve is related to a particular user. Session state information, by its very nature, is tied to the current user's session. However, session state information is lost when the user's session expires. ASP.NET 2.0 provides a new feature called **profile properties**, which allows an application to permanently store user-specific data.

Profile properties provide an infrastructure that allows an application to manage user information without requiring the developer to create and maintain a custom database for this information. The ASP.NET profile feature makes the user information available using a strongly typed API. As well, because this feature uses a generic storage system, a profile can contain objects of any type.

The profile system has many uses. For instance, it can be used to personalize a Web application for your user or store a permanent shopping cart or wish list. The profile system does require the capability to identify a user. This requires the authentication and authorization of the users. For this reason, we do not cover the profile feature now, but in Chapter 14, after we cover user authorization in Chapter 13.

ASP.NET Cache

In the last section's discussion on session state, it was mentioned that in-process session data is stored within the application's in-memory cache. A *cache* is simply an area of memory where frequently used data can be rapidly accessed. Caching is a very important way to improve the performance of Web applications that need to access external resources such as databases or Web services. For instance, in the earlier section on application state, we imagined a site using the information in the books database. In this site, there are many pages that display information from the series and book publishers tables. Because there are less than a dozen items for each of these, you can improve page performance by storing these two collections in cache memory as a way of reducing the number of queries that must be handled by the DBMS.

Like session state, the ASP.NET cache is contained within the memory space of a single ASP.NET worker process. Also, like the application or session state, the ASP.NET cache is a dictionary-style collection that can contain any type of object. However, the cache is different than the application state mechanism in ASP.NET. Application state data exists as long as the process for the application domain is running; cache data items have a more variable lifespan. The cache is of flexible size and eliminates items that are less recently used. To this end, items within the cache are time stamped and removed after a certain time period (although an item can be configured to have no expiry time).

There are two different caching mechanisms in ASP.NET. The first is *application data caching*, which allows you to programmatically cache data. The second is *page output caching*, which saves the rendered output of a page or user control and reuses the output instead of reprocessing the page when a user requests the page again.

Application Data Caching

The cache in ASP.NET is represented by the `Cache` class in the `System.Web.Caching` namespace. The cache for an application can be programmatically accessed via the `Cache` property of the `Page` class, via `HttpContext.Current.Cache`, or via `HttpRuntime.Cache`. The ASP.NET cache is implemented internally by the class `CacheSingle` or `CacheMultiple` depending upon whether the Web server is running on a single process or multiple work processes. If multiple worker processes are being used, each process has its own cache. Internally, the cache's data is stored within a `Hashtable`.

You add an object to the cache by specifying both its key and its value. For instance, to cache a collection of publishers, you could use the following.

```
BookCatalogLogic bcl = new BookCatalogLogic();
publishers = bcl.GetAllPublishers();

Cache["PublisherKey"] = publishers;
```

Alternately, you could use the `Insert` method of `Cache`.

```
Cache.Insert("PublisherKey", publishers);
```

The advantage of using `Insert` is that you can customize the cache expiry of the inserted item. One of the overloads for `Insert` allows you to specify a cache dependency (which is covered later, so here we just use a `null` for the `CacheDependency` object), an absolute expiry time, or a sliding expiry time. When an absolute expiry time arrives, the cached item is removed. A sliding expiry time is relative to the current time and is reset if it is accessed before it is expired. You cannot specify both an absolute and a sliding expiry time. If a sliding expiry is being used, the absolute expiry must be set to `Cache.NoAbsoluteExpiration`. If an absolute expiry is being used, the sliding expiry must be set to `Cache.NoSlidingExpiration`.

```
// Cache class is in this namespace
using System.Web.Caching;
...
// Expire this item two minutes after it is last used
Cache.Insert("PublisherKey", publishers, null,
   Cache.NoAbsoluteExpiration, TimeSpan.FromMinutes(2));
...
// Expire this item in two minutes
Cache.Insert("SeriesKey", series, null,
   DateTime.Now.AddMinutes(2.0), Cache.NoSlidingExpiration);
```

To retrieve an item from the cache, you simply use the key name along with a cast to the appropriate type.

```
publishers = (EntityCollection<Publisher>)Cache["PublisherKey"];
```

Remember that there is no guarantee that the cache contains the item associated with the key, because the item may have timed out and been removed. As a result, you should always check if the retrieved item is `null` before attempting to use it. If the item is `null`, the typical approach is to reretrieve the item, as shown in the following.

```
EntityCollection<Publisher> publishers;

// Retrieve collection from cache
publishers = (EntityCollection<Publisher>)Cache["PublisherKey"];
if (publishers == null)
{
```

```
    // Item no longer in cache, so refetch collection
    publishers = BookCatalogLogic.GetAllPublishers();

    // Place collection back in the cache
    Cache["Publishers"] = publishers;
}
```

Integrating the Cache with a Layered Design

The capability to cache a frequently used set of data can dramatically improve the performance and scalability of a Web application. Because the Page class provides easy access to the ASP.NET cache through its Cache property, it is very tempting to use it in your code-behind classes. The trouble with this approach is that it adds a form of data or application logic into the presentation layer. Perhaps a better solution is to use the cache within the application logic layer, or within the data access layer.

For instance, in the BookCatalogLogic class in Listing 11.3 on page 701, there was a GetBooksByIsbn method. You could integrate the cache into that method, so that it first tries to retrieve the book from the cache; if it is not there, it can retrieve it from the data access layer and then place it in the cache.

```
public Book GetBookByIsbn(string isbn)
{
    // Caching a null raises an exception
    if (isbn == null)
      return null;

    // First try to get book from cache using ISBN as key
    Book b = (Book)HttpRuntime.Cache[isbn];
    if (b == null)
    {
      BookDAO dao = new BookDAO();
      b = dao.GetByKey(isbn);

      // Save book into cache
      if (b != null)
          HttpRuntime.Cache[isbn] = b;
    }
    return b;
}
```

CORE NOTE

You must reference the cache via the HttpRuntime.Cache property because this code is not contained within a Web Form's code-behind class. This also requires you to link to the System.Web namespace.

As an alternative to (or in conjunction with) this approach, you might decide to use the cache in your data access layer. Because the ASP.NET cache is an externality, you might decide to create a wrapper class that encapsulates the ASP.NET cache, as shown in Listing 12.1. This static wrapper class only is used to store entity collections and entities, so you can use generics to make sure that its methods are strongly typed.

Listing 12.1   DataCache.cs

```
using System;
using System.Web;

using FourLayer.BusinessEntity;

namespace FourLayer.DataAccessObject
{
    /// <summary>
    /// Encapsulates the ASP.NET cache
    /// </summary>
    public static class DataCache<T> where T : AbstractEntity
    {
        public static void Add(string key,
            EntityCollection<T> item)
        {
            // You could define the expiry time as well
            HttpContext.Current.Cache.Insert(key, item);
        }

        public static EntityCollection<T> Retrieve(string key)
        {
            return (EntityCollection<T>)
                HttpContext.Current.Cache[key];
        }

        public static void AddEntity(string key, T entity)
        {
            HttpContext.Current.Cache.Insert(key, entity);
        }

        public static T RetrieveEntity(string key)
        {
            return (T)HttpContext.Current.Cache[key];
        }
        public static void Remove(string key)
        {
            HttpContext.Current.Cache.Remove(key);
        }
    }
}
```

It is now up to the developer to decide which data in the data access layer needs to be cached. In your sample application, there might be thousands of books and authors, but no more than a few dozen publishers and book series, and perhaps two to three dozen book categories. Thus, you could boost performance to cache all the publishers, series, and categories without using up too much server memory. Caching all the books and authors is not wise, however, because it take up way too much memory.

You can modify your `AbstractDA` class in the data access layer by adding two abstract properties dealing with the cache that are implemented by each data access subclass. The first returns a Boolean value indicating whether the data access class should cache the collection returned in the `GetAll` method. The second provides the cache key name to be used when storing the collection in the cache. With these properties defined, you can modify the `GetAll` method so that it uses your DataCache.

```
public abstract class AbstractDA<T> where T : AbstractEntity
{
    ...
    /// <summary>
    /// Should the GetAll method cache the collection?
    /// </summary>
    public abstract bool IsGetAllCached
    {
        get;
    }

    /// <summary>
    /// The key name to be used by this data layer for caching
    /// </summary>
    public abstract string CacheName
    {
        get;
    }

    /// <summary>
    /// Returns all the records for this entity
    /// </summary>
    public EntityCollection<T> GetAll()
    {
        EntityCollection<T> collection = null;
        if (IsGetAllCached)
            collection =
                DataCache<T>.RetrieveCollection(CacheName);
        if (collection == null)
        {
            collection = GetCollection(SelectStatement,
                CommandType.Text, null);
```

```
    if (IsGetAllCached)
        DataCache<T>.AddCollection(CacheName,
            collection);
    }
    return collection;
    }
}
```

All you need to do now is add the implementations for the new abstract properties to each of your data access classes. For the `PublisherDA` class, this might look like the following.

```
public class PublisherDAO: AbstractDAO<Publisher>
{
    ...
    public override bool IsGetAllCached
    {
        get { return true; }
    }
    public override string CacheName
    {
        get { return "Publishers"; }
    }
}
```

For the `BookDA` or `AuthorDA`, you set the `IsGetAllCached` property so that it returns `false`. You could also introduce caching in a similar way to other retrieval methods defined in `AbstractDA` or in the various concrete data access classes.

Cache Dependencies

A cache dependency lets you make a cache's expiry conditional upon the physical status of the item. Rather than make a cache item invalid after a set time, you can make the cached item's validity dependent upon whether a file, folder, or a SQL Server table changes via the `CacheDependency` or `SqlCacheDepencency` class. Making a cached item dependent upon changes in a SQL Server database prior to SQL Server 2005 requires a bit of extra administrative work. It requires using the `aspnet_regsql.exe` tool to enable change notification support for any table that requires it. The following command line enables dependency notification for the `Publishers` table in the `BookCatalog` database using Windows authentication.

```
aspnet_regsql -E -d BookCatalog -et Publishers
```

This command adds a special table named `AspNet_SqlCacheTablesFor-ChangeNotification` to the specified database. It also generates a database trigger that updates this table whenever the watched table (`Publishers` in our case) is changed.

You also need to add a `sqlCacheDependency` element to the `Web.config` file.

```xml
<configuration>
  <appSettings/>
  <connectionStrings>
    <add name="BookCatalog" connectionString="..."
      providerName="..."/>
  </connectionStrings>

  <system.web>

    ...

    <caching>
      <sqlCacheDependency enabled="true">
        <databases>
          <add name="BookCatalogSystem"
            connectionStringName="BookCatalog"
            pollTime="500"/>
        </databases>
      </sqlCacheDependency>
    </caching>
  </system.web>
</configuration>
```

This tells ASP.NET to poll the specified database every half second to see if the `AspNet_SqlCacheTablesForChangeNotification` table has been changed. Of course, one might argue that polling the database every half second might negate the performance benefits from caching the data in the first place!

At any rate, after all this setup is finished, you can use a `SqlCacheDependency` object when adding items to the cache. The constructor for this class takes the database name that you just defined in the `Web.config` file as well as the watched table name.

```
// Create cache dependency
SqlCacheDependency depend = new SqlCacheDependency(
  "BookCatalogSystem", "Publishers");

Cache.Insert("PublisherKey", publishers, depend,
  Cache.NoAbsoluteExpiration, TimeSpan.FromMinutes(2));
```

SQL Server 2005 introduced a cleaner change notification approach that does not require any `aspnet_regsql` setup, no special tables and stored procedures, and no polling settings in the `Web.config` file. SQL Server 2005 has a CREATE EVENT NOTIFICATION command that allows SQL Server to push a notification message to ASP.NET when the specified table or even record changes. If you have SQL Server 2005, all you need to do is use a different constructor for the `SqlCacheDependency` class that accepts a `SqlCommand` object that indicates the data whose status is to be watched.

You could use this `SqlCacheDependency` class in your data access layer (although doing so changes the layer so it no longer is database provider independent) in the manner similar to that shown in the following example.

```
EntityCollection<T> collection = new EntityCollection<T>();
...
SqlCommand cmd = new SqlCommand(SelectStatement, conn);
...
DbDataReader reader = cmd.ExecuteReader();
...
while (reader.Read())
{
    collection.Add(CreateAndFillEntity(reader));
}

SqlCacheDependency dep = new SqlCacheDependency(cmd);
HttpContext.Current.Cache.Insert(CacheName, collection, dep);
```

Page Output Caching

The previous section examined the programmatic caching of application data. ASP.NET also supports page output caching. In this type of caching, the contents of the rendered ASP.NET page are cached in memory. This can be particularly helpful because it allows ASP.NET to send a page response to a client without going through the entire page processing lifecycle again. Page output caching is especially useful for pages whose content does not change frequently, but requires significant processing to create.

There are two models for page caching: *full page caching* and *partial page caching*. In full page caching, the entire contents of a page are cached. In partial page caching, only specific parts of a page are cached, whereas the other parts are dynamically generated in the normal manner.

Full Page Caching

Full page caching is quite easy to set up. It simply requires adding the `OutputCache` directive to a page.

```
<%@ OutputCache Duration="60" VaryByParam="None" %>
```

This instructs ASP.NET to cache the entire page for 60 seconds. However, remember that the page may not actually last for 60 seconds in the cache, because it may be removed early due to memory constraints or other content being added to the cache. Nonetheless, for a busy page with dozens or hundreds of requests a minute, being able to potentially serve all those requests during that minute from the cache (rather than by executing the code and perhaps interacting with the database) is a substantial performance gain. Of course, this only makes sense for a page whose content is the same for all requests and is thus not being customized for a specific user or session.

However, the caching mechanism does allow you to cache different versions of the page depending upon the value of the page's querystring parameters. This is controlled by the `VaryByParam` attribute, which is in fact required (or an exception is generated). In the preceding example, the `None` indicates that the caching for this page does not vary by the querystring parameters.

You can instruct ASP.NET to cache versions of the page for all querystring or form parameters via `VaryByParam="*"`. It should be noted that if there are a large number of possible querystring parameters, this setting undoubtedly fills up the cache quite quickly and thus negates any possible performance benefits gained by full page caching. You can also specify just the querystring or form parameter name in the `VaryByParam`.

```
<%@ OutputCache Duration="60" VaryByParam="id" %>
```

This caches a separate version of the page for each requested `id` parameter. That is, each time ASP.NET receives a request for this page, it examines the value of the `id` parameter. If there is a version of the page already for this `id`, it serves the cached version; if there is not, it generates the page output normally and then saves that output in the cache along with the `id`.

CORE NOTE

If a page contains any type of postback event handling, it should not be full page cached. Although you can maintain event handling, specifying the relevant control `id` in the `VaryByParam` attribute forces the caching of each possible permutation of the page with that control.

Partial Page Caching

With partial page caching, ASP.NET caches only a portion of the page. This is often the most workable page caching mechanism for the typical Web application, because it allows some parts of the page to be cached while other parts can be dynamically generated.

There are actually two ways of working with partial page caching: ***control caching*** and ***post-cache substitution***. With control caching, you cache part of the page output by placing some of page's content into a user control and then marking the user control as cacheable using the `OutputCache` directive. Thus, control caching makes the page dynamically generated for each request, but with some parts of that page retrieved from the cache.

Post-cache substitution (new to ASP.NET 2.0) is the opposite. The page as a whole is cached, but fragments within the page are dynamic. With post-cache substitution, you use the `OutputCache` directive to cache the entire page, and then mark certain sections of the page to be dynamically generated through the use of the `Substitution` control. The `Substitution` control specifies a section on an output-cached Web page where you want dynamic content substituted for the control.

For instance, imagine that you have a search page for your site that displays almost exactly the same content for all users or sessions and that has no postback event handling. The one part that does vary is a box that displays the current content of the shopping cart.

You can improve this page's performance by adding the `OutputCache` directive to the page, and then use a `Substitution` control where you want the shopping cart's content to be displayed.

```
<div id="cartBox">
  <h2>Your Shopping Cart</h2>
  <asp:Substitution id="subCart" runat="server"
    MethodName="GetCart" />
</div>
```

The `Substitution` control requires the name of a method that returns the content to be displayed in the control. This method *must* have a specific signature. It must be `static`, return the content as a `string`, and accept a `HttpContent` parameter. For instance, the following example `GetCart` method retrieves the shopping cart from session state and outputs the cart items as <p> elements to a string. Thus, each time your search page is requested, all of the page are retrieved from the cache, except for the content of the `Substitution` control, which contains the current contents of the session's shopping cart.

```
public static string GetCart(HttpContext context)
{
    ShoppingCart cart = (ShoppingCart)context.Session["Cart"];

    // Handle missing cart
    ...

    // Output the cart item markup for this session to a string
    string output = "";
    foreach (CartItem item in cart)
    {
        output += "<p class='cartRow'>";
        output += item.Name + "</p>";
    }
    return output;
}
```

CORE NOTE

You can customize how page output caching works in a Web application via output caching profiles. For more information, see J. Ambrose Little's article, "Output Caching Profiles and Custom Caching," listed in the References section.

Summary

Most Web sites larger than a few pages eventually require some manner of persisting information on one page (generally referred to as "state") so that it is available to other pages in the site. This chapter examined the options for managing state on the client (view state, control state, hidden fields, querystrings, and cookies), as well as those for managing state on the server (application state and session state).

The chapter finished with caching, an important technique for optimizing real-world Web applications. Because busy Web sites have to deal with hundred or thousands of simultaneous requests, it is vital for these types of sites to optimize their use of processing and database handling. The judicious storing of database data or page output in a memory cache can substantially decrease the time needed to process and handle a user request.

The next chapter covers another essential topic, that of Web application security in ASP.NET.

Exercises

The solutions to the following exercises can be found at my Web site, http://www.randyconnolly.com/core. Additional exercises only available for teachers and instructors are also available from this site.

1. Add a class called `CartItem` and a class called `ShoppingCart` to the domain layer from the last chapter. The `CartItem` class should contain properties for the ISBN and the quantity. The `ShoppingCart` class should contain an entity collection of `CartItem` objects, as well as methods for clearing the cart, adding an item, and removing the item.

2. Using the classes created in Exercise 1, create a new `OrderLogic` class in the application logic layer that allows the user to clear the cart, add a book, remove a book, count the number of books in the cart, and return the cart as a collection. This requires the use of session state.

3. Create a test page that demonstrates the functionality of Exercises 1 and 2. The first page should be called `BookCatalogList.aspx`, and should use a `GridView` and `ObjectDataSource` to display a list of book ISBNs and titles. The `GridView` should contain a button column that adds the specified book to the cart. There should be a link on this page to `ViewCart.aspx`, which displays the ISBNs and titles of each item in the cart. As well, this page should have a button to remove the item from the cart.

Key Concepts

- Application data caching
- Attributes
- Cache
- Control caching
- Control state
- Deserialization
- Full page caching
- In-process session provider
- Lazy initialization
- Page output caching
- Partial page caching
- Post-cache substitution
- Profile properties
- Serialization
- Session ID
- SQL Server session provider
- State
- State provider
- State server session provider
- URL encoding
- View state
- Web farm
- Web garden

References

Esposito, Dino. "Underpinnings of the Session State Implementation in ASP.NET."
   `http://msdn.microsoft.com`.

Little, J. Ambrose, "Output Caching Profiles and Custom Caching."
   `http://dotnettemplar.net`.

Meier, J. D., *et al*, *Improving .NET Application Performance and Scalability*. Microsoft Corporation, 2004.

Normén, Fredrik. "Introduction to the Control State Feature." `http://fredrik.nsquared2.com`.

Onion, Fritz. "Speed Up Your Site with the Improved View State in ASP.NET 2.0." *MSDN Magazine* (October 2004).

Salysle. "Using Control State in ASP.NET 2.0." `http://www.codeproject.com`.

Part III

IMPLEMENTING WEB APPLICATIONS

Chapter 13

SECURITY, MEMBERSHIP, AND ROLE MANAGEMENT

"If thou be'st not immortal, look about you: security gives way to conspiracy. The mighty gods defend thee!"

—William Shakespeare, *Julius Caesar*, Act II, Scene 3

In this quote from *Julius Caesar*, Artemidorus tries to warn the general on the Ides of March what fate awaits him within the Senate building. In a similar vein, moving an ASP.NET application from your development machine to a more public and open production server also seems like a transition from complacent security to the nasty conspiracy and many knives of hackers and unscrupulous users. Luckily, you do not have to rely on the mighty gods to defend your ASP.NET sites. Instead, you can rely on the security features of ASP.NET.

This chapter begins by examining how security is built into ASP.NET. It introduces the concepts of authentication, authorization, and trust, as well as describes the different levels of security in an ASP.NET Web application. The chapter also examines the two principal forms of authentication available to ASP.NET developers: Windows Authentication and forms authentication.

The chapter continues by examining the provider model, which is one of the chief new architectural features of ASP.NET 2.0. Two of the examples of the provider model are the focus for the most of the remainder of the chapter: these being the

Membership and the Role Management systems. Finally, the chapter also examines the login controls introduced with ASP.NET 2.0. These controls simplify the process of creating and logging into user accounts.

Introduction to ASP.NET Security

One of the most important and (unfortunately) complex issues facing Web developers is security. By default, a Web application is available to anyone who can access its Web server. However, almost every Web site has some resources within the site that are not meant to be publicly available. Configuration files, subscription-only content, and administration pages are examples of site content that should not be openly available to all visitors. As such, the principal focus of Web application security is to restrict access to site resources to the appropriate users.

Protecting a site's content does require careful planning and a clear understanding of the options for securing a site. ASP.NET provides a multilayered approach to security. Its security system works in concert with the .NET Framework as well as Microsoft Internet Information Server (IIS). Part of the complexity with ASP.NET security is that there are these multiple layers of security, each with its own nomenclature and configuration options.

Nonetheless, you cannot go far wrong by beginning with the two fundamental functions of any security system: authentication and authorization.

Authentication refers to the process of verifying the identity of the user. This is typically achieved by having the user enter *credentials*, such as a user name and password. If the credentials are valid (usually by checking them against a database or a list of operating system user accounts), the entity that submitted the credentials is considered an *authenticated identity*.

Authorization refers to the process of determining whether the authenticated identity (i.e., the user) has permission to access certain resources. The most common approach for authorization is *role-based authorization*, which is authorization based not on the user but on the role or group to which the user belongs. Thus, permissions are assigned to different roles, and then users are assigned to different roles. Typical roles in a Web application might be guest, registered user, content editor, moderator, and administrator. Each role has a different set of permissions. For instance, users with the guest role can only visit the front home page and a few marketing pages; registered users can view most of the publicly viewable pages; whereas the administrator can view and modify all of the content in the site. A given user, for example, `randy91248`, might be assigned to more than one role: registered user, content editor, and administrator.

ASP.NET does not operate by itself but in conjunction with IIS, the .NET Framework, and the underlying Windows operating system. Each of these provides a level of security.

Overview of IIS Security

The first level of security checks is that imposed by IIS. Recall that all HTTP requests for ASP.NET Web application resources are initially handled by IIS. The request is first checked by IIS to see if the IP address of the request is allowed access to the domain of the requested resource. The next check is to authenticate the user if necessary. If successful, the request is passed on to ASP.NET. If either of these two checks fails, the user receives an access denied response, as shown in Figure 13.1.

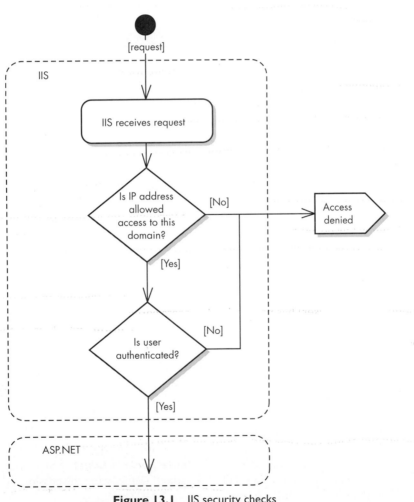

Figure 13.1 IIS security checks

By default, IIS allows ***anonymous access*** to a Web application, which means the user of the request does not actually have to be authenticated. However, a Web application can be configured to require IIS authentication (see Figure 13.2).

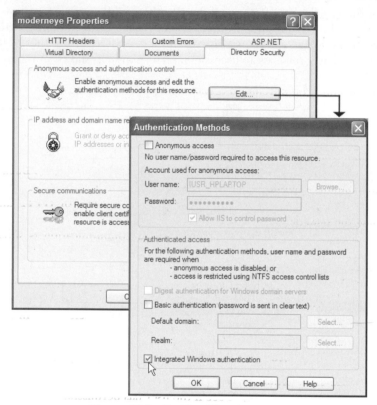

Figure 13.2   Enabling IIS authentication

IIS supports several types of authentication, including basic, digest, certificate-based, and integrated Windows Authentication.

With ***basic authentication***, the user name and password are encoded and transmitted in an HTTP header. The user and password are checked to see if they match a Windows account on the server.

Because the user name and password are not encrypted, basic authentication should only be used in conjunction with ***Secure Sockets Layer*** (SSL). SSL encrypts all communications sent using HTTPS (see the following discussion on certificate-based authentication).

With ***digest authentication,*** the password is subjected to a special calculation (a hash), the result of which is sent to the server; the server performs the same calculation and compares it to the received value. If it is a match, it assumes the passwords match. The advantage of this approach is that the password is never sent over the network. However, the hashing mechanism is not completely secure and does not work with all browsers.

Certificate-based authentication uses certificates as a means of verifying the identity of a given site. In public-key cryptography, a *certificate* uses a digital signature to bind together a public key with an identity (information such as the name of a person or an organization, his address, and so on). The certificate is then used to verify that a public key belongs to an individual.

Certificates must be purchased (generally for about $100 to $500 a year) from a known certificate authority, such as www.VeriSign.com, www.geotrust.com, www.thawte.com, or www.instantssl.com. Most of these certificate authorities also offer free limited-time trial certificates. After you have a certificate, it must be installed and configured for the site in IIS (go to the site properties, click the Directory Security tab, and then click the Server Certificate button). Because each certificate contains a public key, your site can use SSL to communicate with the client. SSL communication uses the HTTPS protocol instead of HTTP and safely encrypts all the data passed between the client and the server. Due to the encryption and communication of a certificate, HTTPS communication is substantially slower than regular HTTP. As a result, it generally makes sense to only use it for the transmission of sensitive information, such as a login session or registering credit cards. However, sites that traffic almost exclusively in sensitive information, such as a bank, might use SSL for its pages. For more information on using certificates in ASP.NET, see the Michele Leroux Bustamante article listed in the References section at the end of the chapter.

In *integrated Windows Authentication*, IIS authenticates the user against a Windows user account. When used within a corporate intranet, Windows Authentication allows IIS to determine the requester's identity based on her Windows login. As well, IIS can use that identity to see if the user has permission to access files protected by the Windows's access control list (ACL).

When the user first requests a resource from a Web application with integrated Windows Authentication, IIS tries to authenticate the user. If the requesting user doesn't match an account on the server or on a trusted domain, the browser displays a dialog box asking the user for credentials (see Figure 13.3).

Integrated Windows Authentication is available in two flavors: NTLM (NT LAN Manager, also sometimes called Windows NT Challenge/Response) and Kerberos. The latter uses a stronger encryption method than the former. However, the requirements for using Kerberos can be difficult to meet. It requires the server to be member of an Active Directory domain, that the requesting client is part of a trusted domain, that the Web application is registered with Kerberos, and that the client's browser supports Kerberos. Kerberos Windows Authentication is necessary if you want to enable the delegation of Window's user identities to other machines "behind" the Web server (and thus access remote resources). For more information on using Kerberos authentication, see the Microsoft article, "Developing Identity-Aware ASP.NET Applications," listed in the References section at the end of the chapter.

Figure 13.3   Windows Authentication

The ASP.NET Security Process

Whether IIS authentication is enabled, ASP.NET can also be configured to perform its own security checks. Like IIS, there is a process of checks within ASP.NET, as shown in Figure 13.4.

The first check is whether ASP.NET impersonation is enabled. ***Impersonation*** refers to the process by which a Web application "pretends" to be a different account than the actual account that is running the application. By default, impersonation is disabled. This means the Web application is run using the permissions of a predefined user account, typically either ASPNET (for IIS 5) or NETWORK SERVICE (for IIS 6). The ASPNET user account is a local account created when the .NET Framework is installed; the NETWORK SERVICE account is predefined in Windows Server 2003 and has the same set of somewhat limited permissions as the ASPNET account.

When impersonation is enabled for a Web application, the application runs under an identity specified by a security token that is passed by IIS. This might be used in Web applications that rely on IIS to authenticate the user, or for server environments that host applications from different customers. Impersonation is often used in such a situation, because each Web application could be provided with a separate Windows account to absolutely prevent one application from accessing another application's resources. You can specify that an application should impersonate via a setting in the `Web.config` file. This might also require specifying the specific user and password of the identity under which the application is to run, as shown here.

```
<configuration>
  <system.web>

    ...
    <identity impersonate="true" userName="JohnLocke"
      password="aj3*a2hd" />
  </system.web>
</configuration>
```

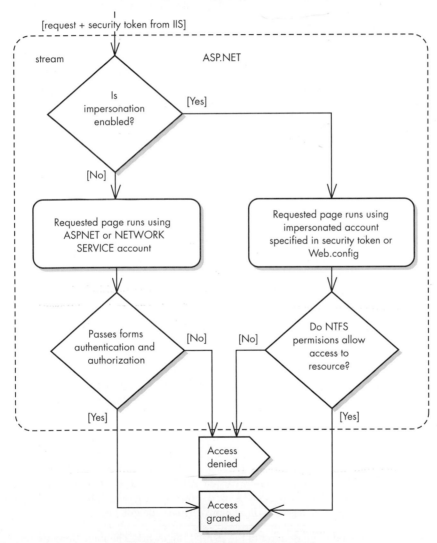

Figure 13.4   ASP.NET security checks

Alternately, if the user and password are *not* specified in the `identity` element, the application runs under the account specified in the security token provided by IIS. This typically is the case if the user has already authenticated with IIS. If impersonation is enabled, any resource request still must pass the underlying operating system NTFS permission check that happens for all requests, whether impersonated or not. Finally, if you are not using Windows Authentication and you enable impersonation, ASP.NET acts under the configured anonymous identity in IIS, typically the `IUSR_machinename` account. Some Web site hosts take this approach so that they can set up multiple accounts for applications to run under IIS.

If impersonation is not enabled, the request runs under the default process identity for ASP.NET applications (i.e., ASPNET or NETWORK SERVICE). As well, ASP.NET can authenticate the user using its own forms authentication mechanism, which is covered in much more detail later in the chapter. If the request passes these final checks, the request for the page is granted, and the page can execute.

Code Access Security and ASP.NET Trust Levels

One of the principal security features in the .NET Framework is the support in the CLR for **code access security**. With this feature, code in an assembly is given a security zone classification that constrains what types of things the code can do when executing. Because ASP.NET assemblies are dynamically generated, security policies can be specified declaratively in a trust level. Thus, a **trust level** is a declarative set of rules that define what .NET Framework classes your ASP.NET application can use. Trust levels can be set using the `trust` element in the application's `Web.config` file.

```
<system.web>
    . . .
    <trust level="Medium"/>
</system.web>
```

The possible values for the trust level are described in Table 13.1.

Table 13.1   Trust Levels

Trust Name	Description
Full	The application is fully trusted. All .NET code is allowed to run and thus any .NET classes can be used (however, still subject to operating system and Windows ACL limitations). This is the default.
High	Code can use most of the .NET Framework. The limitations are no unmanaged code, no enterprise services, and limited use of reflection.

```
        PublicKeyToken=b77a5c561934e089" />
</SecurityClasses>
```

How do you know the needed content for the `Description` string? If you try to create a page that uses any classes in the `Data.OleDb` namespace with the site's trust set to the Medium trust level, you see the error message shown in Figure 13.5.

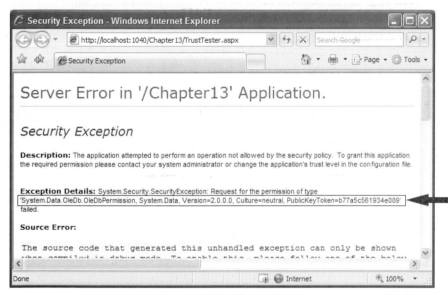

Figure 13.5   Trust exception

Notice that the exact string you need for the description is there in the exception details. You simply need to copy it from the browser and paste it into the `Description` string.

After specifying this `SecurityClass` entry, you now need to modify the ASP.NET permission set so that the `OleDbPermission` class is allowed. This is accomplished by adding the following `IPermission` element.

```
<PermissionSet class="NamedPermissionSet" version="1"
    Name="ASP.Net">
    ...
    <IPermission class="OleDbPermission" version="1"
        Unrestricted="true" />
<PermissionSet>
```

Now all you need to do is apply the new custom trust file in your own site's or the machine's `Web.config` file.

```
<trust level="CustomMedium" originUrl=""/>
```

ASP.NET Authentication

Like IIS, ASP.NET has its own authentication methods. When IIS receives a request for an ASP.NET resource such as an `.aspx` file, it performs its own authentication (if the Web application is configured in IIS to do so), and then passes on the request and a security token to the ASP.NET runtime.

You can specify which authentication mode to use in your Web application within the `authentication` element of the application's `Web.config` file.

```
<system.web>

  ...
  <authentication mode="Windows" />
</system.web>
```

ASP.NET supports the following authentication modes:

- `None`—ASP.NET does not perform any authentication (and thus relies on IIS for authentication).
- `Windows`—ASP.NET Windows Authentication treats the user identity supplied in the security token by IIS as the authenticated user. That is, ASP.NET Windows Authentication uses the result of the configured IIS authentication mechanism. When the user first requests an ASP.NET resource from a Web application with Windows Authentication, IIS tries to authenticate the user. If the user is successfully authenticated, the request and a security token is passed onto ASP.NET.

  This authentication approach generally only makes sense for intranet applications with a known set of users existing in the operating system's user list. Windows Authentication is also used in applications that want to use the underlying Windows access control lists (ACLs) for determining whether a given user is allowed to access specific files.

- `Passport`—This mode uses the Microsoft Passport system running on a separate Passport server for authentication. As well, you need to install the Passport .NET SDK on the Web server. The setup and use of *Passport authentication* is not covered in this book. For more information on Passport authentication, see the Siddiqui article in the References section.

- `Forms`—This authentication mode allows you to authenticate the user via a login Web Form that you create. Unauthenticated requests are redirected to this login page, where the user can provide credentials and submit the form. With this mode, the Web application, not the underlying operating system, must authenticate the request. After authentication, ASP.NET issues its own authentication "ticket" that contains a key for reestablishing the identity for subsequent requests.

Forms authentication is generally the most practical authentication system for public Web sites. As such, this chapter examines it in much more detail in the next section.

Each of these different authentication modes is implemented in ASP.NET as different HTTP modules: `FormsAuthenticationModule`, `PassportAuthentication-Module`, and `WindowsAuthenticationModule`. As you may recall from Chapter 2, all incoming requests pass through the events in the `HttpApplication` pipeline. As part of this process, different HTTP modules can register their own event handlers with the events in the pipeline. All three of these modules perform their processing during the `AuthenticateRequest` event of `HttpApplication`.

Forms Authentication

With forms authentication, the Web application itself collects credentials such as the name and password directly from the user via a login Web Form and determines their authenticity. Unauthenticated requests are automatically redirected to this login page by the `FormsAuthenticationModule`. Because the Web application will perform the authentication, you generally configure IIS to enable anonymous access for this application.

Using Forms Authentication

Using forms authentication in your Web application requires changing the authentication mode in the `Web.config` file to `Forms`. As well, you must specify the name of the page that contains the login form, as shown in the following.

```
<system.web>
    ...
    <authentication mode="Forms" >
        <forms loginUrl="Login.aspx" />
    </authentication>

    <authorization>
        <deny users="?"/>
    </authorization>
</system.web>
```

Notice in this example configuration that there is also an `authorization` element. This element is used to specify user access rights to resources in the application. In this example, the `deny users="?"` specifies that all unauthenticated users are denied access to ASP.NET resources in the site. The `?` wildcard character matches all unauthenticated users. You can also specify users by name, or use the `*` character, which matches all authenticated and unauthenticated users. The other element that you can use within the authorization element is allow, which can be used to specify the resources that users are allowed to access.

The consequence of the preceding sample configuration is that the first time a user requests any ASP.NET resource in the Web application, the user is redirected to the page Login.aspx.

You can customize the authentication approach used in your Web application on a folder-by-folder basis by using a separate Web.config file in each folder in your application. For instance, imagine that most of the pages in your site are available to all users, anonymous or authenticated. However, you do have some member-only pages that are available to only authenticated users. In that case, you can create a separate folder and place all content that is member-only in that folder. The Web.config file for the main application contains the authentication element as well as an authorization element that allows all users. The member-only folder has another Web.config file that does not contain an authentication element but contains a different authorization element that denies all unauthenticated users, as shown in Figure 13.6.

As an alternative to multiple Web.config files in different folders, you can centralize your authorization rules by using the location element. With this option, the application has only a single Web.config file, but it contains multiple location elements nested within the configuration element, as shown in the following example.

```
<configuration>
    <connectionStrings>…</connectionStrings>
    <location path="membersOnly">
        <system.web>
            <authorization>
                <deny users="?"/>
            </authorization>
        </system.web>
    </location>

    <system.web>
        …
        <authentication mode="Forms" >
            <forms loginUrl="Login.aspx" >
            </forms>
        </authentication>
        <authorization>
            <allow users="*"/>
        </authorization>
    </system.web>
</configuration>
```

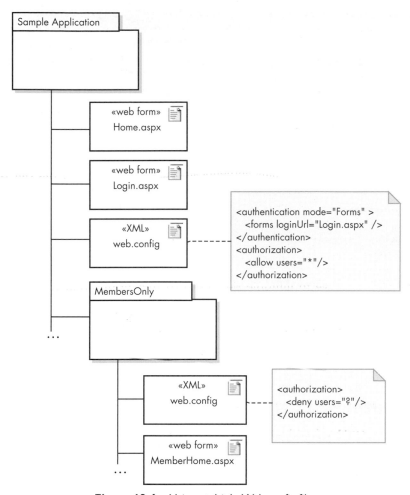

Figure 13.6   Using multiple Web.config files

Whether you use multiple `Web.config` files or multiple `location` elements within a single `Web.config` file, it is important to remember that the `authentication` element can appear just once in the main `Web.config` file. If you use multiple `authentication` elements, ASP.NET generates the error shown in Figure 13.7.

CORE NOTE

You can also use the Website Administration Tool to set up your `Web.config` files (covered in Walkthrough 13.1 on page 794).

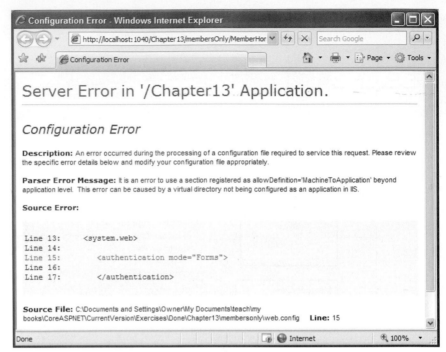

Figure 13.7   Error due to multiple authentication elements

Creating a Login Form

So what can your login form contain? Listing 13.1 illustrates the markup for a very simple login form. Notice that it uses both `RequiredFieldValidator` and `RegularExpressionValidator` controls. Figure 13.8 illustrates how this form appears in the browser.

Listing 13.1   Login.aspx

```
<h1>Login Page</h1>
<p>
You were automatically redirected to this page by the forms
authentication system.
Notice how the query string for this page contains the page name of
the originally requested page.
</p>
<asp:Panel ID="panLogin" runat="server" GroupingText="Log-in"
   CssClass="panel">
```

```
<p>
User:<br />
<asp:TextBox ID="txtUser" runat="server" /><br />
<asp:RequiredFieldValidator ID="reqUser" runat="server"
   ControlToValidate="txtUser" Display="dynamic"
   ErrorMessage="User must be entered" />
<asp:RegularExpressionValidator ID="regUser" runat="server"
   ControlToValidate="txtUser" Display="dynamic"
   ValidationExpression="^\w{0,8}$"
   ErrorMessage="Invalid user name" />
</p>
<p>
Password:<br />
<asp:TextBox ID="txtPassword" runat="server"
   TextMode="Password"/>
<br />
<asp:RegularExpressionValidator ID="regPassword" runat="server"
   ControlToValidate="txtPassword" Display="dynamic"
   ValidationExpression="^\w{8,16}$"
   ErrorMessage="Invalid password" />
<asp:RequiredFieldValidator ID="reqPass" runat="server"
   ControlToValidate="txtPassword" Display="dynamic"
   ErrorMessage="Password must be entered" />
</p>
<p>

<asp:ImageButton ID="ibtnLogin" runat="server"
   ImageUrl="images/btn_login.gif" OnClick="btnLogin_Click" />
</p>
<p>

<asp:Label ID="labError" runat="server" CssClass="error" />
</p>
</asp:Panel>
```

Because you are using the forms authentication approach, you must write the code that performs the actual authentication yourself. In this example, the authentication happens in the event handler for the login button. Listing 13.2 illustrates the typical pattern followed when using forms authentication. The event handler for the button retrieves the user-entered values and then calls a local private method to see if this user is valid. If it is valid, it calls the static `FormsAuthentication.Redirect-FromLoginPage` method to redirect control back to the originally requested page.

Figure 13.8   Sample login form

Listing 13.2   Login.aspx.cs

```
using System;
using System.Data;
using System.Configuration;
using System.Collections;
using System.Web;
using System.Web.Security;
using System.Web.UI;
using System.Web.UI.WebControls;
using System.Web.UI.WebControls.WebParts;

public partial class Login : System.Web.UI.Page
{
    /// <summary>
    /// Event handler for the login button
    /// </summary>
    protected void btnLogin_Click(object sender, EventArgs e)
    {
        string user= txtUser.Text;
        string password = txtPassword.Text;
```

```
    // Check to see if this is a valid user
    if (IsValidUser(user, password))
        // Redirect back to the originally requested page
        FormsAuthentication.RedirectFromLoginPage(user, true);
    else
        labError.Text = "User not found, try again";
}

/// <summary>
/// Is this a valid user?
/// </summary>
private bool IsValidUser(string user, string password)
{
    // To simplify, hard-code a sample valid user
    if (user == "plato" && password == "abcdabcd")
        return true;
    else
        return false;
}
}
```

Of course, the IsValidUser method in Listing 13.2 is unrealistic in that it simply
checks for a hard-coded username and password. Obviously, a more likely scenario is
to compare the user input against values in a database, perhaps by using some application logic or business object class, as shown in the following.

```
private bool IsValidUser(string user, string password)
{
    CustomerServiceLogic cs = new CustomerServiceLogic();

    if ( cs.AuthenticateUser(user,password) )
        return true;
    else
        return false;
}
```

Finally, note that in this type of form authentication, the user name and password
are sent over the network as plain text; as such, they can potentially be intercepted by
packet or wireless sniffer software. If the site is a public site and the security of the
user's login information is important, you can encrypt the transmission of this information using SSL.

CORE NOTE

If you run the example in Listings 13.1 and 13.2 on the personal Web server that comes with Visual Studio, you may notice that the login page does not use the external style sheet, nor does it display the button image. However, if you use IIS, you will see the styles and the image. The reason for this behavior is that with the personal Web server *all* file requests (including requests for the `.css` and the `.gif` files) are handled by ASP.NET; thus, any restrictions made in the `Web.config` file are applied to these files as well.

After the user has successfully been authenticated, then all allowed ASP.NET resources are available to that user. Any given page in the site can retrieve the identity of the logged-in user via the `User.Identity` property of the page.

```
labUser.Text = User.Identity.Name;
```

A typical approach for a site that allows authentication is to provide a mechanism (typically, a `LinkButton` or `ImageButton`) for the user to log out. You can log a user out via the static `SignOut` method of the `FormsAuthentication` class. After the user logs out, the site typically redirects the user back to the home page as in the following.

```
protected void lnkLogOut_Click(object sender, EventArgs e)
{
    FormsAuthentication.SignOut();
    Response.Redirect("~/Home.aspx");
}
```

Alternately, you can redirect back to the login page via the following.

```
FormsAuthentication.RedirectToLoginPage();
```

Figure 13.9 illustrates how this process might appear in the browser.

CORE NOTE

Later in the chapter, we examine the built-in login controls that come with ASP.NET. One of these controls is the `Login` control that provides similar functionality as that shown in Listing 13.1.

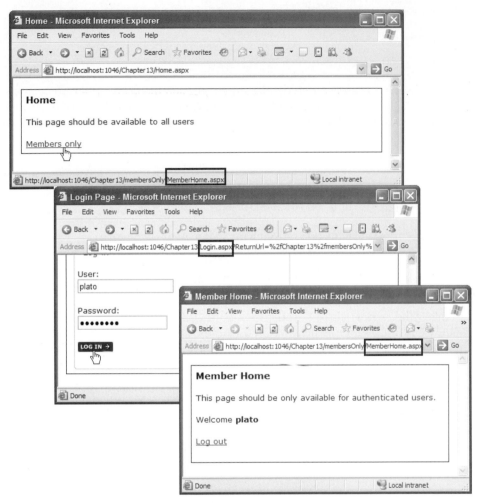

Figure 13.9   Forms authentication

Storing User Credentials in the Web.config File

Rather than store the user credentials in an external data source such as a database, you can alternately store them within the Web.config file. To do so requires adding user elements to the credentials element.

```
<authentication mode="Forms" >
  <forms loginUrl="Login.aspx" >
    <credentials passwordFormat="Clear">
      <user name="plato" password="abcdabcd"/>
```

```
        <user name="aristotle" password="efghefgh"/>
        <user name="kant" password="ijklijkl"/>
    </credentials>
 </forms>
</authentication>
```

Because in this case your credential store is in the `Web.config` file, you can use the built-in `Authenticate` method of `FormsAuthentication` to determine whether the user's credentials match a credential in the `Web.config` file, as shown here.

```
protected void btnLogin_Click(object sender, EventArgs e)
{
    string user= txtUser.Text;
    string password = txtPassword.Text;

    if ( FormsAuthentication.Authenticate(user,password) )
        FormsAuthentication.RedirectFromLoginPage(user, true);
    else
        labError.Text = "User not found, try again";
}
```

Using the credential store in the `Web.config` file is not practical for sites with many users or for sites that dynamically add users. However, it can be useful for a site in which the vast majority of the content is publicly available to all users, but that has a very limited number of resources, which are only available to a select group of users such as administrators. In such a case, you can use these user credentials in the `authorization` section within the `Web.config` file's `location` element or within a subdirectory's `Web.config` file.

```
<authorization>
    <allow users="plato,aristotle"/>
    <deny users="*"/>
</authorization>
```

Notice the `deny` element here uses a * rather than a ?. The ? signifies all unauthenticated users, whereas the * indicates all users, authenticated or unauthenticated. You want to deny all anonymous users as well as all authenticated users except for `plato` and `aristotle`, so you have to use `users="*"`.

CORE NOTE

The order of the `allow` and `deny` elements is important. The first authorization element that matches the user is used; so if `deny` is placed first in the list, it denies everyone.

For sites that require the capability to handle a larger numbers of users, a better solution is to use the built-in membership system in ASP.NET 2.0, which is covered a bit later in the chapter. But before we look at the membership system, we need to first understand how the form authentication system actually works.

How Forms Authentication Works

After the user has been authenticated, any subsequent requests for allowable ASP.NET resources are processed without requiring authentication again. Figure 13.10 illustrates the process in which a user requests pageA.aspx, is forced to authenticate, and, when successful, receives pageA.aspx. When the user makes a request for another page (pageB.aspx), the server provides it without requiring authentication. Of course, this is the behavior that you expect; after all, you hardly want the user to authenticate for every single request!

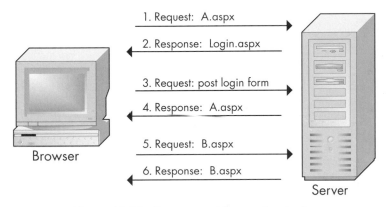

Figure 13.10   Requests and form authentication

The question that this process should raise is this: When the server receives the request for pageB.aspx, how does the server "know" that the user has already been authenticated? Remember that HTTP is a stateless protocol, so some type of state mechanism must be working behind the scenes with forms authentication.

By default, forms authentication in ASP.NET makes use of a browser cookie to maintain the state of the user's authentication across requests (see Chapter 12 for a review on cookies and on state management in general). Figure 13.11 illustrates how this authentication cookie is transmitted between client and server to serve the request flow illustrated in Figure 13.10.

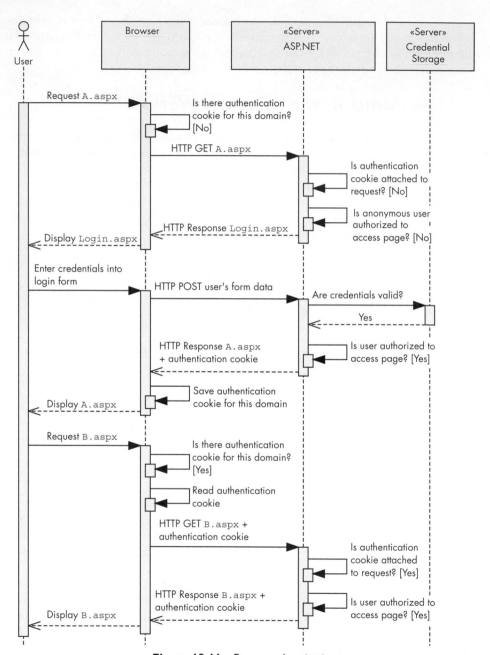

Figure 13.11 Forms authentication

What information is contained in this authentication cookie? It contains an encrypted and hashed instance of something called a ***forms authentication ticket***. This ticket contains information that is used by the forms authentication module to identify a previously authenticated user.

By default, this ticket is persisted across requests using cookies. In ASP.NET 2.0, the application can be configured to use cookieless authentication tickets. In this case, the ticket information is embedded within the URL. Nonetheless, using cookies for the authentication ticket does have a key advantage. A cookie-based ticket can be persistent; that is, it can last far beyond the individual user session. This can be a great usability improvement for sites in which their users infrequently visit (and who frequently forget their credentials for the site). In ASP.NET 1.1 and earlier, the authentication cookie had a lifetime of 50 years. In ASP.NET 2.0, the default lifetime of this cookie is only 30 minutes. This means that after 30 minutes, the user must reauthenticate.

Although the 50-year expiration in ASP.NET 1.1 was probably far too long from a security standpoint, a 30-minute expiration may very well be too short for sites that want to persist the ticket across multiple sessions spread over time. Luckily, the expiration timeout value can be changed via a configuration setting in the `Web.config` file, as shown in the following example.

```
<forms loginUrl="Login.aspx" timeout="86400"
   slidingExpiration="true">
```

In this example, the authentication cookie times out 60 days after it was last used. Setting the `slidingExpiration` attribute to `true` means the expiration of the cookie is reset each time the user makes a request of the site. Thus, if the user accesses the site and authenticates on January 1, the user can access the site without needing to authenticate any time until early March. But if the user accesses the site, for example, on February 1, the user can access the site without authentication anytime until early April.

CORE NOTE

If you are using sessions along with forms authentication, the timeout value should be the same for both.

Table 13.2 contains the other possible configuration options for the `forms` element.

Table 13.2   Forms Authentication Options

Attribute Name	Description
cookieless	Defines whether the authentication ticket is transported via HTTP cookies. The default is `UseDefaultProfile`, which uses cookies if the browser supports them (according to the device profile settings in `machine.config`); otherwise, it encodes the ticket in the URL.
	Other possible values are `UseCookies` (which always uses cookies), `UseUri` (which always embeds ticket in URL), and `AutoDetect`.
	You should strongly consider using the `AutoDetect` option. It tries to use cookies if the default profile for the requesting device indicates support for cookies. However, it first probes the requesting device to see if cookies are enabled. Only if they are enabled does it use a cookie-based ticket; otherwise, it uses URL encoding.
defaultUrl	If the user browses to the login page, after a successful authentication, the user is redirected to this URL.
domain	Specifies the domain for the authentication cookie. Changing this attribute can allow the authentication cookie to be used by multiple Web applications in a given domain.
enableCrossAppRedirects	If set to `true`, it permits the use of a different Web application on the same server for authentication. Default is `false`.
loginUrl	Specifies the URL through which the user can log in when no valid authentication ticket is found.
name	The cookie name for the authentication ticket. If multiple Web applications are running on the same server, and each requires a unique cookie, each Web application should use a unique cookie name.
path	The path for the application's cookies.
protection	The type of encryption to use for the authentication ticket. The possible values are `All` (use both hash data validation and encryption), `Encryption` (ticket is only encrypted), `None` (neither validated nor encrypted), and `Validation` (ticket is only checked for modification). The default is `All`.

Table 13.2 Forms Authentication Options *(continued)*

Attribute Name	Description
requireSSL	If `true`, an SSL connection is required to transmit the ticket. The default is `false`.
slidingExpiration	If `true`, the expiration time for a cookie is reset with each request during a single session. The default is `false`.
timeout	The number of integer minutes before the authentication cookie expires. The default is `30` minutes.

Using Cookieless Authentication Tickets

By default, ASP.NET uses cookies to transport the authentication ticket if the browser supports cookies. That is, if the device profile settings in `machine.config` indicate that the requesting device supports cookies, it uses them; otherwise, it embeds the ticket in the URL. You can change this behavior so that it always embeds the ticket in the URL by changing the `cookieless` attribute of the forms element in the `Web.config` file.

```
<forms loginUrl="Login.aspx" … cookieless="UseUri">
```

Another interesting option for the `cookieless` attribute is `AutoDetect`. When set to this value, ASP.NET tries to use cookies if the default profile for the requesting device indicates support for cookies. However, it first probes the requesting device to see if cookies are enabled. Only if they are enabled does it use a cookie-based ticket; otherwise, it uses URL encoding.

Security Concerns with Authentication Tickets

Both cookie-based and cookieless authentication tickets are potentially vulnerable to so-called ***replay attacks***. In a replay attack, authentication information for a given user is captured without proper authorization by a different user and then retransmitted later by the different user, thus allowing this rogue user unauthorized access to the first user's session. Thus, a replay attack does not require the breaking of keys or passwords.

Reply attacks can come from cross-site scripting hoaxes that give a third-party site access to another domain's cookies. Cookieless authentication tickets are especially vulnerable to replay attacks. If the user bookmarks a page in which the authentication ticket is embedded in the URL on a public computer or copies the URL and pastes it into an email sent to another, and if the timeout for the authentication ticket is quite long, someone else can access the URL and be logged in to the other person's account!

As a consequence, if you are allowing cookieless authentication tickets, it is advisable to make the timeout value as low as possible, probably somewhere in the 60-minute range. Alternately, if for usability reasons you need a longer-lasting, persistent authentication ticket, consider forcing the user to reauthenticate for pages with important security information, such as a payment page or a page that views credit card information.

Provider Model

The **provider model** is one of the chief architectural features of ASP.NET 2.0. The idea behind the provider model is that instead of programming directly against data stores, key ASP.NET services such as site maps, session state, and the membership service use providers to read and write data. A **provider** is a software class (or classes) that provide a uniform programming interface between a service and a data source. Thus, a provider is a contract between the service and its implementation in that it implements a guaranteed interface.

Like the data access layer in some of the previous chapters, providers are an abstraction of the physical storage medium. As such, the use of providers makes a given service very extensible, because you can create your own providers or purchase them from third-party sources. For instance, while ASP.NET 2.0 ships with an SQL Server and an Active Directory membership provider, you could create an Oracle membership provider and the rest of the membership system in ASP.NET could work with it. Or, if you already have an existing user account system that works via Web services, you could adopt it to work with the new membership features in ASP.NET 2.0 by creating a provider for this existing system. Figure 13.12 illustrates the architecture of the provider model.

The benefits of the provider model are similar to the benefits of using a layered architecture in general. First among these is that it enforces a separation between the code for accessing a service and the code that implements the service. Doing so isolates the page developer from changes in the back-end implementation of a given service. The provider model can also make it easier to implement a division of labor amongst the developers on a project. Back-end developers can work on custom providers, whereas page developers need only worry about working with the API of the provider. Finally, because the provider model is built-in to ASP.NET 2.0, you can change the specific provider used by a Web application for a service declaratively in the `Web.config` file without any programming changes.

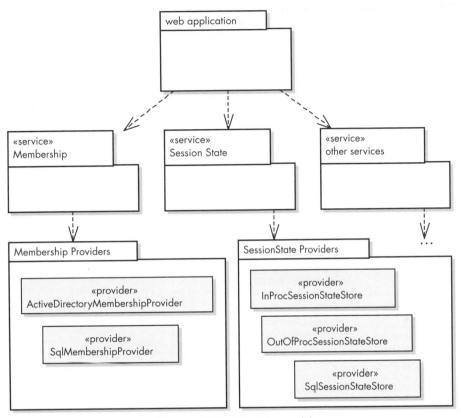

Figure 13.12 Provider model

Provider Model Architecture

For those readers who are familiar with the common Gang of Four design patterns, the provider model is principally based on the Strategy and Factory Method design patterns. In the **Strategy design pattern**, a given algorithm or feature can be replaced by another by encapsulating the two features into two separate classes that have a common interface defined by a common abstract base class or interface. We have already encountered the Factory Method design pattern (in Chapter 9). In the **Factory Method design pattern,** the creation of instances of an object is separated from its use. This is typically implemented by having a static method that is responsible for instantiating instances of a given object. Given that the Strategy pattern requires the instantiation of just one class out of several possible classes to implement a feature, the Factory Method is used in conjunction with it to determine which feature class to create. The provider model uses reflection along with

XML-based configuration files to determine which class to instantiate. For instance, in the `machine.config` file, the different installed providers for the membership service are configured as shown here.

```
<membership>
   <providers>
      <add name="AspNetSqlMembershipProvider"
         type="System.Web.Security.SqlMembershipProvider,
            System.Web, Version=2.0.0.0,
            Culture=neutral,
            PublicKeyToken=b03f5f7f11d50a3a"
         connectionStringName="LocalSqlServer"
         enablePasswordRetrieval="false"
         enablePasswordReset="true"
         requiresQuestionAndAnswer="true"
         applicationName="/"
         requiresUniqueEmail="false"
         passwordFormat="Hashed"
         maxInvalidPasswordAttempts="5"
         minRequiredPasswordLength="7"
         minRequiredNonalphanumericCharacters="1"
         passwordAttemptWindow="10"
         passwordStrengthRegularExpression="" />
      ...
   </providers>
</membership>
```

In the individual Web application's `Web.config` file, you can add providers.

```
<membership defaultProvider="myCustomMemberProvider">
   <providers>
      <add name="myCustomMemberProvider"
         type="MyProviders.CustomOracleMembershipProvider,..." ... />
   </providers>
</membership>
```

In this case, you have configured your application to use the custom Oracle membership provider. The provider system handles the instantiation of the correct Strategy class, which in this case is `CustomOracleMembershipProvider`.

Provider-Based Services

Membership is just one of the services in ASP.NET that uses the provider model. Table 13.3 lists the other provider-based services in ASP.NET.

Table 13.3   Provider-Based Services

Service	Description
Encryption	Handles encryption and decryption of sections of the ASP.NET configuration files.
Membership	Manages user accounts.
Profile	Manages user preferences and user information across visits.
Role management	Handles role-based security.
Session state	Maintains user state between requests.
Site map	Provides a description of a site's structure.
Web events	Used by ASP.NET health monitoring subsystem that allows the monitoring of a Web application.
Web parts	Manages the special set of controls for creating Web sites that enable end users to modify the content, appearance, and behavior of Web pages directly within the browser.

CORE NOTE

If you do not want to use the default SQL Server membership provider (perhaps because you do not want to incur the extra cost that a hosting company may charge you), you might be interested in downloading a Microsoft Access version of the Membership, Role Manager, Profile, and Web Parts providers from `http://msdn.microsoft.com/asp.net/ downloads/providers`. Although Access is not suitable for most real-world Web applications, for sites with a small number of simultaneous users (under 20 to 30), using the Microsoft Access version of these providers may be a cost-effective solution.

Figure 13.13 illustrates the relationship between some of the classes that make up these provider services. Notice that all providers share a common base class, and that each provider-based service is defined by a common base type as well.

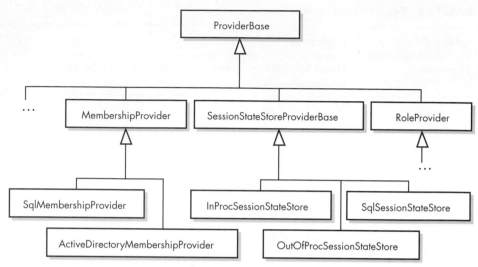

Figure 13.13   Provider classes

Creating Custom Providers

One of the main benefits of the provider model is that it is extensible. You can define a new provider that is based on an existing provider service, or you can define an entirely new provider-based service.

CORE NOTE

This section on creating custom providers is intended for readers already comfortable with the provider model, as well as the membership provider in particular. You may want to skip this section and return to it later as needed.

Defining a Custom Provider for Existing Provider Service

If you want to create a new provider for an existing provider service, you only need to implement the functionality defined in the interface to its base class. For instance, imagine that you want to create an XML-based membership service or a new membership service that makes use of existing tables of user information. In both cases, you create a subclass of the `MembershipProvider` base class. In your `Customer-Management` database, there is a `Customers` table with `Email` and `Password` fields. If you want the membership service to use this information, you define a new custom membership provider that looks similar to the following.

CORE NOTE

The custom membership provider is too long to show in this chapter. However, you can download the complete version from my Web site at `http://www.randyconnolly.com/core`.

```csharp
public class CustomerMembershipProvider: MembershipProvider
{
    // Only 2 of 27 members are shown here
    ...

    public override MembershipUser CreateUser(string username,
        string password, string email, string passwordQuestion,
        string passwordAnswer, bool isApproved,
        object providerUserKey,
        out MembershipCreateStatus status)
    {
        // Use existing application logic and business entities
        CustomerServiceLogic cs = new CustomerServiceLogic();
        Customer cust = new Customer();
        cust.LastName = username;
        cust.Email = email;
        cust.Password = password;

        if ( cs.SaveCustomer(cust) )
            status = MembershipCreateStatus.Success;
        else
            status = MembershipCreateStatus.UserRejected;
    }


    public override bool ValidateUser(string username,
        string password)
    {
        // Use existing application logic and business entities

        CustomerServiceLogic cs = new CustomerServiceLogic();
        Customer cust = cs.GetCustomer(username, password);
        if (cust == null)
            return false;
```

```
        else
            return true;
    }
}
```

To use this custom membership provider, all you need to do is indicate in your `Web.config` file that you want to use it with the `defaultProvider` attribute as shown here.

```
<system.web>
    ...
    <membership defaultProvider="CustomerMembershipProvider">
      <providers>
        <add name=" CustomerMembershipProvider"
            type="CustomerMembershipProvider,…" … />
      </providers>
    </membership>
</system.web>
```

Defining a New Custom Provider Service

Creating an entirely new provider service is a bit more complicated. First, you need to define a new abstract class that inherits from `ProviderBase`. For instance, imagine that you want to create a service that retrieves or stores customer book reviews based on the book's ISBN. You might then define the following class.

```
public abstract class BookReviewProvider : ProviderBase
{
    public abstract void SaveReview(string isbn, Review review);
    public abstract EntityCollection<Review>
      GetReviews(string isbn);
}
```

Because it is possible to have more than one `BookReviewProvider`, you also need to define a collection class for these providers.

```
public class BookReviewProviderCollection : ProviderCollection
{
    public new BookReviewProvider this[string name]
    {
        get { return (BookReviewProvider) base[name]; }
    }

    public override void Add(ProviderBase provider)
    {
        if (provider == null)
            throw new ArgumentNullException("provider");
```

```
        if (!(provider is ImageProvider))
            throw new ArgumentException
                ("Invalid provider type", "provider");

        base.Add(provider);
    }
}
```

You can then define concrete implementations of this new provider class. For instance, you might decide to define a version of the book review provider that retrieves reviews from a SQL Server database.

```
public class SqlBookReviewProvider : BookReviewProvider
{
    public override string Name
    {
        get { return " SqlBookReviewProvider"; }
    }
    public override string Description
    {
        get {
            return
                "Retrieve or stores book review objects from
                    SQL Server database table"; }
    }

    public override EntityCollection<Review>
        GetReviews(string isbn)
    {
        // Implement this functionality
        ...
    }
    public override void SaveReview(string isbn, Review review)
    {
        // Implement this functionality
        ...
    }
    public override void Initialize (string name,
        NameValueCollection config)
    {
        // Implement this functionality
        ...
    }
}
```

You might also define another concrete provider that retrieves reviews from the Amazon.com Web service.

```
public class AmazonBookReviewProvider : BookReviewProvider
{
   public override string Name
   {
      get { return " AmazonBookReviewProvider"; }
   }
   public override string Description
   {
      get {
         return "Retrieve or stores book review objects from the
            amazon.com web service"; }
   }

   // Implement the required members
   ...
}
```

To use a new provider-based service, consumers must be able to configure the service, register providers for it, and designate which provider is the default. The following Web.config snippet registers the SqlBookReviewProvider as a provider for the image service and makes it the default provider.

```
<system.web>
   ...
   <reviewService defaultProvider="SqlReviewProvider">
      <providers>
        <add name="SqlReviewProvider"
           type="SqlBookReviewProvider" … />
      </providers>
   </reviewService>
</system.web>
```

Unfortunately, you still need to do a bit more work. Because this is a brand new service, ASP.NET knows nothing about this reviewService element in the Web.config file. Thus, you must define the infrastructure that recognizes this new configuration element.

The first step is to write a custom configuration class that derives from System.Configuration.ConfigurationSection. This class must add two properties (Providers and DefaultProvider), which are described by [Configuration-Property] attributes, as shown here.

```
using System;
using System.Configuration;

public class ReviewServiceSection : ConfigurationSection
{
   [ConfigurationProperty("providers")]
   public ProviderSettingsCollection Providers
   {
```

```
    get { return (ProviderSettingsCollection)
        base["providers"]; }
}

[StringValidator(MinLength = 1)]
[ConfigurationProperty("defaultProvider",
    DefaultValue = "SqlReviewProvider")]
public string DefaultProvider
{
    get { return (string) base["defaultProvider"]; }
    set { base["defaultProvider"] = value; }
}
}
```

The next step is to register the reviewService configuration section in the Web.config file and designate ReviewServiceSection as the handler for it.

```
<configuration >
    <configSections>
        <sectionGroup name="system.web">
            <section name="reviewService"
                type="ReviewServiceSection, CustomSections"
                allowDefinition="MachineToApplication"
                restartOnExternalChanges="true" />
        </sectionGroup>
    </configSections>
    ...
    <system.web>
        ...
    </system.web>
</configuration>
```

Note that the preceding markup assumes that the ReviewServiceSection class is within an assembly named CustomSections. If you use a different assembly name, you need to modify the markup accordingly.

The final step is to create a class that provides a programmatic interface to the review service and that loads and initializes the providers registered in reviewService's providers element. Like ASP.NET's Membership class, which represents the membership service and contains static methods for performing membership-related tasks, ReviewService class represents the review service and contains static methods for working with the book reviews. A sample implementation of this class is shown in Listing 13.3.

Listing 13.3 ReviewService.cs

```
using System;
using System.Drawing;
using System.Configuration;
```

```csharp
using System.Configuration.Provider;
using System.Web.configuration;
using System.Web;

public class ReviewService
{
    private static BookReviewProvider _provider = null;
    private static object _lock = new object();

    public BookReviewProvider Provider
    {
        get { return _provider; }
    }

    public BookReviewProviderCollection Providers
    {
        get { return _providers; }
    }

    public static EntityCollection<Review>
        RetrieveReviews(string isbn)
    {
        // Make sure a provider is loaded
        LoadProviders();

        // Delegate to the provider
        return _provider.GetReviews(isbn);
    }

    public static void SaveReview(string isbn, Review review)
    {
        // Make sure a provider is loaded
        LoadProviders();

        // Delegate to the provider
        _provider.SaveImage(image);
    }

    private static void LoadProviders()
    {
        // if already loaded providers then exit
        if (_provider != null)
            return;

        // lock code in case multiple threads try to do this
        lock (_lock)
        {
            // Do this again to make sure _provider is still null
            if (_provider == null)
```

```
    {
        // Get a reference to the <reviewService> section
        ReviewServiceSection section = (ReviewServiceSection)
          WebConfigurationManager.GetSection(
          "system.web/reviewService");

        // Load registered providers
        BookReviewProviderCollection provs =
            new BookReviewProviderCollection ();

        ProvidersHelper.InstantiateProviders(
            section.Providers,
            provs,typeof(ReviewProvider));

        // Get default review provider
        _provider = provs[section.DefaultProvider];

        if (_provider == null)
            throw new ProviderException
              ("Unable to load default BookReviewProvider");
    }
  }
 }
}
```

The private `LoadProviders` method ensures the providers registered in reviewService's providers element have been loaded and initialized. It uses the `ProvidersHelper.InstantiateProviders` method to load and initialize the registered review providers—that is, the providers exposed through the `Providers` property of the `ReviewServiceSection` object that `LoadProviders` passes to `ProvidersHelper.InstantiateProviders`.

Although defining a new provider service is not exactly trivial, it does follow a well-defined process. For many situations, it might seem easier to simply use the layered approach demonstrated in Chapter 11. The one advantage with the provider approach is that it provides an infrastructure for changing the concrete provider type declaratively through the `Web.config` file.

Membership

As you saw in an earlier section, the forms authentication approach is the only realistic ASP.NET authentication approach for sites that deal with a larger number of users. With forms authentication, the Web application itself is responsible for determining the validity of the user-supplied credentials, which typically involves querying a database or some type of business component. After the validity is determined, the forms authentication infrastructure handles the persistence of the authentication via cookie-based or cookieless authentication tickets.

If you have ever worked on more than one ASP.NET application that has user accounts that need to be managed, you may have found that the development needed to implement user account management to be quite similar. Indeed, you may have found yourself copying from the one application and pasting into another application. As a way to avoid having to recreate the typical user account management solution over and over again, ASP.NET 2.0 introduced the membership API along with several new login controls.

Overview of Membership System

The *Membership API* is a set of classes built on top of the forms authentication system that allows the developer to more easily implement the typical functionality a site needs for managing and authenticating users. In particular, the ASP.NET membership system provides the following functionality:

- Creates new users
- Stores membership information in Microsoft SQL Server, Active Directory, or some other data source
- Authenticates users
- Uses role-based security
- Manages passwords, which includes creating, changing, and resetting them

The new ASP.NET login controls work in conjunction with the membership system and provide a quick solution to the typical user interface features needed for authenticating users. These new login controls (`Login`, `LoginView`, `LoginStatus`, `LoginName`, and `PasswordRecovery`) encapsulate virtually all of the logic required to prompt users for credentials and validate the credentials in the membership system.

By using these login controls, your application can be shielded from all the implementation details (i.e., programming) of retrieving, comparing, and saving credentials. How do these controls work? The login controls use, behind the scenes, the membership API to implement standard operations such as validating a user's credentials, adding a new user, and displaying login error messages.

The membership API makes use of something called membership providers to perform the actual communication with the data sources used to store the user accounts. *Membership providers* are classes with a well-defined interface that have the responsibility of interacting with the specific user account data storage mechanism used by the application. Thus, there is a layer of abstraction between the membership API and the actual membership storage. This layer of abstraction means that you can use any data source, such as SQL Server, Oracle, Active Directory, or a Web service, with the membership API as long as there is a membership provider that can work with that data source.

The .NET Framework ships with two different membership providers: the `SqlMembershipProvider` and the `ActiveDirectoryMembershipProvider`. The `SqlMembershipProvider` stores user information in a Microsoft SQL Server database, whereas the `ActiveDirectoryMembershipProvider` provides membership services using an Active Directory or Active Directory Application Mode (ADAM) server. As well, you can create a custom membership provider to communicate with an existing alternate data source.

CORE NOTE

The `ActiveDirectoryMembershipProvider` only works in full trust mode.

The default membership provider is the `SqlMembershipProvider` (which is actually named `AspNetSqlMembershipProvider`).

Configuring the SqlMembershipProvider

Unlike most of the features of ASP.NET covered so far in this book, the membership API requires some configuration steps before you can use it in your site. In this chapter, we will only demonstrate how to configure the `SqlMembershipProvider`.

To use this provider, you must first create the database that is used by the provider. There are two ways of doing this:

1. Use the **ASP.NET SQL Server Registration Tool** (`aspnet_regsql.exe`). You encountered this command-line program in the last chapter where we used it to configure the SQL Server session state database.
2. Use the **ASP.NET Website Administration Tool (WAT)**. This is a browser-based application that can be launched from Visual Studio that allows you to view and modify security, application, and provider configuration settings in the application's `Web.config` file.

CORE NOTE

The Website Administration Tool creates a SQL Server 2005 database file in the Web application's `APP_DATA` folder. If you want to store this database in a different location or you need to use a different version of SQL Server, you must use the SQL Server Registration Tool.

When using the `SqlMembershipProvider` in conjunction with the WAT, user information is stored in two tables: `aspnet_Users` and `aspnet_Membership`. In Walkthrough 13.1, we demonstrate how to use the WAT.

CORE NOTE

Your Web application must be configured in full trust mode to use the Website Administration Tool. As such, this tool generally is only run in a development, nonproduction environment.

Walkthrough 13.1 *Using the Website Administration Tool*

1. Start the Website Administration Tool for the current Web application by using the Web Site | ASP.NET Configuration menu option in Visual Studio.

   This starts the browser and displays the WAT, as shown in Figure 13.14.

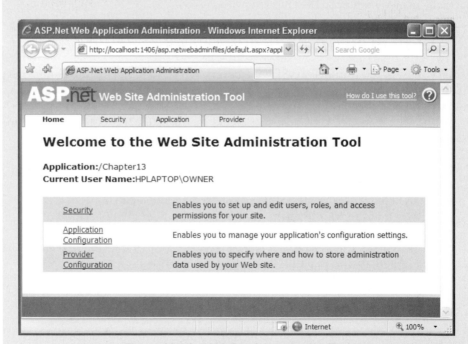

Figure 13.14   Web Site Administration Tool

2. Click the Provider tab. Notice that the `AspNetSqlMembership-Provider` is already configured for use.

3. Click the Security tab.

   If you have SQL Server 2005 (either the Express edition or the full edition) already installed on your computer, you can start adding users to the database.

4. Click the Create User link. This displays the Create User page, as shown in Figure 13.15.

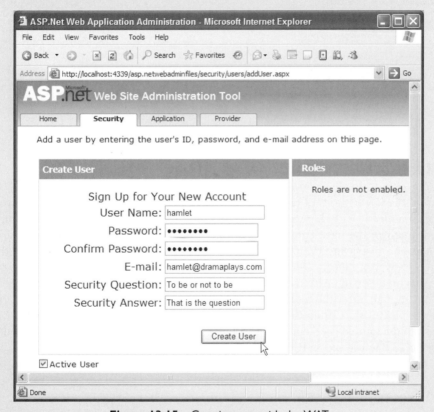

Figure 13.15   Creating user with the WAT

5. Fill in the form and click the Create User button.

6. Add two or three more users.

You can examine the data added by the WAT in the Server Explorer in Visual Studio. Each time you add or create a user with the WAT, it adds a record to each of the `aspnet_Users` and `aspnet_Membership` tables, as shown in Figure 13.16.

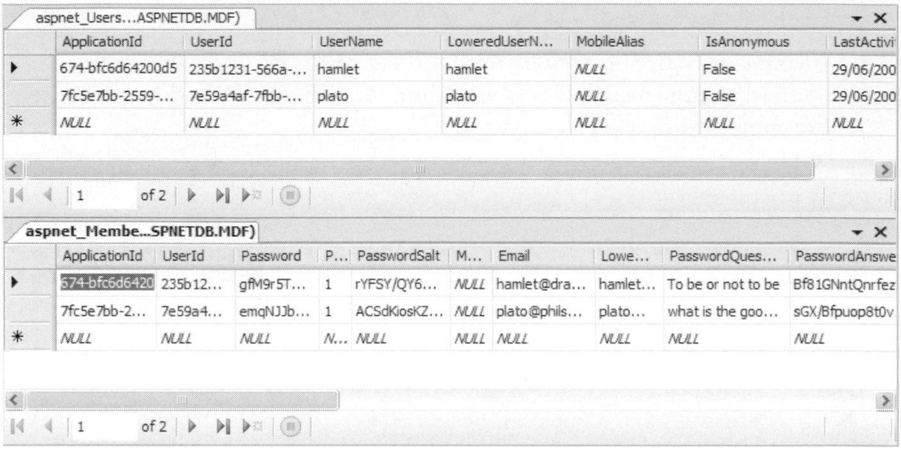

Figure 13.16 Viewing user data

Using the Membership API

One of the key benefits of using this new membership infrastructure is that it works quite seamlessly with the ASP.NET login controls. As a result, it is possible to implement many of the most common security-related user display tasks (such as logging in and out, displaying the current user, and creating a user) without any programming. However, before we encounter these controls, it might be instructive to first see this membership API in action.

At any rate, after the membership database is created and you have added a few users, you can start using the membership API. Back in Listings 13.1 and 13.2, we presented a sample user login form. You can easily change the authentication code in Listing 13.2 to use the ASP.NET membership infrastructure, as shown here.

```
protected void btnLogin_Click(object sender, EventArgs e)
{
    // Use the membership system to authenticate user
    if ( Membership.ValidateUser(txtUser.Text,txtPassword.Text) )
        FormsAuthentication.RedirectFromLoginPage(user, true);
    else
        labError.Text = "User not found, try again";
}
```

Due to the provider model architecture, your Web pages can remain indifferent to whether it is using the SQL Server membership provider, your own custom membership provider, or some other provider.

The `Membership` class has a variety of static methods that you can use to validate users, create or update users, and retrieve a list of users. Table 13.4 lists the methods of the `Membership` class.

Table 13.4　Methods of the Membership Class

Name	Description
`CreateUser`	Adds a new user to the membership data store.
`DeleteUser`	Deletes an existing user from the membership data store.
`FindUsersByEmail`	Returns a `MembershipUserCollection` of users whose email matches the passed email.
`FindUsersByName`	Returns a `MembershipUserCollection` of users whose user name matches the passed user name.
`GeneratePassword`	Generates a random password of the specified length.
`GetAllUsers`	Returns a `MembershipUserCollection` of all users.
`GetNumberOfUsersOnline`	Gets the number of users that is currently accessing the application.
`GetUser`	Returns a `MembershipUser` object for the current logged on user.
`GetUserNameByEmail`	Returns the user name for the specified email.
`UpdateUser`	Updates the data source with the information contained in the specified `MembershipUser` object.
`ValidateUser`	Returns `true` if the specified user name and password are valid (i.e., exist in the data store).

To illustrate the use of some of these methods, imagine that you need to create a page with some similar functionality to that exposed in the WAT. This page allows the site administrator to manage the users for the site. It provides a list of existing users in a `GridView` control. The administrator can delete or select users from this `Grid-View`, as well as edit or create new users via other Web server controls.

This page needs to use some classes in the membership API. Ideally, you should isolate your page's access to this API by wrapping the use of these membership classes within a business object or an application logic class. However, for clarity sake, the example code directly uses the membership classes.

The first of these is an `ObjectDataSource` control to be used by the `GridView` control that uses the `Membership` class to retrieve the users as well as delete a selected user.

```
<asp:ObjectDataSource ID="odsUsers" runat="server"
   TypeName="System.Web.Security.Membership"
   SelectMethod="GetAllUsers"
   DeleteMethod="DeleteUser">

   <DeleteParameters>
     <asp:ControlParameter ControlID="grdUsers" Type="string"
        PropertyName="SelectedDataKey.Values[1]"
          Name="username" />
   </DeleteParameters>
</asp:ObjectDataSource>
```

Notice that this `ObjectDataSource` control interfaces to the `Membership` class and uses its `GetAllUsers` and `DeleteUser` static methods. Because the `DeleteUser` requires a `username` parameter, you fill this parameter from the second of two data keys of the `GridView`, which is shown here.

```
<asp:GridView ID="grdUsers" runat="server"
   DataSourceID="odsUsers"
   AutoGenerateColumns="false"
   AutoGenerateDeleteButton="true"
   AutoGenerateSelectButton="true"
   CellPadding="5"
   DataKeyNames="ProviderUserKey,UserName"
   OnSelectedIndexChanged="grdUsers_SelectedIndexChanged" >

   <Columns>
      <asp:BoundField HeaderText="Name" DataField="UserName" />
      <asp:BoundField HeaderText="Email" DataField="Email" />
      <asp:BoundField HeaderText="Create Date"
         DataField="CreationDate" />
      <asp:BoundField HeaderText="Last Login"
         DataField="LastLoginDate" />
   </Columns>
</asp:GridView>
```

This `GridView` control automatically contains select and delete buttons on each row. Notice that it also defines two data key names. But to what properties do they refer? Similarly, to which object properties are the `DataField` attributes in the `BoundField` elements referring? You may have noticed from Table 13.4 that the `Membership.GetAllUsers` method returns a `MembershipUserCollection` object. This is simply a collection of `MembershipUser` objects. Thus, your `GridView` is referring to properties of the `MembershipUser` class.

Table 13.5 lists the properties of the `MembershipUser` class.

Table 13.5 Properties of the MembershipUser Class

Name	Description
Comment	Custom information for membership user that is specific to an application.
CreationDate	The date and time when user was added to membership data store. Read-only.
Email	The email address for the membership user.
IsApproved	Specifies whether the membership user can be authenticated.
IsLockedOut	A `bool` value indicating whether the member is locked out and unable to be authenticated. Read-only. Members can be locked out by the `Membership.ValidateUser` method.
IsOnline	A `bool` value indicating whether the member is currently online. Read-only.
LastActivityDate	The date and time when the member was last authenticated.
LastLockoutDate	The date and time when the member was locked out. Read-only.
LastLoginDate	The date and time when the member was last authenticated.
LastPasswordChangedDate	The date and time when the member's password was last updated. Read-only.
PasswordQuestion	The password question for the member. Read-only.
ProviderName	The name of the membership provider being used. Read-only.
ProviderUserKey	The unique user identifier from the membership data source for the member. Read-only.
UserName	The logon name for the membership user. Read-only.

Notice that there are no properties for retrieving the password or the password question's answer; notice as well that most of these properties are read-only. Instead, password manipulation is provided by methods of the `MembershipUser` class, which are shown in Table 13.6.

Table 13.6   Methods of the MembershipUser Class

Name	Description
ChangePassword	Updates the password for the member.
ChangePasswordQuestionAndAnswer	Updates the password question and answer for the member.
GetPassword	Returns the password for the member. This method generates an exception if the `Membership.EnablePasswordRetrieval` property is set to `false`.
ResetPassword	Resets the member's password to a new, system-generated password.
UnLockUser	Clears the locked-out status of the user.

The `GridView` controls defined in the preceding table also reference an event handler for the selection event. What do you do when the user selects a `MembershipUser` in the grid? You can allow the user to edit the writeable properties of `MembershipUser` (i.e., `Comments`, `Email`, `IsApproved`, `LastActivityDate`, `LastLoginDate`). The code for this might look similar to the following.

```
protected void grdUsers_SelectedIndexChanged(object sender,
   EventArgs e)
{
   // Retrieve the provider user key of selected user
   object userKey = grdUsers.SelectedDataKey.Values[0];

   // Retrieve the user
   MembershipUser user = Membership.GetUser(userKey);

   if (user != null)
   {
      txtEditEmail.Text = user.Email;
      txtEditComments.Text = user.Comment;
      ...
   }
}
```

Notice that this code uses the `GetUser` method of `Membership` to retrieve the selected `MembershipUser`. This method requires the provider user key of the member. For the default `SqlMembershipProvider`, this is the data in the `UserId` field of the `Membership` table.

If your page is going to provide a way to update the writeable properties, it also needs some way of saving these updates. The code for this might look like the following.

```
protected void btnEdit_Click(object sender, EventArgs e)
{
    // Retrieve the selected user
    object userKey = grdUsers.SelectedDataKey.Values[0];
    MembershipUser user = Membership.GetUser(userKey);

    // Modify its properties based on form values
    user.Email = txtEditEmail.Text;
    user.Comment = txtEditComments.Text;
    …

    // Perform the update
    Membership.UpdateUser(user);
}
```

You may wonder why we defined an event handler and didn't simply get the `ObjectDataSource` to call its `UpdateUser` method. You may recall from the discussion on using business objects with the `ObjectDataSource` control in Chapter 11 that when you pass an object to the method specified by the `ObjectDataSource`'s `UpdateMethod` or `InsertMethod` properties, the object must have a parameterless constructor. `MembershipUser` does not have a parameterless constructor because its internal state is not populated by the developer but by the membership provider.

For this same reason, you must also programmatically perform the creation of a new user yourself and not simply rely on the `ObjectDataSource`. The code for this might look like the following.

```
protected void btnAdd_Click(object sender, EventArgs e)
{
    // Retrieve values from form
    string user = …
    string password = …
    string email = …
    string passQuestion = …
    string passAnswer = …

    // Define the status variable
    MembershipCreateStatus status;
```

```
// Try to create the user
Membership.CreateUser(
    user,password,email,passQuestion,passAnswer,
    true, out status);

// See if it worked
if (status == MembershipCreateStatus.Success)
    labStatus.Text = "User created successfully";
else
    labStatus.Text = GetErrorMessage(status);
}
```

Notice that the `Membership.CreateUser` method takes an `out` parameter. The `out` keyword causes arguments to be passed by reference. This is similar to the `ref` keyword, except that `ref` requires that the variable be initialized before being passed. To use an `out` parameter, both the method definition and the calling method must explicitly use the `out` keyword.

The `out` parameter in this case is of type `MembershipCreateStatus`, which is an enumerated type. You could output a different message for each possible value in `MembershipCreateStatus`, as shown in the sample `GetErrorMessage` helper method.

```
public string GetErrorMessage(MembershipCreateStatus status)
{
    switch (status)
    {
        case MembershipCreateStatus.DuplicateUserName:
            return "Username already exists";

        case MembershipCreateStatus.DuplicateEmail:
            return
                "A username for that e-mail address already exists";

        // The rest of the cases would continue here
        ...

        default:
            return "An unknown error occurred";
    }
}
```

In the next section, we examine the other provider-based service involved with user management, the role management API.

Role Management

ASP.NET 2.0 introduced a role management infrastructure that allows developers to associate users with roles and performs role checks declaratively and programmatically. Role management lets you treat groups of users as a unit by assigning users to roles that you create, such as administrator, editor, or member.

After roles are defined within an application, the developer can then create access rules based on those roles. For example, your site might include a set of pages that you want visible only to members. Similarly, you might want to show or hide a part of a page based on whether the current user is an administrator. With roles, you can establish these types of rules independent from the actual site members. Thus, you do not have to grant individual members of your site access to member-only pages; instead, you can grant access to the member role and then simply add and remove users from that role (note that users can belong to more than one role).

Even if your application has only a few users, you might still find it useful to create roles. As you define more access rules for your application, roles become a more convenient way to apply the changes to groups of users.

Role Provider

Like the membership API, the role management API uses the provider model. ASP.NET 2.0 ships with the following role providers:

- `SqlRoleProvider`—Stores role information in the same SQL Server database as the SQL Server membership provider.
- `WindowsTokenRoleProvider`—Retrieves role information for a Windows user based on Windows security groups. This provider may be useful if you are using Windows Authentication. You cannot, however, use this provider to create or delete roles or modify the membership of a role, because this functionality is managed by the Windows operating system.
- `AuthorizationStoreRoleProvider`—Manages role information that is stored in an authorization-manager policy store, such as Active Directory or an XML file.

The default role provider is the `SqlRoleProvider`. You can specify the role provider you want to use directly in the `Web.config` file or you can do so via the WAT tool. Just like with any of the providers, you can also create your own custom role provider.

Managing Roles

You can add the ability to work with roles in your application by adding the following to your `Web.config` file.

```
<system.web>
   ...
   <roleManager enabled="true" />
</system.web>
```

After roles are enabled in your application, the Role Management API is available to it. Using this API, you can programmatically create and delete roles and assign users to roles. You can also manage the application's roles by using the WAT (Web Site Administration Tool, introduced in Walkthrough 13.1 on page 794).

In the WAT, you must first click the `Security` tab and click the `Enable roles` link, as shown in Figure 13.17.

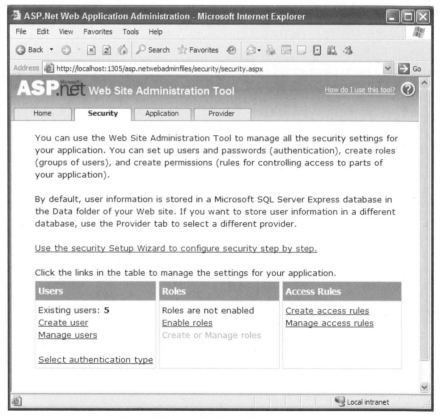

Figure 13.17   Enabling roles management

After roles have been enabled, you can click the `Create or Manage roles` link to begin defining roles (see Figure 13.18).

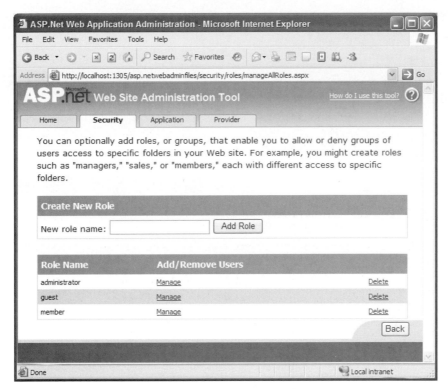

Figure 13.18   Adding new roles

After the roles have been defined, all you need to do is assign users to roles. The WAT makes this process very straightforward (see Figure 13.19).

Role-Based Authorization

Earlier in the chapter, we examined how to set up file or URL-based authorization by nesting `deny` and `allow` elements within the `authorization` element in the `Web.config` file. You also can use role names in the `authorization` element to establish additional access rules for pages and folders in your application.

```
<authorization>
   <deny users="?" />
   <allow roles="Administrators" />
   <deny users="*" />
</authorization>
```

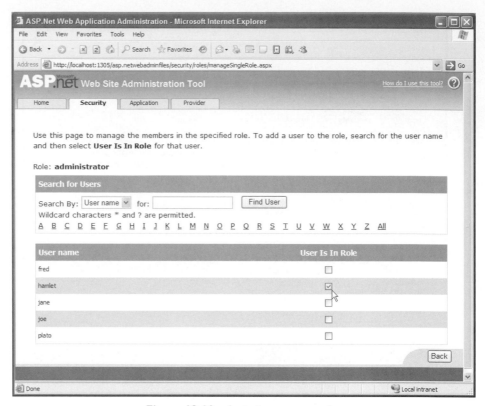

Figure 13.19 Assigning users to roles

Perhaps the easiest way to establish these access rules is to use the WAT (see Figure 13.20).

Using the Role Management API

Although this discussion on role management has used the WAT to create and manage roles, it should be stressed that you can also perform role management tasks programmatically via the `Roles` class. Table 13.7 lists the methods of the `Roles` class.

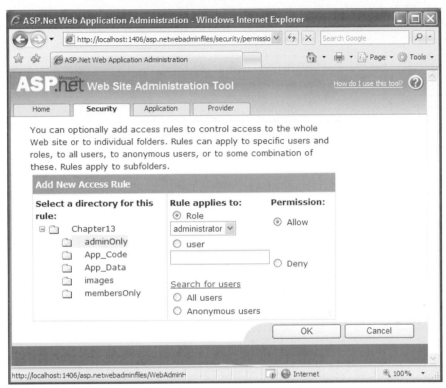

Figure 13.20   Adding a new access rule

Table 13.7   Methods of the Role Class

Name	Description
AddUsersToRole	Adds a list of users to a single role.
AddUsersToRoles	Adds a list of users to a list of roles.
AddUserToRole	Adds a single user to a single role.
AddUserToRoles	Adds a single user to a list of roles.
CreateRole	Adds a new role to the underlying data source.
DeleteCookie	Clears the contents of the cookie that is used to cache role names.
DeleteRole	Deletes an existing role from the underlying data source.

Table 13.7   Methods of the Role Class *(continued)*

Name	Description
FindUsersInRole	Returns an array of user names that matches a user name search string and a specified role.
GetAllRoles	Returns an array of role names.
GetRolesForUser	Returns an array of role names for the specified user.
GetUsersInRole	Returns an array of user names for the specified role.
IsUserInRole	Returns a `bool` value that indicates if the user is in the specified role.
RemoveUserFromRole	Removes a single user from a single role.
RemoveUserFromRoles	Removes a single user from a list of roles.
RemoveUsersFromRole	Removes a list of users from a single role.
RemoveUsersFromRoles	Removes a list of users from a list of roles.
RoleExists	Returns a `bool` value that indicates if the specified role already exists.

Listings 13.4 and 13.5 illustrate a simple role manager page that uses both the `Role` and `Membership` classes. It allows the administrator to select an existing user, view or change its role membership, as well as add new roles or delete existing roles. Figure 13.21 illustrates how this listing appears in the browser.

CORE NOTE

Of course, it is easier to use the WAT for this type of functionality. The example in Listing 13.4 is intended to simply illustrate the usage of the Role Management API.

The markup for this example is fairly straightforward. It uses two `ObjectData-Source` controls to retrieve a list of users and a list of roles, which are in turn bound to a `ListBox` and a `CheckBoxList`, respectively.

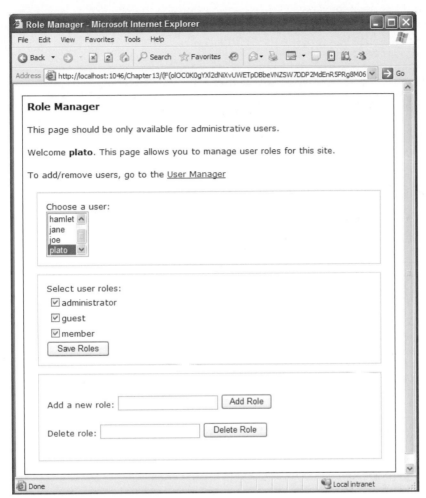

Figure 13.21 RoleManager.aspx

Listing 13.4 RoleManager.aspx

```
<h1>Role Manager</h1>
<p>
This page should be only available for administrative users.
</p>
<p>
Welcome <b><asp:Label ID="labName" runat="server" /></b>.
This page allows you to manage user roles for this site.
</p>
```

```
<p>To add/remove users, go to the <a href="UserManager.aspx">User
Manager</a></p>
<div class="box">
   Choose a user:<br />
   <asp:ListBox ID="drpUsers" runat="server"
     AutoPostBack="True" DataSourceID="odsUsers"
     OnSelectedIndexChanged="drpUsers_SelectedIndexChanged" />
</div>
<asp:Panel ID="panRoles" runat="server" CssClass="box" >
   Select user roles: <br/>
   <asp:CheckBoxList ID="chkRoles" runat="server"
      DataSourceID="odsRoles" />
   <asp:Button ID="btnSaveRoles" runat="server" Text="Save Roles"
      OnClick="btnSaveRoles_Click" />
</asp:Panel>

<div class="box">
   <p>
   Add a new role:
   <asp:TextBox ID="txtRole" runat="server" />
   <asp:Button ID="btnAddRole" runat="server" Text="Add Role"
      OnClick="btnAddRole_Click" />
   </p>
   <p>
   Delete role:
   <asp:TextBox ID="txtDeleteRole" runat="server" />
   <asp:Button ID="btnDeleteRole" runat="server"
      Text="Delete Role"
      OnClick="btnDeleteRole_Click" />
   </p>
</div>

<asp:ObjectDataSource ID="odsUsers" runat="server"
   TypeName="System.Web.Security.Membership"
   SelectMethod="GetAllUsers" />
<asp:ObjectDataSource ID="odsRoles" runat="server"
   TypeName="System.Web.Security.Roles"
   SelectMethod="GetAllRoles" />
```

The code-behind in Listing 13.5 does all the event handling. Whenever the user selects a different user from the list of users, you must loop through the items in the CheckBoxList of all existing roles and either check or uncheck the role depending upon the current roles for that user. When the user clicks the Save Roles button, you must loop through all the roles in the CheckBoxList and add any checked roles to the user's saved role in the role data store, as well as remove any unchecked user roles from that same data store. The code for this is a bit complicated because an exception is raised if you try to add a role to a user that already has that role. For that reason, you first must use the `IsUserInRole` method before adding or removing a role from the user.

The event handler for the add role button is also straightforward. The handler for the delete role is a bit more complicated, because the role name must be removed from all users before it can be deleted.

Listing 13.5   RoleManager.aspx.cs

```csharp
using System;
using System.Data;
using System.Configuration;
using System.Collections;
using System.Web;
using System.Web.Security;
using System.Web.UI;
using System.Web.UI.WebControls;
using System.Web.UI.WebControls.WebParts;

public partial class RoleManager : System.Web.UI.Page
{
    protected void Page_Load(object sender, EventArgs e)
    {
        labName.Text - User.Identity.Name
        if (! IsPostBack)
            btnSaveRoles.Visible = false;
    }

    /// <summary>
    /// Selects a user from list, so check roles in list
    /// </summary>
    protected void drpUsers_SelectedIndexChanged(object o,
        EventArgs e)
    {
        btnSaveRoles.Visible = true;

        // Find out which user is selected
        string username = drpUsers.SelectedValue;

        // Retrieve roles for selected user
        string[] userRoles = Roles.GetRolesForUser(username);

        // Loop through each item in check box list of roles
        foreach (ListItem item in chkRoles.Items)
        {
            string rolename = item.Value;
```

```csharp
        // If this role is a user role, select it
        if (Roles.IsUserInRole(username, rolename))
            item.Selected = true;
        else
            item.Selected = false;
    }
}


/// <summary>
/// Save the user's roles
/// </summary>
protected void btnSaveRoles_Click(object o, EventArgs e)
{
    // Find out which user is selected
    string username = drpUsers.SelectedValue;

    // Loop through each check box
    foreach (ListItem item in chkRoles.Items)
    {
        string rolename = item.Value;
        if (item.Selected)
        {
            // Only need to add user if not already in data store
            if (! Roles.IsUserInRole(username, rolename))
                Roles.AddUserToRole(username, rolename);
        }
        else
        {
            // Only need to remove user if already in data store
            if (Roles.IsUserInRole(username, rolename))
                Roles.RemoveUserFromRole(username, rolename);
        }
    }
}


/// <summary>
/// Add a new role
/// </summary>
protected void btnAddRole_Click(object o, EventArgs e)
{
    string rolename = txtRole.Text;
    if (rolename.Length == 0) return;

    // Only add role if it doesn't already exist
    if (!Roles.RoleExists(rolename))
    {
        Roles.CreateRole(rolename);
        chkRoles.DataBind();
    }
```

```
    }

    /// <summary>
    /// Delete an existing role
    /// </summary>
    protected void btnDeleteRole_Click(object o, EventArgs e)
    {
        string rolename = txtDeleteRole.Text;
        if (rolename.Length == 0) return;

        // Only delete role if it exists
        if (Roles.RoleExists(rolename))
        {
            // Remove any users from this role
            MembershipUserCollection users =
                Membership.GetAllUsers();

            foreach (MembershipUser user in users)
            {
                string username = user.UserName;
                // Only need to remove user if already in data store
                if (Roles.IsUserInRole(username, rolename))
                    Roles.RemoveUserFromRole(username, rolename);
            }

            // Now delete role
            Roles.DeleteRole(rolename);
            chkRoles.DataBind();
        }
    }
}
```

The advantage of the membership and role management APIs is that they provide a simple but well-rounded interface for programmatically managing user accounts. Because both use the provider architecture, you can declaratively change the membership or role provider for your application in the `Web.config` file without requiring any changes in your programming code. But in your sample uses of these two APIs, you still needed programming code to perform common user account management chores. In the next section of this chapter, you shall examine the new login controls that provide a programming-free approach to working with user accounts.

Login Controls

The *login controls* introduced in ASP.NET 2.0 simplify the process of working with user accounts. These controls work in conjunction with the membership API and with the forms authentication infrastructure in ASP.NET. Table 13.8 lists the login controls and summarizes their functionality.

Table 13.8   Login Controls

Name	Description
ChangePassword	Lets users change their password.
CreateUserWizard	Based on the Wizard control covered in Chapter 4. A multistep process for gathering the user name, password, email address, and password question and answer.
Login	Displays a customizable user interface for gathering user credentials.
LoginName	Displays the name of the authenticated user.
LoginStatus	Displays a login link for nonauthenticated users and a logout link for authenticated users.
LoginView	Displays one of two possible interfaces: one for authenticated users and one for anonymous users.
PasswordRecovery	Allows user passwords to be retrieved and sent to the email for that account.

Although each of these controls has its own events that allow you to programmatically customize how they operate, by default, they work behind the scenes with the membership API and thus do not necessarily require any programming.

Login Control

The Login control displays a customizable user interface for gathering user credentials. It renders as two TextBox controls for the user name and password and a button to begin the authentication process. As well, you can add some optional controls: a CheckBox control to toggle whether to automatically authenticate the next time the user needs to login, a link to a page for creating a user, a link to a help page, and a link to a page that allows the user to recover a forgotten password. Figure 13.22 illustrates some sample Login controls.

Figure 13.22   Sample Login controls

As Figure 13.22 illustrates, the Login control can be extensively styled and customized. Yet adding the basic Login control is simple.

```
<asp:Login ID="logSignin" runat="server" />
```

The top example in Figure 13.22 illustrates how this basic login form appears in the browser. Of course, you probably want to improve the appearance of this control.

Styling and Customizing the Login Control

Like many of the other controls that we have examined in this book, the appearance of the Login control is fully customizable through templates and style settings, as well as through CSS. For instance, the second control shown in Figure 13.22 uses the following style elements.

```
<asp:Login ID="logSignin2" runat="server"
   TextLayout="TextOnTop" CssClass="loginStyle">

   <TitleTextStyle CssClass="loginTitle" />
   <InstructionTextStyle Font-Italic="True" ForeColor="Black" />
   <TextBoxStyle Font-Size="0.8em" />
   <LoginButtonStyle CssClass="buttonStyle" />

</asp:Login>
```

Table 13.9 lists the style elements that are supported by the Login control. Like the others encountered in this book, each of these style elements allows you to specify the size of the control as well as the appearance of borders, colors, and fonts.

Table 13.9   Login Style Templates

Name	Description
CheckBoxStyle	Defines the appearance of the check box for the Remember Me option.
FailureTextStyle	Defines the appearance of the text displayed when a login attempt fails.
HyperLinkStyle	Defines the appearance of any hyperlinks that appear in the control.
InstructionTextStyle	Defines the appearance of the instructional text for the control.
LoginButtonStyle	Defines the appearance of the login button.
TextBoxStyle	Defines the appearance of TextBox controls used in the control.
TitleTextStyle	Defines the appearance of title text.
ValidatorTextStyle	Defines the appearance of validation control error messages.

The Login control can be further customized via properties of the Login control. Table 13.10 lists the notable properties of the Login control.

Table 13.10   Notable Properties of the Login Control

Name	Description
`CreateUserIconUrl`	The URL of the image to display next to the link that takes the user to a page for creating/registering users.
`CreateUserText`	The text of the link that takes the user to a page for creating/registering users.
`CreateUserUrl`	The URL of the page for creating/registering users.
`DestinationPageUrl`	The URL of the page to be redirected to when the login attempt is successful.
`DisplayRememberMe`	Specifies whether to display a check box that lets the user indicate whether to persist the authentication cookie so that the user is automatically authenticated on future visits to the site. Default is `true`.
`FailureAction`	Specifies the action to take when a login attempt fails. Possible values are described by the `LoginFailureAction` enumeration (`RedirectToLoginPage` and `Refresh` (default)).
`FailureText`	The text to display in the control when a login attempt fails.
`HelpPageIconUrl`	The URL of the image to display next to the link to the help page.
`HelpPageText`	The text for the link to the help page.
`HelpPageUrl`	The URL of the help page.
`InstructionText`	The instructional text for the control.
`LoginButtonImageUrl`	The URL of the image to use for the login button.
`LoginButtonText`	The button text for the login button
`LoginButtonType`	The type (`Button`, `Image`, `Link`) of the login button.
`MembershipProvider`	The membership provider to use (if different than the default specified in the `Web.config` file).

Table 13.10   Notable Properties of the Login Control *(continued)*

Name	Description
Orientation	Specifies whether the controls are to be horizontally positioned (all on a single row) or vertically positioned (one on top of the other).
Password	Retrieves the password entered by the user.
PasswordLabelText	The text of the label for the password text box.
PasswordRecoveryIconUrl	The URL of the image to display next to the password recovery page link.
PasswordRecoveryText	The text of the link to the password recovery page.
PasswordRecoveryUrl	The URL of the password recovery page.
PasswordRequiredErrorMessage	The error message text to be displayed if the user does not enter anything into the password text box.
RememberMeSet	The value of the Remember Me check box.
RememberMeText	Specifies the text of the Remember Me check box.
TextLayout	Specifies the position of the user name and password labels relative to their text boxes. Possible values are TextOnLeft (default) and TextOnTop.
TitleText	The text to display in the title area of the control.
UserName	Retrieves the user name entered by the user.
UserNameLabelText	The text to be displayed for the user name text box.
UserNameRequiredErrorMessage	The error message text to be displayed if the user does not enter anything into the user name text box.
VisibleWhenLoggedIn	Specifies whether the control is visible after the user is authenticated. Default is true.

Similar to the data controls covered in Chapter 10, the actual layout of the Login control can be completely customized by using the LayoutTemplate element. For instance, you might use the LayoutTemplate element to change the layout of the Login control so that it does not render as an HTML <table> element, but uses a standards-oriented XHTML+CSS approach instead.

```
<asp:Login ID="logSignin" runat="server" >
    <LayoutTemplate>
        <fieldset>
            <legend>Login</legend>
            <label >User:</label>
            <asp:TextBox ID="UserName" runat="server" />
            <label >Password:</label>
            <asp:TextBox ID="Password" runat="server" />
            <br />

            <asp:Button ID="btnLogin" runat="server"
                CommandName="Login"
                Text="Log in" />
            <asp:Label ID="FailureText" runat="server"
                CssClass="error" />

            <asp:RequiredFieldValidator ID="reqUser" runat="server"
                ControlToValidate="UserName"
                ErrorMessage="Please enter a user name" />

            <!-- Other validators here -->
        </fieldset>
    </LayoutTemplate>
</asp:Login>
```

The LayoutTemplate does have some minimal expectations about what is contained within it. It must have

- A TextBox control with an Id of UserName
- A TextBox control with an Id of Password
- A Button or LinkButton or ImageButton control with a CommandName of Login

It can also have an optional CheckBox control with an Id of RememberMe and an optional Label or Literal control with an Id of FailureText.

Event Handling with the Login Control

When using the default membership provider, you generally do not need to perform any event handling. However, there may be times when you need to customize the authentication procedure or perform some type of custom behavior when logging in. In those cases, you can handle one of the events listed in Table 13.11 (which are listed in the order that they fire).

Table 13.11   Login Events

Name	Description
LoggingIn	Raised before the user gets authenticated.
Authenticate	Raised to allow the page to perform its own authentication.
LoggedIn	Raised after the user has been authenticated.
LoginError	Raised if the login fails.

For instance, imagine that you want to display help text as well as display links to the create user and password recovery pages *only* after the user fails a login attempt. You can define the Login control with the hookup to the event method as follows.

```
<asp:Login ID="logSignin" runat="server"
   CreateUserUrl="newUser.aspx"
   HelpPageUrl="help.aspx"
   PasswordRecoveryUrl="getPass.aspx"
   OnLoginError="logSignin_LoginError" … />
```

The event handler simply assigns the text to the appropriate properties.

```
protected void logSignin_LoginError(object sender, EventArgs e)
{
   logSignin.HelpPageText = "Help with logging in";
   logSignin.PasswordRecoveryText = "Forgot your password?";
   logSignin.CreateUserText = "Create new user";
}
```

LoginName Control

The LoginName control displays the name of the authenticated user. It displays this information regardless of whether the user authenticated using ASP.NET controls or integrated Windows Authentication. If the user has not authenticated yet, the control is not rendered.

The LoginName control has one principal unique property, the FormatString property, which defines the format item string. The following example illustrates a typical LoginName control. If the user Plato has already authenticated, it displays the text Welcome Plato to our site.

```
<asp:LoginName id="logWelcome" runat="server"
   FormatString ="Welcome {0} to our site." />
```

LoginStatus Control

The LoginStatus control displays a login link for nonauthenticated users and a logout link for authenticated users. Its properties are described in Table 13.12.

Table 13.12 LoginStatus Properties

Name	Description
LoginImageUrl	The URL of the image to be used for the login link.
LoginText	The text of the login link. The default is login.
LogoutAction	The action to perform when the user logs out with this control. Possible values are described by the LogoutAction enumeration (Redirect (redirects to URL specified by LogoutPageUrl), RedirectToLoginPage (redirects to login page specified in Web.config file), Refresh (reloads the page)).
LogoutImageUrl	The URL of the image to be used for the logout link.
LogoutPageUrl	The URL of the page to be redirected to after logout.
LogoutText	The text of the logout link. The default is logout.

The LoginStatus and the LoginName controls are often used together, as shown in the following.

```
<asp:LoginName ID="logName" runat="server"
   FormatString="Welcome {0}" />

<asp:LoginStatus ID="logStat" runat="server"
   LoginImageUrl="images/btn_login.gif"
   LogoutImageUrl="images/btn_logout.gif"
   LogoutAction="Refresh" />
```

The result in the browser is shown in Figure 13.23. Notice that the first time the page is requested, it displays the login image. Clicking this image redirects to login page; after the successful authentication, it returns to the original page, but now it displays both the LoginName control and the logout button.

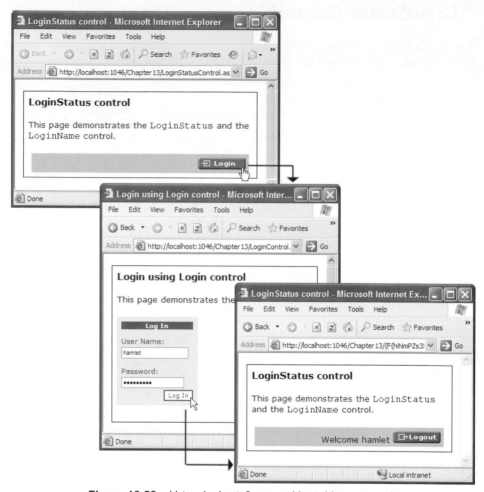

Figure 13.23   Using the LoginStatus and LoginName controls

LoginView Control

The LoginView control allows you to specify a user interface for authenticated users and a different user interface for anonymous users. The LoginView control also allows you to customize the user interface based on the authenticated user's role. For instance, this control could allow you to define content for administrators, content for members, and content for unauthenticated visitors.

You define the different content via different templates. The content within the AnonymousTemplate is displayed for unauthenticated users, whereas the content within the LoggedInTemplate is displayed for authenticated users. The following example illustrates a sample `LoginView` control. It displays a login button for unauthenticated users and displays a rating option for authenticated users. Figure 13.24 illustrates the result in the browser.

```
<asp:LoginView ID="logView" runat="server">

  <AnonymousTemplate>
    <strong>For more features</strong><br />
    <asp:LoginStatus ID="logStat" runat="server"
        LoginImageUrl="images/btn_login.gif"
        LogoutImageUrl="images/btn_logout.gif"
        LogoutAction="Refresh" />
  </AnonymousTemplate>

  <LoggedInTemplate>
      <strong>Rate this book</strong><br />
      <asp:RadioButtonList ID="radList" runat="server">
        <asp:ListItem Selected="true">No Rating</asp:ListItem>
        <asp:ListItem>
            <img src='images/stars1.gif'/></asp:ListItem>
        <asp:ListItem>
            <img src='images/stars2.gif'/></asp:ListItem>
        <asp:ListItem>
            <img src='images/stars3.gif'/></asp:ListItem>
        <asp:ListItem>
            <img src='images/stars4.gif'/></asp:ListItem>
        <asp:ListItem>
            <img src='images/stars5.gif'/></asp:ListItem>
      </asp:RadioButtonList>
      <p>
      <asp:Button ID="btnRate" runat="server" Text="Rate Book" />
      </p>
  </LoggedInTemplate>

</asp:LoginView>
```

You can also add templates for different user roles via the `RoleGroups` element. This element contains any number of `RoleGroup` elements; each `RoleGroup` can define the content to be displayed for the specified roles.

```
<asp:LoginView ID="logView" runat="server">
  <AnonymousTemplate>
    ...
  </AnonymousTemplate>
  <LoggedInTemplate>
    ...
  </LoggedInTemplate>
```

```
<RoleGroups>
  <asp:RoleGroup Roles="Administrator">
    <ContentTemplate>
      <asp:LinkButton ID="lnkEdit" runat="server"
        Text="Edit this book" />
    </ContentTemplate>
  </asp:RoleGroup>
</RoleGroups>
</asp:LoginView>
```

If the user belongs to one of the roles indicated within the RoleGroups, it takes precedent over the LoggedInTemplate.

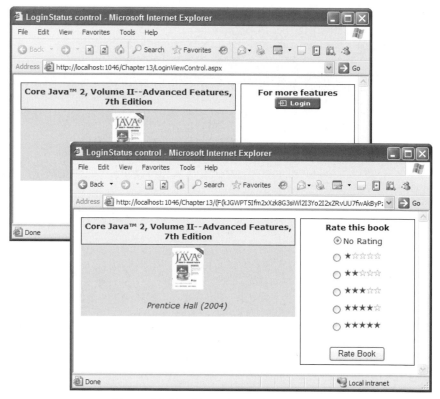

Figure 13.24   Using the LoginView control

ChangePassword Control

The ChangePassword control allows users to change their password. The control works regardless of whether the user is or is not already authenticated. To handle the latter scenario, the control can ask the user for the user name as well as the old and new passwords. Like the `Login` control, the `ChangePassword` control can contain style elements as well as a `ChangePasswordTemplate` to completely customize the appearance and content of the control.

```
<asp:ChangePassword ID="chngPass" runat="server"
   CssClass="passChangeStyle" >

   <CancelButtonStyle CssClass="buttonStyle" />
   <ChangePasswordButtonStyle CssClass="buttonStyle" />
   <ContinueButtonStyle CssClass="buttonStyle" />
   <TitleTextStyle CssClass="titleStyle" />
   <TextBoxStyle CssClass="textboxStyle" />

</asp:ChangePassword>
```

The result in the browser is shown in Figure 13.25.

Figure 13.25   Using the ChangePassword control

You can configure the `ChangePassword` control so that it emails a confirmation message to the email for this member. You can add this capability via the `MailDefinition` element.

```
<asp:ChangePassword ID="chngPass" runat="server" >
  ...
  <MailDefinition From="abc@abc.net"
    Subject="Password Change" />

</asp:ChangePassword>
```

You can also specify the regular expression that the passwords must satisfy via the NewPasswordRegularExpression property.

```
<asp:ChangePassword ID="chngPass" runat="server" ...
    PasswordHintText="Password must be at least 7 characters long,
        contain a number and one special character."
    NewPasswordRegularExpression=
        '@\"(?=.{7,})(?=(.*\d){1,})(?=(.*\W){1,})'
    NewPasswordRegularExpressionErrorMessage=
        "Password must be at least 7 characters long,
        contain a number and one special character">
```

PasswordRecovery Control

The PasswordRecovery control allows a member's passwords to be retrieved and sent to the email address for that account. However, users can only recover passwords when the membership provider supports clear text or encrypted passwords. Hashed passwords, on the other hand, cannot be recovered. Users at sites that use hashed passwords can only reset their passwords. Like the other login controls covered in this chapter, the PasswordRecovery control supports style elements and templates.

```
<asp:PasswordRecovery ID="passRec" runat="server"
    CssClass="passRecovStyle">

    <InstructionTextStyle CssClass="instructionStyle" />
    <SuccessTextStyle CssClass="instructionStyle" />
    <TextBoxStyle CssClass="textboxStyle" />
    <TitleTextStyle CssClass="titleStyle" />
    <SubmitButtonStyle CssClass="buttonStyle" />

    <MailDefinition From="abc@abc.net"
        Subject="Password Recovery"  />

</asp:PasswordRecovery>
```

Notice that this example also includes a MailDefinition element that defines some of the fields in the email that are sent to the user's email account. The result in the browser is shown in Figure 13.26.

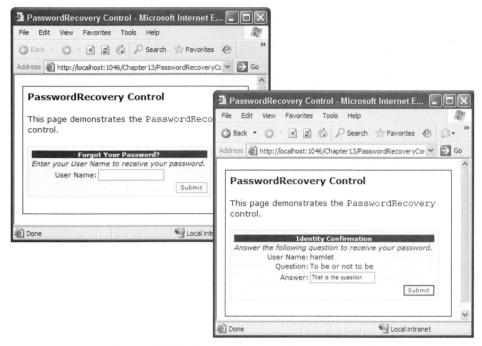

Figure 13.26   Using the PasswordRecovery control

CORE NOTE

Your `Web.config` file must be properly configured with the appropriate SMTP information for this control to actually send the email message. For instance, the following example configures the Web server to send emails on port 25. Notice that it uses the `system.net` element.

```
<system.net>
   <mailSettings>
      <smtp deliveryMethod="Network"
            from="webmaster@yoursite.net">
         <network port="25" host="mail.yoursite.com"/>
      </smtp>
   </mailSettings>
</system.net>
```

You can also configure the Web server for email delivery using the WAT.

CreateUserWizard Control

The CreateUserWizard control provides a multistep process for creating a new user. It is a subclass of the Wizard control covered in Chapter 4. By default, the control has two wizard steps: one step for gathering the user name, password, email address, and password question and answer, and another step for the completion of the wizard. Like the other login controls, it supports style elements and templates, as in the following example. (The result in the browser can be seen in Figure 13.27.)

```
<asp:CreateUserWizard ID="createUser" runat="server"
   ActiveStepIndex="0" CssClass="wizardStyle">

   <TitleTextStyle CssClass="titleStyle" />
   <NavigationButtonStyle CssClass="buttonStyle" />
   <HeaderStyle CssClass="headerStyle" />
   <CreateUserButtonStyle  CssClass="buttonStyle" />
   <ContinueButtonStyle  CssClass="buttonStyle" />

</asp:CreateUserWizard>
```

Like the Wizard control, the CreateUserWizard control allows you to define custom steps via the WizardSteps element.

```
<asp:CreateUserWizard ID="createUser" runat="server" … >

   <WizardSteps>
      <asp:WizardStep >
        …
      </asp:WizardStep>
      <asp:WizardStep >
        …
      </asp:WizardStep>
   </WizardSteps>

</asp:CreateUserWizard>
```

For more information, see "Wizard Control" on page 200 of Chapter 4.

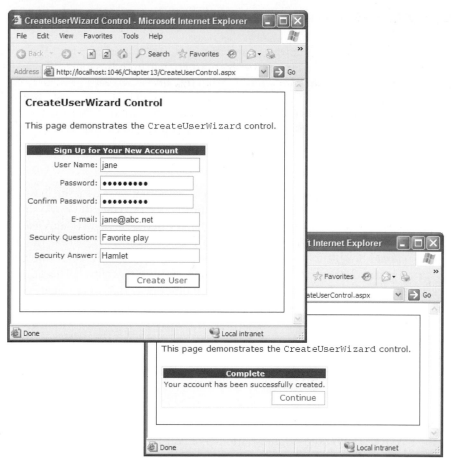

Figure 13.27   Using the CreateUserWizard control

Summary

This chapter has examined the security features in ASP.NET. It described how an ASP.NET Web application's security is constructed in different layers, as both IIS and ASP.NET have their own security features. The chapter principally focused on the security features unique to ASP.NET: namely forms authentication as well as the membership and roles management systems introduced in ASP.NET 2.0. The chapter also explored the other security-related features added in version 2.0, the various login controls that simplify the process of gathering and validating user credentials.

The next chapter introduces the personalization features in ASP.NET. These personalization features make use of the security infrastructure covered in this chapter.

Exercises

The solutions to the following exercises can be found at my Web site, http://www.randyconnolly.com/core. Additional exercises only available for teachers and instructors are also available from this site.

1. Create a page named ChangeUserPassword.aspx that uses the membership API (and not the ChangePassword control) to change the logged-in user's password.

The next exercise uses the ModernEyeCatalog database.

2. Create a page named SingleArtWork.aspx that displays a single work of art. The page should allow all authenticated users to rate the work, similar to the example shown earlier in the chapter in the section "LoginView Control" on page 822. As well, if the user belongs to the Editor role, the user should be able to write and save a review for the work. Finally, if the user is unauthenticated, the page should display the Login control. This Login control should allow the user to go to another page that you must also create named RegisterUser.aspx that allows the user to create a user account. This page should use the CreateUserWizard control.

Key Concepts

- Anonymous access
- ASP.NET SQL Server Registration Tool
- ASP.NET Website Administration Tool (WAT)
- Authenticated identity
- Authentication
- Authorization
- Basic authentication
- Certificate
- Certificate-based authentication
- Code access security
- Credentials
- Digest authentication
- Factory Method design pattern
- Forms authentication ticket
- Impersonation
- Integrated Windows Authentication
- Login controls
- Membership API

- Membership providers
- Passport authentication
- Provider
- Provider model
- Replay attacks
- Role-based authorization
- Secure Sockets Layer
- Strategy design pattern
- Trust level

References

Bustamante, Michele Leroux. "Working with Certificates." *asp.netPRO Magazine* (October 2006).

Esposito, Dino. "A Provider-Based Service for ASP.NET Tracing." *MSDN Magazine* (June 2006).

Meier, J.D., *et al*, "How to: Use Code Access Security in ASP.NET 2.0." `http://msdn.microsoft.com`.

Microsoft. "Custom Provider-Based Services." `http://msdn.microsoft.com`.

Microsoft. "Developing Identity-Aware ASP.NET Applications." `http://msdn.microsoft.com`.

Mitchell, Scott. "Examining ASP.NET 2.0's Membership, Roles, and Profile, Part 1-5." `http://aspnet.4guysfromrolla.com`.

Siddiqui, Bilad. "Set up Passport Authentication in ASP.NET." `http://www.devx.com`.

Stahl, Rick. "Understanding ASP.NET Impersonation Security." `http://westwind.com`.

PERSONALIZATION WITH PROFILES AND WEB PARTS

Web applications often need to track user information over time. Sometimes, this information is mission critical, such as customer orders, shipping addresses, and so on. A site may also want to track information that is not absolutely essential to the application, but is helpful in terms of the overall user experience with the site. This type of information is often referred to as *personalization information*. Examples of personalization information can include user preference information such as the language or theme to use in the site, the size of the font, shopping interests, and so on. Personalization can also include information that is visit oriented, but which needs to be more persistent than session state. Some examples of this type of information are a shopping cart, a wish list, or a list of the last N products viewed by the user.

Prior to ASP.NET 2.0, developers needed to create this functionality from scratch, typically using tables relationally linked to a user table. ASP.NET 2.0 introduced two new features that help developers manage and implement personalization in their sites. These features are the profile system and the Web parts framework and are the subject of this chapter.

ASP.NET Profiles

The profile feature is a way of easily associating and persisting application information with users. You can use profiles to track any user-related information, from personalization data to more mission-critical information such as customer names, addresses, financial information, and so on.

The profile feature is yet another ASP.NET subsystem that is built using the provider model (see Chapter 13 for more information on the provider model). As such, the actual data storage mechanism for the profile information is independent of its usage. By default, ASP.NET uses the `SqlProfileProvider`, which uses the same SQL Server database as the membership and role management features examined in the previous chapter (i.e., `ASPNETDB.MDF` in the `App_Data` folder). However, if you have an existing database of user or personalization data, you might decide instead to create your own custom profile provider.

Profile data can be easily defined within the `Web.config` file and is consumed using the familiar properties programming model. It can be used to store data of any type, as long as it is serializable. Unlike session state data, which must be cast to the appropriate type, profile data is made available via strongly typed properties.

Defining Profiles

Perhaps the best thing about the profile feature is how easy it is to set up. You define the data that is to be associated with each user profile via the `profile` element in the `Web.config` file. Within this element, you simply define the properties whose values you want to persist. Each property consists of a name, a type, and perhaps a default value as well as a flag indicating whether this property is available to anonymous users. For instance, Listing 14.1 illustrates the configuration of three string properties.

Listing 14.1   Web.config

```
<configuration>
  <system.web>
    <authentication mode="Forms" >
      <forms loginUrl="LoginSimple.aspx" timeout="2" />
    </authentication>
    <authorization>
      <deny users="?"/>
    </authorization>
    ...
    <profile>
      <properties>
        <add name="BackgroundColor" type="string"
```

```
            defaultValue="White"
            allowAnonymous="false" />
        <add name="TextColor" type="string"
            defaultValue="Black"
            allowAnonymous="false"/>
        <add name="Region" type="string"
            defaultValue="NorthAmerica"
            allowAnonymous="false"/>
      </properties>
    </profile>
  </system.web>
</configuration>
```

CORE NOTE

It is important to remember that if you do not explicitly allow anonymous use, the user must be logged in before using the page's `Profile` property; otherwise, a runtime exception is generated.

Table 14.1 lists the notable configuration properties for the profile properties `add` element.

Table 14.1 Configuration for the Profile add Element

Name	Description
allowAnonymous	Indicates whether the property can be set by anonymous users. The default is `false`.
customProviderData	A string of custom data to be used by the profile provider. Individual providers can implement custom logic for using this data.
defaultValue	The initial default value used for the property.
name	The name of the property.
provider	The profile provider to use (if not using the default profile provider). By default, all properties are managed using the default provider specified for profile properties, but individual properties can also use different providers.
readOnly	Indicates whether the property is read-only. The default is `false`.

Table 14.1   Configuration for the Profile add Element *(continued)*

Name	Description
serializeAs	Specifies the serialization method to use when persisting this value. Possible values are described by the Serialization-Mode enumeration: Binary, ProviderSpecific (the default), String, and Xml.
type	The data type of the property. You can specify any .NET class or any custom type that you have defined. If you use a custom type, you must also specify how the provider should serialize it via the serializeAs property.

Using Profile Data

After the profile properties are configured, you can store and retrieve this data within your pages via the Profile property (which is an object of type ProfileCommon), of the Page class. Each profile defined via the add element is available as a property of this Profile property. For instance, to retrieve the Region value, you could use the following.

```
string sRegion = Profile.Region;
```

Notice that you do not have to do any typecasting, because the profile properties are typecast using the value specified by the type attribute for each property in the Web.config file.

You can save this profile value in a similar manner as shown in the following.

```
Profile.Region = txtRegion.Text;
```

This line (eventually) results in the profile value being saved by the profile provider for the current user. Where might you place these two lines of code? A common pattern is to retrieve the profile values in the Page_Load handler for the page and then set the profile value in some type of event handler as a result of user action.

Listings 14.2 and 14.3 illustrate a sample page that makes use of the three profile properties defined in Listing 14.1. You may recall that the Web.config file in Listing 14.1 requires that the user must first log in. After authentication, the page uses the default region, background color, and text color defined in Listing 14.1. The user can then change these profile values via three drop-down lists (see Figure 14.1). When the user clicks the Save Settings button, the event handler for the button changes the page's colors as well as saves the values in the profile object for the page.

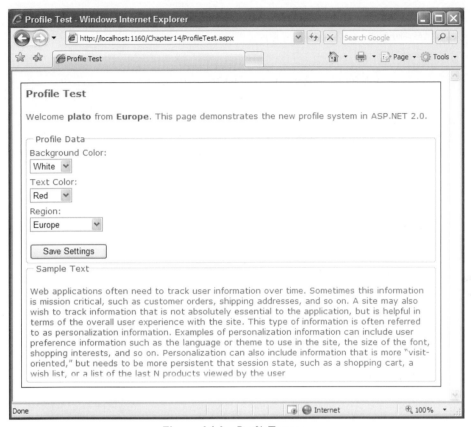

Figure 14.1   ProfileTest.aspx

Listing 14.2   ProfileTest.aspx

```
<h1>Profile Test</h1>
<p>Welcome
<asp:LoginName ID="logName" runat="server" Font-Bold="true" /> from
<asp:Label ID="labWhere" runat="server" Font-Bold="true" />.
This page demonstrates the new profile system in ASP.NET 2.0.
</p>
<asp:Panel ID="panForm" runat="server" GroupingText="Profile Data">
   <asp:label ID="labBack" runat="server"
      AssociatedControlID="drpBackColor"
      Text="Background Color:" />
   <asp:DropDownList ID="drpBackColor" runat="server" >
      <asp:ListItem>Black</asp:ListItem>
      <asp:ListItem>Green</asp:ListItem>
      <asp:ListItem>Red</asp:ListItem>
```

```
        <asp:ListItem>Yellow</asp:ListItem>
        <asp:ListItem>White</asp:ListItem>
    </asp:DropDownList><br />

    <asp:label ID="labText" runat="server"
      AssociatedControlID="drpTextColor" Text="Text Color:" />

    <asp:DropDownList ID="drpTextColor" runat="server" >
        <asp:ListItem>Black</asp:ListItem>
        <asp:ListItem>Green</asp:ListItem>
        <asp:ListItem>Red</asp:ListItem>
        <asp:ListItem>Yellow</asp:ListItem>
        <asp:ListItem>White</asp:ListItem>
    </asp:DropDownList><br />
    <asp:label ID="labRegion" runat="server"
        AssociatedControlID="drpRegion" Text="Region:" />

    <asp:DropDownList ID="drpRegion" runat="server" >
        <asp:ListItem>Africa</asp:ListItem>
        <asp:ListItem>Asia</asp:ListItem>
        <asp:ListItem>Europe</asp:ListItem>
        <asp:ListItem>North America</asp:ListItem>
        <asp:ListItem>Oceania</asp:ListItem>
        <asp:ListItem>South America</asp:ListItem>
    </asp:DropDownList>
    <p>
    <asp:Button ID="btnSave" runat="server" Text="Save Settings"
        OnClick="btnSave_Click" />
    </p>
</asp:Panel>
<asp:Panel ID="panSample" runat="server"
    GroupingText="Sample Text">

    <p>
    Web applications often need to track user information over time.
Sometimes this information is mission critical, such as customer
orders, shipping addresses, and so on. A site may also wish to track
information that is not absolutely essential to the application, but
is helpful in terms of the overall user experience with the site.
This type of information is often referred to as personalization
information. Examples of personalization information can include
user preference information such as the language or theme to use in
the site, the size of the font, shopping interests, and so on.
Personalization can also include information that is more "visit-
oriented," but needs to be more persistent than session state, such
as a shopping cart, a wish list, or a list of the last N products
viewed by the user
    </p>
</asp:Panel>
```

The code-behind for this page is reasonably straightforward. The first time the page is requested, it sets the page's colors based on the current profile values, and sets the default values of the page's controls to these same profile values. The event handler for the Save Settings button simply sets the profile properties to the new user-chosen values. Everything else is handled by the profile system and its provider, so that the next time this user requests this page, whether in five minutes or five years, it uses these saved profile values.

Listing 14.3 ProfileTest.aspx.cs

```
using System;
using System.Data;
using System.Configuration;
using System.Collections;
using System.Web;
using System.Web.Security;
using System.Web.UI;
using System.Web.UI.WebControls;
using System.Web.UI.WebControls.WebParts;
using System.Web.UI.HtmlControls;

public partial class ProfileTest : System.Web.UI.Page
{
    protected void Page_Load(object sender, EventArgs e)
    {
        if (! IsPostBack)
        {
            SetPageData();

            // Set initial values of controls to profile values
            drpRegion.SelectedValue = Profile.Region;
            drpBackColor.SelectedValue = Profile.BackgroundColor;
            drpTextColor.SelectedValue = Profile.TextColor;
        }
    }
    protected void btnSave_Click(object sender, EventArgs e)
    {
        // Save the profile values based on user input
        Profile.Region = drpRegion.SelectedValue;
        Profile.BackgroundColor = drpBackColor.SelectedValue;
        Profile.TextColor = drpTextColor.SelectedValue;

        SetPageData();
    }
    private void SetPageColors()
    {
        labWhere.Text = Profile.Region;
```

```
        body1.Attributes["bgcolor"] = Profile.BackgroundColor;
        body1.Attributes["text"] = Profile.TextColor;
    }
}
```

Profile Groups

You can define hierarchical data within the profile element using the `group` element. For instance, you could define the following two profile groups in the `Web.config` file.

```
<profile>
    <properties>
        <group name="UserPreferences">
            <add name="MasterPage" type="string"
                defaultValue="Main"/>
            <add name="Theme" type="string" defaultValue="Cool" />
        </group>
        <group name="Visit">
            <add name="Last5Products"
                type=
                "System.Collections.Specialized.StringCollection" />
        </group>
    </properties>
</profile>
```

You can access grouped properties using dot notation, as shown here.

```
StringCollection products = Profile.Visit.Last5Products;
Profile.UserPreferences.Theme = "CoolTheme";
```

CORE NOTE

You cannot nest profile groups within another profile group.

How Do Profiles Work?

The profile system uses the provider model introduced in Chapter 13 so that some type of profile provider handles the actual responsibility of saving and retrieving items from the data store. But how does the `Profile` property of the page "know" about the profile properties defined in the `Web.config` file?

When a page is requested from a Web application that has profile properties defined in its `Web.config` file, ASP.NET automatically generates a class named `ProfileCommon` in the `Temporary ASP.NET Files` directory. In the following example, you can see the `ProfileCommon` class that was generated from the profiles in Listing 14.1.

```
// <auto-generated>
//    This code was generated by a tool.
//    Runtime Version:2.0.50727.42
//
//    Changes to this file may cause incorrect behavior and will
//    be lost if the code is regenerated.
// </auto-generated>

using System;
using System.Web;
using System.Web.Profile;

public class ProfileCommon : System.Web.Profile.ProfileBase {

    public virtual string Region {
        get {
            return ((string)(this.GetPropertyValue("Region")));
        }
        set {
            this.SetPropertyValue("Region", value);
        }
    }

    public virtual string BackgroundColor {
        get {
            return ((string)(this.GetPropertyValue(
                "BackgroundColor")));
        }
        set {
            this.SetPropertyValue("BackgroundColor", value);
        }
    }

    public virtual string TextColor {
        get {
            return ((string)(this.GetPropertyValue(
                "TextColor")));
        }
        set {
            this.SetPropertyValue("TextColor", value);
        }
    }

    public virtual ProfileCommon GetProfile(string username) {
        return ((ProfileCommon)(ProfileBase.Create(username)));
    }
}
```

As you can see, this generated class is a subclass of the `ProfileBase` class and contains strongly typed properties for each profile property defined in the `Web.config` file. This class is available to the page via a `Profile` property that is added to the Web Form by the page parser.

Saving and Retrieving Profile Data

One of the real benefits of using the profile system is that the values for each user are automatically saved and retrieved by the system. The profile system works via an `HttpModule` named `ProfileModule`. You may recall from Chapter 2, all incoming requests pass through the events in the `HttpApplication` pipeline and, as part of this process, different HTTP modules can register their own event handlers with the events in the pipeline.

The `ProfileModule` registers its event handlers for the `AcquireRequestState` and `EndRequest` events of the pipeline, as well as registers its own `Personalization` event (which is called before the profile data is loaded and which can be handled in the `global.asax` file). The `ProfileModule` does *not* populate the profile object with data during the `AcquireRequestState` event, because this necessitates retrieving data from the profile provider for every request, regardless of whether the page used profile data. Instead, an instance of `ProfileCommon` is created and populated with data (via the `ProfileBase.Create` method) from the provider by `HttpContext` during the page's first request for the `Profile` property.

The data within the `ProfileCommon` object is potentially saved during the `EndRequest` event of the request pipeline. The data in this object is serialized and then saved by the provider if the data has been changed by the page. For the default SQL Server profile provider, simple primitive data is serialized into a string; for more complex data types, such as arrays and custom types, the data is serialized into XML. For instance, the sample profile properties from Listing 14.1 are serialized into the following string and then saved into the `PropertyValuesString` field of the `aspnet_Profile` table.

```
YellowRedEurope
```

As well, there is a `PropertyNames` field in this table that specifies how to deserialize this string data (it indicates the starting position for each property and its length).

```
BackgroundColor:S:0:6:TextColor:S:6:3:Region:S:9:6:
```

In summary, using profiles in your page potentially adds two requests to the data source. A page that uses profile data always reads the profile data at the beginning of the request. Because the profile system uses the lazy initialization pattern (see Chapter 12), if your page does not access the `Profile` object, it does not read the profile data from the data source. When the page has finished the request processing, it checks to see if the profile data needs to be saved. If all the profile data consists of strings or simple primitive data types such as numbers or Booleans, the profile system checks if any of the properties of the page's `ProfileCommon` object are *dirty* (that is, have been modified) and only saves the data if any of them has been modified. If your profile object does contain any complex type, the page *always* saves the profile data, regardless of whether it has been changed.

Controlling Profile Save Behavior

If your profile data includes nonprimitive data types, the profile system assumes the profile data is dirty and thus saves it, even if it hasn't been modified. If your site includes many pages that use complex profile data, but few that actually modify it, your site will do a lot of unnecessary profile saving. In such a case, you may want to disable the automatic saving of profile data and then explicitly save the profile data only when you need to.

To disable autosaving, simply make the following change to the `profile` element in your application's `Web.config` file.

```
<profile automaticSaveEnabled="false" >
```

After the automatic profile saving is disabled, it is up to the developer to save the profile data by explicitly calling the `Profile.Save` method. For instance, you could change the code-behind in your example in Listing 14.3 to the following.

```
protected void btnSave_Click(object sender, EventArgs e)
{
    Profile.Region = drpRegion.SelectedValue;
    Profile.BackgroundColor = drpBackColor.SelectedValue;
    Profile.TextColor = drpTextColor.SelectedValue;
    Profile.Save();

    SetPageColors();
}
```

Using Custom Types

Profile properties can be any .NET type or any custom type that you have defined. The only requirement is that the type must be serializable. For instance, imagine that you have a custom class named `WishListCollection` that can contain multiple `WishListItem` objects. If you want to store this custom class in profile storage, both it and its contents must be serializable. You can do so by marking both classes with the `Serializable` attribute, as shown here.

```
[Serializable]
public class WishListCollection
{
```

```
    ...
}

[Serializable]
public class WishListItem
{
    ...
}
```

Along with allowing the use of custom types for profile properties, the profile system allows you to define the profile structure programmatically using a custom type
rather than declaratively in the Web.config file. You can do this by defining a class
that inherits from the ProfileBase class and then referencing it via the inherits
attribute of the profile element in the Web.config file. For instance, Listing 14.4
illustrates a sample derived profile class. Notice that it inherits from the Profile-
Base class. Notice as well that each property is marked with the SettingsAllow-
Anonymous attribute; this is equivalent to the AllowAnonymous attribute that was
used in the Web.config example in Listing 14.1.

Listing 14.4 CustomProfile.cs

```
using System;
using System.Collections.Generic;
using System.Web;
using System.Web.UI;
using System.Web.UI.WebControls;
using System.Web.Profile;
using System.IO;

public class CustomProfile: ProfileBase
{
    [SettingsAllowAnonymous(false)]
    public List<WishListItem> WishList
    {
        get {
            if (base["WishList"] == null)
                base["WishList"] = new List<WishListItem>();
            return (List<WishListItem>)base["WishList"];
        }
        set { base["WishList"] = value; }
    }

    [SettingsAllowAnonymous(true)]
    public string Theme
    {
        get {
            string theme = (string)base["Theme"];
```

```csharp
        // Set up a default theme if necessary
        if (theme.Length == 0)
        {
            theme = "Cool";
            base["Theme"] = theme;
        }
        return theme;
    }
    set
    {
        string newThemeName = value;
        string path =
            HttpContext.Current.Server.MapPath("~/App_Themes");
        if (Directory.Exists(path))
        {
            // Retrieve array of theme folder names
            String[] themeFolders =
                Directory.GetDirectories(path);

            // See if the specified theme name actually exists
            // as a theme folder
            bool found = false;
            foreach (String folder in themeFolders)
            {
                DirectoryInfo info = new DirectoryInfo(folder);
                if (info.Name == newThemeName)
                    found = true;
            }
            // Only set the theme if this theme exists
            if (found)
                base["Theme"] = newThemeName;
        }
    }
}

[SettingsAllowAnonymous(true)]
public ViewedProducts Last5Products
{
    get {
        if (base["Last5Products"] == null)
            base["Last5Products"] = new ViewedProducts();
        return (ViewedProducts)base["Last5Products"];
    }
    set { base["Last5Products"] = value;   }
}

// This property is explained shortly
// in section on migrating anonymous profiles
[SettingsAllowAnonymous(false)]
```

```
public bool MigratedAlready
{
    get { return (bool)base["MigratedAlready"]; }
    set { base["MigratedAlready"] = value; }
}
}
```

With this custom profile class defined, you can use it by changing your `Web.config` file as shown in the following example. Notice that you can still supply additional declarative properties to the profile if you want.

```
<profile inherits="CustomProfile">
    <properties>
        <add name="BackgroundColor" type="string" />
        ...
    </properties>
</profile>
```

The main advantage of using a custom provider class is that the developer can better control what happens when the profile's accessors (i.e., the getters and setters) are used. For instance, in Listing 14.4, the setter for the `Theme` property first verifies that the specified theme actually exists as a real theme folder before setting the value. Just like we saw back in Chapter 11 with custom business objects and entities, a custom profile class allows you to implement some type of business logic with your profile data. As well, another advantage of using a custom provider class is that you can define a profile property that uses a generic collection, as illustrated in Listing 14.4.

Working with Anonymous Users

As you have seen, by default, the profile properties in ASP.NET are only available to authenticated users. However, you can make profiles available to anonymous users. This involves two steps. The first step is to mark individual properties as allowing **anonymous access**. You can do this declaratively using the `allowAnonymous` attribute.

```
<profile>
    <properties>
        <add name="BackgroundColor" type="string"
            allowAnonymous="true" />
        <add name="TextColor" type="string"
            allowAnonymous="false" />
        ...
    </properties>
</profile>
```

If you are using a custom profile class, you can change the `SettingsAllow-Anonymous` attribute to each property in the class.

```
public class CustomProfile: ProfileBase
{
    [SettingsAllowAnonymous(true)]
    public string BackgroundColor
    {
        ...
    }

    [SettingsAllowAnonymous(false)]
    public string TextColor
    {
        ...
    }
    ...
}
```

The second step is to enable the ***anonymous identification*** feature for the Web application as a whole via the `anonymousIdentification` element.

```
<system.web>
    ...
    <anonymousIdentification enabled="true" />
    <profile>
        ...
    </profile>
</system.web>
```

By default, anonymous identification is disabled. By enabling it, ASP.NET ensures that the `AnonymousIdentificationModule` is involved in the request pipeline. This module creates and manages anonymous identifiers for an ASP.NET application. When an anonymous user makes a request for a resource in an application that has anonymous identification enabled, the `AnonymousIdentificationModule` generates a ***globally unique identifier*** (this is universally referred to as a GUID). A ***GUID*** is a 128-bit integer (16 bytes) that can be used across all computers and networks wherever a unique identifier is required. Such an identifier has a very low probability of being duplicated. At any rate, after generating the GUID, the module writes it to a persistent cookie and this GUID becomes the anonymous user's name.

CORE NOTE

Although each new anonymous user session is assigned a new GUID (because the GUID is written to a cookie on the computer), if a different person accesses the site using this same computer, the site uses the same anonymous GUID issued to the first user.

Deleting Anonymous Profiles

Because every new anonymous user session generates a new GUID, a site that receives many anonymous requests may end up with many profile records for all these anonymous requests, most of which are inactive. In this case, you may need to run some type of scheduled task that deletes these inactive profiles because there is no automatic built-in mechanism for doing so. You can do this via the `ProfileManager` class. This class can be used to manage profile settings, search for user profiles, and delete user profiles that are no longer in use. Table 14.2 lists the methods of the `ProfileManager` class.

Table 14.2   Methods of the ProfileManager Class

Method	Description
DeleteInactiveProfiles	Deletes user profiles for which the last activity date occurred before the specified date.
DeleteProfile	Deletes the profile for the specified user name.
DeleteProfiles	Deletes the specified list of profiles.
FindInactiveProfilesByUserName	Retrieves a collection of `ProfileInfo` objects in which the last activity date occurred on or before the specified date and the user name for the profile matches the specified user name.
FindProfilesByUserName	Retrieves a collection of `ProfileInfo` objects that matches the specified user name.
GetAllInactiveProfiles	Retrieves a collection of `ProfileInfo` objects in which the last activity date occurred on or before the specified date.
GetAllProfiles	Retrieves a collection of `ProfileInfo` objects that represents all the profiles in the profile data source.
GetNumberOfInactiveProfiles	Gets the number of profiles in which the last activity date occurred on or before the specified date.
GetNumberOfProfiles	Gets the total number of profiles in the profile data source.

For instance, imagine that you have some type of administrative page in which you want to display all the authenticated profiles and all the anonymous profiles in two separate `GridView` controls. The code for this might look like the following.

```
protected void Page_Load(object sender, EventArgs e)
{
    // Get all the authenticated profiles
    grdProfiles.DataSource = ProfileManager.GetAllProfiles(
        ProfileAuthenticationOption.Authenticated);
    grdProfiles.DataBind();

    // Get all the anonymous profiles
    grdAnonProfiles.DataSource = ProfileManager.GetAllProfiles(
        ProfileAuthenticationOption.Anonymous);
    grdAnonProfiles.DataBind();
}
```

Notice that the `ProfileManager.GetAllProfiles` method uses the `ProfileAuthenticationOption` enumeration to specify which profiles to retrieve. If you want to delete the anonymous profiles in which there has been no activity for the last day, you could use the following.

```
// Delete everything created one day ago or later
DateTime dateToDelete = DateTime.Now.Subtract(new TimeSpan(1,0,0));
ProfileManager.DeleteInactiveProfiles(
    ProfileAuthenticationOption.Anonymous, dateToDelete);
```

You can also delete just a specific profile as well. For instance, if the `GridView` of authenticated users has a delete command column, you could allow the user to delete a specific authenticated user using the following.

```
protected void grdProfiles_RowCommand(object sender,
    GridViewCommandEventArgs e)
{
    if (e.CommandName == "Delete")
    {
        // Retrieve user name to delete
        int rowIndex = Convert.ToInt32(e.CommandArgument);
        string username = grdProfiles.Rows[rowIndex].Cells[1].Text;

        ProfileManager.DeleteProfile(username);
    }
}
```

CORE NOTE

In the code samples that can be downloaded for this book, there is a completed profile manager page that allows an administrator to view and delete authenticated and anonymous user profiles. Figure 14.2 illustrates how this sample profile manager appears in the browser.

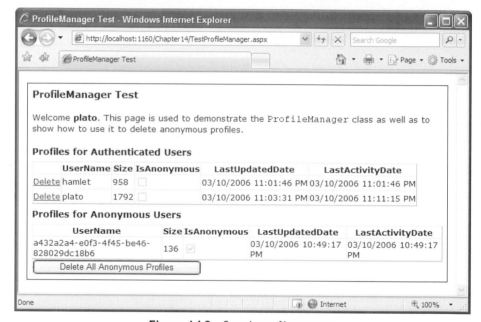

Figure 14.2   Sample profile manager

Migrating Anonymous Profiles

If your site supports profiles for both authenticated and anonymous users, you might want the ability to migrate a user's anonymous profile to his authenticated profile. That is, if an anonymous user sets some profile values, then registers and logs on, the profiles the user set while anonymous should be copied to the new profile the user has as an authenticated user.

The profile system provides a mechanism for this scenario. You can handle this situation by creating a `MigrateAnonymous` event handler for the `ProfileModule` in the `global.asax` file. This handler copies the profile properties from the anonymous profile into the profile for the just-logged-in user. However, there is a potential problem with this mechanism. Recall that before the user can log in, the system considers the user to be an anonymous user. Unfortunately, the `MigrateAnonymous` event is triggered every time the user logs in. This means you would likely overwrite the user's actual profile with the anonymous profile each time the user logs in. One way to handle this situation is to add some type of flag to the profile to indicate whether the profile has already been migrated. The custom profile class in Listing 14.4 has such a flag property, named `MigratedAlready`.

You can set up the `MigrateAnonymous` event handler in the `global.asax` file as shown in the following example. Notice that it also deletes the anonymous profile and its cookie.

```
<%@ Application Language="C#" %>

<script runat="server">
   void Application_Start(object sender, EventArgs e)
   {
      …
   }
   …
   public void Profile_OnMigrateAnonymous(object sender,
      ProfileMigrateEventArgs args)
   {
      // Retrieve the anonymous profile
      ProfileCommon anonymousProfile =
         Profile.GetProfile(args.AnonymousID);

      // Only migrate the values if the logged in profile hasn't
      // already been migrated
      if (!Profile.MigratedAlready)
      {
         // Copy the anonymous profile values to
         // the logged in profile
         Profile.Theme = anonymousProfile.Theme;
         Profile.WishList = anonymousProfile.WishList;
         Profile.Last5Products = anonymousProfile.Last5Products;
      }

      // Because the user is now logged on, make sure you don't
      // overwrite the profile in the future by setting the
      // MigratedAlready flag
      Profile.MigratedAlready = true;

      // Delete the anonymous profile. If the anonymous ID is not
      // needed in the rest of the site, remove the
      // anonymous cookie.
      ProfileManager.DeleteProfile(args.AnonymousID);
      AnonymousIdentificationModule.ClearAnonymousIdentifier();
   }

</script>
```

When to Use Profiles

The profile system is ideal for user-related data in which you do not have an already existing database schema. If you already have an existing database of user or personalization data, you may prefer instead to use a similar approach to that covered in Chapter 11—namely, create entity or business object classes for this data along with necessary data access classes, rather than design a custom profile provider for this existing data. Even if you do not already have an existing database schema for user information, you might want to avoid using the default profile provider for mission-critical or large amounts of data, because the profile system is not exactly the most optimized way to store data. Although the profile system can serialize its data into string or XML or binary format, serialization is never as efficient as the pure binary approach used by a database.

In my opinion, the profile system is best used for tracking user information that is generated by the application itself, and not for data that is actually entered by the user. For instance, in a site that contains forms for the user to enter her mailing addresses, credit card information, shoe size, and so on, it is best to design database tables for containing this information, and then use business objects/entities and data access classes for working with this data. This way, you can add any validation, application-logic processing, or other behaviors to these classes.

The profile system is ideal for customizing the site based on the user's preferences and the user's behavior within the site, because this type of data either necessitates little validation or logic (e.g., use preferences) or can be generated by the system itself without the user's knowledge (e.g., tracking user behaviors).

In the extended example that you can download for this chapter, you can see both types of customization demonstrated. This sample site (see Figures 14.3, 14.4, and 14.5) uses roughly the same master page-based theme selection mechanism used in the listings at the close of Chapter 6, except here it uses the profile mechanism rather than session state to preserve the user's theme choice.

The site also keeps track of (and displays) the last five books browsed by the user in the single book display page (see Figure 14.4). Both this tracking and the user's theme selection are enabled for both authenticated and unauthenticated users.

Finally, if the user is authenticated, the profile system is used to maintain the user's wish list of books (shown in Figure 14.5).

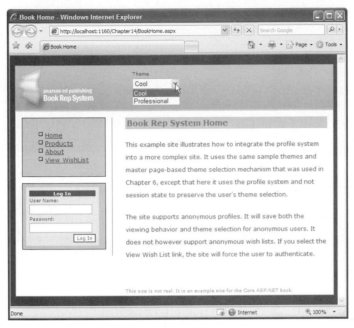

Figure 14.3   Setting the site theme

Figure 14.4   Tracking the user's page visits with the profile system

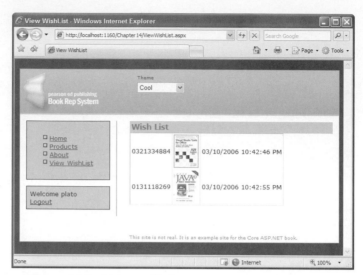

Figure 14.5   Using profile feature to maintain a user wish list

Web Parts Framework

In the last section, we examined how you can use the profile system in ASP.NET to programmatically customize Web content for specific users. In this section, we examine the Web parts framework that was introduced in ASP.NET 2.0. The **Web parts framework** is the name for the infrastructure and controls that allow you to create pages that provide end users with the ability to modify the content, appearance, and behavior of these pages directly within the browser. When users modify pages and controls, the settings are saved so as to retain the user's personal preferences across future browser sessions. Thus, the Web parts framework lets you let develop sites that can be customized by users at runtime without developer or administrator intervention. Figure 14.6 illustrates a sample page that is using Web parts. Each of these rectangular boxes of content can be moved into different locations on the page by the user, as well as minimized, restored, and closed.

This type of personalized Web site is sometimes called a portal. A **portal** is a type of Web application that displays different types of information, usually based on some type of prior user setup. A portal site may provide a unified interface to an organization's information or it may aggregate information from multiple organizations. Microsoft's My MSN and Google's Personalized Home Page are examples of very general-purpose portals.

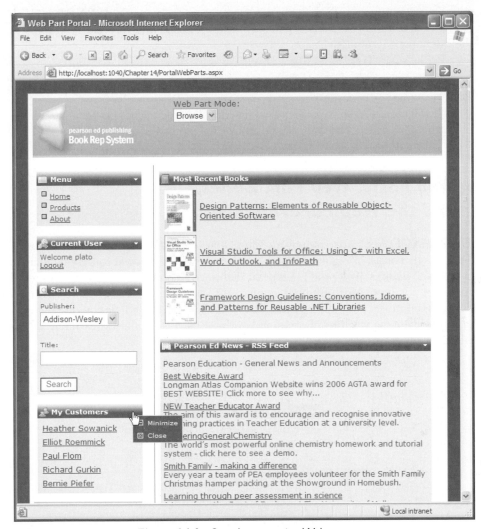

Figure 14.6   Sample page using Web parts

Microsoft has a dedicated product named SharePoint 2003 that can be used to create portal sites for managing collaboration between geographically dispersed team members. A SharePoint portal is constructed using something called SharePoint Web parts, which (in the current version) are extensions of ASP.NET 1.1 controls that can interact with the SharePoint framework. The rest of this chapter covers the ASP.NET 2.0 Web parts framework, which is different than the SharePoint Web parts framework but has a similar functionality. Finally, to muddy the waters further, with SharePoint Service Pack 2, SharePoint Services can now use ASP.NET 2.0 Web parts; as well, future versions of SharePoint are to use ASP.NET 2.0 Web parts as their default content model.

CORE NOTE

If you require Web part-like portal functionality, you might also want to consider instead Microsoft Sharepoint or the open-source DotNetNuke.

Web Parts, Web Part Zones, and the Web Part Manager

The ASP.NET Web parts framework allows you to create user-customizable pages. These pages consist of regular ASP.NET content as well as special content containers called Web parts. A **Web part** is a type of Web server container control; it is a special container for both ASP.NET and regular HTML content. A Web part is thus a user-customizable "box" of displayable content that is provided with additional user interface elements such as chrome and verbs. Figure 14.7 illustrates many of the additional elements that are added to a Web part.

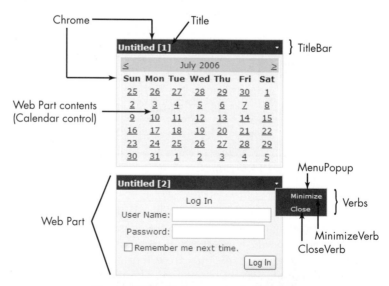

Figure 14.7   Components of a Web part

The **verbs** of a Web part are the actions that a user can instruct the Web part to perform. By default, the Web part framework adds the minimize/restore and close verbs to each Web part. Depending upon the display mode of the Web parts, other verbs may be available, such as edit, connect, and export. As well, it is possible to define custom verbs for a Web part.

The **chrome** of a Web part refers to the common user interface elements rendered around each Web part. The chrome for a Web part includes a border, a title bar, and the icons, title text, and verb menu that appear within the title bar.

Web parts are placed into one or more **Web part zones**, which is yet another specialized container control (named `WebPartZone`). It is the Web part zone that defines the chrome and verbs for the Web parts that it contains. Figure 14.8 illustrates the relationship between parts and zones.

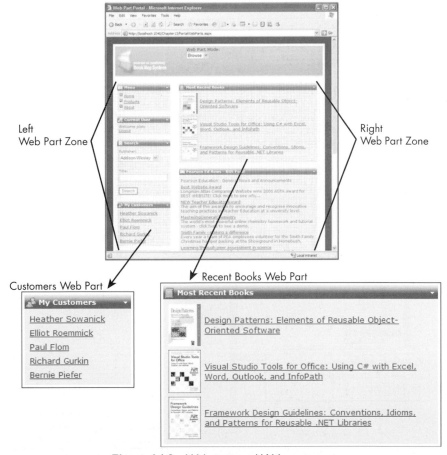

Figure 14.8 Web parts and Web part zones

Finally, there is the **Web part manager**, which manages the entire Web part infrastructure on a page. This manager is a nonrendered control named `WebPart-Manager`. This control must be present on any page that uses the Web part infrastructure. The manager control can also be used to programmatically change the display mode of the Web parts or to set up communication between Web parts.

Figure 14.9 illustrates some (but not all) of the different display modes available to the Web part manager. These different display modes may also require the use of different types of zones: for instance, the `CatalogZone`, `EditorZone`, and `ConnectionsZone`.

Figure 14.9   Web part manager display modes

Internally, a Web part is a server control that ultimately inherits from the `Web-Part` abstract base class. As you can see from Figure 14.10, Web parts are specializations of the `Panel` server control. As can also be seen from this diagram, Web parts are one of three different part types in the Web parts framework. The editor part allows users to modify the appearance of a Web part, whereas the catalog part provides a catalog or list of Web parts that a user can add to a page.

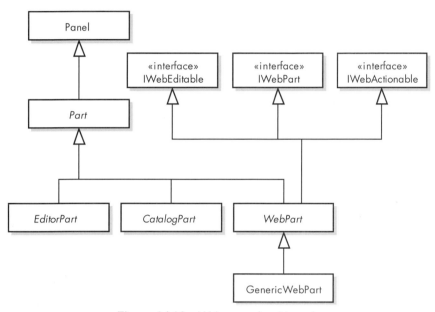

Figure 14.10   Web parts class hierarchy

Web Parts Personalization

Another feature of the Web parts infrastructure is its support for personalization. **Web parts personalization** refers to the capability of the current state of Web part property values to be identified with users and saved in long-term storage. It should be stressed that Web parts personalization stores user-specific state data for controls on a particular Web page only. Information that relates to the user as a person or that is intended to be used across multiple pages in a Web application should be kept in a profile.

The Web parts personalization system is based on the provider model, and by default, uses the same database as the membership and profile systems. Just as with the other provider-based subsystems in ASP.NET, it is possible to create your own customized personalization provider so as to use any data store.

Web parts personalization requires authenticated users. Although Web parts are visible for anonymous users, the personalization of Web parts requires the user to be logged in first. Normally, any personalization changes that the user makes to the Web parts in a page are saved just for that user, so that the next time the user visits the page, the previous changes are visible. In Web parts terminology, this is called *user scope*.

The other possible scope is shared scope. With ***shared scope***, any changes that the user makes are visible to all users. By default, all users (authorized or anonymous) are denied access to shared scope. It might make sense, however, for site administrators to have shared scope so that they can make changes that are visible to all users. We illustrate how to set up shared scope later in the chapter in the section "Making the BehaviorEditorPart Appear" on page 884.

Creating and Using Web Parts

There are three basic approaches to creating a Web part:

- Use *any* Web server control or HTML server control within a WebPartZone control. When you add a server control to a WebPartZone, the runtime wraps the control as a GenericWebPart object, and thus is treated as a WebPart control and has the same consistent Web part user interface elements such as verbs, icons, a title, and a header.
- Create a user control that implements the IWebPart interface.
- Create a custom control that derives from the WebPart abstract class.

In this chapter, we begin with the first approach and then move onto the second approach, because it provides us with more control and cleaner markup. We then finish with the third approach, because it provides the highest degree of customization and control.

Because we begin by letting ASP.NET convert normal server controls into Web parts, let us examine the steps necessary for creating a page with Web parts.

1. Add a WebPartManager control to the page, as shown in the following.

   ```
   <asp:WebPartManager ID="partManager" runat="server" />
   ```

2. Add one or more WebPartZone controls to the page. This control is the container that will hold the Web parts. Each WebPartZone control contains a ZoneTemplate, which contains the Web parts. As well, each WebPartZone control can contain various style elements, such as HeaderStyle and PartChromeStyle, which allow you to define and customize the appearance of the Web parts within the zone.

   ```
   <asp:WebPartZone ID="wpzOne" runat="server" >
     <ZoneTemplate>
   ```

```
      ...
   </ZoneTemplate>

   style elements can go here
   <PartChromeStyle ... />
      ...
</asp:WebPartZone>
```

Most pages have at least two different zones, which correspond broadly to the different layout areas for the page. For instance, in Figure 14.7, the page structure contains two columns. Each of these columns contains a separate WebPartZone control. Some developers place different zones into different columns of an HTML `<table>` element; other developers place the different zones into different HTML `<div>` elements and then use CSS to position the zones. The latter approach is used in this chapter.

3. Add one or more Web parts to the different zones. Recall that any ASP.NET control, whether a standard control—such as a `GridView` or a `Label` control, a user control, or even a custom control—can be used as a Web part. In the following example, two Web parts (a `Calendar` control and a `LoginView` control) are added to a Web part zone.

```
<asp:WebPartZone ID="wpzOne" runat="server" >
   <ZoneTemplate>
      <asp:Calendar ID="calOne" runat="server"  />
      <asp:LoginView ID="logView" runat="server">
         <AnonymousTemplate>
            <asp:Login ID="logSignin" runat="server" />
         </AnonymousTemplate>
         <LoggedInTemplate>
            <asp:LoginName ID="logName" runat="server"
               FormatString="Welcome {0}" />
         </LoggedInTemplate>
      </asp:LoginView>
   </ZoneTemplate>
</asp:WebPartZone>
```

4. Optionally add specialized zones and parts, such as the `CatalogZone` or the `EditorZone`.

The result in the browser is shown in Figure 14.11. Notice how the chrome for the Web parts changes after the user is authenticated. Anonymous users still see the Web parts; however, they do not see the verb menu, nor are they able to view the page in anything other than the default browse display mode.

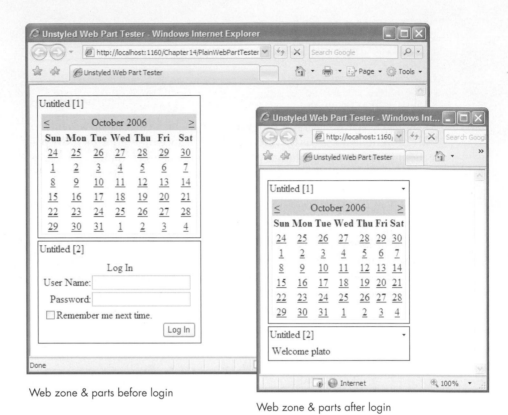

Web zone & parts before login

Web zone & parts after login

Figure 14.11   Simple Web part example

Of course, the example Web parts shown in Figure 14.11 are quite plain. You can style the Web parts by adding style elements to the `WebPartZone` (and by setting properties of the `WebPartZone` control). As well, within the Visual Studio designer, you can use the AutoFormat option to apply a prebuilt set of formatting options to a zone. Table 14.3 lists the different style elements available to the `WebPartZone`, whereas Table 14.4 lists the different properties of the `WebPartZone` control.

Table 14.3   WebPartZone Style Elements

Name	Description
`EmptyZoneTextStyle`	The style for the text that appears in an empty zone.
`ErrorStyle`	The style for any error messages that are displayed if Web part cannot be loaded or created.

Table 14.3 WebPartZone Style Elements *(continued)*

Name	Description
FooterStyle	The style of the text that appears in the footer of the zone.
HeaderStyle	The style of the text that appears in the header of the zone.
MenuCheckImageStyle	The style of the check mark that may appear beside a verb in the verb menu.
MenuLabelHoverStyle	The style of the text label for the verb menu when user positions the mouse pointer over the label.
MenuLabelStyle	The style of the text label for the verb menu.
MenuPopupStyle	The style of the pop-up verb menu for each Web part in the zone.
MenuVerbHoverStyle	The style of the verb menu items when user positions the mouse pointer over the text.
MenuVerbStyle	The style of the verb menu items.
PartChromeStyle	The style of the borders for each Web part in the zone.
PartStyle	The style of the title bar for each Web part in the zone.
PartTitleStyle	The style of the title in the title bar for each Web part in the zone.
SelectedPartChromeStyle	The style of the chrome for the selected Web part in a zone. A Web part is selected when it is in edit mode.
TitleBarVerbStyle	The style of the verbs in the title bar.
VerbStyle	The style for the verbs for each Web part in the zone.

Table 14.4 Notable WebPartZone Properties

Property	Description
AllowLayoutChange	Indicates whether the user is allowed to change the layout of Web parts within the zone. Default is true.
BackImageUrl	The URL of an image to display in the background of a zone.
DragHighlightColor	The color to be displayed around the border of a Web zone and its drop-cue when a user is dragging a Web part.

Table 14.4   Notable WebPartZone Properties *(continued)*

Property	Description
EmptyZoneText	The text to be displayed when a Web zone contains no Web parts.
HeaderText	The text to display in the header of the zone.
LayoutOrientation	Indicates whether the controls in a zone are to be arranged horizontally or vertically.
MenuCheckImageUrl	The URL of image to display when a verb is checked.
MenuLabelText	The text label for the pop-up verb menu in each Web part.
MenuPopupImageUrl	The URL for image that opens the drop-down menu in the title bar of each Web part.
Padding	The cell padding for the table that contains the Web parts in the zone.
ShowTitleIcons	Indicates whether title icons are to be displayed in the title bar of each Web part in the zone.
TitleBarVerbButtonType	Indicates what type of button to use (Button, Image, or Link) for the verbs in the title bar.
VerbButtonType	The type of button to use for the zone when rendered in an older browser.
WebPartVerbRenderMode	Specifies how to render verbs on the Web parts in the zone. Possible values are WebPartVerbRenderMode.Menu (verbs appear in a drop-down menu) and WebPartVerb-RenderMode.TitleBar (verbs appear as links in title bar).

All Web parts within a zone inherit the visual appearance defined by the zone. Thus, if you move the Web part from one zone to another, its appearance may change if the styling of the zone is different.

CORE NOTE

Perhaps the easiest way to ensure that the Web parts in each zone have the same consistent appearance is to set the properties and style elements for the WebPartZone control in a skin file.

Verbs

Verbs are an important part of the Web part framework. They are the actions that a user can instruct a Web part to perform. When displayed with the default Browse display mode, a Web part has two verbs: Minimize/Restore and Close. When viewing a page anonymously, there is no user interface to represent these verbs. After a user is authenticated, however, the different verbs are available as either a pop-up menu or a series of text or image links in the title bar of each Web part, depending upon the value of the zone's `WebPartVerbRenderMode` property and of its verb setting elements, as shown in Figure 14.12.

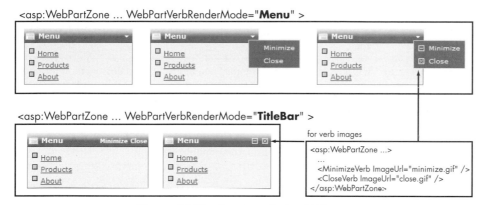

Figure 14.12   Sample verbs in a Web part

CORE NOTE

Verbs can only be displayed in the pop-up menu if the user's browser is Internet Explorer. For other browsers, the verbs are displayed in the title bar.

As shown in Figure 14.12, each zone has its own verb setting element. Table 14.5 lists the verbs that are provided by the Web part framework. You can also create your own verbs; we illustrate how to do so later when we create a custom Web part control.

Table 14.5   Web Part Verbs

Name	Description
Close	Closes the Web part. After a Web part is closed, the only way to bring it back is via the catalog.
Connect	Allows a connection to be made to another Web part.
Delete	Deletes a control permanently from a page. This verb is not allowed for Web parts added declaratively.
Edit	Allows the user to edit the Web part. When editing, the user can personalize the appearance, properties, layout, and content of the Web part.
Export	Allows the user to export an XML definition file for each Web part in a zone.
Help	Displays help for the Web part in a modal or modeless window, or by navigating to a help page.
Minimize	Minimizes the Web part. When minimized, only the title bar of the part is visible.
Restore	Restores a Web part from the minimized state.

You can customize the settings for each verb in the zone via the verb setting elements, as shown in the following.

```
<asp:WebPartZone … >
   …
   <CloseVerb Enabled="false" />
   <MinimizeVerb Text="Min" Description="Shrinks this box"/>
   <RestoreVerb Text="Res" Description="Restores this box"/>
</asp:WebPartZone>
```

Each verb setting element supports the properties listed in Table 14.6.

Table 14.6   Notable Verb Properties

Property	Description
Checked	Indicates whether custom state for the verb is currently active. If it is selected, a check box appears next to the verb. This property is not used with the system-provided verbs; it is only available for custom verbs.
Description	A short description of the verb that is displayed in the tool tip for the verb.

Table 14.6   Notable Verb Properties *(continued)*

Property	Description
Enabled	Indicates whether the verb is enabled.
ImageUrl	The URL of the image to display for the verb.
Text	The text label for the verb.
Visible	Indicates whether the verb is visible.

Making Web Parts from User Controls

You may have noticed from the example shown in Figure 14.11 that the title for each Web part begins with "Untitled." Why is this? You may remember that when you add a regular Web server control to a Web part zone, it is wrapped as a `GenericWebPart` control so that the control can exhibit the same functionality as true `WebPart` controls. As you can see from Figure 14.10, this control inherits from the `WebPart` base control, which in turn implements the `IWebPart` interface. This interface, which is described in Table 14.7, defines the minimal user interface properties needed by any Web part. If you want to change the default implementations of any of these `IWebPart` properties in your Web parts, you need to either create your own custom control for the Web part or create a user control for the Web part that implements the `IWebPart` interface.

Table 14.7   IWebPart Properties

Property	Description
CatalogIconImageUrl	The URL of the image used to represent the Web part in the catalog.
Description	The summary description of the Web part for use in tool tips and the catalog.
SubTitle	The string that is concatenated with the `Title` property and displayed in the title bar of the Web part.
Title	The title of the Web part, which is displayed in the Web part's title bar.
TitleIconImageUrl	The URL of the image that is displayed in the Web part's title bar.
TitleUrl	The URL of a page that contains more information about the Web part. When set, the title in the title bar becomes a hyperlink.

As you may recall from Chapter 6, a user control encapsulates the appearance and behavior of a part of a page's user interface. User controls have an extension of .ascx and their code-behind classes inherit from the UserControl rather than the Page class.

If you want to be able to display a different title as well as a title bar image—for example, the LoginView Web part shown earlier—you could define the following user control.

```
<%@ Control Language="C#" AutoEventWireup="true"
   CodeFile="LoginControl.ascx.cs" Inherits="LoginControl" %>

<asp:LoginView ID="logView" runat="server">
   <AnonymousTemplate>
      <asp:Login ID="logSignin" runat="server"
         DisplayRememberMe="True"
         TitleText="" TextLayout="TextOnTop"
         RememberMeText="Remember me">
      </asp:Login>
   </AnonymousTemplate>
   <LoggedInTemplate>
      <asp:LoginName ID="logName" runat="server"
         FormatString="Welcome {0}" /><br/>
      <asp:LoginStatus ID="logStatus" runat="server" />
   </LoggedInTemplate>
</asp:LoginView>
```

The code-behind for this user control might look like the following. Notice how the user control class definition must also implement the IWebPart interface. The implementation of this interface simply consists of properties as well as the data members to contain the state for these properties.

```
public partial class LoginControl : UserControl, IWebPart
{
   // Data members necessary for IWebPart properties
   private string _description = "";
   private string _title = "";
   private string _subtitle = "";
   private string _titleIconImageUrl = "";
   private string _catalogIconImageUrl = "";
   private string _titleUrl = "";

   // Implement IWebPart

   public string CatalogIconImageUrl
   {
      get { return _catalogIconImageUrl; }
      set { _catalogIconImageUrl = value; }
   }
```

```
public string Description
{
   get { return _description; }
   set { _description = value; }
}

public string Subtitle
{
   get { return _subtitle; }
}

public string Title
{
   get { return _title; }
   set { _title = value; }
}

public string TitleIconImageUrl
{
   get { return _titleIconImageUrl; }
   set { _titleIconImageUrl = value; }
}

public string TitleUrl
{
   get { return _titleUrl; }
   set { _titleUrl = value; }
}

   // Any additional properties or behaviors go here
}
```

After this user control is defined, it can be used within a Web part zone. Remember that to use a user control in a Web page, you must first register the tag name and prefix via the Register page directive. You can then declaratively add the control via this tag name and prefix as well as set any of the Web part properties defined by the control.

```
<%@ Register Src="controls/LoginControl.ascx"
   TagName="LoginControl" TagPrefix="uc" %>
...
<asp:WebPartZone ID="zoneSample" runat="server"  >
   <ZoneTemplate>
      ...
      <uc:LoginControl ID="myLogin" runat="server"
         Title="Current User"
         Description=
            "Necessary to login in order to modify web parts"
         TitleIconImageUrl="images/webpartLogin.gif"
```

```
                    CatalogIconImageUrl="images/webpartLogin.gif"   />
   </ZoneTemplate>
</asp:WebPartZone>
```

If your Web site is to have more than two or three Web parts created from user controls, you may find that you are uncomfortable with the fact that the code-behind classes for each of these user controls looks almost identical. That is, because a Web part user control must implement IWebPart, you will find that each of these user controls have the identical data members and property definitions necessary to implement this interface. A better approach is to define a custom base class that implements the IWebPart interface, and then use it as the base class for your Web part user controls. Listing 14.5 contains a sample implementation of this custom base class.

Listing 14.5 CustomWebPartBase.cs

```csharp
using System;
using System.Web;
using System.Web.UI;
using System.Web.UI.WebControls;
using System.Web.UI.WebControls.WebParts;

/// <summary>
/// Base class for my user control-based Web parts
/// </summary>
public abstract class CustomWebPartBase : UserControl, IWebPart
{
   private string _description = "";
   private string _title = "";
   private string _titleIconImageUrl = "";
   private string _catalogIconImageUrl = "";
   private string _titleUrl = "";

   // IWebPart interface requires Subtitle to be read-only; thus
   // to allow subclasses to initialize it, you must make it a
   // protected data member
   protected string _subtitle = "";

   public string CatalogIconImageUrl
   {
      get { return _catalogIconImageUrl; }
      set { _catalogIconImageUrl = value; }
   }

   public string Description
   {
      get { return _description; }
```

```
      set { _description = value; }
   }

   public string Subtitle
   {
      get { return _subtitle; }
   }

   public string Title
   {
      get { return _title; }
      set { _title = value; }
   }

   public string TitleIconImageUrl
   {
      get { return _titleIconImageUrl; }
      set { _titleIconImageUrl = value; }
   }

   public string TitleUrl
   {
      get { return _titleUrl; }
      set { _titleUrl = value; }
   }
}
```

Your user control code-behind classes simply inherit from this base class and set up the default values for the properties, as shown in Listing 14.6.

Listing 14.6 LoginControl.ascx.cs

```
using System;
using System.Web;
using System.Web.UI;
using System.Web.UI.WebControls;
using System.Web.UI.WebControls.WebParts;

public partial class LoginControl : CustomWebPartBase
{
   public LoginControl()
   {
      // Set default values for properties
      Title = "Current User";
      Description =
        "Necessary to login in order to modify web parts";
```

```
        TitleIconImageUrl = "images/webpartLogin.gif";
        CatalogIconImageUrl = "images/webpartLogin.gif";

        // IWebPart interface requires Subtitle to be read-only;
        // thus, must initialize it via protected data member
        // of CustomWebPartBase
        _subTitle = "Login";
    }

    // any additional properties or behaviors go here
}
```

Making Web Parts from Custom Controls

Although creating Web parts from user controls is quite straightforward, there may be times when you want to instead create a Web part as a custom control. The advantage of using custom controls for your Web parts is that you have complete control over the rendering and behavior of the control. As well, you can add custom verbs and make it easier to create communication links between Web parts when you create Web parts from custom controls. As well, if you want to add personalization attributes to properties within the Web part (we do this later when we work with the PropertyGridEditorPart control), you can avoid a potential deserialization error if your property uses enumerated types by using a custom Web part control.

Creating a custom Web part control is by no means difficult. You must create a new class that inherits from the WebPart class. You can then add any custom properties that your Web part requires. Finally, you must provide the rendering for the control, either by overriding the RenderContents or the CreateChildControls method. You should override RenderContents when you want to exactly control the rendered output of the Web part; when you want to use the functionality and rendering of other controls, you should override CreateChildControls. In this section's example, you use the RenderContents approach. For an example of the Create-ChildControls approach, you can examine Listing 14.8 later in the chapter.

The following listing illustrates the code for a custom Web part that displays the first 10 books in the books database. Eventually, you add custom verbs to the Web part so that the user can filter the list by a publisher. The code for a basic custom control is shown in Listing 14.7.

Listing 14.7   BookListViewer.cs

```
using System;
using System.Data;
using System.Configuration;
using System.Web;
```

```
using System.Web.Security;
using System.Web.UI;
using System.Web.UI.WebControls;
using System.Web.UI.WebControls.WebParts;
using System.Web.UI.HtmlControls;

using FourLayer.ApplicationLogic;
using FourLayer.BusinessEntity;

namespace Chapter14
{
    public class BookListViewer : WebPart
    {
        private Publisher _publisher = null;

        public BookListViewer()
        {
            Title = "View Books";
            Description = "Views all books";
            TitleIconImageUrl = "images/webpartBooks.gif";
            CatalogIconImageUrl = "images/webpartBooks.gif";
        }

        /// <summary>
        /// Outputs the HTML content for the control
        /// </summary>
        protected override void RenderContents(
            HtmlTextWriter writer)
        {
            EntityCollection<Book> books;
            if (PublisherToUse == null)
                books = BookCatalogLogic.GetAllBooks();
            else
                books =
                    BookCatalogLogic.GetBooksByPublisher(Publisher.Id);

            int max = 10;
            if (max > books.Count) max = books.Count;

            string output = "<div id='listContainer'>";
            for (int i = 0; i < max; i++)
            {
                Book book = books[i];
                output += "<p><a href=BookDetails.aspx?id=";
                output += book.Isbn + ">";
                output += book.Title;
                output += "></p>";
            }
            output += "</div>";
```

```
        writer.Write(output);
    }

    [Personalizable, WebBrowsable]
    public Publisher PublisherToUse
    {
        get { return _publisher; }
        set {
            _publisher = value;
            Title = "View Books for " + _publisher.Name;
        }
    }
  }
}
```

Notice that this custom control inherits from the WebPart base class. This base class has the Web part functionality already defined. The custom control also initializes the Web part properties within its constructor. The RenderContents method outputs the actual HTML content that appears within the Web part. This method uses some classes from Chapter 11 to retrieve the data, loop through it, and output the appropriate HTML using the passed in HtmlTextWriter object. The control also defines a Publisher property, which we use later to allow the user to filter the books by a publisher. This property is marked with two attributes. The Personalizable attribute ensures that the value of this property is saved to the data store by the personalization system, whereas the WebBrowsable attribute makes this property visible to the PropertyGridEditorPart editor part (covered later in the chapter).

After this class is defined, you can then use it in a Web part page. Just as with user controls, you have to register the class in your markup through the Register directive.

```
<%@ Register Namespace="Chapter14" TagPrefix="ch14" %>
```

This Register directive is a bit different than with user controls, in that you do not specify the filename but the namespace and/or assembly name. Using the control is now simply a matter of using this tag prefix along with the class name.

```
<ch14:BookListViewer id="myViewer" runat="server" />
```

Adding a Custom Verb

To make your custom Web part control more useful, you can change it so that the user can filter the displayed books by a publisher selected by the user in the verb menu. To create a custom verb, your Web part control must override the Verbs property (which is defined by the IWebActionable interface). In your version of

Verbs, you create and return a collection of `WebPartVerb` objects. Each of these `WebPartVerb` objects needs to reference the handler method that runs when the user selects the verb (from the verb menu or the verb list in the title bar).

In our example, we create a verb for each publisher in the database (obviously, this might cause some visual problems if there are many publishers and our web part zone uses `WebPartVerbRenderMode="TitleBar"`). The code for creating these custom verbs is as follows.

```
public override WebPartVerbCollection Verbs
{
    get
    {
        // Create new collection of verbs
        ArrayList verbs = new ArrayList();
        // Get all the publishers
        EntityCollection<Publisher> pubs =
            BookCatalogLogic.GetAllPublishers();

        // Make each publisher a verb
        foreach (Publisher p in pubs)
        {
            WebPartVerb verb = new WebPartVerb(p.Id.ToString(),
                new WebPartEventHandler(ChangePublisher));
            verb.Text = p.Name;
            verb.Description = "See books for " + p.Name;

            // If this is the current publisher, check it
            if (PublisherToUse != null &&
                p.Name == PublisherToUse.Name)
            {
                verb.Checked = true;
            }
            // Add new verb to collection
            verbs.Add(verb);
        }
        // Create new verb collection with the new verbs added
        // to any existing verbs
        return new WebPartVerbCollection(base.Verbs, verbs);
    }
}
```

Notice that the constructor for `WebPartVerb` requires a reference to the handler method that executes when the verb is selected. All your example needs to do is set the `Publisher` property to the name of the publisher in the verb, as shown in the following.

```
public void ChangePublisher(object o, WebPartEventArgs e)
{
    WebPartVerb verb = (WebPartVerb)o;
    PublisherToUse =
        BookCatalogLogic.GetPublisherByName(verb.Text);
}
```

The result in the browser is shown in Figure 14.13.

Figure 14.13   Custom control Web part with custom verbs

Changing the Different Display Modes

If you have been following the examples so far in this chapter, you may have wondered what exactly is the benefit of web parts. If all you want is to display content within boxes, the Web parts framework might seem to be more bother than it is worth. However, the real benefit of Web parts can be realized after you allow the user to modify your Web part pages. To do this requires that the user be able to change the **Web part display mode** of the page via the WebPartManager.DisplayMode property. Table 14.8 lists the available display modes for the Web parts framework.

Table 14.8   Display Modes

Name	Description
Browse	Displays Web parts in the normal mode. This is the only display mode available for anonymous users.
Catalog	Displays the catalog user interface that allows end users to add and remove page controls. Allows dragging of controls, just as with design mode.
Connect	Displays the connections user interface that lets users connect Web parts.

Table 14.8 Display Modes *(continued)*

Name	Description
Design	Makes each Web zone visible and enables users to drag Web parts to change the layout of a page.
Edit	Enables the Edit verb in Web parts. Choosing the Edit verb displays editing elements and lets end users edit the Web parts on the page. Also allows the dragging of Web parts, just as with design mode.

You must provide the user interface yourself for changing the `DisplayMode` property. In the example that follows, we use a `DropDownList` (you can see the result in Figure 14.14), but you could use buttons or some other control type. You could also encapsulate the markup and event handling for this list within a user or custom control. Your definition for this list is as follows.

```
<asp:WebPartManager ID="partManager" runat="server" />

Web Part Mode:
<asp:DropDownList ID="drpWebPartMode" runat="server"
   AutoPostBack="true"
   OnSelectedIndexChanged="drpWebPartMode_SelectedIndexChanged" />
```

Notice that we have not statically populated the list with the available modes. You should not statically fill the list because the items in the list vary depending upon the user's permissions (e.g., an anonymous user should only see the Browse mode, an authenticated user might see Design and Catalog, whereas a user with the administrator role might see the Edit mode). Instead, we programmatically fill the list when the page loads.

```
protected void Page_Load(object sender, EventArgs e)
{
    if (!IsPostBack)
    {
        // Loop through all the supported display modes
        foreach (WebPartDisplayMode mode in
            partManager.SupportedDisplayModes)
        {
            // Only display the mode if it is enabled for
            // the current user
            if (mode.IsEnabled(partManager))
            {
                // Create list item and add to list
                ListItem item = new ListItem(mode.Name);
```

```
        // If this item matches the current display mode,
        // make it the selected item in the list
        if (mode == partManager.DisplayMode)
            item.Selected = true;

        drpWebPartMode.Items.Add(item);
        }
    }
}
}
```

The event handler for the list simply needs to change the display mode of the WebPartManager control on the page to that chosen by the user.

```
protected void drpWebPartMode_SelectedIndexChanged(object sender,
    EventArgs e)
{
    // Retrieve the user's selection
    string mode = drpWebPartMode.SelectedValue;

    // Retrieve the WebPartDisplayMode object for this mode
    WebPartDisplayMode display =
        partManager.SupportedDisplayModes[mode];

    // Set the display mode if this mode is enabled
    if (display != null && display.IsEnabled(partManager))
        partManager.DisplayMode = display;
}
```

Design Mode

When the Web parts page is in Design mode, each Web part zone is visible with its name and a border around it. The user can then drag and drop Web parts from one zone to another, as shown in Figure 14.14.

CORE NOTE

This drag-and-drop behavior is currently *only* available to users using Internet Explorer as their browser. For non-IE browsers, Web parts can only be moved using the Catalog Zone (covered shortly). You can also add this drag-and-drop behavior for other uplevel browsers if you use ASP.NET AJAX, which is covered in the Appendix.

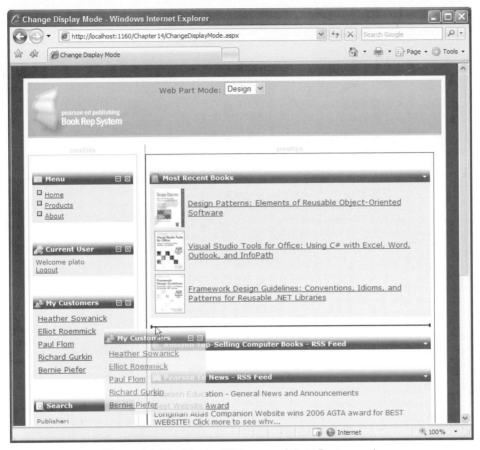

Figure 14.14   Moving Web parts while in Design mode

To provide this design functionality to your Web part page, you need a page that contains more than one `WebPartZone`. The following example illustrates the markup for the page shown in Figure 14.14.

```
<div id="sideArea">
   <asp:WebPartZone ID="zoneSide" runat="server"
        Padding="6" WebPartVerbRenderMode="TitleBar"
        PartChromeType="TitleOnly" Width="14em">
     <ZoneTemplate>
        <uc:MainMenuControl ID="myMenu" runat="server"
           Title="Menu"/>
        <uc:LoginControl ID="myLogin" runat="server"
           Title="Current User" />
        <uc:SearchControl ID="mySearch" runat="server"
```

```
                    Title="Search"/>
            <uc:CustomersControl ID="myCustomers" runat="server"
                Title="My Customers" />
        </ZoneTemplate>
    </asp:WebPartZone>
</div>

<div id="mainArea">
    <asp:WebPartZone ID="zoneMain" runat="server"
        WebPartVerbRenderMode="TitleBar"
        Padding="6" PartChromeType="TitleOnly">
        <ZoneTemplate>
            <uc:RecentBooksControl ID="myRecentBooks" runat="server"
                Title="Most Recent Books" />
            <uc:RSSControl ID="myAmazon" runat="server"
                Title="Amazon Top-Selling Computer Books"
              Description="Amazon Top Computer Books"

                XmlUrl="~/amazonRSS.xml"
                XsltUrl="~/RssTransformAmazon.xsl" />
            <uc:RSSControl ID="myPearson" runat="server"
                Title="Pearson Ed News"
                Description="Pearson Ed News"
                CatalogIconImageUrl="~/images/webpartNews.gif"
                TitleIconImageUrl="~/images/webpartNews.gif"
                XmlUrl="~/pearsonRSS.xml"
                XsltUrl="~/RssTransformPearson.xsl" />
        </ZoneTemplate>
    </asp:WebPartZone>
</div>
```

Notice that the zones in this example contain no formatting markup; instead, all of the styling elements and properties are contained in a separate skin file for the theme used in the page, while the actual positioning of the zones is contained within a CSS file for the theme. Notice as well that the different web parts are all encapsulated as user controls.

Catalog Mode

Catalog mode allows the user to add Web parts to the page at runtime. It also allows the user to move parts from zone to zone in the same manner as Design mode. A *catalog* is simply a list of Web parts that is visible when a page is in Catalog mode.

When the page is switched to Catalog mode, the catalog user interface appears. The user interface for this catalog is provided by a CatalogZone control, which can be declaratively added to the page. The CatalogZone can only contain Catalog-Part controls. Table 14.9 lists the available CatalogPart controls.

Table 14.9 CatalogPart Controls

Name	Description
`DeclarativeCatalogPart`	Provides a way for developers to define a set of possible (but not initially visible) Web parts declaratively to a catalog. A user can select controls from the list and add them to the page, which effectively gives users the ability to change the set of controls and the functionality on a page.
`ImportCatalogPart`	Provides the user interface for a user to upload a definition file (an XML file with a `.WebPart` extension that imports settings for a control) to a catalog, so that the control can be added to the page. The control must be present on the server before the definition file can be imported. The description file is not the same as the control itself. It is an XML file that contains name/value pairs that describe the state of the control.
`PageCatalogPart`	Maintains references to Web parts that have been previously added to the page but have been subsequently closed by the user. This part lets the user reopen (add back to the page) closed Web parts.

After the `CatalogZone` control is added declaratively to the page, `CatalogPart` controls can be added to the zone. For instance, in the following example, we add a catalog zone to the side area of our page that contains both a `PageCatalogPart` and a `DeclarativeCatalogPart`.

```
<div id="sideArea">
   <asp:CatalogZone ID="catZone" runat="server" Padding="6" >
      <ZoneTemplate>
         <asp:PageCatalogPart ID="pageCatalog"
            runat="server" />
         <asp:DeclarativeCatalogPart ID="decCatalog"
               runat="server" Title="Optional Parts">
            <WebPartsTemplate>
               <uc:CalendarControl ID="myCalendar" runat="server"
                  Title="Calendar"/>
               <uc:RecentViewsPartControl ID="myRecentViews"
                  runat="server"
                  Title="Recently Viewed Products"/>
            </WebPartsTemplate>
         </asp:DeclarativeCatalogPart>
      </ZoneTemplate>
   </asp:CatalogZone>
```

```
<asp:WebPartZone ID="zoneSide" runat="server" >
    ...
</asp:WebPartZone>
</div>
```

Notice that the `DeclarativeCatalogPart` control contains two user controls. These define two optional Web parts that are not part of the initial page, but can be added later by the user via the catalog. The result in the browser is shown in Figure 14.15.

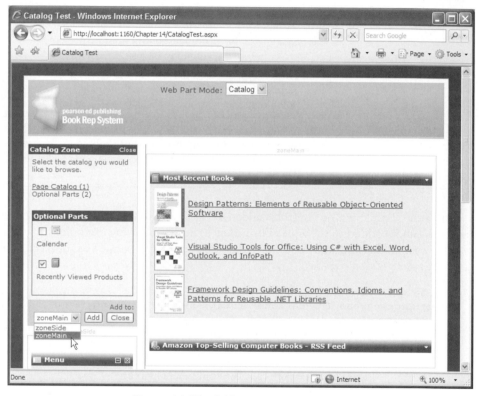

Figure 14.15   Adding parts via the catalog

The `PageCatalogPart` and a `DeclarativeCatalogPart` appear within the browser as choices within the catalog zone. For both of these parts, a list of possible Web parts appears as check boxes and labels. The user can then select a part, choose the zone, and then click the Add button. After the controls have been added to the page via the catalog, they appear in normal browse mode.

Edit Mode

The Edit design mode lets users edit or modify the properties of a Web part control. After the user switches the page to Edit mode, all Web parts in which editing is enabled display the edit verb. After the user selects the edit verb for a Web part, that Web part is then in Edit mode and the editing user interface appears for editing the selected Web part.

Similar to the approach used by Catalog mode, the user interface for editing is provided by an `EditorZone` control, which is declaratively added to the page. The `EditorZone` control can contain only `EditorPart` controls. Table 14.10 lists the available controls that are subclasses of the `EditorPart` class.

Table 14.10   EditorPart Controls

Name	Description
`AppearanceEditorPart`	Provides a user interface for editing appearance properties of a Web part.
`BehaviorEditorPart`	Provides a user interface for editing behavioral properties of a Web part.
`LayoutEditorPart`	Provides a user interface for editing the chrome state and the zone of a Web part. This part allows non-Internet Explorer users to change the layout of Web parts.
`PropertyGridEditorPart`	Provides a user interface for editing properties of a Web part that are marked in the source code with the `WebBrowsable` attribute.

Figure 14.16 illustrates how these controls might appear when rendered in the browser.

After the `EditorZone` control is added declaratively to the page, `EditorPart` controls can be added to the zone. For instance, in the following example, we have added an editor zone to the main area of our page that contains an `Appearance-EditorPart`, `BehaviorEditorPart`, and a `LayoutEditorPart`.

```
<asp:EditorZone ID="editZone" runat="server" >
   <ZoneTemplate>
      <asp:AppearanceEditorPart ID="partAppear" runat="server" />
      <asp:BehaviorEditorPart ID="partBehave" runat="server" />
      <asp:LayoutEditorPart ID="partLayout" runat="server" />
   </ZoneTemplate>
</asp:EditorZone>
```

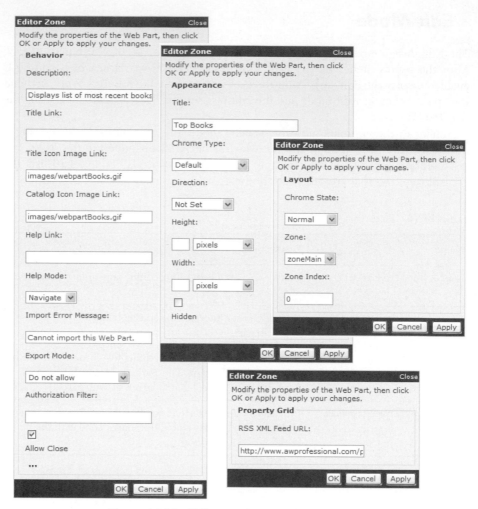

Figure 14.16   Different editor parts in the browser

Making the BehaviorEditorPart Appear

However, when you view this in the browser, only the `AppearanceEditorPart` and the `LayoutEditorPart` are actually visible. The reason for this is that changes made to the properties of a Web part via the `BehaviorEditorPart` affect not only the current user but *all* users. As such, the user must have shared scope before the `BehaviorEditorPart` control is visible.

You may recall from the earlier discussion on Web part personalization that, with shared scope, any changes that the user makes to the state of a Web part are visible to all users. By default, all users are denied access to shared scope. It might make sense, however, for site administrators to have shared scope so that they can make universal changes to a Web part with the `BehaviorEditorPart`.

There are two steps you must follow to have the `BehaviorEditorPart` control visible in your pages. First, you must allow users in the administrator role to have access to shared scope. You do this by adding the following section to your `Web.config` file.

```
<system.web>
    ...
    <webParts>
        <personalization>
            <authorization>
                <allow roles="Administrator"
                    verbs="enterSharedScope"/>
            </authorization>
        </personalization>
    </webParts>
</system.web>
```

Rather than allowing shared scope on a role basis, you could instead do so on a user-by-user basis.

```
<allow users="Hamlet,Plato" verbs="enterSharedScope"/>
```

The next step is to change the personalization scope of the page from user to shared scope. Perhaps the easiest way to do this is to add the following to the `Page_Load` method of the page.

```
protected void Page_Load(object sender, EventArgs e)
{
    ...

    // For users who are authorized to enter shared
    // personalization scope (that is, users who are allowed to
    // make changes that affect all users), change the page scope
    // from user scope to shared scope

    if (partManager.Personalization.Scope ==
        PersonalizationScope.User &&
        partManager.Personalization.CanEnterSharedScope)
    {
        partManager.Personalization.ToggleScope();
    }

}
```

Using the PropertyGridEditorPart

The `PropertyGridEditorPart` is a bit different from the other editor parts in that it does not present the user with a predefined set of properties. Instead, the `Property-GridEditorPart` allows the developer to display a list of custom properties to the user. This control displays all the properties in the Web part that have been marked with the `WebBrowsable` attribute (thus, the Web part has to be a user control or a custom control). When a property is marked with this attribute, a `PropertyGridEditorPart` creates the editing user interface based on the type of the property. For instance, strings, dates, and numbers are displayed in a `TextBox`, Booleans are displayed with a `Check-Box`, whereas enumerated types are displayed in a `DropDownList`.

You can add some other attributes to the properties of your Web part class to further customize how the control displays the editing interface. These include

- `WebDisplayName`—Allows you to specify the text for the label that appears with each control in the editing interface.
- `WebDescription`—Allows you to specify a string that appears as a `Tool-Tip` for each control.
- `Personalizable`—Allows you to specify the personalization scope for the property. If set to `PersonalizationScope.Shared`, the property is only displayed for users in shared scope (e.g., administrators).

Listing 14.8 contains a sample Web part custom control that illustrates the use of some of these attributes. This Web part displays an RSS feed. Unlike the custom control created in Listing 14.7, this one does not override the `RenderContents` method, but instead overrides the `CreateChildControls` method. The `Create-ChildControls` method allows you to programmatically create and set up existing server controls and then add them to the child control collection of the Web part; by doing so, you can let the child controls handle their own rendering. In the example shown in Listing 14.8, the `CreateChildControls` method uses an `Xml` server control along with an XSLT file to read and display several sample external RSS feeds. This control also presents two `WebBrowsable` properties: one for specifying which publisher's RSS feed to use, the other the filename of the XSLT file to use. The former is modifiable by all users, whereas the later is only available to administrators (i.e., users with shared scope).

Listing 14.8   PressReleaseRSS.cs

```
using System;
using System.Web;
using System.Web.UI;
using System.Web.UI.WebControls;
using System.Web.UI.WebControls.WebParts;
```

```
using System.Xml;
using System.Xml.XPath;
using System.Xml.Xsl;

namespace Chapter14
{
    /// <summary>
    /// Specifies the possible press release RSS feeds
    /// </summary>
    public enum PressReleaseRssFeeds
    {
        AddisonWesley, PeachPit, PrenticeHall, QuePublishing,
          SamsPublishing
    }

    public class PressReleaseRSS: WebPart
    {
        private string _xsltUrl =
            "~/RssTransformPressRelease.xslt";
        private PressReleaseRssFeeds _whichFeed =
            PressReleaseRssFeeds.AddisonWesley;

        // For simplicity's sake, we will hardcode the URLs for the
        // RSS feed, but it is better and more realistic
        // to extract from database or config file
        private string[] _rssUrls = {
            "http://www.awprofessional.com/press/press_rss.asp",
            "http://www.peachpit.com/press/press_rss.asp",
            "http://www.phptr.com/press/press_rss.asp",
            "http://www.quepublishing.com/press/press_rss.asp",
            "http://www.samspublishing.com/press/press_rss.asp"
        };

        public PressReleaseRSS()
        {
            Title = "Press Releases";
            Description = "Press releases from Pearson Ed";
            TitleIconImageUrl = "images/webpartNews.gif";
            CatalogIconImageUrl = "images/webpartNews.gif";
        }

        [Personalizable(PersonalizationScope.Shared),
          WebBrowsable, WebDisplayName("XSLT filename")]
        public string XsltUrl
        {
            get { return _xsltUrl; }
            set { _xsltUrl = value; }
        }
```

```
[Personalizable(PersonalizationScope.User),
  WebBrowsable, WebDisplayName("Press Release RSS Feed")]
public PressReleaseRssFeeds WhichFeed
{
    get { return _whichFeed; }
    set { _whichFeed = value; }
}

/// <summary>
/// Responsible for creating the content of the control
/// </summary>
protected override void CreateChildControls()
{
    // Create an XML Web server control
    Xml myXml = new Xml();

    // Get URL for selected feed
    string xmlurl = _rssUrls[(int)WhichFeed];

    // Create the XPathNavigator object
    XPathDocument xpdoc = new XPathDocument(xmlurl);
    XPathNavigator xnav = xpdoc.CreateNavigator();

    // Set up the XML control and apply XSLT transformation
    myXml.XPathNavigator = xnav;
    myXml.TransformSource =
      HttpContext.Current.Server.MapPath(XsltUrl);

    // Add XML control to the Web part's collection
    // of child controls
    Controls.Add(myXml);
    }
  }
}
```

With this control defined, you can now add it to a Web part page.

```
<%@ Register Namespace="Chapter14" TagPrefix="ch14" %>

…

<ch14:PressReleaseRSS ID="myPressRelease" runat="server"
   Title="Press releases"
   Description="Press releases from Pearson Ed"
   CatalogIconImageUrl="~/images/webpartNews.gif"
   TitleIconImageUrl="~/images/webpartNews.gif"
   WhichFeed="AddisonWesley"
   XsltUrl="~/RssTransformPressRelease.xsl" />
```

Figure 14.17 illustrates how the `PropertyGridEditorPart` editor part appears for the `PublisherRSSControl` Web part depending upon the scope of the user.

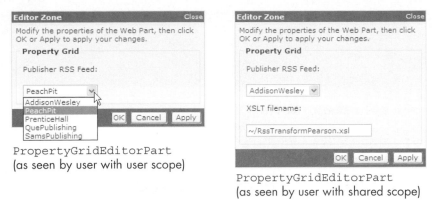

PropertyGridEditorPart
(as seen by user with user scope)

PropertyGridEditorPart
(as seen by user with shared scope)

Figure 14.17   PropertyGridEditorPart in the browser

Web Part Connections

The Web parts framework allows connections to be made between Web parts. When a part is enabled for connections, a user can create dynamic communication connections between the parts at runtime, as well as static, predefined connections declared in the markup of the page. You can also declare a user interface that enables users to manage connections and to connect or disconnect Web parts at runtime.

A **Web parts connection** is a link between two Web parts that enables them to share data. A connection always involves exactly two parts: one is the provider of data, and the other is the consumer of the data from the provider. A **provider Web part** can establish connections with multiple consumers at the same time. A **consumer Web part** connects to only one provider at a time. Any changes made to a provider are immediately consumed by any Web part consumers. Figure 14.18 illustrates a sample usage of Web parts connections. The provider in this example is the Select Publisher Web part; whenever the user selects a different publisher, the two consumer Web parts (View Books and News) are updated and display new data based on the user's selection.

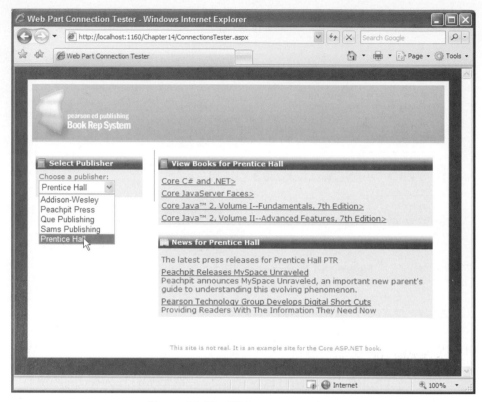

Figure 14.18   Web part connections

Creating a Static Connection

A Web part connection is either static or dynamic. **Static connections** are declared in the markup of the page by adding a `StaticConnection` element to the `WebPartManager`. Creating a static connection requires that you complete these four steps.

1. Define a C# `interface` that is the shared connection contract between the two Web parts. This interface defines the data that is passed between the two parts.

2. The provider Web part must implement this connection interface. As well, the provider must define a **connection point**. A connection point is a method that returns an instance of the class that implements the connection interface; in other words, it must return the provider object itself. This method must be marked with the `ConnectionProvider` attribute.

3. The consumer Web part must also define a connection point. In this case, it is a `void` method that accepts an object of the type defined by the `interface` from step 1. This object can then be used by the consumer to retrieve data from the provider Web part. This method must be marked with the `ConnectionConsumer` attribute.

4. You must declaratively define the static connections in the markup of the Web parts page by adding a `StaticConnection` element to the `WebPartManager`.

Figure 14.19 provides a visualization of how data flows via connection points between provider and consumer Web parts.

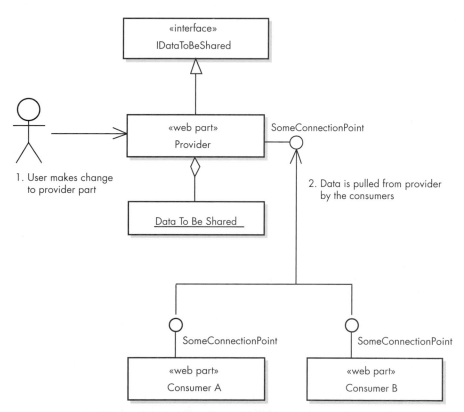

Figure 14.19 Data flow with Web part connections

Walkthroughs 14.1 through 14.3 demonstrate how to set up two Web part connections. These create the controls and the connections necessary to implement the example shown in Figure 14.18.

Walkthrough 14.1   *Defining the Interface and the Provider Web Part*

In this example, we pass a `Publisher` object that represents the selected publisher from part to part.

1. Create a new class in the `App_Code` folder named `ISelectPublisher.cs`.

2. Change the code to that shown in the following. As you can see, the `interface` defines a single property named `ChosenPublisher` that returns a `Publisher` object (defined in the `FourLayer.Business-Entity` namespace).

```
using FourLayer.BusinessEntity;

namespace Chapter14
{
    /// <summary>
    /// Defines the shared connection contract between the
    /// SelectPublisherProvider and its consumers
    /// </summary>
    public interface ISelectPublisher
    {
        Publisher ChosenPublisher { get; }
    }
}
```

3. Create a new class in the `App_Code` folder named `SelectPublisher-Provider.cs`. This custom control is the provider in your example.

4. Change the code to the following. It consists of a drop-down list of publishers in your books database. Notice that this class inherits not only from the `WebPart` class but also from the `ISelectPublisher` interface that you just defined.

```
using System;
using System.Web;
using System.Web.UI;
using System.Web.UI.WebControls;
using System.Web.UI.WebControls.WebParts;

using FourLayer.ApplicationLogic;
using FourLayer.BusinessEntity;

namespace Chapter14
{
    public class SelectPublisherProvider : WebPart,
        ISelectPublisher
    {
```

```
        DropDownList _drpPublishers;

        public SelectPublisherProvider()
        {
            Title = "Select Publisher";
            Description =
                "Select publisher for connections testing";
            TitleIconImageUrl = "images/webpartBooks.gif";
            CatalogIconImageUrl = "images/webpartBooks.gif";
        }

        protected override void CreateChildControls()
        {
            _drpPublishers = new DropDownList();
            _drpPublishers.AutoPostBack = true;

            // Get all the publishers
            EntityCollection<Publisher> pubs =
                BookCatalogLogic.GetAllPublishers();

            // Set up the drop-down list. Notice that its value
            // field is the integer publisher ID, whereas the
            // text field is the publisher name
            _drpPublishers.DataTextField = "Name";
            _drpPublishers.DataValueField = "Id";
            _drpPublishers.DataSource = pubs;
            _drpPublishers.DataBind();

            Literal lit = new Literal();
            lit.Text = "Choose a publisher: ";

            Controls.Add(lit);
            Controls.Add(_drpPublishers);
        }
    }
}
```

5. You must now add the property defined in the `ISelectPublisher` interface. This property returns a populated `Publisher` object based on the current value of the publisher drop-down list.

```
/// <summary>
/// Implementation of method defined in ISelectPublisher
/// </summary>
public Publisher ChosenPublisher
{
    get {
```

```
      // Return a publisher object for the selected ID
      int pubId = Convert.ToInt32(
         _drpPublishers.SelectedValue);
      return BookCatalogLogic.GetPublisherById(pubId);
   }
}
```

6. Finally, you must define a connection point for this provider class. This method simply returns this instance of the provider as defined by your connection interface. It must also be marked with the `Connection-Provider` attribute.

```
/// <summary>
/// Defines the connection point
/// </summary>
[ConnectionProvider("SelectedPublisherConnectionPoint")]
public ISelectPublisher SupplyProvider()
{
   return this;
}
```

CORE NOTE

It does not matter what name you give the connection point method in either the provider or the consumer class. It only matters that they are marked with the `ConnectionProvider` and `ConnectionConsumer` attributes, respectively.

Walkthrough 14.2 *Defining a Consumer Web Part*

This consumer Web part displays a list of books for the publisher selected by the user in the `SelectPublisher` Web part.

1. Create a new class in the `App_Code` folder named `BookListConsumer.cs`.

2. Change the code to the following. This Web part handles its own rendering. It renders a list of book title links that match the selected publisher. Notice that the selected publisher is contained in a private data member available via the `PublisherToUse` property.

```
using System;
using System.Collections;
using System.Web;
using System.Web.UI;
```

```
using System.Web.UI.WebControls;
using System.Web.UI.WebControls.WebParts;

using FourLayer.ApplicationLogic;
using FourLayer.BusinessEntity;

namespace Chapter14
{
    public class BookListConsumer : WebPart
    {
        private Publisher _publisher = null;

        public BookListConsumer()
        {
            Title = "View Books";
            Description = "Views all books";
            TitleIconImageUrl = "images/webpartBooks.gif";
            CatalogIconImageUrl = "images/webpartBooks.gif";
        }

        public Publisher PublisherToUse
        {
            get { return _publisher; }
            set {
                _publisher = value;
                Title = "View Books for " + _publisher.Name;
            }
        }

        protected override void RenderContents(
            HtmlTextWriter writer)
        {
            // Retrieve books for the selected publisher
            EntityCollection<Book> books =
                BookCatalogLogic.GetBooksByPublisher(
                    PublisherToUse.Id);

            // Display no more than the first 10 matches
            int max = 10;
            if (max > books.Count) max = books.Count;
            string output = "<div id='listContainer'>";
            for (int i = 0; i < max; i++)
            {
                Book book = books[i];
                output += "<p><a href=BookDetails.aspx?id=";
                output += book.Isbn + ">";
                output += book.Title;
```

```
            output += "></p>";
        }
        output += "</div>";
        writer.Write(output);
    }


}
}
```

Notice that in the `RenderContents` method defined in the preceding, it retrieves a collection of books that match the `Id` of the `_publisher` data member (via the `PublisherToUse` property). What populates this data member? You must define a connection point that populates this member.

3. You must now define the connection point shown here for this consumer. It simply saves in a data member the reference (i.e., the interface) to your provider.

```
private ISelectPublisher _pubInterface;

[ConnectionConsumer("SelectedPublisherConnectionPoint")]
public void GetProvider(ISelectPublisher pubInterface)
{
    _pubInterface = pubInterface;
}
```

4. You now need to retrieve the `Publisher` object from the provider using this `_pubInterface` data member. When should you do this? You need to retrieve the `Publisher` object before the `RenderContents` method is invoked (because it uses this object). Perhaps the best choice is to perform this retrieval in the `OnPreRender` event of the control, which is invoked before `RenderContents`. Add this method, shown in the following, to your class.

```
/// <summary>
/// Retrieves the Publisher from the provider
/// </summary>
protected override void OnPreRender(EventArgs e)
{
    if (_pubInterface != null)
    {
        PublisherToUse = _pubInterface.ChosenPublisher;
    }
}
```

Walkthrough 14.3 *Defining Another Consumer Web Part*

This consumer Web part displays the RSS feed defined for the publisher selected by the user in the `SelectPublisher` Web part.

1. Create a new class in the `App_Code` folder named `PublisherRSS-Consumer.cs`.

2. Change the code to the following. Notice that this control is using `CreateChildControls` rather than rendering the contents itself. Instead of using an `OnPreRender` handler to retrieve the `Publisher` object from the provider, it does so directly within the `CreateChild-Controls` method.

```
using System;
using System.Web;
using System.Web.UI;
using System.Web.UI.WebControls;
using System.Web.UI.WebControls.WebParts;

using System.Xml;
using System.Xml.XPath;
using System.Xml.Xsl;

using FourLayer.ApplicationLogic;
using FourLayer.BusinessEntity;

namespace Chapter14
{
    public class PublisherRSSConsumer : WebPart
    {
        private string _xsltUrl =
            "~/RssTransformPressRelease.xsl";
        private ISelectPublisher _pubInterface;

        public PublisherRSSConsumer()
        {
            Title = "News";
            Description = "News for Publisher";
            TitleIconImageUrl = "images/webpartNews.gif";
            CatalogIconImageUrl = "images/webpartNews.gif";
        }

        [Personalizable(PersonalizationScope.Shared),
          WebBrowsable, WebDisplayName("XSLT filename")]
        public string XsltUrl
        {
```

```
      get { return _xsltUrl; }
      set { _xsltUrl = value; }
   }

   protected override void CreateChildControls()
   {
      // Create an XML Web server control
      Xml myXml = new Xml();

      // Set up the XML control using the select
      // publisher provider
      if (_pubInterface != null)
      {
         // Get the publisher from the provider
         Publisher p = _pubInterface.ChosenPublisher;
         if (p != null)
         {
            Title = "News for " + p.Name;

            // Use the RSS URL defined for the publisher
            XPathDocument xpdoc =
               new XPathDocument(p.RssUrl);

            // Set up the path navigator for this XML
            // document
            XPathNavigator xnav = xpdoc.CreateNavigator();
            myXml.XPathNavigator = xnav;

            // Specify XSLT file
            myXml.TransformSource =
               HttpContext.Current.Server.MapPath(XsltUrl);
         }
      }
      // Add XML control to the Web part's collection
      // of controls
      Controls.Add(myXml);
   }

   [ConnectionConsumer("SelectedPublisherConnectionPoint")]
   public void GetProvider(ISelectPublisher pubInterface)
   {
      _pubInterface = pubInterface;
   }
  }
}
```

Walkthrough 14.4 *Creating the Web Part Page with Static Connections*

Finally, you are ready to create the Web part page that uses these Web parts and which demonstrates how static connections are declared.

1. Create a new page named `ConnectionsTester.aspx`.

2. Change the markup so that it is similar to that shown here. Although you can create any layout you want, the bolded markup in the code that follows is necessary.

```
<%@ Page Language="C#" AutoEventWireup="true"
    Theme="WebPartDemo"
    CodeFile="ConnectionsTester.aspx.cs"
    Inherits="ConnectionsTester" %>

<%@ Register Namespace="Chapter14" TagPrefix="ch14" %>

<!DOCTYPE html PUBLIC "-//W3C//DTD XHTML 1.0 Transitional//EN"
    "http://www.w3.org/TR/xhtml11/DTD/xhtml11-transitional.dtd">
<html xmlns="http://www.w3.org/1999/xhtml">
<head id="Head1" runat="server">
    <title>Web Part Connection Tester</title>
    <link href="chapterStyles.css" type="text/css"
rel="stylesheet"  />
</head>
<body id="body1" runat="server" >
    <form id="form1" runat="server">
    <asp:WebPartManager ID="partManager" runat="server" >
    </asp:WebPartManager>
    <div id="container">
        <div id="header">
           <div id="theme"></div>
           <div id="logo">
              <asp:Image runat="server" ID="imgLogo"
                 SkinID="logo" />
           </div>
        </div>
        <div id="sideArea">
           <asp:WebPartZone ID="zoneSide" runat="server">
              <ZoneTemplate>
                 <ch14:SelectPublisherProvider
                    ID="mySelectPublisher"
                    runat="server" />
              </ZoneTemplate>
           </asp:WebPartZone>
        </div>
```

```
        <div id="mainArea">
            <asp:WebPartZone ID="zoneMain" runat="server">
                <ZoneTemplate>
                    <ch14:BookListConsumer id="myBookViewer"
                        runat="server"/>
                    <ch14:PublisherRSSConsmer ID="myPublisherRSS"
                        runat="server" />
                </ZoneTemplate>
            </asp:WebPartZone>
        </div>
        <div id="footer">
            <p>…</p>
        </div>
    </div>
    </form>
</body>
</html>
```

3. Modify the `WebPartManager` by adding the following static connection information.

```
<asp:WebPartManager ID="partManager" runat="server" >
    <StaticConnections>
        <asp:WebPartConnection ID="conn1"
            ProviderID="mySelectPublisher"
            ConsumerID="myBookViewer" />
        <asp:WebPartConnection ID="conn2"
            ProviderID="mySelectPublisher"
            ConsumerID="myPublisherRSS" />
    </StaticConnections>
</asp:WebPartManager>
```

4. Test in browser. The result should look similar to that shown in Figure 14.18 on page 890.

After examining the code for these sample provider and consumers Web parts, you may wonder when the connection between the provider and consumer is made during the page's lifecycle. It is made during the page's `LoadComplete` event. This event fires after all postback data and view-state data is loaded into the page and its controls. This means that your page cannot rely on the connection within the page's `PreInit`, `Init`, `PreLoad`, or `Load` event handlers.

Making Static Connections with Master Pages

When I introduced the Web parts framework, I mentioned that each page must have one and only one `WebPartManager`. This can be a problem for some designs, particularly those using master pages. When designing a site with master pages, it is usual to put elements that are common to all pages within a master page. In such a situation, it might make sense to place the `WebPartManager` within the master page. How then can you define Web part connections in your content pages if the `WebPartManager` exists in a separate file?

The `ProxyWebPartManager` control exists for this particular situation in which you need to declare static connections in content pages when a `WebPartManager` control has already been declared in a master page. The `ProxyWebPartManager` control takes the place of the `WebPartManager` control in this scenario. By declaring a `ProxyWebPartManager` element instead of a `WebPartManager` element within content pages, you can still define static connections, as shown in the following example.

```
<asp:ProxyWebPartManager ID="myProxy" runat="server">
   <StaticConnections>
      <asp:WebPartConnection ID="conn3"
         ProviderID="someProvider"
         ConsumerID="someConsumer" />
   </StaticConnections>
</asp:ProxyWebPartManager>
```

At runtime, the connections in the `ProxyWebPartManager` control are simply added to the `StaticConnections` collection of the `WebPartManager` control and treated like any other connection.

Creating a Dynamic Connection

Although static connections make sense for most situations, there are times when a page is unable to create static connections. For instance, recall that it is possible for the user to add a Web part that requires a connection via the Web part catalog. In such a case, you are unable to statically predefine the connection because static connections can only be made between Web parts that are declared within `WebPartZone` elements. Another situation in which you might need to use *dynamic connections* is a page whose Web parts have been programmatically added.

To allow the user to make dynamic connections, you must still follow the first three steps indicated in the section on setting up static connections. Instead of adding the declarative `StaticConnections` element, however, all you must do here as a developer is add a `ConnectionsZone` control to the page. This control can be styled like the other Web parts controls. After this control is added to the page, the user must follow these steps for each connection.

1. Change the page to Connect mode (of course, this presumes that the page contains some mechanism for doing so).

2. From the consumer Web part, choose the Connect verb. This displays the Connection Zone part.

3. In the Connection Zone part, the user must choose the provider connection from the list of available provider connections for the page and click the Connect button. This connects just the two parts.

4. The user can optionally disconnect the connection or close the Connection Zone.

Figure 14.20 illustrates how this process appears in the browser.

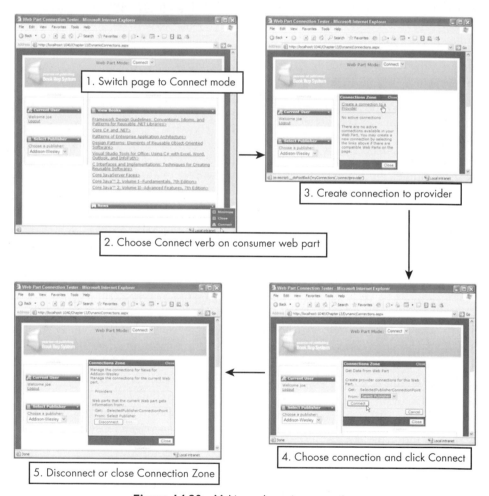

Figure 14.20 Making a dynamic connection

Summary

This chapter examined two mechanisms in ASP.NET 2.0 for integrating user personalization into a Web application. The profile system allows an application to persist user information across time and across multiple pages. The Web part framework provides the developer with a mechanism for creating pages in which the user can customize the placement, appearance, and possibly the behavior of the page's content.

The next chapter examines Web services, a powerful feature that has been an integral part of ASP.NET since its introduction. Web services are often used in conjunction with Web parts.

Exercises

The solutions to the following exercises can be found at my Web site, http://www.randyconnolly.com/core. Additional exercises only available for teachers and instructors are also available from this site.

1. Create a profile-based shopping cart. This requires a products listing page, a single product page in which the user can add to the cart, and a view cart page in which the user can view and remove items from the cart. You can use the book catalog database as the data source.

2. Create a page that allows administrators to view, edit, or delete anonymous and authenticated profiles. This page should allow the user to filter the profiles by some type of user-entered date range.

3. Make a new RSS user control that displays one of the Amazon RSS feeds (see www.amazon.com/exec/obidos/subst/xs/syndicate.html). This control should have a property named RssFeed, which contains the RSS URL and can be changed by the user via a PropertyGrid-EditorPart. Integrate this control with the Web part page created in Walkthrough 14.4.

The next exercises use the ModernEyeCatalog database.

4. Create a Web part page that displays information from the Modern-EyeCatalog database. It must consist of the following Web parts that you must create (using either user or custom controls): a Menu part, a Login part, an Artist List part, a List of the Top 10 Keywords part, and a List of the Top 10 Works of Art part. Finally, this page should contain a catalog.

5. Create a Select Keyword part and a Art Words By Keyword part. Implement a static connection between the two parts, with the Select Keyword part the connection provider.

Key Concepts

- Anonymous access
- Anonymous identification
- Catalog
- Chrome
- Connection point
- Consumer Web part
- Dynamic connections
- Globally unique identifier (GUID)
- Personalization information
- Portal
- Provider Web part
- Shared scope
- Static connections
- User scope
- Verbs
- Web part display mode
- Web part manager
- Web parts
- Web parts connection
- Web parts framework
- Web parts personalization
- Web part zone

References

Allen, K. Scott. "Profiles in ASP.NET 2.0." http://www.odetocode.com.

Esposito, Dino. "Personalization and User Profiles in ASP.NET 2.0." *MSDN Magazine* (October 2005).

Onion, Fritz. "Asynchronous Web Parts." *MSDN Magazine* (July 2006).

Pattison, Ted. "Introducing ASP.NET Web Part Connections." *MSDN Magazine* (February 2006).

Pattison, Ted and Onion, Fritz. "Personalize Your Portal with User Controls and Custom Web Parts." *MSDN Magazine* (September 2005).

Walther, Stephen. "Introducing the ASP.NET 2.0 Web Parts Framework." http://msdn.microsoft.com.

Chapter 15

WEB SERVICES

"Small service is true service while it lasts. Of humblest friends, bright
Creature! scorn not one . . . "
—William Wordsworth, "To a Child. Written in her Album," 1834

The typical Web service is indeed a small but true service and it plays an important part in the networked and cooperating Web application architecture of the present day. And far from being scorned, Web services are one of the hottest—or certainly the most hyped—new technologies within the software application world. But what exactly are Web services?

This chapter introduces the technologies behind Web services as well as explains the role that Web services play in the present day application development environment. The chapter then moves on to demonstrate how to use Web services synchronously and asynchronously with ASP.NET. The examples in this chapter illustrate how to consume a mapping service from Microsoft, a weather service from WebserviceX, and a book service from Amazon. The chapter also covers how to create your own Web services. It demonstrates how to create a Web service that retrieves famous quotes from an XML file, as well as a book information service that uses our own database and application infrastructure from Chapter 11.

Introduction to Web Services

At the most general level, Web services refers to a computing paradigm that utilizes something called "services" as a key element in the development and operation of applications. A ***service*** is a piece of software with a platform-independent interface that can be dynamically located and invoked. ***Web services*** are thus a standardized mechanism by which one software application can connect to and communicate with another software application. Web services make use of the HTTP protocol so that they can be used by any computer with Internet connectivity. As well, Web services use standard XML to encode data within HTTP transmissions so that almost any platform should be able to encode or retrieve the data contained within a Web service.

Besides HTTP and XML, Web services are usually built on two additional platform-independent XML-based grammars: WSDL and SOAP. ***WSDL (Web Services Description Language)*** describes the operations provided by a service. It is an XML document that uses XML Schema to describe the data types and signatures of the operations provided by a Web service. ***SOAP (Simple Object Access Protocol)*** is the message protocol used by Web services; it is an XML-based protocol that encodes the service invocations and their return values within the HTTP header. Figure 15.1 illustrates how WSDL and SOAP are used in the consumption of a Web service.

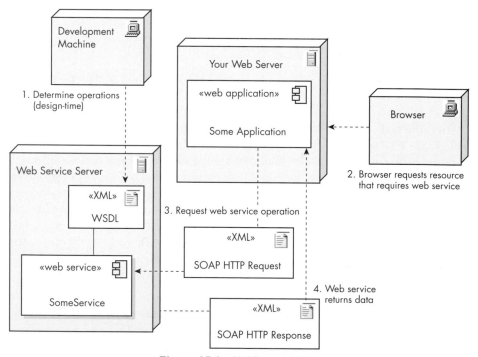

Figure 15.1   WSDL and SOAP

Besides WSDL and SOAP, there are additional Web services specifications. Representational State Transfer (REST) provides an alternative to SOAP for passing information to and from a Web service. Some other optional specifications define functionality for Web services discovery, adding binary attachments, and implementing security and transactions.

Although Web services are by design platform-independent, some platforms make it easier to construct and consume them. One of the great strengths of the .NET Framework in general and ASP.NET in particular is its strong support for SOAP-based Web services and the ease with which you can consume or create Web services.

Benefits of Web Services

The benefit of Web services is that they potentially provide interoperability between different software applications running on different platforms. Because Web services use common and universally supported standards (HTTP and XML), they can be supported on a wide variety of platforms. Another key benefit of Web services is that they can be used to implement something called a ***service-oriented architecture (SOA)***. This type of software architecture aims to achieve very loose coupling among interacting software services. The rationale behind an SOA is one that is familiar to computing practitioners with some experience in the enterprise: namely, how to best deal with the problem of application integration. Due to corporate mergers, longer-lived legacy applications, and the need to integrate with the Internet, getting different software applications to work together has become a major priority of IT organizations. SOA provides a very palatable potential solution to application integration issues. Because services are independent software entities, they can be offered by different systems within an organization as well as by different organizations. As such, Web services can provide a computing infrastructure for application integration and collaboration within and between organizations, as shown in Figure 15.2.

CORE NOTE

For more information on SOA, see Thomas Erl's *Service-Oriented Architecture*, listed in the References at the end of the chapter.

So who is using Web services? It is important to remember that Web services are not a consumer product, but a series of technologies that enable heterogeneous software applications to communicate. As such, the use of Web services is not usually visible to the end-user, although the end result of an application using Web services may be visible.

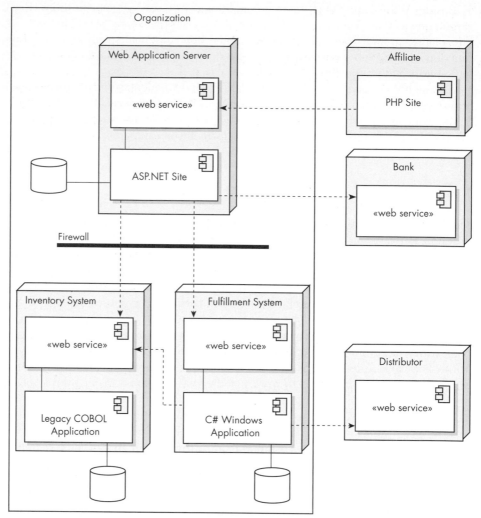

Figure 15.2 Web services-enabled integration

Sites that you visit may well be using Web services from other providers behind the scenes. Some of these providers offer useful discrete bits of functionality that other sites can use, such as the current weather, financial stock lookups, and current news flashes. Other sites, such as Amazon, eBay, Google, and PayPal, offer more comprehensive Web services that provide a programmatic interface to the key functionality of these sites. For instance, by using Amazon Web Services (AWS), developers can access Amazon's entire product data line as well as several business processes, ranging from retrieving information about a set of products, adding an item to a shopping cart, and storing and retrieving data objects up to five gigabytes in size.

As illustrated in Figure 15.2, Web services are also used as a means of integrating different computer systems within an organization. A single organization might add Web service interfaces to their existing applications so that these applications can share data between them and facilitate interapplication workflow. Web services are also used to enable process integration and data sharing between organizations. For instance, the Xbox Live subscription-based online gaming Web service for Xbox and Xbox 360 video game consoles exposes a collection of Web services that are used by game publishers and developers to store and retrieve game data and manage user accounts.

Consuming Web Services

Consuming (i.e., using) a Web service in your ASP.NET Web application is quite painless and straightforward to implement. Fortunately, your applications do not have to worry about parsing and decoding the XML in the WSDL and SOAP streams. Instead, your application interacts with something called a local proxy class that is generated at design time by the .NET Framework from the service's WSDL document. A *proxy* is a class that functions as an interface to some other thing. This local proxy class acts as a surrogate for the Web service and handles the actual interaction with the external Web service. Thus, your application interacts with the Web service as if it were a local object by instantiating and using the proxy, as shown in Figure 15.3.

How to Consume a Web Service Using Visual Studio

The first step in using a Web service in your ASP.NET application is to add a *Web reference* in Visual Studio. When you add a Web reference in Visual Studio, it generates the Web service proxy class and creates a reference to it. This proxy class contains methods that replicate the functionality described by the service's WSDL document. For instance, in the example shown in Figure 15.3, the sample Web service has two operations; the proxy generates a method for each operation in the service (as well as a version that allows the developer to asynchronously invoke the operation). Similarly, the proxy also contains any complex data types needed to represent any complex type defined by the Web service. The proxy also handles the marshalling of the method arguments back and forth between the Web service and your application.

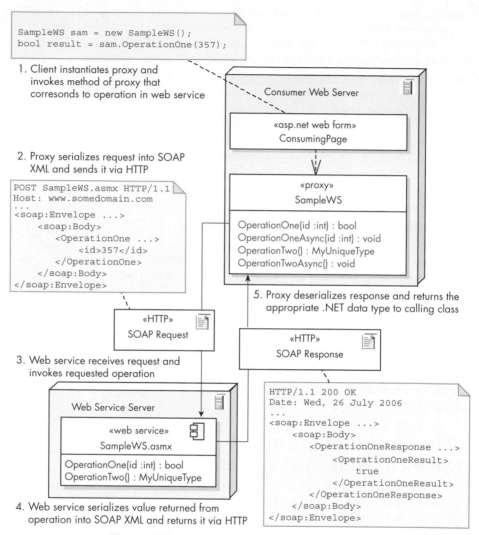

Figure 15.3   Consuming Web services in ASP.NET

To illustrate this process, let us consume Microsoft's TerraService. TerraService is operated by the Microsoft Corporation as a database research project. The Terra-Service Web site provides free public access to a vast SQL Server database of maps and aerial photographs of the United States. The site provides a Web service interface to this data, thus allowing Web developers to integrate TerraServer data into their own applications.

CORE NOTE

As with any external Web service, it is possible that the URL or the API for the TerraService could change in the future.

As mentioned, the first step in using a Web service is to add a Web reference. This is done by right-clicking the solution or project in the Solution Explorer, and choosing the Add Web Reference menu option. Visual Studio then displays the Add Web Reference dialog. In the URL box, you must enter the URL of the Web service to be consumed. This is generally the URL of the WSDL document; for this example, enter `http://terraservice.net/TerraService2.asmx`. After entering the URL of the Web service, click the Go button to see the operations provided by the service (see Figure 15.4). If this is the Web service you require, simply clicking the Add Reference button finishes the process.

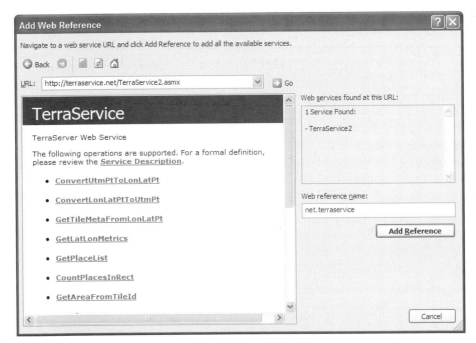

Figure 15.4   Adding a Web reference

CORE NOTE

If your development machine is behind a firewall, and your application is consuming a Web service found outside of the firewall, you may also need to include the address and port of your network's proxy server in the URL.

Visual Studio creates a folder named `App_WebReferences` to your application that contains all Web references for your application, and within that folder, another folder for the particular Web service. As well, Visual Studio also generates three other files: a local copy of the external Web service's WSDL document as well as one or two files to aid in the discovery of the Web service. The proxy class for this service is also generated, but is not visible within Visual Studio; instead, it is generated, compiled, and placed within an assembly within the `Temporary ASP.NET Files` folder for the application. As well, an entry is added to the application's `Web.config` file that records the URL of the WSDL document for this Web reference.

CORE NOTE

You can also create the proxy without using Visual Studio by using the .NET Framework `WSDL.EXE` command-line program.

After adding the Web reference, you can use it in your application. For instance, let us create a sample page that uses the `GetPlaceFact` operation of the Terra-Service Web service to retrieve the latitude and longitude of a city in the United States. The markup for this page might look like the following.

```
City:   <asp:TextBox ID="txtCity" runat="server" /><br />
State:  <asp:TextBox ID="txtState" runat="server" /><br />

<asp:Button ID="btnLookup" runat="server" Text="Lookup"
  OnClick="btnLookup_Click" />
<br />
<asp:Label ID="labResult" runat="server" />
```

The code-behind for this page contains the following.

```
using System;
...

using net.terraservice;

public partial class TerraServiceTester : System.Web.UI.Page
{
```

```
protected void btnLookup_Click(object sender, EventArgs e)
{
    try
    {
        // Create the TerraService proxy
        TerraService ts = new TerraService();

        // Create and populate a TerraService place
        Place aPlace = new Place();
        aPlace.City = txtCity.Text;
        aPlace.State = txtState.Text;
        aPlace.Country = "USA";

        // Get facts about this place from Web service
        PlaceFacts facts = ts.GetPlaceFacts(aPlace);

        // Output the results
        labResult.Text += "Place Location: ";
        labResult.Text += facts.Center.Lat + "&deg; / ";
        labResult.Text += facts.Center.Lon + "&deg;";
    }
    catch (Exception ex)
    {
        labResult.Text = ex.Message;
        return;
    }
}
}
```

Notice the reference to the `web.terraservice` namespace. This namespace is defined in the proxy class and is visible with the Solution Explorer (see Figure 15.5).

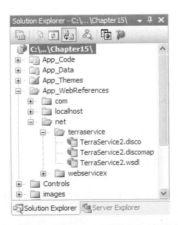

Figure 15.5   Web references within the Solution Explorer

As you type in this code, Visual Studio makes all the methods and data types in the service available via its Intellisense feature. Notice as well that this code uses exception handling. Any time your application needs to access an externality such as a Web service or a database, you should always code defensively and wrap the usage of the externality within a try...catch block.

At any rate, that is all the coding you need to do. The result when run in the browser is shown in Figure 15.6.

Figure 15.6   Consuming Microsoft's TerraService Web service

The complete simplicity of programming the consumption of Web services in ASP.NET masks the fact that the proxy class and the various other .NET classes it is using are doing a great deal of work behind the scenes. When I first started teaching Web services in 2001 (before ASP.NET), it took almost half a semester to get my students to the point where they could consume a Web service. They first had to learn how to parse XML, how to decode a SOAP envelope, and how to use reflection to dynamically create objects from a WSDL document. Now with the .NET Framework and its tools, you can work with external Web services easily and simply as if they were local objects.

Consuming Web Services in a User Control

Because a Web service is a discrete block of external functionality that clients can utilize, it makes sense to encapsulate the retrieval and display of data from a Web service within either a user or a custom control. The next two examples illustrate the use of Web services in user controls. Walkthrough 15.1 is a more detailed example that displays the current weather of the user's city based upon the user's profile; the second is a series of listings for an example that displays data from Amazon about a book selected from our book database.

CORE NOTE

Walkthrough 15.1 uses a weather service from an external provider. It is possible that the URL or API for this service could change in the future. As a result, this code may not always work in the future.

Walkthrough 15.1 *Creating a Current Weather User Control*

In this example, we create a user control that displays the current weather based on a user profile setting. It uses a free Web service available from WebserviceX.NET.

1. Add the following entries to the `Web.config` file.

```
<anonymousIdentification enabled="true" />
<profile>
    <properties>
        <add name="City" defaultValue="Denver"
            allowAnonymous="true"
            type="string" />
    </properties>
</profile>
```

2. Create a Web reference in Visual Studio by right-clicking the solution or project in the Solution Explorer, and choosing the Add Web Reference menu option.

3. Enter `http://www.webservicex.net/WeatherForecast.asmx?WSDL` into the URL, click Go, and then click Add Reference.

4. Create a user control named `ShowWeatherControl.ascx`.

5. Add the following markup to this user control.

```
<div class="box">
    <div id="weatherBox">
        <asp:Image ID="imgWeather" runat="server" />
        <div id="weatherText">
            <h2><asp:Label ID="labWeather" runat="server" /></h2>
            <asp:Label ID="labCity" runat="server" />
        </div>
        <div id="weatherDate">
```

```
            <asp:Label ID="labDate" runat="server" />
        </div>
        <p class="error">
        <asp:Label ID="labError" runat="server" />
        </p>
    </div>
</div>
```

6. Add the following namespace reference to your code-behind class.

```
// This namespace set up for us via Add Web Reference
using net.webservicex.www;
```

7. Add the following to the control's `Page_Load` event handler.

```csharp
public partial class ShowWeatherControl :
System.Web.UI.UserControl
{
    protected void Page_Load(object sender, EventArgs e)
    {
        if (!IsPostBack)
        {
            try
            {
                // Create the weather forecast proxy
                WeatherForecast weatherService =
                    new WeatherForecast();

                // Use current city profile setting for this user
                string city = Profile.City;

                // Get the weather forecast for this city
                WeatherForecasts forecasts =
                    weatherService.GetWeatherByPlaceName(city);

                // Only interested in today's date
                WeatherData today = forecasts.Details[0];
                labCity.Text = city;
                labWeather.Text = today.MinTemperatureF;
                imgWeather.ImageUrl = today.WeatherImage;
                labWeather.Text += "&deg;F / " +
                    today.MaxTemperatureF + "&deg;F";
                labDate.Text = today.Day;
            }
            catch (Exception ex)
            {
            labError.Text = ex.Message;
            return;
            }
        }
    }
}
```

8. Create a test page named `ControlTester.aspx`.

9. Register the user controls as follows.

```
<%@ Register Src=" ShowWeatherControl.ascx"
    TagName="ShowWeatherControl" TagPrefix="uc" %>
```

10. Add the user control to your page.

```
<uc:ShowWeatherControl ID="myWeather" runat="server" />
```

11. Add the following styles to your page.

```
<style type="text/css">
    div.box { border: solid 1pt silver; margin: 1em;
        padding: 0.5em; width: 14em;
    }

    #weatherBox { margin: 0; padding: 0.5em;
        background-color: #CEDCE7;}
    #weatherBox  img { float:left; width:55px; }
    #weatherText { float:right; width:8em; }
    #weatherDate { clear:both; font-size: 0.7em;
        margin-top: 0.25em; }
</style>
```

Test in browser. The result should look similar to that shown in Figure 15.7.

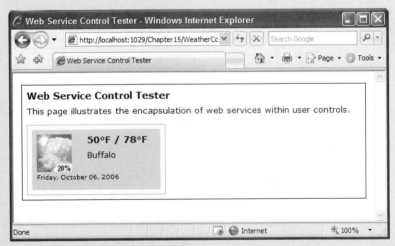

Figure 15.7   Weather Web service user control in browser

Consuming the Amazon Web Service

In the next example, we are going to create a user control that uses the more complex *Amazon Web Services (AWS)* to display a book cover and a link to a detail page at www.amazon.com. As well, the control has the option to display some user reviews. Figure 15.8 illustrates how this control appears in the browser.

Figure 15.8   Amazon Web service user control in browser

Although it is free to use the AWS, you must first apply for your own unique developer's access key (via https://aws-portal.amazon.com/gp/aws/developer/registration/index.html). There are a variety of rules and conditions that must be followed when using AWS, such as not exceeding one Web service call per second per IP address, not saving the data to a database, and not caching data for more than 24 hours.

After you have obtained your AWS access key, you can create your user control. As with our previous examples, the first step is to add a Web reference in Visual Studio to the Amazon WSDL. At the time of writing this chapter, the URL for this document is:

```
http://webservices.amazon.com/AWSECommerceService/
AWSECommerceService.wsdl
```

Amazon does occasionally update and modify the WSDL document for its services. By the time you are reading this book, it is possible that the chapter's Amazon example may no longer work with the most recent WSDL. Fortunately, Amazon maintains older versions of its WSDL documents. If you do need to use the WSDL that was current when this chapter was written, you can use the following URL:

```
http://webservices.amazon.com/AWSECommerceService/2006-05-17/
AWSECommerceService.wsd
```

Your Amazon user control displays information from Amazon about a particular book. This user control needs access to the developer's access key. For this example, you place this key within the `Web.config` file in the `appSettings` section, as shown in the following.

```
<configuration>
   <system.web>
     ...
   </system.web>
   <appSettings>
     ...
     <add key="AWSaccessKey"
        value="your access key goes here" />
   </appSettings>
</configuration>
```

You can then retrieve this key value via the `WebConfigurationManager` class (which is in the `System.Web.configuration` namespace), as shown in the following.

```
string myKey = WebConfigurationManager.AppSettings["AWSaccessKey"];
```

Listing 15.1 contains the straightforward markup for this control. Other than some structural `<div>` elements, the user control consists of an `Image`, `HyperLink`, `LinkButton`, and `Panel` controls. The `Image` control eventually displays the book image from Amazon, whereas the `HyperLink` contains the book title and a link to the details page on the Amazon site for the book. The `Panel` control contains a `Repeater` that displays customer reviews for the book from Amazon. This `Panel` is initially hidden; the user can toggle its visibility via the `LinkButton`.

Listing 15.1 AmazonBookControl.ascx

```
<%@ Control Language="C#" AutoEventWireup="true"
    CodeFile="AmazonBookControl.ascx.cs"
    Inherits="AmazonBookControl" %>
```

```
<div class="box">
   <div id="amazonBox">
      <h2>Amazon</h2>
      <div id="amazonImage">
         <asp:Image ID="imgBook" runat="server" />
      </div>
      <asp:HyperLink ID="hypTitle" runat="server"
            CssClass="amazonTitle"/>
      <p>
      <asp:LinkButton ID="lnkReviews" runat="server"
            OnClick="lnkReviews_Click" CssClass="amazonButton"/>
      </p>
      <asp:Panel ID="panReviews" runat="server"
            CssClass="amazonReviewPanel">
         <asp:Repeater ID="rptReviews" runat="server">
            <HeaderTemplate>
               <ul class="amazonReviewList">
            </HeaderTemplate>
            <ItemTemplate>
               <li><%# Eval("Summary") %></li>
            </ItemTemplate>
            <FooterTemplate>
               </ul>
            </FooterTemplate>
         </asp:Repeater>
      </asp:Panel>
      <p class="error">
      <asp:Label ID="labError" runat="server" />
      </p>
   </div>
</div>
```

Listing 15.2 contains the code-behind class for this user control. It exposes a public property named ISBN that is used to specify the book to display. As well, it contains a public method (RefreshControlFromAmazon) that refreshes the user control with data from the AWS.

Listing 15.2 AmazonBookControl.ascx.cs

```
using System;
using System.Data;
using System.Configuration;
using System.Collections;
using System.Web;
using System.Web.configuration;
using System.Web.UI;
using System.Web.UI.WebControls;
using System.Web.UI.WebControls.WebParts;
```

```csharp
using com.amazon.webservices;

public partial class AmazonBookControl : System.Web.UI.UserControl
{
    // Data member for storing ISBN
    private string _isbn = "";

    /// <summary>
    /// When control is first loaded, retrieve data and
    /// hide review Panel
    /// </summary>
    protected void Page_Load(object sender, EventArgs e)
    {
        if (! IsPostBack)
        {
            lnkReviews.Text = "See Reviews";
            panReviews.Visible = false;
            RefreshControlFromAmazon();
        }
    }

    /// <summary>
    /// Specifies the ISBN to look up
    /// </summary>
    public string ISBN
    {
        get { return _isbn; }
        set { _isbn = value; }
    }

    /// <summary>
    /// Loads the control with data for the book specified by ISBN
    /// </summary>
    public void RefreshControlFromAmazon()
    {
        try
        {
            // Create the Amazon Web service proxy class
            AWSECommerceService ecs = new AWSECommerceService();

            // Create an Amazon item lookup object
            ItemLookup itemLookup = new ItemLookup();

            // Populate the Amazon access key from your Web.config
            itemLookup.AWSAccessKeyId =
                WebConfigurationManager.AppSettings["AWSaccessKey"];

            // Create an Amazon item lookup request object
            // and populate it
            ItemLookupRequest amazonRequest =
                new ItemLookupRequest();
```

```csharp
// Indicate what kind of info you want back
amazonRequest.ResponseGroup = new string[] {
   "ItemAttributes", "Reviews", "Images" };

// Indicate which item to look up
amazonRequest.ItemId = new string[] { ISBN };
amazonRequest.IdType = ItemLookupRequestIdType.ASIN;
amazonRequest.IdTypeSpecified = true;

// Add request to look up
itemLookup.Request =
   new ItemLookupRequest[] { amazonRequest };

// Perform the request and retrieve response object
ItemLookupResponse amazonResponse =
   ecs.ItemLookup(itemLookup);

// If response object is empty, display error and quit
if (amazonResponse == null)
{
   labError.Text =
      "Amazon Error - no response received!";
   return;
}

// Now work your way down through the object model
// for this response object to get at the book data
Items[] itemsArray = amazonResponse.Items;

// Check for errors; exit if error encountered
if (itemsArray == null)
{
   labError.Text = "Amazon Error - empty response!";
   return;
}
if (itemsArray[0].Request.Errors != null)
{
   labError.Text =
      itemsArray[0].Request.Errors[0].Message;
   return;
}

// Finally, you can get the retrieved book data
Item book = amazonResponse.Items[0].Item[0];
if (book != null)
{
   // Set up the controls based on the book data
   imgBook.ImageUrl = book.MediumImage.URL;
   hypTitle.Text = book.ItemAttributes.Title;
   hypTitle.NavigateUrl = book.DetailPageURL;
```

```
        // Data bind the Repeater to the array of reviews
        CustomerReviews customerReviews =
            book.CustomerReviews;
        if (customerReviews != null)
        {
            Review[] reviewArray = customerReviews.Review;
            rptReviews.DataSource = reviewArray;
            rptReviews.DataBind();
        }
    }
}
catch (Exception ex)
{
    labError.Text = ex.Message;
    return;
}
}

/// <summary>
/// Handler for See/Hide Reviews LinkButton
/// </summary>
protected void lnkReviews_Click(object sender, EventArgs e)
{
    if (lnkReviews.Text == "See Reviews")
    {
        panReviews.Visible = true;
        lnkReviews.Text = "Hide Reviews";
    }
    else
    {
        panReviews.Visible = false;
        lnkReviews.Text = "See Reviews";
    }
}
}
```

Just as with the two previous Web services, consuming the AWS is a matter of instantiating the proxy object, setting up the input parameters for the Web service operation you will be using, calling the appropriate method in this proxy for this operation, and then using the data returned from the method. As Listing 15.2 illustrates, the data sent to or returned from the Web service might be quite complex and might require ample perusing of the Web service's documentation to fully comprehend its usage.

CORE NOTE

A great tool for experimenting with and understanding the AWS is the AWS scratch pad at http://awszone.com/index.aws.

Finally, you need to use the user control in Listings 15.1 and 15.2 within a Web page. Listings 15.3 and 15.4 demonstrate how to use this `AmazonBookControl` user control as well as the `ShowWeatherControl` created earlier. Figure 15.9 illustrates how this page (`ControlTester.aspx`) appears in the browser.

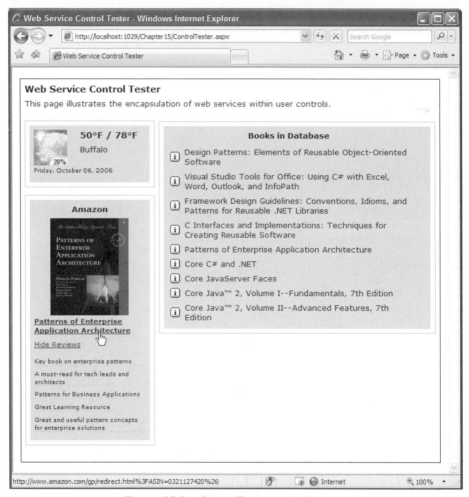

Figure 15.9 ControlTester.aspx in browser

Besides the two Web service user controls, this page also contains a `GridView` control that displays the books in your own Books database. Each time the user selects a book from this `GridView`, the selection event handler for the `GridView` changes the ISBN property of the `AmazonBookControl` user control and has it reload itself based on the new ISBN.

Listing 15.3   ControlTester.aspx

```
<%@ Page Language="C#" AutoEventWireup="true"
    CodeFile="ControlTester.aspx.cs" Inherits="ControlTester" %>

<%@ Register Src="Controls/AmazonBookControl.ascx"
    TagName="AmazonBookControl" TagPrefix="uc" %>
<%@ Register Src="Controls/ShowWeatherControl.ascx"
    TagName="ShowWeatherControl" TagPrefix="uc" %>

<!DOCTYPE html PUBLIC "-//W3C//DTD XHTML 1.0 Transitional//EN"
    "http://www.w3.org/TR/xhtml1/DTD/xhtml1-transitional.dtd">
<html xmlns="http://www.w3.org/1999/xhtml">
<head id="Head1" runat="server">
  <title>Web Service Control Tester</title>
  <link href="chapterStyles.css" type="text/css" rel="stylesheet" />
</head>
<body>
  <form id="form1" runat="server">
    <div id="container">
    <h1>Web Service Control Tester</h1>
    <p>
    This page illustrates the encapsulation of Web services
    within user controls</p>
      <div id="sideArea">
        <uc:ShowWeatherControl ID="myWeather"
          runat="server" />
        <uc:AmazonBookControl ID="myBook" runat="server"
          ISBN="0131472275" />
      </div>
      <div id="mainArea">
        <div class="box">
          <div id="bookListBox">
            <h2>Books in Database</h2>
            <asp:GridView ID="grdBookList" runat="server"
              DataSourceID="dsBooks"
              AutoGenerateColumns="False"
              AllowPaging="false" PageSize="4"
              DataKeyNames="Isbn" GridLines="None"
              Width="30em"
              CellPadding="4" ShowHeader="false"
              OnSelectedIndexChanged=
                "grdBookList_SelectedIndexChanged">

              <Columns>
                <asp:CommandField ShowSelectButton="true"
                  ButtonType="Image"
                    SelectImageUrl=
                      "images/btn_select.gif"/>
```

```
                              <asp:BoundField DataField="Title" />
                          </Columns>
                      </asp:GridView>
                  </div>
              </div>
          </div>
          <div id="footer">
              <p> <asp:Label ID="labFooter" runat="server" /> </p>
          </div>
      </div>
      <asp:SqlDataSource ID="dsBooks" runat="server"
          ProviderName="System.Data.SqlClient"
          ConnectionString="<%$ ConnectionStrings:BookCatalog %>"
          SelectCommand="SELECT ISBN,Title FROM Books" />
   </form>
</body>
</html>
```

Listing 15.4   ControlTester.aspx.cs

```
using System.Data;
using System.Collections;
using System.Web;
using System.Web.UI;
using System.Web.UI.WebControls;

public partial class ControlTester : System.Web.UI.Page
{
   protected void grdBookList_SelectedIndexChanged(object sender,
      EventArgs e)
   {
      // Retrieve the ISBN of the selected book
      string isbn = (string)grdBookList.SelectedDataKey.Value;

      // Change the user control's ISBN
      myBook.ISBN = isbn;

      // Get user control to refresh its data from Web service
      myBook.RefreshControlFromAmazon();
   }
}
```

Consuming Web Services and Performance

Consuming a Web service is generally quite slow in comparison to other operations within a Web application. The request must be serialized into XML, transmitted via HTTP to some other computer, deserialized by the Web service upon receiving the request, and then the requested operation must be executed (which may very well involve some type of database request). After the request is finished executing, the data to be returned must be serialized by the service, transmitted using HTTP to the requesting computer, deserialized by the requesting computer, and finally returned to the requesting class.

As a result, you should always take care to reduce the total number of Web service requests made by your applications. For instance, it is quite possible that the Show-WeatherControl that you created in Walkthrough 15.1 might appear on multiple pages within a site. After you have retrieved the current weather data for the user's city at the beginning of the user's session, do you really need to reretrieve this data for every other page the user visits that has this control? Certainly, some cities have weather that changes frequently, but not so frequently that you need to update the weather control every few seconds!

Preserving Web Service Data

One way that you can reduce the total number of Web service requests made by your application is to use ASP.NET session state or the ASP.NET cache for temporarily storing the data returned from frequently used, but infrequently changing Web services.

Listing 15.5 illustrates how you could change the code-behind for the Show-WeatherControl so that it tries to retrieve the data first from session state, and only use the Web service if the data is not in session state.

Listing 15.5   ShowWeatherControl.ascx.cs

```
public partial class ShowWeatherControl : UserControl
{
    protected void Page_Load(object sender, EventArgs e)
    {
        if (!IsPostBack)
        {
            // Use the current city profile setting for this user
            string city = Profile.City;

            // First try to retrieve this data from session
            WeatherData today = (WeatherData)Session["Weather"];
```

```csharp
        // If not in session state, retrieve from service
        if (today == null)
            today = GetWeatherData(city);

        DisplayWeatherData(today);
    }
}

private WeatherData GetWeatherData(string city)
{
    WeatherData today = null;
    try
    {
        // Create the weather forecast proxy
        WeatherForecast weatherService = new WeatherForecast();

        // Get the weather forecast for this city
        WeatherForecasts forecasts =
            weatherService.GetWeatherByPlaceName(city);

        // Return weather for today's date
        return forecasts.Details[0];
    }
    catch (Exception ex)
    {
        labError.Text = ex.Message;
    }
    return today;
}

public void DisplayWeatherData(WeatherData today)
{
    // If I have weather data, display it
    if (today != null)
    {
        string city = Profile.City;
        labCity.Text = city;
        labWeather.Text = today.MinTemperatureF;
        imgWeather.ImageUrl = today.WeatherImage;
        labWeather.Text += "&deg;F / " + today.MaxTemperatureF +
            "&deg;F";
        labDate.Text = today.Day;

        // Save weather data in session
        Session["Weather"] = today;
    }
}
}
```

As an alternative to saving the weather data in session state, you could store it instead in the ASP.NET cache. Because cache data is available to all sessions within the worker process, this allows weather data from the same city to be stored just once on the server. If the data returned from a Web service is the same for multiple users, it certainly makes more sense to use the cache rather than session state to preserve data from the service.

You can change the code in Listing 15.5 to use the cache by making the following change to its `Page_Load` method. Notice that the cache key for this item is constructed from the city name so that the application can cache the weather for multiple cities.

```
protected void Page_Load(object sender, EventArgs e)
{
    if (!IsPostBack)
    {
        ...
        // First try to retrieve this data from cache
        WeatherData today = (WeatherData)Cache["Weather" + city];
        ...
        if (today != null)
        {
            ...
            // Save weather data in cache
            // It times out in 10 minutes
            Cache.Insert("Weather" + city, today, null,
                DateTime.Now.AddMinutes(10.0),
                System.Web.Caching.Cache.NoSlidingExpiration);
        }
    }
}
```

You also need to change your `DisplayWeatherData` method so that it saves the weather data in the cache rather than in the session, as shown here.

```
// Save weather data in cache
Cache.Insert("Weather" + city, today, null,
    DateTime.Now.AddMinutes(10.0),
    System.Web.Caching.Cache.NoSlidingExpiration);
```

Setting the Proxy Timeout

The generated proxy class that your Web applications use to interact with a Web service contains more members than just the methods and types defined by the Web service. One of the most useful of these members is the `Timeout` property. This property is used to set the length of time, in milliseconds, until a synchronous call to a Web service request times out. The default is 100,000 milliseconds (100 seconds). You probably want to reduce this time out from the default length, because it is unlikely that you can expect your application's users to wait that long. The following example illustrates how to reduce the timeout for requests to the weather forecast Web service to a more realistic 10 seconds.

```
WeatherForecast weatherService = new WeatherForecast();

// Set timeout to 10 seconds (10000 milliseconds)
weatherService.Timeout = 10000;
```

CORE NOTE

The `Timeout` property should always be less than the `executionTimeout` attribute of the `httpRuntime` element in the `machine.config` file. This value controls how long ASP.NET continues processing a request before it returns a timed out error. The default `executionTimeout` value is 90 seconds, so your proxy timeout should be less than 90 seconds.

Asynchronous Web Services

As was mentioned earlier, a Web service operation is comparatively slow. This relative slowness can be a noticeable problem for Web pages like the example in Listing 15.3 that consume multiple Web services. The principal problem here is that when your application makes a request from one Web service, it must wait until it receives a response from this service before it can make a request of the next service. Figure 15.10 illustrates this flow for a sample page consuming three different Web services encapsulated within three different user controls. After each user control is loaded by its containing page, it then invokes the Web service it uses.

The problem with the scenario shown in Figure 15.10 is that although these Web services are independent of each other, the service calls to the user controls loaded later must wait for the earlier service calls. For instance, imagine that each of these Web service requests takes five seconds to respond. This means that the page takes more than 15 seconds to be displayed.

You could improve performance if you could issue Web service requests in parallel (that is, at the same time, or **asynchronously**). Figure 15.11 illustrates what the program flow might look like when invoking Web services asynchronously. Notice that the user controls in this case no longer wait to receive responses from the services. When the response finally does arrive back from the service, the control or page can continue its rendering. In the mean time, the page can continue its processing (which in this example means that it can make other Web service requests). In our hypothetical example in which each of these services takes five seconds to respond, the entire page would only take somewhat more than five seconds to be displayed instead of the 15 seconds with the synchronous approach.

Asynchronous development is often feared by developers because it can be quite difficult and complicated. However, with ASP.NET, Web service requests can be made asynchronously without a great deal of programming or intellectual strain. There are only three steps to using a Web service asynchronously.

1. Enable asynchronous processing in the Web Form via the `Async` attribute of the `Page` directive.
2. Register with the proxy the handler method that is invoked when the asynchronous service is completed.
3. Call the proxy's asynchronous version of the method.

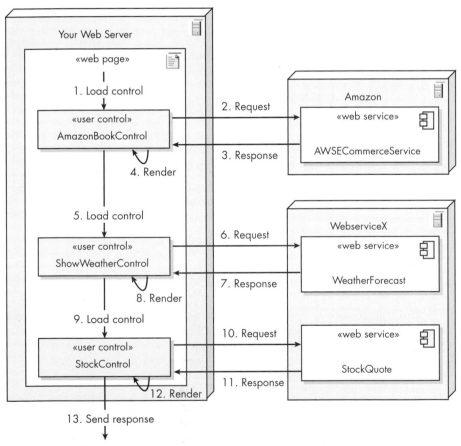

Figure 15.10   Program flow with synchronous Web services

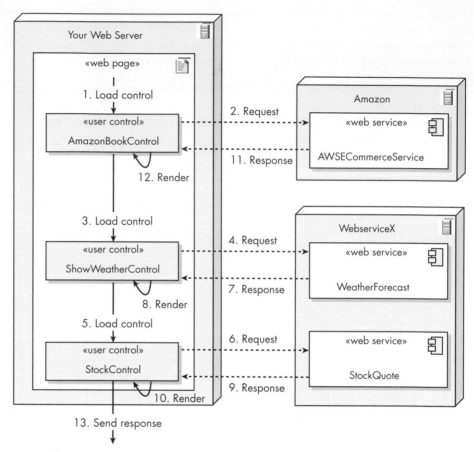

Figure 15.11   Program flow with asynchronous Web services

The first step is easily accomplished. You must mark any Web Forms that will be invoking any Web service asynchronously via the `Async="true"` attribute of the Page directive, as shown in the following example.

```
<%@ Page Language="C#" Async="true" … />
```

The next two steps require changes in how you access a service. Recall that in the generated proxy class, it contains a method for each operation exposed by the service and that this method name matches exactly the operation name in the Web service. This generated proxy class also contains asynchronous versions of each of these methods.

For instance, in the previous Web services consumption example from Listing 15.5, you used the `GetWeatherByPlaceName` method from the proxy to retrieve weather data from the service. To invoke any Web service operation asynchronously, you can use the XxxxAsync method of the proxy, where Xxxx is the name of the operation (e.g., GetWeatherByPlaceName**Async**). This XxxxAsync method takes the same parameters as the synchronous version, as shown here.

```
WeatherForecast weatherService = new WeatherForecast();
…
weatherService.GetWeatherByPlaceNameAsync(city);
```

Notice that unlike the synchronous version, the asynchronous version of a service's method does not return a value. How then do you retrieve the returned value of this Web service? You can do so within a special event handler method for this operation that will be invoked by the proxy when the service finally returns a value. This handler method must follow the signature that is defined for it in the proxy. The basic form of this handler looks similar to the following.

```
public void WhatEverYouWant(object o, XxxxCompletedEventArgs e)
{
    // Get the requested data
    … = e.Result;

    // Use the data
    …
}
```

This handler must be registered with the proxy. Each asynchronous method in the proxy also contains an event property named XxxxCompleted that takes a delegate of the type XxxxCompletedEventHandler that can be used as follows.

```
myProxy.XxxxCompleted +=
    new XxxxCompletedEventHandler(WhatEverYouWant);
```

For instance, to invoke your weather service asynchronously, your code might look like the following.

```
protected void Page_Load(object sender, EventArgs e)
{
    …
    // Create the weather forecast proxy
    WeatherForecast weatherService = new WeatherForecast();

    // Register event method (with your proxy class) that
    // executes when service operation finally responds
    weatherService.GetWeatherByPlaceNameCompleted +=
      new GetWeatherByPlaceNameCompletedEventHandler(
        WeatherServiceDone);
```

```
    // Make asynchronous request for the service operation
    weatherService.GetWeatherByPlaceNameAsync(city);
    ...
}


/// <summary>
/// Called by proxy when asynchronous request finally
/// returns with data
/// </summary>
public void WeatherServiceDone(object sender,
    GetWeatherByPlaceNameCompletedEventArgs e)
{
    // Get the requested weather forecast
    WeatherForecasts forecasts = e.Result;
    // Display the forecast
    DisplayWeatherData( forecasts.Details[0] );
}
```

If you are consuming a Web service in a user control, it is sensible to design the control so that it tries consuming it asynchronously only if the parent page has enabled asynchronous processing. If asynchronous processing has not been enabled, the service can be consumed in the regular, synchronous fashion. You can check this state via the IsAsync property of the page. In the following example, you have modified Listing 15.5 so that it first tries to retrieve the data from the cache. If not there, it gets the weather data asynchronously if the parent page for the user control supports it; otherwise, it uses the synchronous approach.

```
public partial class ShowWeatherControl : System.Web.UI.UserControl
{
    protected void Page_Load(object sender, EventArgs e)
    {
        if (!IsPostBack)
        {
            // Use the current city profile setting for this user
            string city = Profile.City;

            // First try to retrieve this data from cache
            WeatherData today =
                (WeatherData)Cache["Weather" + city];
            if (today == null)
            {
                if (this.Page.IsAsync)
                    AsynchronousGetWeatherData(city);
                else
                    DisplayWeatherData( GetWeatherData(city) );
            }
            else
                DisplayWeatherData(today);
```

```
      }
   }

   private void AsynchronousGetWeatherData(string city)
   {
      try
      {
         // Create the weather forecast proxy
         WeatherForecast weatherService =
            new WeatherForecast();

         // Register event method (with your proxy class) that
         // executes when service operation finally responds
         weatherService.GetWeatherByPlaceNameCompleted +=
            new GetWeatherByPlaceNameCompletedEventHandler(
               WeatherServiceDone);

         // Make asynchronous request for the service operation
         weatherService.GetWeatherByPlaceNameAsync(city);

      }
      catch (Exception ex)
      {
         labError.Text = ex.Message;
      }
   }

   /// <summary>
   /// Called by proxy when asynchronous request finally
   /// returns with data
   /// </summary>
   public void WeatherServiceDone(object sender,
      GetWeatherByPlaceNameCompletedEventArgs e)
   {
      // Get the requested weather forecast for this city
      // from the parameter
      WeatherForecasts forecasts = e.Result;

      // Display the forecast
      DisplayWeatherData( forecasts.Details[0] );
   }

   ...
}
```

You can demonstrate the difference in time between the synchronous and asynchronous version of the `ControlTester.aspx` page from Listing 15.3, by adding the following event handlers to the code-behind class for `ControlTester`.

```
public partial class ControlTester : System.Web.UI.Page
{
    private DateTime _start;
    protected void Page_PreLoad(object o, EventArgs e)
    {
        _start = DateTime.Now;
    }

    protected void Page_LoadComplete(object o, EventArgs e)
    {
        TimeSpan timeTaken = DateTime.Now.Subtract(_start);
        labFooter.Text =
            "Page took " + timeTaken.TotalMilliseconds;
        labFooter.Text += " ms to display";
    }

    ...
}
```

If you test this yourself, you will probably find that by accessing both the weather and Amazon Web service asynchronously, the page is displayed roughly twice as fast as accessing the services synchronously.

Creating Web Services

Consuming external Web services is an important way of expanding the functionality of a Web application. There may be times, however, when you may need to create and offer your own Web service for the rest of the world (or maybe just the rest of your organization) to consume. Fortunately, the .NET Framework and Visual Studio make the process of creating your own Web services quite pain free.

There is one important difference between creating a Web service and creating a Web application in Visual Studio: You cannot use the Web server that is built into Visual Studio to simultaneously host the Web service and the Web application for testing (i.e., consuming) that Web service. As a consequence, you must host Web services the old fashioned way (that is, the pre-Visual Studio 2005 way) and create an IIS virtual directory for the Web service. Because you may have become familiar with using the built-in Web server in Visual Studio 2005, let us go through the steps necessary for creating and using a virtual directory. You can create a virtual directory using the IIS Manager or you can create it directly in Visual Studio. In Walkthrough 15.2, you shall demonstrate the latter approach.

Walkthrough 15.2 *Creating a Web Service on the Local Machine*

The first step is to create a Web service project in its own virtual directory.

1. In Visual Studio, use the File → New Web Site menu command.

2. In the New Web Site dialog, choose the ASP.NET Web Service template. Change the Location option to HTTP. Click the Browse button.

3. In the Choose Location dialog, click the Local IIS button.

4. Click the Default Web Site node in the virtual directory tree. This displays all the existing virtual directories on your machine. Because you are creating a new virtual directory, you can click either the Create New Web Application or the Create New Virtual Directory button (see Figure 15.12). Choosing the former option ultimately creates a virtual directory in the `C:\Inetpub\wwwroot` folder; the latter option lets you choose the location of your virtual directory. However, depending upon the security settings with your computer, you might not be able to access a local Web service that is not in the `C:\Inetpub\wwwroot` folder.

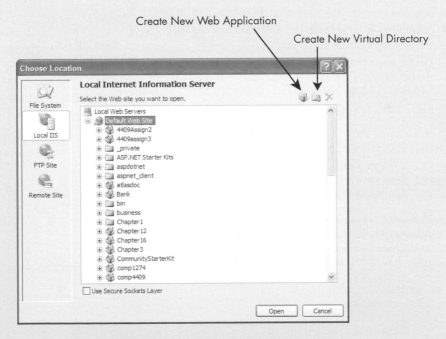

Figure 15.12 Creating an HTTP Web site

5. Click the Create New Virtual Directory button.

6. In the New Virtual Directory dialog, enter `CoreASPNETservices` as the alias name and use the Browse button to select the location of the virtual directory (you may want to make a folder named `CoreASPNETservices` in the same location as the other examples in this book; or you can place it in the `C:\Inetpub\wwwroot` folder). Click OK.

7. Select the `CoreASPNETservices` virtual directory in the virtual directory tree. Click Open. This returns you to the New Web Site dialog.

8. Click OK. Visual Studio creates a sample `.asmx` file as well as an `App_Code` folder with the code-behind class for the `.asmx` file.

9. Right-click the solution in the Solution Explorer and choose the Add New Item command.

10. Choose Web Service from the template list and name the service `Quote-Service`. Click OK.

Creating a Simple Quote Service

When you create a Web service using Visual Studio, you create two source files. The Web service file itself has an extension of `.asmx`. This file contains only a `@Web-Service` directive. Like the `@Page` directive for `.aspx` pages, the `@WebService` directive specifies the class name and the filename for this Web service. Because a Web service does not contain any user interface, there is no other markup necessary for this `.asmx` file. Instead, the code-behind class for the Web service contains the methods and operations that define the operations that the Web service provides. The initial class created by Visual Studio looks similar to the following.

```
using System;
using System.Web;
using System.Web.Services;
using System.Web.Services.Protocols;

[WebService(Namespace = "http://tempuri.org/")]
[WebServiceBinding(ConformsTo =
   WsiProfiles.BasicProfile1_1)]
public class QuoteService : System.Web.Services.WebService
{
    public QuoteService () {     }
    [WebMethod]
    public string HelloWorld() {
        return "Hello World";
    }
}
```

As you can see from the preceding example, the code-behind class for the Web service created by Visual Studio inherits from the `WebService` class (in the `System.Web.Services` namespace). This `WebService` class provides access to the same `Application`, `Context`, `Server`, `Session`, and `User` properties as the `Page` class.

You will also notice that this Web service class is marked with two attributes. The `WebService` attribute can be used to add a textual description to the service, which is visible when someone examines the WSDL file for the service, and to specify the namespace for the service. Each Web service requires a unique namespace to make it possible for client applications to differentiate this Web service from another service that might use the same name. When you create a Web service in Visual Studio, it assigns `http://tempuri.org/` as the namespace for the service. This value is meant to be changed; although the namespace for a Web service is conventionally a URL, it is by no means necessary. URLs are typically used as the namespace for a service only because you need to use some type of universally unique identifier. You could optionally use an email address as well.

The `WebServiceBinding` attribute in the preceding example is used to indicate that the SOAP and WSDL created by this service conforms to something called the Basic Profile Version 1.1 specification. This specification is from **WS-I**, the **Web Services Interoperability Organization**. WS-I is an open industry organization that promotes open standards so that Web services work on different platforms and with different languages.

Like any method, the code-behind class can contain any number of public methods. However, the methods of a Web service class do not automatically become operations of the Web service. How do you specify which methods of the class are available as an operation to this Web service? To add this capability, you must apply the `WebMethod` attribute to any public methods that are to be available as operations in your Web service. The `WebMethod` attribute can also be used to add a description to your operation that is visible in the WSDL generated by the service, as shown here.

```
[WebMethod(Description = "Returns a randomly-selected quotation")]
public string GetQuoteText()
{
    // Get the quote from somewhere
    string quote = …

    return quote;
}
```

Listing 15.7 demonstrates a simple Web service named `QuoteService`. You first need to define a virtual directory and create a Web service project as shown in Walkthrough 15.2. This service returns a famous quote randomly selected from a collection of quotes contained in an XML file in the `App_Data` subfolder for the service. This XML file has the following structure.

```
<Quotes>
  <Quote>
    <Text>
      The web of our life is of a mingled yarn,
      good and ill together.
    </Text>
    <Author>William Shakespeare</Author>
    <Source>All's Well That Ends Well</Source>
    <Keyword>Web</Keyword>
  </Quote>
  ...
</Quotes>
```

This service contains two operations: GetQuoteText, which simply returns the quotation as a string, and GetQuoteFull, which returns the quotation as a Quote object. This Quote class is defined in Listing 15.6. Notice that the classes in the two listings are defined within a C# namespace named Chapter15.Services. Due to this different namespace, you also have to change the class reference in your Quote-Service.asmx file, which is shown in Listing 15.8.

Listing 15.6 Quote.cs

```
using System;

namespace Chapter15.Services
{
    /// <summary>
    /// Encapsulates a single quote
    /// </summary>
    public class Quote
    {
        private string _author = "";
        private string _source = "";
        private string _text = "";
        private string _keyword = "";

        public Quote() {  }

        public Quote(string author, string source, string keyword,
                string text)
        {
            _author = author;
            _source = source;
            _keyword = keyword;
            _text = text;
        }
```

```
      public string Author
      {
         get { return _author; }
         set { _author = value; }
      }
      public string Source
      {
         get { return _source; }
         set { _source = value; }
      }
      public string Keyword
      {
         get { return _keyword; }
         set { _keyword = value; }
      }
      public string Text
      {
         get { return _text; }
         set { _text = value; }
      }
   }
}
```

Listing 15.7   QuoteService.cs

```
using System;
using System.Web;
using System.Web.Services;
using System.Web.Services.Protocols;

using System.Data;

namespace Chapter15.Services
{
   [WebService(Namespace = "http://www.coreASPNETbook.com/",
      Description =
         "<b>A web service that returns famous quotes</b>")]
   [WebServiceBinding(ConformsTo = WsiProfiles.BasicProfile1_1)]
   public class QuoteService : System.Web.Services.WebService
   {
      public QuoteService() { }

      [WebMethod(Description =
         "Returns a randomly-selected quotation")]
      public string GetQuoteText()
      {
         Quote quote = GetQuoteFull();
```

```csharp
        return quote.Text;
    }

    [WebMethod(Description="Returns a randomly-selected
        <code>Quote</code> object")]
    public Quote GetQuoteFull()
    {
        DataSet ds = RetrieveQuoteDataSet();

        // Get a random number based on number of
        // quotes in data set
        Random rg = new Random();
        int ranNum = rg.Next(0, ds.Tables[0].Rows.Count);

        // Get the row for this random number
        DataRow quoteRow = ds.Tables[0].Rows[ranNum];

        // Return a quote object for this row
        return MakeQuoteFromRow(quoteRow);
    }

    /// <summary>
    /// Returns a DataSet populated from quotes.xml file
    /// </summary>
    private DataSet RetrieveQuoteDataSet()
    {
        // First try to retrieve DataSet from cache
        DataSet ds = (DataSet)Context.Cache["Quotes"];

        // If not in cache, read in from XML file ...
        if (ds == null)
        {
            ds = new DataSet();
            string filename =
                Server.MapPath("~/App_Data/quotes.xml");
            ds.ReadXml(filename);

            // ... and save it in cache
            Context.Cache["Quotes"] = ds;
        }
        return ds;
    }

    /// <summary>
    /// Extract a Quote object from the passed-in DataRow
    /// </summary>
    private Quote MakeQuoteFromRow(DataRow row)
    {
```

```
        // Create a Quote object for transport …
        Quote q = new Quote();

        // … and HTML encode its contents
        q.Text = Server.HtmlEncode(row[0].ToString());
        q.Author = Server.HtmlEncode(row[1].ToString());
        q.Source = Server.HtmlEncode(row[2].ToString());
        q.Keyword = Server.HtmlEncode(row[3].ToString());
        return q;
      }
    }
}
```

Listing 15.8   QuoteService.asmx

```
<%@ WebService Language="C#" CodeBehind="~/App_Code/QuoteService.cs"
    Class="Chapter15.Services.QuoteService" %>
```

Testing the Quote Service

After you have compiled and built the Web service project in Visual Studio, it is ready to be consumed. Perhaps the easiest way to do so is to access the WSDL directly from a browser. Assuming that this service is contained in a virtual directory named `CoreASPNETservices`, you enter the following URL into the browser to view the WSDL for this service.

```
http://localhost/CoreASPNETservices/QuoteService.asmx
```

The result in the browser is shown in Figure 15.13. Notice that the text you supplied via the `Description` attributes is visible on this page.

You can test the Web service operations from this page. For instance, if you click the `GetQuoteText` operation in the browser, you see more information about this operation, including the ability to invoke the service. If you click the Invoke button, you see the SOAP data actually returned from the method, as shown in Figure 15.14.

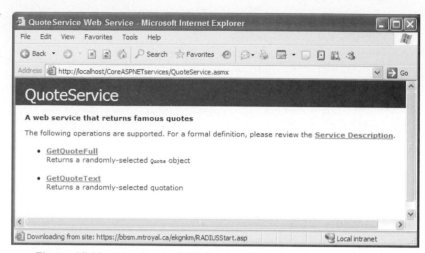

Figure 15.13   Viewing the WSDL for the QuoteService in the browser

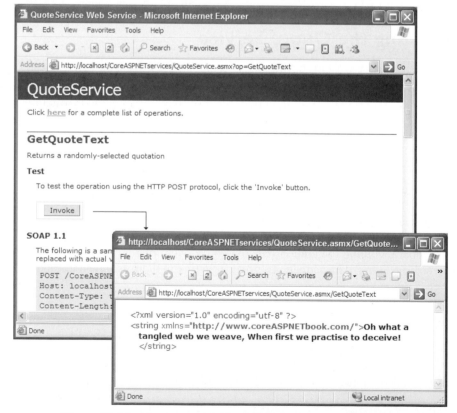

Figure 15.14   Viewing the SOAP result from a service operation

To consume this service in an ASP.NET page (not in the same Visual Studio solution as the service but in a different Visual Studio solution, such as your `Chapter15` solution), you need to follow the same steps that you followed at the beginning of the chapter. That is, you first need to add a Web reference in Visual Studio to this service (`http://localhost/CoreASPNETservices/QuoteService.asmx`). You could then consume this service by instantiating the proxy (be sure to also reference the namespace of the proxy) and then use its methods, as shown in the following.

```
using System;
using System.Data;
using System.Web;
using System.Web.UI;
using System.Web.UI.WebControls;

using localhost;

public partial class MyServicesTester : System.Web.UI.Page
{
    protected void Page_Load(object sender, EventArgs e)
    {
        // Instantiate the proxy
        QuoteService qs = new QuoteService();

        // Retrieve a quote
        Quote quote = qs.GetQuoteFull();

        // Display the quote
        labRandomQuote.Text = quote.Text + "<br/>";
        labRandomQuote.Text += "-- " + quote.Author;
    }
}
```

Creating a Web Service Front-End for Business or Application Logic Classes

In the previous example, your quote Web service contained all the coding necessary for implementing the service. For a more complex service, however, you do not want to make your Web service class contain all the programming necessary to implement the service. As you saw in Chapter 11, it often makes sense to keep your Web page code-behind classes focused only on the presentation-level details and use related classes grouped into logical layers to perform data-access and business and application logic. A similar approach makes sense for Web services as well. Web service classes should ideally be fairly "thin" classes with most of the "real" functionality performed by your business or application logic classes. In this way, a Web service is perhaps best understood as a special type of interface to your business or application logic classes, as shown in Figure 15.15.

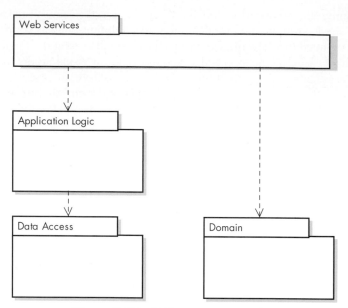

Figure 15.15   Web services as interface

Web services align well with the application logic classes covered in the four-layer model shown in Chapter 11. You may recall that the application logic layer provides a set of available operations for the application as a whole and that the operations in this layer often align with specific use cases. Web services also provide an interface to the available operations of an application; the difference is that Web services make these operations available to other external applications.

For instance, Listing 15.9 defines a Web service that returns a populated Book business entity object for the specified ISBN.

Listing 15.9   BookService.cs

```
using System;
using System.Web;
using System.Collections;
using System.Web.Services;
using System.Web.Services.Protocols;

using FourLayer.ApplicationLogic;
using FourLayer.BusinessEntity;

namespace Chapter15.Services
{
    [WebService(Namespace = "http://www.coreASPNETbook.com/",
```

```
    Description =
        "Sample service interface to Application Layer")]
[WebServiceBinding(ConformsTo = WsiProfiles.BasicProfile1_1)]
public class BookService : System.Web.Services.WebService
{
    public BookService() { }

    [WebMethod(Description=
        "Returns a book object for an ISBN")]
    public Book GetBook(string isbn)
    {
        return BookCatalogLogic.GetBookByIsbn(isbn);
    }
}
}
```

As you can see, the Web service is delegating all the functionality to another existing class (in this case, the BookCatalogLogic class).

Guidelines for Creating Web Services

I should mention a few guidelines to remember when creating Web services. Perhaps the most important point to remember about Web services is that the client that is requesting the Web service is no more to be trusted than that with any other type of HTTP request. An ASP.NET Web service is hosted in ASP.NET and is just as vulnerable to attacks as a regular ASP.NET application. As a consequence of this fact, a Web services developer must be as aware as the Web page developer of potential security risks. For instance, just as with a regular ASP.NET Web page, if you are passing sensitive information between the client and a Web service, you may need to encrypt and protect this information by using SSL (i.e., HTTPS rather than HTTP).

There is one considerable problem with constructing secure Web services. A Web application can use the presentation layer to construct and implement its security (for instance, by using the login controls and membership feature covered in Chapter 13). A Web service, by contrast, has no user interface; so, if authentication and authorization is needed by the service, you must "build" it into your Web service.

There are different ways to approach this problem. Amazon, for instance, requires that each request for any of its Web services include a unique Amazon access key and, for any of its nonfree services, an Amazon secret key. Another approach is to use authentication. Like any ASP.NET Web application, an ASP.NET Web service can enable Windows Authentication or forms authentication. Because Web services are not used by users but by other applications, the requesting applications must provide the user's credentials to the service.

Finally, another approach is available via **_Web Service Enhancements_** (WSE), which is an extensibility mechanism that allows third parties to add features to the Web services standards by adding information via SOAP extensions. For SOAP extensions to be useful, both the client and the server need to be able to expect the same thing in the SOAP messages. Various WSE standards have been have proposed or defined, such as WS-Security and WS-Attachments, to aid in this process.

Microsoft Web Services Enhancements Toolkit is a free download that lets developers add some of these WSE features (including WS-Security) to their Web services; however, the same version of the WSE must be installed on both the client (the requester) and the server hosting the Web service for this mechanism to work.

There is one additional guideline that you should remember when creating Web services: Be very cautious using .NET-specific types such as the `DataSet` for return values or input parameters for Web service operations that might be consumed by non-.NET clients. As you saw in the quote service that you created in Listing 15.7 or the Book service shown earlier, a Web service can return a custom type. For instance, you had the `GetQuoteFull` method return a `Quote` object and the `GetBook` method return a `Book` object. In both cases, the returned object data is ultimately based on types defined by the XML Schema standard, and as a result, can be consumed by any client. However, if you return .NET types that are not defined in the XML Schema standard, a non-.NET client will have a difficult time creating a proxy to consume this service; instead, the client must parse the returned XML data in the SOAP envelope to extract the data. On the other hand, if you are sure that all clients for your service will be .NET applications, you can use .NET types for input parameters or return types (although you may still want to avoid using `DataSet` objects because they are extremely verbose when serialized).

The final guideline to keep in mind when creating Web services is to remember that calling a Web service is very slow in comparison to an in-process method call. Web services are not meant to be a replacement for a normal business object or application logic class. Rather, Web services provide a standardized interface that allows external applications to consume selected behaviors in your application. That is, within an application, Web services should only be used if there is a good reason to do so. Web services should not be used for communication within an application; instead, Web services should only be used for interapplication communication.

Summary

This chapter provided a quick overview of Web services in general, and illustrated in detail how to consume and create Web services in ASP.NET. As this chapter demonstrated, both consuming and creating simple Web services is straightforward and painless.

The next chapter covers the internationalization and deployment of Web applications.

Exercises

The solutions to the following exercises can be found at my Web site, http://www.randyconnolly.com/core. Additional exercises only available for teachers and instructors are also available from this site. It is possible that some of the external Web services mentioned in these exercises may not be always available in the future.

1. Create a user control named StockControl that consumes the stock quote Web service from WebserviceX (available from http://www.webservicex.net/stockquote.asmx?WSDL). This user control should contain a text box for entering the stock symbol and a button that invokes the GetQuote operation of the Web service; it then should display the current price returned from the service. Be sure to create a Web Form to test the service.

2. Change the AmazonBookControl user control so that it retrieves the data from the Amazon Web service either synchronously or asynchronously based on the state of the parent page's IsAsync property.

3. Create a new user control named AmazonDetailsBookControl that uses the Amazon Web service (synchronously or asynchronously based on the state of the parent page's IsAsync property) to display the following information from Amazon about a book specified by the control's ISBN property: Title, Author, ISBN, Publisher, PublicationDate, ListPrice, and LargeImage. Be sure to create a Web Form to test the service.

4. Add a Web service method to the BookService class that returns a collection of all Publisher objects. Be sure to create a Web Form to test the service.

The next exercise uses the Bank database.

5. Create a new Web service named BankService. This service contains a method named Verify, which takes a credit card number, credit card holder name, credit card type, expiry date, and a purchase amount as parameters. This method verifies if the purchase request is valid by verifying that the card number exists (in the database), that the card number, holder's name, card type and expiry date all match, that the card hasn't expired or been cancelled, and that the card balance (with this purchase) is not over limit. By using the supplied CustomerServiceLogic, CustomerCard, and CustomerCardDAO classes, you can perform most of these checks. This method must return an object of type CustomerServiceCardErrors, which is defined within the CustomerServiceLogic class.

Key Concepts

- Amazon Web Services
- Asynchronous Web services
- Proxy
- Service
- Service-oriented architecture
- SOAP (Simple Object Access Protocol)
- Web reference
- Web services
- Web Service Enhancements (WSE)
- Web Services Interoperability Organization (WS-I)
- WSDL (Web Services Description Language)

References

Ballard, Paul. "Top 5 Web Service Mistakes." http://www.theserverside.net.

Chatterjee, Sandeep and Webber, James. *Developing Enterprise Web Services: An Architect's Guide*. Prentice Hall, 2003.

Erl, Thomas. *Service-Oriented Architecture*. Prentice Hall, 2004.

He, Hao. "What Is a Service-Oriented Architecture?" http://webservices.xml.com.

Mitchell, Scott. "An Extensive Examination of Web Services: Part 1-10." http://aspnet.4guysfromrolla.com.

Onion, Fritz. "Asynchronous Web Parts." *MSDN Magazine* (July 2006).

Prosise, Jess. "Asynchronous Pages in ASP.NET 2.0." *MSDN Magazine* (October 2005).

Shodjai, Payam. "Web Services and the Microsoft Platform." http://msdn.microsoft.com.

Skonnard, Aaron. "A Survey of Publicly Available Web Services at Microsoft." *MSDN Magazine* (December 2003).

Wahlin, Dan. "Calling Web Services Asynchronously." *www.aspnetPro.com Magazine* (July 2006).

Chapter 16

INTERNATIONALIZATION AND DEPLOYMENT

"The trouble with foreign languages is, you have to think before your speak."
—Swedish proverb, *The Columbia World of Quotations*
(Columbia World of Quotations, 1996)

To adopt the proverb that begins this chapter, the trouble with adapting a Web application for an international audience is that you must plan for it from the very beginning. Ideally, when you are planning your ASP.NET application, you decide which languages your application will support. Doing so allows you to implement your Web application so that it supports these languages. The first part of this chapter demonstrates how to plan and adapt an ASP.NET application for an international audience.

Happily for us, the other focus of this chapter—the deployment of ASP.NET applications—does not require any real planning ahead of time. ASP.NET provides several ways to move a Web application from the developer's machine to a production server. One of the great strengths of ASP.NET is that an application can be installed simply by copying or FTPing the files to a destination machine. ASP.NET also provides additional deployment mechanisms to handle situations where simple file-copy installations are not ideal or even possible.

Internationalizing a Web Application

One of the principal advantages of hosting an application in a Web browser is that the potential audience for that application can be worldwide. Yet, despite this potential global reach, ASP.NET developers sometimes ignore the fact that not everyone in their target audience necessarily lives in the same country as themselves. Although it is certainly unfeasible to have a different version of a given Web application for every possible language and/or culture in the world, it is quite possible that you want to make your Web application usable for a small number of select languages. However, having multiple language versions for each page and control in a Web site is unfortunately error-prone and inefficient due to the massive code and markup duplication that this entails. A better approach for improving the user experience for international users is to use the globalization and localization features in ASP.NET 2.0.

Globalization is the process of designing an application so that it can adapt to different cultures. I should mention here that a *culture* is more specialized than a language. For instance, Canada, England, and the United States all speak the same language, but for the context of internationalization, these are three different cultures. Globalization is the process of designing and developing an application so that it supports user interfaces and regional data for users in target cultures. Some examples of the types of things that can vary from culture to culture are currency symbols, units of measure, and date and number formatting.

Ideally, globalization should start before you even begin to design the application. Right at the start of your design process, you should determine which cultures your application will support. Doing so allows you to design and implement your application to support these cultures. This is done by developing your application so that it is culture-neutral and language-neutral. In ASP.NET, you do this by placing culture and language-specific content into separate culture-specific resource files.

Localization is the process of creating a localized version of the application's resources. This typically involves translating each resource for each culture that the application will support. Unless your development team is universally multilingual, this process involves professional translators who are fluent in the base language and the localized language as well as localization testers who can test the application in the context of the target cultures.

Figure 16.1 illustrates the relationship between globalization and localization.

Introducing Resource Files

In ASP.NET, developers can globalize their applications by creating each page so that it obtains its content and data based on the preferred language setting for the browser or the user's explicit choice of language. This culture- or language-specific content and data are referred to as *resources*. This resource data can be stored in separate resource

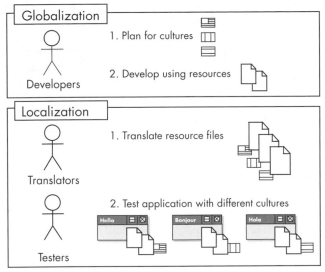

Figure 16.1   Globalization and localization

files or contained directly within the application's deployed assembly files. These resource files contain any number of key-value pairs and are encoded using XML that follows a particular predefined schema and have the .resx extension.

Resource files reside in one of two special ASP.NET folders in your application: App_LocalResources and App_GlobalResources. Resource files for individual pages, user controls, or master pages are stored in the App_LocalResources folder, whereas resource files that contain content to be used in multiple places in the site should be stored in the App_GlobalResources folder. For each supported culture in the application, there is a separate version of each resource. These resource files are automatically compiled into a binary form and then stored in an assembly by the ASP.NET runtime. Figure 16.2 illustrates the relationship between site content and resource files.

What sort of things need to be localized in a Web application? In a Windows application, you typically place *all* textual content (e.g., text for labels, buttons, windows, and so on) within resource files. For a content-oriented Web application that pulls all of its content from a centralized database, localizing all the textual content in the site can be difficult unless you have all the content in the database localized as well (which typically requires different versions of the database for different cultures). However, for Web applications that are task-oriented rather than content-oriented, it is quite possible to make your application fully localized. Doing so requires placing the textual content for the site's user interface within resource files.

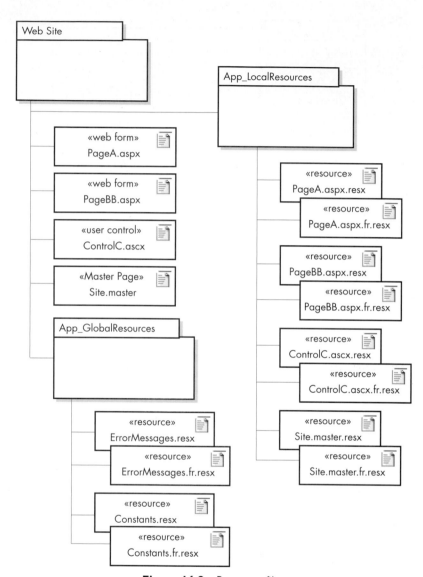

Figure 16.2   Resource files

Generating Resource Files

Visual Studio 2005 and ASP.NET 2.0 make this process significantly easier than in previous versions. To localize an .aspx page, a user control, or a master page, switch the file to Design view and then choose the Tools →Generate Local Resource menu option. Visual Studio generates a resource file for the current Web page, user control, or master page in the App_LocalResources folder (and creates that folder, if necessary). The truly convenient thing about this approach is that Visual Studio automatically generates an entry in the resource file for every page and control property that is marked with the Localizable attribute. The Localizable attribute is used to indicate that a property should be localized. You can also add this attribute to those properties in your user controls that contain localizable text.

To demonstrate the generation of local resources, imagine that you have the page shown in Listing 16.1, which illustrates a sample page named Localization-Demo.aspx. Notice the properties that have been emphasized in the listing. Because these properties contain English text, they are the ones that need to be localized.

Listing 16.1   LocalizationDemo.aspx

```
<%@ Page Language="C#" MasterPageFile="~/Site.master"
   CodeFile="LocalizationDemo.aspx.cs"
   Inherits="LocalizationDemo"
   Title="Localization Demonstration" %>

<asp:Content ID="Content2" ContentPlaceHolderID="mainContent"
      Runat="Server">
  <asp:Panel ID="panReg" runat="server"
    GroupingText="Registration" >

    <p>
    <asp:Label ID="labName" runat="server" Text="Name:" /><br />
    <asp:TextBox ID="txtName" runat="server" />
    <asp:RequiredFieldValidator ID="reqName" runat="server"
      ControlToValidate="txtName" ValidationGroup="main"
      ErrorMessage="Please enter a name" />
    </p>
    <p>
    <asp:Label ID="labHired" runat="server" Text="Hired Date:" />
    <br />
    <asp:TextBox ID="txtHired" runat="server" />
    </p>
    <p>
    <asp:Label ID="labSalary" runat="server" Text="Salary:" />
    <br />
    <asp:TextBox ID="txtSalary" runat="server" />
    </p>
    <asp:Button ID="btnSubmit" runat="server" Text="Save"
      ValidationGroup="main" />
  </asp:Panel>
</asp:Content>
```

When you generate the local resource file in Visual Studio for this page, Visual Studio generates a file named `LocalizationDemo.aspx.resx` in the `App_LocalResources` folder. This file represents the ***default resource values*** for this page. Default resource values are those that are used in lieu of any culture-specific resource values.

You can open this generated resource file in Visual Studio so as to examine or edit its contents, as shown in Figure 16.3. Notice how the emphasized text properties from Listing 16.1 are now contained in this resource file.

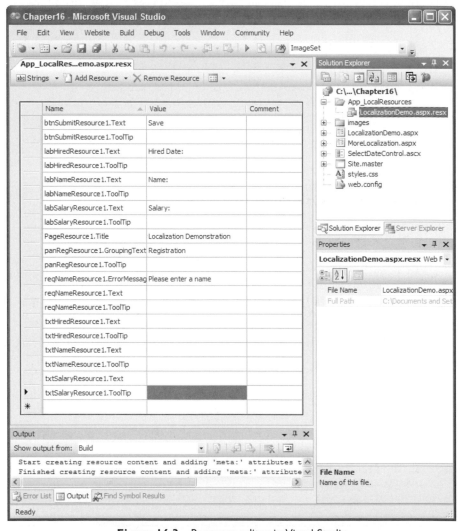

Figure 16.3 Resource editor in Visual Studio

CORE NOTE

To improve the efficiency of localization, you should remove all unused entries in the generated resource file. For instance, in the previous example, you can remove the resource entries for the Text and ToolTip properties of the three TextBox controls.

When Visual Studio generates local resources, it also modifies control declarations in the original source file. For instance, after generating local resources, the code in Listing 16.1 is modified as shown here (modifications are shown in bold).

```
<%@ Page Language="C#" MasterPageFile="~/Site.master"
  CodeFile="LocalizationDemo.aspx.cs"
  Inherits="LocalizationDemo"
  Title="Localization Demonstration"
  Culture="auto" meta:resourcekey="PageResource1"
  UICulture="auto" %>

<asp:Content ID="Content2" ContentPlaceHolderID="mainContent"
    Runat="Server">
  <asp:Panel ID="panReg" runat="server"
    GroupingText="Registration"
    meta:resourcekey="panRegResource1" >
  <p>
  <asp:Label ID="labName" runat="server" Text="Name:"
    meta:resourcekey="labNameResource1" /><br />
  <asp:TextBox ID="txtName" runat="server"
    meta:resourcekey="txtNameResource1" />
  <asp:RequiredFieldValidator ID="reqName" runat="server"
    ControlToValidate="txtName"
    ErrorMessage="Please enter a name"
    meta:resourcekey="reqNameResource1" />
  </p>
  <p>
  <asp:Label ID="labHired" runat="server" Text="Hired Date:"
    meta:resourcekey="labHiredResource1" /><br />
  <asp:TextBox ID="txtHired" runat="server"
    meta:resourcekey="txtHiredResource1" />
  </p>
  <p>
  <asp:Label ID="labSalary" runat="server" Text="Salary:"
    meta:resourcekey="labSalaryResource1" /><br />
  <asp:TextBox ID="txtSalary" runat="server"
    meta:resourcekey="txtSalaryResource1" />
  </p>
  <asp:Button ID="btnSubmit" runat="server" Text="Save"
```

```
        meta:resourcekey="btnSubmitResource1" />
  </asp:Panel>
</asp:Content>
```

Visual Studio adds something called an ***implicit resource expression*** to each control that has a property that is `Localizable`. Resource expressions were introduced in ASP.NET 2.0; they provide a design-time mechanism for referencing a value that is contained in a resource file. There are two types of resource expression: implicit and explicit (which are covered a bit later in the chapter). Implicit resource expressions are declaratively added to a control as a property (in the preceding example, the property name is `meta:resourcekey`). The value for the resource attribute specifies a ***resource key prefix value***, which is used to perform property assignments for the control. As can be seen in Figure 16.3, a given control may have multiple properties that can be localized. For instance, the save button (`btnSubmit`) has two localizable properties: `Text` and `ToolTip`. In the resource file, there are two keys (`btnSubmitResource1.Text` and `btnSubmitResource1.ToolTip`) defined for these two localizable properties. The key name for each of these localizable properties is constructed by concatenating the resource key prefix value with the property name.

As you have seen, the Generate Local Resources command in Visual Studio generates a resource file and adds implicit resource expressions for each server control that has localizable properties. But what do you do with content that should be localized but that is not contained within a server control? For instance, imagine that you have the following HTML content.

```
<p>
This is an example.
</p>
```

The Generate Local Resources command can generate a resource for static HTML content such as this if it is wrapped within the `Localize` control. The `Localize` control was introduced in ASP.NET 2.0 and is a subclass of the `Literal` control covered in Chapter 3. It is used to reserve a location on the page or control that retrieves its content from a resource file. For instance, you could change the previous code snippet to the following.

```
<p>
<asp:Localize ID="locEx" runat="server">
This is an example.
</asp:Localize>
</p>
```

This code is then transformed by the Generate Local Resources command to the following.

```
<p>
<asp:Localize ID="locEx" runat="server"
   meta:resourcekey="locEx1" Text="Select a Date" >
</asp:Localize>
</p>
```

Localizing Resource Files

It should be stressed that the resource file created by the Generate Local Resources command represents only the default resources for the page or control. You still must manually create different versions of the resource file for any additional languages or cultures that your application is going to support. If your site is going to support English, French, and Arabic, you are going to need separate resource files for each of these languages (although you could use the generated default resource file for English). That is, the developer must manually create copies of each generated resource file for each supported language or culture.

ASP.NET uses a naming convention to differentiate different resource files. Localized versions of resource files must have the appropriate *culture ID* appended to the original filename. Culture IDs are standardized identifiers in the format `languagecode-regioncode`, where `languagecode` is a lowercase two-letter code derived from ISO 639-1 and `regioncode` is an optional uppercase two-letter code derived from ISO 3166. For example, the culture ID for general English is `en`, whereas the culture ID for U.S. and Canadian English is `en-US` and `en-CA`, respectively. There are some culture IDs, however, that do differ from this format. The MSDN documentation for the `CultureInfo` class contains a listing of all the pre-defined culture IDs supported by ASP.NET localization.

In an earlier example, you used Visual Studio to generate the default resource file for `LocalizationDemo.aspx`, which was named `LocalizationDemo.aspx.resx`. The general English version of the resource file is named `Localization-Demo.aspx.en.resx`, whereas the general French version is named `Localiza-tionDemo.aspx.fr.resx`. Figure 16.4 illustrates a sample general French version for the resource file shown in Figure 16.3.

If you require different versions of the resource for more specific cultures, the name for each of these files contains not only the language code but the region code as well. For instance, if you need your French resources to also have a more specialized Québécoise version, you would also have a resource file named `Localiza-tionDemo.aspx.fr-CA.resx`. Figure 16.5 illustrates the possible hierarchy of local resources for an application.

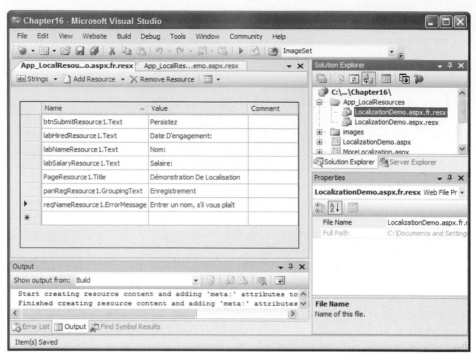

Figure 16.4   French version of resource

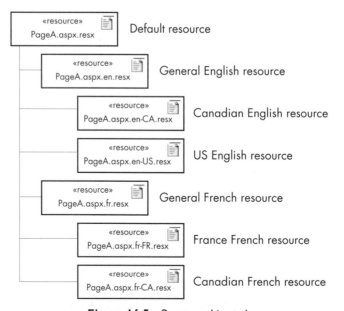

Figure 16.5   Resource hierarchy

ASP.NET uses the appropriate resource file based on the value of the
`Accept-Language` HTTP header value for each request. As a result, you can test
the localization capabilities of your site by changing the preferred language in your
browser. For instance, in Internet Explorer, you can set the language via the Internet
Options menu command, as shown in Figure 16.6.

Figure 16.6 Setting preferred language in Internet Explorer

Adding Resources

The resource editor in Visual Studio can be used to change, add, or remove entries
from this or any other resource file. For instance, imagine that you have a master
page with a logo displayed in an `Image` control and that you want a different image
file displayed for the different languages supported by your site. You can use the
resource editor to add a new resource entry that contains the filename of the appropriate logo image, as shown in Figure 16.7.

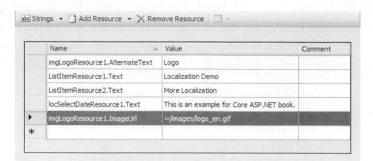

Figure 16.7   Adding a new resource entry

Unfortunately, you cannot simply rely on an implicit resource expression, because the `ImageUrl` property of the `Image` control is not marked with the `Localizable` attribute. As a result, you must instead use an ***explicit resource expression***. Like the data-binding expressions covered in Chapter 8, explicit resource expressions provide a way to declaratively assign a resource entry to a control property. The syntax for an explicit resource expression is as follows.

```
<%$ Resources: resource-file, resource-key %>
```

The `resource-file` specifies the name of the global resource file in the `App_GlobalResources` folder and is optional. The `resource-key` specifies the name of the resource key in the file. If the `resource-file` is not specified, ASP.NET looks for the `resource-key` in the local resource file. For instance, given the resources defined in Figure 16.7, you can use explicit resource expressions to set the image URL and alternate text.

```
<asp:Image runat="server" ID="imgLogo"
   ImageUrl="<%$ Resources: imgLogoResource1.ImageUrl %>"
   AlternateText="<%$ Resources: imgLogoResource1.AlternateText %>" />
```

CORE NOTE

You cannot combine an explicit resource expression for a local resource and an implicit resource expression within the same control. However, you can combine an implicit resource expression with an explicit resource expression for a *global* resource.

The result in the browser is shown in Figures 16.8 and 16.9; the former shows the result when the browser language is set to English, whereas the latter shows the result when the browser language is set to French. Notice how the `Calendar` control automatically changes the month and day labels for the language setting.

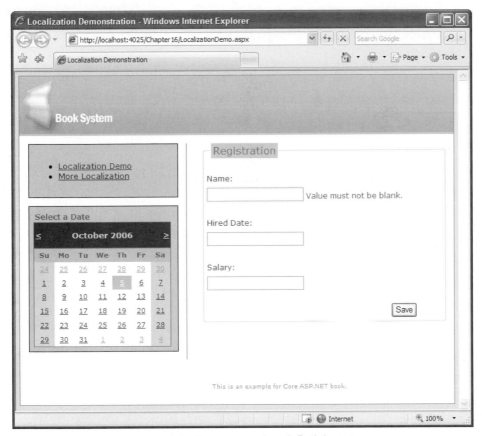

Figure 16.8   Browser result with English setting

CORE NOTE

Resource files can contain data other than strings. You can also embed images and other files, such as style sheets and XML site maps, within a resource file.

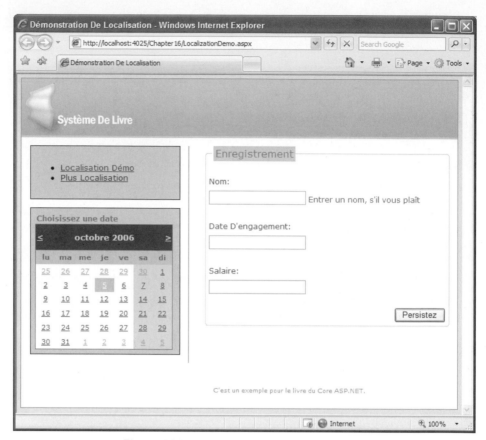

Figure 16.9   Browser result with French setting

Global Resources

Although the capability of Visual Studio to automatically generate local resources for Web Forms, user controls, and master pages is very useful, it is quite possible that it may lead to duplicate entries for common values, and thus to unnecessary additional translation efforts. To prevent this duplication, you can consolidate common resource entries into global resources.

Global resource files must be manually created in the special ASP.NET App_GlobalResources folder. As well, all references to global resources must use explicit resource expressions. For instance, if you have a resource named EntryNotBlank in a global resource file named ErrorMessages.resx (or with

`ErrorMessages.fr.resx` or any other culture ID), the resource expression for accessing this resource needs to reference the prefix of the global resource file.

```
<%$ Resources: ErrorMessages, EntryNotBlank %>
```

One possible use for global resources is to specify the overall directionality for the Web application. ***Directionality*** refers to the reading order of the text within the application. Most languages have left-to-right directionality, but some languages (e.g., Arabic, Hebrew, Urdu) have right-to-left directionality. In ASP.NET 2.0, the `Panel` control has a `Direction` property used to indicate the directionality of the controls contained within it. As well, the `html` or the `body` element also has the `dir` attribute, which controls whether text flows from right to left (`dir="rtl"`) or left to right (`dir="ltr"`).

Perhaps the best approach for handling directionality is to define a global resource that indicates the overall directionality of the application. Pages in the site can then add a `dir` attribute that references this resource to each page's `html` element. A similar approach can be used for the `Direction` attribute of the `Panel`. These global directionality resources could be customized for each culture's version of the global resource file, as shown in Figure 16.10.

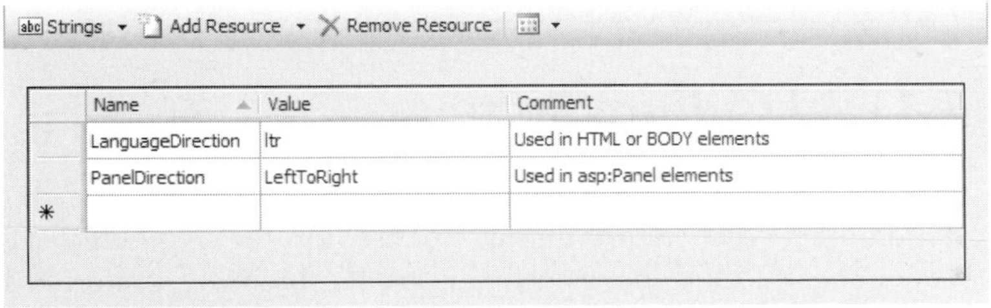

Figure 16.10　Creating global directionality resource elements

With these two elements defined, you can reference them in your Web Forms, as shown here. The `runat` attribute in the `html` element is necessary to use a resource expression.

```
<html runat="server"
    dir="<%$ Resources:ApplicationConstants,LanguageDirection %>">
...
<asp:Panel ID="panReg" runat="server"
    Direction="<%$ Resources:ApplicationConstants,
        PanelDirection %>">
```

CORE NOTE

You probably need to make additional changes to an application to completely support both left-to-right and right-to-left languages. Typical changes include the regular expressions in validation controls for date, decimal, and currency values, as well as changes to the layout (which are much easier if the site uses CSS rather than tables for layout).

An interesting feature of global resources is that when the Web site is built they are compiled into a strongly typed class. This class's name is the same as the prefix of the global resource file and is contained in the `Resources` namespace. All entries in the global resource file are available as properties of this class, as shown here.

```
labMessage.Text = Resources.ErrorMessages.EntryNotBlank;
```

You can also access local resources programmatically. Local resources are not, however, available via an external class. Instead, you must use the `GetLocalResourceObject` method of the code-behind class, as shown in the following example.

```
labMessage.Text =
    (string)GetLocalResourceObject("PageResource1.Title");
```

Page-Level Culture Settings

As you have seen, ASP.NET uses the `Accept-Language` setting in the HTTP header to determine the culture setting to use for the requested page. This `Accept-Language` HTTP value is set based on the browser's preferred language setting. However, users may prefer to view certain sites in a language different than the one specified in their browser preferences. For instance, a user using a browser in an Internet café in a foreign country does not want to use the browser's language setting. In such a case, it is best for the site itself to provide a language choice option; this user-selected choice could then be persisted in a cookie or in the ASP.NET 2.0 user profile.

You can set the cultures of a page via the `UICulture` and `Culture` properties of the `Page` class. The `Culture` property controls various culture-dependent functions, such as the date, number, and currency formatting for the page. The `UICulture` property sets the user interface culture for the thread executing the page; this property determines which culture's resource files are loaded. Both of these properties accept a `string` containing a valid culture ID.

The two culture settings do not have to have the same value. In fact, depending on your application, it might make sense to set them independently. For instance, a site dealing with money might want to always display money values in US dollars, regardless of the culture setting of the user. In such a case, you want the UICulture property to be set to the user's culture, but the Culture property to be always set to en-us.

These two properties can be set declaratively or programmatically. One way to declaratively set these properties is via the page's Page directive, as shown here.

```
<%@ Page … Culture="en-US" UICulture="auto:en-US" %>
```

In this example, culture formatting uses US English norms and the thread culture uses the language settings in the HTTP header; if none is specified in the header, it defaults to US English culture.

Rather than setting the culture in every page, you can set it for the site as a whole via the globalization element in the web.config file.

```
<configuration >
   <system.web>
      …
      <globalization culture="en-US" uiCulture="auto:en-US" />
   </system.web>
</configuration>
```

If you want to provide users with the option to set the page's culture themselves, you need to do so programmatically. The page's culture must be set quite early in the page's lifecycle, during its InitializeCulture event. Thus, you need to override the InitializeCulture method so that it sets the page's culture properties based on the user's choice, as shown here.

```
protected override void InitializeCulture()
{
    // First call the version defined in Page
    base.InitializeCulture();

    // Now retrieve the user's culture choice …
    string myCulture = …

    // … and set the page culture to this value
    if (myCulture != null)
    {
        this.Culture = myCulture;
        this.UICulture = myCulture;
    }
}
```

The one problem with this approach is that each page in your site needs to override this InitializeCulture method. To avoid this code duplication, you can use the same approach that you used when setting the page theme back in Chapter 6: namely, define a base class that inherits from the Page class and that contains the overridden InitializeCulture method. All the code-behind classes for the site's pages then inherit from this new base class.

The next set of walkthrough exercises demonstrates how to use this technique for gathering and setting the user's culture preference. As can be seen in the finished version shown in Figure 16.11, the user can now choose which language to use via a user control added to the header of the site.

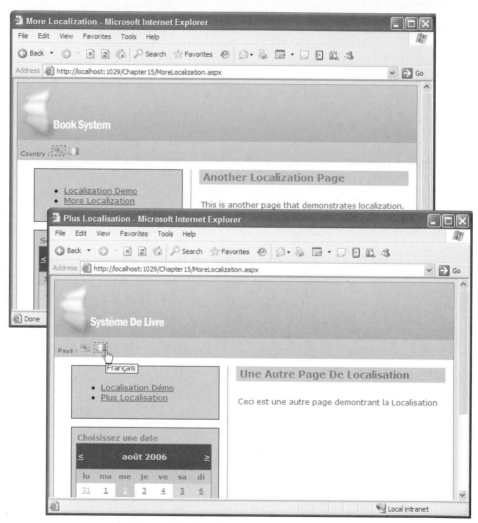

Figure 16.11   Choosing the site's language

Walkthrough 16.1 creates a user control that displays several image buttons that allow the user to specify which the language and culture to use for the site. In this example, the user's choice is persisted in a user profile setting, so you must begin by defining the profile name that will be used to store the language preferences of the user (who can be authenticated or anonymous).

Walkthrough 16.1 *Letting the User Control the Site's Culture*

1. Add the following entries to the `web.config` file.

   ```
   <anonymousIdentification enabled="true" />
   <profile>
      <properties>
         <add name="Culture" type="string" allowAnonymous="true"
            defaultValue="auto"/>
      </properties>
   </profile>
   ```

2. Create a new user control named `ChooseCultureControl.ascx`.

3. Add the following markup to the control.

   ```
   <div id="cultureStyle">
      <asp:Localize ID="locCountry" runat="server"
         Text="Country :" />

      <asp:ImageButton ID="imgUS" runat="server"
         CssClass="cultureFlag" BorderWidth="1"
         CommandName="US"
         OnCommand="imgCommand"
         ImageUrl="images/flag_us.gif" />

      <asp:ImageButton ID="imgFR" runat="server"
         CssClass="cultureFlag" BorderWidth="1"
         CommandName="France"
         OnCommand="imgCommand"
         ImageUrl="images/flag_fr.gif"/>
   </div>
   ```

4. Switch to Design view and choose the Tools →Generate Local Resource menu command.

5. Add the following event handlers to the user control's code-behind class.

   ```
   using System;
   using System.Web;
   using System.Web.UI;
   using System.Web.UI.WebControls;

   public partial class ChooseCultureControl :
      System.Web.UI.UserControl
   {
   ```

```
protected void Page_Load(object sender, EventArgs e)
{
    // Draw border around current culture's flag image
    if (Profile.Culture == "fr-FR")
    {
        imgFR.BorderStyle = BorderStyle.Dotted;
        imgUS.BorderStyle = BorderStyle.None;
    }
    else
    {
        imgUS.BorderStyle = BorderStyle.Dotted;
        imgFR.BorderStyle = BorderStyle.None;
    }
}


protected void imgCommand(object sender, CommandEventArgs e)
{
    // Set the profile based on which button was selected
    if (e.CommandName == "France")
        Profile.Culture = "fr-FR";
    else
        Profile.Culture = "en-US";

    // Re-request this page so it uses language
    // selected by user
    Response.Redirect(Request.Url.AbsolutePath);
}
}
```

6. You have to add the text for the entries in the ChooseCultureControl.ascx.resx resource file, as shown in Figure 16.12. You also have to make a French version of this resource file named ChooseCultureControl.ascx.fr.resx, which has the values shown in Figure 16.12.

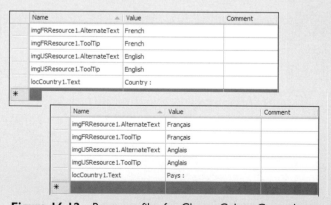

Figure 16.12   Resource files for ChooseCultureControl.ascx

Walkthrough 16.2 demonstrates how to dynamically set the page's culture based on the user's profile settings. Rather than implement this logic in each page in your site, this example places it within a new base class.

Walkthrough 16.2 *Letting the User Control the Site's Culture*

1. Create a new class in the `App_Code` folder named `BasePage.cs`.

2. Change the class as shown here.

```csharp
using System;
using System.Web;
using System.Web.UI;
using System.Web.UI.WebControls;

public class BasePage: Page
{
    protected override void InitializeCulture()
    {
        // First call the version defined in Page
        base.InitializeCulture();

        // Now set the culture based on the profile
        ProfileCommon myProfile =
            (ProfileCommon)Context.Profile;
        string myCulture = myProfile.Culture;
        if (myCulture != null)
        {
            this.Culture = myCulture;
            this.UICulture = myCulture;
        }
    }
}
```

3. Change the code-behind classes for all pages in your site so that they inherit from `BasePage` rather than `Page`, as shown in the following example.

```csharp
public partial class MySamplePage : BasePage
{
    ...
}
```

4. Set up the resource files for the site's pages and other controls, then test.

Deployment

Although Visual Studio 2005 makes it easy to develop and test a Web application on your local machine, it is important to remember that eventually the application must be deployed on a real Web server. This section examines three possible ways of deploying an ASP.NET Web application. These deployment options are

- Manually copy files from development machine to target machine, using XCOPY, FTP, Visual Studio's Copy Web Site command, or some other file management program.
- Precompile the application and deploy, using either command-line tools or Visual Studio's Publish Web Site command. You can completely control the precompilation and deployment of a Web application using the **Web Deployment Project** add-in to Visual Studio. This requires the add-in to be first downloaded and installed.
- Use Visual Studio's **Web Setup Project** or **Setup Wizard Project** to create an .msi installation file that can be run on the target machine.

The rest of this chapter examines each of these options. But before looking at these options, we should first briefly examine one important step that needs to be taken before deployment begins: namely, turning off debugging in the application's Web.config file. When developing an application, it is not uncommon to have used the debugger when tracking down a bug or a nonoperational piece of code. To enable debugging on a site-wide basis, either the developer or Visual Studio must have enabled it in the Web.config file. Unfortunately, this adds debugging symbols to the compiled code, which increases the size of the resulting assembly; as well, these extra debugging symbols decreases runtime performance. So, for a site that is being deployed to a production server, you should disable debugging in its Web.config file, as shown here.

```
<configuration>
   <system.web>

      ...
      <compilation debug="false" />
   </system.web>
</configuration>
```

Manually Copy Files from Development to Deployment Machine

This is certainly the easiest way to deploy a Web application. It requires copying all the files in the project to some location on the destination Web server, using FTP, Windows Explorer, the DOS XCOPY command, or some other file management program. The great advantage of this approach is that if a file changes in the future, all you need to do is upload the changed file to the server. The ASP.NET runtime and the .NET CLR handles the rest (i.e., the parsing, compilation into assemblies, and Just-In-Time (JIT) compilation) automatically for you.

You can also copy files from the development machine to the server within Visual Studio using the Copy Web Site command, which is available in the Solution Explorer and within the Website menu (see Figure 16.13).

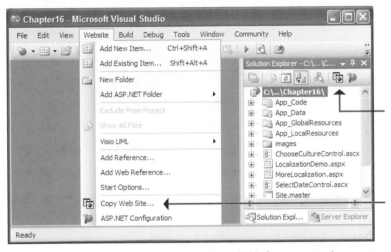

Figure 16.13 Invoking the Copy Web Site command

When the Copy Web Site command is invoked, Visual Studio displays an interface (see Figure 16.14) that is familiar to anyone who has used an FTP program such as WS_FTP.

On the left side of the Copy Web Site interface is a list of the files for the Web application on the development machine; on the right side is a list of files on the destination machine. You must connect to the destination machine first by using the Connect button. Doing so displays the familiar Open Web Site dialog (see Figure 16.15), by which you can connect to a local or remote IIS virtual directory or to a remote FTP location.

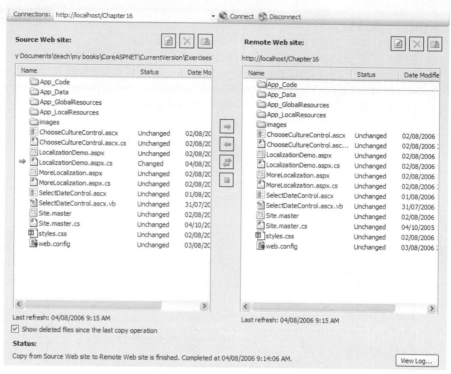

Figure 16.14   Copy Web Site interface

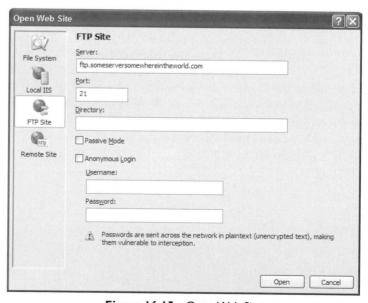

Figure 16.15   Open Web Site

After you have connected to the site, you can upload selected files from the local machine to the destination, download selected files from the destination to the local machine, or synchronize the site. Synchronizing examines the dates on files on both the local and remote sites and makes sure that all files on both sites are up-to-date. Synchronization can also be useful for multideveloper environments where developers keep copies of the Web site on their local computers. Individual developers can copy their latest changes to a shared remote server and at the same time update their local computer with changed files from other developers. However, because there is no check-in/check-out mechanism with this synchronization feature (which prevents two developers from making changes to the same file), it is no replacement for a true version control system such as Microsoft SourceSafe.

The main strength of this upload-and-forget approach to deployment, whether using Visual Studio or some other program to do so, is also its main drawback. Recall that with this approach, you are relying on the ASP.NET runtime to parse and compile pages and classes as they are requested. As you no doubt have noticed many times already, there is a noticeable time delay the first time a page is requested due to this on-the-fly compilation step. Although the developer might try to work around this issue by immediately manually requesting all changed pages right after deployment, this might be unmanageable for updates involving many pages and controls.

Another drawback to the simple upload deployment approach is that the source code for the site must be deployed to the server. Although this may not be a problem for the majority of ASP.NET sites, there are occasions when a developer may want to protect his intellectual property or some proprietary algorithms. Fortunately, there is a solution to these drawbacks: precompilation deployment, which is covered next.

Precompiling a Web Site

ASP.NET provides two options for precompiling a site. The site can be precompiled on the deployment machine into assemblies (also called *in-place precompilation*), or it can be precompiled on the development machine and then deployed to the server (also called *precompilation for deployment*).

In-Place Precompilation

In-place precompilation effectively performs the same compilation that occurs when users request pages from the site. Doing so eliminates the performance penalty for the first request to the site, as well as verifies that the site's code on the server is free of compile-time errors. In-place precompilation requires running the *aspnet_compiler.exe* command-line program on the server (which resides in `\[Windows folder]\Microsoft.NET\Framework\[version]`). The syntax for in-place precompilation is as follows.

```
aspnet_compiler -v virtualPath -OtherSwitches
```

Table 16.1 lists some of the notable command-line switches for the `aspnet_compiler` tool.

Table 16.1 Notable aspnet_compiler.exe Switches for In-Place Precompilation

Switch	Description
-?	Displays help for the `aspnet_compiler` tool.
-c	Entire application is completely recompiled.
-fixednames	Compiler does not generate unique names for assemblies each time it is run.
-p	The physical path of the root directory that contains the application to be compiled. Must be combined with the –v switch.
-v	The virtual path (the virtual directory name in IIS) of the application to be compiled.

For instance, if you had your application in a virtual directory named `Chapter16` on the server, you could use the following command to precompile the site.

```
aspnet_compiler -v /Chapter16
```

The `aspnet_compiler` creates assemblies for all executable output and places them in a special folder under the `\[Windows folder]\Microsoft.NET\Framework\ [version]\Temporary ASP.NET Files` folder, as shown in Figure 16.16. ASP.NET uses the assemblies in this folder for all subsequent requests for this application. Notice that all the Web Forms in the folder are placed in a single assembly, whereas each user control is contained in its own assembly. As well, the classes in the `App_Code` folder are contained in a single assembly, and the global and local resources are also compiled into separate assemblies.

In-place precompilation does require command-line execution access on the deployment server, which is not always available to the developer. As well, in-place precompilation still leaves the source files on the server. It is possible to have the benefits of compilation, but avoid having source files on the server by precompiling on the development machine, which is covered next.

Precompilation for Deployment

Precompiling for deployment creates an executable-only version of your site. You typically precompile for deployment on your development machine, and then deploy the resulting files to the server.

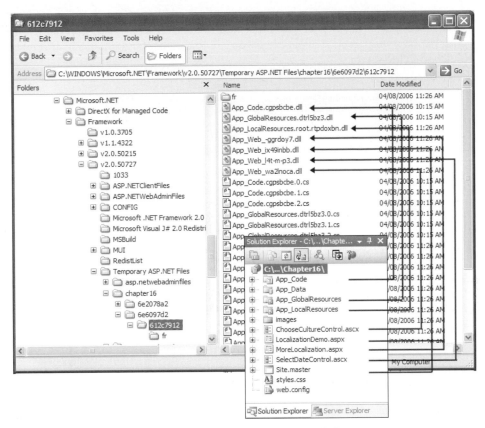

Figure 16.16   The in-place precompiled site

You can perform precompilation for deployment using the `aspnet_compiler.exe` command-line program or use the Publish Web Site command in Visual Studio. To precompile for deployment using the `aspnet_compiler`, you must specify the target directory for the output generated by the compiler.

```
aspnet_compiler -v virtualPath -OtherSwitches target_folder
```

For instance, you could change your previous example to the following to precompile for deployment.

```
aspnet_compiler -v /Chapter16 c:/staging/Chapter16
```

The compiler produces the same number of assemblies as before from the ASP.NET source files and places them within a bin folder within the target folder, as shown in Figure 16.17. Although it may appear that source files still exist in the compiled output, they are in fact only marker files for IIS; they are almost empty and contain the text, "This is a marker file generated by the precompilation tool, and should not be deleted!". This target folder can now be deployed to the server.

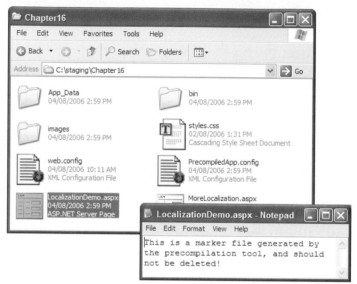

Figure 16.17 Contents of target folder after precompilation for deployment

If you want to make any future changes to the Web site, you must make changes on the development machine, recompile the site, and redeploy the target folder. The only exception is the Web.config file; it can be changed on the production server without having to recompile the site.

You can also precompile for deployment in Visual Studio using the Publish Web Site command (within the Build menu), as shown in Figure 16.18.

Notice that in Figure 16.18, the fixed name option has been enabled. This prevents the compiler from generating unique names for the generated .dll files every time the compiler is run; instead, it uses a fixed name for each generated assembly, as shown in Figure 16.19. This option is a sensible one because it prevents the bin folder on the server from accidentally becoming littered with unused assemblies.

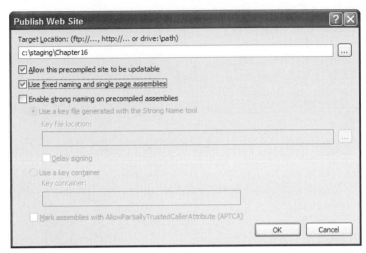

Figure 16.18 Using Visual Studio to precompile for deployment

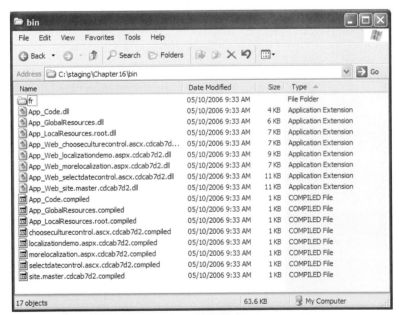

Figure 16.19 Using fixed names for assemblies

Controlling Deployment with the Web Deployment Project Add-In

Soon after Visual Studio was released, Microsoft released an add-in to Visual Studio called the Web Deployment Project, which provides more control over the deployment process than the Publish Web Site command. This add-in is available from `http://msdn.microsoft.com/asp.net/reference/infrastructure/wdp/default.aspx`. After downloading, the add-in must be installed. When installed, the next time you start Visual Studio and open your Web site, a new Add Web Development Project option is available from the Build menu, as shown in Figure 16.20. After choosing this option, you have to specify the name of the new project and its location.

The Add Web Development Project option adds a new project to the solution, as shown in Figure 16.21.

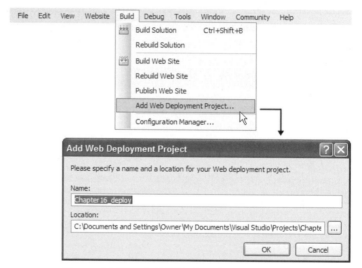

Figure 16.20   Add Web Development Project

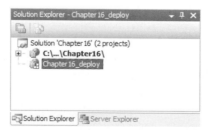

Figure 16.21   The new project in the Solution Explorer

Right-clicking this project and choosing the Property Pages option displays the property pages for this deployment project (see Figure 16.22), which allow you to customize the deployment for this project. After the deployment project is configured, you can build a new deployment with these options via the Build menu.

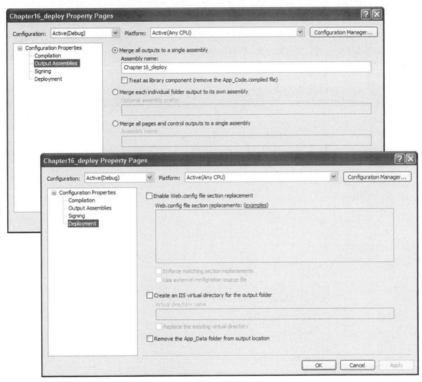

Figure 16.22   Web Deployment Project Property Pages

Creating an Installation Program Using Web Setup Project

There may be situations in which the developer cannot deploy the Web application on a server. For instance, a developer might create a Web application that must be bought and installed by the customers on their own Web servers. In such a case, the developer can distribute and deploy the application as a setup program or ***installer***. This installer, when run on the client machine, can run database scripts, change the registry, check if the host machine has the appropriate version of the .NET Framework installed, or perform other setup tasks.

There are two ways of creating this installer in Visual Studio: the **Web Setup Project** and the **Setup Wizard Project** in Visual Studio. The Setup Wizard provides a friendly, wizard-style interface to creating an installer, whereas the Web Setup Project lets you create the installer manually. In the following discussion, we examine the manual Web Setup Project.

To create a Web Setup Project, you must first have the Web application solution open in Visual Studio. You can then choose the File → Add → New Project menu command. From the New Project dialog, choose the Web Setup Project option from the Setup and Deployment project types, as shown in Figure 16.23.

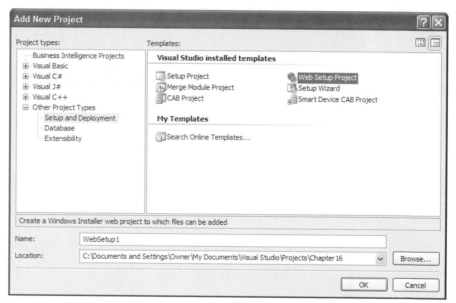

Figure 16.23   Creating a Web Setup Project in Visual Studio

After you have added the Web Setup Project, Visual Studio displays the two panes of the File System Editor window. The Web Application Folder in the leftmost pane represents what is to be installed on the target machine (see Figure 16.24).

Creating the installer principally requires specifying what files need to be included in the installer and where to install them on the target computer. You do this by adding items to the installer via the File System editor (shown in Figure 16.24). You can add the following types of items to an installer: Visual Studio projects (called project outputs), files, merge modules, and assemblies.

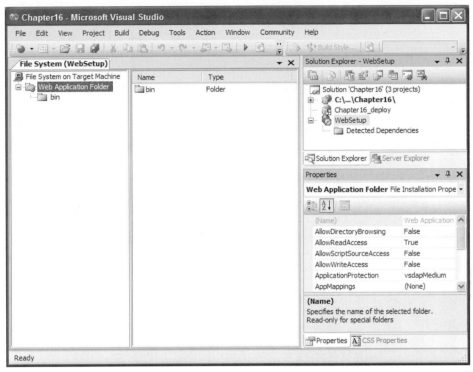

Figure 16.24 File system editor window

To add an existing Visual Studio project to your installer, right-click the Web Application Folder in the leftmost File System pane and choose Add →Project Output (or simply choose Project → Add → Project Output menu command). This displays the Add Project Output Group dialog, as shown in Figure 16.25. You can simply select the project in the current Visual Studio solution that you want to add to the installer (in this example, you are adding the Chapter16 Web project).

After adding a Visual Studio project to the installer, you can now add content to the installer. As well, you can specify setup conditions, registry changes, database scripts, or change the user interface of the installer. You can specify these via new buttons present on the Solution Explorer window, as shown in Figure 16.26.

After you have added all your content to the installer, be sure to set the properties for the Web Application Folder and the Setup Project, as shown in Figure 16.27.

Figure 16.25 Add Project Output Group dialog

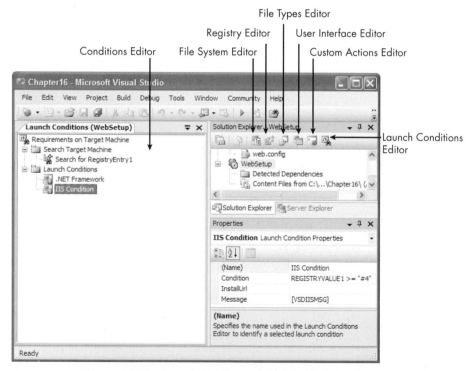

Figure 16.26 Launch Conditions Editor and Solution Explorer

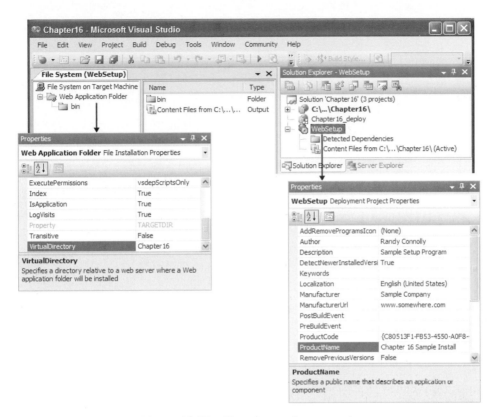

Figure 16.27   Changing installer properties

After the project is set up as required, you are ready to build the installation file via the Build → Build Websetup (or whatever you have named your Web Setup Project) menu command. You can customize how this installation file is generated by changing the project's properties, as shown in Figure 16.28. Be sure to change the Configuration setting to Release, as shown in Figure 16.28.

The end result after building are two files: setup.exe (for client machines without the Windows Installer) and an .msi file with the same name as the Web Setup Project, which is the setup program to be used on client machines with the Windows Installer present. These two installation files by default are generated in a subfolder within My Documents\Visual Studio\Projects\SolutionName.

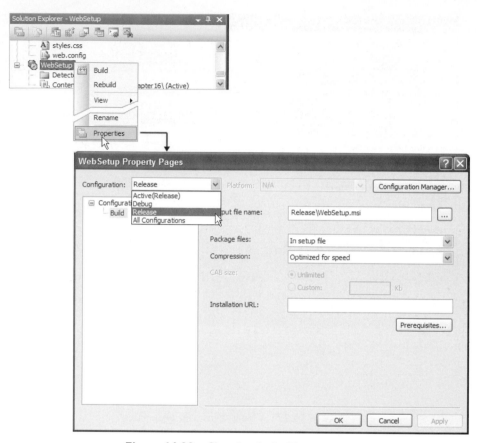

Figure 16.28   Changing the build properties

Executing the `.msi` file installs the Web site on the client machine using the familiar Windows setup dialog boxes, as shown in Figure 16.29.

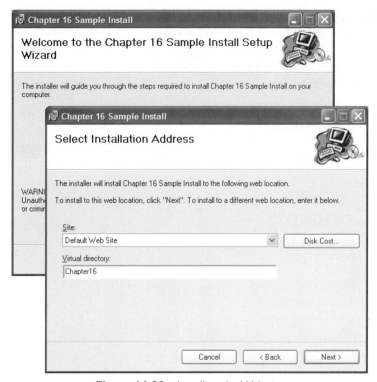

Figure 16.29   Installing the Web site

Summary

This chapter examined two important but often overlooked parts of ASP.NET development. The first of these was how to plan and adapt an ASP.NET application for an international audience. The chapter examined how to use both local and global resource files as part of the process of globalizing an application. The second focus of this chapter was on the deployment of ASP.NET applications. Several different approaches to deployment are possible with ASP.NET and Visual Studio. These include simple manual copying of files, precompiling the application for additional security, and creating a setup installation file.

Exercises

The solutions to the following exercises can be found at my Web site, http://www.randyconnolly.com/core. Additional exercises only available for teachers and instructors are also available from this site.

1. Change Listing 4.1 from Chapter 4 so that it uses resources rather than hard-coded English strings.

2. Perform a precompilation for deployment for the solution for the preceding exercise.

Key Concepts

- aspnet_compiler.exe
- Culture
- Culture ID
- Default resource values
- Deployment project
- Directionality
- Explicit resource expression
- Globalization
- Implicit resource expression
- In-place precompilation
- Installer
- Localization
- Precompilation for deployment
- Resource expression
- Resource key prefix value
- Resources
- Setup Wizard Project
- Web Deployment Project
- Web Setup Project

References

Allen, Scott. "Precompilation in ASP.NET 2.0." http://www.odetocode.com.

Bustamante, Michèle Leroux. "ASP.NET 2.0 Localization Features: A Fresh Approach to Localizing Web Applications." http://msdn.microsoft.com.

Bustamante, Michèle Leroux. "Localization Practices for .NET 2.0: It's Still About the Architecture." `http://www.theserverside.net`.

Esposito, Dino. "Inside Site Precompilation and No-Compile Pages." `http://www.vsj.co.uk`.

Pattison, Ted. "Resources and Localization." *MSDN Magazine* (May 2006).

Pattison, Ted. "Resources and Localization in ASP.NET 2.0." *MSDN Magazine* (August 2006).

Appendix

ASP.NET AJAX Sneak Peek

ASP.NET AJAX is a free framework from Microsoft that adds Asynchronous Java-Script and XML (AJAX) support to ASP.NET. Up until the fall of 2006, ASP.NET AJAX was known by the code-name of Atlas. Though the product has been rebranded, all the code and documentation still refers to the product as Atlas; as a result, the rest of this chapter also refers to Atlas. Thus, this appendix contains a brief overview of Atlas and provides some examples of Atlas integration with ASP.NET using the July 2006 CTP of Atlas.

At the time of this book's printing (February 2007), ASP.NET AJAX is still in beta testing. It is possible that ASP.NET AJAX may be rebranded again in the near future. It is also quite likely that some of the examples in this appendix may no longer work by the time Atlas is finally released. A revised version of this appendix is available in electronic format from my Web site, `http://www.randyconnolly.com/core`, when Atlas moves from beta to final release.

Atlas encompasses a fairly large set of functionality that integrates client script (Javascript) libraries with ASP.NET server-based pages. It provides an API for working with Javascript, a declarative alternative to working with Javascript, rich client-script components, along with special Atlas server-side controls. Fully describing and demonstrating Atlas is the job of an entire book, not a single appendix. Nonetheless, this appendix endeavors to provide an overview of Atlas as well as several examples that demonstrate what a developer can achieve with this framework.

Introducing Atlas

Atlas is an extension to ASP.NET 2.0 that allows developers to create Web applications with a richer user interface and that appear to be quicker and more responsive to the user. Atlas is also Microsoft's response to the very strong interest in AJAX in the Web development community.

AJAX is not a product. Rather, it is the most common name given to a style of Web development that makes fuller use of Javascript and the browser Document Object Model (DOM) in the construction of Web application user interfaces. AJAX Web applications also make use of all the current browsers' capability to asynchronously request and receive information from the browser independently of the usual page request/page receive/page display cycle. This capability to asynchronously communicate with the server makes it possible to create pages that are more responsive and less disruptive. Google Suggest and Yahoo Flickr are prominent examples of sites that use both client scripting and asynchronous communication with the server as a way of improving the user experience. This type of site is sometimes also referred to as Web 2.0.

Figures A.1 and A.2 illustrate the difference between a traditional ASP.NET Web application and an AJAX-enabled ASP.NET application.

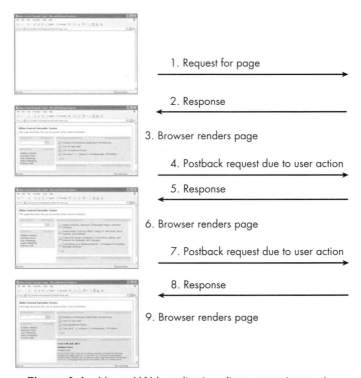

Figure A.1 Normal Web application client-server interaction

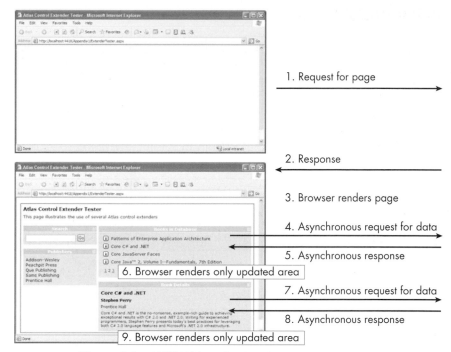

1. Request for page

2. Response

3. Browser renders page

4. Asynchronous request for data

5. Asynchronous response

6. Browser renders only updated area

7. Asynchronous request for data

8. Asynchronous response

9. Browser renders only updated area

Figure A.2 AJAX Web application client-server interaction

An important feature of most AJAX applications is their capability to communicate asynchronously with the server. This capability is typically achieved in Javascript using the XMLHttpRequest object (although some sites use hidden IFrame elements instead). This object was initially offered in Internet Explorer 5 as an ActiveX component; FireFox, Opera, and Safari subsequently have added native support for XMLHttpRequest. However, because Internet Explorer 5 and 6 XMLHttpRequest support is via an ActiveX component, it is possible for the user to disable it via browser settings. Internet Explorer 7, like the other browsers, now supports XMLHttpRequest natively.

Although richer AJAX Web applications are a real boon for the user, creating them can be a real nightmare for the developer. Javascript as a language lacks the kind of object-oriented features developers expect. As well, Javascript can be quite difficult to debug. As a consequence, there has been a proliferation of frameworks and toolkits to simplify the process of developing AJAX applications. Atlas is Microsoft's official framework for developing AJAX Web applications.

Installing Atlas

Atlas must be installed on the developer's machine. At the time of writing this appendix, the installation program for Atlas was available from `http://ajax.asp.net`. The installation of Atlas is straightforward. Running the downloaded setup file steps the user through a standard setup wizard, as shown in Figure A.3.

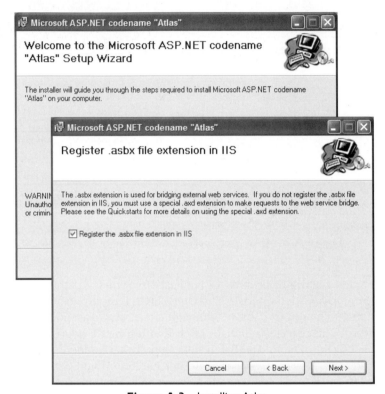

Figure A.3 Installing Atlas

CORE NOTE

Even though Atlas has been rebranded, the downloaded file and its contents at the time of writing are still called Atlas.

The installation program locates Atlas at `C:\Program Files\Microsoft ASP.NET\Atlas\[version]\Atlas`. The principal content of this `Atlas` folder is the `Microsoft.Web.Atlas.dll` assembly. This assembly must be added to the `bin` folder of any Web application that makes use of Atlas. The folder also contains a `web.config` file that contains the configuration settings that also must be added to any application that uses Atlas. Finally, the folder contains a `ScriptLibrary` folder that contains all the Javascript files (`.js`) that make up the client script libraries that are the foundation of Atlas.

The setup program also adds a new template to Visual Studio. This template lets you create a new Atlas-enabled Web site in Visual Studio 2005, as shown in Figure A.4.

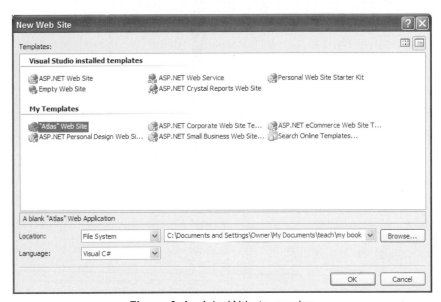

Figure A.4   Atlas Web site template

This template sets up the `Web.config` file for Atlas use as well as adds the Atlas assembly to the `bin` folder, as shown in Figure A.5.

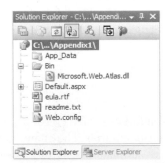

Figure A.5   Atlas template files

The documentation and the control toolkit for Atlas are also available from the same location as the Atlas setup file, and both of these should be installed.

Atlas Architecture

Unlike many other AJAX frameworks, which are usually client-side only, Atlas is both a client- and a server-side framework. It integrates with ASP.NET so that developers can leverage their existing ASP.NET knowledge. Figure A.6 illustrates the basic architecture of Atlas, and how it resides on both the client and the server.

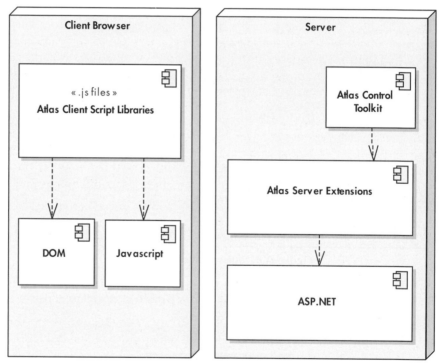

Figure A.6   Atlas architecture

Atlas Client Features

Because the whole purpose of Atlas is to provide a toolset for developers to create complex and responsive user interfaces for Web clients, it should be no surprise that the core of Atlas is its client script libraries. The client script libraries are a number of Javascript files (.js) that are ultimately sent to browsers that request ASP.NET pages created with Atlas. These Javascript files, along with the rest of Atlas, are installed on the developer's machine. The Javascript client script library can be visualized as five separate logical layers.

- Cross-browser compatibility—Provides a foundation of cross-browser compatibility so that the rest of the Atlas client library can work with Internet Explorer, FireFox, and Safari. At the time of writing this appendix, Atlas is still weak in regards to its compatibility, especially with Safari. As well, the Opera browser is not currently supported by Atlas.
- Javascript extensions—Various functions, objects, and data types added to Javascript that allow the developer to work with Javascript in a more object-oriented way.
- Base class library—Useful Javascript classes for debugging, event handling, working with Web services, interacting with timers, and so on.
- Core UI framework—Infrastructure classes for constructing user interfaces.
- UI Toolkit—Client-side controls with a richer user interface than the standard HTML controls. Some of these client-side controls are the listview, dataview, select, button, and counter controls.

Perhaps the best way to approach the client features is via a rather simple example. Imagine that you have a simple form that contains a search text box and button; when the user clicks the button, you want the page to asynchronously call a method in some external Web service and pass it the text entered by the user. When the Web service finally returns a value, you want the page to display this value. The base markup for this page might look like the following.

```
<form id="Form1" runat="server">
   Search for
   <input id="myText" type="text" />
   <input id="myButton" type="button" />
   <span id="myResults"></span>
</form>
```

You should note here that this page does require a special additional Atlas element called the ScriptManager. The ScriptManager must be included on all Web Forms that use Atlas. Analogous to the WebPartManager control from Chapter 13, the ScriptManager control manages any Atlas controls on the page, handles any partial page updates, and renders all necessary client scripts. In this example, you can use it to define the reference to the Web service.

```
<atlas:ScriptManager runat="server" ID="scriptManager">
   <services>
       <atlas:servicereference path="…/ServiceSomewhere.asmx" />
   </services>
</atlas:ScriptManager>
```

There are two ways of performing this task in an AJAX-like way with Atlas.

1. You can use the Atlas Javascript client library directly within Javascript that you add to your page.
2. You can use the same client functionality in the Atlas Javascript client library indirectly via a new XML-based declarative language sometimes referred to as xml-script. This parallel language is contained within `script` elements that are added to your Web Forms. This language can reduce or even eliminate the need to work with Javascript, but increases the downloaded size of the page.

Developers who are already familiar with Javascript probably are most comfortable with the first approach. In this approach, you can simply add a Javascript event handler along with a reference to it in the button's markup. For instance, you can change the markup for the button to the following.

```
<input id="myButton" type="button" OnClick="InvokeWebService" />
```

You can then define a Javascript event handler similar to the following.

```
<script type="text/javascript">

 function InvokeWebService()
 {
   var textElem = document.getElementById("myText");
   SomeServiceSomewhere.SomeMethod(textElem.value,
     OnRequestComplete);
 }

 function OnRequestComplete(result)
 {
   var resultElem = document.getElementById("myResults");
   resultElem.innerHTML = result;
 }

</script>
```

The emphasized code in the `InvokeWebService` function refers to a function that is dynamically defined by Atlas. This function is a client-side Web service proxy. Because you are making an asynchronous call, you must also define an event handler to be called when the service returns a value. This function is passed the return value from the Web service and simply sets the content of the specified `<span>` element.

CORE NOTE

In Chapter 15, you were consuming Web services on the server. That is, the proxy class existed on the server and was executed on the server. In this Atlas example, the Web service is being consumed on the client.

You can also perform this same task using Atlas client markup (i.e., xml-script). In this case, you do not need to define any Javascript event handlers (nor do you need to reference any in the `input` element). Atlas client markup is contained within a special `script` element, as shown in the following.

```
<script type="text/xml-script">
...
</script>
```

For your example, the client markup looks like the following.

```
<script type="text/xml-script">
   <page xmlns:script="http://schemas.microsoft.com/
         xml-script/2005">
     <components>

         <textBox id="myText" />

         <serviceMethod id="myServiceMethod"
             url=".../SomeServiceSomewhere.asmx"
             methodName="SomeMethod">

             <bindings>
                 binding dataContext="myText"
                 dataPath="text"
                 property="parameters"
                 propertyKey="query" />
             </bindings>
             <completed>
               <invokeMethod target="resultsBinding"
                   method="evaluateIn" />
             </completed>
         </serviceMethod>

         <button id="SearchButton">
           <click>
               <invokeMethod target="SomeServiceSomewhere"
                   method="invoke" />
           </click>
         </button>
```

```
        <label id="results">
           <bindings>
               <binding id="resultsBinding"
                   dataContext="myServiceMethod"
                   dataPath="result"
                   property="text"
                   automatic="false" />
           </bindings>
        </label>
     </components>
  </page>
</script>
```

Certainly, in this case, this client markup approach is significantly less concise than the Javascript approach! Unfortunately, Atlas client markup is yet another language/syntax for developers to learn. It is now possible for your `aspx` page to contain all of the following: HTML, CSS, Javascript within a client-side `script` element, C# within a server-side `script` element, ASP.NET server controls, and now Atlas server controls, as well as Atlas client markup within a client-side `script` element. As a consequence, the source code for ASP.NET pages using Atlas can become quite busy and complicated. Fortunately, the longer-term plan for Atlas client markup is that it is principally emitted by Atlas server controls as well as created and consumed by developer tools.

The possible content within this declarative Atlas client markup appears to be quite varied, and it is beyond the scope of this appendix to examine it or the Javascript client library in any depth. As well, at the time of this appendix's writing, there is no documentation available for xml-script, only examples of how to use it. As a result, the rest of the chapter focuses on the more familiar and immediately useful Atlas server features.

Atlas Server Features

As the diagram in Figure A.6 illustrates, Atlas also contains new server-side controls. These Atlas server controls can be used as well as (or as an alternative to) the new client-side controls in the client script library. The Atlas server controls encapsulate some of the functionality available in the client script library. Some of the key tasks these Atlas server controls allow you to perform include

- Render and update only a part of a page (instead of the normal postback cycle) using the `UpdatePanel` control
- Use control extender controls to add special client behavior to ASP.NET Web server controls.
- Create custom extender controls for defining new behaviors for server controls. Other developers can then use these custom extender controls to get additional client behaviors without writing any Atlas client script or Javascript. The Atlas Control Toolkit is a set of Atlas server controls and custom extenders.

The next section examines several of these Atlas server features in more detail.

Using Atlas

Perhaps the best way to understand Atlas is to use it. In this section, there are several walkthrough exercises that illustrate the type of interaction possible with Atlas. By the end of this section, you will have created a reasonably complex Atlas page.

Setting Up the Test Page

You begin with the sample ASP.NET page shown in Listing A.1. This page does not yet contain any Atlas. Figure A.7 illustrates how it appears in the browser.

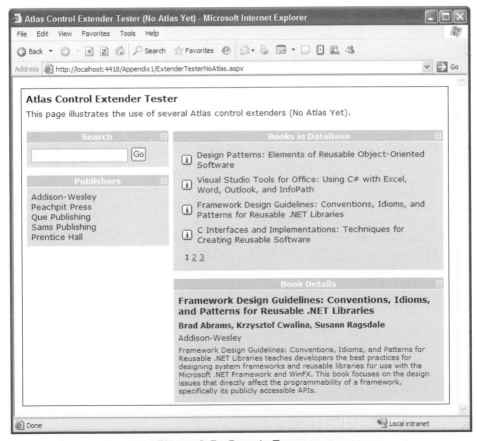

Figure A.7   ExtenderTester.aspx

Listing A.1 ExtenderTester.aspx

```
<div id="container">
  <h1>Atlas Control Extender Tester </h1>
  <p>
  This page illustrates the use of several Atlas
  control extenders
  </p>
  <div id="sideArea">
    <asp:Panel ID="panSearchHeader" runat="server" >
      <h2 class="boxHeading">Search</h2>
      <div class="headerButton">
        <asp:Image ID="imgHeaderSearch" runat="server"
          ImageUrl="~/images/minimize.gif"/>
      </div>
    </asp:Panel>
    <asp:Panel ID="panSearch" runat="server" CssClass="box">
      <div class="insideBox">
        <asp:TextBox ID="txtSearch" runat="server" />
        <asp:button ID="btnSearch" runat="server" Text="Go"
          OnClick="btnSearch_Click" /><br />
        <asp:Label ID="labNotFound" runat="server" />
      </div>
    </asp:Panel>

    <asp:Panel ID="panPublisherHeader" runat="server" >
      <h2 class="boxHeading">Publishers</h2>
      <div class="headerButton">
        <asp:Image ID="imgHeaderPublisher" runat="server"
          ImageUrl="~/images/minimize.gif"/>
      </div>
    </asp:Panel>
    <asp:Panel ID="panPublisher" runat="server" CssClass="box">
      <div class="insideBox">
        <asp:Repeater ID="rptPublishers" runat="server"
          DataSourceID="dsPublishers">
          <ItemTemplate>
            <asp:Panel ID="panRepeaterItem" runat="server"
              CssClass="publisherItems">
              <%# Eval("PublisherName") %>
            </asp:Panel>
          </ItemTemplate>
        </asp:Repeater>
      </div>
    </asp:Panel>
  </div>

  <div id="mainArea">
    <asp:Panel ID="panBookListHeader" runat="server" >
      <h2 class="boxHeading">Books in Database</h2>
```

```
        <div class="headerButton">
           <asp:Image ID="imgHeaderBookList" runat="server"
               ImageUrl="~/images/minimize.gif"/>
        </div>
     </asp:Panel>
     <asp:Panel ID="panBookList" runat="server" CssClass="box">
        <div class="insideBox">
           <asp:GridView ID="grdBookList" runat="server"
               DataSourceID="dsBooks"
               AutoGenerateColumns="False"
               AllowPaging="true" PageSize="4"
               DataKeyNames="Isbn" GridLines="None"
               CellPadding="4" ShowHeader="false"
               OnSelectedIndexChanged="grdBookList_Selected">

               <Columns>
                  <asp:CommandField ShowSelectButton="true"
                      ButtonType="Image"
                      SelectImageUrl="images/btn_select.gif"/>
                  <asp:BoundField DataField="Title" />
               </Columns>
           </asp:GridView>
        </div>
     </asp:Panel>

     <asp:Panel ID="panBookHeader" runat="server" >
        <h2 class="boxHeading">Book Details</h2>
        <div class="headerButton">
           <asp:Image ID="imgHeaderBook" runat="server"
               ImageUrl="~/images/minimize.gif"/>
        </div>
     </asp:Panel>
     <asp:Panel ID="panBook" runat="server" CssClass="box">
        <div class="insideBox">
           <h2>
              <asp:Label ID="labBookTitle" runat="server" />
           </h2>
           <p class="bookAuthors">
              <asp:Label ID="labBookAuthors" runat="server" />
           </p>
           <p class="bookPublisher">
              <asp:Label ID="labBookPublisher" runat="server" />
           </p>
           <p class="bookDesc">
              <asp:Label ID="labBookDesc" runat="server" />
           </p>
        </div>
     </asp:Panel>
   </div>
</div>
```

```
<asp:SqlDataSource ID="dsBooks" runat="server"
   ProviderName="System.Data.SqlClient"
   ConnectionString="<%$ ConnectionStrings:BookCatalog %>"
   SelectCommand="SELECT ISBN,Title FROM Books" />
<asp:SqlDataSource ID="dsPublishers" runat="server"
   ProviderName="System.Data.SqlClient"
   ConnectionString="<%$ ConnectionStrings:BookCatalog %>"
   SelectCommand="SELECT PublisherId,PublisherName
      FROM Publishers" />
```

The structure of this document is illustrated in Figure A.8. Notice that the content of the page is contained within `Panel` controls. Many of the Atlas server controls allow you to manipulate a block of ASP.NET content when it is contained within a `Panel` control.

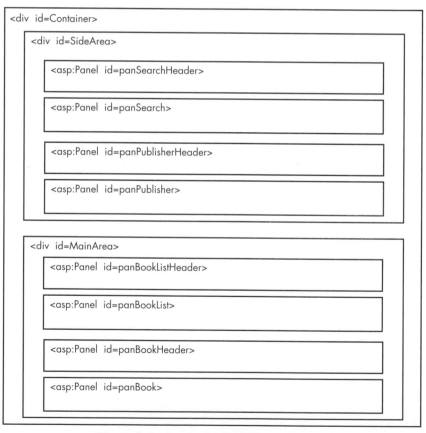

Figure A.8　Structure of ExtenderTester.aspx

This page also contains some code-behind logic, which is shown in Listing A.2.

Listing A.2   ExtenderTester.aspx.cs

```csharp
using System;
using System.Data;
using System.Configuration;
using System.Collections;
using System.Web;
using System.Web.Security;
using System.Web.UI;
using System.Web.UI.WebControls;

using FourLayer.ApplicationLogic;
using FourLayer.BusinessEntity;

public partial class ExtenderTester : System.Web.UI.Page
{
    /// <summary>
    /// Handles user selection events for the GridView of Books
    /// </summary>
    protected void grdBookList_Selected(object sender,
        EventArgs e)
    {
        string isbn = (string)grdBookList.SelectedDataKey.Value;

        Book book = BookCatalogLogic.GetBookByIsbn(isbn);
        if (book != null) DisplayBook(book);
    }

    /// <summary>
    /// Click event for search button
    /// </summary>
    protected void btnSearch_Click(object sender, EventArgs e)
    {
        // Try to retrieve book for entered text
        EntityCollection<Book> books =
            BookCatalogLogic.GetBooksByTitle(txtSearch.Text);

        // If found a book, display it in Book Panel
        if (books == null || books.Count <= 0)
            labNotFound.Text = "Book Not Found";
        else
            DisplayBook(books[0]);
    }

    /// <summary>
    /// Displays the book contents in the Book Panel
```

```
/// </summary>
private void DisplayBook(Book book)
{
    labNotFound.Text = "";
    labBookTitle.Text = book.Title;
    labBookAuthors.Text = book.AuthorsCommaList;
    labBookPublisher.Text = book.BookPublisher.Name;
    labBookDesc.Text = book.BriefDescription;
}
}
```

Enabling Partial Page Updates

You are now ready to Atlas-ize this page. The first walkthrough demonstrates how to improve the general responsiveness of this page by using the Atlas `UpdatePanel` control. This control allows part of a page to be updated and rendered independently of the rest of the page. Figures A.1 and A.2 at the start of this appendix illustrate the contrast between normal postback page updates and partial asynchronous updates. Partial updates generally make the user experience of the page less disruptive, because there are fewer postback requests. Remember that each time there is a postback request, the page must be redrawn by the browser. This creates the so-called flicker (caused by the browser blanking the page and then rerendering it as it receives the new page) that is the bane of all AJAX applications.

Enabling partial page updates in Atlas is quite painless. First, you must add a `ScriptManager` control that enables partial rendering. Then, you only need to embed the Web server content that you want to be asynchronously updated within Atlas `UpdatePanel` controls. Finally, you can define any conditions that trigger a refresh of that content.

Walkthrough A.1 illustrates how to enable partial page updates in your sample page. In it, you are going to wrap the single book details `Panel` within an `UpdatePanel`. This way, every time the user selects a new book, only the contents of this panel are updated and rerendered. As well, you wrap the paged `GridView` in an `UpdatePanel` so that paging it only causes a partial page refresh.

Walkthrough A.1   *Enabling Partial Page Refreshes*

1. Add the following `ScriptManager` to the page. Notice that it sets the `EnablePartialRendering` property, which enables asynchronous partial page updates.

```
<atlas:ScriptManager ID="mySM" runat="server"
    EnablePartialRendering="true" />
```

2. Wrap the book details `Panel` within an `UpdatePanel` as shown here.

```
<atlas:UpdatePanel ID="upBook" runat="server">
   <ContentTemplate>
      <asp:Panel ID="panBook" runat="server" CssClass="box">
         <div class="insideBox">
            ...
         </div>
      </asp:Panel>
   </ContentTemplate>
</atlas:UpdatePanel>
```

This `UpdatePanel` still needs to be refreshed and rerendered, however, when the user selects a book in the `GridView` or when the user enters a title string into the search box. Thus, you need to indicate these refresh conditions via *triggers*.

There are two types of triggers: control event triggers and control value triggers. Control event triggers indicate that the `UpdatePanel` should be refreshed when a certain *control event occurs*. The other type of trigger is a control value trigger, which indicates that the `UpdatePanel` should be refreshed when a certain control *property value changes*. In your example, you will use control event triggers.

3. Add the following triggers to this `UpdatePanel`.

```
<atlas:UpdatePanel ID="upBook" runat="server">
   <ContentTemplate>
      <asp:Panel ID="panBook" runat="server" CssClass="box">
         <div class="insideBox">
            ...
         </div>
      </asp:Panel>
   </ContentTemplate>
   <Triggers>
      <atlas:ControlEventTrigger ControlID="btnSearch"
         EventName="Click" />
      <atlas:ControlEventTrigger ControlID="grdBookList"
         EventName="SelectedIndexChanged" />
   </Triggers>
</atlas:UpdatePanel>
```

4. Wrap the book list `Panel` within an `UpdatePanel`. Because this control is not dependent upon other controls on the page, you do not need to specify any triggers.

```
<atlas:UpdatePanel ID="upBookList" runat="server">
    <ContentTemplate>
        <asp:Panel ID="panBookList" runat="server"
            CssClass="box">
            <div class="insideBox">
                <asp:GridView ID="grdBookList" runat="server"
                    ...
                </asp:GridView>
            </div>
        </asp:Panel>
    </ContentTemplate>
</atlas:UpdatePanel>
```

5. Test in browser. Keep a close eye on the browser's status bar as you select books from the GridView; notice that there are no visible postbacks as you select.

Using an UpdateProgress Control

The capability to asynchronously update just a part of a page can make that page appear much more responsive. Nonetheless, asynchronous requests are still requests that must travel across the Internet to the server and then return back at some point with the response. As a consequence, there are still time delays as the page waits to receive the response back from the server.

When working with normal non-AJAX Web pages, users receive visual feedback via the browser's progress bar while the browser is waiting for a response (see Figure A.9).

However, the browser progress bar does not appear for asynchronous requests. Thus, from a usability standpoint, you may want to add a progress indicator to your pages to let the user know when an asynchronous request is being made. Atlas comes with an UpdateProgress control to handle this need.

The UpdateProgress control provides visual feedback in the browser window while the contents of one or more UpdatePanel controls are being updated. The UpdateProgress control contains a ProgressTemplate that contains the markup that appears when the browser is waiting for the UpdatePanel to be updated. For instance, in the following example, the UpdateProgress control displays an animated .gif and a text message.

```
<atlas:UpdateProgress ID="upProd" runat="server" >
    <ProgressTemplate>
        <asp:Image runat="server" id="imgProgress"
            ImageUrl="~/images/progressBar.gif" />
        Loading ...
    </ProgressTemplate>
</atlas:UpdateProgress>
```

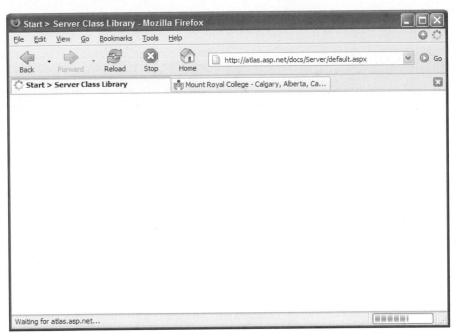

Figure A.9   Browser progress bar

The result in the browser is shown in Figure A.10.

Figure A.10   UpdateProgress example

CORE NOTE

There can be only one `UpdateProgress` control per page.

Using Atlas Control Extenders

Control extenders in Atlas provide a way to attach Javascript functionality to regular ASP.NET server controls. At the time of writing, there are two available extenders in Atlas: the `AutoCompleteExtender` (for adding auto-completion drop-down lists to a control) and the `DragOverlayExtender` (for adding drag-and-drop behavior to a control). As well, the Atlas Control Toolkit contains many additional extenders.

AutoCompleteExtender

The next walkthrough exercise demonstrates how to add an `AutoComplete-Extender` to your example. This extender allows a text box to display a drop-down list of suggestions as the user enters text into the box, as shown in Figure A.11.

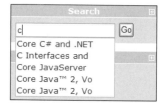

Figure A.11   AutoCompleteExtender in action

Where do these suggestions come from? The content for these suggestions are retrieved asynchronously from a service on the server. Perhaps the easiest way to do this is via Web services.

As we saw earlier in the discussion on client features in Atlas, it is relatively easy to consume Web services from the client using Atlas. In fact, you can specify the Web service to consume directly within the definition of the `AutoCompleteExtender`, as shown in Walkthrough A.2.

Walkthrough A.2   *Adding an AutoCompleteExtender*

1. Add the following markup to your `ExtenderTester.aspx` file. Because an extender "extends" an existing control, it makes no difference where you place it in the markup. You may want to place it close to the control it is extending or instead place it at the end of your page.

```
<atlas:AutoCompleteExtender runat="server"
    MinimumPrefixLength="1"
    ServiceMethod="GetTitleSuggestions"
    ServicePath="BookService.asmx" >

    <atlas:AutoCompleteProperties TargetControlID="txtSearch"
        Enabled="true" />

</atlas:AutoCompleteExtender>
```

This `AutoCompleteExtender` has two properties (`ServiceMethod` and `ServicePath`) that indicate which Web service and which method in that service are to be called to retrieve the suggestions that are used to fill the auto-complete list. The `MinimumPrefixLength` property specifies the minimum number of elements the user must type before invoking the auto-complete lookup.

Notice as well that this extender requires a nested `AutoComplete-Properties` element to specify the control that is being extended (that is, the control to which you are adding the auto-complete list). Almost all of the extenders in Atlas work in the same way.

2. You must now define the Web service. Add a Web service named `Book-Service.asmx` to the same Web site as your `ExtenderTester.aspx` file.

3. Add the following references to your Web service.

```
using FourLayer.ApplicationLogic;
using FourLayer.BusinessEntity;
```

4. Add the following method definition to the Web service.

```
[WebMethod]
public string[] GetTitleSuggestions(string prefixText,
    int count)
{
    // First get a list of books that match the user's entry
    EntityCollection<Book> books =
        BookCatalogLogic.GetBooksByTitle(prefixText);

    // If no matches, simply return null
    if (books == null || books.Count == 0)
        return null;
    else
    {
        // You must return no more than that specified
        // by the count parameter
        int countOfTitles = books.Count;
        if (countOfTitles > count) countOfTitles = count;

        // Create your return array
        string[] titles = new string[countOfTitles];

        // Fill return array from list of books
        for (int i = 0; i < countOfTitles; i++)
        {
```

```
        // Return only the first 16 characters of title
        // (otherwise, drop-down list is too wide)
        int maxLen = 16;
        if (maxLen > books[i].Title.Length)
            maxLen = books[i].Title.Length;
        titles[i] = books[i].Title.Substring(0, maxLen);
    }
    return titles;
  }
}
```

The signature for this method *must* be as shown here. That is, the method used by the AutoCompleteExtender must return an array of `string` objects and have both the `string` and `int` parameters.

5. Test in browser. The auto complete behavior should now work.

Atlas Control Toolkit Extenders

The Atlas Control Toolkit is being developed separately from the rest of Atlas. Microsoft is using a collaborative, open-source model to develop it, in that both Microsoft and non-Microsoft developers can work on the toolkit. The goal is to create a large number of Atlas controls and extenders that allow developers to add rich AJAX support to an application without too much effort.

At the time of writing, the Atlas Control Toolkit contains 21 controls and extenders of varying quality and usefulness. In Walkthrough A.4, you use an extender from the Atlas Control Toolkit in a page. But before you can use an extender from this Toolkit, you first install it, which is covered in Walkthrough A.3.

Walkthrough A.3   *Installing the Atlas Control Toolkit*

The Atlas Control Toolkit requires a separate download and install before it can be used.

1. Download the current version of the Atlas Control Toolkit from the `http://ajax.asp.net` Web site.

2. Extract the contents from the downloaded ZIP file into some location (perhaps the `C:\Program Files\Microsoft ASP.NET\Atlas\ [version]\AtlasControlToolkit` folder).

3. Copy the `Microsoft.AtlasControlExtender.dll` file from the `Binaries` folder of `AtlasControlToolkit` to the `bin` folder of your application.

Walkthrough A.4　*Using an Extender from the Atlas Control Toolkit*

In this example, you use the `CollapsiblePanelExtender` extender. This extender makes an element of your page (typically, a `Panel`) collapsible, that is, it can be easily hidden or displayed by the user simply by a user click.

1. Add the following extender somewhere in your page.

```
<atlasToolkit:CollapsiblePanelExtender ID="cpe"
   runat="server">
</atlasToolkit:CollapsiblePanelExtender>
```

2. You can now add nested `CollapsiblePanelProperties` elements to this extender. Each `CollapsiblePanelProperties` element defines which control you are extending with this extender. Begin by expanding your search panel by adding the following. Notice that you specify which panel is being expanded/collapsed with the `TargetControlID` property, as well as which panel controls (via a mouse click) the current state of the expanded/collapsed panel with the `ExpandControlID` and `Collapse-ControlID` properties. There are other properties for adding images and/or text to indicate the current state of the panel as well as the `Collapsed` property for specifying the initial state of the panel.

```
<atlasToolkit:CollapsiblePanelExtender ID="cpe"
   runat="server">

   <atlasToolkit:CollapsiblePanelProperties
      Collapsed="False"
      TargetControlID="panSearch"
      ExpandControlID="panSearchHeader"
      CollapseControlID="panSearchHeader"
      ExpandDirection="Vertical"
      ImageControlID="imgHeaderSearch"
      ExpandedImage="~/images/restore.gif"
      ExpandedText="Collapse"
      CollapsedImage="~/images/minimize.gif"
      CollapsedText="Expand"
      SuppressPostBack="true" />

</atlasToolkit:CollapsiblePanelExtender>
```

3. Test in browser. The Search panel should now be collapsible, as shown in Figure A.12.

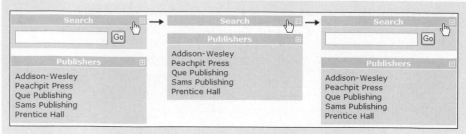

Figure A.12   CollapsiblePanelExtender in action

4. Make the rest of the panels in your page collapsible, by adding the following.

```
<atlasToolkit:CollapsiblePanelExtender ID="cpe"
    runat="server">

    <atlasToolkit:CollapsiblePanelProperties
        Collapsed="False"
        TargetControlID="panSearch"
        ExpandControlID="panSearchHeader"
        CollapseControlID="panSearchHeader"
        ExpandDirection="Vertical"
        ImageControlID="imgHeaderSearch"
        ExpandedImage="~/images/restore.gif"
        ExpandedText="Collapse"
        CollapsedImage="~/images/minimize.gif"
        CollapsedText="Expand"
        SuppressPostBack="true" />

    <atlasToolkit:CollapsiblePanelProperties
        Collapsed="False"
        TargetControlID="panBookList"
        ExpandControlID="panBookListHeader"
        CollapseControlID="panBookListHeader"
        ExpandDirection="Vertical"
        ImageControlID="imgHeaderBookList"
        ExpandedImage="~/images/restore.gif"
        ExpandedText="Collapse"
        CollapsedImage="~/images/minimize.gif"
        CollapsedText="Expand"
        SuppressPostBack="true" />
```

```
        <atlasToolkit:CollapsiblePanelProperties
           Collapsed="False"
           TargetControlID="panBook"
           ExpandControlID="panBookHeader"
           CollapseControlID="panBookHeader"
           ExpandDirection="Vertical"
           ImageControlID="imgHeaderBook"
           ExpandedImage="~/images/restore.gif"
           ExpandedText="Collapse"
           CollapsedImage="~/images/minimize.gif"
           CollapsedText="Expand"
           SuppressPostBack="true" />

        <atlasToolkit:CollapsiblePanelProperties
           Collapsed="False"
           TargetControlID="panPublisher"
           ExpandControlID="panPublisherHeader"
           CollapseControlID="panPublisherHeader"
           ExpandDirection="Vertical"
           ImageControlID="imgHeaderPublisher"
           ExpandedImage="~/images/restore.gif"
           ExpandedText="Collapse"
           CollapsedImage="~/images/minimize.gif"
           CollapsedText="Expand"
           SuppressPostBack="true" />

   </atlasToolkit:CollapsiblePanelExtender>
```

5. Test in browser.

Summary

ASP.NET AJAX is still very much in a state of development and change. This appendix endeavored to provide an overview of what it does as well as some demonstrations of it at work. ASP.NET AJAX technology promises to play an increasingly important part in ASP.NET development in the future.

References

Gibbs, Matt. "ASP.NET Atlas Powers the AJAX-Style Sites You've Been Waiting For." *MSDN Magazine* (July 2006).

Index

informIT

YOUR GUIDE TO IT REFERENCE

Articles

Keep your edge with thousands of free articles, in-depth features, interviews, and IT reference recommendations – all written by experts you know and trust.

Online Books

Answers in an instant from **InformIT Online Book's** 600+ fully searchable on line books. For a limited time, you can get your first 14 days **free**.

POWERED BY
Safari
TECH BOOKS ONLINE®

Catalog

Review online sample chapters, author biographies and customer rankings and choose exactly the right book from a selection of over 5,000 titles.